Samuel T. Gladding Kevin G. Alderson
Wake Forest University University of Calgary

Canadian Edition

Counselling

A Comprehensive Profession

Pearson Canada
Toronto

Library and Archives Canada Cataloguing in Publication

Gladding, Samuel T.

Counselling : a comprehensive profession / Samuel T. Gladding, Kevin G. Alderson.—Canadian ed.

Includes bibliographical references and indexes.
ISBN 978-0-13-800989-2

1. Counseling. I. Alderson, Kevin, 1956– II. Title.
BF636.6.G63 2011   158'.3   C2011-900442-9

ISBN 978-0-13-800989-2

Vice President, Editorial Director: Gary Bennett
Editor-in-Chief: Ky Pruesse
Acquisitions Editor: David S. Le Gallais
Signing Representative: Duncan MacKinnon
Marketing Manager: Loula March
Senior Developmental Editor: Patti Altridge
Project Manager: Cheryl Noseworthy
Production Editor: Raj Singh/MPS
Copy Editor: Patricia Jones
Proofreader: Sally Glover
Composition: MPS Limited, a Macmillan Company
Art Director: Julia Hall
Photo Researcher: Joanne Tang
Cover Design: Anthony Leung
Cover Image: Veer Inc.

For permission to reproduce other copyrighted material, the publisher gratefully acknowledges the copyright holders listed on page 636, which is considered an extension of this copyright page.

7 2022

I dedicate this book to the thousands of clients I have worked
with over the years. Without you, there would
be no need for this book or this profession.

Dr. Kevin Alderson

Contents

Note: Every effort has been made to provide accurate and current Internet information in this book. However, the internet and information posted on it are constantly changing, so it is inevitable that some of the internet addresses listed in this textbook will change.

Preface

When I was approached to co-author this book with the distinguished and highly regarded Samuel Gladding, something inside me soared like an eagle! Truthfully, I have never felt more privileged than to be part of something I believe in ever more strongly, and that is Canada and the profession I deeply cherish. The more I read in preparation for this book, the more excited I became to share with you what Samuel and I have learned.

Counselling is an amazing profession, and those who enter it are richly rewarded with knowing that they are applying the best of what we know about people in the interest of helping them. It is difficult to deny the interconnectedness that underlies the human condition, and counselling brings us into the core of that connection.

If you have not already had the privilege of counselling someone who, at the end of it, shows you a level of gratitude that you feel is undeserving, then just wait! Likewise, if you have not felt the pain, frustration, and sadness that emerges when you have not been helpful to someone, then also wait—you cannot have yin without yang, success without failure. Like Yoda said to Luke in one of the *Star Wars* movies, you will not be ready to become a Jedi until you have learned to face failure.

In becoming a counsellor, your own imperfections stare at you—and brilliantly so— as you uncover your own unfinished business that must be addressed. I strongly believe that you cannot help your client grow further than you have yourself.

So much of what we do in relationships occurs unconsciously. When we have created a real relationship with our client, he or she sees through the façade that we might conjure in order to hide something that is not helpful to the counselling process. Alas, our client feels the momentary pause, the vacant look in our eye, or the pulling away that signifies that a minor breach has occurred in our ability to strengthen the working alliance. A teacher only appears when you are ready, and you only become that teacher when you have the wisdom that earns the title.

You can certainly learn a lot from a textbook like this one, but wisdom develops over time as you learn more about yourself, your profession, and your clients, and as you live so that your challenges can keep you humble through it all. Without this, you may become a great technician, but you will never become a great counsellor.

ORGANIZATION OF TEXT

Materials in *Counselling: A Comprehensive Profession*, Canadian Edition, have been divided into four main sections.

Part 1, Historical and Professional Foundations of Counselling, contains chapters dealing with an overview of the development of counselling and important competencies of contemporary counsellors. Specific chapters that will orient you to the counselling profession as it was and is are

- Chapter 1   History of and Trends in Counselling
- Chapter 2   Personal and Professional Aspects of Counselling
- Chapter 3   Ethical and Legal Aspects of Counselling
- Chapter 4   Counselling in a Multicultural Society
- Chapter 5   Counselling with Diverse Populations

In Chapter 1, counselling is defined and examined historically, including trends in the 21st century. Chapter 2 explores personal and professional aspects involved in counselling and discusses ways of promoting practitioners' competencies. Chapter 3 focuses on the ethical and legal domains of counselling, especially counsellor responsibilities to clients and society. Chapter 4 highlights the importance of being sensitive to and responsible for clients from distinct cultures, and Chapter 5 looks at diversity factors in counselling such as old age, gender, sexual orientation, and spirituality.

As you read these five chapters, I hope you will recognize both overt and subtle aspects of counselling, including ways in which it differs from other mental health disciplines and some of the major events in its historical evolution. This section should help you understand the importance of a counsellor's personhood and education as well as emphasize the knowledge necessary to work ethically and legally with various clients in multiple settings and situations.

Part 2, Counselling Processes and Theories, highlights the main processes, stages, and theories of the counselling profession. This section addresses the universal aspects of popular counselling approaches and zeros in on specific theories and ways of dealing with client concerns. The seven chapters are

- Chapter 6   Building Counselling Relationships
- Chapter 7   Working in a Counselling Relationship
- Chapter 8   Termination of Counselling Relationships
- Chapter 9   Psychoanalytic and Psychodynamic Theories of Counselling
- Chapter 10 Behavioural and Cognitive Theories of Counselling
- Chapter 11 Humanistic Theories of Counselling
- Chapter 12 Postmodern Theories of Counselling

Chapters 6, 7, and 8 highlight three major stages of counselling: building, working in, and terminating a relationship. For each stage, the universal qualities and problems associated with it are outlined. Regardless of their theoretical orientation, counsellors must be aware of the process of counselling.

Chapters 9 and 10 describe and briefly discuss the importance of theory in counselling and the nature of eclectic counselling. Thirteen major theories or approaches of counselling are examined in a uniform manner for comparison purposes on the following seven factors: founders and developers, view of human nature, role of the counsellor, goals, techniques, strengths and contributions, and limitations. The theories included are psychoanalytic and psychodynamic, Adlerian, Jungian, behavioural, cognitive, humanistic, systemic, narrative, solution-focused, collaborative, and crisis. They are among the most popular in the profession.

Part 3, Core Counselling Activities in Various Settings, emphasizes universal skills required in almost all counselling environments. Counsellors use group counselling, consultation, research, and assessment skills in various areas. The four chapters in this section include

- Chapter 13   Groups in Counselling
- Chapter 14   Consultation
- Chapter 15   Evaluation and Research
- Chapter 16   Testing, Assessment, and Diagnosis in Counselling

Professional counsellors work in a variety of settings and with many different populations. Nevertheless, some of the activities in which they are regularly engaged overlap. This common core of functions unites counsellors in a way similar to that in which the history and foundations of the profession, examined in Part I, do. Some of the most prevalent practices of counsellors include conducting groups, offering consultation, participating in evaluation and research, and utilizing tests and assessment methods to diagnose and treat clients.

The four chapters in this section (Chapters 13–16) deal with these vital tasks. Almost all counsellors find themselves immersed in these activities as a part of their responsibilities. Thus, it is not surprising that there is considerable interest in these topics at professional meetings and continuing education seminars. Counsellors must lead groups, consult, evaluate the services they offer, and assess those they work with so as to give everyone the services they need and deserve.

Finally, **Part 4, Counselling Specialties**, contains five chapters that focus on specific populations with whom counsellors work or professional practices in which they are engaged that are unique. The chapters are titled

- Chapter 17   Career Counselling Over the Lifespan
- Chapter 18   Marriage, Couple, and Family Counselling
- Chapter 19   Counselling Children, Adolescents, and Young Adults
- Chapter 20   Mental Health Counselling and Addictions
- Chapter 21   Counselling the Economically Disadvantaged in Canada

Counsellors usually specialize in doing therapeutic work with the populations they most enjoy or with whom they have the most expertise. Specialization benefits counsellors and the public because those who specialize can delve deeply into a particular body of knowledge and as a result know the subtleties of disorders or distress. Therefore, they may pick up on signs or symptoms in clients that would be missed by others. In so doing, they may offer assistance to the person or persons involved that they would not otherwise receive. Just as in medicine, counsellors may acquire unique or deep knowledge that makes their role more valuable.

There are not nearly as many specialties in counselling as in medicine; however, in Chapters 17 to 20, the specialties most notable in counselling are covered. Chapter 21 is a unique chapter to the Canadian edition, focused on the growing problem of the economically disadvantaged.

A COMMON THEME

A common theme woven throughout this book is that counselling is both a generic and a specialized part of the helping field. Although it is a profession that has come of age, it is still growing. It is best represented in professional organizations such as the Canadian Counselling and Psychotherapy Association, the counselling psychology section of the Canadian Psychological Association, and the Canadian Association of Social Workers. There are numerous other professional groups—psychiatric nurses, psychiatrists, marriage and family counsellors, and pastoral counsellors—that use and practise counselling procedures and theories on a daily basis. In essence, no one profession owns the helping process.

Please note that all names and other pertinent details have been changed in all practice reflections and case examples included in the text. If someone's story reminds you of someone you know, he or she is *not* that person. Of sacrosanct importance is that, as counsellors, we protect our clients by keeping them anonymous and confidential. Without them, we have no profession. They deserve our highest respect.

This text is the result of a lifetime of effort on the part of Samuel Gladding and Kevin Alderson to understand the counselling profession as it was, as it is, and as it will be. Our journey has included a wide variety of experiences—working with clients in all ages and stages of life in counselling and clinical settings and with students who are interested in learning more about the essence of how counselling works. Research, observation, dialogue, assimilation, and study have contributed to the growth of the content contained in these pages.

Your introduction to the counselling profession begins in a few pages. I welcome you inside to a most incredible journey.

ACKNOWLEDGMENTS

No book of this magnitude occurs without the contribution of many, many people. How does one pay homage to the thousands of mental health professionals and researchers who have contributed to our profession? Well, I guess you simply acknowledge that without them, our field would still be where it was 50 years ago—that is, in its infancy stages. What struck me in meeting some of the great leaders in counselling in workshops and seminars, including big names like Albert Ellis, Virginia Satir, Donald Meichenbaum, Insoo Kim Berg, and many others, is that they, like you, are just people.

They each have strengths and weaknesses that sometimes glare in their own mirrors, just like the rest of us. Ultimately, we each have to do something with what we are and become someone we can respect, despite our human condition.

I am indebted to those closer to me who have shaped my life in deeper ways; these are the people who have been part of my personal journey through life. Deepest appreciation goes out to my parents: my late father, "Ted" Alderson, and my mother, Hazel Alderson. Thank you for giving me a chance to have life. I also provide a special dedication to my ex-wife and continuing best friend, Bess Alderson. Without you, I would have never learned that loving needed to begin from within. I also share this gratitude with my husband, Manuel Mendoza, who continues to teach me more everyday about diversity and the joy of living in a country that provides us full legal rights to be proud, strong, and free.

I hope you hear the thunder of our Canadian identity as you read this book. Without this, little here would really matter to me.

My thanks go to the team at Pearson Canada, which has seen this book through from manuscript to finished product, including David Le Gallais, Acquisitions Editor; Patti Altridge, Developmental Editor; Richard Di Santo, Production Manager; and Patricia Jones, Copyeditor. I would also like to thank Raj Singh and his team at MPS.

Pearson Canada and the authors would like to thank the many colleagues who served as reviewers for their valuable comments and suggestions on this Canadian edition:

Jason Brown, *University of Western Ontario*
Joseph Roy Gillis, *University of Toronto*
Colleen Haney, *University of British Columbia*
Chris Harris, *Durham College*
Pam Hirakata, *University of British Columbia*
Sara Menzel, *Vancouver Community College*
Leanne Rose Sladde, *Vancouver Island University*
Susan L. Tasker, *University of Victoria*
Kevin G. Alderson, *with contributions added from Samuel T. Gladding's original preface*

ABOUT THE AUTHORS

 Samuel T. Gladding is a professor of counselling and chair of the Department of Counseling at Wake Forest University in Winston-Salem, North Carolina. He has been a practising counsellor in both public and private agencies since 1971. His leadership in the field of counselling includes service as president of the American Counseling Association (ACA), the Association for Counselor Education and Supervision (ACES), the Association for Specialists in Group Work (ASGW), and Chi Sigma Iota (counselling academic and professional honour society international).

Gladding is the former editor of the *Journal for Specialists in Group Work* and the author of over 100 professional publications. In 1999, he was cited as being in the top 1% of contributors to the *Journal of Counseling and Development*, 1978–1993. Some of Gladding's other recent books are *Community and Agency Counseling* (with Debbie Newsome) (3rd ed., 2009); *Group Work: A Counseling Specialty* (5th ed., 2008); *Family Therapy: History, Theory, and Practice* (4th ed., 2007); *Becoming a Counselor: The Light, The Bright, and the Serious* (2nd ed., 2008); *The Counseling Dictionary* (2nd ed, 2006); and *The Creative Arts in Counseling* (3rd ed., 2004).

Gladding's previous academic appointments have been at the University of Alabama at Birmingham and Fairfield University (Connecticut). He received his degrees from Wake Forest, Yale, and the University of North Carolina–Greensboro. He is a National Certified Counselor (NCC), a Certified Clinical Mental Health Counselor (CCMHC), and a practising Licensed Professional Counselor (North Carolina). Gladding is a Fellow in the American Counseling Association and a recipient of the Gilbert and Kathleen Wrenn Award for a Humanitarian and Caring Person.

Dr. Gladding is married to Claire Tillson Gladding and is the father of three children—Ben, Nate, and Tim. Outside of counselling, he enjoys tennis, swimming, and humour.

Kevin G. Alderson is an associate professor of counselling psychology at the University of Calgary (UC). Following a BA in psychology (UC), Dr. Alderson earned an MSc in clinical, school, and community psychology (UC), and finally a PhD in counselling psychology (University of Alberta).

Dr. Alderson has been a counsellor for more than 30 years and a licensed practising psychologist for 25. His experiences have included working as a child and youth care worker, a caseworker, a mental health worker, and a psychologist in diverse settings. Before joining the university in July 2001, Dr. Alderson was Head of Counselling and Health Services at Mount Royal College (now a university) in Calgary for several years.

Alderson is the current editor of the *Canadian Journal of Counselling and Psycho-therapy* and the author of five previous books, including *Beyond Coming Out* (2000), *Breaking Out* (2002), *Same-Sex Marriage: The Personal and the Political* (co-authored with Kathy Lahey; 2004), *Grade Power: The Complete Guide to Improving Your Grades through Self-Hypnosis* (2004), and a self-published smoking cessation book. Three soon-to-be released books include *"Breathe, Freedom!"A Comprehensive and Hypnotic Approach to Quitting Smoking, Counseling GLBT Individuals*, and *Breaking Out II*, the second edition, that will be inclusive of GLBT individuals.

Dr. Alderson is married to Manuel Mendoza, and is the father of two adult children. Outside of counselling, he enjoys racket sports, beach volleyball, dancing, hiking, camping, and weight training.

Chapter 1

History of and Trends in Counselling

PRACTICE REFLECTION

While this chapter is about the history of the counselling profession, it is also important to know that each counselling approach places different value on having a thorough *client* history. For example, in the newer postmodern approaches to counselling, client history is not given much weight at all, while in psychoanalytic and psychodynamic approaches, it is sacrosanct. In my own practice, I have been guided by the presenting concern of the client and/or by his or her stated desire to examine the past.

Sylvia, a 33-year old client, came to see me and said she felt unlovable because her relationships never lasted more than a few months. Sylvia really wanted to marry and have children—she also felt time was running out. I thought it was important to assess what thoughts and behaviours might be contributing to this perception. I began, "Would it be okay to begin by looking at your relationship history up to this point?" She concurred, so I asked her to write down a list of all the relationships she had had in chronological order and to record how long each relationship had lasted. Sylvia listed 10 relationships she felt were somewhat important to her, leaving the many short dating episodes off the list.

I then asked her to write down beside each name whether he or she had ended the relationship. Of the 10 relationships, one was mutually dissolved, one was ended by the man, and the remaining eight were ended by her! Consequently, her relationship history would not indicate that she was unlovable. This was an important thought for Sylvia to remember. Next, we began talking about her dating behaviour. Typically, Sylvia responded to her physical attractions for men by first sleeping with them and then quickly developing feelings if the sex was good. So I asked, "Besides good looks, what criteria do you use to look for a man suitable to marry?" I first watched her jaw drop as she uttered, "You know something, I don't use any!"

Next, we collaboratively created a list of criteria for Sylvia. The list included (a) between 28- and 40-years old, (b) financially stable, (c) has already had long-term relationships in his adult life, and (d) is not on the rebound from a recent breakup. We then looked retrospectively at whether any of the men she had had relationships with would have met these criteria. Sadly, not one would have qualified.

With this realization, Sylvia began to change her dating behaviour by first finding out if the man she was physically attracted to also met her criteria. This had the double benefit of keeping her from becoming emotionally involved by becoming sexually involved too quickly. Sylvia understood that it would still take some time to find what she was looking for, but at least now, she knew how to change her relationship history into something that was more likely to fulfill her goal of having a family.

A profession is distinguished by having a specific body of knowledge, accredited training programs, a professional organization of peers, credentialing of practitioners such as licensure, a code of ethics, legal recognition, and other standards of excellence (Myers & Sweeney, 2001). Counselling meets all of the standards for a profession and is unique from, as well as connected with, other mental health disciplines by both its emphasis and its history. Counselling emphasizes growth as well as remediation. Counsellors work with persons, groups, families, and systems that are experiencing situational and long-term problems. Counselling's focus on development, prevention, and treatment makes it attractive to those seeking healthy life-stage transitions and productive lives free from disorders.

Counselling has not always been an encompassing and comprehensive profession. It has evolved over the years from very diverse disciplines "including but not limited to anthropology, education, ethics, history, law, medical sciences, philosophy, psychology, and sociology" (Smith, 2001, p. 570). Many people associate counselling with schools or equate the word guidance with counselling because they are unaware of counselling's evolution. As a consequence, old ideas linger in their minds in contrast to reality, and they misunderstand the profession. Even among counsellors themselves, those who fail to keep up in their professional development may become confused.

Therefore, it is important to examine the history of counselling because a counsellor who is informed about the development of the profession is likely to have a strong professional identity and make real contributions to the field. This chapter covers the people, events, and circumstances that have been prominent and have shaped modern counselling as well as current directions. By understanding the past, you may better appreciate present and future trends of the profession.

DEFINITION OF COUNSELLING

THERE HAVE ALWAYS BEEN "COUNSELLORS"—PEOPLE WHO LISTEN TO OTHERS AND HELP THEM resolve difficulties—but the word counsellor has been misused over the years by connecting it with descriptive adjectives to promote products. Thus, one hears of carpet counsellors, colour coordination counsellors, pest control counsellors, financial counsellors, and so on. These counsellors are mostly glorified salespersons or advice givers. They are to professional counselling what furniture doctors are to medicine (see Figure 1.1).

Counselling as a profession grew out of the guidance movement, in opposition to traditional psychotherapy. Yet today professional counselling focuses on growth and wellness as well as the remediation of mental disorders. To understand what counselling is now, it is important first to understand the concepts of guidance and psychotherapy and the history of the profession.

Guidance

Guidance is the process of helping people make important choices that affect their lives, such as choosing a preferred lifestyle. Although the decision-making aspect of guidance has long played an important role in the counselling process, the term *guidance* has more of a historical significance than a present-day usage. Nevertheless, it sometimes distinguishes a way of helping that differs from the more encompassing word *counselling*.

One distinction between guidance and counselling is that guidance focuses on helping individuals choose what they value most, whereas counselling focuses on helping

"Essentially, what I hear you saying is, you've resolved your sugar/saccharin conflict, but you're still not secure with your role as a decaf drinker."

Figure 1.1 The coffee counsellor

Source: From a cartoon by J. Millard, 1987, *Chronicle of Higher Education, 33*, p. 49. Reprinted with permission.

them make changes. Much of the early work in guidance occurred in schools and career centres where an adult would help a student make decisions, such as deciding on a course of study or a vocation. That relationship was between unequals and was beneficial in helping the less experienced person find direction in life. Similarly, children have long received "guidance" from parents, religious leaders, and coaches. In the process they have gained an understanding of themselves and their world. This type of guidance will never become passé; no matter what the age or stage of life, a person often needs help in making choices. Yet such guidance is only one part of the overall service provided by professional counselling.

Psychotherapy

Traditionally, psychotherapy (or *therapy*) focused on serious problems associated with intrapsychic, internal, and personal issues and conflicts. It dealt with the "recovery of adequacy" (Casey, 1996, p. 175). As such, psychotherapy, especially analytically based therapy, emphasized (a) the past more than the present, (b) insight more than change, (c) the detachment of the therapist, and (d) the therapist's role as an expert. In addition, psychotherapy was seen as involving a long-term relationship (20 to 40 sessions over a period of six months to two years) that focused on reconstructive change. Psychotherapy was also viewed as being provided more through inpatient settings (residential treatment facilities such as mental hospitals) as opposed to outpatient settings (nonresidential buildings such as community agencies).

However, in more modern times, the distinction between psychotherapy and counselling has blurred and professionals who provide clinical services often determine whether clients receive counselling or psychotherapy. Some counselling theories are commonly referred to as therapies as well and can be used in either counselling or therapy settings. Therefore, the similarities in the counselling and psychotherapy processes often overlap, as Figure 1.2 shows.

Counselling

The Canadian Counselling and Psychotherapy Association (CCPA, 2009c) defines counselling as "... the skilled and principled use of relationship to facilitate self-knowledge, emotional acceptance and growth, and the optimal development of personal resources" (para. 1).

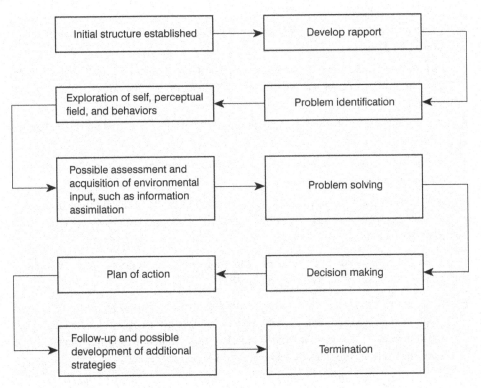

Figure 1.2 The work of counsellors and psychotherapists have similar processes

Counselling is intended to help people live more successful and satisfying lives. The possibility of presenting issues is nearly endless, but often centres on (a) development issues, (b) overcoming specific problems, (c) coping better with a crisis situation, (d) improving relationships with others, or (e) overcoming feelings associated with inner conflicts (CCPA, 2009c).

Several members of the Canadian Psychological Association (Beatch et al., 2009) have recently written an extensive Canadian definition and description of counselling psychology, a specialty that combines the two disciplines of counselling and psychology. Their definition includes mention of the following aspects:

1. *Broad practice and research focus.* Counselling psychologists (CPs) work with a very diverse clientele within diverse settings (e.g., community agencies, private practices, universities). They also research in a wide range of areas.

2. *Promoting wellness.* CPs promote growth, well-being, and the mental health of individuals, families, groups, and the community at large.

3. *Collaborative research and practice.* CPs work in collaboration with their clients to promote wellness as mentioned above.

4. *Prevention.* Some CPs are focused on helping to prevent psychological and emotional disturbances.

5. *Overlap with other specialities.* The work of CPs overlaps with clinical psychologists, industrial and organizational psychologists, and other mental health professionals.

6. *Advocacy.* Some CPs are involved in advocacy efforts on behalf of their clients or society.

7. *Multicultural approach.* CPs take a multicultural approach both in providing counselling and in conducting research.

8. *Adherence to core values.* CPs believe in (a) clients' strengths and their own ability to make personal changes, (b) a holistic and client-centred focus, and (c) a sensitivity to diversity and multiculturalism.

These definitions contain a number of implicit and explicit points that are important for counsellors as well as consumers to realize.

- *Counselling deals with wellness, personal growth, career, and pathological concerns.* In other words, counsellors work in areas that involve relationships. These areas include intra- and interpersonal concerns related to finding meaning and adjustment in such settings as schools, families, and careers.

- *Counselling is conducted with persons who are considered to be functioning well and those who are having more serious problems.* Counselling meets the needs of a wide spectrum of people. Clients seen by counsellors have developmental or situational concerns that require help in regard to adjustment or remediation. Their problems often require short-term intervention, but treatment may be extended to encompass disorders included in the *Diagnostic and Statistical Manual of Mental Disorders* of the American Psychiatric Association.

- *Counselling is theory based.* Counsellors draw from a number of theoretical approaches, including those that are cognitive, affective, behavioural, and systemic. These theories may be applied to individuals, groups, and families.

- *Counselling is a process that may be developmental or intervening.* Counsellors focus on their clients' goals. Thus, counselling involves both choice and change. In some cases, "counselling is a rehearsal for action" (Casey, 1996, p. 176).

Counselling psychology and social work are closely related fields, although their origins are different and so are some of their central tenets. Social work has always promoted human rights and social justice, often from an advocacy perspective. This has become a more recent development in the field of counselling psychology. Counselling psychologists are also trained extensively in the psychology field and consequently are more likely to administer and interpret psychological tests, albeit not usually of the more "clinical" variety utilized extensively by clinical and school psychologists.

Social Work

Here is the most recent definition from the Canadian Association of Social Workers (2009):

> Social work is a profession concerned with helping individuals, families, groups and communities to enhance their individual and collective well-being. It aims to help people develop their skills and their ability to use their own resources and those of the community to resolve problems. Social work is concerned with individual and personal problems but also with broader social issues such as poverty, unemployment and domestic violence.
>
> Human rights and social justice are the philosophical underpinnings of social work practice. The uniqueness of social work practice is in the blend of some particular values, knowledge and skills, including the use of relationship as the basis of all interventions and respect for the client's choice and involvement.
>
> In a socio-political-economic context which increasingly generates insecurity and social tensions, social workers play an important and essential role.

For more information, refer to the *CASW National Scope of Practice Statement* (March 2000), available from the CASW office and website.

HISTORY OF COUNSELLING

In relation to other professions, counselling is relatively new, having been developed in the late 1890s and early 1900s. During this time, Europe and to a greater extent the

United States exerted an important influence over the developing profession in Canada. The best way to chart the evolution of counselling in Canada is to trace important events and personal influences through the 20th century both globally and domestically.

Before 1900 Prior to the 1900s, most counselling was in the form of advice or information. In the United States, counselling developed out of a humanitarian concern to improve the lives of those adversely affected by the Industrial Revolution of the mid- to late 1800s (Aubrey, 1983). The social welfare reform movement (now known as social justice), the spread of public education, and various changes in population makeup (e.g., the enormous influx of immigrants) also influenced the growth of the emerging profession (Aubrey, 1977; Goodyear, 1984). Humanitarian concerns were also coming to the forefront in Europe in a response to reform the asylum system. These situations influenced the Canadian counselling landscape in the early development of child and youth counselling (Herman, 1981). In particular, it was the Moral Therapy Movement in France that migrated to Canada around 1850 that promoted a humane approach as the best way to treat psychological problems (Hayduk & Jewell, 2005).

Although these developments were taking place, "no mention of counseling was made in the professional literature until 1931" (Aubrey, 1983, p. 78) and most of the pioneers in counselling identified themselves as teachers and social reformers or advocates. They focused on teaching children and young adults about themselves, others, and the world of work. Initially, these helpers were involved primarily in child welfare, educational/vocational guidance, and legal reform. Their work was built on specific information and lessons, such as moral instruction on being good and doing right, as well as a concentrated effort to deal with intra- and interpersonal relations (Nugent & Jones, 2005).

1900 to 1909 Between 1900 and 1909, two movements were underway in the United States that found their way into Canada—the mental health movement and the vocational guidance movement. While vocational guidance was emerging as an important field for dealing with problems resulting from the Industrial Revolution, humane mental health treatment was rising in popularity. During this decade, two Americans emerged as leaders in counselling history, Frank Parsons and Clifford Beers.

Frank Parsons, often called the founder of guidance, focused his work on growth and prevention. His influence was great in his time, and it is "Parson's body of work and his efforts to help others [that] lie at the center of the wheel that represents present day counseling" (Ginter, 2002, p. 221). Parsons had a colourful life career in multiple disciplines, being a lawyer, an engineer, a college teacher, and a social worker before ultimately becoming a social reformer and working with youth (Hartung & Blustein, 2002; Pope & Sweinsdottir, 2005; Sweeney, 2001). He has been characterized as a broad scholar, a persuasive writer, a tireless activist, and a great intellect (Davis, 1988; Zytowski, 1985). However, he is best known for founding Boston's Vocational Bureau in 1908, a major step in the institutionalization of vocational guidance.

At the Bureau, Parsons worked with young people who were in the process of making career decisions. He "envisioned a practice of vocational guidance based on rationality and reason with service, concern for others, cooperation, and social justice among its core values" (Hartung & Blustein, 2002, p. 41). He theorized that choosing a vocation was a matter of relating three factors: a knowledge of work, a knowledge of self, and a matching of the two through "true reasoning" (Drummond & Ryan, 1995).

Clifford Beers, a former Yale student, was hospitalized for mental illness several times during his life for depression (Kiselica & Robinson, 2001). He found conditions in mental institutions deplorable and exposed them in his book, *A Mind That Found Itself* (1908), which became a popular bestseller. Beers used the book as a platform to advocate for better mental health facilities and reform in the treatment of people with mental illness by making friends with and soliciting funds from influential people of his day, such as the Fords and the Rockefellers. His work had an especially powerful influence on the fields of psychiatry and clinical psychology. "Many people in these fields referred to what they were doing as counseling," which was seen "as a means of helping people adjust to themselves and society" (Hansen, Rossberg, & Cramer, 1994, p. 5). Beers's work was the impetus for the mental health movement in the United States and Canada. In conjunction with Clarence Hincks, a Canadian physician who had himself experienced mental health problems, he founded the Canadian National Committee for Mental Hygiene in 1918, which is today called the Canadian Mental Health Association (Canadian Mental Health Association, 2009).

1910s to 1940s Some important developments occurred during these decades. For example, in the United States, the congressional passage of the *Smith-Hughes Act* of 1917 provided funding for public schools to support vocational education. This had a positive effect on the growth of the counselling profession in Canada in that many early counsellors received their graduate training in the United States, and the textbooks used were American (Herman, 1981). The other major events during these times that contributed to the emerging profession were World Wars I and II.

During World War I, "counseling became more widely recognized as the military began to employ testing and placement practices for great numbers of military personnel" (Hollis, 2000, p. 45). Aubrey (1977) observes that, because the vocational guidance movement developed without an explicit philosophy, it quickly embraced psychometrics to gain a legitimate foundation in psychology. Reliance on psychometrics had both positive and negative effects. On the positive side, it gave vocational guidance specialists a stronger and more "scientific" identity. On the negative side, it distracted many specialists from examining developments in other behavioural sciences, such as sociology, biology, and anthropology.

Less stressful times in the 1920s saw vocational guidance begin in Canadian junior and senior high schools (Marshall & Uhlmann, 1996), an initiative that was also underway in the United States (Conklin, 1985). The 1920s in the United States also saw the development of the first standards for the preparation and evaluation of occupational materials (Lee, 1966). Along with these standards came the publication of new psychological instruments, such as Edward Strong's Strong Vocational Interest Inventory (SVII) in 1927. The publication of this instrument set the stage for future directions for assessment in counselling (Strong, 1943).

The 1930s were not as quiet as the 1920s, in part because the Great Depression influenced researchers and practitioners, especially in university and vocational settings, to emphasize helping strategies and counselling methods that related to employment. A highlight of the decade was the development of the first theory of counselling, which was formulated by E. G. Williamson and his colleagues (including John Darley and Donald Paterson) at the University of Minnesota. Williamson modified Parsons's theory and used it to work with students and the unemployed. His emphasis on a direct, counsellor-centred approach came to be known by several names—for example, as the Minnesota point of view and as trait-factor counselling. His pragmatic approach emphasized the counsellor's teaching, mentoring, and influencing skills (Williamson, 1939).

One premise of Williamson's theory was that individuals had traits (e.g., aptitudes, interests, personalities, achievements) that could be integrated in a variety of ways to form factors (constellations of individual characteristics). Counselling was based on a scientific, problem-solving, empirical method that was individually tailored to each client to help him or her stop nonproductive thinking/behaviour and become an effective decision maker (Lynch & Maki, 1981). Williamson thought the task of the counsellor was to ascertain a deficiency in the client, such as a lack of knowledge or a skill, and then to prescribe a procedure to rectify the problem. Williamson's influence dominated counselling for the next two decades, and he continued to write about his theory into the 1970s (Williamson & Biggs, 1979).

By the late 1930s, World War II had created a role for counsellors and psychologists in Canada, largely in the area of test construction for selecting and classifying military personnel (Ferguson, 1992). In 1938, Ferguson (1992) himself was in Munich when Hitler and Chamberlain were there to sign the Munich Pact. A few months earlier, several psychologists met in Ottawa while attending a conference to look at how psychology could make a contribution to the impending war.

In April 1939, another meeting occurred in Toronto with only three people present: E. A. Bott of the University of Toronto, George Humphrey of Queen's University, and Roy Liddy of the University of Western Ontario. Ferguson (1992) identifies this meeting as the beginning of the Canadian Psychological Association (CPA): "This meeting was a major event in the history of psychology in Canada" (Ferguson, 1992, p. 698). The CPA formed in the same year (Paivo & Ritchie, 1996).

The three psychologists who met in Toronto (who justifiably could be considered the three "wisemen" of Canadian psychology) decided to publish a newsletter, known as the *Bulletin* of the CPA. The first issue, published in October 1940, set the stage for a publication that was between a newsletter and a journal. After a few years, the *Bulletin* transformed into the *Canadian Journal of Psychology* (Ferguson, 1992).

In education, another major occurrence was the broadening of counselling beyond occupational concerns in America. The seeds of this development were sown in the 1920s, when Edward Thorndike began to challenge the vocational orientation of the guidance movement (Lee, 1966). The work of John Brewer completed this change in emphasis. Brewer published a book titled *Education as Guidance* in 1932. He proposed that every teacher be a counsellor and that guidance be incorporated into the school curriculum as a subject. Brewer believed that all education should focus on preparing students to live outside the school environment. His emphasis made counsellors see vocational decisions as just one part of their responsibilities.

Growing from this in the 1940s, Canadian vocational guidance counsellors began to replace teachers in the areas of testing and counselling (Marshall & Uhlemann, 1996). Provincial guidance associations also began to form in the middle of this decade, including the L'Association des orienteurs de la province de Quebec (OCCOPPQ, 2009) and the Maritime Guidance Association, which was later renamed the Atlantic Chapter of the Canadian Counselling Association (Hayduk & Jewell, 2005). Post-secondary counselling also emerged soon after WWII as the Canadian government recognized its importance (Hayduk & Jewell, 2005).

In counselling psychotherapy, Carl Rogers rose to prominence in 1942 with the publication of his book *Counselling and Psychotherapy*, which challenged the counsellor-centred approach of Williamson as well as major tenets of Freudian psychoanalysis. Rogers emphasized the importance of the client, espousing a nondirective approach to counselling. His ideas were both widely accepted and harshly criticized. Rogers advocated giving clients responsibility for their own growth. He thought that if clients had an opportunity to be accepted and listened to, then they would begin to know themselves better and become more congruent (genuine). He described the role of the professional helper as being nonjudgmental and accepting. Thus, the helper served as a mirror, reflecting the verbal and emotional manifestations of the client.

Aubrey (1977, p. 292) has noted that, before Rogers, the literature in guidance and counselling was quite practical, dealing with testing, cumulative records, orientation procedures, vocations, placement functions, and so on. In addition, this early literature dealt extensively with the goals and purpose of guidance. With Rogers, there was a new emphasis on the importance of the relationship in counselling, research, refinement of counselling technique, selection and training of future counsellors, and the goals and objectives of counselling. Guidance, for all intents and purposes, suddenly disappeared as a major consideration in the bulk of the literature and was replaced by a decade or more of concentration on counselling. The Rogers revolution had a major impact on both counselling and psychology. Not only did Rogers's ideas come to the forefront, but a considerable number of alternative systems of psychotherapy emerged as well (Corsini, 2008).

1950s to 1980s Before 1950, four main theories influenced the work of counsellors: (a) psychoanalysis and insight theory (e.g., Sigmund Freud); (b) trait-factor or directive theories (e.g., E. G. Williamson); (c) humanistic and client-centred theories (e.g., Carl Rogers); and, to a lesser extent, (d) behavioural theories (e.g., B. F. Skinner). During the 1950s and 1960s, Canadian schools saw vocational guidance work decrease and personal counselling increase as Roger's person-centred approach spread far and wide (Marshall

& Uhlmann, 1996). This also led school boards to begin hiring full-time school counsellors (Marshall & Uhlmann, 1996). With the four main theories, debates among counsellors usually centred on whether directive or nondirective counselling was most effective, and almost all counsellors assumed that certain tenets of psychoanalysis (e.g., defense mechanisms) were true.

As the 1950s progressed, however, debate gradually shifted away from this focus as new theories of helping began to emerge. Applied behavioural theories, such as Joseph Wolpe's systematic desensitization, began to gain influence. Cognitive theories also made an appearance, as witnessed by the growth of Albert Ellis's rational-emotive therapy, Eric Berne's transactional analysis, and Aaron Beck's cognitive therapy. Learning theory, self-concept theory, Donald Super's work in career development, and advances in developmental psychology made an impact as well (Aubrey, 1977). By the end of the decade, the number and complexity of theories associated with counselling had grown considerably.

Some powerful influences that emerged during the 1960s were the humanistic counselling theories of Dugald Arbuckle, Abraham Maslow, and Sidney Jourard. Also important was the phenomenal growth of the group movement (Gladding, 2008). The emphasis of counselling shifted from a one-on-one encounter to small-group interaction. Behavioural counselling grew in importance with the appearance of John Krumboltz's *Revolution in Counseling* (1966), in which learning (beyond insight) was promoted as the root of change. Thus, the decade's initial focus on development became sidetracked. As Aubrey notes, "the cornucopia of competing counseling methodologies presented to counsellors reached an all-time high in the late 1960s" (1977, p. 293).

Another noteworthy milestone was the establishment of the ERIC Clearinghouse on Counselling and Personnel Services (CAPS) at the University of Michigan. Founded in 1966 by Garry Walz and funded by the Office of Educational Research and Improvement at the U.S. Department of Education, ERIC/CAPS was another example of the impact of government on the development of counselling. Through the years ERIC/CAPS has become one of the largest and most used resources on counselling activities and trends in the United States and throughout the world. It also sponsors conferences on leading topics in counselling that bring national leaders together.

Canada had its own milestone with the creation of the Canadian Guidance Counsellors Association (CGCA) in 1965 with Dr. Myrne B. Nevison from the University of British Columbia as one of its founders (Paterson & Janzen, 1993). Mryne was also the first editor of the *Canadian Journal of Counselling* (renamed the *Canadian Journal of Counselling in Psychotherapy* in July 2010), the national peer-reviewed journal dedicated to counselling theory and practice. The name of CGCA was changed to CCA (Canadian Counselling Association) in 1999 (Hayduk & Jewell, 2005) and then CCPA (Canadian Counselling and Psychotherapy Association) in 2009 (CCPA, 2009a).

The rapid growth of counselling outside educational institutions began in the 1970s when mental health centres and community agencies began to employ counsellors. This hiring occurred for several reasons, including the passage of new U.S. federal legislation that opened up human services activities more to girls and women, minorities, and persons with disabilities. Canada's focus began to shift as it moved more to a preventative developmental approach (Paterson, Robertson, & Bain, 1979). Nonetheless, most Canadian counsellors continued providing educational and vocational counselling (Brown, 1980).

The 1970s also saw the development of helping skills programs that concentrated on relationship and communication skills. Begun by Truax and Carkhuff (1967) and Ivey (1971), these programs taught basic counselling skills to professionals and nonprofessionals alike. The emphasis was humanistic and eclectic. It was assumed that certain fundamental skills should be mastered to establish satisfactory personal interaction. A bonus for counsellors who received this type of training was that they could teach it to others rather easily. Counsellors could now consult by teaching some of their skills to those with whom they worked, mainly teachers and paraprofessionals. In many ways, this trend was a new version of Brewer's concept of education as guidance.

In 1973, the Association of Counsellor Educators and Supervisors (ACES), a division of APGA, outlined the standards for a master's degree in counselling. Robert Stripling of the University of Florida spearheaded that effort. In 1977, ACES approved guidelines for doctoral preparation in the discipline (Stripling, 1978). During the 1970s, APGA membership increased to almost 40 000. Four new divisions (in addition to AMHCA) were chartered: the Association for Religious and Value Issues in Counselling, the Association for Specialists in Group Work, the Association for Non-white Concerns in Personnel and Guidance, and the Public Offender Counsellor Association.

Among the most noteworthy events of the 1980s were those that standardized the training and certification of counsellors, recognized counselling as a distinct profession, increased the diversification of counsellor specialties, and emphasized human growth and development.

The U.S. National Board for Certified Counsellors (NBCC), which was formed in 1982, began to certify counsellors on a national level. It developed a standardized test and defined eight major subject areas in which counsellors should be knowledgeable: (a) human growth and development, (b) social and cultural foundations, (c) helping relationships, (d) groups, (e) lifestyle and career development, (f) appraisal, (g) research and evaluation, and (h) professional orientation. To become a National Certified Counsellor (NCC), examinees have to pass a standardized test and meet experiential and character-reference qualifications. By the end of the 1980s, there were approximately 17 000 NCC professionals.

Counselling became a distinct profession in this decade. Division 17—the division devoted to counselling psychology—of the American Psychological Association continued to grow at a steady rate (Woody, Hansen, & Rossberg, 1989). In 1987, a professional standards conference was assembled by its president, George Gazda, to define further the uniqueness of counselling psychology and counselling in general.

During the 1980s, counsellors became more diversified. Large numbers of counsellors continued to be employed in primary and secondary schools and in higher education in a variety of student personnel services. Mental health counsellors and community/agency counsellors were the two largest blocks of professionals outside formal educational environments. In addition, the number of counsellors swelled in mental health settings for business employees, the aging, and married persons and families.

The first counselling section of the Canadian Psychological Association was formed in 1986, and in 1989 the CPA established accreditation criteria for doctoral programs, modelled after the American Psychological Association (Lalande, 2004). The formation of a counselling section within CPA in effect created the discipline in Canada called "counselling psychology," anchoring counselling in this case as a field within the psychology profession instead of the converse (Beatch et al., 2009). Counselling psychology had already existed in the United States as a recognized discipline since 1951 (Beatch et al., 2009).

In the United States, counselling psychology grew out of professional psychology, while in Canada its roots were primarily in educational counselling (Young & Nichol, 2007). Notable is the fact that counselling psychology is housed within education faculties throughout Canada and not within psychology departments, reflecting its unique Canadian history (Beatch et al., 2009).

Counselling's emphasis on human growth and development grew during the 1980s as well. For example, a new spotlight was placed on developmental counselling across the lifespan (Gladstein & Apfel, 1987). New behavioural expressions associated with Erik Erikson's first five stages of life development were formulated, too (Hamachek, 1988), and an increased emphasis on the development of adults and the elderly resulted in the formation of the Association for Adult Aging and Development (AAAD).

A second way that human growth and development was stressed was through increased attention to gender issues and sexual preferences (see, for example, O'Neil & Carroll, 1988; Pearson, 1988; Weinrach, 1987). Carol Gilligan's (1982) landmark study on the development of moral values in females, which helped introduce feminist theory into the counselling arena, forced human growth specialists to examine the differences between genders.

There was also a renewed emphasis on models of moral development, such as Lawrence Kohlberg's theory (1969), and increased research in the area of enhancing moral development. In counsellor education, it was found that moral development was closely related to both cognitive ability and empathy (Bowman & Reeves, 1987).

Finally, the challenges of working with different ethnic and cultural groups received more discussion (Ponterotto & Casas, 1987). In focusing on multicultural issues, the Association for Multicultural Counselling and Development (AMCD) took the lead, but multicultural themes, such as the importance of diversity, became a central issue among all groups, especially in light of the renewed racism that developed in the United States in the 1980s (Carter, 1990).

1990s An important event that originated in 1992 was the writing of the multicultural counselling competencies and standards by Sue, Arredondo, and McDavis (1992). Although these competencies mainly applied to counselling with people of colour, they set the stage for a larger debate about the nature of multicultural counselling—for instance, inclusion within the definition of other groups, such as people with disabilities. Thus, a lively discussion occurred throughout the decade about what diversity and counselling within a pluralistic society entail (Weinrach & Thomas, 1998).

A renewed interest regarding counselling issues related to the whole person also emerged in the 1990s. Counsellors became more aware of social factors important to the development and maintenance of mental disorders and health, including the importance of organism-context interaction (i.e., contextualism) (Thomas, 1996). These factors include spirituality, family environment, socioeconomic considerations, the impact of groups and group work, and prevention (Bemak, 1998).

Case Example: What Would *You* Do?

Psychology is interesting in that certain "fads" emerge at certain times, but like other fads, they later disappear. There was a time when some clients would ask me if I did "inner-child" work. If I said no, I would lose that potential client. If I said yes, I would need to offer this type of work to them. I decided to follow the higher ground by telling these potential clients that I considered inner-child work to be the new lingo for the need that many people have to do unfinished business from the past. If they were interested, I would help them become more accepting of their pasts and of themselves. I still lost some potential clients, but that is always going to happen no matter what approach you take.

1. Would you be more inclined to simply tell clients that you did inner-child work, or whatever the latest fad therapy was called, and then work with them in the way that you thought was best? Why or why not?

2. Would your answer vary at all depending on whether you were in private practice and needed more clients or if you worked as a salaried employee?

3. What potential problems arise when clients tell psychologists what it is they expect or want? What happens if you don't agree with your client?

CURRENT TRENDS IN THE NEW MILLENNIUM

The Registry of Marriage and Family Therapists in Canada (RMFT) was formed in 2001 to promote the counselling profession in Canada. In 2002, the Council of Canadian Child and Youth Care Associations began meeting to establish Canadian standards for child and youth care workers (Hayduk & Jewell, 2005).

Regulation of professional counselling is currently being pursued in Ontario, British Columbia, New Brunswick, and Prince Edward Island, and some regulation of counselling occurred in Nova Scotia in 2009 with the establishment of the Nova Scotia College of Counselling Therapists (CCPA, 2009b). Regulation of counselling is the current hot topic in counselling across Canada. As remains true in any profession, it is necessary to ensure credibility.

Psychological practice is regulated at the provincial or territorial level, and consequently there are some differences between regions in Canada. Since the turn of the millennium, provincial psychologists' regulatory bodies have established a Mutual Recognition Agreement, allowing psychologists in one jurisdiction to become registered more easily in another (Canadian Psychological Association, 2004). This agreement has also created Canadian standards to facilitate this movement from one jurisdiction to another; over time, this will likely result in fewer differences between Canadian jurisdictional registration requirements.

In the United States, counselling formally celebrated its 50th anniversary as a profession under the umbrella of the American Counseling Association in 2002. However, accompanying the celebration was a realization that counselling is ever changing and that emphases of certain topics, issues, and concerns at the beginning of the 21st century would most likely change with the needs of clients and society. The changing roles of men and women, innovations in media and technology, poverty, homelessness, trauma, loneliness, and aging, among other topics, captured counselling's attention as the new century began (Lee & Walz, 1998; Webber, Bass & Yep, 2005). Among the most pressing topics were dealing with violence, trauma, and crises; managed care; wellness; social justice; technology; leadership; and identity.

Dealing with Violence, Trauma, and Crises

Concerns about conflict and safety from both a prevention and treatment standpoint emerged in the United States in the 1990s in a rash of school shootings and the Oklahoma City bombing, where a number of innocent people were killed (Daniels, 2002). School shootings are rare in Canada, but they are equally as violent as in the United States. The most famous occurred in Montreal on December 6, 1989. Armed with a semi-automatic rifle and a hunting knife, 25-year old Marc Lépine went on a 20-minute rampage. He targeted women, uttering that he was fighting feminism. By the end of it, 28 people had been shot before he killed himself, with 14 women dead, 10 others injured, and 4 men who were likely shot unintentionally (Tonso, 2009). This event has become known as the École Polytechnique Massacre, and December 6 is now recognized as a day of mourning in many post-secondary schools in Canada. Following the shooting, several of the witnesses and those injured experienced post-traumatic stress disorder. A few even took their own lives (Parent & Cousineau, 2003).

Is Canada as violent a country as the United States? There was a consecutive decline in the numbers of reported crimes in Canada between 2003 and 2008. Approximately one in five crimes reported to police is violent, and although homicides (which only constitute 1% of violent crimes) went up 2 percent between 2007 and 2008, the homicide rate has actually been quite stable over the past decade. The youth (ages 12 to 17) crime rate decreased by 3 percent between 2007 and 2008, but overall it, too, has been relatively stable since 2000 (Statistics Canada, 2009).

Researchers have been interested in bullying for about 25 years, but it is only now recognized as a global problem (Konishi et al., 2009). The World Health Organization recently reported that Canada ranks 26th and 27th in a survey of 35 countries on measures of bullying and victimization, respectively (Craig & Peplar, 2007); in other words, we outrank most countries in prevalence of bullying. In a study published in 1992 of 4000 Canadian high school students, 45 percent of the teens surveyed knew someone who had been physically assaulted at school (Carter & Lewin, 1999). Another study, using data from the Canadian National Longitudinal Survey of Children and Youth 1996 to 2001, found that 46 percent of the children experienced harassment and victimization at school and 40 percent outside of school (Abada, Hou, & Ram, 2008).

Finally, researchers are aware that "bullying is wrong and hurtful" (Pepler, Craig, Jiang, & Connolly, 2008, p. 113; Ryan & David, 2009). Children who are bullied are more likely to have achievement problems (Beran, Hughes, & Lupart, 2008) and they report poorer health status and more depression (Abada et al., 2008). Bullying is most evident with children between Grades 5 and 7 (Konishi et al., 2009).

In the area of dealing with trauma, a renewed emphasis has been focused in recent years on the treatment of stress, acute stress disorder (ASD), and post-traumatic stress disorder (PTSD) (Jordan, 2002; Marotta, 2000; Taylor & Baker, 2007). Both ASD and PTSD develop as a result of being exposed to a traumatic event involving actual or threatened injury (American Psychiatric Association, 1994). Events include such things as physical abuse, natural disasters, accidents, or incidents connected with wars. Threats are associated with intense fear, helplessness, or horror. ASD is more transient; people develop symptoms within about four weeks of a situation and resolve them within about another four weeks (Jordan, 2002). However, PTSD differs in that; except in cases of delayed onset, symptoms occur within about a month of an incident, and they may last for months or years if not treated. People who develop PTSD may display a number of symptoms including re-experiencing the traumatic event again through flashbacks, avoidance of trauma-related activities, and emotional numbing, as well as other disorders such as substance abuse, obsessive-compulsive disorders, and panic disorders.

Counsellors who are employed in the area of working with ASD or PTSD clients need specialized training to help these individuals. Crises often last in people's minds long after the events that produced them. Crisis counselling as well as long-term counselling services are often needed, especially with individuals who have PTSD. For example, psychosocial and moral development may be arrested in PTSD war veterans, making it more difficult for them to have successful relationships and to cope by themselves "with the trauma, confusion, emotion, brutality, and fear associated with combat" (Taylor & Baker, 2007, p. 368). "It is only by recognizing and treatment of PTSD that trauma victims can hope to move past the impact of trauma and lead healthy lives" (Grosse, 2002, p. 25).

The terrorist attack of 9/11 forever changed our world. One of the most important developments in the counselling field in the United States was the beginning of an active and new emphasis in counselling on preparing and responding to trauma and tragedies such as those associated with Hurricane Katrina, the Iraq War, and the Virginia Tech shootings (Walz & Kirkman, 2002; Webber et al, 2005). Within this new emphasis is a practical focus on activities such as developing crisis plans and strategies for working with different age groups, from young children to the elderly, in order to provide psychological first aid and facilitate the grieving and healing process.

Promoting Wellness

In recent years, the idea of promoting wellness within the counselling profession has grown (Lawson, Venart, Hazler, & Kottler, 2007; Myers & Sweeney, 2005). Wellness involves many aspects of life, including the physical, intellectual, social, psychological, emotional, and environmental facets. Myers, Sweeney, and Witmer (2000) define wellness as a way of life oriented toward optimal health and well-being in which body, mind, and spirit are integrated by the individual to live life more fully within the human and natural community. "Ideally, it is the optimum state of health and well-being that each individual is capable of achieving" (p. 252).

A model for promoting wellness was developed by Myers et al. (2000). It revolves around five life tasks: spirituality, self-direction, work and leisure, friendship, and love. Some of these tasks, such as self-direction, are further subdivided into a number of subtasks, such as sense of worth, sense of control, problem solving and creativity, sense of humour, and self-care. The premise of this model is that healthy functioning occurs on a developmental continuum, and healthy behaviours at one point in life affect subsequent development and functioning as well.

One of the tenets of counselling psychology since its inception has been its commitment to personal growth and mental wellness. Calling this ideology "positive psychology" is more recent, however (Beatch et al., 2009), and the concept is now mainstream, meaning that psychologists in other disciplines are now aware that applied psychology has taken a pathology approach for too long. Renowned researchers like Albert Bandura (famous for his work with social learning theory and self-efficacy) and Martin Seligman (who studied learned helplessness years ago) seem to have become less deterministic in their later years and now embrace the study of positive psychology. The message of positive psychology is "to remind our field that psychology is not just the study of pathology, weakness, and damage; it is also the study of strength and virtue" (Seligman & Czikszentmihalyi, 2000, p. 7).

Concern for Social Justice and Promotion of Diversity

Early pioneers in what evolved to be counselling were interested in the welfare of people in society. Therefore, it is not surprising that counsellors today are drawn to social justice causes. Social justice "reflects a fundamental valuing of fairness and equity in resources, rights, and treatment for marginalized individuals and groups of people who do not share the power in society because of their immigration, racial, ethic, age, socioeconomic, religious heritage, physical abilities, or sexual orientation status groups" (Constantine, Hage, Kindaichi, & Bryant, 2007, p. 24). Major elements of a social justice approach include "helping clients identify and challenge environmental limits to their success," "challenging systematic forms of oppression through counsellor social action," and "liberating clients from oppressive social practices" (Astramovich & Harris, 2007, p. 271).

Among the active involvement counsellors are taking in social justice causes now are advocacy (for the profession and for clients), along with community outreach and public policy-making (Constantine et al., 2007). Advocacy involves "helping clients challenge institutional and social barriers that impede academic, career, or personal-social development" (Lee, 1998, pp. 8–9). The purpose is to "increase a client's sense of personal power and to foster sociopolitical changes that reflect greater responsiveness to the client's personal needs" (Kiselica & Robinson, 2001, p. 387).

To be an effective advocate, counsellors need to have "the capacity for commitment and an appreciation of human suffering; nonverbal and verbal communications skills; the ability to maintain a multisystems perspective"; individual, group, and organizational intervention skills; "knowledge and use of the media, technology, and the Internet; and assessment and research skills" (p. 391). Advocates must also be socially smart, knowing themselves, others, and the systems around them. Likewise, they must know when to be diplomatic as well as confrontational. They must have a knowledge and passion for the cause or causes they advocate for and be willing to be flexible and to compromise to obtain realistic goals.

Promotion of diversity is a fundamental value of counselling psychology in Canada and is reflected in graduate training programs throughout the country (Beatch et al., 2009). A current example of promoting diversity is the work of some individuals within the Sexual Orientation and Gender Identity Issues section of CPA, who are preparing fact sheets and a policy statement regarding how individuals with varying degrees of gender dysphoria ought to be treated in society. These documents will soon be brought forward to CPA's Board of Directors for ratification.

Greater Emphasis on the Use of Technology

Technology use has grown rapidly in counselling (e.g., Shaw & Shaw, 2006). What once was considered promising has now become reality, and technology "is having a profound impact on almost every aspect of life, including education, business, science, religion, government, medicine, and agriculture" (Hohenshil, 2000, p. 365). For example, technology, particularly the internet, is now a major tool for career planning (Harris-Bowlsbey, Dikel, & Sampson, 2002).

Initially, technology was used in counselling to facilitate record keeping, to manipulate data, and to do word processing. More attention is now being placed on factors affecting technology and client interaction, especially on the internet and on telephones

(Reese, Conoley, & Brossart, 2006). "The number of network-based computer applications in counseling has been increasing rapidly" (Sampson, Kolodinsky, & Greeno, 1997, p. 203). Listservs and bulletin board systems (BBSs) have become especially popular for posting messages and encouraging dialogue between counsellors.

E-mail is also used in counsellor-to-counsellor interactions as well as counsellor-to-client conversations. Websites are maintained by counselling organizations, counsellor education programs, and individual counsellors (Pachis, Rettman, & Gotthoffer, 2001). There are even "online" professional counselling journals, the first being the *Journal of Technology in Counseling* (Layne & Hohenshil, 2005; http://jtc.colstate.edu/WhatisJTC. htm). The similarities between working with certain aspects of technology (e.g., computers or telephones) and working with clients are notable (e.g., establishing a relationship, learning a client's language, learning a client's thought process, setting goals, and taking steps to achieve them). However, the practice is fraught with ethical and legal risks, such as (a) the issue of confidentiality, (b) how to handle emergency situations, (c) the lack of nonverbal information, (d) the danger of offering online services over provincial judicial lines, (e) the lack of outcome research on the effectiveness of online counselling services, (f) technology failures, and (g) the difficulties of establishing rapport with a client who is not visually seen (Pollock, 2006; Shaw & Shaw, 2006).

A number of counsellors and counselling-related organizations do offer services across the internet (such as suicide prevention) (Befrienders International, 2007) and through the telephone (such as adolescent smokers cessation help) (Tedeschi, Zhu, Anderson, Cummins, & Ribner, 2005). This trend is understandable given the fact that people are pressed for time, phone services are readily available, and internet use is ubiquitous.

Psychologists can use web technology to enhance the services they offer if they follow guidelines adopted by the Canadian Psychological Association on internet counselling (see Appendix B). Clients who may be especially well served through the use of online counselling are those who (a) are geographically isolated, (b) are physically disabled, (c) would ordinarily not seek counselling, and (d) are more prone to writing than speaking (Shaw & Shaw, 2006).

Competencies for counsellors continue to be developed in regard to the use of technology in therapy. These competencies include skills they should master, such as being able to use word processing programs, audiovisual equipment, e-mail, the internet, Listservs, and CD-ROM databases. Although the internet, the telephone, and other technologies will never fully replace face-to-face counselling, clearly they are here to stay. They offer a unique experience with both benefits and limitations (Haberstroh, Duffey, Evans, Gee, & Trepal, 2007). Streaming video and wireless connectivity are two of the more cutting-edge technologies that will affect how counsellors will function in the future (Layne & Hohenshil, 2005). Counsellors "would be wise to educate themselves on the ethical and technical issues emerging in this new arena" (Pollock, 2006, p. 69).

Leadership

With the rapid changes in society and counselling, there is an increased need for counsellors to develop leadership and planning skills. By so doing, they become a more positive and potent force in society. Although many counselling skills can be readily applied to effective leadership, such as empathy, group processing, and goal setting, other "specific leadership practices, such as completing performance reviews, communicating compensation philosophies and practices, addressing colleagues' performance problems, and being accountable for team camaraderie and productivity, are not taught in traditional counseling programs" (Curtis & Sherlock, 2006, p. 121). Therefore counsellors are particularly challenged in agencies and schools to move beyond clinical supervision and into managerial leadership roles. In such roles they influence "a group of individuals to achieve a goal" (p. 120). Managerial leadership is an important topic in counselling because there is considerable evidence that "it makes a difference in an organization's performance" (p. 121).

In the United States, the ACA is engaged in leadership activities through working nationally and regionally to provide new leaders training and legislative training for counsellors. Divisions within the ACA also focus on leadership development and legislative training. Chi Sigma Iota (Counseling Academic and Professional Honor Society International) is especially strong in providing leadership training and services to counsellors through workshops and seminars.

One area of leadership, strategic planning, involves envisioning the future and making preparations to meet anticipated needs. Similar to the counselling skill of leading, it is usually accomplished in a group and involves hard data as well as anticipations and expectations (C. Kormanski, personal interview, June 20, 1994). In 2005, the ACA and 28 other counselling groups initiated the 20/20 Futures of Counseling initiative in order to map the future of the profession for the year 2020. By the fall of 2007, the group had agreed on over 50 areas that counsellors had in common that would help propel individual counsellors and the profession into the future. The skill of strategic planning is greatly needed in leading and promoting the profession of counselling.

Identity

Since 1952, most counsellors in the United States and a number in other countries have held membership in ACA. The composition of ACA has been mixed, "like a ball of multicolored yarn," and sometimes within ACA there has been an emphasis on the specialties of counselling as opposed to the overall profession (Bradley & Cox, 2001, p. 39). Other professions, such as medicine, have overcome the divisiveness inherent in a profession where there is more than one professional track that practitioners can follow. ACA has not been as fortunate.

In Canada, most counsellors and psychologists consider belonging to either the Canadian Psychological Association or the Canadian Counselling and Psychotherapy

Association. Neither is required, however, in order to practise in their respective jurisdictions. Again, psychologists and social workers in Canada are regulated through their jurisdictional bodies, and professional counsellors are regulated in some jurisdictions but not in others.

SUMMARY AND CONCLUSION

Counselling is a distinct profession. It is concerned with wellness, development, and situational difficulties as well as with helping dysfunctional persons. It is based on principles and a definition that has evolved over the years. It contains within it a number of specialties. An examination of the history of counselling shows that the profession has an interdisciplinary base. In the United States, it began with the almost simultaneous concern and activity of Frank Parsons, Jesse B. Davis, and Clifford Beers to provide, reform, and improve services in vocational guidance, character development of school children, and mental health treatment.

Canada has become a world leader, especially in the area of promoting human rights. Clifford Beers was an influential man, and after he met Dr. Clarence Hincks, the two of them founded what is now known as the Canadian Mental Health Association. The Canadian Association of Social Workers formed in 1926, followed by the Canadian Psychological Association in 1939, and then what is now known as the Canadian Counselling and Psychotherapy Association in 1965.

Counselling became interlinked early in its history with psychometrics, psychology, anthropology, ethics, law, philosophy, and sociology. In addition to the development of theory and the generation of practical ways of working with people, important events in the development of counselling include the involvement of the government in counselling during and after World War I, the Great Depression, and World War II.

Ideas from innovators such as Frank Parsons, E. G. Williamson, Carl Rogers, Gilbert Wrenn, Donald Super, Leona Tyler, Thomas J. Sweeney, Myrne Nevison, E. A. Bott, George Humphreys, and Roy Liddy have shaped the development of the profession and broadened its horizon. The emergence and growth of the Canadian and American Counselling Associations and the Canadian and American Psychological Associations have been major factors in the growth of the counselling profession. Challenges for the profession in the 21st century include dealing with violence, trauma, and crises; promoting wellness; using technology wisely and effectively; providing leadership; and working on establishing a stronger identity for the profession. Canadian counsellors also continue to work toward regulation across the provinces and territories.

Your Personal Reflections

1. What do you know about your family history that has helped you in your life? Why do you find this type of information valuable? What parallels do you see between knowing your family history and the history of counselling?

2. What special talents do you have? How did they develop from your overall definition of yourself as a person? How do you see your personal circumstances paralleling the general definition of counselling and counselling specialties?

3. Much of the growth of counselling in the 1950s came as a reaction to external events or pressures. What other positive outcomes have you seen emerge from crises, such as natural or person-initiated disasters? For example, the state of New York passed legislation licensing counsellors as mental health professionals after September 11, 2001.

4. What's in a name? Think of your own name and how it has influenced your relationships. If you have changed your name, write down some of the impacts of that change. What might be some of the ramifications of a counselling organization changing its name?

Classroom Activities

1. How do you distinguish between counselling, guidance, and psychotherapy? How do you think the public perceives the similarities and differences in these three ways of helping? Discuss your ideas with your classmates.

2. What decade do you consider the most important for the development of counselling? Is there a decade you consider least important? Be sure to give reasons for your position.

3. What do you know about counselling now that you have read this chapter? Describe how it is like and unlike what you expected. What did you discover about the profession? Explain your answer fully. Investigate in more detail the life and influence of a historical or contemporary figure in counselling. You may choose one of the innovators mentioned in this chapter or a person suggested by your instructor. Share your information with the class.

4. What do you consider pressing future issues for the profession of counselling? How do you think counsellors should address these concerns? See whether there is a consensus of topics and ways to address them within your class.

5. Break into dyads before sharing some aspect of your personal history with each other. Then ask the question of each other, "Why is history important in understanding you?" Next, ask the question, "Why is it important to understand the history of the counselling profession?"

Chapter 2
Personal and Professional Aspects of Counselling

PRACTICE REFLECTION

Several years ago I saw a client who himself was a fellow counsellor. Cliff was 45 years old and was a registered social worker. He had found that over the previous few weeks, he had been losing "steam," as he called it. Increasingly, Cliff was sliding into a state of burnout and couldn't understand why, as he loved his work in the correctional justice system. So I asked him, "What do you do for fun?" With a surprised look in his face, he said, "Well, really nothing—I don't have time for that right now. I started a part-time private practice a year ago and see 10 clients a week or so in the evening. I also work at a residential program for impaired drivers one weekend out of every three. I barely have enough time to see my girlfriend or my friends for that matter."

I looked at Cliff and said, "Do you have any idea what might be causing your problem of losing steam right now?" He sighed. "I guess that isn't too hard to figure out, is it?" "No, it is quite clear—you have allowed your life to get out of balance."

Unfortunately Cliff did not feel able to relinquish any of his work commitments at that time, and after another six weeks, he became completely unable to work. Upon his return to work after a short-term sick leave, he resumed his duties in corrections, but cut his private practice in half and resigned from the impaired driving program. He came to appreciate that no one can be all work and no play.

Counselling is "an altruistic and noble profession." For the most part, "it attracts caring, warm, friendly and sensitive people" (Myrick, 1997, p. 4), yet individuals aspire to become counsellors for many reasons. Some motivators, like the people involved, are healthier than others are, just as some educational programs, theories, and systems of counselling are stronger than others are. It is important that persons who wish to be counsellors examine themselves before committing their lives to the profession. Whether they choose counselling as a career or not, people can be helped by studying their own lives as well as the field of counselling. By doing so they may gain insight into their thoughts, feelings, and actions, learn how to relate better to others, and understand how the counselling process works. They may also develop further their moral reasoning and empathetic abilities.

The effectiveness of a counsellor and of counselling depends on numerous variables, including

- *the personality and background of the counsellor;*
- *the formal education of the counsellor; and*
- *the ability of the counsellor to engage in professional counselling-related activities, such as continuing education, supervision, and advocacy.*

The counsellor and the counselling process have a dynamic effect on others; if it is not beneficial, then it most likely is harmful (Carkhuff, 1969; Ellis, 1984; Mays & Franks, 1980). In this chapter, personal and professional factors that influence the counselling profession are examined.

THE PERSONALITY AND BACKGROUND OF THE COUNSELLOR

A COUNSELLOR'S PERSONALITY IS AT TIMES A CRUCIAL INGREDIENT IN COUNSELLING. Counsellors should possess personal qualities of maturity, empathy, and warmth. They should be altruistic in spirit and not easily upset or frustrated. Unfortunately, such is not always the case and some people aspire to be in the profession of counselling for the wrong reasons.

Negative Motivators for Becoming a Counsellor

Not everyone who wants to be a counsellor or applies to a counsellor education program should enter the field. The reason has to do with the motivation behind the pursuit of the profession and the incongruent personality match between the would-be counsellor and the demands of counselling.

A number of students "attracted to professional counseling . . . appear to have serious personality and adjustment problems" (Witmer & Young, 1996, p. 142). Most are weeded out or decide to pursue other careers before they finish a counsellor preparation program. However, before matriculating into graduate counselling programs, candidates should explore their reasons for doing so. According to Guy (1987), dysfunctional motivators for becoming a counsellor include the following:

- *emotional distress*—individuals who have unresolved personal traumas
- *vicarious coping*—persons who live their lives through others rather than have meaningful lives of their own
- *loneliness and isolation*—individuals who do not have friends and seek them through counselling experiences
- *a desire for power*—people who feel frightened and impotent in their lives and seek to control others
- *a need for love*—individuals who are narcissistic and grandiose and believe that all problems are resolved through the expression of love and tenderness
- *vicarious rebellion*—persons who have unresolved anger and act out their thoughts and feelings through their clients' defiant behaviours

A recent meta-analysis found that the personality of the counsellor accounted for more of the variability in outcome than did the treatment factors themselves (Ahn & Wampold, 2001)! This is probably not that surprising to you. You have known people you have turned to in times of need who were not professional counsellors yet were immensely helpful. If you are one of those people that others turn to, you might well have the "right stuff."

Nonetheless, you do not have to be a near-perfect individual to become an effective counsellor. There are many different kinds of individuals who enter the counselling profession, and the counsellor who is a "good fit" for one particular client might not be a good fit for someone else. Paul (1967) asked the critical question in the sixties: "What treatment, by whom, is most effective for this individual with that specific problem, under which set of circumstances?" (p. 111). Surprisingly, the question has still not been sufficiently answered (Reupart, 2006).

For example, famed Dr. Albert Ellis was known for using profanity in his workshops. He was also frequently abrasive toward his clients. Did his clients improve through rational emotive behaviour therapy (REBT), which he founded? REBT has well established effectiveness (see Chapter 10).

Most people who do eventually become counsellors and remain in the profession have healthy reasons for pursuing the profession, and a number even consider it to be a "calling" (Foster, 1996). Counsellors and counsellors-in-training should always assess themselves in regard to who they are and what they are doing. Such questions may include those that examine their development histories, their best and worst qualities, and personal and professional goals and objectives (Faiver, Eisengart, & Colonna, 1995).

Personal Qualities of an Effective Counsellor

Among the functional and positive factors that motivate individuals to pursue careers in counselling and make them well suited for the profession are the following qualities as delineated by Foster (1996) and Guy (1987). Although this list is not exhaustive, it highlights aspects of a person's personal life that make him or her best suited to function as a counsellor.

- *curiosity and inquisitiveness*—a natural interest in people
- *ability to listen*—the ability to find listening stimulating
- *comfort with conversation*—enjoyment of verbal exchanges
- *empathy and understanding*—the ability to put oneself in another's place, even if that person is totally different from you
- *emotional insightfulness*—comfort dealing with a wide range of feelings, from anger to joy
- *introspection*—the ability to see or feel from within
- *capacity for self-denial*—the ability to set aside personal needs to listen and take care of others' needs first
- *tolerance of intimacy*—the ability to sustain emotional closeness
- *comfort with power*—the acceptance of power with a certain degree of detachment
- *ability to laugh*—the capability of seeing the bittersweet quality of life events and the humour in them

In addition to personal qualities associated with entering the counselling profession, a number of personal characteristics are associated with being an effective counsellor over time (Patterson & Welfel, 2005). They include stability, harmony, constancy, and purposefulness. Overall, the potency of counselling is related to counsellors' personal togetherness (Carkhuff & Berenson, 1967; Gladding, 2002; Kottler, 1993). The personhood or personality of counsellors is as important, if not more crucial in bringing about client change, than their mastery of knowledge, skills, or techniques (McAuliffe & Lovell, 2006; Rogers, 1961). Education cannot change a person's basic characteristics. Effective counsellors are growing as persons and are helping others do the same both personally and globally. In other words, effective counsellors are sensitive to themselves and others. They monitor their own biases, listen, ask for clarification, and explore racial and cultural differences in an open and positive way (Ford, Harris, & Schuerger, 1993).

Related to this sensitive and growth-enhancing quality of effective counsellors is their appropriate use of themselves as instruments in the counselling process (Brammer & MacDonald, 2003; Combs, 1982). Effective counsellors are able to be spontaneous, creative, and empathetic. "There is a certain art to the choice and timing of counseling interventions" (Wilcox-Matthew, Ottens, & Minor, 1997, p. 288). Effective counsellors choose and time their moves intuitively and according to what research has verified works best. It is helpful if counsellors' lives have been tempered by multiple life experiences that have enabled them to realize some of what their clients are going through and to therefore be both aware and appropriate.

The ability to work from a perspective of resolved emotional experience that has sensitized a person to self and others in a helpful way is what Rollo May characterizes as being a wounded healer (May, Remen, Young, & Berland, 1985). It is a paradoxical phenomenon. Individuals who have been hurt and have been able to transcend their pain and gain insight into themselves and the world can be helpful to others who struggle to overcome emotional problems (Miller, Wagner, Britton, & Gridley, 1998). They have been where their clients are now. Thus, "counsellors who have experienced painful life events and have adjusted positively can usually connect and be authentic with clients in distress" (Foster, 1996, p. 21).

Effective counsellors are also people who have successfully integrated scientific knowledge and skills into their lives. That is, they have achieved a balance of interpersonal and technical competence (Cormier & Cormier, 1998). Qualities of effective counsellors over time other than those already mentioned include the following:

- *intellectual competence*—the desire and ability to learn as well as think fast and creatively
- *energy*—the ability to be active in sessions and sustain that activity even when one sees a number of clients in a row
- *flexibility*—the ability to adapt what one does to meet clients' needs
- *support*—the capacity to encourage clients in making their own decisions while helping engender hope
- *goodwill*—the desire to work on behalf of clients in a constructive way that ethically promotes independence
- *self-awareness*—a knowledge of self, including attitudes, values, and feelings and the ability to recognize how and what factors affect oneself

According to Holland (1997), specific personality types are attracted to and work best in certain vocational environments. The environment in which counsellors work well is primarily social and problem oriented. It calls for skill in interpersonal relationships and creativity. The act of creativity requires courage (Cohen, 2000) and involves a selling of new ideas and ways of working that promote intra- as well as interpersonal relations

(Gladding, 2004). The more aligned counsellors' personalities are to their environments, the more effective and satisfied they will be.

In one study, Wiggins and Weslander (1979) found empirical support for Holland's hypothesis. They studied the personality traits and rated the job performance of 320 counsellors in four U.S. states. In general, those counsellors who were rated "highly effective" scored highest on the social (social, service oriented) and artistic (creative, imaginative) scales of the John Holland's Vocational Preference Inventory. Counsellors who were rated "ineffective" generally scored highest on the realistic (concrete, technical) and conventional (organized, practical) scales. Other factors, such as gender, age, and level of education, were not found to be statistically significant in predicting effectiveness. The result of this research and other studies like it affirms that the personality of counsellors is related to their effectiveness in the profession.

Recent studies have demonstrated that Holland's theory is appropriate for people choosing nonprofessional occupations (Miller, Scaggs, & Wells, 2006) and it has been found applicable to ethnically diverse clients as well (Spokane & Cruza-Guet, 2005). Nevertheless, the relationship of persons and environments is complex: Individuals with many different personality types manage to find places within the broad field of counselling and to make significant contributions to the profession.

Case Example: What Would *You* Do?

In one counselling setting, I was asked to job shadow a colleague for the first week of my employment there. This meant sitting in on counselling sessions and observing my colleague's day-to-day routine. A depressed young woman came for a session and after some disclosure on her part, the counsellor asked, "When was the last time you had sex?" After she replied that it had been quite some time, the counsellor looked at her and retorted, "What you need to do is go out and make some man happy." I was completed astounded by his comment and didn't know how to react. He was assigned as my "mentor," and reporting him would have meant both losing his support and likely creating some fear with others that I could not be trusted. I decided not to do anything about it. I later discovered that he was not well regarded by the others at this place.

1. What would you do if you had been in my shoes? Was there any action I could have taken that would not have been perceived in an unfavourable light by other colleagues?

2. What difference would it make if the counsellor had been female? Why?

3. From your reading so far, what qualities of an effective counsellor were not being demonstrated that day?

Maintaining Effectiveness as a Counsellor

Persons who become counsellors experience the same difficulties as everyone else. They must deal with aging, illness, death, marriage, parenting, job changes, divorce, and a host of other common problems. Some of these life events, such as marrying for the first time late in life or experiencing the death of a child, are considered developmentally "off time," or out of sequence, and even tragic (Skovholt & McCarthy, 1988). Other events consist of unintended but fortuitous chance encounters, such as meeting a person with whom one develops a lifelong friendship (Bandura, 1982; Krumboltz & Levin, 2004).

Both traumatic and fortunate experiences are problematic because of the stress they naturally create. A critical issue is how counsellors handle these life events. As Roehlke (1988) points out, Carl Jung's idea of synchronicity, "which [Jung] defined as two simultaneous events that occur coincidentally [and that] result in a meaningful connection," is perhaps the most productive way for counsellors to perceive and deal with unexpected life experiences (p. 133).

Besides finding meaning in potentially problematic areas, other strategies used by counsellors for coping with crisis situations include remaining objective, accepting and confronting situations, asserting their own wishes, participating in a wellness lifestyle, and grieving (Lenhardt, 1997; Myers & Sweeney, 2005; Witmer & Young, 1996). Counsellors who have healthy personal lives and learn both from their mistakes and from their successes are more likely than others to grow therapeutically and to be able to concentrate fully and sensitively on clients' problems. Therefore, counsellors and those who wish to enter the profession need to adapt to losses as well as gains and to remain relatively free from destructive triangling patterns with persons, especially parents, in their families of origin. Such a stance enables them to foster and maintain intimate yet autonomous relationships in the present as desired (Gaushell & Lawson, 1994).

Other ways effective counsellors maintain their health and well-being include taking preventive measures to avoid problematic behaviours, such as burnout (Grosch & Olsen, 1994). *Burnout* is the state of becoming emotionally or physically drained to the point that one cannot perform functions meaningfully. In a burnout state, counsellors develop a negative self-concept, a negative job attitude, and even loss of concern, compassion, and feeling for others (Lambie, 2007). Burnout is the single most common personal consequence of working as a counsellor. It is estimated that approximately 39 percent of school and community counsellors experience a high to moderate amount of burnout during their careers (Emerson & Markos, 1996; Lambie, 2007).

To avoid burnout, counsellors need to modify the environmental as well as the individual and interpersonal factors associated with it (Wilkerson & Bellini, 2006). For example, counsellors need to step out of their professional roles and develop interests outside counselling. They must avoid taking their work home, either mentally or physically. They also must take responsibility for rejuvenating themselves through such small but significant steps as refurbishing their offices every few years; purging, condensing, and creating new files; evaluating new materials; and contributing to the counselling profession through writing or presenting material with which they are comfortable (McCormick, 1998). Counsellors can also avoid or treat burnout by

- associating with healthy individuals
- working with committed colleagues and organizations that have a sense of mission

- being reasonably committed to a theory of counselling

- using stress-reduction exercises

- modifying environmental stressors

- engaging in self-assessment (i.e., identifying stressors and relaxers)

- periodically examining and clarifying counselling roles, expectations, and beliefs (i.e., working smarter, not necessarily longer)

- obtaining personal therapy

- setting aside free and private time (i.e., balancing one's lifestyle)

- maintaining an attitude of detached concern when working with clients

- retaining an attitude of hope

Despite such attempts, there may still be times when a counsellor becomes overwhelmed and the usual strategies of self-care are unsuccessful. Imagine a psychologist working in downtown Manhattan on 9/11. After that, the psychologist moves to a "safer" place, let's say New Orleans, only to soon be in the middle of hurricane Katrina—from devastation to devastation. One such unlucky psychologist was Lynn Schechter (2008). Even when writing about her experience for publication, she continued to experience unresolved anger and painful emotions and memories at the anniversaries of these events. What has been most helpful to her? Having a network of friends and colleagues proved invaluable. A recent article by Barlow and Phelan (2007) also speaks to the importance of peer collaboration as a form of self-care. Embracing spirituality can also have beneficial effects (Collings, 2005).

In summing up previous research about the personalities, qualities, and interests of counsellors, Auvenshine and Noffsinger (1984) concluded, "Effective counsellors must be emotionally mature, stable, and objective. They must have self-awareness and be secure in that awareness, incorporating their own strengths and weaknesses realistically" (p. 151).

PROFESSIONAL ASPECTS OF COUNSELLING
Levels of Helping

There are three levels of helping relationships: nonprofessional, paraprofessional, and professional. To practise at a certain level requires that helpers acquire the skills necessary for the task (see Figure 2.1).

The first level of helping involves *nonprofessional helpers*. These helpers may be friends, colleagues, untrained volunteers, or supervisors who try to assist those in need in whatever ways they can. Nonprofessional helpers possess varying degrees of wisdom and skill. No specific educational requirements are involved, and the level of helping varies greatly among people in this group.

A second and higher level of helping is encompassed in the field known as *generalist human services workers* (paraprofessionals). These individuals are usually human

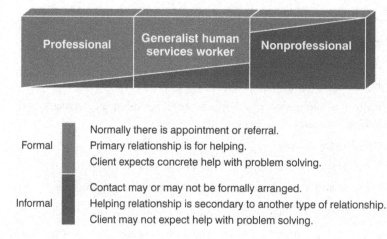

| Formal | Normally there is appointment or referral.
Primary relationship is for helping.
Client expects concrete help with problem solving. |
| Informal | Contact may or may not be formally arranged.
Helping relationship is secondary to another type of relationship.
Client may not expect help with problem solving. |

Figure 2.1 Kinds of helping relationships

Source: From *Effective Helping: Interviewing and Counseling Techniques*, 5th edition by Barbara R. Okun. © 1997. Reprinted with permission of Wadsworth, a division of Thomson Learning: **www**.thomsonrights. com. Fax 800-730-2215.

services workers who have received some formal training in human relations skills but work as part of a team rather than as individuals. People at this level often work as mental health technicians, child care workers, probation personnel, and youth counsellors. When properly trained and supervised, generalist human services workers such as residence hall assistants can have a major impact on facilitating positive relationships that promote mental health throughout a social environment (Waldo, 1989).

Finally, there are *professional helpers*. These persons are educated to provide assistance on both a preventive and a remedial level. People in this group include counsellors, psychologists, psychiatrists, social workers, psychiatric nurses, and marriage and family therapists. Workers at this level have a specialized advanced degree and have had supervised internships to help them prepare to deal with a variety of situations.

In regard to the education of helpers on the last two levels, Robinson and Kinnier (1988) have found that self-instructional and traditional classroom training are equally effective at teaching skills.

Professional Helping Specialties

Each helping profession has its own educational and practice requirements. Counsellors need to know the educational backgrounds of other professions in order to use their services, to communicate with them in an informed manner, and to collaborate with them on matters of mutual concern. Although many counsellors are themselves psychologists or social workers, they will frequently interact with other psychologists, social workers, and psychiatrists in performing their duties.

Psychiatrists earn a medical degree (MD) and complete a residency in psychiatry. They are specialists in working with people who have major psychological disorders. They are schooled in the biomedical model, "which focuses on the physical processes thought to underlay mental and emotional disorders" (MacCluskie & Ingersoll, 2001, p. 8). Frequently, they prescribe medications and then evaluate the results, especially in agencies such as mental health clinics. Generally, psychiatrists take almost an exclusive biopsychological approach in treatment, and as a group they are not heavily engaged in counselling activities. They are regulated through provincial and territorial colleges of physicians and surgeons. Their clients are called patients.

Psychologists in Canada are regulated within the province or territory where they practise, which means that credentials and requirements for registration differ across the country. Although the Canadian Psychological Association recommends a doctoral degree for independent practice, several provinces allow psychologists to register (and consequently practise independently) with a master's degree (e.g., Alberta, Sasksatchewan, Newfoundland and Labrador, Nova Scotia). Some provinces (e.g., British Columbia) allow doctoral registrants to practise independently as psychologists, while master's registrants can practise independently as psychological associates (Beatch et al., 2009).

There are different kinds of doctoral degrees that psychologists may hold, including a doctor of philosophy (PhD), a doctor of education (EdD), or a doctor of psychology (PsyD). Their coursework and internships may be concentrated in clinical, counselling, or school-related areas. Graduates of counselling psychology programs follow a curriculum that includes courses in scientific and professional ethics and standards, counselling theory, counselling interventions, multicultural aspects of counselling, research design and methodology, qualitative or qualitative data analysis, psychological assessment, and other courses that are sometimes completed at the undergraduate level (e.g., biological bases of behaviour, cognitive-affective bases of behaviour, social bases of behaviour, individual behaviour). Graduates have also completed practicums during their training and had an internship before they can become licensed to practise independently.

Often applicants, students, the general public, and even practitioners themselves are confused by the differences and similarities between professional counselling, counselling psychology, and clinical psychology. Tables 4 and 5 in Beatch et al. (2009) are excellent in showing the differences between the three disciplines (these are contained in the *Note Supplement*).

Social workers in Canada are also regulated within the province or territory where they practise. You need a bachelor's degree in social work (BSW) for registration in all provinces (except Alberta) and the Northwest Territories. Saskatchewan usually requires a bachelor's degree (Service Canada, 2007b). Earning a master's degree (MSW) is often advisable, and this generally takes one additional year for those with a BSW or two years for those with their degree in another discipline (Canadian Institute for Health Information, 2006b). There is also advanced training at the doctoral level.

Regardless of their educational background, social workers at all levels have completed one or more practicums in social agency settings. Social workers vary in how they function. Some administer government programs for the underprivileged and disenfranchised. Others engage in counselling activities. "Social work differentiates itself from counselling, psychology, and psychiatry in that its mission includes mandates to negotiate social systems and advocate for change, to understand clients' habitats (physical and social settings within cultural contexts) and niches (statuses and roles in community) and to provide social services" (MacCluskie & Ingersoll, 2001, p. 13).

EDUCATION AND CREDENTIALING

Few people, if any, have the ability to work effectively as counsellors without formal education in human development and counselling (Kurpius, 1986). The level of education needed is directly related to the intensity, expertise, and emphasis of work in which one engages.

Professional Counsellors

Professional counsellors have varying credentials in Canada, and as noted in Chapter 1, regulation of the word *counsellor* is the current hot topic in the field. Most professional counsellors in Canada are either social workers or counselling psychologists and are consequently regulated through their professional associations. Practicums and internships may be focused on school counselling, community/agency counselling, mental health counselling, career counselling, gerontological counselling, addiction counselling, or marriage and family counselling.

While American counsellors are certified by the National Board of Certified Counselors (NBCC) as National Certified Counselors (NCC), some Canadian professional counsellors without registration as social workers or psychologists voluntarily become Canadian Certified Counsellors (CCC) through the Canadian Counselling and Psychotherapy Association (Beatch et al., 2009). This is not, however, a legislative requirement, as is the case with psychologists and registered social workers.

The Canadian Counselling and Psychotherapy Association (CCPA) accredits master's programs in Canada that are counselling-related. Such accreditation, however, is not currently required of counselling schools in Canada.

Although accreditation standards change periodically, the following broad standards must be met for accreditation by CCPA (Canadian Counselling and Psychotherapy Association, 2003):

- The program must require a minimum of 48 semester hours of all students, whether full-time or part-time.

- The following core competencies must be met: (a) counselling as a profession; (b) ethical and legal issues in counselling; (c) counselling and consultative processes; (d) group counselling; (e) human development and learning; (f) diversity; (g) lifestyle and career development; (h) assessment processes; (i) research methods; and (j) program evaluation.

- Students must complete both an initial 100-hour practicum and a 400-hour practicum.
- Students' progress through the program is systematically reviewed.
- Three full-time faculty members must be assigned to the academic unit in counsellor education.

Counselling Psychology

Accreditation is also available to doctoral programs in clinical, counselling, and neuro-psychology through the Canadian Psychological Association (CPA). Currently, there are four CPA-accredited doctoral programs in counselling psychology: the University of Alberta, the University of British Columbia, McGill University, and the Ontario Institute for Studies in Education (part of the University of Toronto) (Beatch et al., 2009). Requirements for CPA accreditation can be found at www.cpa.ca/accreditation. Applied psychology graduates from a CPA-accredited doctoral program have an advantage over graduates from non-accredited programs in (a) meeting the educational requirements for psychologist licensure and certification, and (b) obtaining employment as a psychologist, whether in practice or in academia.

Social Work

Social work schools (both graduate and undergraduate programs) in Canada can become accredited voluntarily through the Canadian Association for Social Work Education (CASWE), and its list of accredited schools would suggest that most have availed them-selves of this opportunity (Canadian Association for Social Work Education, 2009). Details concerning the accreditation requirements and procedures can be found at www.caswe-acfts.ca/en/Board_of_Accreditation_33.html.

The Special Case of Québec

Due to the linguistic diversity inherent in Canada and the fact that most Canadians (except in New Brunswick and Québec) are not bilingual in Canada's two official lan-guages, counselling developments in Francophone Canada are different from those in Anglophone Canada (Beatch et al., 2009). The counselling literature in English does not generally get read by individuals who speak only French, and vice versa.

Interestingly, there is no French translation for *counselling psychology*. In Québec, you are either a *psychologue* or *conseillers d'orientation* (guidance counsellor), and each profession is regulated by different bodies. As a result, the evolution of counselling psy-chology in Québec is at "a premature stage" (Beatch et al., 2009, p. 44), despite the accreditation of McGill University's counselling psychology program. Many students and practitioners in Québec have limited awareness of counselling psychology as a field (Beatch et al., 2009).

ATTRIBUTION AND SYSTEMATIC FRAMEWORK OF THE COUNSELLOR

Attribution and the systematic framework of counsellors make a difference in what counsellors do and how effectively they do it. Attribution is what the counsellor attributes the cause of a client's problem to (e.g., an external circumstance or an internal personality flaw). A system is a unified and organized set of ideas, principles, and behaviours. Systems associated with counselling are concerned with how the counsellor approaches clients and are interrelated to attributes and theories. Two systems, one based on developmental issues and one based on the diagnosis of disorders, will be examined here; it is from these two perspectives (and the places in between) that counsellors work.

Attributes

Both counsellors and clients enter a relationship with some assumptions about what may have caused a problem. Often these personal perceptions are far apart. However, "diagnostic decisions, symptom recognition, and predictions concerning treatment response and outcome can be [and often are] influenced by counselors' explanations for the cause [or causes] of clients' presenting problems" (Kernes & McWhirter, 2001, p. 304). For example, if clients are seen as being responsible for their problems, such as bad decision making, they may be blamed, whereas if the cause of a problem is viewed as beyond their control, such as the trauma of an unexpected death, they may be treated sympathetically.

There are four main attribution models that counsellors use on either a conscious or unconscious level (Kernes & McWhirter, 2001), as follows:

1. *Medical model.* "In this model, clients are not held responsible for either the cause of their problem or its solution" (p. 305). Counsellors who adopt this model act basically as experts and provide the necessary services for change. Although clients are not blamed, they may become dependent.

2. *Moral model.* This model is best typified by the self-help movement and is basically the opposite of the medical model. "Clients are seen as responsible for both causing and solving their problems" (p. 305). Counsellors are viewed primarily as coaches or motivators. The drawback to this model is that those who may be victims of circumstances may be held responsible for their own victimization.

3. *Compensatory model.* In the compensatory model, clients are held "responsible only for solving their problems but not for causing them" (p. 304). Essentially, clients are viewed as "suffering from the failure of their social environments to meet their needs" (p. 304). Therefore, counsellors and clients form a partnership to overcome

problems, with the counsellor taking a subordinate role and acting as a teacher who provides education, skills, and opportunities for clients. The drawback to this model is that clients may "feel undue pressure at having to continually solve problems they did not create" (p. 304).

4. *Enlightenment model.* This model holds "clients responsible for causing their problems but not for solving them" (p. 304). Clients are seen as "guilty individuals whose lives are out of control" (p. 304). They need enlightenment into the nature of their problems and ways of resolving these problems that the counsellor can provide. Whereas clients may feel relief in such an approach, the disadvantage in this model is that they may become dependent on the counsellor, who acts in the role of an authority figure, or they may structure their lives around external sources of authority after they have completed counselling.

Systems of Counselling

Effective counsellors adhere to certain systems and theories of counselling; indeed, the strength of counselling ultimately depends on a continuation of that process. That counselling is not governed by one dominant system approach is hardly surprising considering its historical development. Counselling started like a person who mounted a horse and rode off in all directions—that is, with no focus or planned direction (Ungersma, 1961).

As far back as the late 1940s, professionals noticed the lack of a system for counselling. Robert Mathewson (1949) observed that counselling was in "a search for a system . . . to win free from inadequate frames borrowed from traditional philosophy and education, from psychology, from political formulations underlying democratic government, from the concepts of physical science, etc." (p. 73).

Until the late 1940s, counselling used a variety of systems. Because the profession was without an organizational base, different factions defined what they did according to the system that suited them best. Competition among points of view, especially those connected with theories, was often spirited. For example, E. G. Williamson and Carl Rogers debated the merits of their approaches with passion. Some counsellors recognized the need for a unifying systematic approach to their discipline, but the unplanned growth of the profession proved an obstacle. However, by the 1990s, several systems of counselling had emerged, the two most dominant being the developmental/wellness approach and the medical/pathological approach.

The Developmental/Wellness Approach The developmental/wellness perspective to counselling is based on stages, outlined by various personality theorists, that people go through as a normal part of human growth. Counselling from this perspective is based on whether a problem a client is having is based on a developmental task of life. Behaviours that are appropriate at one stage of life may not be seen as healthy at another stage of life. Allen Ivey (1990) was not the first to suggest that counselling systems be based on a developmental perspective, but his integration of developmental growth with counselling strategies stands out as one of the most unique expressions of this approach. Basically, Ivey suggests applying Piagetian concepts of cognitive levels (i.e., sensorimotor, concrete, formal, and postformal) to clinical interviews with adults and children. If clients do not initially recognize their feelings, counsellors will work from a sensorimotor level to bring out emotions. In a similar way, clients who are interested in planning strategies for change will be helped using a formal pattern of thought. *Developmental counselling and therapy (DCT)* "specifically addresses the sequence and process of development as it occurs in the natural language of the interview" (Ivey & Ivey, 1990, p. 299).

Wellness goes even further than development in emphasizing the positive nature and health of human beings (Myers & Sweeney, 2005). "Counselors have historically been in the business of helping their clients identify their strengths and build on their strengths" (Rak & Patterson, 1996, p. 368). In this perspective, individuals are seen as having the resources to solve their own problems in a practical, immediate way. "Problems are not evidence of an underlying pathology" (Mostert, Johnson, & Mostert, 1997, p. 21). Indeed, as Rak and Patterson (1996) point out, even most at-risk children show resilience and become coping adults.

An example of a counselling approach based on the wellness model is *solution-focused theory. Stress inoculation training (SIT)* (Meichenbaum, 1993), a proactive, psychoeducational intervention that can be used in schools and with adults, is another example of a present and future wellness emphasis approach (Israelashvili, 1998). In this model individuals are helped to understand their problematic situations, to acquire skills for coping with them, and to apply this knowledge to present and even future events through the use of imagery or simulated rehearsal.

A cornerstone of the developmental/wellness approach is an emphasis on prevention and education (Kleist & White, 1997). Counsellors and clients function best when they are informed about the mental, physical, and social spheres of human life. Through such a process they recognize how they can focus on avoiding or minimizing disruptive forces that are either internal or external in nature.

The Medical/Pathological Model In contrast to the developmental/wellness view of counselling, the *medical/pathological model* of human nature is represented by those who base treatment plans in accordance with the *Diagnostic and Statistical Manual of Mental Disorders (DSM)* (American Psychiatric Association, 2000). The DSM is compatible with the *International Classification of Diseases* manual (ICD-10), published by the World Health Organization, in codifying psychiatric disorders. The fourth edition text revision of the DSM (DSM-IV-TR) contains 297 different clinical diagnoses (as opposed to 106 in the initial edition of this manual published in 1952). Besides being thicker, it is culturally more sensitive than its predecessors. For example, "14 of the 16 major diagnostic classes (e.g., mood disorder, anxiety disorder) include some discussion of cultural issues" (Smart & Smart, 1997, p. 393). The DSM also provides "information about the course, prevalence . . . gender, and familial issues related to each diagnosis—information that may be helpful to counselors who are struggling to fully understand their clients' experiences" (Eriksen & Kress, 2006, p. 203).

A unique feature of the DSM system since 1980 is the use of five axes to describe client diagnoses.

- *Axis I* includes clinical syndromes and other conditions that may be a focus of clinical attention. It is usually thought of as the axis on which a client's presenting problem and principal diagnosis appear.

- *Axis II* contains diagnostic information only on personality disorders and mental limitations.

- *Axis III* describes information about general medical conditions of the client, such as chronic pain.

- *Axis IV* contains information on psychosocial and environmental problems that may affect the diagnosis, treatment, and prognosis of mental disorders, such as a lack of friends and inadequate housing.

- *Axis V* gives a Global Assessment of Relational Functioning (GARF) for the client on a scale from 0 to 100 (Ginter, 2001). (Higher numbers on the scale indicate a better level of functioning.) The assessment can be used in relationship to the past or the present.

When all of the axes are combined, the result might look like the following:

- Axis I: 305.00; alcohol abuse, moderate

- Axis II: 317.00; mild mental retardation

- Axis III: chronic pain

- Axis IV: divorced, unemployed, no friends

- Axis V: GARF = 40 (present)

Overall, the DSM is an extremely interesting but controversial systemic model (Eriksen & Kress, 2006; Hinkle, 1994; Lopez et al., 2006). It is atheoretical and frames mental disorders as dispositional "(i.e., something that is within the individual and part of his or her psychological makeup)" (Lopez et al., 2006, p. 259). Social problems such as racism, discrimination, patriarchy, homophobia, and poverty may "become lost in the DSM's focus on disorders being rooted in the individual" (Kress, Eriksen, Rayle, & Ford, 2005, p. 98). Furthermore, the DSM does not substantially deal with anything but individual diagnoses, many of which are severe. Therefore, this classification system is of limited value to group workers, marriage and family counsellors, and counselling professionals who are not working with highly disturbed populations or who work from a humanistic orientation. However, the DSM-IV-TR is logically organized and includes a good network of decision trees (see Appendix C for DSM-IV-TR classifications).

Counsellors should not be naive to the limitations of the DSM or to alternatives to it, which have been discussed comprehensively by Eriksen and Kress (2006). However, they should master DSM terminology regardless of their setting, specialty, or even agreement with the classification system for the following reasons (Geroski, Rodgers, & Breen, 1997; Kress et al., 2005; Seligman, 1997, 1999):

1. The DSM system is universally used in other helping professions and forms the basis for a common dialogue between counsellors and other mental health specialists.

2. The DSM system helps counsellors recognize patterns of mental distress in clients who need to be referred to other mental health professionals or treated in a certain way.

3. By learning the DSM system, counsellors establish accountability, credibility, uniform record keeping, informed treatment plans, research, and quality assurance.

ENGAGING IN PROFESSIONAL COUNSELLING-RELATED ACTIVITIES

Becoming a counsellor is a lifelong process (Gladding, 2002). It continues well past the formal education of obtaining a master's or doctoral degree and includes participation in professional counselling-related activities. Most psychologists and social workers practising in Canada must obtain continuing education units (CEUs) to continue their licensure. This also ensures that professionals stay up-to-date, get needed supervision to ensure excellence in treatment, and advocate for both their clients and the profession of counselling.

Continuing Education

There is a need for continuing education for all counsellors, especially after graduation from a counselling program. New ideas in the practice and treatment of clients are always evolving and must be evaluated, incorporated, and, if necessary, mastered. Counsellors who stop reading professional publications or stop attending in-service workshops and conventions quickly become dated in the delivery of skills. Therefore, competent counsellors stay abreast of the latest and best methods of working with their clients.

Supervision

Supervision is another way of improving professional counselling skills. *Supervision* is an interactive and evaluative process in which someone with more proficiency oversees the work of someone with less knowledge and skill to enhance the professional functioning of the junior member (Bernard & Goodyear, 2004). At its best, supervision is a facilitative experience that combines didactic and experiential learning in the context of a developmental relationship. It allows the acquiring of expertise in theory and practice that is not possible to gain in any other way (Borders & Leddick, 1988). Supervision is a required area of instruction in all CPA-accredited doctoral programs.

To be effective, supervision must be given on a counsellor's developmental level and help the novice counsellor conceptualize better what counselling is like. For beginning graduate students who have a noticeable gap between their knowledge of theory and practice, supervisors are most potent if they assume a highly structured teaching role (Ronnestad & Skovholt, 1993). For example, supervisors may be more authoritarian, didactic, and supportive in their interactions with beginning counsellors in supervision. Thus, a supervisor might help counsellor trainees increase their case note conceptual skills by using Prieto and Scheel's (2002) format for organizing and structuring thinking about a case using the acronym STIPS, in which the letters stand for the following:

S = signs and symptoms
T = topics discussed in counselling
I = counselling interventions used
P = clients' progress and counsellors' continuing plan for treatment
S = any special issues of importance regarding clients (e.g., suicidality) (p. 11)

By using this acronym, counsellor trainees enhance their "ability to acquire relevant facts about clients, better understand clients' presenting problems, better monitor counseling processes, and better evaluate and adjust treatment interventions" (p. 11). They also may gain enhanced skills in becoming more methodical in monitoring relevant elements of the counselling process, such as diagnosis and treatment planning. These skills can help them become more verbally interactive and astute in their interactions with supervisors.

With advanced graduate students or experienced counsellors, such a teaching modality is usually not appropriate. Instead, supervisors are more confrontive and consultative. In essence, supervision, like counselling, may increase one's self-awareness. However, this process is focused on professional rather than personal growth (Ronnestad & Skovholt, 1993).

In setting up supervisory situations, one must address several myths and many realities. Myths are made up of extreme views; for example, "one supervisor can perform all supervisory roles," "individual supervision is best," or "individuals do not need training to supervise" (McCarthy, DeBell, Kanuha, & McLeod, 1988). Realities include the following facts:

- There is not just one theoretical model of supervision but several (e.g., behavioural, facilitative, dynamic, systemic) (Landis & Young, 1994).

- Before a productive supervisory relationship can be established, the developmental level of the supervisee must be verified and a written plan of realistic goals must be completed (Borders & Leddick, 1987).

- There is a significant relationship between a supervisor's credibility, such as trustworthiness, and a supervisee's performance (Carey, Williams, & Wells, 1988).

- Supervision relationships may last for years and there are potential challenges, including transference, countertransference, anxiety, and resistance that must be addressed when this happens (Pearson, 2000).

Overall, the literature and the sophistication of supervisory techniques in counselling are growing (Borders & Brown, 2005; Dye & Borders, 1990). For example, the *reflective team model* is an innovative way of providing group supervision, especially in working with couples and families (Landis & Young, 1994). In this model, graduate students are asked to collaborate, brainstorm, and take their clients' perspectives as they advance hypotheses about client behaviours, view situations from the clients' framework, and work cooperatively.

Counsellors who take advantage of supervisory opportunities, especially opportunities for peer supervision (supervision among equals), can both gain and give information about themselves and their clinical abilities. This increased awareness is the bedrock on which other positive professional experiences can be built.

Advocacy

Social justice advocacy has become a new buzzword in professional counselling, as it already has been in social work for years. The summer issue of the *Journal of Counseling and Development* in 2009 devoted a special section to promoting advocacy work in the counselling profession. Roysircar's motivational article (Roysircar, 2009) reminds us that we do not need to be born advocates—Martin Luther King, Jr., himself was at times a "reluctant" leader.

"Advocacy can be defined simply as promoting an idea or a cause through public relations. It involves networking and education" (Tysl, 1997, p. 16). Counsellors need to support and actively espouse client concerns and the profession of counselling. By doing so they correct injustices and improve conditions for an individual or group (Osborne et al., 1998). This process can be achieved in a number of ways, such as making presentations to clubs and civic groups, writing articles for newspapers, and focusing on community issues through giving one's time and effort. It is especially important to make others aware of social concerns of needy populations, since such groups do not usually have a voice or recognition. At times advocacy involves speaking on the behalf of such people and promoting ways of ensuring that their rights are respected and that their needs are taken care of through social action (McClure & Russo, 1996).

Another form of advocacy is working through the political process. Not only must counsellors be knowledgeable about social matters, they must also influence the passage of laws when conditions adversely affect either their clients or the profession of counselling. Counsellors can do this by staying informed and knowing what bills are being considered and by writing letters or visiting with legislators.

A second way to advocate is to know the rules for effective communication with legislators. The use of jargon, exaggeration, or rambling hurts a counsellor's presentation.

Therefore, it is important to be organized, concise, and concrete in advocating for certain actions. Flexibility and anticipation of opposite points of view are crucial to being successful.

Finally, it is important to be persistent. As in counselling, follow-up is essential in dealing with legislative situations. Initiatives may require years of lobbying before they are enacted.

If, as a professional counsellor, counselling psychologist, or social worker, you have a particular expertise that could affect a social justice issue, recognize that knowledge is power. You need to speak up and be heard.

Case Example: What Would *You* Do?

The Alberta government recently defunded surgeries for people requiring gender reassignment surgery. Perhaps inadvertently, they picked a very vulnerable group to target through this decision, a group whose members suffer intense negative emotions and psychological distress because of severe gender dysphoria. Most transpeople want to pass, a state called *going stealth*. The last thing most of them want is the publicity of going public. Nonetheless, several did go public after the government defunded surgeries for them.

I contacted the Canadian Psychological Association (CPA) and asked if they would support some social justice action regarding this issue. They concurred, so I wrote a letter to the Alberta premier, the minister of Health, and the minister of Finance that was co-signed on CPA letterhead by the president of CPA. The written response back from the minister of Health explained why they had made the decision but offered little in the way of reinstating these funds.

Next, I co-authored fact sheets about gender dysphoria, drafted a policy statement, and wrote out possible responses to the media, all negotiated in consort with CPA. After the board of directors officially endorses these documents, I will encourage CPA to send out a media release.

1. What else would you think would be appropriate actions for a counsellor to take in this matter?

2. Do you already have a group that you would advocate for?

3. What would you do if that group's rights or privileges were being removed?

A CAREER IN THE COUNSELLING FIELD

Service Canada (2007a) does not break down psychologists by subdisciplines, so their report is an aggregate. Regarding all types of psychologists, 73% work in health care and social assistance, 21% in educational services, and 7% in public administration. More specifically, they work in (a) clinics and hospitals, (b) correctional centres, (c) mental health facilities, (d) community service organizations, (e) businesses, (f) schools and universities, (g) government and private research agencies, and (h) private practice. While clinical psychologists and counselling psychologists may work either part-time or full-time in private practice, clinical psychologists are found more plentifully in clinics and hospitals while counselling psychologists are more commonly found in schools and universities and community service organizations.

Work prospects for psychologists as of 2010 are considered good, partly due to the retirement rate (which is above average). Reportedly, the wage for psychologists is considered higher than average compared to all professional occupations lumped together (Service Canada, 2007a). Although wages vary across the country, the average salary for psychologists in Alberta in 2007 was $78 600 a year (Alberta Learning Information Service, 2008). The Psychologists Association of Alberta (2010) recommends that Alberta psychologists in private practice charge $170 per hour. Again, such recommendations are only for Alberta and the consumer will still find a significant range of fees among psychologists.

Regarding social workers, 71% work in health care and social assistance, 19% in public administration, 6% in other services (except public administration), and 3% in educational services (Service Canada, 2007b). More specifically, they work in (a) hospitals and clinics, (b) school boards, (c) social service agencies and child welfare organizations, (d) correctional facilities and community agencies, (e) employee assistance programs, (f) Aboriginal band councils, and (h) private practice.

Work prospects for social workers as of 2010 are considered good, partly again due to the retirement rate (which is above average). Reportedly, the wage for social workers is considered about average compared to all professional occupations lumped together (Service Canada, 2007b). Although wages vary across the country, the average salary for social workers in Alberta in 2007 was $57 800 a year (Alberta Learning Information Service, 2009). Fees for seeing a social worker in private practice vary widely in Canada, but generally social workers charge less than counselling psychologists.

SUMMARY AND CONCLUSION

The qualities and behaviours necessary to become an effective counsellor will probably increase as counselling evolves as a profession. Yet there will always be some basic qualities and abilities that all counsellors must embody to become effective.

One such quality is related to the core personality of counsellors. Individuals feel comfortable working in counselling environments because of their interests, backgrounds, and abilities. The majority of effective counsellors have social and artistic interests and enjoy working with people in a variety of problem-solving and developmental ways. Effective counsellors are generally characterized as warm, friendly, open, sensitive, patient, and creative. They are consistently working on their own mental health and strive to avoid becoming burned out and ineffective.

Education is a second quality related to the effectiveness of counsellors. One can become a professional counsellor in several different ways in Canada. The most common educational pursuit is within counselling psychology or social work. These also happen to be the two counselling professions that are regulated in most jurisdictions.

A third area related to effectiveness in counselling is theory and systems. Effective counsellors know that theory is the *why* behind the *how* of technique and practice and that nothing is more practical than mastering major theoretical approaches to counselling. These counsellors are not unsystematic and capricious in using theories and methods in their practice; many use a healthy type of eclecticism in their work. They operate systematically from a developmental/wellness approach, a medical/pathological model, or someplace in between. Regardless, effective counsellors know how individuals develop over the lifespan and also know the terminology and uses of the latest edition of the *Diagnostic and Statistical Manual.*

Finally, effective counsellors are active in counselling-related activities. They realize the importance of keeping their knowledge up-to-date by participating in continuing education programs and supervisory activities. Furthermore, they advocate both for the needs of their clients and for the profession of counselling.

Your Personal Reflections

1. What do you do that invigorates you or that you enjoy? What other activities or hobbies would you like to include in your life? What keeps you from doing so? How might you get around any real or potential barriers?

2. Think of difficulties you have had in your life. Which of the attribution models discussed do you think you would feel most comfortable with had you gone to a counsellor for help with most of these problems?

3. How exciting is diagnosing clients through the DSM to you? Did you expect that you would have to diagnose when you decided to become a counsellor? What appeals to you most in regard to the two models presented (medical vs. wellness)? More specifically, which do you like best and why?

Classroom Activities

1. Research indicates that some personality types are more suited to be counsellors than are others. Suppose you do not possess the ideal personality for this profession (i.e., social, artistic, and enterprising). What are some ways in which you could compensate? In groups of three, discuss your reaction to the qualities of personality associated with effective counselling.

2. Review the personal, theoretical, and educational qualities that ideal counsellors possess. Discuss how you think these qualities might differ if you were counselling outside Canada—for example, in India, Sweden, Israel, Australia, or Argentina. Share your opinions with the class.

3. Discuss with another classmate how you might help each other grow professionally if you were unequal in ability as counsellors. After you have made your list, share it with another group of two and then with the class as a whole. As a class, discuss how the strategies you have formulated might be helpful in your lifetime development as counsellors.

4. With another classmate, discuss how you would approach clients differently and similarly if you were coming from a developmental/wellness perspective as opposed to a medical/pathological model. Report your results to the class.

5. Investigate how counselling associations or counsellors have advocated for their clients' needs and for the profession of counselling itself. A good place to begin is to consult the policy statements of the Canadian Psychological Association (www.cpa.ca/aboutcpa/policystatements) and the social justice/advocacy section of the Canadian Association of Social Workers (www.casw-acts.ca).

CASE EXAMPLES

1. Robert had been a business student pursuing an MBA. However, he found dealing with facts and figures boring, so he quit. "What now?" he wondered. After a few months of floundering, he went to see a career specialist. In examining his interests, he found he liked working with people. "That's it!" he said excitedly. "I'll become a counsellor! That way I can 'assist' all those overwrought and overeducated business types who are bored to death with their jobs. And all I'll have to do is listen. Sweet!"

   Would you want Robert in your counselling program? Why? What else do you think he should consider?

2. Patricia grew up in a comfortable environment. She went to private schools, was tutored and toasted by her parents' associates, and was on the path to succeeding her father as CEO of a large corporation when she realized she wanted to work with people in a therapeutic way. She applied to a number of counselling programs and was accepted. However, she decided that before she entered a program she would take a year to work with poor people in a developing country so that she could "suffer" some. What do you think of her idea? Do you think it would help her?

3. When he moved to a new province, Ajay set about making sure he was licensed. He worked hard and in time the provincial licensure board granted him a license. Ajay was thrilled, but when he showed his new business cards to his friend Luke, Luke's response was "Why do you want to put the alphabet after your name? Who cares about letters like 'RSW'?"

   Ajay was taken aback initially but then he thought: "I want to do it because it indicates my professional status. I have earned it and the credential is important not only to me but to my clients."

   What do you think of Luke's reaction? How about Ajay's answer?

Chapter 3
Ethical and Legal Aspects of Counselling

PRACTICE REFLECTION

Jared, aged 39, used to be a professional football player. During those years, he was promiscuous with innumerable women. For the past 12 years, however, he has been married and raising two preschool-aged children with his wife. He showed up at my office and said, "My problem is that I am still acting promiscuously—I have had several one-nighters and affairs since I got married. I am currently seeing Roberta on the side, and my feelings for her have become very strong."

I have long believed that honesty in a serious relationship—particularly in marriage—is crucial. With honesty, many things are negotiable that otherwise would remain secretive. In Jared's case, his wife knew nothing of his proclivities. We met weekly for maybe eight or nine sessions, and Jared was stuck—he could not give up Roberta and he could not give up his wife either. I remember feeling very uncomfortable with this because I believe very strongly in open and honest communication.

One day he came to see me and said, "I don't feel that counselling is helping me. I am still stuck." I replied, "Jared, we have talked extensively about the pros and cons of maintaining this façade. It seems that, overall, this behaviour has hurt you and your relationship with your wife. Still, it is only you that can take action concerning it."

He left that day, and my intuition said we were both frustrated. How could I possibly get him to act without imposing my own values? The next session opened my eyes, however. His wife had found Roberta's phone number in his wallet, and without questioning him about it, had called her. Roberta said they should meet, and when Jared arrived home that day, both were sitting at the kitchen table waiting for him. Everything about his affair had been disclosed already.

In the ensuing months, Jared faced a nasty divorce, His business partners were so disgusted by his affairs that they bought him out of their lucrative operation. I saw him years later working at a fast food restaurant, but he did not seem to recognize me in the bustle of a busy lunch hour.

I have questioned many times if I did the right thing, and, more importantly, what could I have done differently to have perhaps helped Jared have a better outcome? Should I have expressed my deep values from the beginning? Should I have pushed him to disclose to his wife despite his reluctance to do so? Was I ethical in my counselling with Jared?

There are few events more stressful in counsellors' lives than facing a formal ethics complaint lodged against them by a client or someone associated with the client (Shapiro, Walker, Manosevitz, Peterson, & Williams, 2008). "Doing hard time" in a remand centre—an expression often used by inmates to describe the increased anxiety and fear caused by not knowing what will happen to them when they finally get their case heard in court—is a good analogy for what counsellors face when a similar uncertainty awaits them Licensing and regulatory bodies have several disciplinary measures they can take, ranging from no action on one end to levying huge fines and in some cases permanent revocation of the ability to practise within the profession on the other. Best practice, of course, is to avoid engaging in activities that could be construed as unethical.

In this chapter, ethical standards and legal constraints under which counsellors operate are explored. Both ethics and the law are crucial in the work and well-being of counsellors and the counselling process. They promote the professionalism of counselling both directly and indirectly. In some cases, ethical and legal considerations overlap (Wilcoxon et al., 2007). However, counselling and the law may be quite different and may operate according to different premises (Rowley & MacDonald, 2001).

DEFINITIONS: ETHICS, MORALITY, AND LAW

ETHICS INVOLVES "MAKING DECISIONS OF A MORAL NATURE ABOUT PEOPLE AND THEIR interaction in society" (Kitchener, 1986, p. 306). The term is often used synonymously with *morality*, and in some cases the two terms overlap. Both deal with "what is good and bad or the study of human conduct and values" (Van Hoose & Kottler, 1985, p. 2). Yet each has a different meaning.

"*Ethics* is generally defined as a philosophical discipline that is concerned with human conduct and moral decision making" (Van Hoose & Kottler, 1985, p. 3). Ethics are normative in nature and focus on principles and standards that govern relationships between individuals, such as those between counsellors and clients. *Morality*, however, involves judgment or evaluation of action. It is associated with such words as *good, bad, right, wrong, ought,* and *should* (Brandt, 1959; Grant, 1992). Counsellors have morals, and the theories counsellors employ have embedded within them moral presuppositions about human nature that explicitly and implicitly question first "what is a person and second, what should a person be or become?" (Christopher, 1996, p. 18).

Law is the precise codification of governing standards that are established to ensure legal and moral justice (Hummell, Talbutt, & Alexander, 1985; Remley & Herlihy, 2005). Law is created by legislation, court decision, and tradition, as in English common law (Wheeler & Bertram, 2008). The law does not dictate what is ethical in a given situation but what is legal. Sometimes what is legal at a given time (e.g., matters pertaining to race, age, or sex) is considered unethical or immoral by some significant segments of society.

An example is the internment of Japanese Canadians during World War II in 1942 after Pearl Harbor was bombed. Their property was confiscated and sold by the Canadian government, and even after the war, they were not allowed to live wherever they wanted in Canada until April 1, 1949. Prime Minister Brian Mulroney provided an official apology in 1988, admitting that the government at the time was influenced by racial discrimination. He authorized the provision of $21 000 to each survivor of the wartime detention (Breti, 1998; Wordpress.com, 2007).

ETHICS AND COUNSELLING

As a group, professional counsellors are concerned with ethics and values. Indeed, many counsellors treat ethical complaints with the same seriousness that they treat lawsuits (Chauvin & Remley, 1996). However, some counsellors are better informed or more attuned to these issues. Patterson (1971) has observed that counsellors' professional identity is related to their knowledge and practice of ethics. According to Welfel (2006), the effectiveness of counsellors is connected to their ethical knowledge and behaviour as well.

Unethical behaviour in counselling can take many forms. The temptations common to people everywhere exist for counsellors. They include "physical intimacy, the titillation of gossip, or the opportunity (if the gamble pays off) to advance one's career" (Welfel & Lipsitz, 1983b, p. 328). Some forms of unethical behaviour are obvious and willful, whereas others are more subtle and unintentional; regardless, the harmful outcome is the same. The following are some of the most prevalent forms of unethical behaviours in counselling (Canadian Association of Social Workers, 2005a, 2005b; Canadian Counselling and Psychotherapy Association, 2007; Canadian Psychological Association, 2000):

- violation of confidentiality
- exceeding one's level of professional competence
- negligent practice
- claiming expertise one does not possess
- imposing one's values on a client
- creating dependency in a client
- sexual activity with a client
- certain conflicts of interest, such as a dual relationship—where the role of the counsellor is combined with another relationship, either personal or professional (Moleski & Kiselica, 2005)
- questionable financial arrangements, such as charging excessive fees
- improper advertising
- plagiarism

PROFESSIONAL CODES OF ETHICS AND STANDARDS

To address ethical situations, counsellors have developed professional codes of ethics and standards of conduct "based upon an agreed-on set of values" (Hansen et al., 1994, p. 362). Professionals in counselling voluntarily abide by such codes for many reasons. "Among its many purposes, a code of ethical conduct is designed to offer formal statements for ensuring protection of clients' rights while identifying expectations of practitioners" (Wilcoxon, 1987, p. 510). Another reason for ethical codes is that "without a code of established ethics, a group of people with similar interests cannot be considered a professional organization" (Allen, 1986, p. 293). Ethics not only help professionalize an association on a general level but "are designed to provide some guidelines for the professional behaviour of members on a personal level" (Swanson, 1983a, p. 53). Three other reasons for the existence of ethical codes, according to Van Hoose and Kottler (1985), are as follows:

1. Ethical codes protect the profession from government. They allow the profession to regulate itself and function autonomously instead of being controlled by legislation.

2. Ethical codes help control internal disagreements and bickering, thus promoting stability within the profession.

3. Ethical codes protect practitioners from the public, especially in regard to malpractice suits. If counselling professionals behave according to ethical guidelines, the behaviour is judged to be in compliance with accepted standards.

In addition, ethical codes help increase public trust in the integrity of a profession and provide clients with some protection from charlatans and incompetent counsellors (Vacc, Juhnke, & Nilsen, 2001). Like counsellors, clients can use codes of ethics and standards as a guide in evaluating questionable treatment.

Limitations of Ethical Codes

Remley (1985) notes that ethical codes are general and idealistic; they seldom answer specific questions. Furthermore, he points out that such documents do not address "foreseeable professional dilemmas" (p. 181). Rather, they provide guidelines, based on experiences and values, of how counsellors should behave. In many ways, ethical standards represent the collected wisdom of a profession at a particular time.

A number of specific limitations exist in any code of ethics. Here are some of the limitations most frequently mentioned (Corey, Corey, & Callanan, 2007; Talbutt, 1981):

- Some issues cannot be resolved by a code of ethics.
- Enforcing ethical codes is difficult.
- There may be conflicts within the standards delineated by the code.
- Some legal and ethical issues are not covered in codes.
- Ethical codes are historical documents. Thus, what may be acceptable practice at one time may be considered unethical later.
- Sometimes conflicts arise between ethical and legal codes.
- Ethical codes do not address cross-cultural issues.
- Ethical codes do not address every possible situation.
- There is often difficulty in bringing the interest of all parties involved in an ethical dispute together systematically.
- Ethical codes are not proactive documents for helping counsellors decide what to do in new situations.

Thus, ethical codes are useful in many ways, but they do have their limitations. Counsellors need to be aware that they will not always find all the guidance they want when consulting these documents. Nevertheless, whenever an ethical issue arises in counselling, the counsellor should first consult ethical codes to see whether the situation is addressed.

Conflicts Within and Among Ethical Codes

The adoption of ethical codes and the emphasis placed on them has paralleled the increased professionalism of counselling (Remley & Herlihy, 2005). But the presence of such standards poses a potential dilemma for many counsellors, for three reasons. First, as Stadler (1986) points out, to act ethically, counsellors must be aware of ethical codes and be able to differentiate an ethical dilemma from other types of dilemmas, a differentiation that is not always easy. For example, a person may take a stand on a controversial issue, such as homosexuality, that he or she seemingly supports with ethical principles but in reality supports only with personal beliefs or biases.

Second, sometimes different ethical principles in a code offer conflicting guidelines about what to do in a given situation. An example is the potential conflict over confidentiality and acting in a client's best interest where a client reveals that he or she is going to attempt to harass someone or inflict self-harm. In such a situation, the counsellor who keeps this information confidential may actually act against the best interests of the client and the community in which the client resides.

Third, conflicts may occur when counsellors belong to two or more professional organizations whose codes of ethics differ, such as the codes of the College of Alberta Psychologists (CAP), CPA, and CCPA. Such counsellors may become involved in situations in which ethical action is unclear. For instance, the CAP *Standards of Practice* (College of Alberta Psychologists, 2005) states that psychologists cannot engage in sexually intimate relationships with former clients for at least two years after cessation or termination of treatment, and the CCPA *Code of Ethics* requires a minimum three-year waiting period post-counselling (Canadian Counselling and Psychotherapy Association, 2007). The *Canadian Code of Ethics for Psychologists* (Canadian Psychological Association, 2000), however, states that sexual relations cannot occur either during therapy or later unless the power differential would no longer reasonably affect the client's decision making (thereby leaving more discretion in this matter). If a professional belongs to all three organizations and is dealing with this dilemma, which code should he or she follow?

MAKING ETHICAL DECISIONS

Ethical decision making is not always easy, yet it is a part of being a counsellor. It requires virtues such as character, integrity, and moral courage as well as knowledge (Welfel, 2006). Some counsellors operate from personal ethical standards without regard to the ethical guidelines developed by professional counselling associations. They usually function well until faced with a dilemma "for which there is no apparent good or best solution" (Swanson, 1983a, p. 57). At such times, ethical issues arise and these counsellors experience anxiety, doubt, hesitation, and confusion in determining their conduct. Unfortunately, when they act, their behaviour may turn out to be unethical because it is not grounded in an ethical code or it is grounded in only part of a code that they have extracted to justify their behaviour.

In a study conducted in New York (Hayman & Covert, 1986), researchers found five types of ethical dilemmas most prevalent among the university counsellors they surveyed there: (a) confidentiality, (b) role conflict, (c) counsellor competence, (d) conflicts with employer or institution, and (e) degree of dangerousness. The situational dilemmas that involved danger were the least difficult to resolve, and those that dealt with counsellor competence and confidentiality were the most difficult. The surprising finding of this study, however, was that less than one third of the respondents indicated that they relied on published professional codes of ethics in resolving dilemmas. Instead, most used "common sense," a strategy that at times may be professionally unethical and at best unwise.

It is in difficult, murky, and personally troubling situations that counsellors need to be aware of resources for ethical decision making, such as books and articles on ethics and the advice of more experienced colleagues (Welfel, 2006). Such resources are especially important when questions arise over potentially controversial behaviours such as setting or collecting fees, conducting multiple relationships, or working with individuals whose beliefs and styles counsellors do not agree with. *Ethical reasoning*, "the process of determining which ethical principles are involved and then prioritizing them based on the professional requirements and beliefs," is crucial (Lanning, 1992, p. 21).

In making ethical decisions, counsellors should take actions "based on careful, reflective thought" about responses they think are professionally right in particular situations (Tennyson & Strom, 1986, p. 298). Several ethical principles relate to the activities and ethical choices of counsellors:

- *beneficence* (doing good and preventing harm)
- *non-maleficence* (not inflicting harm)
- *autonomy* (respecting freedom of choice and self-determination)
- *justice* (fairness)
- *fidelity* (faithfulness or honouring commitments) (Remley & Herlihy, 2005; Wilcoxon et al., 2007)

All these principles involve conscious decision making by counsellors throughout the counselling process. Of these principles, some experts identify non-maleficence as the primary ethical responsibility in the field of counselling. Non-maleficence not only involves the "removal of present harm," but also the "prevention of future harm, and passive avoidance of harm" (Thompson, 1990, p. 105). It is the basis on which counsellors respond to clients who may endanger themselves or others and why they respond to colleagues' unethical behaviour (Daniluk & Haverkamp, 1993).

Other Guidelines for Acting Ethically

Swanson (1983a) lists guidelines for assessing whether counsellors act in ethically responsible ways. The first is *personal and professional honesty*. Counsellors need to operate openly with themselves and with those with whom they work. Hidden agendas or unacknowledged feelings hinder relationships and place counsellors on shaky ethical ground. One way to overcome personal or professional honesty problems that may get in the way of acting ethically is to receive supervision (Kitchener, 1994).

A second guideline is *acting in the best interest of clients*. This ideal is easier to discuss than achieve. At times, a counsellor may impose personal values on clients and ignore what they really want (Gladding & Hood, 1974; Nassar-McMillan, 1995). At other times, a counsellor may fail to recognize an emergency and too readily accept the idea that the client's best interest is served by doing nothing.

A third guideline is that counsellors *act without malice or personal gain*. Some clients are difficult to like or deal with, and it is with these individuals that counsellors must be especially careful. However, counsellors must be careful to avoid relationships with likable clients on either a personal or professional basis. Errors in judgment are most likely to occur when the counsellor's self-interest becomes a part of the relationship with a client (St. Germaine, 1993).

A final guideline is whether counsellors can *justify an action* "as the best judgment of what should be done based upon the current state of the profession" (Swanson, 1983a, p. 59). To make such a decision, counsellors must keep up with current trends by reading professional literature, attending in-service workshops and conventions, and becoming actively involved in local, state, and national counselling activities.

The CCPA counselling ethics casebook (Schulz, Sheppard, Lehr, & Shepard, 2006) contains examples in which counsellors are presented with issues and case studies of questionable ethical situations and given both guidelines and questions to reflect on in deciding what an ethical response would be. Each situation involves a standard of the ethical code.

As helpful as the casebook may be, in many counselling situations the proper behaviour is not obvious (Wilcoxon et al., 2007). For example, the question of confidentiality in balancing the individual rights of a person with AIDS and society's right to be protected from the spread of the disease is one with which some counsellors struggle (Harding, Gray, & Neal, 1993). Likewise, there are multiple ethical dilemmas in counselling adult survivors of incest, including those of confidentiality and the consequences of making decisions about reporting abuse (Daniluk & Haverkamp, 1993). Therefore, when they are in doubt about what to do in a given situation, it is crucial for counsellors to consult and talk over situations with colleagues, in addition to using principles, guidelines, casebooks, and professional codes of ethics.

THE MAJOR CANADIAN CODES OF ETHICS AND STANDARDS FOR COUNSELLORS

Professional counsellors in Canada who are regulated must adhere to the ethical codes, standards of practice, and other prescriptive documents that are issued by their provincial or territorial regulatory bodies. Furthermore, those who belong to one or more of the voluntary national counselling organizations must comply with theirs as well.

Most of these codes and standards say more or less the same thing, albeit with differing details. For the most up-to-date information, visit the website of the provincial or territorial regulatory body for that profession (psychologist, social worker, or professional counsellor, where regulated).

The Canadian Code of Ethics for Psychologists

The ethical decision-making model recommended by the CPA contains four principles, listed in hierarchical order. These principles apply to counsellors working directly with clients as well as other roles that counsellors perform, such as research, consultation, and teaching. Principle I is given the highest weighting in making an ethical decision, while principle IV receives the lowest priority. By following this model, most ethical decisions become easier to make. However, if the best decision remains unclear, it is best to consult with a supervisor, or if in private practice to contact one of the practice consultants authorized by the regulatory body.

Principle I is *respect for the dignity of persons*. This principle takes the highest precedence, except when there is clearly imminent danger to the physical safety of a person. This moral imperative means that each person must be treated as an individual with their own particular worldview. The greatest responsibility is to the person who is most vulnerable, and usually this is the client.

Principle II is *responsible caring*. To be responsible means a counsellor needs to provide competent services such as obtaining informed consent, discerning the harm versus the benefit of potential interventions, and by becoming self-aware and reflective about the treatment of those who are different. In principle II, the concern is for the well-being of clients, while in principle I, it is more about their human rights.

Principle III is *integrity in relationship*, and is given the third highest weight. Psychologists should demonstrate the highest levels of integrity in their work with clients by being straightforward, honest, and objective, and by avoiding conflicts of interest whenever possible. Sometimes in counselling work, however, absolute honesty must be tempered, particularly if it would violate principles I or II.

Principle IV is *responsibility to society*. This principle is given the lowest weighting. Psychologists are not empowered police a society—instead, they are expected to work in ways that help clients become better citizens.

How do these principles of ethical decision making play out in real-life scenarios? For example, ask yourself the following questions:

1. If a client wants to commit suicide tomorrow, what are you expected to do?

2. If a client plans to rob a bank tonight when no one is expected to be there and he has no weapons, do you have to report it?

3. A client tells you he abused children 10 years ago but no longer has access to children or any interest. What do you do with that information?

4. You are addicted to cocaine and a client offers you a line—do you snort it? What else should you do?

5. You live in a small rural town and are the only psychologist. Your ex-partner of 10 years ago comes to you and wants help getting over a present relationship. Do you agree to see him or her?

College of Alberta Psychologists' (2005) Standards of Practice

Informed Consent   Providing informed consent is not only an important part of beginning work with a new client; it is also imperative that psychologists inform clients of the potential risks and benefits of their ongoing work. This is particularly true if counselling is changing direction in some manner. Counselling is most effective when the counsellor and the client have formed a strong working and therapeutic alliance. In effect, this means they collaborate on the goals and tasks of counselling and they establish a respectful, trusting relationship. Informed consent helps to facilitate these processes.

Informed consent means keeping the client informed of important details regarding the service you intend to provide before it is provided. Similar to the medical profession, informed consent means that clients know the potential consequences of what you have in mind for them.

You are a wonderful therapist and you just know the best approach to take with Celina is to shock her foot until she stops shaking uncontrollably. You tell her this is what you are going to do before you attach the electrodes. After several unsuccessful sessions of this, she asks, "Are you sure there aren't other ways to treat my anxiety condition? After the shocks, I often end up vomiting for the next hour or so." You reply, "Well, yes there are. There is systematic desensitization for your fear of snakes, or perhaps flooding. However, I prefer shocks because they often work faster."

1. What are the main problems with the way you have conducted therapy?

2. What should you do now that you have told her about other ways of treating the problem?

3. If she complains to your professional association, what will be your defense?

Competence Psychologists are expected to limit their practice to those areas in which they have demonstrated competence and to stay abreast of advancements in these areas. There are various ways a counsellor can develop new areas of competency, but generally it involves ongoing consultation and appropriate education or training. The best approach is to receive supervision from someone with demonstrated competence and to take courses, attend continuing education (such as seminars, workshops, and conferences), and read in this new area.

Case Example: What Would *You* Do?

You are working in a small Inuit community in the Northwest Territories. A client comes to you concerned about his attraction to pre-pubescent boys. He lives alone and he has no access to boys within his immediate social milieu. Nonetheless, you do not have the skills to treat people with this presenting concern. The nearest city is more than a five-hour drive away, and, in the dead of winter, driving is out of the question.

1. Would you have to report this person to the authorities?

2. Should you offer counselling? If not, what alternative will you choose?

3. Are you liable if you counsel him and he is later apprehended for sexually assaulting an underage boy?

Impaired Objectivity It is unethical to work or continue working with a client if your judgment is impaired because of physical, emotional, or mental conditions, including substance abuse or adverse effects caused by pharmaceuticals. If you need to limit, suspend, or terminate counselling, you are responsible for helping the client obtain professional services from someone else.

Relationship with Supervisees Supervisors have a responsibility to be ethical in their practice with supervisees, and this includes not discriminating against them or exploiting them. They are expected to provide "appropriate" and competent supervision.

Violations of Law Violations of law means that you cannot attempt to obtain the registration of another psychologist. In effect, this regulation is about not engaging in fraudulent practices.

Aiding Illegal Practice This standard is specifically about not knowingly aiding or abetting another person's misrepresentation of professional credentials or registration status. If someone is not registered as a psychologist, for example, but uses the title, you are required to take action. The first step is to bring this infraction to the offending individual and ask that he or she stop misrepresenting himself or herself. If that is not sufficient, then you are to formally report the individual to their respective regulatory body.

Dual Relationships Several dual relationship types are prohibited, while others are not but are highly discouraged. You cannot counsel someone where a potentially harmful conflict of interest exists due to either a current or previous professional, familial, social, sexual, emotional, financial, supervisory, political, administrative, or legal relationship.

In some instances dual relationships are unavoidable, such as when the psychologist lives in a rural community or when he or she has special attributes that are relatively uncommon, such as belonging to the same minority group as the client. In such cases, the psychologist must discuss with the client the possible consequences and record the nature of the dual relationship in file notes.

Case Example: What Would *You* Do?

You are counselling a client and the two of you have much in common. Your share a mutual attraction for each other. After 10 sessions, your work together is done.

1. Can you suggest seeing each other socially?

2. If the client initiates it, is it okay to begin seeing each other socially?

3. Assume you said "yes" to question 1 or 2. What potential problems may arise?

Discussions among professional groups have concluded that nonsexual multiple relationships should be avoided. The reason is that, no matter how harmless such relationships seem, a conflict of interest can easily occur. For example, if you become friends with a former client, how will the two of you successfully transition from the therapeutic relationship, which is one-sided in most respects? First, you know far more about your client than your client knows about you. Second, you were always expected to show empathy and compassion toward your client, while the reverse was not expected.

In a friendship, there are times when you don't feel like caring, or you are exhausted. In an honest friendship, you will share your reason for not wanting to talk or for needing time alone. Not showing empathy now to your friend will seem odd because, when he or she was your client, you needed to show empathy and caring as part of your job regardless of your inner state. Therefore, as a matter of ethics, counsellors should remove themselves from socializing or doing business with present or former clients, should not accept gifts from them, and should not enter into a counselling relationship with a close friend, family member, student, lover, or employee.

Maintenance and Retention of Records   You need to keep notes from your sessions with clients, and these must contain (a) appropriate identifying information; (b) the presenting problem or problems; (c) the fee arrangement; (d) the date and substance of each session, including information regarding interventions, progress, and issues about informed consent or termination; (e) test results or other evaluative results and the test data itself; (f) notations from consults with other service providers; and (g) a copy of all test or evaluative reports. In Alberta, for example, you are required to keep your professional record for a minimum of 10 years from the date of your last contact with the client. Your clients have the right to read the contents of their files, and they can ask you to correct factual information.

Fees and Statements Psychologists must provide full information regarding their billing practices at the outset, including fees for missed appointments. They must also provide receipts or itemized statements to clients.

Providing Supportable Services Psychologists are expected to provide services based on sound psychological theory and demonstrated effectiveness (where this information exists). If they are providing some form of "innovative" service, they must inform their client(s). Furthermore, they are expected to refer when they are not the best person for a particular client or clients. Lastly, when psychologists render opinions about someone in which their legal or civil rights may be affected, they are required to have a substantial amount of contact with the person.

Representation of Service As a registered professional, you are not permitted to misrepresent yourself either directly or by implication. As in the above example, you could not call yourself a doctor with the word "psychologist" after your name because it implies that your PhD is in psychology, not English literature. Second, you cannot say you are a specialist unless you have demonstrated competence to be one.

Protecting Confidentiality of Clients Psychologists must inform their clients of the limits to confidentiality at the outset. You cannot release information about the booking of a session with someone without the client agreeing to this release. When information is to be released to a third party, a psychologist requires the client to sign a release of information form.

Working with Adults. Everything said to a psychologist by a client who is of the age of majority (18 years and older) must be kept confidential from everyone, with the following exceptions.

1. *Imminent risk to self or others.* If the client or another person is at immediate risk and at grave harm of being hurt mentally or physically, the psychologist must break confidentiality. If the client is planning to commit suicide after he or she leaves your office, you must make every reasonable attempt to stay with the person until appropriate help arrives. In the instance where the client is willing to go to hospital, you should arrange for a responsible person (e.g., spouse, parent, sibling, friend) to take the client there, or call for an ambulance. If the person is unwilling to get help, call the police. They are the only ones with the authority to apprehend an unwilling individual.

    If the client is homicidal, do not attempt to stay with the person or you may become the first victim! Instead, you have a dual responsibility to notify the individual(s) whose life is threatened and to inform the police.

2. *Admission of child abuse, child neglect, or abuse of vulnerable adults.* If your client admits to child abuse, child neglect, or abuse of vulnerable adults (e.g., elderly individuals who can no longer care for themselves, mentally or physically challenged individuals), you must report this person in accordance with the provincial or territorial laws governing duty to report. This duty applies to *all* citizens. You will also need to determine whether there is a statute of limitations (a period of time since the abuse occurred where reporting is no longer required by law) in your jurisdiction.

3. *Records subpoenaed by a court of law.* Under judicial order, you are required to surrender your records. This may occur in serious situations where your client is involved with the judicial system in some way (e.g., charged with a criminal offense, victim of a serious accident).

Working with Minors. If the client is under the age of 18, signed consent from the legal guardians is required in order for you to provide counselling. This can become particularly "messy" if the child or children have two parents—both with legal custody—who are now estranged. In some instances, only one parent is the legal guardian, in which case only this individual's consent is required.

Furthermore, a psychologist is required to establish at the outset with both the minor and the legal guardian what information will be kept confidential from the legal guardian(s) and what information can be shared. It is helpful to have this laid out in a document to be signed by both the legal guardian(s) and the child.

One way of protecting both client and counsellor is to suggest that the guardian(s) will be provided information only if the counsellor assesses there is *moderate* risk to the well-being of the minor or another person. Moderate risk includes such things as having frequent and serious suicidal thoughts, making suicidal gestures, continuing use of dangerous illicit drugs (e.g., heroin, crack, crystal meth), or having a strong desire to hurt someone else.

It is also important to check the standards of practice for your particular jurisdiction if there are other reporting functions that take precedence over confidentiality. In Alberta, for example, a psychologist must report if a minor is being exploited, sexually or otherwise.

There are two exceptions to the general rule of requiring consent from legal guardians to provide counselling to a minor. First, a counsellor can provide counselling to a minor in the case of an emergency. Second, school counsellors generally do not require parental consent as "counselling" is likely listed under the provincial or territorial school act as an educational activity, which is then subsumed under the rubric of classroom instruction.

Case Example: What Would *You* Do?

In the first session, your client, Clyde, tells you that he is dealing with a legal issue. While leaving a department store, two store detectives allegedly used excessive force to push Clyde to the ground, believing that he had stolen some merchandise. Clyde is seeing you because he has complained of regular headaches since then, and he wants your help in dealing with the pain and the trauma he claims he experienced. You tell him you will work with him, but that you refuse to go to court or release your records. Clyde agrees to this. A few months later, however, you receive a letter from Clyde's lawyer requesting a photocopy of the entire contents of your file. The request is accompanied by a release of information form signed by Clyde.

1. Are you obligated to release your records?

2. If you are called as a witness, do you have to attend court?

3. How could you write notes in a way that would minimize the risk that they would be "torn apart" by the defense lawyer for the store detectives?

Assessment Procedures   If you are conducting an assessment of a client, you must ensure that the assessment is valid. For this condition to be met, the assessment needs to be based on extensive personal contact with the client and often backed up with results from valid psychological tests. It is one thing to report observable behaviour—it is an entirely different thing to give someone a diagnostic label, particularly one that carries the potential for serious consequences to the client.

The Code of Ethics of the Canadian Counselling and Psychotherapy Association

Ethical conduct in the CCPA (2007) *Code of Ethics* contains six fundamental principles: (a) *beneficence*—proactively promoting the best interests of the client, (b) *fidelity*—maintaining integrity and honouring commitments made to clients, (c) *non-maleficence*—refraining from actions that could harm clients, (d) *autonomy*—respecting clients' need to be self-determining, (e) *justice*—respecting the dignity and fair treatment of all people, and (f) *societal Interest*—maintaining respect and responsibility toward society.

CCPA (2007) also offers three different models to help counsellors make ethical decisions and resolve ethical dilemmas. First is *principle-based ethical decision making*. Second is *virtue-based ethical decision making*. Third is called the *quick check*.

Principle-based Ethical Decision Making   This six-step decision-making model is intended to help counsellors make better decisions. The steps are as follows:

1. What are the key ethical issues in this situation?
2. What ethical articles from the CCPA *Code of Ethics* are relevant to this situation?
3. Which of the six ethical principles are of major importance in this situation?
4. How can the relevant ethical articles be applied in this circumstance and any conflict between principles be resolved, and what are the potential risks and benefits of this application and resolution?
5. What do my feelings and intuition tell me to do in this situation?
6. What plan of action will be most helpful in this situation? (p. 4)

Virtue-based Ethical Decision Making Ask yourself the following five questions to help make virtuous decisions. The goal is to do what you believe is the right thing.

1. What emotions and intuition am I aware of as I consider this ethical dilemma, and what are they telling me to do?
2. How can my values best show caring for the client in this situation?
3. How will my decision affect other relevant individuals in this ethical dilemma?
4. What decision would I feel best about publicizing?
5. What decision would best define who I am as a person? (CCPA, 2007, p. 5)

Quick check. Ask yourself three questions:

1. *Publicity.* Would I want this ethical decision announced on the front page of a major newspaper?
2. *Universality.* Would I make the same decision for everyone? If every counsellor made this decision, would it be a good thing?
3. *Justice.* Is everyone being treated fairly by my decision? (CCPA, 2007, p. 5)

Although the CCPA *Code of Conduct* (CCPA, 2007) is arranged and titled differently from the *College of Alberta Psychologists' Standards of Practice (2005)*, the two documents cover essentially the same issues. Additionally, a special section in the CCPA code addresses the responsibility to screen prospective members before inviting them into group counselling.

In one other regard, the CCPA code (CCPA, 2007) differs from the other codes and standards of practice discussed here: When terminating counselling relationships, the code specifies that counsellors should do so when either "the client or another person with whom the client has a relationship threatens or otherwise endangers the counsellor" (CCPA, 2007, p. 12).

Case Example: What Would *You* Do?

You are counselling a woman who has been physically abused by her husband. You assist her by beginning to look into a room at a local emergency shelter. The next day, the husband calls you and says that if you see his wife again and either attempt to put her in the shelter or counsel her, he will kill you.

1. Are you ethically allowed to see this woman again?

2. If you decide not to see her, what alternative would you choose?

3. If you don't see her, to what extent are you collaborating with patriarchy and male privilege?

The Canadian Association of Social Workers' Code of Ethics 2005 and Guidelines for Ethical Practice 2005

The preamble to the CASW *Code of Ethics 2005* (CASW, 2005a) acknowledges that the social work profession "has a particular interest in the needs and empowerment of people who are vulnerable, oppressed, and/or living in poverty" (p. 3). The promotion and achievement of social justice has been a primary concern of the social work profession since its inception.

Social workers are expected to uphold the following social work values:

1. Respect for the inherent dignity and worth of persons

2. Pursuit of social justice

3. Service to humanity

4. Integrity of professional practice

5. Confidentiality in professional practice

6. Competence in professional practice (CASW, 2005a, p. 4)

The CASW *Guidelines for Ethical Practice 2005* (CASW, 2005b) again cover more or less the same standards of practice as noted earlier, but specify a few guidelines that are not spelled out in the other codes. Under the heading *Protect Privacy and Confidentiality,* they specify that one must protect the confidentiality of deceased clients. Under *Ethical Responsibilities in Professional Relationships,* they note that physical contact with clients (e.g., hugs, kisses on cheeks, hand on hand or on shoulder) should be avoided if it might be harmful to the client. If the social worker does intend to display physical contact, he or she must ensure that is considered culturally and personally appropriate.

ETHICS IN SPECIFIC COUNSELLING SITUATIONS

Ethical behaviour is greatly influenced by the prevalent attitudes in the setting in which one works, by one's colleagues, and by the task the counsellor is performing (e.g., diagnosing). Therefore, implementing ethical decisions and actions in counselling sometimes involves substantial personal and professional risk or discomfort (Faiver, Eisengart, & Colonna, 2004). The reasons are multiple, but as Ladd (1971) observes, the difficulty in making ethical decisions can sometimes be attributed to the environments in which counsellors work. "Most organizations that employ counselors are organized not collegially or professionally, as is in part the case with universities and hospitals, but hierarchically. In a hierarchical organization, the administrator or executive decides which prerogatives are administrative and which are professional" (p. 262).

Counsellors should check thoroughly the general policies and principles of an institution before accepting employment; employment in a specific setting implies that the counsellor agrees with its policies, principles, and ethics. When counsellors find themselves in institutions that misuse their services and do not act in the best interests of their clients, they must act either to change the institution through educational or persuasive means or find other employment.

Case Example: What Would *You* Do?

A counselling relationship is one-sided: The counsellor listens intensely and attempts to engage in a therapeutic conversation. The focus is not on the therapist but is instead with the client. Clients are often appreciative of having someone give them undivided attention—a practice many do not often experience in their daily lives.

Zara was a client who brought me home-baked cookies and bread after only three sessions with her. In some counselling theoretical orientations, counsellors are clearly advised not to accept gifts from their clients. As a counsellor with a strong humanistic orientation, I have not felt that this is necessarily a problem. I accepted her gift.

The next week, however, she brought me more baked goods and this time I felt uncomfortable. I shared my discomfort with her and asked her not to do this again. I believed that she looked disappointed and so we then talked further about the accuracy of my observation. Indeed, Zara said that this had hurt her feelings and that her only intent had been to share with me as I was doing with her.

1. What are your thoughts regarding accepting gifts from clients?

2. Assuming that you too would have accepted her first gift, how would you have dealt with gifts being brought to you a second time?

3. If you had refused the first gift, how would you have done so? What would you have said if Zara was disappointed with your refusal?

School Counselling and Ethics

The potential for major ethical crises between a counsellor and his or her employer exists in many school settings (Davis & Ritchie, 1993; Stone, 2005). School counsellors are often used as tools by school administrators (Boy & Pine, 1968). When the possibility of conflict exists between a counsellor's loyalty to the employer and the client, "the counsellor should always attempt to find a resolution that protects the rights of the client; the ethical responsibility is to the client first and the school [or other setting] second" (Huey, 1986, p. 321). One way school counsellors can assure themselves of an ethically sound program is to realize that they may encounter multiple dilemmas in providing services to students, parents, and teachers. Colleagueship may be particularly helpful, allowing consultation with other Canadian school counsellors through membership and participation in the School Counsellors Chapter of the Canadian Counselling and Psychotherapy Association (see www.ccpa-accp.ca/en/chapters/details.php?ID=8).

Computers, Counselling, and Ethics

The use of computers and technology in counselling is another area of potential ethical difficulty. With over 300 websites now being run by individual counsellors (Ainsworth, 2002), the possibility exists for a breach of client information when computers are used to transmit information among professional counsellors.

Other ethically sensitive areas include client or counsellor misuse and even the validity of data offered over computer links (Sampson et al., 1997). The problem of *cyber counselling* or *webcounselling*—that is, counselling over the internet, in which the counsellor may be hundreds of miles away—is fraught with ethical dilemmas. Thus, the Canadian Counselling and Psychotherapy Association has issued ethical guidelines regarding such conduct, as has the Canadian Psychological Association. (Both of these ethical codes and the code for the Canadian Association of Social Workers can be found in the Notes, the student supplement to this text.)

Marriage/Family Counselling and Ethics

Another counselling situation in which ethical crises are common is marriage and family counselling (Corey et al., 2007; Margolin, 1982; Wilcoxon et al., 2007). The reason is that counsellors are treating a number of individuals together as a system, and it is unlikely that all members of the system have the same goals (Wilcoxon, 1986). To overcome potential problems, Thomas (1994) has developed a dynamic, process-oriented framework for counsellors to use when working with families. This model discusses six values that affect counsellors, clients, and the counselling process: (a) responsibility, (b) integrity, (c) commitment, (d) freedom of choice, (e) empowerment, and (f) right to grieve.

Other Counselling Settings and Ethics

Other counselling settings or situations with significant potential for ethical dilemmas (and often legal consequences) include counselling the elderly (Myers, 1998), multicultural counselling (Baruth & Manning, 2007), working in managed care in the United States (Murphy, 1998), diagnosis of clients (Braun & Cox, 2005; Rueth, Demmitt, & Burger, 1998), and counselling research (Jencius & Rotter, 1998). In all of these areas, counsellors face new situations, some of which might not be addressed by existing ethics codes.

In working with older adults, counsellors often must make ethical decisions. They must assess the unique needs of the aging, who may have cognitive impairments, terminal illnesses, or perhaps are victims of abuse (Schwiebert, Myers, & Dice, 2000). Counsellors may apply principle ethics that are based on a set of obligations that focus on finding socially and historically appropriate answers to the question: "What shall I do?" (Corey et al., 2007). In other words, "Is this action ethical?" They may employ virtue ethics, too, which focus on the "character traits of the counselor and nonobligatory ideals to which professionals aspire" (p. 13). Rather than solving a specific ethical dilemma, virtue ethics focus on the question: "Am I doing what is best for my client?" Counsellors are wise to integrate both forms of ethical reasoning into their deliberations if they wish to make the best decisions possible.

In making ethical decisions where there are no guidelines, it is critical for counsellors to stay abreast of current issues, trends, and even legislation related to the situation they face. In the process, counsellors must take care not to stereotype or otherwise be insensitive to clients with whom they are working. For instance, "a primary emphasis of research ethics is, appropriately, on the protection of human subjects [people] in research" (Parker & Szymanski, 1996, p. 182). In the area of research in particular, there are four main ethical issues that must be resolved:

1. Informed consent
2. Coercion and deception
3. Confidentiality and privacy
4. Reporting the results (Robinson & Gross, 1986, p. 331)

All of these areas involve people whose lives are in the care of the researcher. Anticipation of problems and implementation of policies that produce humane and fair results are essential.

WORKING WITH COUNSELLORS WHO MAY ACT UNETHICALLY

Although most counsellors are ethical, occasional situations arise where such is not the case. In these circumstances, counsellors must take some action; by condoning or ignoring a situation they risk eroding their own sense of moral selfhood and may find it easier to condone future ethical breaches, a phenomenon known as the "slippery slope effect." Herlihy (1996) suggests several steps to take in order to work through potential ethical dilemmas, especially with impaired professionals. The first is to identify the problem as objectively as possible and the counsellor's relationship to it. Such a process is best done on paper to clarify thinking.

The second step in the process is for a counsellor to apply the current code of ethics and standards of practice of the particular professional associations or regulatory bodies to which the counsellor belongs. In such cases, clear guidance as to a course of action may emerge. Next, a counsellor should consider moral principles of the helping profession discussed earlier in this chapter, such as beneficence, justice, and autonomy. Consultation with a colleague is also an option.

If action is warranted, the colleague in question should first be approached informally. This approach involves confrontation in a caring context, which hopefully will lead to the counsellor in question seeking help. If it does not, the confronting counsellor should consider the potential consequences of all other options and then define a course of action. This might include filing an ethical complaint with the particular professional association and/or regulatory body to which the colleague belongs. A complaint may be filed by either the professional who has queried his or her colleague or by a client who believes he or she has been treated unethically.

In examining courses of action, a counsellor must evaluate where each potential action might lead. Criteria for judgment include comfort surrounding (a) publicity (i.e., if the actions of the confronting counsellor were reported in the press), (b) justice (i.e., fairness), (c) moral traces (i.e., lingering feelings of doubt), and (d) universality (i.e., is this a course I would recommend others take in this situation?).

Finally, a course of action is chosen and implemented. When this happens, the counsellor must realize that not everyone will agree; therefore, he or she needs to be prepared to take criticism as well as credit for what has been done.

THE LAW AND COUNSELLING

The profession of counselling is also governed by legal standards. Legal refers to "law or the state of being lawful," and law refers to "a body of rules recognized by a state or community as binding on its members" (Shertzer & Stone, 1980, p. 386). Contrary to popular opinion, "law is not cut and dried, definite and certain, or clear and precise" (Van Hoose & Kottler, 1985, p. 44). Rather, it always seeks compromise between individuals and parties. It offers few definite answers, and there are always notable exceptions to any legal precedent.

There is "no general body of law covering the helping professions" (Van Hoose & Kottler, 1985, p. 45), but there are a number of court decisions and statutes that influence legal opinions on counselling, and counsellors need to keep updated. Likely the best and easiest way to do this is to read the newsletter that is mailed or e-mailed regularly from your regulatory body. A less efficient way is to check the website of your regulatory body regularly for updates.

In most cases, the law is "generally supportive or neutral" toward professional codes of ethics and counselling in general (Stude & McKelvey, 1979, p. 454). It supports licensure or certification of counsellors as a means of ensuring that those who enter the profession attain at least minimal standards. It also supports the general "confidentiality of statements and records provided by clients during therapy" (p. 454). In addition, the law is neutral "in that it allows the profession to police itself and govern counsellors' relations with their clients and fellow counsellors" (p. 454). The only time the law overrides a professional code of ethics is when it is necessary "to protect the public health, safety, and welfare" (p. 454). This is most likely a necessity in situations concerning confidentiality, when disclosure of information is necessary to prevent harm. In such cases, counsellors have a duty to warn potential victims about the possibility of a client's violent behaviour (Costa & Altekruse, 1994).

GENERAL LEGAL CONSIDERATIONS

Counsellors have considerable trouble in situations in which the law is not clear or in which a conflict exists between the law and professional counselling ethics. Nevertheless, it is important that providers of mental health services be fully informed about what they can or cannot do legally. Such situations often involve the sharing of information among clients, counsellors, and the court system.

Sharing may be broken down into confidentiality, privacy, and privileged communication. *Confidentiality* is "the ethical duty to fulfill a contract or promise to clients that the information revealed during therapy will be protected from unauthorized disclosure" (Arthur & Swanson, 1993, p. 7). Confidentiality becomes a legal as well as an ethical concern if it is broken, whether intentionally or not. It is annually one of the most inquired about ethical and legal concerns received by the American Counseling Associations' Ethics Committee, including "dilemmas/questions regarding right to privacy, clients' right to privacy, and counsellors avoiding illegal and unwarranted disclosures of confidential information (exceptions, court ordered disclosure and records)" (Williams & Freeman, 2002, pp. 253–254).

Privacy is "an evolving legal concept that recognizes individuals' rights to choose the time, circumstances, and extent to which they wish to share or withhold personal information" (Herlihy & Sheeley, 1987, p. 479). Clients who think they have been coerced into revealing information they would not normally disclose may seek legal recourse against a counsellor.

Privileged communication, a narrower concept, regulates privacy protection and confidentiality by protecting clients from having their confidential communications disclosed in court without their permission. It is defined as "a client's legal right, guaranteed by statute, that confidences originating in a therapeutic relationship will be safeguarded"

(Arthur & Swanson, 1993, p. 7). Most American states recognize and protect privileged communication in counsellor–client relationships (Glosoff, Herlihy, & Spence, 2000). Every Canadian jurisdiction recognizes and protects privileged communication. However, there are nine categories of exceptions (this list is more specific than the exceptions to confidentiality mentioned earlier):

1. In cases of a dispute between counsellor and client
2. When a client raises the issue of mental condition in legal proceedings
3. When a client's condition poses a danger to self or others
4. In cases of child abuse or neglect (in addition to mandated reporting laws)
5. When the counsellor has knowledge that the client is contemplating commission of a crime
6. During court-ordered psychological evaluations
7. For purposes of involuntary hospitalization
8. When the counsellor has knowledge that a client has been a victim of a crime
9. In cases of harm to vulnerable adults (p. 455)

As opposed to individuals, the legal concept of privileged communication generally does not apply in group and family counselling (Wheeler & Bertram, 2008). However, counsellors should consider certain ethical concerns in protecting the confidentiality of group and family members.

One major difficulty with any law governing client and counsellor communication is that laws vary from one Canadian jurisdiction to another. It is essential that counsellors know and communicate to their clients potential situations in which confidentiality may be broken (Glosoff et al., 2000; Woody, 1988).

EXAMPLES OF LEGAL DECISIONS THAT IMPACT COUNSELLING RELATIONSHIPS IN CANADA

Counsellors have a legal obligation under all child abuse laws to report suspected cases of abuse to proper authorities, usually specific personnel in provincial and territorial child welfare offices in Canada and state social welfare offices in the United States (Henderson, 2007). Such situations may be especially difficult when counsellors are working directly with families in which the abuse is suspected (Stevens-Smith & Hughes, 1993).

A landmark court case in the United States that reflects the importance of limiting confidentiality is *Tarasoff v. Board of Regents of the University of California* (1976). The result of this case applies throughout Canadian jurisdictions. In this case, Prosenjit Poddar, a student who was a voluntary outpatient of the student health services department of the University of California at Berkeley, informed the psychologist who was counselling him that he intended to kill his former girlfriend, Tatiana Tarasoff, when she arrived back on campus. The psychologist notified the campus police, who detained and questioned the student about his proposed activities. The student denied any intention of killing Tarasoff, acted rationally, and was released. Poddar refused further treatment from the psychologist, and no additional steps were taken to deter him from his intended action. Two months later, he killed Tarasoff. Her parents sued the Regents of the University of California for failing to notify the intended victim of a threat against her. The California Supreme Court ruled in their favour, holding, in effect, that a therapist has a duty to protect the public that overrides any obligation to maintain client confidentiality (Haggard-Grann, 2007).

Although there is no identical case law in Canada to the Tarasoff decision, McDonald (2000) provides a similar ruling in Canada:

> Furthermore, across Canada, the 1998 *Cuerrier 145* decision of the Supreme Court of Canada held that if serious danger to health exists, there is a duty to warn (HIV–prospective partner) . . . Likewise in 1999, that Court in the *Jones 146* case would allow a breach of solicitor–client privilege where the risk of serious bodily harm to another was clear and imminent. Interestingly, this decision [which involved a psychiatrist also under a duty of confidentiality warning the solicitor of the intentions of his client (a sexual rapist)], considered a similar 1975 American case [note: the 1975 case referred to is Tarasoff]. (p. 113)

The ethical codes of regulated mental health professionals include wording that requires breaching confidentiality in such matters where there is duty to warn both the police and likely victims. An example of this is found in the Canadian Psychological Association Code of Ethics under article I.45 and II.39 (Canadian Psychological Association, 2000).

Thus, there is a limit to how much confidentiality a counsellor can or should maintain. When it appears that a client is dangerous to him- or herself or to others, laws specify that this information must be reported to the proper authorities. For example, when a child is suicidal, the courts hold that school personnel, including counsellors, are in a position to make a referral and "have a duty to secure assistance from others" (Maples et al., 2005, p. 401).

Knapp and Vandecreek (1982) suggest that when there is a risk of client violence, a counsellor should try to defuse the danger while also satisfying any legal duty. They recommend consulting with professional colleagues who have expertise in working with violent individuals and documenting the steps taken. In addition, Haggard-Grann (2007) advocates using risk-assessment tools whenever possible and appropriate. She also recommends in risk assessment that a number of variables be included, such as situational aspects including life situation (e.g., living conditions), behavioural patterns (e.g., substance abuse, medication), and foreseeable events or stressors (e.g., child custody, dilemmas, separation/divorce).

Several Canadian Supreme Court decisions also affect the practice of psychologists (see College of Alberta Psychologists, 2009). The results from several of these are listed below:

1. *McInerney v. MacDonald [1992].* A patient has access to information about himself/herself while in the custody of a health care provider.

2. *R. v. Mohan [1994].* This decision affects the conditions under which individuals can provide expert evidence to the Courts.

3. *R. v. Mills [1999].* The counselling records of rape victims are now protected from disclosure in criminal proceedings against alleged assailants.

4. *Smith v. Jones [1999].* Public safety considerations may override the otherwise privileged communications between a psychiatrist and a defense lawyer.

5. *Young v. Bella [2006].* This decision concerns the obligations for mandatory reporting (e.g., child abuse or neglect) and the legal protections provided to those making such reports.

Sheppard (n.d.) discussed a few interesting cases from case law in Canada. In 1995, a mother residing in British Columbia requested access to her two children's counselling sessions from an elementary school counsellor. The counsellor refused, and after several decisions by the school district and the Information and Privacy Commissioner of British Columbia, the case went to court. The judge ruled that, in the case of a child, the parent or guardian normally has the right to consent to the release of a child's counselling record.

In 1979–1981, a social worker was working as a youth counsellor at a detention centre in St. John's, Newfoundland. One of the counsellor's clients was a 14-year-old girl. When the girl was 16 years old, she was living in a community group home. The counsellor and the girl began having consensual sex, which continued for three years. The girl did not disclose this sexual relationship until 1995, but by this time the counsellor was working as a regional supervisor at the detention centre where the two of them had first met. The counsellor was fired, but he sued for wrongful dismissal. In July 2000, the Newfoundland Supreme Court dismissed the claim and ruled that the dismissal "was not an unreasonable consequence for this type of conduct" (Sheppard, n.d., p. 2).

In 1994 in Ontario, parents wanted to challenge a school psychologist's decision that their daughter was not gifted. The parents wanted to see the answers and scoring procedures for the test that was used to make this determination—in this case, the Stanford Binet Intelligence Scales. After refusal by the school board, the parents brought this to the Information and Privacy Commissioner. The Commissioner concurred that this information should be released, but the school board again refused and went to court. The court agreed with the school board and overturned the Commissioner's decision on the grounds that a release of this information would affect the validity of the test (Sheppard, n.d.).

CIVIL AND CRIMINAL LIABILITY

The Tarasoff case raises the problem of counsellor liability and malpractice. Basically, *liability* in counselling involves issues concerned with whether counsellors have caused harm to clients (Wilcoxon et al., 2007). The concept of liability is directly connected with malpractice. *Malpractice* in counselling is defined as "harm to a client resulting from professional negligence, with *negligence* defined as the departure from acceptable professional standards" (Hummell et al., 1985, p. 70; emphasis added). Until recently, there were relatively few counsellor malpractice lawsuits, but with the increased number of licensed, certified, and practising counsellors, malpractice suits have become more common. Therefore, professional counsellors need to make sure they protect themselves from such possibilities.

Two ways to protect oneself from malpractice are (a) to follow professional codes of ethics and (b) to follow normal practice standards (Wheeler & Bertram, 2008). Regardless of how careful counsellors are, however, malpractice lawsuits can still occur; therefore, carrying liability insurance is a must (Bullis, 1993).

Counsellors in Canada who want to avoid ethics complaints will find the case example book referred to earlier called *Counselling Ethics: Issues and Cases* published by the CCPA (Schulz et al., 2006) to be a helpful read. Another useful resource in the event that a formal complaint is filed is *Surviving a licensing board complaint: What to do, what not to do: Practical tips from the experts* (Shapiro et al., 2008).

Liability can be classified under three main headings: civil, criminal, and administrative (Leslie, 2005). Liability can also involve a combination of these three. *Civil liability* means that one can be sued for acting wrongly toward another or for failing to act when there is a recognized duty to do so (Wheeler & Bertram, 2008). Usually civil liability results in a lawsuit from a client against the counsellor for professional malpractice (i.e., negligence) or gross negligence. *Criminal liability* involves a counsellor working with a client in a way the law does not allow. Examples of criminal liability are the commitment of a crime by a counsellor, such as failing to report child abuse; engaging in sexual relations with a client; or insurance fraud. *Administrative liability* "means that the therapist's license to practise is threatened by an investigation from the licensing board, which has the power to revoke or suspend a license" (Leslie, 2005, p. 46). Additionally, a client can file a complaint with the ethics committee of a professional association to which the counsellor belongs. The association has the power, among other options, to terminate the counsellor's membership.

The concept of civil liability rests on the concept of *tort*, a wrong that legal action is designed to set right (Wheeler & Bertram, 2008). The legal wrong can be against a person, property, or even someone's reputation and may be unintentional or direct. Counsellors are most likely to face civil liability suits for malpractice in the following instances: (a) malpractice in particular situations (e.g., birth control, abortion, treatment); (b) illegal search; (c) defamation; (d) invasion of privacy; and (e) breach of contract (Wheeler & Bertram, 2008). Three situations in which counsellors risk criminal liability are (a) accessory to a crime, (b) civil disobedience, and (c) contribution to the delinquency of a minor (Wheeler & Bertram, 2008).

LEGAL ISSUES INVOLVED WHEN COUNSELLING MINORS

Minors are children under the age of 18. Many school counsellors work with children in this age group. Other counsellors interact with children in this age range in community agencies. Working with minors in nonschool settings involves legal (and ethical) issues different from those in an educational environment (Lawrence & Kurpius, 2000). For example, since the "client-counsellor relationship is fiduciary it falls under the legal jurisdiction of contract law. Typically, a minor can enter into a contract for treatment in one of three ways: (a) with parental consent, (b) involuntarily at a parent's insistence, or (c) by order of the juvenile court" (p. 133). Whereas court-ordered treatment of a child does not require parental consent, the other two conditions do and, even with court-ordered treatment, parents or guardians should be informed. "If informed parental consent is not obtained, counselors risk the possibility of being sued for battery, failure to gain consent, and child enticement" (p. 133).

In working with minors and their families, Lawrence and Kurpius (2000, p. 135) provide a number of suggestions, including the following:

- "Be thoroughly familiar with state statutes," especially regarding privileged communication. The same advice applies to Canadian provinces and territories.

- "Clarify your policies concerning confidentiality with both the child and parents at the initiation of the therapeutic relationship and ask for their cooperation. Provide a written statement of these policies that everyone signs."

- "Keep accurate and objective records of all interactions and counseling sessions."

- "Maintain adequate professional liability coverage." Such coverage should be above the minimum.

- If you need help, "confer with colleagues and have professional legal help available."

CLIENT RIGHTS AND RECORDS

There are two main types of client rights: implied and explicit (Hansen et al., 1994). Both relate to due process. *Implied rights* are linked to substantive due process. When a rule is made that arbitrarily limits an individual (i.e., deprives the person of his or her constitutional rights), he or she has been denied substantive due process. *Explicit rights* focus on procedural due process (the steps necessary to initiate or complete an action when an explicit rule is broken). An individual's procedural due process is violated when an explicit rule is broken and the person is not informed about how to remedy the matter. A client has a right to know what recourse he or she has when either of these two types of rights is violated.

The records of all clients are legally protected except under special circumstances. For example, an individual has the legal right to inspect his or her record. There are also some cases in which third parties have access to student information without the consent of the student or parent. In the vast majority of cases, counsellors are required by law to protect clients of all ages by keeping records under lock and key, separate from any required business records, and by not disclosing any information about a client without that person's written permission (Mitchell, 2007). The best method to use in meeting a request for disclosing information is a release-of-information form, which can be drawn up by an attorney (Rosenthal, 2005). Counsellors should not release client information they have not obtained firsthand.

Because record keeping is one of the top five areas pertaining to legal liability of counsellors (Snider, 1987), the question often arises about what should go into records. Basically, records should contain "all information about the client necessary for his or her treatment" (Piazza & Baruth, 1990, p. 313). The number and types of forms in a client record vary with the agency and practitioner, but six categories of documents are usually included:

1. *Identifying or intake information*—name, address, telephone number(s), date of birth, sex, occupation, and so on

2. *Assessment information*—psychological evaluation(s), social/family history, health history, and so on

3. *Treatment plan*—presenting problem, plan of action, steps to be taken to reach targeted behaviour, and so on

4. *Case notes*—for example, documentation of progress in each session toward the stated goal

5. *Termination summary*—outcome of treatment, final diagnosis (if any), after-care plan, and so on

6. *Other data*—client's signed consent for treatment, copies of correspondence, notations about rationale for any unusual client interventions, administrative problems, and so on

It is vital for counsellors to check their provincial or territorial legal codes for exact guidelines about record keeping. It is critical for counsellors who receive third-party reimbursement to make sure that their client records refer to progress in terms of a treatment plan and a diagnosis (if required) (Hinkle, 1994). In no case, however, should confidential information about a client be given over the telephone. Counsellors are also ethically and legally bound to ensure that a client's rights are protected by not discussing counselling cases in public. Overall, good record keeping is good for both the client and the counsellor.

Case Example: What Would *You* Do?

Diane kept her records on her computer. It was easier for her to keep up to date, and she figured she could always makes changes or edits without anyone knowing. However, when Diane received a court order regarding one of her clients, she had to appear—and so did her computer. One of the questions asked was "Have you made any modifications of this client's record?" Diane wanted to answer "no" but she knew she that was not true. She was constantly making corrections or inserting new impressions in her notes.

1. If you were Diane, what would you say and how?

2. Do you think that modifying client records on a computer is unethical? Why or why not?

THE COUNSELLOR IN COURT

The court system in Canada is divided into federal and provincial or territorial courts. The Canadian government has the exclusive right to legislate criminal law, while the provinces have the exclusive right to legislate civil law (Department of Justice Canada, n.d.). Almost all cases begin in provincial courts, regardless of whether they are criminal or civil matters, and from there cases may be appealed to higher courts. Most counsellors who appear in court do so at the provincial or territorial level.

Most counsellors end up in court in two main ways. One is voluntary and professional, when the counsellor serves as an expert witness. "An expert witness is an objective and unbiased person with specialized knowledge, skills, or information, who can assist a judge or jury in reaching an appropriate legal decision" (Remley, 1992, p. 33). A counsellor who serves as an expert witness is compensated financially for his or her time.

The other way in which a counsellor may appear in court is through a court order (a subpoena to appear in court at a certain time in regard to a specific case). Such a summons is issued with the intent of having the counsellor testify on behalf of or against a present or former client. Because the legal system is adversarial, counsellors are wise to seek the advice of attorneys before responding to court orders (Remley, 1991; Remley & Herlihy, 2005). By so doing, counsellors may come to understand law, court proceedings, and the options they have in response to legal requests. For example, once a subpoena is issued, counsellors do not have to produce their records or give testimony until the client–counsellor privilege has been waived or the court orders the counsellor "to turn over the records or to testify" (Leslie, 2005, p. 46). Role-playing possible situations before appearing in court may also help counsellors function better in such situations.

ETHICS AND THE LAW: TWO WAYS OF THINKING

In ending this chapter, it should be apparent that attorneys and counsellors tend to think in different ways. The professionals in these specialties live for the most part in two different cultures and base their practices on unique worldviews. For this reason, there is a "strong rationale for considering counseling and the legal system from a cross-cultural perspective" (Rowley & MacDonald, 2001, p. 423). The relative differences in the culture between counsellors and attorneys are outlined in Table 3.1. It should be noted, in considering these differences, that there are notable exceptions.

To be successful in a litigious society, counsellors, who are part of a minority culture, must become acculturated into the majority culture—the law. There are several ways they can accomplish this goal, including

- becoming "knowledgeable with those elements that are common to both mental health and the law"

- understanding and being prepared to "work with those elements of the law that differ from the culture of mental health," such as seeking information from a counsellor without an appropriate release

- reviewing codes of ethics and standards of practice annually

- participating in continuing education programs that review laws pertinent to one's counselling specialty

- learning more about the legal system through "organizations and publications that interface the mental health and legal system" (e.g., Canadian Law and Society Association and their publication, *Canadian Journal of Law & Society*)

- creating a collaborative relationship with a lawyer, a judge, or other legal practitioner

- developing a relationship with a counsellor who is knowledgeable about the world of law

Table 3.1 Relative differences in culture between counselling and law

Counseling	Law
Systemic and linear reasoning	Linear reasoning
Artistic, subjective-objective understandings	Objective, fairness understandings
Growth, therapeutic priorities	Order, protection priorities
Individual or small group focus	Societal focus
Priority on change	Priority on stability
Relativity, contextual understanding	Normative dichotomies understanding
Cooperative, relational emphasis	Adversarial, fact-finding emphasis
Recommendation, consultation emphases	Legal sanctions and guidance emphases
Ethical, experiential, education bases	Legal reasoning basis
Deterministic worldview or unknowns, or both, accepted	Deterministic worldview

Source: Reprinted from "Counseling and the Law: A Cross-Cultural Perspective." (p. 424) by W. J. Rowley & D. MacDonald in the *Journal for Counseling and Development* (2001), 79, 422–429. © ACA. Reprinted with permission. No further reproduction authorized without written permission of The American Psychological Association.

- consulting and receiving feedback on possible decisions when there is an ethical–legal dilemma (Rowley & MacDonald, 2001, pp. 427–428)

Even though thinking styles may differ, there are times when legal and ethical outlooks reach similar conclusions even for different reasons. An American example of this occurred in *Bruff v. North Mississippi Health Services, Inc.*, 2001 (Hermann & Herlihy, 2006). In this situation, a therapist refused on religious grounds to treat an openly lesbian woman who requested assistance in having better sexual relations with her partner. The counsellor assumed that she would have to perform only those duties she found acceptable and within cited sections A.11.b and C.2.a (which deal with competence and boundary issues) of the 2005 ACA *Code of Ethics* to support her referral of the client to another counsellor. The court found that "providing counseling only on issues that do not conflict with a counselor's religious beliefs is an inflexible position not protected by the law" (p. 416). Ethically, the "moral principles of justice (fairness), beneficience (doing good), non-malefience (doing no harm), and respect for autonomy" (p. 417) all applied to this case.

SUMMARY AND CONCLUSION

Counsellors are like other professionals in having established codes of ethics to guide them in the practice of helping others. The main codes of ethics and standards of practice are published by the Canadian Psychological Association, the Canadian Association of Social Workers, and the Canadian Counselling and Psychotherapy Association. Acting ethically is not always easy, comfortable, or clear.

In making an ethical decision, counsellors may rely on personal values as well as ethical standards and legal precedents. They can also consult with professional colleagues, casebooks, and principles. It is imperative that counsellors become well informed in the area of ethics for the sake of their own well-being and that of their clients. It is not enough that counsellors have an academic knowledge of ethics; they must have a working knowledge and be able to assess at what developmental level they and their colleagues are operating.

In addition, counsellors must be informed about provincial or territorial and national legislation and legal decisions. These will affect the ways in which they work. Counsellors are liable for civil and criminal malpractice suits if they violate client rights or societal rules. One way for counsellors to protect themselves legally is to follow the ethical standards of the professional organizations with which they are affiliated and to operate according to recognized normal practices. It is imperative that counsellors be able to justify what they do. Counsellors should also carry malpractice insurance.

Ethical standards and legal codes reflect current conditions and are ever-evolving documents. They do not cover all situations, but they do offer help beyond that contained in counsellors' personal beliefs and values. As counselling continues to develop as a profession, its ethical and legal aspects will probably become more complicated, and enforcement procedures will become stricter. Ignorance of ethics and the law is no excuse for any practising counsellor. It is important that counsellors realize that, with notable exceptions, they think differently from attorneys. Therefore, as the minority culture, they need to take the initiative in learning how to deal with legal matters and lawyers.

Your Personal Reflections

1. Although the 2007 CCPA *Code of Ethics* covers multiple topics, it does not cover all counselling situations. What other topics can you think of that are related to counselling but not mentioned in the six sections of the Code?

2. When have you acted in a way to avoid harm (non-maleficence)? When have you acted in a way that promoted good (beneficence)?

3. Ethical issues in research grew out of experiments where people were deceived into believing they were actually torturing others or acting in ways that they later regretted and were upset about. If someone signs up to do research with you and then changes his or her mind, what do you think you should do? Would it make a difference if you needed only one more person to complete your research, no one else had signed up, and you had only two days left to collect your data or you would fail the research course?

Classroom Activities

1. Obtain copies of early ethical codes for the CCPA. Compare these guidelines to the most recently published CCPA *Code of Ethics*. What differences do you notice? Discuss your observations with fellow class members.

2. In groups of four, use the CCPA's *Counselling Ethics: Issues and Cases* (Schulz et al., 2006) as a guide to enact specific ethical dilemmas before your classmates. Have the other groups write down at least two courses of action they would pursue in solving your enacted situation. Have them justify the personal and professional reasons for their actions. Discuss each of these situations with the class as a whole and with your instructor.

3. Invite three or four professional counsellors to your class to discuss specific ethical and legal concerns they have encountered. Ask what areas they find the most difficult to deal with. After their presentations, question them about the role of ethics and law in the future of counselling.

4. Obtain as many copies as you can of counselling laws in provinces and territories where psychologists are licensed. Check the CPA website (www.cpa.ca) as a starting place in carrying out this assignment. Compare these laws for similarities and differences. What areas do you think the laws need to address that are not being covered?

5. Write down ways that you, as a professional counsellor, can influence the development of counselling ethics and law. Be specific. Share your thoughts with fellow classmates.

Chapter 4
Counselling in a Multicultural Society

PRACTICE REFLECTION

In counselling practice, we often learn as much from our failures as we do from our successes. As you will discover in this chapter, every counsellor–client interaction can be viewed as a multicultural exchange. After all, we are all different and we are all the same in some regard.

I was working at an employee and family assistance firm part-time when George and Samantha came to see me. Before I brought them in, I asked them to complete a two-page questionnaire that asked for some basic demographic information.

I reviewed their answers and discovered that they were struggling with deciding whether to abort Samantha's pregnancy. Both were in their mid-forties and were well educated. This was a second marriage for both of them, and the pregnancy was an accident.

Once they came into my office, Samantha elaborated, "Well, here it is December 22, and I have 10 days to make my decision—after that, I no longer qualify for an abortion because of the gestation period. George and I are completely conflicted about what to do about this. We have children from previous marriages, and we are at a stage in our lives where we prefer to travel and not have childrearing obligations." I asked for clarification from both of them regarding their thinking about this.

They were articulate in describing the extensive intellectual work they had already done in exploring their options. Still, they were in a stalemate; neither could decide. I noted that they both self-described as Catholic, and wondered if that made any difference to them. They said it did to some extent but that it would not be the determining factor.

The 50-minute session was nearly over, leaving us only 15 minutes. I knew that, with my schedule, I would not be able to see them again until after the qualifying period had expired. What should I have done? I reasoned that what was missing for both of them was the religious component—how could they have an abortion without examining the impact of what it would mean spiritually? I was not coming from a religious place, but from a desire to help them.

I wondered about using the empty chair technique, in which I would ask Samantha to have a conversation with the unborn, imagining that the child was sitting in the empty chair in my office. I thought this would evoke a strong emotional response, but I also thought it would be overpowering and would unduly influence her decision to keep the developing fetus. That seemed manipulative to me, so instead I continued my questioning along religious grounds.

Time was up, and I knew I had failed them. I cannot recall ever feeling more on the spot in my counselling work. Furthermore, after the session, they complained to my employer that I had overemphasized spirituality and religion in our conversation. I have wondered many, many times about how I could have been more helpful. Frankly, it still bothers me to some extent.

I now think the best approach would have been to cut them short with their rational reasons for either keeping or not keeping the fetus and to ask, "You have already explored this at the cognitive level *ad nauseum*—there is little else here that I can contribute. How do you think we could best utilize our remaining time here tonight?" After their response, I might have gone with their suggestion or made my own. I could then have told them that what I was missing was the emotional component to their decision making process. If they concurred, I would have obtained informed consent regarding use of the empty chair technique or a related technique where I would have asked them to pretend their spouse was the unborn child and instructed the other respond to him or her. Following this, they could have reversed roles. Both would have needed to understand that it may have evoked a strong emotional response that could influence their decision. Would they have found this acceptable? If not, what would they have preferred as an alternative? As the cliché goes, however, hindsight is always 20/20.

The effectiveness of counselling depends on many factors, but among the most important is that the counsellor and client are able to understand and relate to each other. Such a relationship is usually easier to achieve if the client and counsellor are from the same culture or similar to each other in background. Regardless, it is imperative that counsellors be acutely sensitive to their clients' backgrounds and special needs and equally attuned to their own values, biases, and abilities (Atkinson, 2004; Brinson, 1996; Holiday, Leach, & Davidson, 1994). Otherwise they may misunderstand and frustrate clients and even harm them. Understanding and dealing positively with differences in cultures is a matter of developing self-awareness (from the inside out) as well as developing an awareness of others (from the outside in) (Okun, Fried, & Okun, 1999). Differences between counsellors and clients should never be allowed to influence the counselling process negatively.

This chapter considers distinct populations and issues that impact counselling in a culturally diverse world, especially North America. "As the racial and ethnic diversity of Canada continues to increase, the need for mental health professionals to tailor their mental health services to the needs of various cultural populations has become more germane" (Constantine et al., 2007, p. 24). Culturally neutral counselling does not exist (Coleman, 1998).

Topics covered here focus on working with culturally and ethnically distinct clients. Methods that work best with one population may be irrelevant or even inappropriate for others. Indeed, "a particular characteristic may be valued and desirable in certain cultures and denigrated and seen as a weakness in others" (Harris, Thoresen, & Lopez, 2007, p. 5). Therefore, counsellors must be constant lifelong learners and implementers of new and effective methods of working with clients in distinct cultures.

COUNSELLING ACROSS CULTURE AND ETHNICITY

MANY CULTURAL AND ETHNIC GROUPS LIVE IN CANADA. CANADA'S POPULATION WAS estimated at 33 873 400 on October 1, 2009 (Statistics Canada, 2009c). In 2007, Canada welcomed 236 800 new immigrants, with 56.5% coming from an Asiatic country, constituting a net immigration rate nearly double that of the United States and higher than other G8 countries. In 2008, this figure rose to 247 202 immigrants (Citizenship and Immigration Canada, 2009). Most immigrants are in the most economically active age group of 25 to 44 years (Statistics Canada, 2009d).

The total percentage of immigrants living in Canada is already sizeable—about 20% of the population as of 2006 (Statistics Canada, 2009b). According to projections, up to 23% of the population will belong to a visible minority by 2017 (Statistics Canada, 2010). Furthermore, 75% of visible minorities will be living in Toronto, Vancouver, or

Montreal (Statistics Canada, 2010). As of 2006, 1 172 785 people reported Aboriginal status in Canada (Statistics Canada, 2008), constituting about 3.7% of the population. *Aboriginal identity*, according to Statistics Canada (2008),

> refers to those persons who reported identifying with at least one Aboriginal group, that is, North American Indian, Metis or Inuit, and/or those who reported being a Treaty Indian or a Registered Indian, as defined by the *Indian Act* of Canada, and/or those who reported they were members of an Indian band or First Nation. (p. 1)

Besides those of British, French, and Aboriginal heritage, Canada is also host to peoples of many ethnicities from around the world; approximately 200 were represented in the 2006 census. Table 4.1 will gives a sense of the larger ethnicities living in Canada. Note that many individuals in the census reported more than one ethnicity, so a respondent who reported both "English" and "Scottish" would be included in the "multiple responses" column.

How many times have you been slightly annoyed when someone asked you, "So where are you from?" If you are an immigrant, you have an easy answer to this question. However, if you are part of the 80% of Canada's population who were born here, you want to say, "I'm from Canada—like, I'm Canadian, eh?" Then they annoy you further by asking, "No, I mean where are you *really* from?" They want to know your *ethnicity*—your roots before your ancestors came to Canada.

The question has always struck me as irrelevant. I am Canadian, I am proud to be Canadian, and whether I am a little mongrel of English, Scottish, and Irish, I simply don't care. I live here, we are a multicultural nation, and that is what I care about.

Several factors influence the counselling of cultural and ethnic groups, but the harsh reality is that over 50% of minority-culture clients who begin counselling terminate after

Table 4.1 Top 10 Ethnic Origins, 2006 Counts for Canada, Provinces and Territories

#	Ethnic Origins	Total Responses	Single Responses	Multiple Responses
1	Canadian	10 066 290	5 748 725	4 317 570
2	English	6 570 015	1 367 125	5 202 890
3	French	4 941 210	1 230 535	3 710 675
4	Scottish	4 719 850	568 515	4 151 340
5	Irish	4 354 155	491 030	3 863 125
6	German	3 179 425	670 640	2 508 785
7	Italian	1 445 335	741 045	704 285
8	Chinese	1 346 510	1 135 365	211 145
9	North American Indian	1 253 615	512 150	741 470
10	Ukrainian	1 209 085	300 590	908 495

Note: Data extrapolated from 20% of the sample (Statistics Canada, 2009a).

one session, as compared with about 30% of majority-culture clients (Sue & Sue, 2003). This statistic suggests that, as a rule, minority-culture clients have negative experiences in counselling. As a group, ethnic minorities underutilize counselling services because of the treatment they receive or fail to have been provided. Such results work against these clients, their families, and society in general.

DEFINING CULTURE AND MULTICULTURAL COUNSELLING

Culture may be defined in several ways. Definitions include *"ethnographic variables* such as ethnicity, nationality, religion, and language, as well as *demographic variables* of age, gender, place of residence, etc., *status variables* such as social, economic, and educational background and a wide range of formal or informal memberships and affiliations" (Pedersen, 1990, p. 550; emphasis added). A culture "structures our behaviour, thoughts, perceptions, values, goals, morals, and cognitive processes" (Cohen, 1998, p. B4). It may do so on an unconscious or a conscious level.

A broad definition of *culture* that is inclusive as well as accurate is "any group of people who identify or associate with one another on the basis of some common purpose, need, or similarity of background" (Axelson, 1999, p. 2). Shared elements of a culture include learned experiences, beliefs, and values. These aspects of a culture give coherence and meaning to life. Whereas some cultures may self-define partially in regard to similar physical features, others do so more in terms of a common history and philosophy, and still others combine the two. What people claim as a part of their culture and heritage is not always apparent at first sight.

Just as the word *culture* is multidimensional, the term *multicultural* has been conceptualized in a number of different ways. There is no universal agreement as to what it includes, perhaps leading Canadian accrediting bodies, like CPA and CCPA, to use words like "non-discriminatory" practice and respect for "diversity" instead, respectively. "Respect for diversity" is also the expression used in the ethics code of the Canadian Association of Social Workers. "The lack of a concrete definition for multiculturalism has been a continuing problem" (Middleton, Flowers, & Zawaiza, 1996, p. 19). The most prominent foci of multiculturalism are distinct group uniquenesses and concepts that facilitate attention to individual differences (Locke, 1998).

Therefore, *multicultural counselling* may be viewed generally as counselling "in which the counselor and client differ" (Locke, 1990, p. 18). As it is always the case that clients and counsellors differ in some respects, Arthur and Collins (2009) describe all counselling as multicultural exchanges. The differences between client and counsellor may be the result of socialization in a unique cultural way, developmental or traumatic life events, or the product of being raised in a particular ethnic environment. The debate in the multicultural counselling field is how broad differences should be defined. On one hand, some proponents advocate what is known as an *etic perspective*, stating universal qualities exist in counselling that are culturally generalizable. On the other hand, the *emic perspective* assumes counselling approaches must be designed to be culturally specific.

"The etic approach can be criticized for not taking important cultural differences into account. The emic approach can be criticized for placing too much emphasis on specific techniques as the vehicle for client change" (Fischer, Jome, & Atkinson, 1998, p. 578). Some professionals have tried to find common elements shared by these two approaches. For example, Fischer et al. (1998) proposed four conditions common to any type of counselling treatment:

- the therapeutic relationship,
- a shared worldview between client and counsellor,
- client expectations for positive change, and
- interventions believed by both client and counsellor to be a means of healing (p. 531).

However, this proposal has received only limited support. Thus, in the 21st century, the definition of multicultural counselling continues to be argued. There are those who are more inclusive and more exclusive of others. In this chapter, multiculturalism will be dealt with using an emic approach, which should be combined with diversity factors (covered in the next chapter). In order to really understand clients, counsellors must realize the persons sitting before them are complex and multifaceted. Therefore, combining cultural and diversity factors as a part of understanding is essential.

Furthermore, as Hoskins (2003) has aptly pointed out, the communalities of a cultural group do not tell to what extent, if any, individuals from that group have incorporated these into their beliefs and practices. For example, Hoskins goes on to describe the international reputation of Canadians as agreeable, complacent beer drinkers who watch hockey. But we know for a fact that some aren't agreeable, some aren't complacent, and some even avoid hockey!

HISTORY OF MULTICULTURALISM AND MULTICULTURAL COUNSELLING

As fact, "multiculturalism" in Canada refers to the presence and persistence of diverse racial and ethnic minorities who define themselves as different and who wish to remain so. Ideologically, multiculturalism consists of a relatively coherent set of ideas and ideals pertaining to the celebration of Canada's cultural diversity. Multiculturalism at the policy level is structured around the management of diversity through formal initiatives in the federal, provincial and municipal domains. Finally, multiculturalism is the process by which racial and ethnic minorities compete to obtain support from central authorities for the achievement of certain goals and aspirations. (Dewing & Leman, 2006, p. 4)

According to the *Library of Parliament* (Dewing & Leman, 2006), some analysts have viewed the development of Canadian society as having gone through three "forces." First,

Aboriginal people arrived here around 28 000 BC by crossing over the Bering Strait (EI group, 2010). Second, the so-called "Charter groups" arrived, comprised of French- and English-speaking communities. Third, the arrival of racial and ethnic minorities who fall outside the Charter groups immigrated to Canada.

Multiculturalism

How did Canada become a multicultural nation known as a "cultural mosaic" (i.e., plural cultural identities) instead of as a "melting pot" (i.e., a singular cultural identity)? It began with official policy. Canada's first multiculturalism policy was announced by then–Prime Minister Pierre Trudeau in 1971, making Canada the first country in the world to take this step (Arthur & Collins, 2009). This followed four years after the *Immigration Act* of 1967, which "did not discriminate on the basis of race, national origin, religion, or culture and was thus less discriminatory against non-Europeans" (Esses & Gardner, 1996, p. 147).

Following the 1971 policy, the *Act for the Preservation and Enhancement of Multiculturalism in Canada* was passed in 1988 (Esses & Gardner, 1996, p. 147). This act went further in defining multiculturalism as a part of Canada's collective identity and included measures for implementing the policy.

How effective have Canada's policies been? Berry and Kalin (1995) reported the results of a national representative study conducted in June 1991 with 2500 respondents. They concluded that "there is moderately high and continuing acceptance of the general idea of Canada remaining a culturally diverse society" (Berry & Kalin, 1995, p. 315). That did not mean, however, that everything was fine here. Every culture experiences *ethnocentrism* (Levine & Campbell, 1972), which is the idea that people judge other cultures as less than or inferior to their own, and this judgment (i.e., prejudice) is often extrapolated to individuals living in or emigrating from these other cultures. Berry and Kalin (1995) remarked that groups living in Canada from non-European backgrounds are less accepted than those of European descent. In effect, this is racism, and Canadians are not immune either.

According to the Ethnic Diversity Study completed in 2002 (Statistics Canada, 2003), 8% of the Canadian population (about 1.8 million people) felt out of place or uncomfortable some of the time because of their accent, culture, ethnicity, language, race, religion, or skin colour, and a further 2% felt this way most of the time. Visible minorities reported higher rates of feeling this way most or all of the time—a booming 24%, or 683 000 people. This study did not include Aboriginal people; if it had, the figures likely would have been still higher.

Multicultural Counselling

In a country that prides itself on being pluralistic and that has allowed immigration at record levels, it is not surprising that leaders in the counselling profession became concerned about how to train graduates of counselling programs to deal with the resulting diversity of clientele (Arthur & Collins, 2009). Research had also shown that graduates did not feel adequately prepared to deal effectively with such diversity (Arthur & Collins, 2009). This was experienced not only in Canada, but also in the United States.

The history of offering counselling services for culturally distinct populations in the United States and Canada is rather brief and uneven (Arredondo, 1998). For example, in a survey of experts in the field, Ponterotto and Sabnani (1989) found "only 8.5% of the most frequently cited books in the field [were published] before 1970" (p. 35). Indeed, the focus of multicultural counselling has shifted in its short history from an emphasis on the client (1950s) to an emphasis on the counsellor (1960s), and then to the total counselling process itself (1970s to the present). In the late 1980s, multicultural counselling was described as "the hottest topic in the profession" (Lee, 1989, p. 165).

Throughout the 1990s and into the 21st century it has remained so, with a significant increase in counselling journals that focus on multicultural issues from an exploratory and developmental, rather than a pathology-oriented, view (Arredondo, Rosen, Rice, Perez, & Tovar-Gamero, 2005). Indeed, multicultural issues in counselling now account for 12% of the quantitative articles published in the flagship journal of the American Counseling Association, the *Journal of Counselling and Development*, which is only slightly less than the leading subject published in the journal (career/academic issues, with 14%; (Nisson, Love, Taylor, & Slusher, 2007). From 1999 to 2009, 20% of the articles published in the flagship journal of the Canadian Counselling Association, the *Canadian Journal of Counselling* (CJC), have dealt with multicultural issues, and this number does not include a sizeable percentage of articles that are published in French. This new emphasis is why multicultural counselling is often called "the fourth force," following psychoanalysis, behaviourism, and humanistic concepts of counselling.

Although a number of scholars had previously pointed out the cultural limits of counselling, Gilbert Wrenn (1962) was the first prominent professional to call attention to the unique aspects of counselling people from different cultures. In a landmark work, he described the *culturally encapsulated counsellor* as one who disregards cultural differences and works under the mistaken assumption that theories and techniques are equally applicable to all people. Such a counsellor is insensitive to the actual experiences of clients from different cultural, racial, and ethnic backgrounds and therefore may discriminate against some persons by treating everyone the same. Clemmont Vontress (1966; 1967; 1996) was another early active pioneer in defining culture and showing how it influences counselling relationships. In 1973, Paul Pedersen chaired a panel on multicultural counselling at the American Psychological Association's annual convention, and with his colleagues later published the first book specifically on the subject, *Counseling across Cultures* (Pedersen, Lonner, & Draguns, 1976), now in its 6th edition. Since that time, numerous other publications and workshops have highlighted different aspects of multicultural counselling.

The Association for Multicultural Counseling and Development (AMCD), a division within the American Counseling Association, is dedicated primarily to defining and dealing with issues and concerns related to counselling across cultures in the United States.

Originally known as the Association for Non-white Concerns in Personnel and Guidance (ANWC), the division became part of the ACA in 1972 (McFadden & Lipscomb, 1985). It publishes a quarterly periodical, the *Journal of Multicultural Counselling and Development*, which addresses issues related to counselling in a culturally pluralistic society.

In Canada, CCPA has within it two chapters that address multicultural issues, the Aboriginal Circle Chapter and the Social Justice Chapter, while CPA has sections devoted to both Aboriginal psychology and international and cross-cultural psychology. The number of associations in Canada devoted to multiculturalism is staggering. A perusal of the list for Vancouver alone revealed nearly 300 organizations (Vancouver Community Network, 2009).

The AMCD has also sponsored training to help counsellors understand competencies needed in working with clients from non-European backgrounds and to promote the *Multicultural Competence Standards* (Sue et al., 1992). "Multicultural competence generally is defined as the extent to which counselors possess appropriate levels of self-awareness, knowledge, and skills in working with individuals from diverse cultural backgrounds" (Constantine et al., 2007, p. 24).

DIFFICULTIES IN MULTICULTURAL COUNSELLING

Smith and Vasquez (1985) caution that it is important to distinguish differences that arise from cultural backgrounds from those that are the result of poverty or deprived status. A failure to make this distinction can lead to *over-culturalizing*—that is, "mistaking people's reactions to poverty and discrimination for their cultural pattern" (p. 533). In Canada and the United States, many members of minority culture groups live in poverty. This problem is compounded by persistent second-language patterns in which the primary language of the client is not English. Nonverbal behaviours, especially in immigrant populations, are another problematic area in that clients may not be understood or accepted by counsellors from other than their own cultures.

Racism is a problematic area in working across cultures. *Racism* is prejudice displayed in blatant or subtle ways due to recognized or perceived differences in the physical and psychological backgrounds of people. It demeans all who participate in it. Essentially, racism is a form of projection usually displayed out of fear or ignorance.

Another difficulty in multicultural counselling involves *acculturation*, "the process by which a group of people give up old ways and adopt new ones" (Romero, Silva, & Romero, 1989, p. 499). In the acculturation process, individuals are simultaneously being influenced to some extent by elements of two distinct cultures. The process is not easy, and research indicates difficulties in trying to balance contrasting values of two different cultures include "psychological stress, guilt, apathy, depression, delinquency, resentment, disorientation, and poor self-esteem" (Yeh & Hwang, 2000, p. 425). Therefore, it is crucial to know where clients are located on a continuum of acculturation in order to provide them with appropriate services (Weinrach & Thomas, 1998).

Each of these difficulties in multicultural counselling must be recognized, understood, and empathetically resolved if counsellors are to be effective with clients who are different from them (Ridley, 2005).

ISSUES IN MULTICULTURAL COUNSELLING

A primary issue of concern for some multicultural counsellors in Canada, especially those with an emic perspective, is the dominance of theories based on European/North American cultural values. Some of the predominant beliefs of Europeans and North Americans are the value of individuals, an action-oriented approach to problem solving, the work ethic, the scientific method, and an emphasis on rigid time schedules (Axelson, 1999). A liability of these values in counselling is that theories built around them may not always be applicable to clients from other cultural traditions (Lee, 2006; Nwachuku & Ivey, 1991; Sue, 1992). If this fact is not recognized and dealt with, bias and a breakdown in counsellor–client relationships may occur (Pedersen, 1987).

A second issue in multicultural counselling is sensitivity to cultures in general and in particular. Pedersen (1982) believes that it is essential for counsellors to be sensitive to cultures in three areas:

1. *Knowledge* of the worldviews of culturally different clients,

2. *Self-awareness* of one's own personal worldview and how one is a product of cultural conditioning, and

3. *Skills* necessary for work with culturally different clients.

In the United States, these three areas were used by the AMCD as a basis for developing the Multicultural Counselling Competencies in 1992 and for operationalizing them (Arredondo et al., 1996). In Canada, researchers Nancy Arthur and Sandra Collins have created their own model, which addresses a criticism that the above conceptual framework does not sufficiently address the importance of the working alliance (Collins & Arthur, 2009). Their model, called culture-infused counselling, also includes social justice competencies. Their three core competency domains include the following:

1. Cultural self-awareness
2. Awareness of client cultural identities
3. Culturally sensitive working alliance

Arthur and Collins (2009) then intersect their three domains with the three areas (i.e., knowledge, self-awareness, and skills) outlined by Pedersen (1987) and others, while at the same time adding social justice into the mix. Consequently, the resulting matrix looks something like Table 4.2.

Culture-infused counselling competence is defined as "the integration of attitudes and beliefs, knowledge, and skills essential for awareness of the impact of culture on personal assumptions, values, and beliefs, understanding of the worldview of the client, coming to agreement on goals and tasks in the context of a trusting and culturally sensitive working alliance, and reinforcing that alliance by embracing a social justice agenda" (Collins & Arthur, 2009, p. 55).

Prior to the development of the competency models, Pedersen (1977; 1978) developed a triad model for helping counsellors achieve a deeper understanding of cultures in general. The four areas in the model are "articulating the problem from the client's cultural perspective; anticipating resistance from a culturally different client; diminishing defensiveness by studying the trainee's own defensive responses; and learning recovery skills for getting out of trouble when counselling the culturally different" (1978, p. 481). In this model, an anticounsellor, who functions like an alter ego and deliberately tries to be subversive, works with a counsellor and a client in a videotaped session. The interaction and feedback generated through this process help break down barriers and foster greater understanding and sensitivity in counsellors (Parker, Archer, & Scott, 1992).

Another model for understanding specific cultures was devised by Nwachuku and Ivey (1991). They propose that counsellors first study a culture and its values before trying to adapt a theory to fit a particular client. So the third issue in multicultural

Table 4.2 Arthur and Collins (2009) Multicultural Competence Framework

	Cultural Self-Awareness	Awareness of Client's Culture	Working Alliance	Engage in Social Justice
Attitudes and Beliefs (i.e., Self-Awareness)				
Knowledge				
Skills				

counselling is understanding how cultural systems operate and influence behaviours. Counsellors who have gained knowledge and awareness from within the cultural system are more likely to be skilled in helping members from a specific cultural group. These counsellors are able to share a particular worldview with clients, make skillful and appropriate interventions, and yet maintain a sense of personal integrity. This type of cultural sensitivity requires "active participation on the part of the practitioner," including self-awareness (Brinson, 1996, p. 201).

A fourth issue in multicultural counselling is providing effective counselling services across cultures. Sue (1978) established five guidelines that are still applicable:

1. Counsellors recognize the values and beliefs they hold in regard to acceptable and desirable human behaviour. They are then able to integrate this understanding into appropriate feelings and behaviours.

2. Counsellors are aware of the cultural and generic qualities of counselling theories and traditions. No method of counselling is completely culture-free.

3. Counsellors understand the sociopolitical environment that has influenced the lives of members of minority groups. Persons are products of the milieus in which they live.

4. Counsellors are able to share the worldview of clients and do not question its legitimacy.

5. Counsellors are truly eclectic in counselling practice. They are able to use a wide variety of counselling skills and apply particular counselling techniques to specific lifestyles and experiences.

Sue (1978) further suggests a framework for multicultural counselling based on a two-dimensional concept, with locus of control on the horizontal axis and locus of responsibility on the vertical axis (see Figure 4.1). The four quadrants represent the kinds and degrees of possible interactions among these variables with clients from different cultures.

A final issue in multicultural counselling is the development and employment of counselling theories. Cultural bias is present in majority and minority counsellors (Wendel, 1997) and in the past has spilled over into counselling theories. To deal with culturally limited counselling theories, bias, and transcending cultural limitations, McFadden (1999) and a number of leading counsellor educators have devised ways to overcome ideas and methods developed before there was any awareness of the need for multicultural counselling. McFadden's model is a transcultural perspective that focuses on three primary dimensions counsellors must master:

■ the cultural–historical, where counsellors must possess knowledge of a client's culture;

■ the psychosocial, where counsellors must come to understand the client's ethnic, racial, and social group's performance, speeches, and behaviours in order to communicate meaningfully; and

■ the scientific–ideological, where counsellors must use appropriate counselling approaches to deal with problems related to regional, national, and international environments.

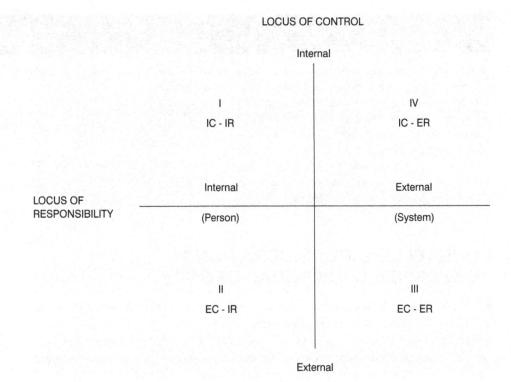

Figure 4.1 Graphic representation of worldviews

Source: From "Counseling Across Cultures," by D. W. Sue, 1978, *Personnel and Guidance Journal, 56*, p. 460.

© 1978 by ACA. Reprinted with permission. No further reproduction authorized without written permission of the American Counseling Association.

Explanations of existing theories and their applicability to certain populations and problems have also become popular (e.g., Corsini & Wedding, 2008; Sue, Ivey, & Pedersen, 1996; Vontress, 1996). Existential counselling is one such approach that, like McFadden's transcultural perspective, is holistic and applicable across "all cultures and socioeconomic groups" (Epp, 1998, p. 7). As a theoretical approach it deals with meaning and human relationships and with the ultimate issues of life and death.

Another exciting development in multicultural counselling is the renewed emphasis on theories specifically designed for different cultures (Lee, 2006). For example, traditional Asian psychotherapies, which have existed for more than 3000 years, have recently become more popular in the West (Walsh, 2000). Many of these traditions stress existential and transpersonal health and development over pathology, employing such techniques as meditation and yoga. They have a beneficial effect on wellness and psychological growth whether used alone or in concert with other approaches.

Katie was a quick study. Her mind was like a machine in being able to size up and solve a task. Therefore, she thought her high intellectual skills would translate well into helping her clients when she became a counsellor. With her first few clients that's exactly what happened. However, her next client was culturally different from Katie in a number of ways. To her credit, Katie listened well and seemed to grasp the client's worldview. However,

after that she felt stuck and the session seemed to go nowhere.

1. What does Katie's situation tell you about the power of knowledge and intellectual understanding?

2. What would you suggest Katie do to become more culturally competent?

COUNSELLING CONSIDERATIONS WITH SPECIFIC CULTURAL GROUPS

In addition to general guidelines for working with culturally different clients, counsellors should keep in mind some general considerations when working with specific cultural groups. In reviewing these considerations, it is crucial that counsellors remind themselves that each individual, like each counselling session, is unique. There are probably more within-group differences than between-group differences in counselling people from specific cultural traditions (Atkinson, 2004; Swartz-Kulstad & Martin, 1999). Therefore, knowing a cultural tradition is only a part of the information counsellors need in order to be effective. They must work to know their clients, problems, and themselves equally well.

In examining themselves, counsellors who are from minority cultures need to be aware that they may harbour "historical hostility" at either a conscious or an unconscious level toward members of majority cultures (Wendel, 1997). On the opposite side, counsellors from majority cultures may carry attitudes of superiority and privilege. Neither attitude is healthy or productive.

European Canadians

Background of British Canadians As mentioned earlier, individuals of British ancestry constitute the largest percentage of Canadians; about 21% of the population report British ancestry only (Statistics Canada, 2003). At the time of Confederation in 1867, Canada's population was mostly British (60%) and French (30%). By 1981, as a result of declining birthrate and immigration, it fell to 40% and 27%, respectively (Dewing & Leman, 2006). British Canadians are more likely than not to espouse a worldview that "values linear, analytical, empirical, and task solutions" and stresses that "rugged individualism should be valued, and that autonomy of the parts and independence of action are more significant than group conformance" (Sue, 1992, p. 8). Consequently, they epitomize the values inherent in an individualistic society.

Approaches that Work with British Canadians Given that most substantial counselling theories that have evolved in the United States were developed by Americans of various European ancestries, British Canadians are one of the groups these approaches were developed for. Suffice it to say that any of the modern and postmodern approaches to counselling will find their partisans within this group. More on this will be discussed under "European Canadians."

Background of French Canadians Just as Canadians whose first language is English are called "anglophones," Canadians whose first language is French are often referred to as "francophones." (Those whose first language is neither French nor English are called "allophones.") Today, only 10% of Canadians report French ancestry only (Statistics Canada, 2003). The numbers are higher than this in actuality, as Statistics Canada (2003) also reported in its study that 8% of the population simply reported themselves as Canadian only, and another 7% reported a mix of English-, French-, and Canadian-only origins. While 59.1% of the population reported that they spoke English in the 2001 Canadian Census, French came next at 22.9% (Dewing & Leman, 2006). Consequently, French Canadians and those who speak French fluently are the second largest percentage of Canadians.

Donnelly (n.d.) stated that "*Québécois* society is divided more than ever along multi-ethnic lines" (p. 2). Québec remains the only French-speaking majority region throughout North America, and it is considered the most distinct region of the country (McCullough, 2010). Because of their diminishing numbers, French Canadians, as a group, have been rightfully concerned about preserving their language and their culture in Canada. This has resulted in a significant minority believing that the best way to maintain the French language and culture is for Québec to separate from the rest of Canada. In this vein, Québec has held two referendums; in 1980, 40% of the voters favoured separating, and in 1995, the percentage rose to 49% (McCullough, 2010).

Although some people believe Québec is a conservative part of Canada because of its long history of Roman Catholicism, nothing could be further from the truth. Instead, it is "the most left-wing region of the entire North American continent" (McCullough, 2010, para. 9). While many Québécois call themselves Catholic for ancestral and nationalistic reasons, church attendance has sunk very low while their support for liberal causes (i.e., same-sex marriage, abortion, cohabitation) is higher than anywhere else in the country.

Approaches that Work with French Canadians The two referendums revealed the ambivalence felt by many Québécois, and for some, like Donnelly (n.d., p. 2), raised the question, "Who is a *Québécois*?" Does it refer to all who live in Québec, regardless of ethnic origin, or only to those who can trace back their ancestry to the first settlers of the French Régime? Some of these descendants no longer speak French—do they count?

Donnelly (n.d.) recommends that cross-cultural counsellors do not assume that their Québécois clients share the same beliefs, values, or even speak the same French dialect. In effect, the Québécois do not form "an ethnically monolithic society" (Donnelly, n.d., p. 6). He suggests that the French Québécois are very buoyant and they are more likely to plan for the future compared to British Canadians. Aside from that, Donnelly (n.d.) provides sage advice to all counsellors: Unless you speak a second language with the same ease and accuracy as your client, stick to counselling in your first language.

Background of Other European Canadians As a group, European Canadians are a diverse population. Although Europe is their common ancestral homeland, there are large differences between the cultural heritages of people from Sweden, Italy, Poland, Germany, Russia, Sweden, and Austria. (In addition, many people from Spain or of Spanish ancestry consider their heritage distinct from other Europeans in general.) Europeans who have recently arrived in Canada differ widely from those whose families settled in North America generations ago, many of whom now identify themselves as simply "Canadian," forsaking their European ancestries (El Nasser & Overberg, 2002). Overall, there is no typical European Canadian.

As a group, European Canadians have blended together more than most other cultural groups. Reasons include a history of intergroup marriages and relationships that have simultaneously influenced the group as a whole and made it more homogeneous.

Approaches That Work with Europeans and European Canadians As mentioned earlier, some professionals argue that the vast majority of counselling theories in Europe and the United States are applicable for either Europeans or European Americans and European Canadians. The reason is that members from this group generated most of the theories used in Western society. Their point has considerable merit. Most counselling theories employed with these populations are more in tune with the lifestyle and values of these groups than not. However, not all theories work well for all European Canadians. Those theories that do work well emphasize many of the shared values of European Canadians. For example, many European Canadians gravitate toward rational or logical methods in understanding themselves and others. Therefore, cognitive and cognitive-behavioural approaches may work well with this group as a whole. However, existential, psychoanalytic, Adlerian, person-centred, and other affective counselling theories may be appropriate for some within this population. Just as there is no typical European Canadian, there is no one counselling theory or approach that will work with all members of this group.

Aboriginal Canadians

Background of Aboriginal Canadians In Canada, Aboriginal people include status Indians, non-Status Indians, Métis, and Inuit (Devin & Leman, 2006). Aboriginal Canadians, mistakenly called Indians by the first European settlers in America, are the indigenous peoples of the Western Hemisphere who were the first inhabitants of the American continents (Garrett & Pichette, 2000). When European settlers arrived in Canada, they entered a land comprised of 56 Aboriginal nations who spoke more than 30 languages (Arthur & Collins, 2009). Unfortunately, "colonialism has left an indelible imprint on the psyche of the First Nations people" (Nuttgens & Campbell, 2010, p. 117). The impact on Aboriginal people has been profound. For over 350 years in Canada (1620 to 1976) (Blue, Darou, & Ruano, 2009), Aboriginal children were sent to residential schools with the goal of purging them of their traditions, their values, and their language (Arthur & Collins, 2009). Close to 40% of Aboriginal Elders living today attended these schools (Arthur & Collins, 2009). These attempts at "*driving the Indianness out of* them" (Blue et el., 2009, p. 266) are arguably the worst form of "genocide" that ever intentionally occurred in Canada. The negative psychological and cultural sequelae will be felt for generations (Blue et al., 2009).

In general, Aboriginal Canadians have strong feelings about the loss of ancestral lands, a desire for self-determination, conflicts with the values of mainstream Canadian culture, and a confused self-image resulting from past stereotyping (Atkinson, 2004). Anger from or about past transgressions of people from other cultures is a theme that must be handled appropriately (Hammerschlag, 1988). Aboriginal Canadians, as a group, have high suicide, unemployment, and alcoholism rates, and they experience high levels of domestic and physical violence (Nuttgens & Campbell, 2010). They also have high rates of involvement with child welfare agencies and correctional services (Nuttgens & Campbell, in press).

Approaches That Work with Aboriginal Canadians "Due to the lack of training Aboriginal counsellors, Aboriginal clients are often referred to Euro-Canadian counsellors for assistance. However, many Aboriginal clients do not access services available to them or terminate counselling early" (Wihak & Price, 2006, p. 1). Most research focused on counselling Aboriginal clients has been conducted in the United States (Wihak & Price, 2006). Wihak and Price (2006) briefly described the themes that emerged from their two independent studies (doctoral dissertation and master's thesis, respectively): Wihak interviewed Euro-Canadian counsellors who worked with Inuit clients, while Price interviewed Aboriginal Elder counsellors. Collectively, the themes that emerged included the need to (a) *develop self-understanding*—both studies emphasized the need to understand white privilege and to find a personal spiritual connection; (b) *understand Aboriginal realities*—counsellors must become familiar with the impact of the past, learn about their collectivist worldview, practice non-interference (in the Aboriginal worldview, you do not tell another what to do), and give them time to speak; (c) *be flexible in structuring counselling*—be flexible, for example, about where and when sessions are held; (d) *build connections with clients*—be willing to self-disclose and be nondirective, (e) *Aboriginal humour*—be careful with the timing of it and appreciate that humour is self-deprecating for many; and (f) *venting anger*—allow clients to vent their anger without it getting out of control.

According to Richardson (1981), four ideas to be considered when counselling Native Americans are silence, acceptance, restatement, and general lead. Richardson has used vignettes to model ways of using these techniques. The use of the vision quest, a rite of passage and religious renewal for adult men, is recommended in some cases (Heinrich et al., 1990). The use of the creative arts is also an approach that has considerable merit because emotional, religious, and artistic expression is "an inalienable aspect of Native culture" (Herring, 1997, p. 105). The creative arts do not require verbal disclosure. In addition, they may focus on rituals and wellness in Native American culture. Using multiple counselling approaches in a synergetic way, such as network therapy, home-based therapy, indigenous-structural therapy, and traditional Native activities such as "the talking circle," "the talking stick," and storytelling, are also recommended (Garrett, 2006; Herring, 1996).

More important than specific ways of working is the crucial nature of a sense of "realness" when in a counselling relationship with an Aboriginal Canadian. Being willing to be a learner and to admit one's mistakes can help a counsellor and an Aboriginal Canadian bond.

Aboriginal peoples have many traditional forms of healing, but as each Aboriginal group shares both similarities and differences with other Aboriginal groups, it is important to find out which traditions apply and which do not. The RCMP, for example, published a guide to help its officers realize that many Native ceremonies are considered sacred (Royal Canadian Mounted Police Public Affairs Directorate [RCMP], 1993).

According to one spiritual advisor, everything Aboriginal people do is in a circle (i.e., the *circle of life*). The belief is that power came from the sacred hoop, and as long as the hoop was not broken, the people would flourish. Tradition says that a flowering tree resided in the middle with four quarters that nourished it; the East gave peace and light, the South provided warmth, the West gave rain, and the North sent the cold and mighty winds of strength and endurance (RCMP, 1993). Native spiritual life is based on a fundamental interconnectedness between all things, with Mother Earth having greatest importance.

According to the RCMP (1993), the following are common Aboriginal traditions:

1. *The medicine wheel.* As everything spiritual is in a circle, the medicine wheel represents the idea that every seeker can find a harmonious way of living with their environment.

2. *The four powers.* The four directions of a compass represents four natural forces. North represents wisdom, South represents warmth and growth, West represents introspection, and East represents enlightenment and its gift of peace and light.

3. *Ceremonies.* Ceremonies are a form of religious expression. Nothing is written; instead, teachings are passed down orally from Elder to Elder.

4. *Elders.* Elders are generally older men and women, but sometimes a young person is given a special gift (e.g., wisdom, healing, dream interpretation) from the Great Creator.

5. *Prayers.* Both individual and group prayers may occur.

6. *Pipes and pipe ceremonies.* These may be used for both private and group ceremonies. The pipe belongs to the community, not to an individual. They may be used for prayers or for the *sacred circle* (whoever holds the pipe gets to speak).

7. *Fasting.* Fasting is meant to quicken spirituality. Such fasting allows no food or drink.

8. *Sweat lodges.* Used mostly for communal prayer purposes, sweat lodges are also for spiritual healing, purification, and fasting.

9. *Feasting.* During feasting ceremonies, there are certain foods that must be eaten by a particular Aboriginal community, and these foods vary between groups.

10. *Rattles.* Rattles are shaken to summon a spirit for spiritual or physical purposes (such as healing a sick person).

11. *Drums.* The drumbeat signifies the heartbeat of the group and the pulse of the universe. Each drum is considered a sacred object.

12. *Eagle whistles.* When a dancer blows an eagle bone whistle, the drum group begins singing an appropriate song. There are rules governing the frequency of this practice.

13. *Herbs/incense.* The four sacred plants are sweetgrass, sage, cedar, and tobacco. Each serves a particular purpose.

14. *Medicine pouches.* An Elder may prescribe that plant material be carried in a pouch. These are not to be concealed.

Aside from the traditions, there are also a host of ceremonial rituals discussed in the RCMP (1993) document. Most commonly known is perhaps the *pow-wow*, a time for celebrating and socializing after religious ceremonies. In some Aboriginal cultures, it is itself a religious event. Interested readers should pull up a copy of the document from the web (www.rcmp-grc.gc.ca/pubs/abo-aut/spirit-spiritualite-eng.htm). If you are interested in taking a closer look at Inuit culture and recommended counselling practices, refer to the Wihak and Meralit (2003) article found at http://cjc-rcc.ucalgary.ca/cjc/index.php/rcc/article/view/238/530.

Case Example: What Would *You* Do?

Offet-Gartner (2009) has worked extensively with Aboriginal Canadians. She described a story that certainly opened my eyes. After testing a young Native boy at a rural school, she contacted the parents to meet with them and added that they could invite whoever they wanted. When she arrived, she found over 20 people present with a celebration underway. When the crowd became silent, Dr. Offet-Gartner began speaking, given that she was the one who had called the "meeting." Before she could react, an Elder swiftly leaped out of her chair and slapped her face. She later learned that the period of silence was out of respect for this Elder.

1. How would you react if you had been Dr. Offet-Gartner?

2. The slap was a form of physical assault. Would you press charges? Why or why not?

3. What would you suggest as an appropriate "next step?"

South Asian Canadians

Background of South Asian Canadians In 2001, almost a million people of South Asian origin lived in Canada, constituting about 3% of the total Canadian population (Statistics Canada, 2007d). *South Asian Canadians* include East Indians (74%), Pakistani (8%), Sri Lankan (6%), Punjabi (5%), and Tamil (4%) (Statistics Canada, 2007d). By 2006, the census revealed that the number of South Asians had surpassed the Chinese to become the largest visible minority in Canada with a population base of 1.3 million, or 4% of Canada's total population, compared to 1.1 million Chinese Canadians (Singh, 2008).

In 2001, 62% of Canada's South Asians lived in Ontario while another 22% lived in British Columbia, with 500 000 living in Toronto and 163 000 living in Vancouver (Statistics Canada, 2007d). South Asian Canadians are almost equally divided between Sikh, Hindu, and Muslim faiths: 28%, 28%, and 22%, respectively.

South Asians are not a homogenous group. In Metro Toronto, for example, there are over 20 different ethnic groups that are part of the South Asian population (Canadian Encyclopedia, 2010). Each ethnic group varies widely in its social and community life, so few generalities can be made about South Asians. As a rule, however, they generally form strong bonds with others of similar background (within their ethnic group), while remaining disconnected from other South Asian ethnic groups (Canadian Encyclopedia, 2010). Those groups that have high ethnic consciousness are generally the most involved in extra-familial cultural activities, such as the Sikhs and Ismaili Muslims. What South Asian communities have in common is that they (a) place a high value on family, (b) maintain social networks within their ethnic group, (c) value religion within their distinct cultures, and (d) preserve their customs, traditions, and language (Tran, Kaddatz, & Allard, 2005).

Approaches That Work with South Asian Canadians There is research indicating that especially women who immigrate to Canada from South Asia are at high risk of experiencing acculturation stress (Ahmad et al., 2004). This is credited to the rigid gender roles that prevent them from becoming integrated into their adopted country. Furthermore, their gender roles mean that they experience many demands for their labour both in and outside the home (Grewal, Bottorff, & Hilton, 2005). Consequently, South Asian Canadian women often experience high levels of anxiety, depression, and loneliness (Ahmad et al., 2004; Grewal et al., 2005). As Tiwari and Wang (2008) have found, Asians are less likely to seek help when troubled compared to whites in Canada, with Chinese being the least likely and South Asians in the middle. Clinicians must also to be aware that South Asians often rely on herbal medicine and folk or religious healers when in need (Hilton et al., 2001).

Shariff (2009) has suggested several interventions that work well with South Asian Canadians. First, for those dealing with acculturation stress, she recommends discussion of the values, beliefs, and behaviours that characterize their own culture and the host culture (i.e., Canada) and encouraging the client to look at what fits, what doesn't fit, and what resides in the middle (ambivalence). Shariff also recommends cognitive behaviour therapy, solution-focused techniques, gestalt methods, and reframing. Second, for those dealing with parenting stress (the other focus of her article), she recommends the above methods in addition to education, particularly to help parents understand the differences between parenting in the two cultures. If a counsellor proceeds too quickly, however, it is likely that the parents will terminate counselling prematurely.

Southeast Asian Canadians

Background of Southeast Asian Canadians   Southeast Asian Canadians include Chinese, Japanese, Filipinos, Indochinese, Indians, and Koreans, among others. They vary widely in cultural background (Atkinson, 2004; Morrissey, 1997). Historically, they have faced strong discrimination in Canada and the United States and have been the subject of many myths (Sue & Sue, 1972, 2003).

Chinese Canadians first arrived on the West Coast in 1788 and began to settle in large numbers in 1858. Of 17 000 Chinese individuals brought to build the Canadian Pacific Railway in the 1880s, 1500 of them died in the process (Victoria Holocaust Remembrance and Education Society [VHRES], 2002). In the 20th century, it was illegal for Chinese Canadian restaurant owners to hire white women (VHRES, 2002), reflecting an example of Canadian racism. As mentioned in Chapter 3, Japanese Canadians were interned and their land confiscated during WWII after the bombing of Pearl Harbor. By 2001, Canadians of Chinese origin comprised the largest non-European ethnic origin in Canada, constituting about 4% of the total Canadian population (Statistics Canada, 2007b). By 2006, however, South Asians had outnumbered them (Singh, 2008). In 2001, 82% of Chinese Canadians lived in either Ontario or British Columbia, with 72% living in either Toronto (436 000) or Vancouver (348 000) (Statistics Canada, 2007b).

A combination of factors has promoted a positive image of Southeast Asian Canadians. They are collectively described as hardworking and successful and not prone to mental or emotional disturbances. Sometimes they are referred to as the "model minority" (Bell, 1985). Like all stereotypes, there are kernels of truth in this last descriptor, but it is still not realistic or accurate. There are many subtleties in Southeast Asian Canadian cultures, and often communication is more indirect and discrete. Traditional Southeast Asian people are expected to exert control over strong emotions. Other expectations include filial piety, stress on family bonds and unity, and respect for roles and status (Sue & Sue, 1991).

Approaches That Work with Southeast Asian Canadians   Due to cultural values, Southeast Asian Canadians are less likely to seek out counselling than European Canadians (Tiwari & Wang, 2008). Counsellors must see and appreciate Southeast Asian Canadians in the context of their cultural heritage or they will be unable to offer them help in mentally healthy ways (Henkin, 1985). One cultural factor in some Southeast Asian

Canadians' worldviews is that psychological distress and disorders are explained within a religious framework. If persons are troubled, they may believe they are possessed by a bad spirit or suffering because they have violated some religious or moral principle. Thus, religious tradition plays a strong role in some of their views about the origins of mental health and mental illness. Similarly, they may see healing take the form of "invoking the help of some supernatural power or restoring the sufferer to a state of well being through prescribing right conduct and belief" (Das, 1987, p. 25). Many references also indicate that Southeast Asian Canadians are more likely to somatize psychological problems, meaning that they develop physical complaints instead of acknowledging that their pain is more psychological than physical (Ryder et al., 2008; Zhang, 1995).

Another important factor, which will have an impact in career counselling, is that many Southeast Asians choose occupations in the investigative and realistic areas (see Chapter 17 under Holland's theory) and their occupational choices are often a compromise between their own interests and the acceptability of that choice to their parents (Tang, Fouad, & Smith, 1999). Most of the 187 college students in Tang et al.'s (1999) study were intending to become engineers, physicians, or computer scientists. In other words, in counselling Southeast Asians, one must be aware that collectivist ideals of fulfilling family obligations, such as having the means to help family in instrumental ways, is of great importance.

It is critical that counsellors appreciate the history and unique characteristics of the different Southeast Asian groups in Canada, such as the Chinese, Japanese, and Vietnamese (Atkinson, 2004; Axelson, 1999; Sandhu, 1997). This sensitivity often enables counsellors to facilitate the counselling process in ways not otherwise possible (Lum, 2007). For example, counsellors may promote self-disclosure with Chinese Canadians through educational or career counselling rather than direct, confrontational psychotherapeutic approaches.

African Canadians

Background of African Canadians "Black people in Canada primarily refer to themselves as Black (a political or cultural concept, not just an adjective) or as African-Canadian (among other possible terms including AfriCanadian and African-Nova Scotian or Jamaican-Canadian)" (Sadlier, n.d., para. 2). According to the 2001 census, the Black population in Canada was the third largest visible minority group with a self-reported population of 662 200 (Statistics Canada, 2004). This represents over 2% of Canada's total population. When counselling African Canadians, counsellors must understand African Canadian history, cultural values, conflicts, and coping mechanisms and be aware of their own attitudes and prejudices about this group (Brown, 2008; Cheboud & France, n.d.; Gerrard, 1991). Brown (2008) stated that the only way she could have come to Canada before 1967 was as a domestic servant. In immigration policies, Brown went on to write that "in immigration policies, Black people were deemed unsuitable, and every effort was made to keep them out of Canada" (p. 376).

It is possible for counsellors from different cultural backgrounds to work effectively with African Canadian clients if they understand the nature of racism; the fact that individual, institutional, and cultural racism are facts of life for people of African descent (Utsey, Ponterotto, Reynolds, & Cancelli, 2000); and that racial discrimination and self-esteem are inversely related. They must further be aware that African Canadians are a diverse group and display a broad range of feelings, thoughts, and behaviours (Baruth & Manning, 2007; Harper, 1994). Therefore, no one single counselling or helping approach works best for everyone.

Counsellors also need to be aware that there is emphasis on the collective in African Canadian traditions (Cheboud & France, n.d.). "In historical times the collective was the clan or tribe" (Priest, 1991, p. 213). Today, it is the family and those who live, work, or worship nearby. This emphasis on the collective and the therapeutic power of the group (i.e., the village concept) is the antithesis of individual responsibility for resolving difficulties (McRae, Thompson, & Cooper, 1999).

Spirituality and the role of the minister and the church in African Canadian culture are factors influencing members of this group, too (Baruth & Manning, 2007; Cheboud & France, n.d.). Rather than a counsellor, a minister is usually sought out as a "source of mental and emotional sustenance" (Priest, 1991, p. 214).

Approaches That Work with African Canadians One place to begin in counselling African Canadians is to carefully identify their expectations. Because there are a number of within-group differences among African Canadians, as with any group, clients come to counselling for different reasons and with different variations of a worldview. Therefore, it is important to determine what has brought clients to seek counselling services now and what, as well as how, they hope to be different as a result of the experience (Parham, 2002; Sue & Sue, 2003). If the client and counsellor are from different cultural and ethnic backgrounds, that factor should be examined (Brammer, 2004; Sue & Sue, 2003). Likewise, the impact of discrimination and racism on African Canadian clients should not be ignored. Racial identity is a further factor to consider.

In practical terms, an egalitarian relationship should be established between African Canadian clients and their counsellors (Sue & Sue, 2003). Beyond the relationship there should be an emphasis on pragmatics. Often Black individuals come to therapy to receive some practical steps to deal with their problems. Consequently, counselling may take the form of education and job training, drug rehabilitation, or learning better parenting skills (Brammer, 2004). What does not work with clients of African descent is "overemphasizing the client's feelings" (p. 53).

In addition to being practical, counsellors should focus on African Canadians' strengths "and address the individual within the context of [his or] her family, neighborhood, and city" (Brammer, 2004, p. 54). Family members or neighbours can often be brought in to help. Likewise, spiritual resources within the client's community should be tapped whenever possible because the church and spirituality are an integral part of African Canadian life (Ahia, 2006; Cheboud & France, n.d.).

Cheboud & France (n.d.) recommend that counsellors need to keep the following in mind when counselling African Canadians:

- avoid presumptions about level of adjustment being tied to one's identity being centred on race

- be aware of how context can effect healthy Black adjustment

- attempt to understand the client's frame of reference

- base social and other interventions on multidimensional model of Black psychological functioning (p. 6).

Counsellors who are not from the African Canadian community need to accept that racism is a crucial part of Black clients' experience (Cheboud & France, n.d.). Even if they have not experienced racism themselves, they are certainly aware of the history of slavery and other violent acts. Consequently, African Canadians have survived in an atmosphere of racial discrimination, and they may appear to counsellors as guarded, challenging, and needing to "size up" their helper (Cheboud & France, n.d.). It is important that the counsellor not become defensive. Building trust is paramount.

Latino Canadians

Background of Latino Canadians.   Most Latino Canadians immigrated to Canada in the latter part of the 20th century. The majority hail from Mexico, El Salvador, Chile, Columbia, and Venezuela, and smaller number come from Cuba, Peru, Guatemala, Ecuador, and elsewhere (Statistics Canada, 2007c). Sometimes referred to as *Hispanic Canadians*, *Latino Canadians* are people of Latin American descent residing in Canada. The common denominator for Latinos is the Spanish language, but they are a very diverse group. In 2001, 244 400 people of Latino origin lived in Canada (Statistics Canada, 2007c), representing about 1% of the total population. Regardless of their background, most Latinos in Canada are bicultural. However, they vary in their degree of acculturation (Baruth & Manning, 2007). Overall, their ethnic histories and cultures play a major part in influencing their worldviews, family dynamics, and health (Miranda, Bilot, Peluso, Berman & Van Meek, 2006). Many within-group differences exist among Latino Canadians (Atkinson, 2004; Romero et al., 1989).

Approaches That Work with Latino Canadians   As a group, Latinos are reluctant to use counselling services. Part of this hesitancy is cultural tradition (e.g., pride), and part is cultural heritage (e.g., reliance on extended family ties). More practical reasons are inadequate transportation, lack of health insurance, and the absence of counselling professionals fluent in Spanish and familiar with Latino culture (Gonzalez, 1997; Ruiz, 1981; Sue & Sue, 2003).

In addition, many Latinos perceive psychological problems as similar to physical problems (Canino, 2004; Lopez-Baez, 2006). Therefore, they expect the counsellor to be active, concrete, and goal-directed. This perception is especially true for clients who are "very" Latino (Ruiz, 1981).

Overall, counsellors of Latinos must address numerous topics and work within cultural concepts and beliefs. This usually means involving families, because family loyalty is very important in Latino culture. It may also involve working in harmony with the client's spiritual or religious tradition, especially since the majority of Latinos are Roman Catholic (Baruth & Manning, 2007; Statistics Canada, 2007c).

It is often helpful if the counsellor is bilingual. Many Latinos prefer Spanish to English, especially when expressing their emotions. Lower socioeconomic status, racism, and discrimination are some of the universal difficulties affecting members of this population that may directly or indirectly come up in counselling (Sue & Sue, 2003). However, as with other groups, Latino individuals, couples, and families have unique and personal problems.

Case Example: What Would *You* Do?

Collin was a counsellor of few words. As a former athlete, he believed in showing rather than telling individuals how to stay mentally healthy. Therefore, when he first came across a client, Margareta, who referred to her family as a crucial part of her life, he was baffled. None of his individualistic techniques worked. Therefore, he asked a colleague for help. "Ah," said the colleague who was about at Collin's same age and level of maturity, "you are doing just the right thing. The client will eventually see that."

1. What do you think of Collin's colleague's remark?

2. What more should Collin do in regard to preparing himself to work with clients who stress the importance of family and their collective identity?

3. What should he do in regard to Margareta now?

Arab Canadians

Background of Arab Canadians Arab Canadians are a mosaic group coming from 22 countries as diverse as Egypt, Lebanon, Morocco, Yemen, Tunisia, and Palestine. In 2001, there were almost 350 000 people of Arab origin living in Canada, representing 1.2% of the Canadian population (Statistics Canada, 2007a). The Lebanese constitute the largest group of Arab Canadians (Statistics Canada, 2007a). In 2001, most Arab Canadians (58%) were born outside of Canada, most having arrived relatively recently; 43% lived in Ontario and another 39% in Québec. Regarding religion, 44% reported being Muslim and another 44% belonged to a Christian denomination (Statistics Canada, 2007a).

Arab Americans vary among themselves. Potential differences include social class, level of education, language (Arabic has distinct dialects), relative conservatism of the country of origin, time of immigration, and level of acculturation (Abudabbeh & Aseel, 1999). Despite such cultural variations, sufficient commonalities exist that special attention from service providers is warranted.

Arab Canadians as a group usually differ significantly from traditional Canadians in that they emphasize social stability and the collective over the individual. The family is the most significant element in most Arab Canadian subcultures, with the individual's life dominated by family and family relations. Men are the patriarchs in family life and women are expected to uphold the honour of the family. Education is valued in Arab Canadian households; twice as many Arab Canadians compared to other Canadians earn a university degree (Statistics Canada, 2007a).

Approaches That Work with Arab Canadians When working with Arab Canadians, especially immigrants, it is crucial for counsellors to remember that there is a sharp delineation of gender roles in such families. Furthermore, patriarchal patterns of authority, conservative sexual standards, and the importance of self-sacrifice prevail. There is also an emphasis on the importance of honour and shame, because people in Arab cultures seek outside help from helpers, such as counsellors, only as a last resort (Abudabbeth & Aseel, 1999). Complicating matters even more is the fallout, tension, and distrust from 9/11 (Beitin & Allen, 2005). This may have affected Arab Americans more than Arab Canadians, but this is only speculation.

Clinical recommendations for working with members of this population include

- being aware of their cultural context
- being mindful of the issue of leadership and the importance that authority figures play in their lives
- being attentive to the part that the extended family plays in decision making
- being sensitive to the large part culture plays as an active and tangible co-participant in treatment
- being conscious of the fact that a strength-based approach to treatment is both desirable and works better
- being active as a counsellor and balancing the role so as not to be seen as a rescuer or a threat

Counsellors can also assist Arab Canadians by helping them access groups where they can find support and become members of a larger community that is dealing with similar issues. Working in and with groups poses

> some potentially problematic issues for particular clients. This is especially true for the war refugees from Iraq, due to the paranoid symptoms that often accompany the diagnosis of PTSD in clients who have experienced wartime trauma. On the other hand, parenting groups and 12-step programs seem to be effective with some nonrefugee Arab immigrant groups, perhaps due to the collectivist nature of the Arab culture in the countries of origin. (Nasser-McMillan & Hakim-Larson, 2003, p. 154)

International Counselling

Canada's cultural perspective regarding counselling is just one among many in the world. Indeed, some continents have their own counselling associations (specifically, Africa—African Counselling Association; and Europe—European Association for Counselling, www.eac.eu.com, and the European Branch of the American Counseling Association, www.online-infos.de/eb-aca/about.htm). A number of other countries have counselling associations as well (e.g., the United Kingdom, Australia, Malaysia, New Zealand, and Turkey). In addition, the practice of counselling is evolving in a number of regions, particularly Hong Kong, where counselling associations are blossoming.

Furthermore, there are worldwide associations of therapists who ascribe to particular theories, such as Adlerian, transactional analysis (TA), and reality therapy. In some countries without formal counselling associations, such as Italy, literally dozens of training institutes for theories exist (Gemignani & Giliberto, 2005). Finally, the International Association for Counselling (IAC, www.iac-irtac.org) holds annual meetings in countries around the world and publishes the *International Journal for the Advancement of Counselling*.

Super (1983) questioned more than 20 years ago whether counselling, as practised in North America, is adaptable to other countries. His analysis of culture and counselling concluded that prosperous and secure countries view counselling as a way of promoting individual interests and abilities. Economically less-fortunate countries and those under threat of foreign domination view counselling services as a way of channeling individuals into areas necessary for cultural survival (Super, 1954). Knowledge about such cultural differences must be considered in international counselling, especially as it relates to counselling specialties (Watkins, 2001).

Such knowledge is crucial in counselling internationally. For instance, in Poland, career counselling is more highly prized than other forms of counselling because of the developing nature of the country (Richard Lamb, personal communication, June 7, 1997). In other countries, such as Japan, counselling is both therapeutic and psychosocial; for example, working with Japanese men on fathering (Seto, Becker, & Akutsu, 2006). However, Japan still lacks a unified licensure standard, and occupational security is an issue (Iwasaki, 2005). On the other hand, in Malaysia, counselling is modelled after counselling in the United States, except the initial terminal degree is the bachelor's (the same as in Japan). Furthermore, almost all graduates are assigned to school settings where they are qualified to teach one subject as well as counsel.

Regardless of their knowledge of counselling, international students who attend colleges and universities in Canada may be reluctant to receive counselling services, and when they do seek it, the majority only attend one session (Arthur, 2009). This reluctance is in spite of the fact that many international students experience a host of stressors beyond those that are mainly developmental in nature. These stressors include "difficulties with linguistics, academic, interpersonal, financial, and intrapersonal problems" (Mori, 2000, p. 137). The networks of family and friends these students have relied in the past on are absent, and the fear of being seen as a failure and sent home adds to their daily stress (Boyer & Sedlacek, 1989). There is empirical evidence that international students experience greater stress than their Canadian and American counterparts, which often reaches a crisis level in the first six months of study (Schneller & Chalungsooth, 2002).

In order to help international students who do use counselling services, Arthur (2009) suggests the following possible areas of foci:

- *Counselling expectations.* Instruct students regarding what they can expect from counselling.

- *Academic concerns.* Assist with academic performance as it represents a major transition issue encountered by international students.

- *Language barriers.* Refer students for improvement in language proficiency.

- *Social support.* Refer students to groups and organizations where they can meet others to improve their social support networks.

- *Financial concerns.* Assist with budgeting.

- *Discrimination and racism.* International students experience discrimination and racism in Canadian schools (Samuels, 2004). Counsellors can teach assertion training and/or promote social justice by empowering students to report this to human rights offices, which are common at the post-secondary level.

- *Canadian gender roles.* Provide instruction regarding gender role expectations in Canada, which are often different from those in a student's home country.

- *Familial issues.* Recognize that family relationships may be strongly impacted when students study abroad, and assist where possible.

- *Career issues.* Teach career- and life-planning skills.

- *Re-entry transition issues.* Demonstrate willingness to talk about re-entry (to their home culture) transition issues.

Arthur (2009) suggests that offering a psychoeducational approach to help students feel more comfortable with counselling services may be important at first, particularly if personal counselling is viewed as socially stigmatizing in the student's home culture. Arthur also suggests using cognitive restructuring where appropriate.

Henkin (1985) proposes a number of practical guidelines for counsellors interacting on an international level as well. Besides establishing a clear-cut structure for the counselling process and explaining the process to the client, Henkin recommends that counsellors educate themselves about the culture of their clients, including the importance of family and community life. Indeed, "a direct application of Western approaches to persons of Eastern descent may have negative consequences" (Raney & Cinarbas, 2005, p. 157). What is needed instead is "an integration of Western and indigenous counselling approaches" that may include family and friends in counselling sessions along with support for a client's religious practices (p. 158).

SUMMARY AND CONCLUSION

In this chapter we examined counselling issues related to a special area: culture. There is a wealth of material in the professional literature on the general concerns of each group discussed here and on the counselling theories and techniques most appropriate for working with these populations. Indeed, specialty courses and counselling approaches that focus on one or more of these groups are offered in all graduate counsellor education programs in Canada.

Although information on special cultural aspects of a population may appear unrelated to other factors in counselling, they are not. A common theme is that counsellors who work with a variety of culturally different clients must be knowledgeable about them collectively, in subgroups, and individually. They must be able to deal effectively with concerns that transcend stereotypes and prescribed roles. Cultural limitations restrict not only the growth of the people involved in them but the larger society as well. Overcoming traditions, prejudices, fears, and anxieties and learning new skills based on accurate information and sensitivity are major parts of counselling in a multicultural society.

International counselling is also growing. As such, it is adding to cultural understanding of how people are helped both within and outside a particular context.

Your Personal Reflections

1. Think of when you have been misunderstood by someone else. What did it feel like? What did it make you want to do or not want to do in regard to the situation? Then think about what you would feel like if misunderstood by a counsellor—a professional who is supposed to be sensitive and attuned to others!

2. Reflect on the sources of encouragement and support you had while growing up (e.g., an adult leader of a group you were in, siblings, friends, parents, etc.). Were these individuals able to support you and/or help you with your problems satisfactorily? Imagine what it would be like to use such people in a therapeutic way if you were working with someone in or from another country. What do you think?

3. What has been your experience in dealing with European Canadians? If you are a European Canadian, how do you see yourself the same as and different from other European Canadians? If you are not European Canadian, ask yourself the question: "How are European Canadians the same as and different from one another?"

Classroom Activities

1. Talk with a person from a different cultural background than your own. Discuss with that person the difficulties he or she faces. How many of these problems are culturally related? How many are unique to the person? Present your findings to the class. What similarities do you and your classmates find in the results? Discuss your personal interviews as they relate to the material presented in this chapter.

2. Investigate ways of counselling that work for members of minority culture groups (other than those mentioned in the text) or study a multicultural procedure described in this book in great detail.

3. Collins and Pieterse (2007) have mentioned a number of ways to increase cultural awareness, including doing "reaction papers, journal writing, role playing, videotaping, cross-cultural immersion experiences, cross-cultural simulation experiences, experiential exercises, fishbowl exercises, small-group processing, and focus groups" (p. 16). Which of these pedagogical methods do you consider most appealing in learning more about a culture and cultural group?

4. Search the internet for counselling associations in other countries (e.g., Malaysia Counselling Association, British Association for Counselling and Psychotherapy). What is emphasized on the websites of these countries in regard to multicultural counselling? How does that emphasis correspond to what you know about multicultural counselling now?

5. Research counselling approaches offered in other countries. How do the theories and techniques generated in these cultures fit the needs of individuals in their societies? How do you think the counselling approach you have researched would work in Canada?

6. Spend half a day visiting different retail outlets and corner stores. While at each store, record the number of staff who are visible minorities compared to those who are European Canadian. Now calculate the percentage who belong to a visible minority. Is there a higher percentage than ought to be expected by their representation in the Canadian population? Why do you think you found whatever you found?

Chapter 5
Counselling with Diverse Populations

PRACTICE REFLECTION

Maurice, age 47, had been married to Claudette for 19 years. Their daughter, Tanya, was 19 years old and living in a neighbouring city. At our first session, Maurice told me that he was desperate. Although he had known he was gay since he was very young, he could not accept it and instead married Claudette after she unexpectedly became pregnant. Sadly, Maurice and Claudette had very little in common. They lived together but only talked when they were both drunk. Instead of communicating, they lived separate lives and focused instead on raising Tanya the best they could.

Maurice came to see me after he fell in love with one of his "hook ups." He knew he needed to act as he had never felt this way before. Our initial sessions focused on what this meant and later on how and when he would tell his wife. After he finally disclosed his feelings, he found out that Claudette was far more understanding than he ever thought possible. She already knew what was happening to her long-term partner. Claudette loved Maurice unconditionally, and she has a brother who is gay so she understood.

A few sessions later, I received an e-mail from Claudette saying she was very worried about Maurice. In one of their drunken conversations, he had disclosed to her that he had been sexually abused twice in his life—experiences he had never shared with her before—and that he hated himself for being gay. She was afraid he would kill himself.

I already had the next session booked with Maurice for a few days later, but nonetheless, I asked her via e-mail if she thought he needed to come in sooner. She did not think so but she wanted me to be aware of thise new information. Two days later, I received a three-page e-mail from Maurice in which he disclosed everything. He stated that he had never shared this with anyone before, except recently with his wife.

After reading his story, I nearly cried with compassion. Now I understood why so much of what I was attempting to do seemed to fall on deaf ears. He didn't want to lose his wife's support because he had no friends, and she was his lifeline. I knew that part already. . . I had reason to be concerned for him. Our next session was more at the heart level than most conversations I ever have with clients. I feel I got through to him in a deep and impactful way. As I write this, the outcome remains unknown.

Diversity is a major aspect of human life, and people differ in many ways. This chapter deals with diversity in counselling. Specifically, it focuses on counselling different populations based on age, gender, sexual minority status, and spirituality and religion. Each of the populations addressed has distinct, unique needs and concerns as well as issues that are universal in nature. All of these groups are at times stereotyped and may become marginalized, discounted, oppressed, or abused. Therefore, persons who are members of one or more of these subgroups of humanity are sometimes not recognized for their talents and possibilities.

Honouring diversity in all of its many forms is fundamental to counselling. Without such a stance, the welfare of clients is endangered and the respect and dignity that should be accorded every person is ignored. Indeed, negative attitudes toward clients because of their age, sex, sexual orientation, ethnicity, or spirituality "have been found to influence counselling processes" for the worse (Miller, Miller, & Stull, 2007, p. 325).

In examining the populations covered here, as well as the ones discussed in the previous chapter, ask yourself what opinions you hold of each. How have those thoughts and feelings influenced your interactions? How are you like and unlike each of the groups explored? How can the research help modify your beliefs and actions?

Fixed opinions are almost always deleterious in counselling those who differ from us. When trying to work with diversity, it is crucial not to reduce individuals to caricatures who are less than human or to pathologize them.

COUNSELLING AGED POPULATIONS

THE AGED—ALSO REFERRED TO IN THIS CHAPTER AS "SENIORS"—ARE DEFINED HERE AS persons over age 65. This is an arbitrary definition given the fact that Canadians are living longer now than at any time in the past (Statistics Canada, 2007b). The average life expectancy of Canadian women and men is currently 82.6 and 77.8 years, respectively (Statistics Canada, 2007b). Nonetheless, 65 is the age chosen here as it is when people who have been living in Canada for at least 10 years can collect the Old Age Security Pension, known as the "cornerstone of Canada's retirement income system" (Service Canada, 2009, para. 1). (Low-income seniors can qualify at age 60.)

Whereas seniors represented one in twenty Canadians in 1921, their ratio increased to one in eight in 2001 (Health Canada, 2002). According to the 2006 census, seniors constitute 13.7% of the total Canadian population (Statistics Canada, 2007a). By 2041, nearly one in four Canadians will be a senior (Health Canada, 2002). Consequently, "by virtue of their numbers, [they] will influence Canadian society for many years to come" (Health Canada, 2002, p. 4).

Given the size of the aging population, counsellor attention needs to focus on this group. There are a number of myths and misconceptions about old age, many of which are negative. Most centre around loss and dysfunctionality. However, the vast majority of individuals who reach old age are active and well functioning. Indeed, Cohen (2000) has found that some of the most significant and creative works of individuals have come after age 65. For example, a recent qualitative study reported on the significant contributions women over age 65 are making in Québec in both the private and public sectors (Charpentier, Queniart, & Jacques, 2008).

With the exception of dementia and delirium, the prevalence of most mental disorders in seniors in Canada is considered to be about the same (Canadian Mental Health Association [CMHA], Ontario, n.d.) or less (Chappell, 2009) when compared to younger age groups. Furthermore, seniors' reports of their well-being or life indicate that satisfaction does not decline with age (Chappell, 2009).

Historically, however, counselling seniors has been a neglected area within the counselling profession, despite the realization that gerontological counselling will grow significantly in the next few years (Maples & Abney, 2006). Although many mental health professionals are reluctant to view counselling older adults as beneficial (Rainsford, 2002), a recent systematic review has shown that counselling seniors is efficacious (Hill & Brettle, 2005).

In the United States, seniors receive only 6% of all mental health services (less than half of what might be expected since approximately 15% of the country's elderly population manifest at least moderate emotional problems) (Hashimi, 1991; Turner & Helms, 1994). In part, this situation stems from the group's unique developmental concerns, especially those involving financial, social, and physical losses.

In the mid-1970s, Blake (1975) and Salisbury (1975) raised counsellor awareness about counselling older adults by respectively noting a lack of articles on this population in the counselling literature and a dearth of counsellor education programs offering an elective course on the aged and their special needs. By the mid-1980s, the situation had changed. Based on a national survey, Myers (1983) reported that 36% of all counselling programs in the United States offered one or more courses on working with older people. That percentage has continued to increase, along with new studies on the aged (Hollis, 1997; Myers, Poidevant, & Dean, 1991). Now there are standards for working with geriatric populations (Myers, 1995).

In Canada, the Canadian Counselling and Psychotherapy Association only accredits counsellor training programs at the master's level that include graduate coursework in human development and learning, which in turn must include an understanding of working with individuals, families, and groups experiencing transitions across the lifespan (Robertson & Borgen, 2001-2002). At the doctoral level, the Canadian Psychological Association (CPA) only accredits counselling psychology programs that include coursework at either the undergraduate or graduate level in *individual behaviour* (Cohen, 2002). The CPA requirement for individual behaviour includes coursework in one of personality theory, human development, individual differences, or abnormal psychology.

Adult Development and Aging is the section of the Canadian Psychological Association that particularly focuses on chronological lifespan growth after adolescence (www.cpa.ca/sections/adultdevelopmentandaging). Currently there are no sections or divisions with the Canadian Association of Social Workers specific to the study of diverse groups.

Old Age

Several prominent theories of aging, many of them multidimensional, have been proposed. For instance, Birren, Schaie, and Gatz (1996) view aging from a biological, psychological, and social perspective, recognizing that the multidimensional process may be uneven. Aging is a natural part of development (DeLaszlo, 1994; Erikson, 1963; Friedan, 1994; Havighurst, 1959). People have specific tasks to accomplish as they grow older. For example, Erikson views middle and late adulthood as a time when the individual must develop a sense of generativity and ego integrity or become stagnant and despairing. Jung believes spirituality is a domain that those over age 40 are uniquely qualified to explore.

While an earlier classification scheme by Neugarten (1978) focused on two periods of old age—the *young-old* (ages 55-75) and the *old-old* (beyond 75)—a more instrumental approach focuses on differentiating *successful* aging from *normal* aging (Depp & Jeste, 2010). In successful aging, for example, an individual's cognitive and emotional health is more important than one's historical age regarding what are considered appropriate interventions (Depp & Jeste, 2010).

Just as some people are "old before their time," others age more slowly. Perhaps a more important concept is one's *functional age*, which is the ability of an individual to perform desired activities. "Functional age research had its origins in Canada [in 1951] with the work of I. M. Murray" (Stones & Kozma, 1981, p. 104).

Despite an increased understanding of aging and an ever-growing number of older adults, those in this category of life have to deal with age-based expectations and prejudices. For instance, "older people often are tagged with uncomplimentary labels such as senile, absent-minded, and helpless" (McCracken, Hayes, & Dell, 1997, p. 385). These negative attitudes and stereotypes, which are known as ageism, prevent intimate encounters with people in different age groups and sometimes lead to outright discrimination (Butler, 1998, 2001; Kimmel, 1988; Levenson, 1981).

Butler (2005) reiterated the continuing impact of *ageism* on American society more than 30 years after he coined the term. Canada is not immune either. A recent study found that Canadian undergraduate students tend to hold negative attitudes toward the elderly (Allan & Johnson, 2009). Studies have also shown that men hold more ageist attitudes than women (Allan & Johnson, 2009; Van Dussen & Weaver, 2009).

Unfortunately, individuals who are growing older often deny and dread the process, a phenomenon that Friedan (1994) calls "the age mystique." Another type of denial that has been written about is that many old people "buy into" ageist stereotypes, accepting the derogatory and patronizing attitudes that others have of them (Nelson, 2009). Despite their complacency, ageism exists, and it helps perpetuate the notion that one is old before notable signs of aging are even present (Nelson, 2009). Even counsellors are not immune to ageist attitudes (Blake, 1982; Maples & Abney, 2006).

Needs of the Aged

Older adults in Canada and the United States must deal with a wide variety of complex issues in their transition from midlife to senior citizen status, including changes in physical abilities, social roles, relationships, and even residential relocation (Cox, 1995; Kampfe, 2002). Many of these changes have the potential to spark an identity crisis within the person. The developmental demands of older adults are probably second only to those of young children. Older adults must learn to cope successfully with (a) the death of friends and spouses, (b) reduced physical vigour, (c) retirement and the reduction of income, (d) more leisure time and the process of making new friends, (e) the development of new social roles, (f) dealing with grown children, and (g) changing living arrangements or making satisfactory ones (Havighurst, 1959; Whalen, n.d.).

Some of the required changes associated with aging are gradual, such as the loss of physical strength. Others are abrupt, such as death. Overall, aging is a time of both "positive and negative transitions and transformations" (Myers, 1990a, p. 249). Positive transitions for older adults involve a gain for the individual, such as becoming a grandparent or receiving a discount on purchases. Transitions that involve a high level of stress are those connected with major loss, such as the death of a spouse, the loss of a job, or the contraction of a major illness. In these situations many older adults struggle because they lack a peer support group through which to voice their grief and work through emotions (Morgan, 1994).

Major problems of the aged include loneliness, physical illness, retirement, idleness, bereavement, and abuse (Morrissey, 1998; Shanks, 1982; Williams, Ballard, & Alessi, 2005). In addition, members of this group suffer more depression, anxiety, and psychosis as they grow older, with approximately 30% of the beds in mental hospitals being occupied by older adults. About 25% of all reported suicides in the United States are committed by persons over age 60, with white males being especially susceptible. In Canada, 16.7% of reported suicides were committed by adults aged 60 and older in 2005 (Statistics Canada, 2009b).

Domestic elder abuse—"any form of maltreatment by someone who has a special relationship with the elderly," including neglect—is problematic, too (Morrissey, 1998, p. 14). Among the most common forms of maltreatment for older adults, with nearly 600 000 cases a year in the United States, are physical abuse, psychological abuse, financial exploitation, and violation of rights, including personal liberty, free speech, and privacy (Welfel, Danzinger, & Santoro, 2000). Data from the 1999 General Social Survey in Canada revealed that approximately 7% of seniors reported some form of emotional or financial abuse in the five-year period preceding the survey (Dauvergne, 2003). In addition, alcohol abuse is a prevalent but often undiagnosed disorder in older adults, occurring in 6% to 16% of the American population (Williams et al., 2005) and between 5% and 11% of the Canadian population (McEwan, Donnelly, Robertson, & Hertzman, 1991).

Case Example: What Would *You* Do?

Frank, 70 years old, came to see me after Cindy, his wife, insisted on the appointment. Frank admitted that he is a poor communicator and that he easily loses his temper. Since he retired, however, his angry outbursts have increased in frequency. Frank told me he wished he could have provided better for Cindy while he was part of the work force. Cindy had told me in her own individual session that she wanted more physical affection from him and to be romanced like she was in their younger years. With her permission, I disclosed her desires to Frank. His response was that he is now arthritic and he cannot provide her the massages that she wants.

1. How would you help Frank?

2. Would you want Frank to have a physical check up? Why or why not?

3. What might be appropriate goals for counselling and what interventions might you attempt in order to achieve these goals?

Counselling the Aged

Most counsellors interested in working with the aged need additional professional training in this specialty (Goodman, 2010; Miller & Reid, 2009). Many simply do not understand older adults and therefore do not work with them. Such may be especially true in regard to new phenomena regarding older adults, such as grandparents raising grandchildren

(Pinson-Milburn, Fabian, Schlossberg, & Pyle, 1996). In such situations, counselling-related services may need to be offered on multiple levels such as direct outreach interventions that teach new coping strategies and skill training. In addition, indirect or supportive interventions may be needed, such as grandparent support groups, family support groups, and the sponsoring of events such as "Grandparents' Day" at school.

Another reason that older people do not receive more attention from mental health specialists is the investment syndrome described by Colangelo and Pulvino (1980). According to these authors, some counsellors feel their time and energy are better spent working with younger people "who may eventually contribute to society" (p. 69). Professionals who display this attitude are banking on future payoffs from the young and may well be misinformed about the possibilities for change in older adults.

A third reason that older adults may not receive attention from counsellors and mental health specialists is the irrational fear of aging and the psychological distancing from older persons that this fear generates (Maples & Abney, 2006).

A fourth reason is that some counsellors do not believe that older adults can benefit from counselling (Rainsford, 2002). The final reason older adults do not receive more or better treatment by counsellors in regard to their needs is that their problems may simply be mistaken for other conditions related to aging (Williams et al., 2005). For example alcohol abuse is frequently misdiagnosed.

One broad and important approach to working successfully with the aged is to treat them as adults (Cox & Waller, 1991). Old age is a unique life stage and involves continuous growth. When counsellors display basic counselling skills such as reflecting feelings, paraphrasing content, identifying patterns, asking open-ended questions, validating feelings and thoughts, and gently confronting inconsistencies, older adults feel free to explore difficulties or adjustment issues and are likely to respond appropriately (Kampfe, 2002). Another approach is to have older adults focus on their resiliency and on their spiritual resources (Langer, 2004).

Another strategy for promoting change in the aged is to modify the attitudes of people within the systems in which they live (Colangelo & Pulvino, 1980; Sinick, 1980). Many societal attitudes negatively influence older people's opinions about themselves. Often, older adults act old because their environments encourage and support such behaviour. American society "equates age with obsolescence and orders its priorities accordingly" (Hansen & Prather, 1980, p. 74). Therefore, counsellors must become educators and advocates for change in societal attitudes if destructive age restrictions and stereotypes are to be overcome. "We need to develop a society that encourages people to stop acting their age and start being themselves" (Ponzo, 1978, pp. 143–144).

In addition to treating the aged with respect and working for changes in systems, counsellors can help older adults deal with specific and immediate problems. Tomine (1986) asserts that counselling services for older adults are most helpful if they are portable and practical, such as being educational and focused on problem solving. For example, Hitchcock (1984) reviewed successful programs that help older adults obtain employment. A particularly successful program was a job club for older job seekers, where participants at regular meetings shared information on obtaining employment.

For older adults with Alzheimer's disease, counselling based on Rogers's theories is beneficial in the early stages of the disease. Group counselling, based on Yalom's existential writings, may be productive in helping family members cope as the disease progresses (LaBarge, 1981).

A structured life-review process has also proven beneficial in working with older adults (Beaver, 1991; Westcott, 1983). This approach helps them integrate the past and prepare themselves for the future.

Cognitive-behaviour therapy and several other approaches have been found efficacious with older adults (Hill & Brettle, 2005, Rainsford, 2002). Although people cannot change their past, they can change how they view it. This can be helpful in working with older clients (Rainsford, 2002). Twelve-step programs and bibliotherapy have also proven successful in helping older adults who abuse alcohol.

The following groups are among the most popular for adults aged 65 and older (Gladding, 2008):

- reality-oriented groups, which help orient confused group members to their surroundings

- remotivation therapy groups, which are aimed at helping older clients become more invested in the present and the future

- reminiscing groups, which conduct life reviews focused on resolving past issues in order to help members become more personally integrated and find meaning in the present (Zalaquett & Stens, 2006)

- psychotherapy groups, which are geared toward specific problems of the aging, such as loss

- topic-specific groups, which centre on relevant areas of interest to the aging, such as health or the arts

- member-specific groups, which focus on particular transition concerns of individual members, such as hospitalization or dealing with in-laws

In working with the aged, counsellors often become students of life and older persons become their teachers (Kemp, 1984). When this type of open attitude is achieved, clients are more likely to deal with the most important events in their lives, and counsellors are more prone to learn about a different dimension of life and be helpful in the process.

GENDER-BASED COUNSELLING

The second population considered in this chapter focuses on counselling according to gender. Clients have distinct needs and concerns that are determined in part by the cultural climates and social groups in which they live and develop (Cook, 1993; Hoffman,

2006; Moore & Leafgren, 1990). Women and men are "basically cultural–social beings" (McFadden, 1999, p. 234). Counsellors who are not fully aware of the influence of societal discrimination, stereotypes, and role expectations based on gender are not likely to succeed in helping their clients. Effective counselling requires special knowledge and insight that focuses on particular and common aspects of sexuality and sexual orientation of people. "This attention to unique and shared experiences of women and men is the paradoxical challenge of counseling" (Lee & Robbins, 2000, p. 488).

There is no longer any debate over the question of whether counsellors need to possess specialized knowledge and skill in counselling women and men as separate groups and genders that have much in common. However, because women and men "experience different developmental challenges," they may need different styles of interaction from professionals (Nelson, 1996, p. 343). Furthermore, counsellors who work more with one gender than another may need in-depth training and experience in particular areas.

For example, women in Canada suffer from major depression at a ratio of 1.64:1 compared to men between ages 18 and 69 (Romans, Tyas, Cohen, & Silverstone, 2007). During their reproductive years, however, the ratio increases to 2:1 (Grigoriadis & Robinson, 2007). This finding holds true across cultures and countries, even when definitions of depression change (Grigoriadis & Robinson, 2007; Romans et al., 2007). Part of the reason may be that women are socialized to suppress anger because it is seen as incompatible with the feminine gender role, whereas "anger has been hypothesized to be one of the few emotions that are compatible with the traditional masculine role" (Newman, Fugua, Gray, & Simpson, 2006, p. 157).

Counselling Women

Women are the primary consumers of counselling services (Wastell, 1996). They have special needs related to biological differences and socialization patterns that make many of their counselling concerns different from men's (Cook, 1993; Hoffman, 2006; Huffman & Myers, 1999). Women still lack the degree of freedom, status, access, and acceptance that men possess, although their social roles and career opportunities have expanded considerably since the 1960s, when the women's movement influenced substantial changes (Kees, 2005).

As a group, women have quite different concerns than men in many areas. For instance, they differ in their interest and involvement in such fundamental issues as intimacy, career options, and life development (Kopla & Keitel, 2003). That is why various journals have devoted special issues of their publications to the subject of women and counselling (see, for instance, the Summer 2005 issue of the *Journal of Counselling and Development*). "Women grow and/or develop in, through, and toward relationship" (Jordan, 1995, p. 52). When they feel connected with others, women have an increased sense of energy and a more accurate view of themselves and others. Furthermore, they feel empowered to act outside their relationships because they are active within them. They also feel a greater sense of worth and desire more connection (Miller & Stiver, 1997). Among the group's major concerns are development and growth, depression, eating disorders and body image, career development, poverty, sexual victimization, widowhood, and multiple roles (Lalande & Laverty, 2010).

Counselling women "is not a simple matter of picking a counselling theory or approach and commencing treatment" (Hanna, Hanna, Giordano, & Tollerud, 1998, p. 181). Rather, counsellors' attitudes, values, and knowledge may either facilitate or impede the potential development of women clients, especially at an international level (Chung, 2005). Women are basically relational beings, and counsellors' approaches should be geared toward that fact (Davenport & Yurich, 1991; Nelson, 1996). An examination of the literature indicates that professionals who counsel women should be "highly empathic, warm, understanding, and sufficiently well developed as a person to appreciate the predicament in which women find themselves" (Hanna et al., 1998, p. 167).

Unfortunately, evidence indicates that some counsellors and health professionals still hold sex-role stereotypes of women (Mollen, 2006; Simon, Gaul, Friedlander, & Heather-ington, 1992), and some counsellors are simply uninformed about particular difficulties that women face in general or at different stages of their lives. On a developmental level, there is "a noticeable gap in the literature with respect to studies on women in midlife who are childless, single, disabled, lesbian, ethnic minorities, or members of extended family networks" (Lippert, 1997, p. 17). For example, in working with voluntarily child-free women, Mollen (2006) stresses the importance of acceptance and empowerment of these women as well as helping them manage the stigma they may face in society because of their choice.

False assumptions, inaccurate beliefs, and a lack of counsellor understanding may all contribute to the problems of women clients (e.g., those who have primary or secondary infertility) (Gibson & Myers, 2000). It is important that counsellors consider sociopoliti-cal as well as other factors when counselling members of this population for "regardless of the presenting problem, women often blame themselves for inadequacies that were [are] actually the products of unrecognized forced enculturation" (Petersen, 2000, p. 70).

Committees and task forces within professional counselling organizations have been formed to address issues related to counselling women. For instance, there is a national Commission on Women within the American Counseling Association, and the *Section on Women and Psychology* (SWAP) within the Canadian Psychological Association is focused on the psychology of women and feminist psychology. SWAP's mandate also includes advancing the status of women in psychology and promoting equity for women in general (see www.cpa.ca/sections/womenandpsychologyswap).

Concerns in Counselling Women One of the major concerns in counselling women revolves around the issue of adequate information about their lives. Many early theories of the nature and development of women, especially those based on psychoana-lytic principles, tended to characterize women as innately "passive, dependent, and mor-ally inferior to men" (Hare-Mustin, 1983, p. 594). Those theories promoted the status quo in regard to women and limited their available options (Lewis, Hayes, & Bradley, 1992).

The general standard of healthy adult behaviour came to be identified with men, and a double standard of mental health evolved with regard to adult females (Lawler, 1990; Nicholas, Gobble, Crose, & Frank, 1992). This double standard basically depicted adult female behaviour as less socially desirable and healthy, a perception that lowered expectations for women's behaviour and set up barriers against their advancement in nontraditional roles. Thankfully, research conducted over the past 23 years reveals that the double standard is slowly eroding in North America and Europe (McCormick, 2010).

The literature in the field of women's studies and female psychology has grown from only three textbooks in the early 1970s to a plethora of texts and articles today. Many of these publications have been written by women, for women, often from a feminist and feminist therapy perspective to correct some older theoretical views generated by men without firsthand knowledge of women's issues (Axelson, 1999; Enns, 1993; Evans, Kincaide, Marbley, & Seem, 2005). For example, some theorists have proposed that women's development is in marked contrast to Erikson's psychosocial stages of development. These theorists stress the uniqueness of women and connectedness rather than separation. Furthermore, they outline female identity development from several points of view and compare and contrast it to ethnic identity models (Hoffman, 2006).

A second major concern in counselling women involves *sexism*, which is the belief (and the behaviour resulting from that belief) that females should be treated on the basis of their sex without regard to other criteria, such as interests and abilities. Such treatment is arbitrary, illogical, counterproductive, and self-serving. In the past, sexism has been blatant, such as limiting women's access to certain professions and encouraging them to pursue so-called pink-collar jobs that primarily employ women (e.g., nursing). Today, sexism is much more subtle, involving acts more of omission rather than commission (Moradi & DeBlaere, 2010). Many acts of omission result from a lack of information or a failure to change beliefs in light of new facts. Sexism is a worldwide phenomenon (Swim, Becker, Lee, & Pruitt, 2010), and a growing body of literature is revealing how daily experiences of sexism are increasing women's psychological distress (Moradi & DeBlaere, 2010). Sexism hurts not only women but society in general.

Issues and Theories of Counselling Women One of the main issues in counselling women involves the counsellor's research knowledge about them and proven ways of responding to them as individuals and in groups (Leech & Kees, 2005). Women are diverse, and it is important for counsellors to react to women in regard to their uniqueness as well as their similarity (Cook, 1993; Kopla & Keitel, 2003; Van Buren, 1992). Counsellors should recognize that specialized knowledge is required for counselling women at various stages of life, such as childhood and adolescence, midlife, and old age. Counsellors must also understand the dynamics of working with females under various conditions, such as eating disorders (Marino, 1994; Saraceni & Russell-Mayhew, 2007), sexual abuse and rape (Enns, 1996; Lalande & Laverty, 2010), suicide (Lalande & Laverty, 2010; Rogers, 1990), and career development (Cook, Heppner, & O'Brien, 2002; Lalande & Laverty, 2010).

Johnson and Scarato (1979) have presented a model that outlines major areas of knowledge about the psychology of women. It proposes seven areas in which counsellors should increase their knowledge of women and thereby decrease prejudice: (a) history and sociology of sex-role stereotyping, (b) psychophysiology of women and men, (c) theories of personality and sex-role development, (d) lifespan development, (e) special populations, (f) career development, and (g) counselling/psychotherapy. In the last area, the authors focus on alternatives to traditional counselling approaches as well as specific problems of women. A more recent Canadian resource is Lalande and Laverty (2010).

Effective counsellors with women will need to become their advocates in order to reduce the social injustices that lead to many of the mental health issues they face (Evans, 2010). Moreover, they need to become multiculturally competent (Arellano-Morales, 2009) and understand and subscribe to feminist principles (Brown & May, 2009).

A major approach to working with women (and even some men) in counselling is feminist theory (Mejia, 2005). Feminist views of counselling sprang from the eruption of the women's movement in the 1960s. Initially, this movement was a challenge to patriarchal power; as it grew, its focus centred on the development of females as persons with common and unique qualities (Okun, 1990). Beginning with the publication of Carol Gilligan's *In a Different Voice* (1982), there has been an increased integration of feminist theory into counselling. This approach encourages individuals to become more aware of socialization patterns and personal options in altering traditional gender roles as they make changes, and encourages clients to become involved in social change activities that stress equality as a way of bringing about change (Enns & Hackett, 1993).

In many respects, feminist theory is more an approach to counselling rather than a well-formulated set of constructs. It is assertive in challenging and questioning attitudes of traditional counselling theories because these models often advocate the maintenance of the status quo of a male-dominated, hierarchical society. "Although a unified model or theory of feminist therapy does not exist, central tenets include (a) the personal is political, (b) the valuing of egalitarian relationships, and (c) the presence of multiple realities" (Lalande & Laverty, 2010, p. 362).

Two main emphases in the feminist position distinguish it from other forms of helping:

1. Its emphasis on equality in the helping relationship, which stems from a belief that women's problems are inseparable from society's oppression of women (Okun, 1997).

2. Its emphasis on valuing social, political, and economic action as a major part of the process of treatment.

Androgyny, the importance of relationships, the acceptance of one's body "as is," and nonsexist career development are also stressed in feminist thought. Overall, "feminist theory starts with the experience of women and uses women's values and beliefs as the assumptive framework" (Nwachuku & Ivey, 1991, p. 106).

I remember well one of the first cases I had in an internship. A middle-aged married couple, John and Susan, came to see me for counselling. John was an established realtor while Susan had worked as a homemaker for the past 19 years. Susan had become aware that John had been having some kind of relationship with his son's 18-year old ex-girlfriend, Jennifer, who, due to unusual circumstances, was living with them. At one point in the session, Susan became very upset and darted out of the office. We chased after her, and she rejoined the session a few minutes later. During that interim, John confessed to me in confidence that he was both sexually and emotionally involved with Jennifer. Despite Susan's pleading, John had no intent on giving up his relationship with Jennifer.

1. If Susan subsequently became your individual client, how would you help her?

2. If Susan decided to leave John, what obstacles will she likely face in becoming independent?

3. If John became your client, how might you help him?

Counselling Men

An outgrowth of the focus on counselling women and eliminating sexism is new attention to the unique concerns and needs of men. In the early 1980s, Collison (1981) pointed out that "there seem to be fewer counselling procedures tailored to men than to women" (p. 220). Since that time, there has been an increase in conducting research on "men, masculinity, and the male experience" (Wade, 1998, p. 349) with "the burgeoning interest in men's psychology" leading "to a greater demand for clinical services tailored explicitly for men" (Johnson & Hayes, 1997, p. 302). Yet most counsellors lack formal education on men's issues (Gold & Pitariu, 2004).

Concerns in Counselling Men Concerns related to counselling men often stem from their socialization. Part of men's general social behaviour can be explained by the fact that men's traditional sex roles are more narrowly defined than women's, and beginning in childhood there are "stricter sanctions against boys adopting feminine behaviours than exist among girls adopting those deemed as masculine"(Robinson & Howard-Hamilton, 2000, p. 196). In addition, during childhood, girls are rewarded for being emotionally or behaviourally expressive; boys are reinforced primarily for unemotional physical actions. Thus, many men internalize their emotional reactions and seek to be autonomous, aggressive, and competitive (Scher & Stevens, 1987). They are oriented to display fighting rather than nurturing behaviour, and they often "perceive themselves as losing power and status by changing in the direction of androgyny," especially in young adulthood (Brown, 1990, p. 11). Therefore, as a group, men operate primarily from a cognitive perspective (Pollack & Levant, 1998). Affective expression is usually eschewed because of a lack of experience in dealing with it and the anxiety it creates.

In such constrictive roles, insensitivity to the needs of others and self often develops, and a denial of mental and physical problems becomes lethal in the form of shorter life-spans (Brooks, 2010). In addition, "men find psychological safety in independence and fear closeness" (Davenport & Yurich, 1991, p. 65). Therefore, counsellors who work with men need to be aware that many of them will be loners and reticent to talk. Because of this isolation, they may minimize their behaviours and others' actions. Most times they are not being obstinate but are simply displaying behaviours for which they have been reinforced. Many men exhibit childhood social taboos about self-disclosure, especially before other men, for it is not seen as "masculine" (Mejia, 2005).

Extensive research has linked traditional masculinity scripts with psychological distress, including externalizing symptoms of depression through alcohol and drug abuse, interpersonal conflict, and other acting-out behaviours (Cochran & Rabinowitz, 2003). Nonetheless, there are also a number of strengths associated with traditional masculinity, including (a) problem solving, (b) logical thinking, (c) risk taking, (d) expressing anger, (e) and assertiveness (Mahalik, Good, & Englar-Carlson, 2003). These skills may be especially helpful during times of crisis.

Scher (1981) provides guidelines to assist counsellors in understanding the realities of men's situations, including (a) an emphasis on the difficulty of change for most men, (b) the constraints imposed by sex-role stereotypes, (c) the importance of asking for assistance and dealing with affective issues, and (d) the need to distinguish between differences of roles and rules in one's personal and work life.

As a group, men are more reluctant than women to seek counselling (Mahalik et al., 2003). Most men enter counselling only in crisis situations, such as in trauma, because they are generally expected to be self-sufficient, to deny needs, and to take care of others (Maija, 2005; Moore & Leafgren, 1990). Different age and stage levels of men may be especially relevant as to whether they consider counselling or not. Race may cause minority men to be particularly vulnerable, especially to gender role identity (Wester, Vogel, Wei, & McLain, 2006). Thus, when working with men, it is important to consult developmental models and culturally related research that underscores developmental and culture-specific themes.

Issues and Theories in Counselling Men Many myths and realities exist about counselling men (Kelly & Hall, 1994). When males are able to break through traditional restrictions, they usually work hard in counselling and see it as if it were another competition. They have high expectations of the process and want productive sessions. Thus, as a group, they are likely to be clear and sincere in the process and to express themselves directly and honestly.

Across cultures, it has been demonstrated that men who subscribe to the traditional masculine gender role are at greater risk of developing alexithymia (Levant et al., 2003). *Alexithymia* is a condition whereby people cannot identify and describe their own and others' emotions and feelings. In such cases, it is important to help men (this condition affects men more than women) refrain from exploring the cognitive domain and instead focus on the feeling tones of their voices, the inconsistencies of their behaviours and feelings, and their ambivalence about control and nurturance. Good and Brooks (2005) make it abundantly clear in their recently revised book that the "cookie-cutter" approach to counselling men is ill-informed; as in all forms of counselling, the approach should be customized to the particular values of each client.

In contrast to eschewing the cognitive domain, Burch and Skovholt (1982) suggest that Holland's (1997) model of person–environment interaction may serve as the framework for understanding and counselling men. In this model, men are most likely to operate in the realistic dimension of functioning. Such individuals usually lack social skills but possess mechanical–technical skills; therefore, the authors recommend that counsellors adopt a cognitive-behavioural approach to establish rapport and facilitate counselling. Giles (1983) disagrees with this idea, pointing out that no conclusive research supports it. He believes that counsellors are not necessarily effective when they alter the counselling approach to fit the personal typology of clients.

Cultural, as well as cognitive, factors must be considered when working with men. For instance, Canadian Aboriginal men are often caught in a conundrum: If they attempt to meet one set of gender roles and values, such as those of the dominant European Canadian culture, they are likely to frustrate the other set of gender roles and values (that of Canadian First Nations), while societal racism often prevents them from fully meeting either set of expectations (Howell & Yuille, 2004). In such cases, counsellors must work with the intersection of identities and male gender-role conflict (i.e., traditional versus nontraditional behaviours) such as that between work and interpersonal relationships.

Furthermore, counsellors themselves are often caught in their own conundrum in working with Aboriginal clients. Due to the importance of interconnectedness in First Nations culture, counsellors may be expected to attend special events within the community and to interact with family members, resulting in a concern that they might be creating a dual relationship (Konrad, 2005).

In working with some some men from diverse communities, group work may be an effective intervention strategy (Andronico, 1996; Jolliff, 1994). The goals of men's groups are to increase personal awareness of sex-role conditioning, practise new desired behaviours, and promote a lifestyle based on the individual's needs. Three types of men—male sex offenders, gay men, and homeless men—may especially benefit from group work (DeAngelis, 1992). Men who do not do well in groups are those who are manic, very depressed, in severe crisis, addicted, inebriated, or paranoid (Horne & Mason, 1991).

Group work for men in general can be powerful in cutting through defenses such as denial and in building a sense of community. To be effective, the counsellor must publicize the availability of such a group, screen potential candidates carefully, identify specific behaviours on which to focus, institute opening and closing rituals, and develop intervention strategies aimed at resolving deep psychological issues such as conflict management (Hetzel, Barton, & Davenport, 1994; Horne & Mason, 1991).

In working with men in groups, Moore and Haverkamp (1989) found, in a well-controlled study, that "men age 30 to 50 are able to increase their level of affective expression, as measured by both self-report and behavioural tests" (p. 513). During this developmental stage of life, many men are seeking to become more intimate, deepen their relationships, and deal directly with their emotions. Thus, a group for men at this level of maturity can be very effective in producing change, especially, as the authors state, when it follows a social-learning paradigm in which other men serve as models and reinforcers for new behaviours. The impact of Robert Bly and the mythopoetic movement (the use of myths and poetry with men in groups) is one example of the power of such a paradigm for change (Erkel, 1990).

While promoting change and an exploration of affective issues, it is crucial that counsellors be aware that the rules of most men's work worlds differ from those of the personal domain. Counsellors must caution men not to naively and automatically introduce newly discovered behaviours that work in their personal lives into what may be a hostile environment—that is, the world of work.

Counselling with men, as with all groups, is a complex phenomenon, but the potential benefits are enormous. They include helping men develop productive strategies for dealing with expectations and changing roles (Moore & Leafgren, 1990). Through counselling, men may also develop new skills applicable to "marital communication, stress-related health problems, career and life decision making, and family interaction" (Moore & Haverkamp, 1989, p. 516). A particularly powerful procedure that may be employed with select men involves having them interview their fathers. Using a series of structured, open-ended questions about family traditions, these men make discoveries about themselves by understanding their fathers more clearly. This new understanding can serve as a catalyst for implementing different behaviours within their own families.

Case Example: What Would *You* Do?

Barry was a middle-aged man who wondered about saving his marriage. Although they had been together for nearly 17 years, he and his wife, Beth, were completely nonsexual with each other. Over time, Barry became increasingly interested in internet pornography, and he claimed he had not been sexual with anyone since this began. Beth, on the other hand, had started a sexual affair with a married man, whom she saw periodically. In disclosing this, I detected no negative affect or emotion from Barry. He spoke about how Beth wanted him to communicate his thoughts and feelings with her, but he found it difficult to share his own. Furthermore, he did not believe that sharing feelings was considered "manly" behaviour. He saw himself as a traditional man and similar to his dad in this regard.

1. What might be realistic goals for Barry and you to establish collaboratively in counselling?

2. If Barry wanted to become a better communicator, what ideas come to your mind for helping him?

3. Barry doesn't want to become more feeling oriented. Would it be ethical to push him in this direction anyway? Why or why not?

COUNSELLING CLIENTS WITH NONDOMINANT SEXUALITIES

Who Are People with Nondominant Sexualities?

A portion of the Canadian mosaic is comprised of individuals who differ with respect to some aspect of their sexuality or felt gender. The term *nondominant sexualities* refers to individuals with non-heterosexual orientations, gender expressions or gender identities, and/or sexual identities. How people experience and express (if they are able to at all) their nondominant sexuality is heavily dependent on numerous psychosocial and historical realities, such as their society, culture, religion, and age.

The first grouping refers to those individuals with differing sexual orientations. *Sexual orientation* refers to the attraction, erotic desire, and philia for members of the opposite gender, the same gender, or both (Alderson, 2010). Philia is the propensity to fall in love romantically with members of a particular sex or gender (or both, as in the case of biphilia). Consequently, individuals can have a heterosexual, homosexual, or bisexual orientation, regardless of the extent to which they acknowledge or accept it. Most gay men and lesbian women, for example, went through a "coming out" process before they accepted their homosexual orientation (Alderson, 2002).

The second grouping is based on those with differing gender expressions or gender identities. *Transsexual individuals* are those who believe "that they are really a member of the other gender trapped in bodies of the wrong gender" (Herring, 1998, pp. 161–162), while *transgendered persons* are "individuals who do not comply with the either/or, female/male construction in society" (Ormiston, cited in Herring, 1998, p. 162). Generally, transsexualism is viewed as a subset of transgenderism, the overarching category that also includes cross-dressers, drag queens, drag kings, transvestites, and other "gender benders."

Lastly, the third group concerns those with differing sexual identities. *Sexual identity* refers to the label individuals use to define their own sexuality (Alderson, 2010). Some intersexed individuals—that is, individuals with chromosomal or physical characteristics of both biological sexes—will define themselves as intersexed. Most people choose a label of heterosexual ("straight"), gay, lesbian, bisexual, or queer, but sometimes transgendered or transsexual individuals will use the same term to describe their gender expression or gender identity (i.e., *transgendered* or *transsexual*) as they use to describe their sexuality.

It is clearer, however, if one realizes that a transsexual or transgendered person may have any of the three sexual orientations (heterosexual, homosexual, or bisexual). A transgendered person who cross-dresses might define as heterosexual, gay, or bisexual. A gay man who cross-dresses, usually for fun or money, is usually referred to as a *drag queen*, whereas a gay or lesbian women cross-dresser is a *drag king*. A transsexual male-to-female is often referred to as a *transwoman*, and a transsexual female-to-male is a *transman*.

Although the term *queer* has not caught on in general usage (Savin-Williams, 2005), it refers to those people who refuse to be classified on the basis of sexuality (Herdt, 1997). *Gay men* are males who self-identify as having primarily homosexual cognition, affect, and/or behaviour, and who have adopted the construct of "gay" as having personal significance to them. *Lesbians* are females who self-identify as having homosexual cognition, affect, and/or behaviour, and who have adopted the construct of "lesbian" as having personal significance to them (Alderson, 2010).

Bisexual individuals are defined as those who self-identify as having primarily bisexual cognition, affect, and/or behaviour. Bisexual individuals have not established a substantive bisexual community (McKirnan, Stokes, Doll, & Burzette, 1995), so many define themselves as gay, lesbian, or heterosexual (McKirnan et al., 1995).

You can see from the above that sexual minorities refer to a significantly diverse group. Furthermore, terminology is often confused by both counsellors and researchers. Note as well that someone who defines as bisexual might be referring to their sexual behaviour, their sexual orientation, and/or their sexual identity, just as a transsexual or transgendered person might be interested sexually in men, women, or both. Due to the confounding of what is meant by the terms in the published literature, it is impossible to answer the question accurately, "What percentage of the population belongs to a sexual minority?"

Along with problems with definition is a larger issue. Much of the sexual minority community remains invisible to researchers (Flowers & Buston, 2001). When Statistics Canada (2009a) conducted its 2006 census and enumerated 45 300 same-sex couples (0.6% of all couples in Canada), the question remained as to how many Canadians were actually involved in a same-sex relationship. The fight for gay rights in Canada has not been an easy battle (*Same sex rights: Canada timeline*, 2007) and it is likely that many same-sex couples would not report their relationship status to an enumerator.

Given the above caveats, most gay and lesbian research has been based on well-educated Caucasian samples of individuals who are relatively accepting of their homosexual orientation (Croteau, Anderson, Distefano, & Kampa-Kokesch, 2000). We still do not know the actual size of the gay population, although various representative American studies have suggested that the percentage is likely between 3% and 10% for both adults and adolescents (Frankowski, 2004; Savin-Williams, 2005). Research done in Calgary, Alberta (Bagley & Tremblay, 1998), found that approximately 10% of the men in the sample had homosexual orientations, but because many gay men relocate to cities to live more open lives, this figure is likely inflated. We know very little about uneducated gay people, about those who have not yet come to identify as gay, and about bisexual individuals.

As a group, individuals who self-report as lesbian or gay exist in all age categories and approximate racial mixes as the population as a whole (Degges-White & Shoffner, 2002). Demographics on the percentage of bisexuals and transgender people are not as clear, although prevalence information from the Netherlands suggests that transsexuality occurs in about 1 in 11 900 males and 1 in 30 300 females (Meyer et al., 2001).

Bisexuality is nearly impossible to estimate because of the many definitions it encompasses. Nonetheless, sexual orientation is currently viewed as a multidimensional construct, and bisexuality prevalence will depend on the dimension that is being considered. Furthermore, the prevalence rate will depend on what temporal period is being considered in people's lives. One estimate suggests that for males, the post-puberty prevalence rate of having sex with both genders is around 14–16%, while the respective rate for females is around 10–12% (Rodriguez Rust, 2002).

Regardless of their actual numbers, sexual minority individuals are often stereotyped and discriminated against (Savage, Harley, & Nowak, 2005). A number of myths and stereotypes have grown over the years; for example, one claims that members of this population are child molesters and another that same-sex relationships never last (Chen-Hayes, 1997). Within the Canadian Psychological Association, the section called *Sexual Orientation and Gender Identity Issues* (SOGII; www.cpa.ca/sections/sexualorientationandgenderidentity) deals with concerns specifically related to these populations.

Difficulties usually begin for sexual minorities early in life. Children who are oriented toward any of the groups discussed frequently have trouble growing up in regard to their identity. They often have feelings of isolation and stigmatization and trouble with peer relationships, as well as family disruptions (Alderson, Orzeck, & McEwen, 2009; Marinoble, 1998). Many are frequently harassed. Even some counsellors are less accepting of members of these populations than one might expect (Matthews, 2005), although recent Canadian research suggests that most high school counsellors, even in conservative Alberta, are not homophobic (Alderson et al., 2009).

Some of the discomfort in working with sexual minorities often reported in earlier American studies may be a holdover from previous times, because up until the mid-1970s the *Diagnostic and Statistical Manual* of the American Psychiatric Association considered homosexuality a disorder. As Rudolph (1989) states, "ministering to the psychotherapy needs of homosexuals [and bisexuals] has historically been an exercise in dissatisfaction and discomfort for many clients and counsellors" (p. 96).

Thankfully, this discomfort appears to be rarely the case today in more recent American studies. Most counsellors have favourable attitudes toward working with clients with varying sexual orientations (Kilgore, Sideman, Amin, Baca, & Bohanske, 2005), and clients report that they are helpful (Liddle, 1999). On the other hand, the research and treatment of individuals with varying gender expressions or gender identities has tended to pathologize them traditionally (Raj, 2002). The extent to which transgendered individuals feel supported by counsellors is presently unknown.

Counselling Persons with Nondominant Sexualities

Persons with nondominant sexualities are diverse in their lifestyles and in the problems they bring to counselling. Therefore, individuals who embrace these lifestyles do not come to counselling with typical concerns. In fact, members of these groups may have many of the same types of problems as those who identify as heterosexual. For instance, in a two-year analysis of the Lesbian Connection's discussion forum, Erwin (2006), found the top five themes important to lesbians were "(a) isolation, safety, and aging; (b) children; (c) lesbian relationships and sexuality; (d) physical and mental health; and (e) political issues" (p. 99). If "lesbian relationships" are simply interpreted to be "interpersonal relationships," the counselling services required are similar to those needed by people from various backgrounds. Therefore, it is important not to make any assumptions before hearing what clients have to say.

However, there are some fairly frequent issues faced by gay, lesbian, and bisexual individuals that may surface in a counselling relationship. These difficulties include "coming out," forming community organizations, following religious practices, and coping with AIDS and relationships (Alderson, 2002; House & Miller, 1997). Coming out—letting others know that one is gay, lesbian, bisexual, or transsexual—may raise strong feelings, such as anger, in one's family and friends and rupture relationships. The same may be true for members of these populations trying to form community organizations or follow religious practices. Therefore, rehearsing how one will act and what one will say prior to such events can be helpful. Cognitive approaches, in regard to modifying the self-talk a person generates, likewise may be therapeutic. An excellent review of cognitive-behavioural interventions is found in Alderson (2002).

Clients with nondominant sexualities may need help in dealing with the stigma that is attached to them. "Society's reactions can lead to internalized homophobia, resulting in guilt, fear, or self-hatred that can affect many other, seemingly unrelated areas of their lives" (Granello, 2004, p. 59). One area where some gay men may have difficulty, outside of external factors, is in the loss of friends and significant others to the AIDS epidemic (Moursund & Kenny, 2002; Springer & Lease, 2000). Bereavement counselling may be needed to avoid developing major depressive episodes or post-traumatic stress disorder (PTSD).

Savage et al. (2005) advocate that a social empowerment model (SEM) be used with lesbian women and gay men, rather than counselling, because it increases this group's collective and personal self-advocacy. In such a model, clients come to know that the origins of sexual orientation "are not clearly understood or completely known" (p. 135). Likewise, they learn that lesbian women and gay men have a variety of lifestyles and "lead fulfilling and satisfying lives" (p. 135). Furthermore, they come to recognize that same-gender sexuality is a natural variation of human behaviour and that counselling is about dealing with concerns rather than focusing on attempts to persuade clients to change their sexual orientation, gender expression and identity, or sexual identity.

Working with clients with nondominant sexualities is an exciting area of counselling practice. It involves not only working with clients who are diverse in terms of sexuality and gender, but also focusing on transforming the cultural contexts in which these clients live (Carroll, Gilroy, & Ryan, 2002). One way to do that is to attend workshops that focus on learning how to provide affirmative therapy for persons with nondominant sexualities (Granello, 2004).

I remember well the day I received the call from the hospital. After three weeks of admission, they were releasing Howard as he was no longer imminently suicidal. The psychiatric nurse asked if I would see him for ongoing counselling. I said yes. A few days later, Howard entered my office and told his story. After 20 years of marriage to Samantha and raising two children, he could no longer continue living his lie. Howard viewed himself as gay, but he could neither accept it nor continue to hide it. He believed Samantha would hate him if she found out. One afternoon while she was at work, after having chugged back several stiff drinks, he had attempted to asphyxiate himself in the garage. Somehow Samantha had known something was suspicious about Howard that day, and she managed to find him before he caused himself brain damage or death.

1. What else would you want to know about Howard?

2. Assuming Howard is now out of danger for suicide, what goals (established between you and Howard) might address his concerns?

3. How might you help him to accept himself?

SPIRITUALITY, RELIGION, AND COUNSELLING

"Spirituality is increasingly recognized as an important cultural and coping factor that may affect counseling relationships, processes, or outcomes" (Harris et al., 2007, p. 4). Luminaries such as Carl Jung, Victor Frankl, Abraham Maslow, and Rollo May have emphasized the importance of spirituality in counselling. It is a complex, multidimensional construct. "At present, there is no generally agreed on definition of spirituality" (Ganje-Fling & McCarthy, 1996, p. 253). However, "spirituality includes concepts such as transcendence, self-actualization, purpose and meaning, wholeness, balance, sacredness, altruism, and a sense of a Higher Power" (Stanard, Sandhu, & Painter, 2000, p. 209). As a concept, spirituality usually refers to a unique, personally meaningful experience of a transcendent dimension that is associated with wholeness and wellness (Hinterkopf, 1998; Westgate, 1996).

Within counselling there is an increased emphasis on the importance of spirituality in the well-being of those seeking help, those wishing to maintain their own health, and those who are aging in a healthy manner (Burke & Miranti, 1995; Hudson, 1998; Snyder, 2005). For many average people who seek out counsellors, spirituality and religion "are significant aspects of their life" (Burke et al., 1999, p. 251). Two thirds of 1000 respondents in a 1992 Gallup poll indicated they would prefer to see a counsellor who held spiritual values and beliefs similar to theirs (Lehman, 1993, pp. B7–B8).

In recent years "a burgeoning literature has emerged concerning religion and spirituality in psychotherapy" (Ottens & Klein, 2005, p. 32). For example, Ingersoll (1994) developed a comprehensive overview of spirituality, religion, and counselling. He pointed out the importance of defining spirituality and listed dimensions that describe it. The following characteristics were included in Ingersoll's definition:

- a concept of the divine or a force greater than oneself
- a sense of meaning
- a relationship with the divine
- openness to mystery
- a sense of playfulness
- engagement in spiritually enhancing activities
- systematic use of spiritual forces as an integrator of life

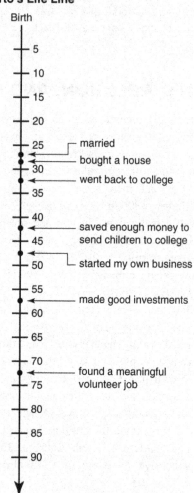

Alberto's Life Line

For most people, a spiritual journey is developmental in nature. It involves an active search toward overcoming one's current centricity to becoming more connected with the meaning of life, including a oneness of ultimate being (Chandler, Holden, & Kolander, 1992; Kelly, 1995). Snyder (2005) relates how personal storytelling is one way aging populations can create community and achieve spirituality simultaneously. She recommends an exercise where aging adults divide their lives into sections of five years and mark how decisions they made altered their fate and helped them reclaim a well-lived life with meaning.

Spirituality and Religion in Canada

According to the 2001 census (Statistics Canada, 2003), 72% of Canadians identify themselves as Roman Catholic (43%) or Protestant (29%). While the number of Canadians reporting Islam (2%), Hinduism (1%), Sikhism (1%), and Buddhism (1%) has increased significantly, the percentage of Canadians reporting no religion has increased as well over a 10-year period (from 12% to 16%). Those who identified themselves as Jewish remained constant over this 10-year period (1.1%).

Attendance at religious services has decreased dramatically over the past 15 years. In 2001, 43% of adults had not attended religious services during the previos 12 months compared to 26% in 1986 (Statistics Canada, 2003).

Spirituality and Religion in the United States

Three events have profoundly affected the attitude about spirituality in America at large and indirectly in counselling. One is the "informal spirituality promulgated by Alcoholics Anonymous, Adult Children of Alcoholics, and other 12-step programs" (Butler, 1990, p. 30). Another is the writings of Scott Peck, whose books, especially *The Road Less Traveled* (1978), bridge the gap between traditional psychotherapy and religion. The final event is a film series featuring Joseph Campbell, as interviewed by Bill Moyers, in which Campbell gives "respectability to the spiritual-psychological quest itself, even in modern times" (Butler, 1990, p. 30).

It is impossible to determine the reasons behind the mass attraction of these three events. However, the Association for Spiritual, Ethical, and Religious Values in Counseling (ASERVIC), a division within ACA, is devoted to exploring the place of spirituality in counselling. (The Canadian equivalent is the Canadian Psychological Association division called *Religion* [www.cpa.ca/sections/religion].)

In 1995, ASERVIC held a "Summit on Spirituality" and generated nine counsellor competencies on spiritual and religious issues in counselling that still influence the counselling profession (Young et al., 2007). There has also been renewed emphasis on the counsellor as a spiritual person from other professionals in the field (Goud, 1990; Kottler, 1986). "Spiritual competencies for counselors have been proposed, distributed nationally, and are beginning to be assimilated into counselor training programs" (Myers & Truluck,

1998, p. 120). The use of clients' values to aid progress in counselling has been a related focus in looking at spirituality and religion (Aust, 1990; Goldberg, 1994).

Counselling Clients with Spiritual and Religious Issues

Ingersoll (1994) states that counsellors interested in working well with clients committed to a particular spiritual view can best do so by

- affirming the importance of spirituality in the client's life,
- using language and imagery in problem solving,
- engaging in treatment that is congruent with the client's worldview, and
- consulting with other "healers" in the client's life such as ministers, priests, or rabbis.

This process calls for cultural sensitivity as well as ethical practices of the highest standard. Thus, asking about a client's spirituality or spiritual resources has become more of a fundamental intake question in many counselling practices, as counsellors address the total person of the client. For example, Moss and Dobson (2006) argue that attending to the spiritual needs of clients is an ethical responsibility of psychologists working in palliative care.

Integrating spiritual practices in working with Native and Inuit people in Canada is also helpful and desirable (McCormick, 1997; 2000; Wihak & Merali, 2005). The symbol of the circle holds a special place in the lives of Aboriginal peoples, for example, and is often referred to as the medicine wheel. Traditional spiritual practices in Native culture occur within or are facilitated through ceremonies, prayers to the Great Creator and spirit helpers, pipes, pipe ceremonies, fasting, sweat lodges, drums, eagle whistles, herbs/incense, medicine pouches, pow-wows, giveaways, honour songs, grand entries, eagle staffs, invocations, flag songs, and various dances (RCMP Public Affairs Directorate, 1993).

Sometimes spirituality is manifested in a particular philosophy or religious belief, such as Taoism or Christianity. At other times, it is more nebulous. When spirituality is in the form of religious beliefs, counsellors need to be respectful and work with clients to maximize the positive nature of their beliefs and values in connection with the difficulties they are experiencing. Counsellors who work best with religious issues in counselling are either pluralistic (i.e., "recognizing the existence of a religious or spiritual absolute reality" but allowing for multiple interpretations and paths toward it") or constructivist (i.e., "recognizing a client worldview that includes God or spiritual realities") (Zinnbauer & Pargament, 2000, p. 167).

Regardless of the form spirituality takes, spiritual aspects of clients' lives can be enhanced through creating rituals (or other ways for clients to focus on their lives) that help them appreciate life rather than deprecate themselves. For example, as one ritual, distraught clients might write down five things for which they are grateful (Hudson, 1998). Such an assignment can help them move away from bitterness and transcend the adversity of the moment. In addition to helping clients, forms of spirituality such as meditation and prayer may also be important aspects of counsellors' lives.

Kelly (1995) found in a nationally representative sample of ACA-affiliated counsellors that the majority of respondents valued spirituality in their lives (even more than institutionalized religion). In many cases, a "counselor's personal spirituality/religiousness may prove a value base for being attuned to clients' spiritual and religious issues" (Kelly, 1995, p. 43). Therefore, counsellors should assess their own spirituality as well as that of their clients.

Case Example: What Would *You* Do?

Like many other Jewish young men, Jeffrey was determined to marry a woman who was also Jewish. While looking for his life mate, Jeffrey met Ruth playing badminton, and their friendship progressed over several months into deep romantic love. Jeffrey was torn: Ruth had Christian beliefs, and although she was not a churchgoer, she was set in her religious convictions. Ruth wanted to marry Jeffrey and have a family with him. She made it clear that she would remain a nonpractising member of the United Church, however, and although willing to raise their children with Jewish beliefs and customs for his sake, she stated firmly that she did not believe in any of it.

1. How would you help Jeffrey?

2. To what extent would your spiritual beliefs become an issue in working with him?

3. If Jeffrey told you that he was willing to forfeit his religious beliefs because he loved Ruth and could not live without her, what response would you have for him? To what extent do you think your response would be helpful?

SUMMARY AND CONCLUSION

This chapter has focused on counselling four different populations based on age, gender, nondominant sexuality status, and spirituality and religion. Each of these areas impacts clients and counsellors for better or worse. When those involved are open to exploring the part that they play in one's personal life, productive insights and behaviours may occur. When there is fear or avoidance of examining any of these aspects of life, people may regress or become stressed. They may even develop disorders.

When counselling the aged, it is important to realize that growing older is a natural part of life. It can be exciting and fulfilling or it can be dreaded.

When working with other specific groups, counsellors need to be aware of unique and common concerns. They must also realize the limitations and appropriateness of counselling theories they employ. Talking and self-disclosure are not valued in many cultures, especially with someone outside one's own tradition. Likewise, gender and sexual orientation are factors in displaying feelings and revealing personal weaknesses. Age and spiritual development also play a part in the counselling process. The aged need to express emotions and resolve past conflicts in their own unique ways if they are to benefit from counselling. Similarly, the spiritually-oriented may wish to resolve difficulties or focus on issues in nontraditional ways.

Counsellors must constantly ask themselves how each of their clients is similar to and different from others. What are within- and between-group universals and uniquenesses? They must concentrate on increasing their sensitivity to global issues as well as individual concerns. When clients differ significantly from counsellors, extra attention and skill must be devoted to establishing and cultivating the counselling relationship.

Your Personal Reflections

1. Aging is a state of mind as well as a physical reality. Think of people you know aged 65 or above. Which ones do you consider to be adjusting well to their age? What factors do you think make that so?

2. A number of distinctions exist between counselling women as opposed to counselling men. What factors do you think you need to be most aware of? What overlap is there in counselling members of both sexes?

3. Sexuality is a controversial subject that stimulates strong views from many sides. What views do you currently hold? Have your views changed or remained the same? Explain.

Classroom Activities

1. Divide the class according to gender. Have the males in the class assume traditional female roles and vice versa. Then discuss making decisions about career and marriage. Talk about what feelings each side of the class has in relation to the decision-making process. Discuss how these feelings would differ if one had a gay, lesbian, bisexual, or transgender, or transsexual sexual identity.

2. Discuss the following question in groups of three: What is the place of spirituality in counselling? Share your opinions with the class.

3. Role-play the following situation with another class member: Imagine that you have reached age 65. What are you doing at this age? What are your needs and expectations? How might a counsellor help you? Do you find your life perspective different from your present outlook? Discuss these questions in relation to Ponzo's (1978) advice that individuals need to be themselves, not act their age.

4. What difficulties do you think persons with homosexual orientations face that those who are heterosexually oriented do not encounter? Find specific examples and share them with your classmates.

5. Examine feminist approaches to counselling. How do they differ from other approaches? How are they the same?

6. Consider bringing in speakers with nondominant sexualities, thereby allowing them to give voice to their experiences.

Chapter 6

Building Counselling Relationships

PRACTICE REFLECTION

I will never forget my experience with Bert. While doing some work with a local Salvation Army, I ended up seeing most of the new residents in one of their short-term residential facilities. Most of these men had significant psychosocial problems. The captain of that facility booked sessions for me so that, when I arrived, I was simply given a sheet with who was coming in to see me next.

Bert came in and I began asking him about his life. He told me a compelling story about how he had been abused as a child and had begun drinking to escape the emotional pain. Over time, he became unable to control his drinking and grew dependent on alcohol. As a young 23-year-old counsellor, I was not a psychologist yet and many would say I had not "earned my stripes," meaning I looked young enough to be the son of many of these men.

After seeing another client after Bert, I waited for my third appointment. As time passed by, I realized he was a no-show. I walked out to the lounge area and saw Bert sitting there watching television. I sat close by and said hi.

Without missing a beat, Bert replied, "You know, everything I told you in there was a lie." Surprised and confused, I asked why. He responded, "You think in your office that you are so high and mighty, thinking you are better than we are, no doubt. The truth is, most of us have lived on the street for many years. Have you ever lived on the street, Kevin?" "No, I can't say that I have." Bert continued, "I know, and I am not blaming you for that. You have had a more privileged life than we have. I don't want to sink your boat by telling you the truth."

I was annoyed with Bert's judgment, so now was my time to be honest. I retorted, "You are correct, Bert. I never slept on the street or was forced to leave my home. However, my family was on welfare through most of my growing years. My dad died when I was young and my mom had few marketable skills. I may not know what it is like to sleep in a back alley, but I do know what it is like to not have clothes that fit properly or to pick welfare frames for the glasses I needed. My peers often laughed at my ugly frames and my flood pants. I had little choice over either."

Bert looked at me and knew I was telling the truth. He said, "Kevin, I was never abused as a child. The fact is, I couldn't hold down a job because of my alcoholism. My wife left me when she couldn't take *my* abuse any longer and no employer wanted to hire me either. I really don't know what to do right now."

Bert and I had a few more sessions after that. He wanted something from a counsellor that he felt he needed: someone who had suffered a little as well and, more importantly, someone who would be real with him. I learned from people like Bert that unless you can get let go of whatever pretense you still have inside, you will lose clients who cannot relate to a façade that they can wear better than you can.

The process of counselling develops in definable stages with recognizable transitions. The first stage involves building a relationship and focuses on engaging clients to explore issues that directly affect them. Two struggles take place at this time (Napier & Whitaker, 1978). One is the battle for structure, which involves issues of administrative control (e.g., scheduling, fees, participation in sessions). The other is the battle for initiative, which concerns the motivation for change and client responsibility. It is essential that counsellors win the first battle and clients win the second. If there are failures at these points, the counselling effort will be prematurely terminated, and the counsellor and client may feel worse for the experience.

Other factors that influence the progress and direction of counselling are the physical setting, the client's background, the counsellor's skill, and the quality of the relationship established. They will be examined here, as will the nature of the first interview and the exploration stage of counselling. Carkhuff (1969; 2000) and Daniel and Ivey (2007) have demonstrated that some counselling responses cut across theoretical and cultural lines in helping build a client–counsellor relationship. These responses are sometimes known as microskills and include atheoretical and social-learning behaviours such as attending, encouraging, reflecting, and listening. When mastered, these abilities allow counsellors to be with their clients more fully and to "act in a culturally appropriate manner, and find positives in life experience" (Weinrach, 1987, p. 533). Thus, part of this chapter will focus on microskills.

THE COUNSELLING RELATIONSHIP

ACCORDING TO GELSO AND CARTER (1985), THE COUNSELLING RELATIONSHIP IS COMPRISED of three key elements: (a) transference and countertransference (these are explained in Chapter 7), (b) the working alliance (explained in the next section), and (c) the real relationship. If helping skills have been used well, a *real relationship* (one that is reality oriented, appropriate, and undistorted) will emerge. The real relationship begins as a two-way experience between counsellors and clients from their first encounter. Counsellors are real by being genuine (owning their thoughts and feelings), trying to facilitate genuineness in their clients, and attempting to see and understand clients in a realistic manner. Clients contribute to the realness of the relationship by being genuine and perceiving their own situations realistically.

The real relationship that exists in counselling has been written about mostly from counsellors' viewpoints and has been misunderstood or incompletely defined. According to Gelso and Carter (1985), there are specific propositions about the nature of a real relationship. One is that the relationship increases and deepens during the counselling process. Another is that counsellors and clients have different expectations and actualizations of what a real relationship is like.

The work of Gelso and Carter has been evaluated by Sexton and Whiston (1994), who have reviewed the clinical literature on counsellor–client relationships. Among other results, they have found that "the alliance between the client and counsellor is a complex interactional phenomenon" (p. 45). Counselling is a dynamic, interactional process, and the strength of relationships between counsellors and clients varies over time.

BUILDING AND MAINTAINING
A WORKING ALLIANCE

Sometimes clients talk to a counsellor and feel little to no connection with that person. Chances are they do not return for another session.

The working alliance is known by several names: the therapeutic alliance, the ego alliance, the counselling alliance, and the helping alliance (Bedi, Davis, & Arvay, 2005). The *working alliance* "refers to the quality and strength of the reciprocal relationship between a client and a counsellor and includes both the affective elements and the collaborative working elements of this reciprocal relationship" (Bedi et al., 2005). In other words, the working alliance is about the quality of the relationship formed between the counsellor and client. Several Canadian researchers are leading experts when it comes to the working alliance, including most of the individuals mentioned in this section.

The concept is very important, as it is arguably the best predictor of treatment outcome (Horvath, 2005). According to Horvath (2001), Edward Bordin named the working alliance and conceptualized it as having three components: agreement on goals (what are the therapeutic goals?), agreement on tasks (how will the goals be accomplished?), and the bond between the client and the counsellor (the relationship). Horvath (2006) reported that large-scale investigations have found that the single best indicator of a positive working alliance is "enthusiastic collaboration," indicating that interpersonal factors are more important than intrapersonal ones (i.e., personal qualities of the counsellor). Nonetheless, certain counsellor qualities—such as warmth, flexibility, and making accurate interpretations—are associated with positive working alliances (Castonguay, Constantino, & Holtforth, 2006).

While researchers have predominantly studied factors related to developing a positive working alliance through observation of counsellors, in actuality it is the client's perspective that is more strongly related to counselling success than the counsellor's perspective (Bedi et al., 2005; Horvath, 2005; 2006). Furthermore, clients usually believe it is the counsellor who is primarily responsible for developing the alliance (Bachelor, 1995; Bedi, Davis, & Williams, 2005)

Interestingly, beginning counsellors often believe a strong working alliance has occurred, while studies have shown that they often misperceive how the client feels the session has gone. Consequently, it is recommended that counsellors have clients complete a rating scale (there are several available) of the strength of the working alliance after their session (Castonguay et al., 2006). Research has shown that if a positive working alliance has not developed early (within three to five sessions), retention of clients is low and they are unlikely to benefit from counselling even if they do persist (Horvath, 2000; 2001).

Horvath (2006) indicated that there is still much to be learned about the working alliance, despite the growth in this field of study over the past 20 years. Nevertheless, its importance is undeniable, and this chapter and the next one are mostly about building and maintaining a strong working alliance and counselling relationship.

FACTORS THAT INFLUENCE THE COUNSELLING PROCESS

A number of factors affect the counselling process for better or worse. Those covered here are the seriousness of the concern presented, structure, initiative, physical setting, client qualities, and counsellor qualities.

Seriousness of the Presenting Problem

Counselling is impacted by the seriousness of the client's presenting problem. "Evidence has suggested a relationship between initial self-reported disturbance level and treatment course. Thus, clients reporting higher initial distress take more sessions to reach clinically significant improvement than clients reporting lower levels of distress" (Leibert, 2006, p. 109).

In addition, research suggests that the largest gains in improvement occur early in treatment but that seriously disturbed individuals benefit from longer term treatment. Furthermore, some conditions, such as schizophrenia, and some clients who exhibit anti-social personality disorders are least likely to improve through traditional talk therapies.

Overall, clients who are in better shape at the onset of treatment seem to improve the most, in the least amount of time, and with the best long-term results. Research, as summarized by Leibert (2006), has found "50% of clients diagnosed with anxiety or depression had improved by Sessions 8–13" and "85% of clients improved after one year of weekly treatment" (p. 109).

Structure

Clients and counsellors sometimes have different perceptions about the purpose and nature of counselling. Clients often do not know what to expect from the process or how to act. Seeing a counsellor is a last resort for many individuals. They are likely to have already sought help from more familiar sources, such as friends, family members, ministers, or teachers (Hinson & Swanson, 1993). Therefore, many clients enter counselling reluctantly and hesitantly. This uncertainty can inhibit the counselling process unless some structure is provided (Ritchie, 1986). *Structure* in counselling is defined as "a joint understanding between the counselor and client regarding the characteristics, conditions, procedures, and parameters of counseling" (Day & Sparacio, 1980, p. 246). Structure helps clarify the counsellor–client relationship and give it direction; helps protect the rights, roles, and obligations of both counsellors and clients; and helps ensure the success of counselling (Brammer, Abrego, & Shostrom, 1993).

Practical guidelines are part of building structure. They include time limits (such as a 50-minute session), action limits (for the prevention of destructive behaviour), role limits (what will be expected of each participant), and procedural limits (in which the client is given the responsibility to work on specific goals or needs) (Brammer & MacDonald, 2003). Guidelines also provide information on fee schedules and other important concerns of clients. In general, structure promotes the development of counselling by providing a framework in which the process can take place. "It is therapeutic in and of itself" (Day & Sparacio, 1980, p. 246).

Structure is provided throughout all stages of counselling but is especially important at the beginning. Dorn (1984) states that "clients usually seek counseling because they are in a static behavior state" (p. 342). That is, clients feel stuck and out of control to change behaviour. To help clients gain new directions in their lives, counsellors provide constructive guidelines. Their decisions on how to establish this structure are based on their theoretical orientation to counselling, the personalities of their clients, and the major problem areas with which they will deal. Too much structure can be just as detrimental as not enough (Welfel & Patterson, 2005). Therefore, counsellors need to stay flexible and continually negotiate the nature of structure with their clients.

The importance of structure is most obvious when clients arrive for counselling with unrealistic expectations (Welfel & Patterson, 2005). Counsellors need to move quickly to establish structure at such times. One way is for counsellors to provide information about the counselling process and themselves. This can be done either verbally or by having something prepared in writing to give to clients.

Initiative

Initiative refers to the motivation to change. Most counsellors and counselling theories assume that clients will be cooperative. Indeed, many clients come to counselling on a voluntary or self-referred basis. They experience tension and concern about themselves or others, but they are willing to work hard in counselling sessions. Other clients, however, are more reserved about participating in counselling.

Vriend and Dyer (1973) estimate that the majority of clients who visit counsellors are reluctant to some degree. Recent research reveals that little has changed since the 1970s. Even students today would rather talk to a friend than a counsellor (Vogel, Wade, & Hackler, 2007). More telling is the fact that most multicultural individuals living in Canada view counselling as highly stigmatizing (Arthur & Collins, 2009).

When counsellors meet clients who seem to lack initiative, they often do not know what to do with them, much less how to go about counselling. Therefore, some counsellors are impatient, irritated, and may ultimately give up trying to work with such persons. The result is not only termination of the relationship but also scapegoating—blaming a person when the problem was not entirely his or her fault. Many counsellors end up blaming themselves or their clients if counselling is not successful. Such recriminations need not occur if counsellors understand the dynamics involved in working with difficult clients. Part of this understanding involves assuming the role of an involuntary client and imagining how it would feel to come for counselling. A role-reversal exercise can promote counsellor empathy as well.

A *reluctant client* is one who has been referred by a third party and is frequently "unmotivated to seek help" (Ritchie, 1986, p. 516). Many schoolchildren and court-referred clients are good examples. They do not wish to be in counselling, let alone talk about themselves. Many reluctant clients terminate counselling prematurely and report dissatisfaction with the process.

Case Example: What Would *You* Do?

I completed half of my internship at a family counselling centre in Edmonton. I remember well the seven-year-old boy who I was supposed to assess. Without doubt, he impressed me with his incredible energy, which frankly helped me fully awaken. As I was escorting him to the playroom, he managed to kick me in the groin. I was supposed to observe him while he played; I was writing observation notes when the next thing I knew my glasses (I wore glasses before laser surgery) went flying, mangled all to hell. So much for wire rims, I figured, but I was angry now. Groin shots are one thing, but wrecking my glasses while I am struggling to make ends meet is another. As I opened the door to get him out of the playroom,

he ran past, saying he needed to use the washroom.

I chased him (I was learning to be a good runner at this internship site, actually) out of the office into the hallway where the washroom was located. He locked himself in a cubicle and then refused to come out. Murphy's law kicked in and the next thing I knew, two men were waiting to use the only cubicle in the washroom.

1. What would you do to try and get the boy out of the cubicle?

2. What if all attempts failed? What would be your next course of action?

3. Would you adopt this child? Why or why not?

A *resistant client* is a person in counselling who is unwilling, unready, or opposed to change (Otani, 1989; Ritchie, 1986). Such an individual may actively seek counselling but does not wish to go through the emotional pain, change in perspective, or enhanced awareness that counselling demands (Cowan & Presbury, 2000). Instead, the client clings to the certainty of present behaviour, even when such action is counterproductive and dysfunctional. Some resistant clients refuse to make decisions, are superficial in dealing with problems, and refuse to take any action to resolve a problem (i.e., to do anything a counsellor says). According to Sack (1988), "the most common form of resistance is the simple statement 'I don't know'" (p. 180). Such a response makes the counsellor's next move difficult and protects the client from having to take any action.

Otani (1989) has proposed four broad categories of resistance: "amount of verbalization; content of message; style of communication; and attitude toward counselors and counseling sessions" (p. 459). The 22 forms of resistance included in these categories are shown in Figure 6.1.

Counsellors can help clients win the battle for initiative and achieve success in counselling in several ways. One is to anticipate the anger, frustration, and defensiveness that some clients display. Counsellors who realize that a percentage of their clients are reluctant or resistant can work with these individuals because they are not surprised by them or their behaviours.

Category A: Response quantity resistance

Definition: The client limits the amount of information to be communicated to the counselor.

Forms
Silence
Minimum talk
Verbosity

Category B: Response content resistance

Definition: The client restricts the type of information to be communicated to the counselor.

Forms
Intellectual talk
Symptom preoccupation
Small talk
Emotional display
Future/past preoccupation
Rhetorical question

Category C: Response style resistance

Definition: The client manipulates the manner of communicating information to the counselor.

Forms
Discounting
Thought censoring/editing
Second-guessing
Seductiveness
Last-minute disclosure
Limit setting
Externalization
Counselor focusing/stroking
Forgetting
False promising

Category D: Logistic management resistance

Definition: The client violates basic rules of counseling.

Forms
Poor appointment keeping
Payment delay/refusal
Personal favor-asking

Figure 6.1 Twenty-two forms of resistance

Source: Reprinted from "Client Resistance in Counsellng: Its Theoretical Rationale and Taxonomic Classification," by A. Otani, 1989, *Journal of Classification and Development, 67*, p. 459. © 1989 by ACA. Reprinted with permission. No further reproduction authorized without written permission of the American Counseling Association.

A second way to deal with a lack of initiative is to show acceptance, patience, and understanding as well as a general nonjudgmental attitude. This stance promotes trust, which is the basis of an interpersonal relationship. Nonjudgmental behaviour also helps clients better understand their thoughts and feelings about counselling. Thus, acceptance opens clients to others, themselves, and the counselling process.

A third way to win the battle for initiative is for counsellors to use persuasion (Kerr, Claiborn, & Dixon, 1982; Senour, 1982). All counsellors have some influence on clients, and vice versa (Dorn, 1984; Strong, 1982). How a counsellor responds to the client, directly or indirectly, can make a significant difference in whether the client takes the initiative in working to produce change. Roloff and Miller (1980) mention two direct persuasion techniques employed in counselling: the "*foot in the door*" and the "*door in the face*." In the first technique, the counsellor asks the client to comply with a minor request and then later follows with a larger request. For example, an initial request might be "Would you keep a journal of your thoughts and feelings for this week?" followed the next week by "I'd like you to keep a journal of your thoughts and feelings from now on." In the second technique, the counsellor asks the client to do a seemingly impossible task and then follows by requesting the client to do a more reasonable task. For instance, the initial request might be "I'd like you to talk briefly to 100 people a day between now and our next session" followed, after the client's refusal, by "Since that assignment seems to be more than you are comfortable in handling, I'd like you to say hello to just three new people each day."

A fourth way a counsellor can assist clients in gaining initiative is through *confrontation*. In this procedure the counsellor simply points out to the client exactly what the client is doing, such as being inconsistent. For example, a parent might be disciplining children for misbehaving sometimes and then letting them act out at other times. In such situations, the client must take responsibility for responding to the confrontation. The three primary ways of responding are denying the behaviour, accepting all or part of the confrontation as true, or developing a middle position that synthesizes the first two (Young, 2005). Doing something differently or gaining a new perception on a problem can be a beneficial result of confrontation, especially if what has previously been tried has not worked.

Counsellors can also use language, especially metaphors, to soften resistance or reluctance. "Metaphors can be used to teach and reduce threat levels by providing stories, by painting images, by offering fresh insights, by challenging rigid thinking, by permitting tolerance for new beliefs, and by overcoming the tension often present between a counselor and the resistant [or reluctant] client" (James & Hazler, 1998, p. 122). For instance, in addressing a client who keeps repeating the same mistake over again, the counsellor might say, "What does a fighter do when he gets badly beaten up every time he fights?" (p. 127).

The sixth way counsellors can help reluctant and resistant clients, and indeed all clients, and strengthen the counselling relationship is through "*mattering*," the perception that as human beings we are important and significant to the world around us and to others in our lives (Rayle, 2006). Research shows that mattering to others directly affects individuals' lives and relationships.

Finally, Sack (1988) recommends the use of pragmatic techniques, such as silence (or pause), reflection (or empathy), questioning, describing, assessing, pretending, and sharing the counsellor's perspective, as ways to overcome client resistance. These techniques are especially helpful with individuals who respond to counsellor initiatives with "I don't know." Depending on one's theoretical orientation, resistance can also be declared officially dead (deShazer, 1984). From such a perspective, change is inevitable and clients are seen as cooperative. The reason change has not occurred is that the counsellor has yet to find a way to help stuck clients initiate a sufficient push to escape patterns that have been troubling them.

The Physical Setting

Counselling can occur almost anywhere, but some physical settings promote the process better than others. Among the most important factors that help or hurt the process is the place where the counselling occurs. Most counselling occurs in a room, although Benjamin (1987) tells of counselling in a tent. He says that there is no universal quality that a room should have "except [that] it should not be overwhelming, noisy, or distracting" (p. 3). Shertzer and Stone (1980) implicitly agree: "The room should be comfortable and attractive" (p. 252). Erdman and Lampe (1996) believe that certain features of a counselling office will improve its general appearance and probably facilitate counselling by not distracting the client. These features include soft lighting, quiet colours, an absence of clutter, harmonious comfortable furniture, and diverse cultural artifacts. They go on to recommend that when working with families who have children or with children apart from families, counsellors need to have furniture that is child-sized.

In an extensive review of the research on the physical environment and counselling, Pressly and Heesacker (2001, p. 156) looked at eight common architectural characteristics of space and their potential impact on counselling sessions. The factors they reviewed and their findings are as follows:

1. *Accessories* (i.e., artwork, objects, plants). People prefer "textually complex images of natural settings, rather than posters of people, urban life, and abstract compositions"; people feel "more comfortable in offices that are clean and have plants and artwork"

2. *Colour* (i.e., hue, value, intensity). "Bright colors are associated with positive emotions and dark colors are linked with negative emotions"

3. *Furniture and room design* (i.e., form, line, colour, texture, scale). "Clients prefer intermediate distance in counseling and . . . more protective furniture layouts . . . than do counselors"

4. *Lighting* (i.e., artificial, natural). "General communication tends to occur in bright environments, whereas more intimate conversation tends to occur in softer light"; "full-spectrum lighting helps to decrease depression symptomalology" (In an experiment with 80 undergraduates in Japan, Miwa and Hanyu [2006] found that dim lighting yielded more pleasant and relaxed feelings, more favourable impressions of the counsellor, and more self-disclosure than bright lighting.)

5. *Smell* (i.e., plants, ambient fragrances, general odours). "Unpleasant smells elicit unhappy memories, whereas pleasant smells trigger happy memories"; "inhaled food and fruit fragrances have resulted in self-reported depressive symptoms"

6. *Sound* (i.e., loudness, frequency). "Sound may enhance or detract from task performance"; "music may enhance the healing process and affect muscle tone, blood pressure, heart rate, and the experience of pain"

7. *Texture* (i.e., floors, walls, ceilings, furniture). "Counselors should consider using soft, textured surfaces to absorb sound and to increase clients' feelings of privacy"

8. *Thermal conditions* (i.e., temperature, relative humidity, air velocity). "Most individuals feel comfortable in temperatures ranging from 69 to 80 degrees F and 30% to 60% relative humidity"

Although an office is usually the best setting for counselling to occur, one needs to remain sensitive to the needs of the client. Sometimes other settings are preferable. For example, some individuals may prefer to meet outside or to take a stroll while talking over issues. In some cultural groups, expecting clients to see you on your "turf" means that most will never seek your help (e.g., traditional Aboriginal clients).

The distance between counsellor and client (the spatial features of the environment, or *proxemics*) can also affect the counselling relationship. Individuals differ about the level of comfort experienced in interactions with others. Among other things, comfort level is influenced by cultural background, gender, and the nature of the relationship (Sussman & Rosenfeld, 1982). A distance of 30 to 39 inches has been found to be the average range of comfort between counsellors and clients of both genders in the United States (Haase, 1970). A study conducted in Canada revealed that the optimal distance for counsellors in training to display the highest level of empathy toward mock clients was 50 inches (1.27 metres) (compared to either 30 or 80 inches), while the optimal lighting situation was in the low range (1 candlepower, compared to 32 and 200 candlepower) (Dumont & LeCompte, 1975). This optimum distance may vary because of room size and furniture arrangement (Haase & DiMattia, 1976) as well. An earlier study published in 1971 found that greater eye contact occurred in smaller rooms (within limits) and diminished as room size increased (Dumont, cited in Dumont & LeCompte, 1975).

Counsellors also need to be aware that optimal distance varies among cultures. Wolfgang (1985) described the *equilibrium theory*, published in 1965 by Argyle and Dean, as an influential theory that assumes there is an appropriate amount of intimacy within individuals, and if transgressed, the individual will compensate for it in some nonverbal way (e.g., decreasing eye contact, moving physically further away). In Japan, individuals do not ordinarily look at higher-status people with direct eye contact (also true of some Aboriginal peoples, such as the Inuit), and too much eye contact is viewed as a threatening gesture. Consequently, the Japanese client may compensate for a British Canadian counsellor's expectation of eye contact by, let's say, moving his chair further away. That may be misinterpreted by a counsellor who does not understand this cultural difference (Wolfgang, 1985).

Another interesting theory mentioned by Wolfgang (1985)—this time from anthropology—is Montagu's idea that people who speak Latin-derived languages (e.g., Italian, French, Spanish) prefer more contact in their social interactions compared to people who speak Anglo Saxon–derived languages (e.g., English). Such contact takes the form of getting physically closer, touching more, and using more expressive gestures. Consequently, the British Canadian counsellor may find a French Canadian client overly emotional, pushy, or loud. On the other hand, a French Canadian counsellor may find a British Canadian client rather distant, cold, and unemotional.

Regarding furniture, how it is arranged depends on the counsellor. Some counsellors prefer to sit behind a desk during sessions, but most do not. The reason desks are generally eschewed by counsellors is that a desk can be a physical and symbolic barrier against the development of a close relationship. Benjamin (1987) suggests that counsellors include two chairs and a nearby table in the setting. The chairs should be set at a 90-degree angle from one another so that clients can look either at their counsellors or straight ahead. The table can be used for many purposes, such as a place to keep a box of tissues. Benjamin's ideas are strictly his own; each counsellor must find a physical arrangement that is comfortable for him or her.

Regardless of the arrangement within the room, counsellors should not be interrupted when conducting sessions. All phone calls should be held. If necessary, counsellors should put "do not disturb" signs on the door to keep others from entering. Auditory and visual privacy are mandated by professional codes of ethics and assure maximum client self-disclosure.

Client Qualities

Counselling relationships start with first impressions. The way that counsellor and client perceive one another is vital to the establishment of a productive relationship, and given that counsellors and clients are unique in a multitude of ways, creating a good working alliance from the beginning is sometimes a challenging undertaking. Some clients themselves are difficult people to work with and may appear to the counsellor as unlikeable. Furthermore, some clients are more likely to be successful in counselling than others. Dated acronyms in the counselling profession, such as the "preferred" YAVIS client (young, attractive, verbal, intelligent, and successful) (Schofield, 1964) and the less "preferred" HOUND client (homely, old, unintelligent, nonverbal, and disadvantaged) or DUD (dumb, unintelligent, and disadvantaged) (Allen, 1977), captured these stereotypes in a cruel but nonetheless heuristic fashion. Counsellors are influenced by the appearance and sophistication of the people with whom they work. More attractive clients are usually viewed as more likeable by counsellors than those deemed physically unattractive (Sharf & Bishop, 1979). Counsellors most enjoy working with clients who they think have the potential to change.

Recent research suggests that clients who are psychologically minded (meaning they have good insight into their own psychological functioning) expect more from counselling, both in terms of process and outcome, compared to those who score low on this trait (Beitel et al., 2009). Several scales are available to counsellors who wish to get a sense of how clients view them and their effectiveness. One recent example is the Client Evaluation of Counseling Inventory (Frey, Beesley, & Liang, 2009).

A number of stereotypes have been built around the physical attractiveness of individuals, and these stereotypes generalize to clients. The physically attractive are perceived as healthiest and are responded to more positively than others.

Goldstein (1973) found that clients who were seen by their counsellors as most attractive talked more and were more spontaneous when compared with other clients. Most likely, counsellors were more encouraging to and engaged with the attractive clients. Therefore, aging clients and those with physical disabilities may face invisible but powerful barriers in certain counselling situations. Ponzo (1985) suggests that counsellors become aware of the importance of physical attractiveness in their own lives and monitor their behavioural reactions when working with attractive clients. Otherwise, stereotypes and unfounded assumptions may "lead to self-fulfilling prophecies" (p. 485).

The nonverbal behaviours of clients are also very important. Clients constantly send counsellors unspoken messages about how they think or feel. Mehrabian (1971) and associates found that expressed like and dislike between individuals could be explained as follows:

> Total liking equals 7% verbal liking plus 38% vocal liking plus 55% facial liking. The impact of facial expression is greatest, then the impact of the tone of voice (or vocal expression), and finally that of the words. If the facial expression is inconsistent with the words, the degree of liking conveyed by the facial expression will dominate and determine the impact of the total message. (p. 43)

Attempting to establish the actual percentages of how much communication is verbal versus nonverbal, however, is likely impossible. As one example, Friedman (1978) found in his study that, although nonverbal cues (i.e., facial cues) had more importance than verbal ones, the percentage greatly varied according to context.

A client who reports that all is going well but who looks down at the ground and frowns while doing so is probably indicating just the opposite if he or she is from the dominant Canadian English or French background. A counsellor must consider a client's body gestures, eye contact, facial expression, and vocal quality to be as important as verbal communication in a counselling relationship. It is also crucial to consider the cultural background of the person whose body language is being evaluated and interpret nonverbal messages cautiously (Sielski, 1979).

Counsellor Qualities

The personal and professional qualities of counsellors are very important in facilitating any helping relationship. Okun and Kantrowitz (2008) note that it is hard to separate the helper's personality characteristics from his or her levels and styles of functioning, as they are interrelated. They then list five important characteristics that helpers should possess: self-awareness, honesty, congruence, ability to communicate, and knowledge. Strong (1968) also described three characteristics that make counsellors initially more influential: perceived expertness, attractiveness, and trustworthiness. These qualities are described below.

Accurate Self-Awareness Counsellors who continually develop their self-awareness skills are in touch with their values, thoughts, and feelings. They are likely to have a clear perception of their own and their clients' needs and accurately assess both. Such awareness can help them be honest with themselves and others. They are able to be more congruent and build trust simultaneously. Counsellors who possess this type of knowledge are more likely to communicate clearly and accurately.

Honesty Rivera, Phan, Hadduv, Wilbur, and Arredondo (2006) reported one of the reasons why non-Caucasian clients avoid pursing counselling: They don't think counsellors are real. Rivera et al.'s study found that honesty is an important aspect of building a positive working alliance, yet counsellors in training are usually taught to be polite, kind, and avoidant of conflict. Being honest is more respected by clients than many counsellors assume.

Case Example: What Would *You* Do?

I had a client who smelled really bad every session I saw him. The odour was that of perspiration and dirty clothing. After he left, I literally had to "air out" my office for 30 minutes before I could bring in my next client.

1. Would you bring this bad odour to the client's attention? Why or why not?

2. How would you confront the client about this without sounding offensive?

3. If you confront the client, what do you think is the likelihood that he will return for another session?

Perceived Expertness *Expertness* is the degree to which a counsellor is perceived as knowledgeable and informed about his or her specialty. Counsellors who display evidential cues in their offices, such as certificates and diplomas, are usually perceived as more credible than those who do not and, as a result, are likely to be effective (Loesch, 1984; Siegal & Sell, 1978). Clients want to work with counsellors who appear to know the profession well.

Attractiveness Attractiveness is more than what lies on the surface, although physical looks are also a factor. Under controlled conditions, research suggests individuals are more willing to self-disclose to an attractive counsellor than to an unattractive one (Harris & Busby, 1998). Furthermore, clients tend to perceive attractive counsellors as more expert and trustworthy (Vargas & Borkowski, 1986). Nonetheless, physical beauty often lies in the eyes of the beholder. *Attractiveness* is a function of perceived similarity between a client and counsellor as well as physical features. Counsellors can make themselves attractive by speaking in clear, simple, jargon-free sentences and offering appropriate self-disclosure (Watkins & Schneider, 1989). The manner in which a counsellor greets the client and maintains eye contact can also increase the attractiveness rating. Counsellors who use nonverbal cues in responding to clients, such as head nodding and eye contact, are seen as more attractive than those who do not (Claiborn, 1979; LaCross, 1975).

Research suggests that the preferred attire of the counsellor may depend on the type of client. Hubble and Gelso (1978) found that when counsellors were dressed in casual and very casual attire, clients (in this case undergraduate students) felt the least anxiety, but client dress was a crucial moderator. When clients dressed casually (e.g., sport shirt and slacks), they felt most comfortable with a similarly dressed counsellor. When they were very casually dressed (e.g., sweat shirt and jeans), they preferred a counsellor who also dressed similarly. Another study with undergraduate students found that informally attired counsellors were perceived as more expert, trustworthy, and helpful compared with formally dressed counsellors (Roll & Roll, 1984). While an experimental study found that clients preferred that their counsellors wore a moderate style of dress (Heitmeyer & Goldsmith, 1990), another undergraduate study found that male clients expressed no difference regarding a male counsellor's attire (Stillman & Resnick, 1972). Consequently, it makes sense to dress in a way that is most respected by the counsellor's clientele.

Trustworthiness *Trustworthiness* is related to the sincerity and consistency of the counsellor. The counsellor is genuinely concerned about the client and shows it over time by establishing a close relationship. "There is and can be no such thing as instant intimacy" or trustworthiness (Patterson, 1985, p. 124). Rather, both are generated through patterns of behaviour that demonstrate care and concern. Most clients are neither completely distrusting nor given to blind trust. But, as Fong and Cox (1983) note, many clients test the trustworthiness of the counsellor by requesting information, telling a secret, asking a favour, inconveniencing the counsellor, deprecating themselves, or questioning the motives and dedication of the counsellor. It is essential, therefore, that the counsellor respond to the question of trust rather than the verbal content of the client in order to facilitate the counselling relationship.

Many beginning counsellors make the mistake of dealing with surface issues instead of real concerns. For example, if a client asks a counsellor, "Can I tell you anything?" a novice counsellor might respond, "What do you mean by anything?" An experienced counsellor might say, "It sounds as if you are uncertain about whether you can really trust me and this relationship. Tell me more." Trust with children, as with adults, is built by listening first and allowing children the freedom to express themselves openly on a verbal or nonverbal level before the counsellor responds (Erdman & Lampe, 1996).

Brigit was 48, bucktoothed, pock-faced, undereducated, and largely avoided by most people. To make matters worse, she was introverted and lonely. Her best friend on the weekend was her television. Therefore, when her sister suggested she try counselling, she agreed and thought "I have nothing to lose." However, she encountered problems from the beginning. Brigit's counsellor, Chanel, acted as if Brigit's bad looks were contagious and seemed to distance herself from Brigit and blame her for not being more extraverted. Brigit became furious and decided to do something about the situation.

During the second session, Brigit pointed out specific behaviours Chanel was doing that made her feel rejected. Chanel was embarrassed and admitted engaging in all of the actions Brigit confronted her with, but then continued to criticize Brigit in a subtle fashion.

1. What else might Brigit do with this situation?

2. What would you suggest Chanel do to help correct her mistakes and make the counselling session productive?

TYPES OF INITIAL INTERVIEWS

The counselling process begins with the initial session. Levine (1983) points out that authorities in the profession have observed that "the goals of counseling change over time and change according to the intimacy and effectiveness of the counseling relationship" (p. 431). How much change happens or whether there is a second session is usually determined by the results of the first session.

In the first session, both counsellors and clients work to decide whether they want to or can continue the relationship. Counsellors should quickly assess whether they are capable of handling and managing clients' problems through being honest, open, and appropriately confrontive (Okun & Kantrowitz, 2008). However, clients must ask themselves whether they feel comfortable with and trust the counsellor before they can enter the relationship wholeheartedly.

Client- Versus Counsellor-Initiated Interviews

Benjamin (1987) distinguishes between two types of first interviews: those initiated by clients and those initiated by counsellors. The way to proceed with counselling depends on who initiates the process.

Client-Initiated Interviews When the initial interview is requested by a client, the counsellor is often unsure of the client's purpose. This uncertainty may create anxiety in the counsellor, especially if background information is not gathered before the session.

One way that counsellors can reduce their own anxiety is to have clients provide background information before their first visit. Having clients complete a history questionnaire before the first appointment, for example, may help counsellors feel more comfortable. (Note: the Personal Functioning Questionnaire (PFQ), an example of a personal history questionnaire, is found in the Note Supplement to this book.) There are many advantages to having clients complete a history questionnaire before the first appointment for both the counsellor and the client, including the following:

1. *Usefulness and reliability.* Useful and reliable information is provided to the counsellor (Guthmann, 1998).

2. *Accuracy.* The information provided is usually more accurate than when counsellors themselves write down a client's history (Hershey & Grant, 2002).

3. *Expediency.* The process is expedient as information about clients is provided by clients in writing (Guthmann, 1998).

4. *Positive experience.* Providers and respondents are overwhelmingly positive in their response to using history questionnaires (Hershey & Grant, 2002).

5. *Cost savings.* Procedures that reduce the counsellor's time in obtaining a history results in time and cost savings to the client (Grady & Ephross, 1977).

6. *Accountability.* Information provided by clients in writing is useful should a counsellor ever need to face a professional liability issue.

7. *Working alliance.* The client often feels that they are being *heard* and *cared about* by the therapist even before they meet with the counsellor.

8. *Reduced number of no-shows.* Because this initial working alliance is already developing before the first session, clients are more likely to show up for their appointment.

9. *Increased focus on process, not content.* Because the counsellor already has the client's basic history, more time in the first few sessions can be focused on actual counselling, which is about *process*, instead of on needing to ask many questions related to *content* (e.g., factual information about the client).

10. *Professional considerations.* The PFQ provides a good glimpse into how well the client is currently functioning, and this helps in making an assessment of their degree of disturbance and whether they are currently suicidal. In some cases, depending on the answers received, an appointment may need to be made sooner than initially booked.

Benjamin (1987) recommends that counsellors work to overcome their anxious feelings by listening as hard as possible to what clients have to say. In such situations, as with counselling in general, listening "requires a submersion of the self and immersion in the other" (Nichols, 1998, p. 1). There is no formula for beginning the session. The helping interview is as much an art as a science, and every counsellor must work out a style based on experience, stimulation, and reflection. The counsellor is probably prudent not to inquire initially about any problem the client may have because the client may not have a problem in the traditional sense of the word and may just be seeking information.

Counsellor-Initiated Interviews When the first session is requested by the counsellor, Benjamin (1987) believes that the counsellor should immediately state his or her reason for wanting to see the client. In the case of a school counsellor, for instance, a session might be requested so that the counsellor can introduce himself or herself to the client. If the counsellor does not immediately give a reason for requesting the session, the client is kept guessing and tension is created.

Communalities Regarding All Interview Types Welfel and Patterson (2005) think that all clients enter counselling with some anxiety and resistance regardless of prior preparation. Benjamin (1987) hypothesizes that most counsellors are also a bit frightened and uncertain when conducting a first interview. Uncertain feelings in both clients and counsellors may result in behaviours such as seduction or aggression (Watkins, 1983). Counsellors can prevent such occurrences by exchanging information with clients. Manthei (1983) advocates that counsellors' self-presentations and functioning be *multimodal*: visual, auditory, written, spoken, and descriptive. Although such presentations may be difficult, they pay off by creating good counsellor–client relationships. Overall, early exchanges of information increase the likelihood that clients and counsellors will make meaningful choices and participate more fully in the counselling process.

Information-Oriented First Interview

Cormier and Hackney (2007) point out that the initial counselling interview can fulfill two functions: (a) It can be an intake interview to collect needed information about the client, or (b) it can signal the beginning of a relationship. Either type of interview is appropriate, and certain tasks are common to both, though the skills emphasized in each differ.

If the purpose of the first interview is to gather information, the structure of the session will be counsellor-focused: The counsellor wants the client to talk about certain subjects. The counsellor will respond to the client predominantly through the use of probes, accents, closed questions, and requests for clarification (Cormier & Hackney, 2007). These responses are aimed at eliciting facts.

The *probe* is a question that usually begins with *who, what, where,* or *how*. It requires more than a one- or two-word response—for example, "What do you plan to do about getting a job?" Few probes ever begin with the word *why*, which usually connotes disapproval, places a client on the defensive (e.g., "Why are you doing that?"), and is often unanswerable (Benjamin, 1987).

An *accent* is highlighting the last few words of the client. For example:

> Client: The situation I'm in now is driving me crazy!
>
> Counsellor: Driving you crazy?

A *closed* question is one that requires a specific and limited response, such as yes or no. It often begins with the word *is, do,* or *are*:

Counsellor: Do you enjoy meeting other people?

Client: Yes.

The closed question is quite effective in eliciting a good deal of information in a short period of time. But it does not encourage elaboration that might also be helpful.

In contrast to the closed question is the *open question*, which typically begins with *what*, *how*, or *could* and allows the client more latitude to respond. Examples are "How does this affect you?" "Could you give me more information?" and "Tell me more about it." The major difference between a closed and open question "is whether or not the question encourages more client talk" (Galvin & Ivey, 1981, p. 539). It is the difference between a multiple-choice inquiry that checks the facts and an essay in which a deeper level of understanding and explanation is encouraged.

Finally, a *request for clarification* is a response the counsellor uses to be sure he or she understands what the client is saying. These requests require the client to repeat or elaborate on material just covered. For example, a counsellor might say, "Please help me understand this relationship" or "I don't see the connection here."

Counsellors wish to obtain several facts in an information-oriented first interview. They often assume this information may be used as a part of a psychological, vocational, or psychosocial assessment. Counsellors employed by medical, mental health, correctional, rehabilitation, and social agencies are particularly likely to conduct these types of interviews. Cormier and Hackney (2008) outline some of the data counsellors gather in these initial sessions (see Figure 6.2).

I. Identifying data
   A. Client's name, address, telephone number through which client can be reached. This information is important in the event the counselor needs to contact the client between sessions. The client's address also gives some hint about the conditions under which the client lives (e.g., large apartment complex, student dormitory, private home, etc.).
   B. Age, sex, marital status, occupation (or school class and year). Again, this is information that can be important. It lets you know when the client is still legally a minor and provides a basis for understanding information that will come out in later sessions.

II. Presenting problems, both primary and secondary
   It is best when these are presented in exactly the way the client reported them. If the problem has behavioral components, these should be recorded as well. Questions that help reveal this type of information include
   A. How much does the problem interfere with the client's everyday functioning?
   B. How does the problem manifest itself? What are the thoughts, feelings, and so on that are associated with it? What observable behavior is associated with it?
   C. How often does the problem arise? How long has the problem existed?
   D. Can the client identify a pattern of events that surround the problem? When does it occur? With whom? What happens before and after its occurrence?
   E. What caused the client to decide to enter counseling at this time?

Figure 6.2 An information-oriented first interview

Source: From *Counselling Strategies and Interventions* (pp. 66–68), by L. S. Cormier and H. Hackney, Boston: Allyn & Bacon, 2008. All rights reserved. Reprinted by permission of Allyn & Bacon.

III. **Client's current life setting**

How does the client spend a typical day or week? What social and religious activities, recreational activities, and so on are present? What is the nature of the client's vocational and/or educational situation?

IV. **Family history**

A. Father's and mother's ages, occupations, descriptions of their personalities, relationships of each to the other and each to the client and other siblings.

B. Names, ages, and order of brothers and sisters; relationship between client and siblings.

C. Is there any history of mental disturbance in the family?

D. Descriptions of family stability, including number of jobs held, number of family moves, and so on. (This information provides insights in later sessions when issues related to client stability and/or relationships emerge.)

V. **Personal history**

A. Medical history: any unusual or relevant illness or injury from prenatal period to present.

B. Educational history: academic progress through grade school, high school, and post-high school. This includes extracurricular interests and relationships with peers.

C. Military service record.

D. Vocational history: Where has the client worked, at what types of jobs, for what duration, and what were the relationships with fellow workers?

E. Sexual and marital history: Where did the client receive sexual information? What was the client's dating history? Any engagements and/or marriages? Other serious emotional involvements prior to the present? Reasons that previous relationships terminated? What was the courtship like with present spouse? What were the reasons (spouse's characteristics, personal thoughts) that led to marriage? What has been the relationship with spouse since marriage? Are there any children?

F. What experience has the client had with counseling, and what were the client's reactions?

G. What are the client's personal goals in life?

VI. **Description of the client during the interview**

Here you might want to indicate the client's physical appearance, including dress, posture, gestures, facial expressions, voice quality, tensions; how the client seemed to relate to you in the session; client's readiness of response, motivation, warmth, distance, passivity, etc. Did there appear to be any perceptual or sensory functions that intruded upon the interaction? (Document with your observations.) What was the general level of information, vocabulary, judgment, and abstraction abilities displayed by the client? What was the stream of thought, regularity, and rate of talking? Were the client's remarks logical? Connected to one another?

VII. **Summary and recommendations**

In this section you will want to acknowledge any connections that appear to exist between the client's statement of a problem and other information collected in this session. What type of counselor do you think would best fit this client? If you are to be this client's counselor, which of your characteristics might be particularly helpful? Which might be particularly unhelpful? How realistic are the client's goals for counseling? How long do you think counseling might continue?

Figure 6.2 *continued*

Relationship-Oriented First Interview

Interviews that focus on feelings or relationship dynamics differ markedly from information-oriented first sessions. They concentrate more on the client's attitudes and emotions. Common counsellor responses include restatement, reflection of feeling, summary of feelings, request for clarification, and acknowledgment of nonverbal behaviour (Cormier & Hackney, 2008).

A *restatement* is a simple mirror response to a client that lets the client know the counsellor is actively listening. Used alone, it is relatively sterile and ineffective:

> Client: I'm not sure if I'll ever find a suitable mate. My job keeps me on the road and isolated.
>
> Counsellor: You don't know if you will ever find a spouse because of the nature of your job.

Reflection of feeling is similar to a restatement, but it deals with verbal and nonverbal expression. Reflections may be on several levels; some convey more empathy than others. An example is this counsellor response to a client who is silently sobbing over the loss of a parent: "You're still really feeling the pain."

Summary of feelings is the act of paraphrasing a number of feelings that the client has conveyed. For example, a counsellor might say to a client, "John, if I understand you correctly, you are feeling depressed over the death of your father and discouraged that your friends have not helped you work through your grief. In addition, you feel your work is boring and that your wife is emotionally distant from you."

Acknowledgment of nonverbal behaviour differs from the previous examples. For instance, acknowledgment comes when the counsellor says to a client, "I notice that your arms are folded across your chest and you're looking at the floor." This type of response does not interpret the meaning of the behaviour.

CONDUCTING THE INITIAL INTERVIEW

There is no one place to begin an initial interview, but experts recommend that counsellors start by trying to make their clients feel comfortable (Cormier & Hackney, 2008). Counsellors should set aside their own agendas and focus on the person of the client, including listening to the client's story and presenting issues (Myers, 2000; Wilcox-Matthew et al., 1997). This type of behaviour, in which there is a genuine interest in and acceptance of a client, is known as *rapport*.

Ivey and Ivey (2007) state that the two most important microskills for rapport building are basic attending behaviour and client-observation skills. A counsellor needs to tune in to what the client is thinking and feeling and how he or she is behaving. In this process, "counsellor sensitivity to client-generated metaphors may help to convey understanding of the client's unique way of knowing and at the same time contribute to the development of a shared language and collaborative bond between the client and counsellor" (Lyddon, Clay, & Sparks, 2001, p. 270). For instance, a client may describe herself as being treated by others as "yesterday's leftovers." This metaphor gives both the client and the counsellor information about the thinking and behaviour going on in the client as she seeks to be seen "as the blue-plate special." Regardless, establishing and maintaining rapport is vital for the disclosure of information, the initiation of change, and the ultimate success of counselling.

Inviting clients to focus on reasons for seeking help is one way in which counsellors may initiate rapport. Such non-coercive invitations to talk are called *door openers* and contrast with judgmental or evaluative responses known as *door closers* (Bolton, 1979). Appropriate door openers include inquiries and observations such as "What brings you to see me?" "What would you like to talk about?" and "You look like you are in a lot of pain. Tell me about it." These unstructured, open-ended invitations allow clients to take the initiative (Cormier & Hackney, 2007 Young, 1998). In such situations, clients are most likely to talk about priority topics.

The amount of talking that clients engage in and the insight and benefits derived from the initial interview can be enhanced by a counsellor who appropriately conveys empathy, encouragement, support, caring, attentiveness, acceptance, and genuineness. Of all of these qualities, empathy is the most important.

Empathy

Rogers (1961) describes *empathy* as the counsellor's ability to "enter the client's phenomenal world, to experience the client's world as if it were your own without ever losing the 'as if' quality" (p. 284). Empathy involves two specific skills: perception and communication (Welfel & Patterson, 2005).

An effective counsellor perceives the cultural frame of reference from which his or her client operates, including the client's perceptual and cognitive process (Weinrach, 1987). This type of sensitivity, if it bridges the cultural gap between the counsellor and client, is known as *culturally sensitive empathy* and is a quality counsellors may cultivate (Chung & Bemak, 2002). Nevertheless, a counsellor who can accurately perceive what it is like to be the client but cannot communicate that experience is a limited helper. Such a counsellor may be aware of client dynamics, but no one, including the client, knows of the counsellor's awareness. The ability to communicate clearly plays a vital role in any counselling relationship (Okun & Kantrowitz, 2008).

In the initial interview, counsellors must be able to convey primary empathy (Welfel & Patterson, 2005). *Primary empathy* is the ability to respond in such a way that it is apparent to both client and counsellor that the counsellor has understood the client's major themes. Primary empathy is conveyed through nonverbal communication and various verbal responses. For example, the counsellor, leaning forward and speaking in a soft, understanding voice, may say to the client, "I hear that your life has been defined by a series of serious losses." *Advanced empathy* is a process of helping a client explore themes, issues, and emotions new to his or her awareness (Welfel & Patterson, 2005). This second level of empathy is usually inappropriate for an initial interview because it examines too much material too quickly. Clients must be developmentally ready for counselling to be beneficial.

Verbal and Nonverbal Behaviour

Whatever its form, empathy may be fostered by *attentiveness* (the amount of verbal and nonverbal behaviour shown to the client). Verbal behaviours include communications that show a desire to comprehend or discuss what is important to the client (Cormier & Cormier, 1998). These behaviours (which include probing, requesting clarification, restating, and summarizing feelings) indicate that the counsellor is focusing on the person of the client. Equally important are the counsellor's nonverbal behaviours. According to Mehrabian (1970), physically attending behaviours such as smiling, leaning forward, making eye contact, gesturing, and nodding one's head are effective nonverbal ways of conveying to clients that the counsellor is interested in and open to them.

Egan (2007) summarizes five nonverbal skills involved in initial attending. They are best remembered in the acronym SOLER. The *S* is a reminder to face the client *squarely*, which can be understood literally or metaphorically depending on the situation. The important thing is that the counsellor shows involvement and interest in the client. The *O* is a reminder to adopt an *open posture*, free from crossed arms and legs and showing nondefensiveness. The *L* reminds the counsellor to *lean* toward the client. However, leaning too far forward and being too close may be frightening, whereas leaning too far away indicates disinterest. The counsellor needs to find a middle distance that is comfortable for both parties. The *E* represents *eye contact*. Good eye contact with most clients is a sign that the counsellor is attuned to the client. For other clients, less eye contact (or even no eye contact) is appropriate. The *R* is a reminder to the counsellor to *relax*. A counsellor needs to be comfortable.

Okun and Kantrowitz (2008) list supportive verbal and nonverbal behavioural aids that counsellors often display (see Table 6.1).

Table 6.1 Helpful Behaviours

Verbal	Nonverbal
Uses understandable words	Tone of voice similar to helpee's
Reflects back and clarifies helpee's statements	Maintains good eye contact
Appropriately interprets	Occasional head nodding
Summarizes for helpee	Facial animation
Responds to primary message	Occasional smiling
Uses verbal reinforcers (for example, "Mm-mm," "I see," "Yes")	Occasional hand gesturing
	Close physical proximity to helpee
Calls helpee by first name or "you"	Moderate rate of speech
Appropriately gives information	Body leans toward helpee
Answers questions about self	Relaxed, open posture
Uses humour occasionally to reduce tension	Confident vocal tone
Is nonjudgmental and respectful	Occasional touching
Adds greater understanding to helpee's statement	
Phrases interpretations tentatively so as to elicit genuine feedback from helpee	

Source: From *Effective Helping: Interviewing and Counseling Techniques* (p. 31) by Barbara F. Okun and R. E. Kantrowitz. Copyright © 2008 by Brooks/Cole Publishing Company. Reprinted by permission of Wadsworth Publishing Company.

One of the last nonverbal behaviours on Okun and Kantrowitz's list, occasional touching, is politically sensitive and somewhat controversial. Although Willison and Masson (1986), in agreement with Okun and Kantrowitz, point out that human touch may be therapeutic in counselling, Alyn (1988) emphasizes that "the wide range of individual motivations for, interpretations of, and responses to touch make it an extremely unclear and possibly a dangerous means of communication in therapy" (p. 433). As a general counselling principle, Young (1998) suggests that touch should be appropriately employed, applied briefly and sparingly, and used to communicate concern. Applying the "Touch Test," which simply asks, "Would you do this with a stranger?" is one way to implement Young's suggestions (Del Prete, 1998, p. 63). Thus, counsellors who use touch in their work should do so cautiously and with the understanding that what they are doing can have adverse effects. This same critical scrutiny is suggested when using any verbal or nonverbal technique.

Non-Helpful Interview Behaviour

When building a relationship, counsellors must also realize what they should *not* do. Otherwise, non-helpful behaviours may be included in their counselling repertoire. Welfel and Patterson (2005) list four major actions that usually block counsellor–client communication and should be generally avoided: advice giving, lecturing, excessive questioning, and storytelling by the counsellor.

Advice giving is the most controversial of these four behaviours. Knowles (1979) found that 70% to 90% of all responses from volunteer helpers on a crisis line consisted of giving advice. When a counsellor gives advice, especially in the first session, it may in effect deny a client the chance to work through personal thoughts and feelings about a subject and ultimately curtail his or her ability to make difficult decisions. A response meant to be helpful ends up being hurtful by disempowering the client. For example, if a client is advised to break off a relationship he or she is ambivalent about, the client is denied the opportunity to become aware and work through the thoughts and feelings that initially led to the ambivalence.

Sack (1985) suggests that advice giving need not always be destructive. He notes that there are emergency situations (as in crisis counselling) when, for the client's immediate welfare and safety, some direct action must be taken, which includes giving advice. He cautions counsellors, however, to listen carefully to make sure the client is really asking for advice or simply being reflective through self-questions. There is a big difference between "What should I do?" and "I wonder what I should do." In addition, Sack advocates the responses developed by Carkhuff (1969) as ways in which counsellors can answer direct requests for advice. In this model, counsellors respond using one of seven approaches: respect, empathy, genuineness, concreteness, self-disclosure, confrontation, and immediacy. Sack (1985) concludes that counsellors must examine their roles in counselling to "free themselves of the limitations and pitfalls of giving advice and move toward employing a variety of responses that can more appropriately address their clients' needs" (p. 131).

Lecturing, or preaching, is really a disguised form of advice giving (Welfel & Patterson, 2005). It sets up a power struggle between the counsellor and client that neither individual can win. For example, if a sexually active girl is told "Don't get involved with boys anymore," she may do just the opposite to assert her independence. In such a case, both the counsellor and client fail in their desire to change behaviours. Counsellors are probably lecturing when they say more than three consecutive sentences in a row to their clients. Instead of lecturing, counsellors can be effective by following the client's lead (Evans, Hearn, Uhlemann, & Ivey, 2008).

Excessive questioning is a common mistake of many counsellors. Verbal interaction with clients needs to include statements, observations, and encouragers as well as questions. When excessive questioning is used, the client feels as though he or she is being interrogated rather than counselled. The client has little chance to take the initiative and may become guarded. Children may especially respond in this way or make a game out of answering a question, waiting for the next one, answering it, waiting, and so on (Erdman & Lampe, 1996). Counselling relationships are more productive when counsellors avoid asking more than two questions in a row and keep their questions open rather than closed.

Storytelling by the counsellor is the final non-helpful behaviour. There are a few prominent professionals who can use stories to benefit clients. Milton Erickson, a legendary pioneer in family counselling, was one. His stories were always metaphorically tailored to his clients' situations. They were beneficial because they directed clients to think about their own situations in light of the stories he told. Most counsellors, however, should stay away from storytelling because the story usually focuses attention on the counsellor instead of the client and distracts from problem solving.

Okun and Kantrowitz (2008) list other non-helpful verbal and nonverbal behaviours (see Table 6.2). Some of these behaviours, such as yawning, clearly show the counsellor's disinterest. Others, such as advice giving, appear to be helpful only at select times (for example, when the client is interested or there is a crisis). As you examine this list, think of when you last experienced the behaviours it mentions.

EXPLORATION AND THE IDENTIFICATION OF GOALS

In the final part of building a counselling relationship, the counsellor helps the client explore specific areas and begin to identify goals that the client wants to achieve. Hill (2004) emphasizes that establishing goals is crucial in providing direction at any stage of counselling. Egan (2007) observes that exploring and ultimately identifying goals often occur when a client is given the opportunity to talk about situations or to tell personal stories. The counsellor reinforces the client's focus on self by providing structure, actively listening (hearing both content and feelings), and helping identify and clarify goals.

Table 6.2 Non-Helpful Behaviours

Verbal	Nonverbal
Interrupting	Looking away from helpee
Advice giving	Sitting far away or turned away from helpee
Preaching	Sneering
Placating	Frowning
Blaming	Scowling
Cajoling	Tight mouth
Exhorting	Shaking pointed finger
Extensive probing and questioning, especially "why" questions	Distracting gestures
	Yawning
Directing, demanding	Closing eyes
Patronizing attitude	Unpleasant tone of voice
Overinterpretation	Rate of speech too slow or too fast
Using words or jargon helpee doesn't understand	Acting rushed
Straying from topic	
Intellectualizing	
Overanalyzing	
Talking about self too much	
Minimizing or disbelieving	

Source: From *Effective Helping: Interviewing and Counseling Techniques* (p. 32) by Barbara F. Okun and R. E. Kantrowitz. Copyright © 2008 by Brooks/Cole Publishing Company. Reprinted by permission of Wadsworth Publishing Company.

Rule (1982) states that goals "are the energizing fabric of daily living" but are often elusive (p. 195). He describes some goals as unfocused, unrealistic, and uncoordinated. Unfocused goals are not identified, are too broad, or are not prioritized. Sometimes counsellors and clients may leave unfocused goals alone because the time and expense of chasing them is not as productive as changing unwanted behaviours. In most cases, however, it is helpful to identify a client's goals, put them into a workable form, and decide which goals to pursue first.

Unrealistic goals, as defined by either counsellor or client, include happiness, perfection, progress, being number one, and self-actualization. They have merit but are not easily obtained or sustained. For example, the client who has worked hard and is happy about being promoted will soon have to settle into the duties of the new job and the reality of future job progress. Unrealistic goals may best be dealt with by putting them into the context of broader life goals. Then the counsellor may encourage the client to devise exploratory and homework strategies for dealing with them.

Uncoordinated goals, according to Rule (1982), are generally divided "into two groups: those probably really uncoordinated and those seemingly uncoordinated" (p. 196). In the first group are goals that may be incompatible with one another or with the personality of the client. A person who seeks counselling but really does not wish to work on changing exemplifies an individual with incompatible goals. These clients are often labelled resistant. Into the second group, Rule places the goals of clients who appear to have uncoordinated goals but really do not. These individuals may be afraid to take personal responsibility and engage any helper in a "yes, but . . ." dialogue.

Dyer and Vriend (1977) emphasize seven specific criteria for judging effective goals in counselling:

1. *Goals are mutually agreed on by client and counsellor.* Without mutuality neither party will invest much energy in working on the goals.

2. *Goals are specific.* If goals are too broad, they will never be met.

3. *Goals are relevant to self-defeating behaviour.* There are many possible goals for clients to work on, but only those that are relevant to changing self-defeating action should be pursued.

4. *Goals are achievement and success oriented.* Counselling goals need to be realistic and have both intrinsic and extrinsic payoffs for clients.

5. *Goals are quantifiable and measurable.* It is important that both client and counsellor know when goals are achieved. When goals are defined quantitatively, achievement is most easily recognized.

6. *Goals are behavioural and observable.* This criterion relates to the previous one: An effective goal is one that can be seen when achieved.

7. *Goals are understandable and can be restated clearly.* It is vital that client and counsellor communicate clearly about goals. One way to assess how well this process is achieved is through restating goals in one's own words.

Case Example: What Would *You* Do?

Benjamin has lived with an overlay of depression all his life. Now that he is in college, he has decided to do something about it. When he visited the College Counselling Centre, his counsellor, Charlene, suggested that he set goals on how he was going to handle his depression. Benjamin listed the following:

- Exercise every morning before class.
- Eat healthy food.
- Get engaged in at least one campus activity, such as playing an intramural sport.
- Keep a journal of my thoughts and feelings and when they come.
- Come to counselling for a month.

1. What do you think of Benjamin's goals? Are they realistic?

2. What else do you think he should do (if anything)?

Egan (2007) cautions that in the exploratory and goal-setting stage of counselling, several problems may inhibit the building of a solid client–counsellor relationship. The most notable include moving too fast, moving too slow, fear of intensity, client rambling, and excessive time and energy devoted to probing the past. Counsellors who are forewarned about such potential problems are in a much better position to address them effectively. It is vital that counsellors work with clients to build a mutually satisfying relationship from the start. When this process occurs, a more active working stage of counselling begins.

SUMMARY AND CONCLUSION

Building a relationship, the first stage in counselling, is a continuous process. It begins by having the counsellor win the battle for structure and the client win the battle for initiative. In such situations, both parties are winners. The client wins by becoming more informed about the nature of counselling and learning what to expect. The counsellor wins by creating an atmosphere in which the client is comfortable sharing thoughts and feelings.

Counselling may occur in any setting, but some circumstances are more likely than others to promote its development. Counsellors need to be aware of the physical setting in which the counselling takes place. Clients may adjust to any room, but certain qualities about an environment, such as the seating arrangement, make counselling more conducive. Other less apparent qualities also affect the building of a relationship. For example, the perception that clients and counsellors have about one another is important. Attractive clients who are young, verbal, intelligent, and social may be treated in a more positive way than clients who are older, less intelligent, and seemingly unmotivated. Clients are likely to work best with counsellors they perceive as trustworthy, attractive, and knowledgeable.

Regardless of the external circumstances and the initial perceptions, a counsellor who attends to the verbal and nonverbal expressions of a client is more likely to establish rapport. The counsellor's conveying of empathy and the use of other helpful microskills, such as restatement and reflection, that cut across counselling theory may further enhance the relationship. When counsellors are attuned to their own values and feelings, they are able to become even more effective. The initial counselling interview can be counsellor- or client-initiated and can centre on the gathering of information or on relationship dynamics. In any situation, it is vital for the counsellor to explore with the client the reasons for the possibilities of counselling. Such disclosures can encourage clients to define goals and facilitate the setting of a mutually agreed-on agenda in counselling. When this step is accomplished, the work of reaching goals can begin.

Your Personal Reflections

1. When have you found structure helpful in your life? What did it provide for you that would not have been there otherwise?

2. When have you seen a situation in which a person either got a foot in the door or used the door-in-the-face technique? How do you think you might use either of these procedures?

3. It has been said that a counsellor who cannot convey empathy is like a tree in a forest that falls with no one around. What do you think of that analogy?

4. When have you found advice helpful? When have you found it harmful? What were the results of each?

Classroom Activities

1. Imagine you are about to conduct your first counselling session in an environment of your own choosing. How would you furnish this setting, and how would you spend your first 10 minutes with an ideal client? Make notes and drawings of this experience and share it with another class member.

2. What are some things you can do to make yourself more attractive (likable) to your client? Share your list with fellow classmates in an open discussion. Does your combined list of behaviours differ from Okun and Kantrowitz's list? How? Which items do you consider most crucial in becoming an effective counsellor?

3. What are your feelings about being a counsellor now that you have some idea about what the process is like? Discuss your feelings and the thoughts behind them with other members of the class. Do those feelings and thoughts differ substantially from what they were at the beginning of the course? How?

4. Persuasion has been mentioned as an appropriate counsellor skill. In groups of three, role-play the following situations in which persuasion might be employed: (a) A small boy is afraid of all dogs, (b) a student has high test anxiety, (c) an elderly person is withdrawn, and (d) a marriage partner will not fight fairly with his or her spouse. How do you experience persuasion differently in these situations? How effective are the persuasive techniques you used? Discuss your feelings with the class as a whole.

5. Write down ways that you think you can tell whether a client is anxious or uncomfortable in a relationship. Then silently enact two or more of your behaviours in front of your classmates and let them describe what you are doing and how they would react to it if they were a counsellor.

6. In pairs, practise the skills of *restatement*, *reflection of feeling*, *summary of feelings*, and/or *acknowledgment of nonverbal behaviour*.

7. In pairs, practise using *closed* and *open questions*.

Chapter 7
Working in a Counselling Relationship

PRACTICE REFLECTION

Dameon, age 29, was a tough nut to crack. Earlier he had completed a BA in philosophy and was now working in a bank doing a repetitive job. When he came to see me, he said he was at his wit's end. He was so unhappy in his life that he wondered what the point was. Immediately I noticed that his mind worked in a manner that is uncommon for most people—he was a true intellectual. His confidence was remarkably low and he did not understand how he had even completed a BA degree. Furthermore, he described himself as having a learning disorder and attention deficit disorder, and potentially as also having bipolar disorder.

I asked him about future career plans and he had none. From a family that did not act in a supportive manner, Dameon truly believed that he was not good enough and never would be, neither for a substantial career nor a long-term relationship. I asked one of my graduate students to give him an intelligence test, and he scored in the 160 range on verbal IQ! (This is four standard deviations above the mean—in other words, he was gifted.) Next, I had him complete the Myers Briggs Type Indicator (this test will be described in a later chapter) and, unsurprisingly, he tested as an INTP, a type that is highly intellectual and easily distracted by working on several projects simultaneously, some of which never get completed.

Career planning had never been completed, and much of our work focused on this. At times I saw his face show signs of irritation and distress as I confronted him on his apathy regarding career planning and on his conflicting resolve to better his life. At the end of some of our sessions, I needed to check in with him. "Dameon, I sense that you are having a hard time with some of my confrontations. I know this is difficult for you. From session to session, I see how your mind wants to intellectualize your lack of progress. I believe what is important here is that you develop a solid career plan. Are you okay with my confrontational style?" Dameon said he was and that this was helpful to him. He knew that his tendency was to avoid important life issues; it was easier to stay where he was and not push himself further.

Besides this, I knew that if I did not address the irritation that Dameon often felt with me, he would not come back. Sustaining a working alliance requires checking in with the client to find out how he or she is doing—it is not enough to assume that all is well.

As discussed in Chapter 6, the successful outcome of any counselling effort depends on a working alliance between counsellor and client (Kottler, Sexton, & Whiston, 1994; Okun & Kantrowitz, 2008). Building this relationship is a developmental process that involves exploring the situation that has motivated the client to seek help. According to Carkhuff and Anthony (1979), the involvement and exploration phases of helping should occur at this time. (See Chapter 6 for a review of how to become involved and build a counselling relationship.) After these phases have been completed, the counsellor works with the client to move into the understanding and action phases. Initially, the client's concerns may be stated broadly and in general terms; as the counselling process continues, specific objectives are defined or refined.

Clients arrive in counselling with certain areas of their lives open or understood and other areas hidden or suppressed. The Johari window, shown in Figure 7.1, is a conceptual device used to represent the way in which most individuals enter the counselling relationship (Luft, 1970).

	Known to Self	Not Known to Self
Known to Others	I. Area of Free Activity	III. Blind Area—Blind to self, seen by others
Not Known to Others	II. Avoided or Hidden Area—Self hidden from others	IV. Area of Unknown Activity

Figure 7.1 The Johari window of the client

Sources: From *Of Human Interaction* (p. 13), by J. Luft, Palo Alto, CA: National Press Books, 1969; and *Group Processes: An Introduction to Group Dynamics* (3rd ed.), by J. Luft, Mountain View, CA: Mayfield Publishing Co., 1984. Copyright 1969 by Joseph Luft. Reprinted by permission of the author.

The objective of the first two phases of counselling is to help clients relax enough to tell their story and discover information located in blind areas of themselves, regions about which they have been unaware (see Figure 7.1). Once they obtain a better understanding of these areas (either verbally or nonverbally), informed clients can decide how to proceed. If they are successful in their work, they extend the dimensions of the area of free activity as represented in the Johari window while shrinking the dimensions of the more restrictive areas (see Figure 7.2).

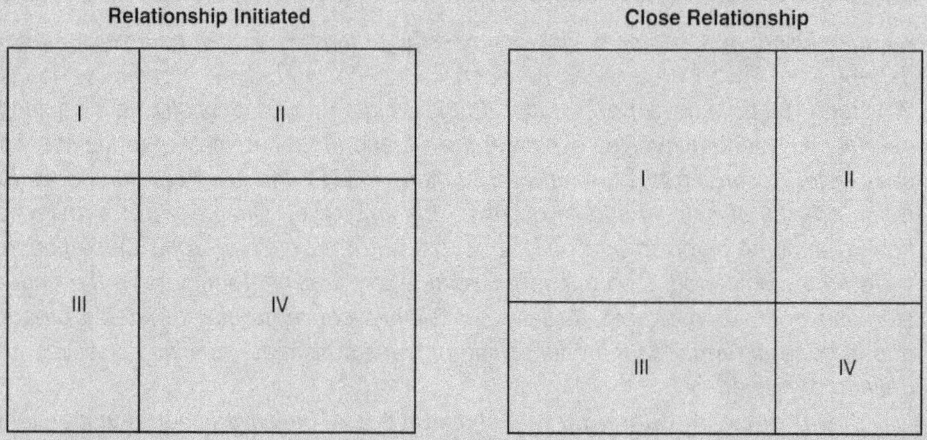

Relationship Initiated

I	II
III	IV

Close Relationship

I	II
III	IV

Figure 7.2 Johari window as modified through the relationship with the counsellor

Source: From *Of Human Interaction* (p. 14), by J. Luft, Palo Alto, CA: National Press Books, 1969; and *Group Processes: An Introduction to Group Dynamics* (3rd ed.), by J. Luft, Mountain View, CA: Mayfield Publishing Co., 1984. Copyright 1969 by Joseph Luft. Reprinted by permission of the author.

It may appear that the counselling process described in this book and repre-
sented in the Johari window is linear, but such is not the case (Moursund & Kenny,
2002). Counselling is multifaceted, with various factors impacting one another con-
tinuously. Therefore, procedures overlap considerably (Egan, 2007). Some tech-
niques used in the involvement and exploration phases are also employed in the
understanding and action phases. Yet as counselling progresses, new and different
skills are regularly incorporated. Counselling requires constant sensitivity to the
status of the relationship and the client's developmental nature. The counsellor
must be alert to new needs and demands as they develop.

In this chapter, we explore the skills commonly associated with the understand-
ing and action phases of counselling. These phases involve a number of counsellor
skills, including changing perceptions, leading, multifocused responding, accurate
empathy, self-disclosure, immediacy, confrontation, contracting, and rehearsal. In
addition, clients and counsellors must work through any transference or counter-
transference issues that arise out of earlier situations or present circumstances
(Gelso & Carter, 1985). There is, of course, a constant need to uncover real
aspects of the counsellor–client relationship (i.e., those not overlaid with defense
mechanisms such as denial or projection) and use them therapeutically.

COUNSELLOR SKILLS IN THE UNDERSTANDING AND ACTION PHASES

Counsellors must be active in helping clients change. After rapport has been established, counsellors need to employ skills that result in clients' viewing their lives differently and thinking, feeling, and behaving accordingly.

Changing Perceptions

Clients often come to counselling as a last resort, when they perceive that the situation is not only serious but hopeless (Watzlawick, 1983). People think their perceptions and interpretations are accurate. When they communicate their view of reality to others, it is commonly accepted as factual (Cavanagh, 1990). This phenomenon, called *functional fixity*, means seeing things in only one way or from one perspective or being fixated on the idea that this particular situation or attribute is the issue (Cormier & Cormier, 1998).

For example, a middle-aged man is concerned about taking care of his elderly mother. He realizes that personal attention to this task will take him away from his family and put a strain on them and him. Furthermore, he is aware that his energy will be drained from his business and he might not receive the promotion he wants. He is torn between caring for two families and sees his situation as an either/or problem. Appropriate and realistic counselling objectives would include finding community and family resources the man could use to help take care of his mother, his family, and himself. In the process the man would discover what he needs to do to relieve himself of sole responsibility in this case and uncover concrete ways he can increase his work efficiency but not his stress. The focus on taking care of self and others as well as using community and family resources woul provide the man with a different perspective about his situation and may help him deal with it in a healthy manner.

Counsellors can help clients change distorted or unrealistic objectives by offering them the opportunity to explore thoughts and desires in a safe, accepting, and nonjudgmental environment. Goals are refined or altered using cognitive, behavioural, or cognitive-behavioural strategies, such as

- redefining the problem,
- altering behaviour in certain situations, or
- perceiving the problem in a more manageable way and acting accordingly (Okun & Kantrowitz, 2008).

By paying attention to both verbal (i.e., language) and nonverbal (i.e., behaviours) metaphors, counsellors can help clients become more aware of both where they are and where they wish to be (Lyddon et al., 2001).

Perceptions commonly change through the process of *reframing*, a technique that offers the client another probable and positive viewpoint or perspective on a situation. Such a changed point of view gives a client a different way of responding (Young, 2005). Effective counsellors consistently reframe life experiences both for themselves and for their clients. For instance, a person's rude behaviour may be explained as the result of pressure from trying to complete a task quickly rather than dislike for the rudely treated person.

Reframing is used in almost all forms of counselling. For example, in family counselling, reframing helps families change their focus from viewing one member of the family as the source of all their problems (i.e., the scapegoat) to seeing the whole family as responsible. In employment counselling, Amundson (1996) has developed 12 reframing strategies that deal with looking back, looking at the present, and looking ahead to help clients widen their perspective of themselves and the labour market. In cases concerning individuals, Cormier and Cormier (1998) point out that reframing can reduce resistance and mobilize the client's energy to do something differently by changing his or her perception of the problem. In short, reframing helps clients become more aware of situational factors associated with behaviour. It shifts the focus from a simplistic attribution of traits, such as "I'm a bum," to a more complex and accurate view, such as "I have some days when things don't go very well and I feel worthless" (Ellis, 1971). Through reframing, clients see themselves and their environments with greater accuracy and insight.

Leading

Changing client perceptions requires a high degree of persuasive skill and some direction from the counsellor. Such input is known as *leading*. The term was coined by Francis Robinson (1950) to describe certain deliberate behaviours counsellors engage in for the benefit of their clients. Leads vary in length, and some are more appropriate at one stage of counselling than another. Robinson used the analogy of a football quarterback and receiver to describe a lead. A good quarterback anticipates where the receiver will be on the field and throws the ball to that spot. (By the way, Robinson worked at Ohio State, a university known for its football and counselling tradition.)

The same kind of analogy of quarterbacks and receivers is true for counsellors and clients. Counsellors anticipate where their clients are and where they are likely to go. Counsellors then respond accordingly. If there is misjudgment and the lead is either too far ahead (i.e., too persuasive or direct) or not far enough (too uninvolved and non-direct), the counselling relationship suffers.

Welfel and Patterson (2005) list a number of leads that counsellors can use with their clients (Figure 7.3). Some, such as silence, acceptance, and paraphrasing, are most appropriate at the beginning of the counselling process. Others, such as persuasion, are directive and more appropriate in the understanding and action phases.

The type of lead counsellors use is determined in part by the theoretical approach they embrace and the current phase of counselling. *Minimal leads* (sometimes referred to as *minimal encouragers*) such as "hmmm," "yes," or "I hear you" are best used in the building phase of a relationship because they are low risk (Young, 2005). *Maximum leads*, however, such as confrontation, are more challenging and should be employed only after a solid relationship has been established.

Multifocused Responding

People have preferences for the way they process information through their senses. Counsellors can enhance their effectiveness by remembering that individuals receive input from their worlds differently and that preferred styles influence perceptions and behaviours. Some clients experience the world visually—they see what is happening. Others are primarily auditory—they hear the world around them. Still others are kinesthetically oriented—they feel situations as though physically in touch with them. (Two of my three children are olfactory—they judge much of their environment through smell, which is especially important in restaurants.) Regardless, Ivey and Ivey (2007) and Lazarus (2000) think that tuning into clients' major modes of perceiving and learning is crucial to bringing about change. Because many clients have multiple ways of knowing the world, counsellors should vary their responses and incorporate words that reflect an understanding of clients' worlds. For example, the counsellor might say to a multimodal sensory person, "I see your point and hear your concern. I feel that you are really upset."

Least leading response

Silence	When the counsellor makes no verbal response at all, the client will ordinarily feel some pressure to continue and will choose how to continue with minimum input from the counsellor
Acceptance	The counsellor simply acknowledges the client's previous statement with a response such as "yes" or "uhuh." The client is verbally encouraged to continue, but without content stimulus from the counsellor.
Restatement (paraphrase)	The counsellor restates the client's verbalization, including both content and affect, using nearly the same wording. The client is prompted to re-examine what has been said.
Clarification	The counsellor states the meaning of the client's statement in his or her own words, seeking to clarify the client's meaning. Sometimes elements of several of the client's statements are brought into a single response. The counsellor's ability to perceive accurately and communicate correctly is important, and the client must test the "fit" of the counsellor's lead.
Approval (affirmation)	The counsellor affirms the correctness of information or encourages the client's efforts at self-determination: "That's good new information," or "You seem to be gaining more control." The client may follow up with further exploration as he or she sees fit.
General leads	The counsellor directs the client to talk more about a specific subject with statements such as "Tell me what you mean," or "Please say some more about that." The client is expected to follow the counsellor's suggestion.
Interpretation	The counsellor uses psychodiagnostic principles to suggest sources of the client's stress or explanations for the client's motivation and behaviour. The counsellor's statements are presented as hypotheses, and the client is confronted with potentially new ways of seeing self.
Rejection (persuasion)	The counsellor tries to reverse the client's behaviour or perceptions by actively advising different behaviour or suggesting different interpretations of life events than those presented by the client.
Reassurance	The counsellor states that, in his or her *judgment,* the client's concern is not unusual and that people with similar problems have succeeded in overcoming them. The client may feel that the reassurance is supportive but may also feel that his or her problem is discounted by the counsellor as unimportant.
Introducing new information or a new idea	The counsellor moves away from the client's last statement and prompts the client to consider new material.

Most leading response

Figure 7.3 Continuum of leads

Source: From *The Counseling Process* (3rd ed., pp. 126–127), by L. E. Patterson and S. Eisenberg, 1983, Boston: Houghton Mifflin. Copyright 1983 by Houghton Mifflin. Reprinted by permission of S. Eisenberg. All rights reserved.

The importance of responding in a client's own language can be powerful, too. Counsellors need to distinguish between the predominantly affective, behavioural, and cognitive nature of speech. *Affective responses* focus on a client's feelings, *behavioural responses* focus on actions, and *cognitive responses* focus on thought. Thus, counsellors working with affectively oriented individuals select words accordingly. Table 7.1 shows some of the most common of these words, as identified by Carkhuff and Anthony (1979).

Table 7.1 Commonly Used Affect Words

			Category of Feeling				
Level of Intensity	Happiness	Sadness	Fear	Uncertainty	Anger	Strength, Potency	Weakness, Inadequacy
Strong	Excited	Despairing	Panicked	Bewildered	Outraged	Powerful	Ashamed
	Thrilled	Hopeless	Terrified	Disoriented	Hostile	Authoritative	Powerless
	Delighted	Depressed	Afraid	Mistrustful	Furious	Forceful	Vulnerable
	Overjoyed	Crushed	Frightened	Confused	Angry	Potent	Cowardly
	Ecstatic	Miserable	Scared		Harsh		Exhausted
	Elated	Abandoned	Overwhelmed		Hateful		Impotent
	Jubilant	Defeated			Mean		
		Desolate			Vindictive		
Moderate	"Up"	Dejected	Worried	Doubtful	Aggravated	Tough	Embarrassed
	Good	Dismayed	Shaky	Mixed up	Irritated	Important	Useless
	Happy	Disillusioned	Tense	Insecure	Offended	Confident	Demoralized
	Optimistic	Lonely	Anxious	Skeptical	Mad	Fearless	Helpless
	Cheerful	Bad	Threatened	Puzzled	Frustrated	Energetic	Worn out
	Enthusiastic	Unhappy	Agitated		Resentful	Brave	Inept
	Joyful	Pessimistic			"Sore"	Courageous	Incapable
	"Turned on"	Sad			Upset	Daring	Incompetent
		Hurt			Impatient	Assured	Inadequate
		Lost			Obstinate	Adequate	Shaken
						Self-confident	
						Skillful	
Weak	Pleased	"Down"	Jittery	Unsure	Perturbed	Determined	Frail
	Glad	Discouraged	Jumpy	Surprised	Annoyed	Firm	Meek
	Content	Disappointed	Nervous	Uncertain	Grouchy	Able	Unable
	Relaxed	"Blue"	Uncomfortable	Undecided	Hassled	Strong	Weak
	Satisfied	Alone	Uptight	Bothered	Bothered		
	Calm	Left out	Uneasy		Disagreeable		
			Defensive				
			Apprehensive				
			Hesitant				
			Edgy				

Source: Reprinted from *The Skills of Helping* written by Carkhuff, R. R. & Anthony, W. A., copyright 1979. Reprinted by permission of the publisher, HRD Press, Amherst Road, Amherst, MA, (413) 253–3488.

Accurate Empathy

There is near-universal agreement among practitioners and theorists that the use of empathy is one of the most vital elements in counselling, one that transcends counselling stages (Clark, 2010a, 2010b; Geist, 2009; Rogers, 1975; Truax & Mitchell, 1971). Not surprisingly, there are also numerous scales to measure empathy (Di Giunta, 2010). A recent conceptualization of empathy describes three types: (a) *subjective empathy*, which enables counsellors to momentarily feel what it is like to be a client; (b) *interpersonal empathy*, which is feeling the client's experience from his or her perspective, and (c) *objective empathy*, which results from having knowledge about the client's problem from reputable sources (Clark, 2010b).

In Chapter 6, two types of empathy were briefly noted. The basic type is called *primary empathy*; the second level is known as *advanced empathy* (Carkhuff, 1969). Accurate empathy on both levels is achieved when counsellors see a client's world from the client's point of view and are able to communicate this understanding back (Egan, 2007). Two factors that make empathy possible are (a) realizing that "an infinite number of feelings" does not exist and (b) having a personal security so that "you can let yourself go into the world of this other person and still know that you can return to your own world. Everything you are feeling is 'as if'" (Rogers, 1987, pp. 45–46).

Primary empathy, when it is accurate, involves communicating a basic understanding of what the client is feeling and the experiences and behaviours underlying these feelings. It helps establish the counselling relationship, gather data, and clarify problems. For example, a client might say, "I'm really feeling like I can't do anything for myself." The counsellor replies, "You're feeling helpless."

Advanced empathy, when it is accurate, reflects not only what clients state overtly but also what they imply or state incompletely. Say, for example, that a counsellor hears a client say: ". . . and I hope everything will work out" while looking off into space. The counsellor responds, "For if it doesn't, I'm not sure what I will do next."

Empathy involves three elements: perceptiveness, know-how, and assertiveness (Egan, 2007). Several levels of responses reflect different aspects of counsellor empathy. A scale formulated by Carkhuff (1969), called Empathic Understanding in Interpersonal Process, is a measure of these levels. Each of the five levels either adds to or subtracts from the meaning and feeling tone of a client's statement.

1. The verbal and behavioural expressions of the counsellor either do not attend to or detract significantly from the verbal and behavioural expressions of the client.

2. Although the counsellor responds to the expressed feelings of the client, he or she does so in a way that subtracts noticeable affect from the communications of the client.

3. The expressions of the counsellor in response to the expressions of the client are essentially interchangeable.

4. The responses of the counsellor add noticeably to the expressions of the client in a way that expresses feelings at a level deeper than the client was able to express.

5. The counsellor's responses add significantly to the feeling and meaning of the expressions of the client in a way that accurately expresses feeling at levels below what the client is able to express.

Responses at the first two levels are not considered empathic; in fact, they inhibit the creation of an empathic environment. For example, if a client reveals that she is heartbroken over the loss of a lover, a counsellor operating on either of the first two levels might reply, "Well, you want your former love to be happy, don't you?" Such a response misses the pain that the client is feeling.

At level three on the Carkhuff scale, a counsellor's response is rated as "interchangeable" with that of a client. The cartoon in Figure 7.4 depicts the essence of such an interchange.

On levels four and five, a counsellor either "adds noticeably" or "adds significantly" to what a client has said. This ability to go beyond what clients say distinguishes counselling from conversation or other less helpful forms of behaviour (Carkhuff, 1972). The following interchange is an example of a higher level empathetic response:

> Client: I have been running around from activity to activity until I am so tired I feel like I could drop.
>
> Counsellor: Your life has been a merry-go-round of activity, and you'd like to slow it down before you collapse. You'd like to be more in charge of your own life.

Means (1973) elaborates on levels four and five to show how counsellors can add noticeably and significantly to their clients' perceptions of an emotional experience, an environmental stimulus, a behaviour pattern, a self-evaluation, a self-expectation, and beliefs about self. Clients' statements are extremely varied, and counsellors must therefore be flexible in responding to them (Hackney, 1978). Whether a counsellor's response

Figure 7.4 Interchangeable client and counsellor reactions

Source: Reprinted from N. Goud [cartoon], 1983, *Personnel and Guidance Journal, 61*, p. 635. © 1983 by ACA.

Reprinted with permission. No further reproduction authorized without written permission of the American Counseling Association.

is empathic is determined by the reaction of clients (Turock, 1978). Regardless, in the understanding and action phases of counselling, it is important that counsellors integrate the two levels of empathy they use in responding to clients seeking help.

Case Example: What Would *You* Do?

When I was in my mid twenties, I worked as a caseworker with individuals in conflict with the law. I began seeing a man, Armano, who had sexually assaulted (i.e., raped) several women viciously. He would tell me details about some of these assaults and express his lack of remorse. I often wondered if he would tell me these disturbing things to simply observe my reaction.

1. How would you demonstrate empathy toward Armano?

2. How would you respond when Armano described these details?

3. In what way could you offer empathy toward his lack of remorse?

4. Would it be appropriate to be honest with Armano and tell him how much his stories bothered you? Why or why not?

Self-Disclosure

Self-disclosure is a complex, multifaceted phenomenon that has generated more than 200 studies (Watkins, 1990). It may be succinctly defined as "a conscious, intentional technique in which clinicians share information about their lives outside the counselling relationship" (Simone, McCarthy, & Skay, 1998, p. 174). Sidney Jourard (1958; 1964) conducted the original work in this area. For him, self-disclosure referred to making oneself known to another person by revealing personal information. Jourard discovered that self-disclosure helped establish trust and facilitated the counselling relationship. He labelled reciprocal self-disclosure the *dyadic effect* (Jourard, 1968).

Client self-disclosure is necessary for successful counselling to occur. Yet it is not always necessary for counsellors to be self-disclosing. "Each counselor–client relationship must be evaluated individually in regard to disclosure," and when it occurs, care must be taken to match disclosure "to the client's needs" (Hendrick, 1988, p. 423).

Clients are more likely to trust counsellors who disclose personal information (up to a point) and are prone to making reciprocal disclosures (Curtis, 1981; Kottler et al., 1994). Adolescents especially seem to be more comfortable with counsellors who are "fairly unguarded and personally available" (Simone et al., 1998, p. 174). Some counsellors use self-disclosure spontaneously in counselling sessions to reveal pertinent personal facts to their clients, especially during the understanding and action phases. Others provide information about themselves and the counselling process in writing. Spontaneous self-disclosure is important in facilitating client movement (Watkins, 1990; Zur, 2009).

According to Egan (2007), counsellor self-disclosure serves two principal functions: modelling and developing a new perspective. Clients learn to be more open by observing counsellors who are open. Counsellor self-disclosure can help clients see that counsellors are not free of problems or devoid of feelings (Cormier & Hackney, 2008). Thus, while hearing about select aspects of counsellors' personal lives, clients may examine aspects of their own lives, such as stubbornness or fear, and realize that some difficulties or experiences are universal and manageable. Egan (2007) stresses that counsellor self-disclosure

- should be brief and focused,
- should not add to the clients' problems, and
- should not be used frequently.

The process is not linear, and more self-disclosure is not necessarily better. Before self-disclosing, counsellors should ask themselves such questions as "Have I thought through why I am disclosing?" "Are there other more effective and less risky ways to reach the same goal?" and "Is my timing right?" (Simone et al., 1998, pp. 181–182).

Kline (1986) observes that clients perceive self-disclosure as risky and may be hesitant to take such a risk. Hesitancy may take the form of refusing to discuss issues, changing the subject, being silent, and talking excessively. Counsellors can help clients overcome these fears by not only modelling and inviting self-disclosure but also exploring negative feelings that clients have about the counselling process, contracting with clients to talk about a certain subject area, and confronting clients with the avoidance of a specific issue.

Case Example: What Would *You* Do?

Imagine you are a marriage counsellor with predominantly a heterosexual clientele, but you have been in a committed and happy same-sex relationship for many years. Many of the problems your clients discuss are problems you have faced with your partner at one time or another. Consequently, you often want to share your experience with the couple you are counselling.

1. By disclosing to the couple something about a past conflict with your partner, are you unnecessarily bringing another potential issue into the counselling that

is not the couple's presenting concern (e.g., their degree of homophobia)? Why or why not?

2. How might you offer counselling to heterosexual individuals without self-identifying as gay or lesbian? Would that be dishonest? Why or why not?

3. Conversely, if you are heterosexual and are working with a gay or lesbian client, is it important to tell them you have a heterosexual identity? Again, why or why not?

Immediacy

"Immediacy . . . is one of the most important skills" in counselling (Wheeler & D'Andrea, 2004, p. 117). It "focuses on the here and now and the therapeutic relationship" from the perspective of how both the client and the counsellor feel (p. 117). At its core, immediacy involves a counsellor's and a client's understanding and communicating what is going on between them in the helping relationship, particularly feelings, impressions, and expectations (Turock, 1980). There are three basic kinds of immediacy:

1. Overall relationship immediacy—"How are you and I doing?"

2. "Immediacy that focuses on some particular event in a session—'What's going on between you and me right now?'"

3. Self-involving statements (i.e., present-tense, personal responses to a client that are sometimes challenging)—"I like the way you took charge of your life in that situation" (Egan, 2007, pp. 180–181).

Egan (2007) believes that immediacy is difficult and demanding. It requires more courage or assertiveness than almost any other interpersonal communication skill.

Turock (1980) lists three fears many counsellors have about immediacy. First, they may be afraid that clients will misinterpret their messages. Immediacy requires counsellors to make a tentative guess or interpretation of what their clients are thinking or feeling, and a wrong guess can cause counsellors to lose credibility with their clients.

Second, immediacy may produce an unexpected outcome. Many counselling skills, such as reflection, have predictable outcomes; immediacy does not. Its use may break down a familiar pattern between counsellors and clients. In the process, relationships may suffer.

Third, immediacy may influence clients' decisions to terminate counselling sessions because they can no longer control or manipulate relationships. Some clients play games, such as "ain't it awful," and expect their counsellors to respond accordingly (Berne, 1964). When clients receive an unexpected payoff, they may decide not to stay in the relationship. Egan (2007) states that immediacy is best used in the following situations:

- in a directionless relationship
- where there is tension
- where there is a question of trust
- when there is considerable social distance between counsellor and client, such as in counselling clients from diverse backgrounds
- where there is client dependency
- where there is counter-dependency
- when there is an attraction between counsellor and client

Humour

Humour involves giving an incongruent or unexpected response to a question or situation. It requires both sensitivity and timing on the part of the counsellor. Humour in counselling should never be aimed at demeaning anyone (Gladding, 1995). Instead, it should be used to build bridges between counsellors and clients. If used properly, it is "a clinical tool that has many therapeutic applications" (Ness, 1989, p. 35). Humour can circumvent clients' resistance, build rapport, dispel tension, help clients distance themselves from psychological pain, and aid in the increase of a client's self-efficacy (Goldin et al., 2006; Vereen, Butler, Williams, Darg, & Downing, 2006). "Ha-ha" often leads to an awareness of "a-ha" and a clearer perception of a situation (i.e., insight) (Kottler, 1991). For instance, when a counsellor is working with a client who is unsure whether he or she wants to be in counselling, the counsellor might initiate the following exchange:

Counsellor: Joan, how many counsellors does it take to change a lightbulb?

Client: (*hesitantly*) I'm not sure.

Counsellor: Just one, but the lightbulb has got to really want to be changed.

Client: (*smiling*) I guess I'm a lightbulb that's undecided.

Counsellor: It's okay to be undecided. We can work on that. Our sessions will probably be more fruitful, however, if you can turn on to what you'd like to see different in your life and what it is we could jointly work on. That way we can focus more clearly.

Overall, humour can contribute to creative thinking; help keep things in perspective; and make it easier to explore difficult, awkward, or nonsensical aspects of life (Bergman, 1985; Goldin et al., 2006; Piercy & Lobsenz, 1994). However, "counselors must remember that to use humor effectively they must understand what is humorous and under what circumstances it is humorous" (Erdman & Lampe, 1996, p. 376). Therefore, they need to realize before attempting humour in a counselling situation that both clients and counsellors are comfortable with it as an activity, that there should be a purpose to it, that trust and respect must have been established before humour is used, and that humour should be tailored or customized to a particular client's specific cultural orientation and uniqueness (Maples et al., 2001). Counsellors can use humour to challenge a client's beliefs, to magnify irrational beliefs to absurdity, or even to make a paradoxical intervention (Goldin & Bordan, 1999). When handled right, humour can open up counsellor–client relationships.

Confrontation

Confrontation, like immediacy, is often misunderstood. Uninformed counsellors sometimes think confrontation involves an attack on clients, a kind of "in your face" approach that is berating. Instead, confrontation is invitational. At its best, confrontation challenges a client to examine, modify, or control an aspect of behaviour that is currently nonexistent or improperly used. Sometimes confrontation involves giving metacommunication feedback that is at variance with what the client wants or expects. This type of response may be inconsistent with a client's perception of self or circumstances (Wilcox-Matthew et al., 1997).

Confrontation can help "people see more clearly what is happening, what the consequences are, and how they can assume responsibility for taking action to change in ways that can lead to a more effective life and better and fairer relationships with others" (Tamminen & Smaby, 1981, p. 42). A good, responsible, caring, and appropriate confrontation produces growth and encourages an honest examination of oneself. Sometimes it may actually be detrimental to the client if the counsellor fails to confront. Avoiding confrontation of the client's behaviour is known as the MUM effect and results in the counsellor's being less effective than he or she otherwise would be (Rosen & Tesser, 1970; Uysal & Oner-Ozkan, 2007).

However, there are certain boundaries to confrontation (Leaman, 1978). The counsellor needs to be sure that the relationship with the client is strong enough to sustain a confrontation. The counsellor must time a confrontation appropriately and remain true to the motives that have led to the act of confronting. It is more productive in the long run to confront a client's strengths than a client's weaknesses (Berenson & Mitchell, 1974), a positive focus that is a foundational principle of the field of counselling psychology (Beatch et al., 2009; Linley, 2006). The counsellor should challenge the client to use resources he or she is failing to employ.

Regardless of whether confrontation involves strengths or weaknesses, counsellors use a "you said . . . but look" structure to implement the confrontation process (Cormier & Hackney, 2008). For example, in the first part of the confrontation, a counsellor might say, "You said you wanted to get out more and meet people." In the second part, the counsellor highlights the discrepancy or contradiction in the client's words and actions—for instance, "But you are now watching television four to six hours a night."

Contracting

There are two aspects of contracting: One focuses on the processes involved in reaching a goal, the other concentrates on the final outcome. In goal setting, the counsellor operates from a theoretical base that directs his or her actions. The client learns to change ways of thinking, feeling, and behaving to obtain goals. It is natural for counsellors and clients to engage in contractual behaviour. Goodyear and Bradley (1980) point out that all interpersonal relationships are contractual, but some are more explicit than others. Because the median number of counselling sessions may be as few as five or six, it is useful and time saving for counsellors and clients to work on goals through a contract system. Such a system lets both parties participate in determining direction in counselling and evaluating change. It helps them be more specific (Brammer et al., 1993).

Other advantages to using contracts in counselling are as follows:

- First, a contract provides a written record of goals the counsellor and client have agreed to pursue and the course of action to be taken.

- Second, the formal nature of a contract and its time limits may act as motivators for a client who tends to procrastinate.

- Third, if the contract is broken down into definable sections, a client may get a clear feeling that problems can be solved.

- Fourth, a contract puts the responsibility for any change on the client and thereby has the potential to empower the client and make him or her more responsive to the environment and more responsible for his or her behaviours.

- Finally, the contract system, by specifically outlining the number of sessions to be held, assures that clients will return to counselling regularly (Sills, 2006; Thomas & Ezell, 1972).

There are several approaches to setting up contracts. Goodyear and Bradley (1980) offer recommendations for promoting maximum effectiveness:

- It is essential that counsellors indicate to their clients that the purpose of counselling is to work. It is important to begin by asking the client, "What would you like to work on?" as opposed to "What would you like to talk about?"

- It is vital that the contract for counselling concerns change in the client rather than a person not present at the sessions. The counsellor acts as a consultant when the client wishes to examine the behaviour of another person, such as a child who throws temper tantrums, but work of this type is limited.

- The counsellor must insist on setting up contracts that avoid the inclusion of client con words such as *try* or *maybe*, which are not specific. Such words usually result in the client's failing to achieve a goal.

- The counsellor must be wary of client goals that are directed toward pleasing others and include words such as *should* or *must*. Such statements embody externally driven goals. For instance, a client who sets an initial goal that includes the statement "I should please my spouse more" may do so only temporarily because in the long run the goal is not internally driven. To avoid this kind of contract goal, the counsellor needs to ask what the client really wants.

- It is vital to define concretely what clients wish to achieve through counselling. There is a great deal of difference between clients who state that they wish to be happy and clients who explain that they want to lose 10 pounds or talk to at least three new people a day. The latter goals are more concrete, and both counsellors and clients are usually aware when they are achieved.

- The counsellor must insist that contracts focus on change. Clients may wish to understand why they do something, but insight alone rarely produces action. Therefore, counsellors must emphasize contracts that promote change in a client's behaviours, thoughts, or feelings.

Another briefer way to think of what to include in a contract is to use the acronym SAFE, where the *S* stands for specificity (i.e., treatment goals), *A* for awareness (i.e., knowledge of procedures, goals, and side effects of counselling), *F* for fairness (i.e., the relationship is balanced and both client and counsellor have enough information to work), and E for efficacy (i.e., making sure the client is empowered in the areas of choice and decision making) (Moursund & Kenny, 2002).

Even though contracts are an important part of helping clients define, understand, and work on specific aspects of their lives, a contract system does have disadvantages. Okun and Kantrowitz (2008) stress that contracts need to be open for renegotiation by both parties. This process is often time-consuming and personally taxing. Thomas and Ezell (1972) list several other weaknesses of a contract system.

- First, a counsellor cannot hold a client to a contract. The agreement has no external rewards or punishments that the counsellor can use to force the client to fulfill the agreement.

- Second, some client problems may not lend themselves to the contract system. For example, the client who wants to make new friends may contract to visit places where there is a good opportunity to encounter the types of people with whom he or she wishes to be associated. There is no way, however, that a contract can ensure that the client will make new friends.

- Third, a contractual way of dealing with problems focuses on outward behaviour. Even if the contract is fulfilled successfully, the client may not have achieved insight or altered perception.

- Finally, the initial appeal of a contract is limited. Clients who are motivated to change and who find the idea fresh and appealing may become bored with such a system in time.

Bartlett (2006) found that suicidal clients rated a no-suicide contract as the *least* effective method of the ones assessed. Of considerably greater help was use of medications, discussion about stress factors and suicidal thoughts, improvement in lifestyle choices, increase in social activities, more frequent sessions, and improvement in problem-solving skills.

In determining the formality of the contract, a counsellor must consider the client's background and motivational levels, the nature of the presenting problems, and what resources are available to the client to assure the successful completion of the contract. Goodyear and Bradley (1980) suggest that the counsellor ask how the client might sabotage the contract. This question helps make the client aware of any resistance he or she harbours to fulfillment of the agreement.

Rehearsal

Once a contract is set up, the counsellor can help the client maximize the chance of fulfilling it by getting him or her to rehearse or practise designated behaviour. The old adage that practice makes perfect is as true for clients who wish to reach a goal as it is for athletes or artists. Clients can rehearse in two ways: overtly and covertly (Cormier & Cormier, 1998). *Overt rehearsal* requires the client to verbalize or act out what he or she is going to do. For example, if a woman is going to ask a man out for a date, she will want to rehearse what she is going to say and how she is going to act before she actually encounters the man. *Covert rehearsal* is imagining or reflecting on the desired goal. For instance, a student giving a speech can first imagine the conditions under which he will perform and then reflect about how to organize the subject matter that he will present. Imagining the situation beforehand can alleviate unnecessary anxiety and help the student perform better.

Sometimes a client needs counsellor coaching during the rehearsal period. Such coaching may take the form of providing temporary aids to help the client remember what to do next (Bandura, 1976). It may simply involve giving feedback to the client on how he or she is doing. Feedback means helping the client recognize and correct any problem areas that he or she has in mastering a behaviour, such as overexaggerating a movement. Feedback works well as long as it is not overdone, whether provided to individuals (Geis & Chapman, 1971) or within groups (Kivlighan & Luiza, 2005). To maximize its effectiveness, feedback should be given both orally and in writing.

Counsellors can also assign clients *homework* (sometimes called "empowering assignments" or "between-session tasks") to help them practise the skills learned in the counselling sessions and generalize such skills to relevant areas of their lives. Homework involves additional work on a particular skill or skills outside the counselling session. It has numerous advantages, such as the following:

- keeping clients focused on relevant behaviour between sessions

- helping them see clearly what kind of progress they are making

- motivating clients to change behaviours

- helping them evaluate and modify their activities

- making clients more responsible for control of themselves

- celebrating a breakthrough achieved in counselling (Hay & Kinnier, 1998; Hutchins & Vaught, 1997)

Cognitive-behavioural counsellors are most likely to emphasize homework assignments. For instance, counsellors with this theoretical background may have clients use workbooks to augment cognitive-behavioural in-session work. Workbooks require active participation and provide a tangible record of what clients have done. Two excellent cognitive-behavioural workbook exercises geared toward children are Vernon's (1989) "Decisions and Consequences," published in her book *Thinking, Feeling and Behaving*, which focuses on cause and effect by having the counsellor do such things as drop an egg into a bowl; and Kendall's (1990) Coping Cat Workbook, which concentrates on the connections between thoughts and feelings by having children engage in such activities as viewing life from a cat's perspective.

However, counsellors from all theoretical perspectives can use homework if they wish to help clients help themselves. For homework to be most effective, it needs to be specifically tied to some measurable behaviour change (Okun & Kantrowitz, 2008). It must also be relevant to clients' situations if it is to be meaningful and helpful (Cormier & Cormier, 1998; Young, 2005). Furthermore, clients need to complete homework assignments if they are to benefit from using a homework method.

"The kinds of homework that can be assigned are limited only by the creativity of the counselor and the client" (Hay & Kinnier, 1998, p. 126). Types of homework that are frequently given include those that are paradoxical (an attempt to create the opposite effect), behavioural (practising a new skill), risk taking (doing something that is feared), thinking (mulling over select thoughts), written (keeping a log or journal), bibliotherapeutic (reading, listening, or viewing literature), and not doing anything (taking a break from one's usual habits).

Case Example: What Would *You* Do?

Max, 38 years old, came to see me complaining of erectile dysfunction (this used to be called impotence) with his wife of several years. As usual, I had him complete my history questionnaire before our first session. Nothing remarkable stood out for me. When we met, Max told me that his family physician did not believe he had anything wrong with him physically. He did, somewhat humourously, give him some advice, however. He said, "Everything will work fine, Max, if you get together with a different woman!"

Max told me that the physician had not given any medical tests. I asked Max if he ever masturbates, and he said he does not for fear his wife, Andrea, would catch him doing it. I suggested Max do this as his homework assignment as a way for both of us to get a better sense of what might be going on. He seemed agreeable to this, and next session, I spent the first 20 minutes talking to his wife to find out her perspective before I asked Max to join us. The first thing she told me is that Max did not complete his homework assignment. She said he must not have told me that both of them are Mormon and masturbating is considered inappropriate.

1. What should we learn from this real experience with a client?

2. What reasons could have led Max not to report his religion on the history questionnaire or in person?

3. What initial hypotheses would you have regarding possible reasons for Max's erectile problems?

4. How would you go about eliminating some of these as reasonable hypotheses?

5. Do you think we need to know the reason for Max's problem before we can treat it successfully? Why or why not? (Note: We will be exploring different theories that speak to this in later chapters).

TRANSFERENCE AND COUNTERTRANSFERENCE

Counsellor skills that help promote development during the counselling process are essential if the counsellor is to avoid *circular counselling*, in which the same ground is covered over and over again. There is an equally important aspect of counselling, however, that influences the quality of the outcome: the relationship between counsellor and client. The ability of the counsellor and client to work effectively with each other is influenced largely by the relationship they develop. Counselling can be an intensely emotional experience (Cormier & Cormier, 1998; Sexton & Whiston, 1994). In a few instances, counsellors and clients genuinely dislike each other or have incompatible personalities (Welfel & Patterson, 2005). Usually, however, they can and must work through transference and countertransference phenomena that result from the thoughts and emotions they feel and express to one another. Although some counselling theories emphasize transference and countertransference more than others, these two concepts occur to some extent in almost all counselling relationships.

Transference

Transference is the client's projection of past or present feelings, attitudes, or desires onto the counsellor (Brammer et al., 1993; Brammer & MacDonald, 2003). It can be used in two ways. Initially, transference reactions help counsellors understand clients better. A second way to use transference is to employ it as a way of resolving the client's problems (Teyber, 2000). Transference as a concept comes from the literature of psychoanalysis. It originally emphasized the transference of earlier life emotions onto a therapist, where they would be worked through. Today, transference is not restricted to psychoanalytic therapy and it may be based on current as well as past experiences (Corey et al., 2007).

All counsellors have what Gelso and Carter (1985) describe as a *transference pull*, an image generated through the use of personality and a particular theoretical approach. A client reacts to the image of the counsellor in terms of the client's personal background and current conditions. The way the counsellor sits, speaks, gestures, or looks may trigger a client reaction. An example of such an occurrence is a client saying to a counsellor, "You sound just like my mother." The statement in and of itself may be observational. But if the client starts behaving as if the counsellor were the client's mother, transference has occurred.

Five patterns of transference behaviour frequently appear in counselling: The client may perceive the counsellor as ideal, a seer, a nurturer, a frustrator, or a nonentity (Watkins, 1983, p. 207). The counsellor may at first enjoy transference phenomena that hold him or her in a positive light, but such enjoyment soon wears thin. To overcome any of the effects associated with transference experiences, Watkins (1983) advocates the specific approaches shown in Table 7.2.

Cavanagh (1990) notes that transference can be either direct or indirect. Direct transference is well represented by the example of the client who thinks of the counsellor as his or her mother. Indirect transference is harder to recognize. It is usually revealed in client statements or actions that are not obviously directly related to the counsellor (e.g., "Talk is cheap and ineffective" or "I think counselling is the experience I've always wanted").

Table 7.2 Conceptualizing and Intervening in Transference Patterns

Transference Pattern	Client Attitudes/Behaviors	Counselor Experience	Intervention Approach
Counselor as ideal	Profuse complimenting, agreements Bragging about counselor to others Imitating counselor's behaviors Wearing similar clothing Hungering for counselor's presence General idealization	Pride, satisfaction, strength Feelings of being all-competent Tension, anxiety, confusion Frustration, anger	Focus on: client's expectations, effects of these expectations intra-punitive expressions trend toward self-negation tendency to give up on oneself
Counselor as seer	Ascribes omniscience, power to counselor Views counselor as "the expert" Requests answers, solutions Solicits advice	Feelings of being all-knowing Expertness, "God-complex" Self-doubt, questioning of self Self-disillusionment Sense of incompetence	Focus on: client's need for advice lack of decision lack of self-trust opening up of options
Counselor as nurturer	Profuse emotion, crying Dependence and helplessness Indecision, solicitation of advice Desire for physical touch, to be held Sense of fragility	Feeling of sorrow, sympathy Urge to soothe, coddle, touch Experiences of frustration, ineptitude Depression and despair Depletion	Focus on: client's need for dependence feeling of independence unwillingness to take responsibility for self behavior–attitudinal alternatives
Counselor as frustrator	Defensive, cautious, guarded Suspicious and distrustful "Enter-exit" phenomenon Testing of counselor	Uneasiness, on edge, tension "Walking on eggshells" experience Increased monitoring of responses Withdrawal and unavailability Dislike for client Feelings of hostility, hate	Focus on: trust building, relationship enhancement purpose of transference pattern consequences of trusting others reworking of early experience
Counselor as nonentity	"Topic shifting," lack of focus Volubility, thought pressure Desultory, aimless meanderings	Overwhelmed, subdued Taken aback Feelings of being used, discounted Lack of recognition Sense of being a "nonperson" Feelings of resentment, frustration Experience of uselessness	Focus on: establishing contact getting behind the client's verbal barrier effects of quietness-reflection on client distancing effects of the transference

Source: Reprinted from "Countertransference: Its Impact on the Counseling Situation," by C. E. Watkins, Jr., 1983, *Journal of Counseling and Development*, *64*, p. 208. © 1983 by ACA. Reprinted with permission. No further reproduction authorized without written permission of the American Counseling Association.

Regardless of its degree of directness, transference is either negative or positive. *Negative transference* is when the client accuses the counsellor of neglecting or acting negatively toward him or her. Although painful to handle initially, negative transference must be worked through for the counselling relationship to get back to reality and ultimately be productive. It has a direct impact on the quality of the relationship. *Positive transference*, especially a mild form, such as client admiration for the counsellor, may not be readily acknowledged because it appears at first to add something to the relationship (Watkins, 1983). Indirect or mild forms of positive transference are least harmful to the work of the counsellor and client.

Cavanagh (1990) holds that both negative and positive transference are forms of resistance. As long as the client keeps the attention of the counsellor on transference issues, little progress is made in setting or achieving goals. To resolve transference issues, the counsellor may work directly and interpersonally rather than analytically. For example, if the client complains that a counsellor cares only about being admired, the counsellor can respond, "I agree that some counsellors may have this need, and it is not very helpful. On the other hand, we have been focusing on your goals. Let's go back to them. If the needs of counsellors, as you observe them, become relevant to your goals, we will explore that issue."

Corey and associates (2007) see therapeutic value in working through transference. They believe that the counsellor–client relationship improves once the client resolves distorted perceptions about the counsellor. If the situation is handled sensitively, the improved relationship is reflected in the client's increased trust and confidence in the counsellor. Furthermore, by resolving feelings of transference, a client may gain insight into the past and become free to act differently in the present and future.

Countertransference

Countertransference refers to the counsellor's projected emotional reaction to or behaviour toward the client (Fauth & Hayes, 2006; Hansen et al., 1994). This reaction may be irrational, interpersonally stressful, and neurotic, emanating from the counsellor's own unresolved issues. Furthermore, countertransference is often "harmful to, threatening, challenging, and/or taxing" to the counsellor's coping resources (Fauth & Hayes, 2006, p. 431). Two examples of countertransference are a counsellor manifesting behaviours toward her client as she did toward her sister when they were growing up or a counsellor overidentifying with her client who has an eating disorder (DeLucia-Waack, 1999). Such interaction can destroy the counsellor's ability to be therapeutic, let alone objective. Unless resolved adequately, countertransference can be detrimental to the counselling relationship.

Kernberg (1975) takes two major approaches to the problem of conceptualizing countertransference. In the classic approach, countertransference is seen negatively and is viewed as the direct or indirect unconscious reaction of the counsellor to the client. The total approach, however, sees countertransference as more positive; from this perspective, countertransference is a diagnostic tool for understanding aspects of the client's unconscious motivations. Blanck and Blanck (1979) describe a third approach. This approach sees countertransference as both positive and negative. Watkins (1985) considers this third approach more realistic than the first two. A fourth and newer approach suggests that different levels of countertransference occur as the analysis unfolds and the *characters* (i.e., the different projections of both analyst and analysand) transform (Ferro, Basile, & Slotkin, 2008).

The manifestation of countertransference takes several forms (Corey et al., 2007). The most prevalent are (a) feeling a constant desire to please the client, (b) identifying with the problems of the client so much that one loses objectivity, (c) developing sexual or romantic feelings toward the client, (d) giving advice compulsively, and (e) wanting to develop a social relationship with the client.

Watkins (1985) thinks that countertransference can be expressed in a myriad of ways. He views four forms as particularly noteworthy: overprotective, benign, rejecting, and hostile. The first two forms are examples of *overidentification*, in which the counsellor loses his or her ability to remain emotionally distant from the client. The latter two forms are examples of *disidentification*, in which the counsellor becomes emotionally removed from the client. Disidentification may express itself in counsellor behaviour that is aloof, non-empathetic, hostile, cold, or antagonistic.

It is vital that counsellors work through any negative or nonproductive countertransference. Otherwise, the progress of the client will lessen, and both counsellor and client will be hurt in the process (Brammer & MacDonald, 2003; Watkins, 1985). It is also important that a counsellor recognize that he or she is experiencing countertransference feelings. Once aware of these feelings, a counsellor needs to discover the reasons behind them. It is critical to develop some consistent way of monitoring this self-understanding, and one way is to undergo supervision (DeLucia-Waack, 1999). Counsellors, like clients, have blind spots, hidden areas, and aspects of their lives that are unknown to them.

Supervision involves working in a professional relationship with a more experienced counsellor so that the counsellor being supervised can simultaneously monitor and enhance the services he or she offers to clients (Bernard & Goodyear, 2004). Among the procedures used in supervision are observing counsellor–client interactions behind one-way mirrors, monitoring audiotapes of counselling sessions, and critiquing videotapes of counselling sessions (Borders, 1994). Analyzing the roles a counsellor plays in sessions is a crucial component of supervision.

SUMMARY AND CONCLUSION

This chapter emphasized the understanding and action phases of counselling, which occur after clients and counsellors have established a relationship and explored possible goals toward which to work. These phases are facilitated by mutual interaction between the individuals involved. The counsellor can help the client by appropriate leads, challenges to perception, multifocused responding, accurate empathy, self-disclosure, immediacy, confrontation, contracts, and rehearsal. These skills are focused on the client, but they also help the counsellor gain self-insight.

Client and counsellor must work through transference and countertransference, which can occur in several forms in a counselling relationship. Some clients and counsellors will encounter less transference and countertransference than others, but it is important that each person recognize when he or she is engaged in such modes of communication. The more aware people are about these ways of relating, the less damage they are likely to do in their relationships with significant others and the more self-insight people are likely to achieve. A successful resolution of these issues promotes realness, and at the root of growth and goal attainment is the ability to experience the world realistically.

Your Personal Reflections

1. When our third child was born, my wife, Claire, looked up at me and said, "The honeymoon is not over. There are just more people on it!" When have you or someone close to you reframed a situation or circumstance? How did it influence your perception of the situation or circumstance?

2. I have a counsellor friend who was completely different in almost every way from a client he saw. Instead of saying to the client something like "We really appear to be different," he lightheartedly said, "If I didn't know better, I would say you must be the other half of me, since we never seem to agree or see things the same way." What do you think of that as a humourous response (on a scale from 1 to 10)? What might you say in such a situation that would be more humourous (unless you rated the response a 10)?

3. When have you met people you immediately seemed to like or dislike? How did you treat them? How did you feel when you interacted with them? How is that like countertransference? How is it different?

Classroom Activities

1. In groups of three, discuss ways of using the counselling skills that you learned about in this chapter. For example, how will you know when to be silent and when to confront?

2. In this chapter as well as previous ones, persuasion was mentioned as an appropriate counsellor skill. In groups of three, role-play the following situations in which persuasion might be employed: (a) A small boy is afraid of all dogs, (b) a student has high test anxiety, (c) an elderly person is withdrawn, and (d) a marriage partner will not fight fairly with his or her spouse. How do you experience persuasion differently in these situations? How effective are the persuasive techniques that you used? Discuss your feelings with the class as a whole.

3. In groups of four, two people should role-play a counsellor and client and two should observe. Enact situations in which the counsellor demonstrates that he or she knows how to display the different levels of empathy. After the counsellor has demonstrated these skills, he or she should receive feedback from the client and the observers about their impressions of each enactment.

4. In the same groups that were formed for the previous activity, practise confrontation and immediacy skills. Discuss among yourselves and then with the class as a whole the differences and similarities between these two counselling skills.

5. Transference and countertransference are still hotly debated issues in counselling. Divide the class into two teams. One team should take the position that these phenomena do occur in counselling, while the other should argue that only real relationships are manifested between counsellors and clients. Select a three-member panel from the class to judge the debate and give the class feedback on the points made by each side.

Chapter 8
Termination of Counselling Relationships

PRACTICE REFLECTION

Janika, aged 45, experienced a progressive deterioration of her vision and at the time I was counselling her, she had little vision left. She knew that her vision would completely vanish within a few more years. Married for 15 years and raising a 12-year-old son, she was very unhappy with her life. Mostly, she wanted to leave her husband, Tony, as she felt he did not care for her at all. They rarely talked and when they did, the tone was hostile. She had also experienced a few affairs; the current lover was married and made it clear that he would not leave his family for her. Despite this, Janika kept asking more of him, and when rebuked, she became angry and sad.

Janika and Tony were very well off, living in a ritzy area and together were worth millions of dollars. Affording to see me was no burden at all. What this also meant was that Janika was content with not making any changes in her life. Each week she poured out her heart and her challenges, but each week she also reported taking no action. After four sessions of this, I confronted her: "Janika, we have gone over your situation several times now and you know what it is that you want to do about it.

Nonetheless, you are choosing not to take action at the moment. Perhaps you need to take more time to decide if you really do want to make any changes in your life?"

Janika replied, "Well, I just know it is going to hurt to have to divide our estate, and I fear that I will then be alone for the rest of my life. Who is going to want a woman who will soon be completely blind?" I chimed back with, "We have gone through all of your options and looked at each one in depth. You concluded that you will never be happy as long as you stay with Tony, and you do appreciate that you are a woman with many gifts to share with a man besides your vision. However, so long as you remain with Tony, you are stuck. You feel guilty when you see other men, and it also increases the animosity between you and Tony." "I know that," Janika replied. I then said, "If I have understood you correctly, you are not feeling that right now is time to make the change you want in your life. To what extent is this accurate?" Janika reflected for a few moments and said, "You are right—I know what to do but am choosing not to do it at the moment."

I said, "It makes sense from my perspective that we conclude our counselling at this point until you are ready to act. I suggest we meet again when that time comes so that I can provide you whatever support you require. What are your thoughts regarding this?" "It does make good sense," she said. I could tell that she was reluctant to stop meeting weekly for our conversations, which were solely focused on her. I had become her trusting, but one-sided, friend.

There are different times when it is appropriate to terminate a counselling relationship. The most mutually satisfying time is when the client has accomplished his or her goal. But another time is when the options have been thoroughly explored, both cognitively and affectively, and the client is not ready yet to take the behavioural "plunge." One of the defining features of counselling is that it is a goal-directed activity, and when counselling becomes nothing more than the type of social conversation you would have with a close friend (i.e., all process and no outcome), it is time to terminate, at least temporarily.

Termination refers to the decision to stop counselling. The decision may be made unilaterally or mutually. Regardless, termination is probably the least researched, most neglected aspect of counselling. Many theorists and counsellors assume that termination will occur naturally and leave both clients and counsellors pleased and satisfied with the results. Goodyear (1981) states that "it is almost as though we operate from a myth that termination is a process from which the counsellor remains aloof and to which the client alone is responsive" (p. 347).

But the termination of a counselling relationship has an impact on all involved, and it is often complex and difficult. Termination may produce mixed feelings on the part of both the counsellor and the client (Kottler, Sexton, & Whiston, 1994). For example, a client may be both appreciative and regretful about a particular counselling experience. Unless it is handled properly, termination has the power to harm as well as heal.

This chapter addresses termination as a multidimensional process that can take any of several forms. Specifically, we will examine the general function of termination as well as termination of individual sessions and counselling relationships. Termination strategies, resistance to termination, premature termination, counsellor-initiated termination, and the importance of terminating a relationship on a positive note will also be discussed. The related areas of follow-up, referral, and recycling in counselling will be covered, too.

FUNCTION OF TERMINATION

HISTORICALLY, ADDRESSING THE PROCESS OF TERMINATION DIRECTLY HAS BEEN AVOIDED for several reasons. Ward (1984) has suggested two of the most prominent. First, termination is associated with loss, a traditionally taboo subject in all parts of society, especially counselling, which is generally viewed as emphasizing growth and development unrelated to endings. Second, termination is not directly related to the microskills that facilitate counselling relationships. Therefore, termination is not a process usually highlighted in counselling. Its significance has begun to emerge, however, because of societal trends such as the aging of the population (Erber, 2005), the wide acceptance of the concept of life stages (Sheehy, 1976), an increased attention to death as a part of the lifespan (Kubler-Ross, 1969; Lefrancois, 1987), and the fact that loss may be associated with re-creation, transcendence, greater self-understanding, and new discoveries (Hayes, 1993).

Termination serves several important functions. First, it signals that something is finished. Life is a series of hellos and goodbyes (Meier & Davis, 2008). Hellos begin at birth, and goodbyes end at death. Between birth and death, individuals enter into and leave a succession of experiences, including jobs, relationships, and life stages. Growth and adjustment depend on an ability to make the most of these experiences and learn from them. To begin something new, a former experience must be completed and resolved (Perls, 1969). Termination is the opportunity to end a learning experience properly, whether on a personal or a professional level (Hulse-Killacky, 1993). In counselling, termination is more than an act signifying the end of therapy; it is also a motivator (Yalom, 2005).

Both client and counsellor are motivated by the knowledge that the counselling experience is limited in time (Young, 2005). This awareness is similar to that of a young adult who realizes that he or she cannot remain a promising young person forever—an event that often occurs on one's 30th birthday. Such a realization may spur one on to hard work while there is still time to do something significant. Some counsellors, such as those associated with strategic, systemic, and solution-focused family therapy, purposely limit the number of counselling sessions so that clients and counsellors are more aware of time constraints and make the most of sessions (Gladding, 2007). Limiting the number of sessions in individual counselling can be effective (Munro & Bach, 1975), although current research suggests that students usually require more sessions than policy allows in order to reach their therapeutic goals (Wolgast, Lambert, & Puschner, 2003)

Second, termination is a means of maintaining changes already achieved and generalizing problem-solving skills acquired in counselling (Dixon & Glover, 1984). Successful counselling results in significant changes in the way the client thinks, feels, or acts. These changes are rehearsed in counselling, but they must be practised in the real world. Termination provides an opportunity for such practice. The client can always go back to the counsellor for any needed follow-up, but termination is the natural point for the practice of independence to begin. It is a potentially empowering experience for the client and enables him or her to address the present in an entirely new or modified way. At termination, the opportunity to put "insights into actions" is created (Gladding, 1990, p. 130). In other words, what seems like an exit becomes an entrance.

Third, termination serves as a reminder that the client has matured (Vickio, 1990). Besides offering the client new skills or different ways of thinking about him- or herself, effective counselling termination marks a time in the client's life when he or she is less absorbed by and preoccupied with personal problems and more able to deal with outside people and events. This ability to handle external situations may result in more interdependent relationships that are mutually supportive and consequently lead to a "more independent and satisfying life" (Burke, 1989, p. 47). Having achieved a successful resolution to a problem, a client now has new insights and abilities that are stored in memory and may be recalled and used as needed.

TIMING OF TERMINATION

When to terminate a relationship is a question that has no definite answer. However, "termination should be planned, not abrupt" (Meier & Davis, 2008, p. 16). If the relationship is ended too soon, clients may lose the ground they gained in counselling and regress to earlier behaviours. However, if termination is never addressed, clients can become dependent on the counsellor and fail to resolve difficulties and grow as persons. There are several pragmatic considerations in the timing of termination (Cormier & Hackney, 2008; Young, 2005).

- *Have clients achieved behavioural, cognitive, or affective contract goals?* When both clients and counsellors have a clear idea about whether particular goals have been reached, the timing of termination is easier to figure out. The key to this consideration is setting up a mutually agreed-upon contract before counselling begins.
- *Can clients concretely show where they have made progress in what they wanted to accomplish?* In this situation, specific progress may be the basis for making a decision about termination.

- *Is the counselling relationship helpful?* If either the client or the counsellor senses that what is occurring in the counselling sessions is not helpful, termination is appropriate.

- *Has the context of the initial counselling arrangement changed?* In cases where there is a move or a prolonged illness, termination (as well as a referral) should be considered.

Overall, there is no one right time to terminate a counselling relationship. The "when" of termination must be figured out in accordance with the uniqueness of the situation and overall ethical and professional guidelines.

ISSUES OF TERMINATION

Termination of Individual Sessions

Termination is an issue during individual counselling sessions. Initial sessions should have clearly defined time limits (Brammer & MacDonald, 2003; Cormier & Hackney, 2008). A range of 45 to 50 minutes is generally considered adequate for an individual counselling session. It usually takes a counsellor five to ten minutes to adjust to the client and the client's concerns. Counselling sessions that terminate too quickly may be as unproductive as ones that last too long.

Benjamin (1987) proposes two important factors in closing an interview. First, both client and counsellor should be aware that the session is ending. Second, no new material should be introduced or discussed during this ending. If the client introduces new material, the counsellor needs to work to make it the anticipated focus of the next session. On rare occasions, the counsellor has to deal with new material on an emergency basis.

A counsellor can close an interview effectively in several ways. One is simply to make a brief statement indicating that time is up (Benjamin, 1987; Cormier & Hackney, 2008). For example, he or she might say, "It looks like our time is up for today." The simpler the statement, the better it is. If a client is discussing a number of subjects in an open-ended manner near the end of a session, the counsellor should remind the client that there are only five or ten minutes left. For example, the counsellor can say: "Lily, it looks like we only have a few minutes left in our session. Would you like to summarize what you have learned today and tell me what you would like to focus on next time?" The client can then focus attention on important matters in the present as well as those that need to be addressed in the future. As an alternative or in addition to the direct statement, the counsellor can use nonverbal gestures to indicate that the session is ending. These include looking at his or her watch or standing up. Nonverbal gestures are probably best used with verbal indicators. Each reinforces the other.

Another approach is to set a timer on one's watch at the 40 minute mark. By telling the client at the outset that, when the alarm sounds, it means there is still 10 minutes left in the session, it prompts both counsellor and client to note this and make the necessary segue into ending the appointment. It also has the advantage that the counsellor does not need to check the time periodically.

As indicated, toward the end of the interview, it is usually helpful to summarize what has happened in the session. Either the counsellor or the client may initiate this summation. A good summary ties together the main points of the session and should be brief, to the point, and without interpretation. If both the counsellor and client summarize, they may gain insight into what each has gotten out of the session. Such a process provides a means for clearing up any misunderstandings.

An important part of terminating any individual session is setting up the next appointment. Most problems are resolved over time. Clients and counsellors need to know when they will meet again to continue the work in progress. It is easier and more efficient to set up a next appointment at the end of a session than to do it later by phone.

Case Example: What Would *You* Do?

You have had two sessions with Martha and she is an endless talker. You can hardly make comments during the session or summarize at the end. Indeed, you find it difficult to interrupt her and even bring the session to a close. Mostly Martha tells you what has occurred over the past week in her life in a story-like fashion.

1. How can you intervene to help Martha move into a process-focused approach instead of a content-focused one?

2. How can you help Martha understand that the interruptions you make are for a good reason?

3. Ultimately, how can you ensure that your sessions with Martha end on time?

Termination of a Counselling Relationship

Counselling relationships vary in length and purpose. It is vital to the health and well-being of everyone that the subject of termination be brought up early so that counsellor and client can make the most of their time together (Cavanagh, 1990). Individuals need time to prepare for the end of a meaningful relationship. There may be some sadness, even if the relationship ends in a positive way. Thus, termination should not necessarily be presented as the zenith of the counselling experience. Cormier and Hackney (2008) stress that it is better to play down the importance of termination rather than play it up.

The counsellor and client must agree on when termination of the relationship is appropriate and helpful (Young, 2005). Generally, they give each other verbal messages about a readiness to terminate. For example, a client may say, "I really think I've made a lot of progress over the past few months." Or a counsellor may state, "You appear to be well on your way to no longer needing my services." Such statements suggest the beginning of the end of the counselling relationship. They usually imply recognition of growth or resolution. A number of other behaviours may also signal the end of counselling. These include a decrease in the intensity of work; more humour; consistent reports of improved abilities to cope; verbal commitments to the future; and less denial, withdrawal, anger, mourning, or dependence (Shulman, 1999; Welfel & Patterson, 2005).

Cormier and Hackney (1999) believe that, in a relationship that has lasted more than three months, the final three or four weeks should be spent discussing the impact of termination. For instance, counsellors may inquire how their clients will cope without the support of the relationship. Counsellors may also ask clients to talk about the meaning of the counselling relationship and how they will use what they have learned in the future. Shulman (1999) suggests that, as a general rule of thumb, one-sixth of the time spent in a counselling relationship should be devoted to focusing on termination.

Maholick and Turner (1979) discuss specific areas of concern when deciding whether to terminate counselling:

- an examination of whether the client's initial problem or symptoms have been reduced or eliminated
- a determination of whether the stress-producing feelings that led to counselling have been eliminated
- an assessment of the client's coping ability and degree of understanding of self and others
- a determination of whether the client can relate better to others and is able to love and be loved
- an examination of whether the client has acquired abilities to plan and work productively
- an evaluation of whether the client can better play and enjoy life

These areas are not equally important for all clients, but it is essential that, before termination of counselling, clients feel confident to live effectively without the relationship (Huber, 1989; Ward, 1984; Young, 2005).

There are at least two other ways to facilitate the ending of a counsellor–client relationship. One involves the use of fading. Dixon and Glover (1984) define fading as "a gradual decrease in the unnatural structures developed to create desired changes" (p. 165). In other words, clients gradually stop receiving reinforcement from counsellors for behaving in certain ways, and appointments are spread out. A desired goal of all counselling is to help clients become less dependent on the counsellor and the counselling sessions and more dependent on themselves and interdependent with others. From counselling, clients should also learn the positive reinforcement of natural contingencies. To promote fading, counselling sessions can be simply shortened (for example, from 50 to 30 minutes) as well as spaced further apart (for example, from every week to every two weeks) (Cormier & Cormier, 1998; MacCluskie & Ingersoll, 2001).

Another way to promote termination is to help clients develop successful problem-solving skills. Clients, like everyone else, are constantly faced with problems. If counsellors can help their clients learn more effective ways to cope with these difficulties, clients will no longer need the counselling relationship. This is a process of generalization from counselling experience to life. At its best, this process includes an emphasis on education and prevention as well as on decision-making skills for everyday life and crisis situations.

RESISTANCE TO TERMINATION

Resistance to termination may come from either the counsellor or the client. Welfel and Patterson (2005) note that resistance is especially likely when the counselling relationship has lasted for a long time or has involved a high level of intimacy. Other factors that may promote resistance include the pain of earlier losses, loneliness, unresolved grief, need gratification, fear of rejection, and fear of having to be self-reliant. Some of these factors are more prevalent in clients, whereas others are more likely to manifest in counsellors.

Client Resistance

Clients resist termination in many ways. Two easily recognized expressions of resistance are (a) asking for more time at the end of a session and (b) asking for more appointments once a goal has been reached. Another more troublesome form of client resistance is the development of new problems that were not part of his or her original concerns, such as depression or anxiety. The manifestation of these symptoms makes termination more difficult; in such situations, a client may convince the counsellor that only he or she can help. Thus, the counsellor may feel obligated to continue working with the person for either personal or ethical reasons.

Regardless of the strategy employed, the termination process is best carried out gradually and slowly. Sessions can become less frequent over time, and client skills, abilities, and resources can be highlighted simultaneously. Sometimes when clients are especially hesitant to terminate, the counsellor can "prescribe" a limited number of future sessions or concentrate with clients on how they will set themselves up for relapse (Anderson & Stewart, 1983). These procedures make the covert more overt and help counsellors and clients identify what issues are involved in leaving a helping relationship.

Vickio (1990) has developed a unique way of implementing a concrete strategy for university students who are dealing with loss and termination. In *The Goodbye Brochure*, he describes what it means to say good-bye and why good-byes should be carried out. He then discusses five Ds for successfully dealing with departure and loss and an equal number of Ds for unsuccessfully dealing with them (Vickio, 1990, p. 576).

Successfully Dealing with Loss

1. Determine ways to make your transition a gradual process.
2. Discover the significance that different activities have had in your life.
3. Describe this significance to others.
4. Delight in what you have gained and in what lies ahead of you.
5. Define areas of continuity in your life.

Unsuccessfully Dealing with Loss

1. Deny the loss.
2. Distort your experience by overglorifying it.

3. Denigrate your activities and relationships.

4. Distract yourself from thinking about departure.

5. Detach yourself abruptly from your activities and relationships.

Lerner and Lerner (1983) believe that client resistance often results from a fear of change. If clients come to value a counselling relationship, they may fear that they cannot function well without it. For example, people who have grown up in unstable or chaotic environments involving alcoholism or divorce may be especially prone to hold on to the stability of counselling and the relationship with the counsellor. It is vital that the counsellor recognize the special needs of these individuals and the difficulties they have in coping with loneliness and intimacy. It is even more critical that the counsellor take steps to help such clients help themselves by exploring with them the advantages of working in other therapeutic settings, such as support or self-help groups. For such clients, counselling is potentially addictive. If they are to function in healthy ways, they must find alternative sources of support.

Counsellor Resistance

Although the "ultimate goal in counseling is for counselors to become obsolete and unnecessary to their clients," some counsellors are reluctant to say goodbye at the appropriate time (Nystul, 2006, p. 36). Clients who have special or unusual needs or those who are very productive may be especially attractive to counsellors. Goodyear (1981) lists eight conditions in which termination may be particularly difficult for counsellors:

1. When termination signals the end of a significant relationship

2. When termination arouses the counselor's anxieties about the client's ability to function independently

3. When termination arouses guilt in the counselor about not having been more effective with the client

4. When the counselor's professional self-concept is threatened by the client who leaves abruptly and angrily

5. When termination signals the end of a learning experience for the counselor (for example, the counselor may have been relying on the client to learn more about the dynamics of a disorder or a particular culture)

6. When termination signals the end of a particularly exciting experience of living vicariously through the adventures of the client

7. When termination becomes a symbolic recapitulation of other (especially unresolved) farewells in the counselor's life

8. When termination arouses in the counselor conflicts about his or her own individuation (p. 348)

It is important that counsellors recognize any difficulties they have in letting go of certain clients. A counsellor may seek consultation with colleagues in dealing with this problem or undergo counselling to resolve the problem. The latter option is quite valuable if the counsellor has a personal history of detachment, isolation, and excessive fear of intimacy. Kovacs (1965; 1976) and Guy (1987) report that some persons who enter the helping professions possess just such characteristics.

PREMATURE TERMINATION

The question of whether a client terminates counselling prematurely is not one that can be measured by the number of sessions the client has completed. Rather, premature termination has to do with how well the client has achieved the personal goals established in the beginning and how well he or she is functioning generally (Ward, 1984).

Premature termination is surprisingly common, with published estimates ranging between 30% and 60% (Lampropoulos, Schneider, & Spengler, 2009). Most studies further suggest that between 65% and 80% of clients will stop attending counselling before the 10th session (Lampropoulos et al., 2009).

Some clients show little, if any, commitment or motivation to change their present circumstances and request that counselling be terminated after the first session. Other clients express this desire after realizing the work necessary for change. Still others make this wish known more indirectly by missing or being late for appointments. Regardless of how clients express a wish for premature termination, it is likely to trigger thoughts and feelings within the counsellor that must be dealt with. Hansen, Warner, and Smith (1980) suggest that the topic of premature termination be discussed openly between a counsellor and client if the client expresses a desire to terminate before specified goals have been met or if the counsellor suspects that premature termination may occur. With discussion, thoughts and feelings of both the client and counsellor can be examined and a premature ending prevented.

Sometimes a client fails to keep an appointment and does not call to reschedule. In such cases, the counsellor should attempt to reach the client by phone or mail. Sending a letter to a client allows him or her more "space" in which to consider the decision of whether to continue counselling or not (MacCluskie & Ingersoll, 2001, p. 179). A model for a "no show" letter is as follows.

Dear _____:

I have missed you at our last scheduled sessions. I would like very much for us to continue to work together, yet the choice about whether to counsel is yours. If you do wish to reschedule, could you please do so in the next 30 days? Otherwise, I will close your chart and assume you are not interested in services at this time.

Sincerely,

Mary Counselor

If the counsellor finds that the client wishes to quit, an exit interview may be set up. Ward (1984) reports four possible benefits from such an interview:

1. An exit interview may help the client resolve any negative feelings resulting from the counselling experience.

2. An exit interview serves as a way to invite the client to continue in counselling if he or she so wishes.

3. Another form of treatment or a different counsellor can be considered in an exit interview if the client so desires.

4. An exit interview may increase the chance that the next time the client needs help, he or she will seek counselling.

In premature termination, a counsellor often makes one of two mistakes. One is to blame either himself or herself or the client for what is happening. A counsellor is more likely to blame the client, but in either case, someone is berated and the problem is compounded. It may be more productive for the counsellor to think of the situation as one in which no one is at fault. Such a strategy is premised on the idea that some matches between clients and counsellors work better than others do.

A second mistake on the counsellor's part is to act in a cavalier manner about the situation. An example is the counsellor who says, "It's too bad this client has chosen not to continue counselling, but I've got others." To avoid making either mistake, Cavanagh (1990) recommends that counsellors find out why a client terminated prematurely. Possible reasons include the following:

■ to see whether the counsellor really cares

■ to try to elicit positive feelings from the counsellor

■ to punish or try to hurt the counsellor

■ to eliminate anxiety

■ to show the counsellor that the client has found a cure elsewhere

■ to express to the counsellor that the client does not feel understood

Counsellors need to understand that, regardless of what they do, some clients terminate counselling prematurely. Such a realization allows counsellors to feel that they do not have to be perfect and frees them to be more authentic in the therapeutic relationship. It also enables them to acknowledge overtly that, no matter how talented and skillful they are, some clients find other counsellors more helpful. Ideally, counsellors are aware of the anatomy of termination (see Figure 8.1). With such knowledge, they become empowered to deal realistically with situations concerning client termination.

Not all people who seek counselling are equally ready to work in such a relationship, and the readiness level may vary as the relationship continues. Some clients need to terminate prematurely for good reasons, and their action does not necessarily reflect on the counsellor's competence. Counsellors can control only a limited number of variables in a

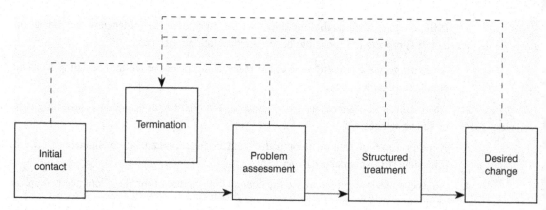

Figure 8.1 The anatomy of termination

Source: From *Contemporary Approaches to Psychotherapy and Counseling* (p. 37), by J. F. Burke, 1989, Pacific Grove, CA: Brooks/Cole. Copyright 1989 by Brooks/Cole Publishing Company, Pacific Grove, CA 93950, a division of Thomson Publishing Company Inc. Based on Gottman and Leiblum's *How to Do Psychotherapy and How to Evaluate It: A Manual for Beginners* (p. 4). Copyright by Holt, Rinehart & Winston. Adapted by permission.

counselling relationship. The following list includes several of the variables most likely to be effective in preventing premature termination (Young, 2005):

- *Appointments.* The less time between appointments and the more regularly they are scheduled, the better.

- *Orientation to counselling.* The more clients know about the process of counselling, the more likely they are to stay with it.

- *Consistency of counsellor.* Clients do not like to be processed from counsellor to counsellor. Therefore, the counsellor who does the initial intake should continue counselling the client if at all possible.

- *Reminders to motivate client attendance.* Cards, telephone calls, or e-mail can be effective reminders. Because of the sensitivity of counselling, however, a counsellor should always have the client's permission to send an appointment reminder.

COUNSELLOR-INITIATED TERMINATION

Counsellor-initiated termination is the opposite of premature termination. A counsellor sometimes needs to end relationships with some or all clients. Reasons include illness, working through countertransference, relocation to another area, the end of an internship or practicum experience, an extended trip, or the realization that client needs could be better served by someone else. These are what Cavanagh (1990) classifies as "good reasons" for the counsellor to terminate.

There are also poor reasons for counsellor-initiated termination. They include a counsellor's feelings of anger, boredom, or anxiety. If a counsellor ends a relationship because of such feelings, the client may feel rejected and even worse than he or she did in the beginning. It is one thing for a person to handle rejection from peers; it is another for that same person to handle rejection from a counsellor. Although a counsellor may have some negative feelings about a client, it is possible to acknowledge and work through those feelings without behaving in an extreme or detrimental way.

Both London (1982) and Seligman (1984) present models for helping clients deal with the temporary absence of the counsellor. These researchers stress that clients and counsellors should prepare as far in advance as possible for temporary termination by openly discussing the impending event and working through any strong feelings about the issue of separation. Clients may actually experience benefits from counsellor-initiated termination by realizing that the counsellor is human and replaceable. They may also come to understand that people have choices about how to deal with interpersonal relationships. Furthermore, they may explore previous feelings and major life decisions, learning more clearly that new behaviours carry over into other life experiences (London, 1982). Refocusing may also occur during the termination process and may help clients see issues on which to work more clearly.

Seligman (1984) recommends a more structured way of preparing clients for counsellor-initiated termination than London does, but both models can be effective. It is important in any situation like this to make sure clients have the names and numbers of a few other counsellors to contact in case of an emergency.

There is also the matter of permanent counsellor-initiated termination. In today's mobile society, "more frequently than before, it is counselors who leave, certain they will not return" (Pearson, 1998, p. 55). In such cases, termination is more painful for clients and presents quite a challenge for counsellors. The timing expected in the counselling process is off.

In permanent counsellor-initiated termination, it is still vital to review clients' progress, end the relationship at a specific time, and make post-counselling plans. A number of other tasks also must be accomplished (Pearson, 1998); among these are counsellors working through their own feelings about their termination, such as sadness, grief, anger, and fear. Furthermore, counsellors need to put clients' losses in perspective and plan accordingly how each client will deal with the loss of the counselling relationship. Counsellors must take care of their physical needs as well and seek professional and personal support where necessary.

In the process of their own termination preparations, counsellors should be open with clients about where they are going and what they will be doing. They should make such announcements in a timely manner and allow clients to respond spontaneously. "Advanced empathy is a powerful means for helping clients express and work through the range of their emotions" (Pearson, 1998, p. 61). Arranging for transfers or referrals to other counsellors is critical if clients' needs are such. Finally, there is the matter of saying goodbye and ending the relationship. This process may be facilitated through the use of immediacy and/or rituals.

Mike enjoyed his work as a counsellor at Family Services. He was enthusiastic and energetic and carried a full case load. However, when his wife received a promotion at work that required a move to another city, he realized he had to end his present counselling practice. Most troubling was the fact that he had only a month to do so, and as a child Mike had had some trauma regarding loss. Thus, Mike was not sure exactly what to do and how. He wanted to be professional and helpful to his clients, but he also wanted to take care of himself.

1. How would you prioritize the actions Mike needs to take first in regard to his clients?

2. Would a letter letting them know that he is leaving be unprofessional or crass?

3. How would you suggest Mike take care of himself?

ENDING ON A POSITIVE NOTE

The process of termination, like counselling itself, involves a series of checkpoints that counsellors and clients can consult to evaluate the progress they are making and determine their readiness to move to another stage. It is important that termination be mutually agreed on, if at all possible, so that all involved can move on in ways deemed most productive. Nevertheless, this is not always possible. Welfel and Patterson (2005, pp. 124–125) present four guidelines a counsellor can use to end an intense counselling relationship in a positive way:

1. *"Be aware of the client's needs and desires and allow the client time to express them."* At the end of a counselling relationship, the client may need time to express gratitude for the help received. Counsellors should accept such expressions "without minimizing the value of their work."

2. *"Review the major events of the counseling experience and bring the review into the present."* The focus of this process is to help a client see where he or she is now as compared with the beginning of counselling and realize more fully the growth that has been accomplished. The procedure includes a review of significant past moments and turning points in the relationship, with a focus on personalizing the summary.

3. *"Supportively acknowledge the changes the client has made."* At this point the counsellor lets the client know that he or she recognizes the progress that has been achieved and actively encourages the client to maintain it. "When a client has chosen not to implement action plans" for issues that emerged in counselling, "the process of termination should also include an inventory of such issues and a discussion of the option of future counseling."

4. *"Request follow-up contact."* Counselling relationships eventually end, but the caring, concern, and respect the counsellor has for the client are not automatically terminated at the final session. Clients need to know that the counsellor continues to be interested in what is happening in their lives. It is an additional incentive for clients to maintain the changes that counselling has produced.

ISSUES RELATED TO TERMINATION: FOLLOW-UP AND REFERRAL

Follow-Up

Follow-up entails checking to see how the client is doing with respect to whatever the problem was sometime after termination has occurred (Okun & Kantrowitz, 2008). In essence, it is a positive monitoring process that encourages client growth (Egan, 2007). Follow-up is a step that some counsellors neglect. It is important because it reinforces the gains clients have made in counselling and helps both the counsellor and the client re-evaluate the experience. It also emphasizes the counsellor's genuine care and concern for the client.

Follow-up can be conducted on either a short- or long-term basis. Short-term follow-up is usually conducted three to six months after a counselling relationship terminates. Long-term follow-up is conducted at least six months after termination.

Follow-up may take many forms, but there are four main ways in which it is usually conducted (Cormier & Cormier, 1998). The first is to invite the client in for a session to discuss any progress he or she has continued to make in achieving desired goals. A second way is through a telephone call to the client; a call allows the client to report to the counsellor, although only verbal interaction is possible. A third way is for the counsellor to send the client a letter asking about the client's current status. A fourth and more impersonal way is for the counsellor to mail the client a questionnaire dealing with his or her current levels of functioning. Many public agencies use this type of follow-up as a way of showing accountability. Such procedures do not preclude the use of more personal follow-up procedures by individual counsellors.

A fifth way to follow-up not mentioned by Cormier and Cormier (1998) is to e-mail past clients about their current status. Although time-consuming, a personal follow-up is probably the most effective way of evaluating past counselling experiences. It helps assure clients that they are cared about as individuals and are more than just statistics.

Sometimes, regardless of the type of follow-up used, it is helpful if the client monitors his or her own progress through the use of graphs or charts. Then, when relating information to the counsellor, the client can do so in a more concrete and objective way. If counsellor and client agree at the end of the last session on a follow-up time, this type of self-monitoring may be especially meaningful and give the client concrete proof of progress and clearer insight into current needs.

Referral and Recycling

Counsellors are not able to help everyone who seeks assistance. When a counsellor realizes that a situation is unproductive, it is important to know whether to terminate the relationship or make a referral. A referral involves arranging other assistance for a client when the initial arrangement is not or cannot be helpful (Okun & Kantrowitz, 2008). There are many reasons for referring, including the following (Cheston, 1991; Goldstein, 1971):

- The client has a problem the counsellor does not know how to handle.
- The counsellor is inexperienced in a particular area (e.g., substance abuse or mental disorders) and does not have the necessary skill to help the client.
- The counsellor knows of a nearby expert who would be more helpful to the client.
- The counsellor and client have incompatible personalities.
- The relationship between counsellor and client is stuck in an initial phase of counselling.

Referrals involve a how, a when, and a who. The *how* involves knowing how to call on a helping resource and handle the client to maximize the chances that he or she will follow through with the referral process. A client may resist a referral if the client feels rejected by the counsellor. Welfel and Patterson (2005) suggest that a counsellor spend at least one session with the client in preparation for the referral. Some clients will need several sessions.

The *when* of making a referral involves timing. The longer a client works with a counsellor, the more reluctant the client may be to see someone else. Thus, timing is crucial. If a counsellor suspects an impasse with a certain client, he or she should refer that client as soon as possible. However, if the counsellor has worked with the client for a while, he or she should be sensitive about giving the client enough time to get used to the idea of working with someone else.

The *who* of making a referral involves the person to whom you are sending a client. The interpersonal ability of that professional may be as important initially as his or her skills if the referral is going to work well. A good question to ask oneself when making a referral is whether the new counsellor is someone you would feel comfortable sending a family member to see (MacCluskie & Ingersoll, 2001).

Recycling is an alternative when the counsellor thinks the counselling process has not yet worked but can be made to do so. It means re-examining all phases of the therapeutic process. Perhaps the goals were not properly defined or an inappropriate strategy was chosen. Whatever the case, by re-examining the counselling process, counsellor and client can decide how or whether to revise and reinvest in the counselling process. Counselling, like other experiences, is not always successful on the first attempt. Recycling gives both counsellor and client a second chance to achieve what each wants: positive change.

SUMMARY AND CONCLUSION

Termination is an important but often neglected and misunderstood phase of counselling. The subjects of loss and ending are usually given less emphasis in counselling than those of growth and development, and the subject of termination is frequently either ignored or taken for granted. Yet successful termination is vital to the health and well-being of both counsellors and clients. It is a phase of counselling that can determine the success of all previous phases and must be handled with skill. Otherwise, everyone in the counselling relationship will become stuck in reviewing data in areas that may be of little use. In addition, termination gives clients a chance to try new behaviours and serves as a motivator.

This chapter has emphasized the procedures involved in terminating an individual counselling session as well as the extended counselling relationship. These processes can be generalized to ending group or family counselling sessions. Both clients and counsellors must be prepared for these endings. One way to facilitate this preparation is through the use of structure, such as time frames, and both verbal and nonverbal signals. Clients need to learn problem-solving skills before a counselling relationship is over so that they can depend on themselves rather than on their counsellors when they face difficult life situations. Nevertheless, it is important that a client be given permission to contact the counsellor again if needed. An open policy does much to alleviate anxiety.

At times, the counsellor, the client, or both resist terminating the relationship. Many times this resistance is related to unresolved feelings of grief and separation. When a client has such feelings, he or she may choose to terminate the relationship prematurely. A counsellor may also initiate termination but usually does so for good reasons. Regardless of who initiates termination, it is vital that all involved know what is happening and prepare accordingly. If possible, it is best to end counselling on a positive note. Once termination is completed, it is helpful to conduct some type of follow-up within a year. Sometimes referrals or recycling procedures are indicated to ensure that the client receives the type of help needed.

Your Personal Reflections

1. Think about times you have voluntarily ended events or relationships. What did termination feel like for you? What did you learn from the experience? What value do you see in concluding an experience?

2. When has education, either formal or self-taught, helped you stop doing something (e.g. smoking, biting your nails, displaying a nervous twitch, talking excessively)? How do you relate doing something new to termination?

3. Almost everyone has a situation in his or her life that ended too soon or that was less than ideal. You may want to explore some of those times in your own life. Could acknowledging those feelings or behaviours help you in working with a client you may not want to terminate?

Classroom Activities

1. In pairs, discuss the most significant termination experience of your life, such as the death of a loved one, graduation, or moving from one life stage to another. Evaluate with your partner the positive things you learned from these experiences as well as the pain you felt.

2. In small groups, take turns role-playing different forms of counsellor–client resistance to termination at the end of a session. Have one person play the part of the counsellor, one person the part of the client, and one person the part of an observer/evaluator. After everyone has had a chance to play the counsellor role, discuss the feelings you had related to resistance as a counsellor and as a client and what strategies you could use in overcoming resistance.

3. Write down ways that you think you can tell whether a counsellor or client is ready to end a relationship, such as using humour, talking positively about upcoming life events, or acting bored. Enact two of your behaviours in front of your classmates and let them describe how they would react to the behaviours you are displaying.

4. Must counselling relationships end on a positive note? What is the rationale for your answer? What benefits might a client or counsellor derive from terminating counselling on a negative note?

5. What are your thoughts and feelings about recycling? How might you refer a difficult client to another professional? What would you say to him or her?

CASE EXAMPLES

1. Tina grew impatient with her client, Molly, as Molly seemed to drone on and on about the misery in her life. Tina was sympathetic and empathetic, but only up to a point. Then she became annoyed and realized she was not doing the kind of work as

a counsellor that was helpful to her or to her client. Therefore, even though only 35 out of 50 minutes had passed since they had begun, Tina decided to end the session. She told Molly that she was having a difficult time following her and she asked if Molly would summarize what she was trying to convey. Molly was startled but when she thought about it, she was able to convey the essence of the session in only a few sentences.

What do you think of Tina's tactic? What else might she have done to make the session with Molly more productive?

2. Flo was an excellent counsellor, but she had one major fault: She never followed up with her clients. As far as she was concerned they were doing fine unless proven otherwise. In her 20 years of counselling, Flo had had only a handful of clients ever return for more therapy. Therefore, Flo hypothesized that she had been able to see and help more people because she was not spending time interacting with those who were better.

Could Flo's philosophy be right? If not, why not? Would you adopt it?

Chapter 9
Psychoanalytic and Psychodynamic Theories of Counselling

PRACTICE REFLECTION

As soon as Carlton entered my office, his eyes swelled with tears. There are times when it is appropriate to ask what the tears are about or what they represent. When tears are the first thing I see with a client, however, I simply move the tissue box closer to him or her and wait. Once the tears subside, I ask, "Are you okay?" This is usually enough of a prompt to summon the story that has brought this person to counselling.

Carlton told me that he was so disappointed that he did not get the job of his dreams for which he believed he was the best candidate. I asked him to explain. He said that he had applied for a job as an employee recruiter for a large nonprofit company. It was a junior position and he had just completed his degree in business administration with a major in human resources. Although Carlton did not strike me as a confident young man, he did seem intelligent and compassionate—traits I would think would be welcome in such a career.

"What happened?" I asked. Carlton said, "I went for the first interview in front of five people. By the end of it, I could tell that I impressed them. I am enthusiastic and eager to learn new things. A week later, they invited me for the second interview, a day-long process where I would meet several managers, have lunch with some key people, and then meet the executive director. Everything went well until my meeting with the executive director. For some reason, I immediately shut down—I could only provide 'yes' and 'no' answers to his questions. Believe me, I tried to engage him, but for some reason I was anxious and mentally blocked."

I asked, "Has this happened to you before in a job interview?" "No, never—that is why I am so pissed at myself. I really wanted that job. It was perfect for me, and I was perfect for it!" I continued, "Have you ever felt so shut down before while trying to talk to someone?" He thought for a moment and I could tell the moment his mind locked onto something. "Of course—he reminds me of my late alcoholic father. His sunken eyes, his bulbous nose, and his raspy voice were almost identical to my dad's."

"What used to happen when you would try and talk to your dad, Carlton?" "The same thing—I would shut down and barely be able to speak. He was usually drunk while verbally attacking me. The executive director seemed like a kind, gentle man . . . completely different from Dad." I said, "I understand that, but the fact remains that he *looks* like your father." "That is true, and my reaction was exactly the same!" replied Carlton.

I said, "Carlton, there are several ways that I can help you overcome this problem. One is to take a cognitive-behavioural approach whereby we systematically reduce your fear through your imagination using a technique called systematic desensitization. Another approach would be hypnotherapy, where the intent is pretty much the same. Still another approach would be to focus on your past relationship with your father with the goal of reducing the turmoil you still feel when you think about him or see someone who reminds you of him. What are your thoughts about these approaches?"

Carlton said, "You know, I've thought a little more about your earlier question while you were talking. I also felt this way before in university with one of my profs. He was a man of slight build, but nonetheless had those same sunken eyes. I could not meet with him to discuss a poor grade I received on a test because I knew he made me feel uncomfortable. I think I should spend some time getting a grip on my past relationship with my father so that this same pattern does not continue emerging."

I said okay, and for the next several sessions, we focused on the verbal abuse he had experienced as a child from his father. At times we also used imagery to have him imagine what he would like to say to his dad if he was still alive. At other times, Carlton cried as he re-enacted some of his encounters with his dad, followed again by having an imaginary therapeutic conversation with him. After six sessions, talking about his father no longer evoked a strong emotional reaction within him. In fact, Carlton told me that he was beginning to view himself as independent from his dad. He recognized his dad as being ill from alcoholism and that much of his behaviour was a consequence of the disease. Carlton did not drink at all, and he associated this as meaning that he had already taken steps to differentiate himself from his dad. Talking through his past relationship with his father changed both the way Carlton viewed him and the way he felt when he thought about him.

Although revisiting the past is sometimes scary, it is also beneficial to work with a trained counsellor through the pain associated with it. Our ghosts are memories that live within the deep recesses called *our mind.*

Counselling, by definition, is a process that involves interpersonal relationships (Canadian Counselling and Psychotherapy Association, 2009). Frequently it is conducted on an individual level in which an atmosphere of trust is fostered between counsellor and client that ensures communication, exploration, planning, change, and growth. In counselling, a client gains the benefit of immediate feedback from the counsellor about behaviours, feelings, plans, and progress.

The following four variables determine the amount of growth and change that takes place in any type of counselling:

- *counsellor*
- *client*
- *setting*
- *theoretical orientation*

We have already examined some of the universal qualities of effective counsellors and the counselling process. Certain characteristics seem to distinguish these aspects of counselling. For example, effective counsellors have a good understanding of themselves and others, an appreciation for the influence of cultures, and a sound educational background. They understand and work with their clients on agreed-upon goals and realize that the personalities of counsellors and clients have a powerful impact on each other and on the counselling process. The setting in which counselling is conducted is also a critical variable. Counsellors respond to client needs in different ways in different settings, such as schools, agencies, and mental health centres. The stages of counselling relationships likewise play a role in how counselling is conducted.

Some theorists view psychology as having developed through four movements, forces, or waves. These movements represent major paradigm shifts in theory and practice. A paradigm is the perspective that is generally accepted within a discipline at a particular time. A paradigm shift has huge consequences, and Pedersen (1999) espoused that we are now in the fourth movement.

Chapter 9 focuses on the first major movement, or force, that dominated counselling practice: psychoanalytic and psychodynamic approaches to counselling. The theories covered in this chapter are among the oldest and most well-known in the profession. Before examining them, however, we will first focus on the nature of and importance of theory within the counselling process.

THEORY

A THEORY IS A MODEL THAT COUNSELLORS USE AS A GUIDE TO HYPOTHESIZE ABOUT THE formation of possible solutions to a problem. "Theoretical understanding is an essential part of effective counselling practice. Theories help counsellors organize clinical data, make complex processes coherent, and provide conceptual guidance for interventions" (Hansen, 2006, p. 291). Counsellors decide which theory or theories to use on the basis of their educational background, philosophy, and the needs of clients. Not all approaches are appropriate for all counsellors or clients. Exceptional practitioners who formulated their ideas on the basis of their experiences and observations were the developers of most counselling theories. Yet most theorists are somewhat tentative about their positions, realizing that no one theory fits all situations and clients (Tursi & Cochran, 2006). Indeed, one theory may not be adequate for the same client over an extended period. Counsellors must choose their theoretical positions carefully and regularly reassess them.

Some theoretical models are more comprehensive than others and "all theories are hopelessly entangled in culture, politics, and language" (Hansen, 2006, p. 293). Effective counsellors realize this and are aware of which theories are most comprehensive and for what reasons. They know that theories determine what they see and how they see it in counselling and that theories can be catalogued in a number of ways, including modernism and postmodernism categories. Hansen, Stevic, and Warner (1986) list five requirements of a good theory:

1. *Clear, easily understood, and communicable.* It is coherent and not contradictory.

2. *Comprehensive.* It encompasses explanations for a wide variety of phenomena.

3. *Explicit and heuristic.* It generates research because of its design.

4. *Specific in relating means to desired outcomes.* It contains a way of achieving a desired end product (i.e., it is pragmatic).

5. *Useful to its intended practitioners.* It provides guidelines for research and practice.

In addition to these five qualities, a good theory for counsellors is one that matches their personal philosophies of helping. Poznanski and Mclennan (2003) found in their study, for example, that each major theoretical orientation was chosen by psychologists based on their own personal characteristics. Counsellors who wish to be versatile and effective should learn a wide variety of counselling theories and know how to apply each without violating its internal consistency (Auvenshine & Noffsinger, 1984).

Importance of Theory

Theory is the foundation of good counselling. It challenges counsellors to be caring and creative within the confines of a highly personal relationship that is structured for growth and insight (Gladding, 1990b). Theory has an impact on how client communication is conceptualized, how interpersonal relationships develop, how professional ethics are implemented, and how counsellors view themselves as professionals. Without theoretical backing, counsellors operate haphazardly in a trial-and-error manner and risk being both ineffective and harmful. Brammer and colleagues (1993) stress the pragmatic value of a solidly formulated theory for counsellors. Theory helps explain what happens in a counselling relationship and assists the counsellor in predicting, evaluating, and improving results. Theory provides a framework for making scientific observations about counselling. Theorizing encourages the coherence of ideas about counselling and the production of new ideas. Hence, counselling theory can be practical by helping to make sense out of the counsellor's observations.

Boy and Pine (1983) elaborate on the practical value of theory by suggesting that theory is the *why* behind the *how* of counsellors' roles, providing a framework within which counsellors can operate. Counsellors guided by theory can meet the demands of their roles because they have reasons for what they do. Boy and Pine point out six functions of theory that help counsellors in a practical way:

1. Theory helps counsellors find unity and relatedness within the diversity of existence.

2. Theory compels counsellors to examine relationships they would otherwise overlook.

3. Theory gives counsellors operational guidelines by which to work and helps them evaluate their development as professionals.

4. Theory helps counsellors focus on relevant data and tells them what to look for.

5. Theory helps counsellors assist clients in the effective modification of their behaviour.

6. Theory helps counsellors evaluate both old and new approaches to the process of counselling. It is the base from which new counselling approaches are constructed.

"The ultimate criterion for all counseling theories is how well they provide explanations of what occurs in counseling" (Kelly, 1988, pp. 212–213). The value of theories as ways of organizing information "hinges on the degree to which they are grounded in the reality of people's lives" (Young, 1988, p. 336).

Theory into Practice

As of 2008, more than 400 systems of psychotherapy and counselling were available worldwide (Corsini, 2008). Thus, counsellors have a wide variety of theories from which to choose. Effective counsellors scrutinize theories for proven effectiveness and match them to personal beliefs and realities about the nature of people and change.

However, as Okun (1990) states, the present emphasis in counselling is on connecting theories instead of creating them. This emphasis is built on the fundamental assumption that "no one theoretical viewpoint can provide all of the answers for the clients we see today" (p. xvi). Furthermore, counsellors seem to be pragmatically flexible in adapting techniques and interventions from different theoretical approaches into their work without actually accepting the premises of some theoretical points of view. This practice seems to be of necessity because counsellors must consider intrapersonal, interpersonal, and external factors when working with clients, and few theories blend all these dimensions together.

Most professional counsellors today (approximately 60% to 70%) identify themselves as *eclectic* in the use of theory and techniques (Lazarus & Beutler, 1993). That is, they use various theories and techniques to match their clients' needs with "an average of 4.4 theories making up their therapeutic work with clients" (Cheston, 2000, p. 254). As needs change, counsellors depart from a theory they are using to another approach (a phenomenon called *style-shift counselling*). Changes made by counsellors are related to the client's developmental level (Ivey, Ivey, Myers, & Sweeney, 2005). To be effective, counsellors must consider how far their clients have progressed in their structural development, as described by Jean Piaget. For example, a client who is not developmentally aware of his or her environment may need a therapeutic approach that focuses on "emotions, the body, and experience in the here and now"; whereas a client who is at a more advanced level of development may respond best to a "consulting–formal operations" approach, in which the emphasis is on thinking about actions (Ivey & Goncalves, 1988, p. 410). The point is that counsellors and theories must start with where their clients are, helping them develop in a holistic manner.

Whereas a strength of eclecticism is its ability to draw on various theories, techniques, and practices to meet client needs, this approach has its drawbacks. For instance, an eclectic approach can be hazardous to the counselling process if the counsellor is not thoroughly familiar with all aspects of the theories involved. In such situations the counsellor may become a technician without understanding why certain approaches work best with specific clients at certain times and certain ways (Cheston, 2000). This unexamined approach of undereducated counsellors is sometimes sarcastically referred to as "electric"; that is, such counsellors try any and all methods that "turn them on." The problem with an eclectic orientation is that counsellors often do more harm than good if they have little or no understanding about what is helping the client.

To combat this problem, McBride and Martin (1990) advocate a hierarchy of eclectic practices and discuss the importance of having a sound theoretical base as a guide. The lowest or first level of eclecticism is really *syncretism*—a sloppy, unsystematic process of putting unrelated clinical concepts together. It is encouraged when graduate students are urged to formulate their own theories of counselling without first having experienced how tested models work. The second level of eclecticism is *traditional*. It incorporates "an orderly combination of compatible features from diverse sources [into a] harmonious whole" (English & English, 1956, p. 168). It is more thought out than syncretism, and theories are examined in greater depth.

On a third level, eclecticism is described as professional or theoretical or as *theoretical integrationism* (Lazarus & Beutler, 1993; Simon, 1989). This type of eclecticism requires that counsellors master at least two theories before trying to make any combinations. The trouble with this approach is that it assumes a degree of equality between theories (which may not be true) and the existence of criteria "to determine what portions or pieces of each theory to preserve or expunge" (Lazarus & Beutler, 1993, p. 382). It differs from the traditional model in that no mastery of theory is expected in the traditional approach.

A fourth level of eclecticism is called *technical eclecticism*, exemplified in the work of Arnold Lazarus (2008) and his multimodal approach to counselling, which assesses what he describes as the seven elements of a client's experience. These vectors are summarized in the acronym BASIC ID:

*B*ehaviour
*A*ffect
*S*ensations (e.g., seeing, hearing, smelling, touching, tasting)
*I*magery
*C*ognitions (e.g., beliefs and values)
*I*nterpersonal relationships
*D*rugs (i.e., any concerns about health, including drug use, fitness, or diet)

In this approach, procedures from different theories are selected and used in treatment "without necessarily subscribing to the theories that spawned them" (Lazarus & Beutler, 1993, p. 384). The idea is that techniques, not theories, are actually used in treating clients. Therefore, after properly assessing clients, counsellors may use behavioural methods (such as assertiveness training) with existential techniques (such as confronting persons about the meaning in their lives) if the situations warrant.

This approach is in line with what Cavanagh (1990) proposes as a healthy eclectic approach to counselling. It requires counsellors to have (a) a sound knowledge and understanding of the counselling theories used, (b) a basic integrative philosophy of human behaviour that brings disparate parts of differing theories into a meaningful collage, and (c) a flexible means of fitting the approach to the client, not vice versa. Counsellors who follow this model may operate pragmatically and effectively within an eclectic framework. The critical variables in being a healthy eclectic counsellor are a mastery of theory and an acute sensitivity to knowing what approach to use when, where, and how (Harman, 1977).

A final type of eclectic approach is the *transtheoretical* model (TTM) of change (Norcross & Beutler, 2008; Prochaska & DiClemente, 1992). This model is developmentally based and has been empirically derived over time. It is "an alternative to technical eclectic approaches that tend to be inclusive to the point that various components are 'poorly' held together" (Petrocelli, 2002, p. 23). The model is direction focused and proposes five stages of change from pre-contemplation to maintenance. There are also five levels of change:

- symptom/situation problems
- maladaptive cognitions
- current interpersonal conflicts
- family system conflicts
- intrapersonal conflicts

"Counseling from a TTM perspective allows for a more *macroscopic approach* (involving a broad and comprehensive theoretical framework) and *personal adaptation* (involving an increase in critical, logical, accurate, and scientific-like thinking) rather than simple *personal adjustment*" (Petrocelli, 2002, p. 25). Its main drawbacks are its comprehensiveness and complexity and the fact that TTM has been tested only among limited groups (for example, addictions populations).

Past the pure theory views and eclectic approaches, counselling theories are now entering a postmodernist perspective. As such they are being seen as prepackaged narratives that help clients create new meaning systems "not by objectively discovering old ones" (Hansen, 2006, p. 295). The essence of such a view is seen in social constructive approaches. For the rest of this chapter and the next, 13 mainline theories that have gained popularity over time will be explained.

Case Example: What Would *You* Do?

Tim was a recently graduated counsellor. As such, he was observant and quick to pick up nuances in various forms of related therapeutic approaches. However, Tim was troubled. He liked most of the theories he had read about and had a hard time deciding which ones he would master. He really began to waffle when he found out that most of the theories worked well when implemented by a master therapist—one who had practised diligently for at least 10 years.

1. Knowing Tim's plight and the fact that he did not want to use only techniques, what might you advise him to do in deciding on a theoretical approach?

2. Would eclecticism work for someone as undecided as Tim? Why or why not?

PSYCHOANALYTIC AND PSYCHODYNAMIC THEORIES

The terms *psychoanalytic* and *psychodynamic* are often used interchangeably by theorists and mental health practitioners (Jacobs, 1994). However, Jacobs (1994) suggested that psychodynamic is a more inclusive term that emphasizes the dynamics of personality more than its structure. Furthermore, dynamics do not pertain to only psychoanalytic theories. As Watt (2000) explained, the Adlerian approach is psychodynamic, but it is not psychoanalytic as commonly believed. For the sake of simplicity, both will be organized together in this section.

From a historical point of view alone, psychoanalytic theories are important. Although these theories have lost favour in recent years in the public, academic, and professional communities (McWilliams, 2009; Rowe, 2009), they were among the first to gain public recognition and acceptance.

Furthermore, there is research suggesting that counsellors are often attracted to a theoretical orientation that fits their own personality type. Varlami and Bayne (2007) found that counsellors with different personality preferences, according to Jungian theory (explained later), preferred to adopt different theoretical orientations. Poznanski and McLennan (2003) found that psychodynamic therapists were older, were higher in emotional expressiveness, and were more interested in "ongoing self-healing" (p. 225), while cognitive-behavioural therapists were younger, were lower on emotional expressiveness and openness to experience, and were more interested in practical problem solving.

Due to its long history, various factions of psychoanalytic theory have developed. Gelso and Fretz (2001), for example, differentiated among four levels of psychoanalytic work (from a few sessions in total to three to five sessions per week for up to seven years) and four psychologies that have developed over time: (a) drive psychology, developed by Sigmund Freud; (b) ego psychology, developed by Heinz Hartmann and Anna Freud (Sigmund's daughter); (c) object relations psychology, developed by Ronald Fairbairn, Melanie Klein, and Harry Stack Sullivan; and (d) self psychology, developed by Heinz Kohut. Only psychoanalysis as developed by Sigmund Freud will be examined in this section, followed by Jung's analytical psychology and Adler's individual psychology. Freud's conceptualization and implementation of psychoanalysis is the basis from which many other theories developed, either by modifying parts of this approach or reacting against it.

Psychoanalysis

Founders and Developers Sigmund Freud, a Viennese psychiatrist (1856–1939), is the person primarily associated with psychoanalysis, especially the classical school of thought. His genius created the original ideas. Anna Freud further elaborated the theory, especially as it relates to children and the development of defense mechanisms.

Sigmund experienced severe emotional problems of his own, and during his early forties he suffered from several psychosomatic disorders and had an excessive fear of dying, which led him to do an extensive analysis of himself and his personality. He had himself felt hostility toward his father and sexual feelings for his mother, ideas that worked themselves into his theorized Oedipal complex. The *Oedipal complex* occurred during the phallic stage (see below), and it represented the conflict that he had experienced (desire and lust for mother, fear and/or dislike toward the competing father). Another important fact about Sigmund is that he had little tolerance for colleagues who disagreed with his view of psychoanalysis (Corey, 2009). Perhaps if it was not for his intellectual stubbornness, other psychodynamic theories would not have developed as quickly.

View of Human Nature Freud's view of human nature is dynamic with the transformation and exchange of energy within the personality (Hall, 1954). People have a *conscious mind* (attuned to an awareness of the outside world), a *preconscious mind* (that contains hidden memories or forgotten experiences that can be remembered), and an *unconscious mind* (containing the instinctual, repressed, and powerful forces). According to Freud, the personality consists of three parts:

1. *Id* (comprised of amoral basic instincts; operates according to the pleasure principle)
2. *Ego* (the conscious, decision-making "executive of the mind," which operates according to the reality principle)
3. *Superego* (the conscience of the mind that contains the values of parental figures and that operates according to the moral principle)

The id and the superego are confined to the unconscious; the ego operates primarily in the conscious but also in the preconscious and unconscious.

Psychoanalysis is also built on what Freud referred to as *psychosexual developmental stages*. Each of the stages focuses on a zone of pleasure that is dominant at a particular time:

1. The *oral stage*, where the mouth is the chief pleasure zone and basic gratification is from sucking and biting
2. The *anal stage*, where delight is in either withholding or eliminating feces
3. The *phallic stage*, where the chief zone of pleasure is the sex organs, and members of both sexes must work through their sexual desires
4. The *latency period*, where energy is focused on peer activities and personal mastery of cognitive learning and physical skills
5. The *genital stage*, where if all has gone well previously, each gender takes more interest in the other and normal heterosexual patterns of interaction appear

Excessive frustration or overindulgence in the first three stages are the main difficulties that can arise going through these stages, in which case the person could become *fixated* (or arrested) at that level of development and/or overly dependent on the use of *defense mechanisms* (i.e., a way of coping with anxiety on the unconscious level by denying or distorting reality). (See Table 9.1; for a thorough review of defense mechanisms, see Blackman, 2003).

Table 9.1 Psychoanalytic Defense Mechanisms

▪ Repression	The most basic of the defense mechanisms, repression is the unconscious exclusion of distressing or painful thoughts and memories. All other defense mechanisms make some use of repression.
▪ Denial	In this process, a person refuses to see or accept any problem or troublesome aspect of life. Denial operates at the preconscious or conscious level.
▪ Regression	When individuals are under stress, they often return to a less mature way of behaving.
▪ Projection	Instead of stating what one really thinks or feels, he or she attributes an unacceptable thought, feeling or motive onto another.
▪ Rationalization	This defense mechanism involves giving an "intellectual reason" to justify a certain action. The reason and the action are connected only in the person's mind after the behaviour has been completed.
▪ Reaction formation	When an individual behaves in a manner that is just the opposite of how he or she feels, it is known as a "reaction formation." This type of behaviour is usually quite exaggerated, such as acting especially nice to someone whom one dislikes intensely.
▪ Displacement	This defense is a redirection of an emotional response onto a "safe target." The substitute person or object receives the feeling instead of the person directly connected with it.

Source: Gladding, S. T. (2008). *Group work: A counseling specialty.* Upper Saddle River, NJ: Prentice Hall.

Role of the Counsellor Professionals who practise classical psychoanalysis function as experts. They encourage their clients to talk about whatever comes to mind, especially childhood experiences. To create an atmosphere in which the client feels free to express difficult thoughts, psychoanalysts, after a few face-to-face sessions, often have the client lie down on a couch while the analyst remains out of view (usually seated behind the client's head). The analyst's role is to let clients gain insight by reliving and working through the unresolved past experiences that come into focus during sessions. The development of transference is encouraged to help clients deal realistically with unconscious material. Unlike some other approaches, psychoanalysis encourages the counsellor to interpret for the client.

Goals The goals of psychoanalysis vary according to the client, but they focus mainly on personal adjustment, usually inducing a reorganization of internal forces within the person. In most cases a primary goal is to help the client become more aware of the unconscious aspects of his or her personality and to work through current reactions that may be dysfunctional (Tursi & Cochran, 2006).

A second major goal, often tied to the first, is to help a client work through a developmental stage not previously resolved. If accomplished, clients become unstuck and are able to live more productively. Working through unresolved developmental stages may require a major reconstruction of the personality.

A final goal of psychoanalysis is helping clients cope with the demands of the society in which they live. Unhappy people, according to this theory, are not in tune with themselves or society. Psychoanalysis stresses environmental adjustment, especially in the areas of work and intimacy. The focus is on strengthening the ego so that perceptions and plans become more realistic.

Techniques Psychoanalytic techniques are most often applied within a specific setting, such as a counsellor's office or a hospital's interview room. Among the most prominent of these techniques are free association, dream analysis, analysis of transference, analysis of resistance, and interpretation. Although each technique is examined separately here, in practice they are integrated.

- *Free association.* In free association, the client abandons the normal way of censoring thoughts by consciously repressing them and instead says whatever comes to mind, even if the thoughts seem silly, irrational, suggestive, or painful. In this way, the id is requested to speak and the ego remains silent (Freud, 1936). Unconscious material enters the conscious mind, and from there the counsellor interprets it.

- *Dream analysis.* Freud believed that dreams were a main avenue to understanding the unconscious, even calling them "the royal road to the unconscious." He thought dreams were an attempt to fulfill a childhood wish or to express unacknowledged sexual desires. In dream analysis, clients are encouraged to dream and remember dreams. The counsellor is especially sensitive to two aspects of dreams: the manifest content (obvious meaning) and the latent content (hidden but true meaning) (Jones, 1979). The analyst helps interpret both aspects to the client.

- *Analysis of transference.* Transference is the client's response to a counsellor as if the counsellor were some significant figure in the client's past, usually a parent figure. The analyst encourages this transference and interprets the positive or negative feelings expressed. The release of feelings is therapeutic, an emotional catharsis. But the real value of these experiences lies in the client's increased self-knowledge, which comes through the counsellor's analysis of the transference. Those who experience transference and understand what is happening are then freed to move on to another developmental stage.

- *Analysis of Resistance.* Sometimes clients initially make progress while undergoing psychoanalysis and then slow down or stop. Their resistance to the therapeutic process may take many forms, such as missing appointments, being late for appointments, not paying fees, persisting in transference, blocking thoughts during free association, or refusing to recall dreams or early memories. A counsellor's analysis of resistance can help clients gain insight into it as well as other behaviours. If resistance is not dealt with, the therapeutic process will probably come to a halt.

- *Interpretation.* Interpretation should be considered part of the techniques we have already examined and complementary to them. When interpreting, the counsellor helps the client understand the meaning of past and present personal events. Interpretation encompasses explanations and analysis of a client's thoughts, feelings, and actions. Counsellors must carefully time the use of interpretation. If it comes too soon in the relationship, it can drive the client away. However, if it is not employed at all or used infrequently, the client may fail to develop insight.

Strengths and Contributions Classical psychoanalysis has several unique emphases:

- The approach emphasizes the importance of sexuality and the unconscious in human behaviour. Before this theory came into being, sexuality (especially childhood sexuality) was denied and little attention was paid to unconscious forces.

- The approach lends itself to empirical studies; it is heuristic. Freud's proposals have generated a tremendous amount of research.

- The approach provides a theoretical base of support for a number of diagnostic instruments. Some psychological tests, such as the Thematic Apperception Test or Rorschach Ink Blots, are rooted in psychoanalytic theory.

- Psychoanalysis continues to evolve and most recently has emphasized adaptive processes and social relations.

- The approach appears to be effective for those who suffer from a wide variety of disorders, including hysteria, narcissism, obsessive-compulsive reactions, character disorders, anxiety, phobias, and sexual difficulties (Luborsky, O'Reilly-Landry, & Arlow, 2008).

- The approach stresses the importance of developmental growth stages.

Limitations The following limiting factors are a part of psychoanalysis:

- The approach is time-consuming and expensive. A person who undergoes psychoanalysis is usually seen three to five times a week over a period of years (Bankart, 1997; Nye, 2000).

- The approach does not seem to lend itself to working with older clients or a large variety of clients. "Patients benefiting most from analysis" are mainly "middle-aged men and women oppressed by a sense of futility and searching for meaning in life" (Bradley & Cox, 2001, p. 35).

- The approach has been claimed almost exclusively by psychiatry, despite Freud's wishes (Vandenbos, Cummings, & Deleon, 1992). Counsellors and psychologists without medical degrees have historically had a difficult time getting extensive training in psychoanalysis. This has changed, however, perhaps due to the diminished number of applicants to these programs (Rowe, 2009). Psychoanalytic institutes today, for example, are "courting social workers in large numbers" (Goldstein, 2009, p. 8).

- The approach is based on many concepts that are not easily communicated or understood—the id, ego, and superego, for instance. Psychoanalytical terminology seems overly complicated.

- The approach is deterministic. For instance, Freud attributed certain limitations in women to be a result of gender—that is, of being female.

- The approach does not lend itself to the needs of most individuals who seek professional counselling. The psychoanalytic model has become associated with people who have major adjustment difficulties or want or need to explore the unconscious.

Case Example: What Would *You* Do?

Travis, aged 22, tells you that he is having difficulty deciding which university to attend. He lives in Halifax and he feels internal pressure to attend Dalhousie University because his mother is ill and he wants to care for her. However, he has always wanted to attend McGill University and practise his French while living in Montreal. Furthermore, Travis is convinced they have a much better program in his area of study at McGill.

Travis tells you that he has also been dreaming about this decision. In his dreams, he keeps seeing himself in Montreal receiving a phone call that his mother has died. He then panics in the dream while noticing that everyone has disappeared.

As you talk further to Travis, you find out that his mother has multiple sclerosis and although her mobility is becoming increasingly limited, she is in good health otherwise.

1. From a psychodynamic perspective, what are the id and the superego telling Travis to do? What does his ego want?

2. Given that his recurring dream is that once his mother dies he is all alone, what significance might this have?

3. What are some ways that you can think of that might help Travis make his decision?

ADLERIAN THEORY

Adlerian theory focuses on social interests as well as the purposefulness of behaviour and the importance of developing a healthy style of life. The therapeutic approach that has grown out of this theory is internationally popular. Watts (2000a; b) argued that this approach will continue to be affirmed through the 21st century, as it is psychoeducational, both present- and future-oriented, and is time-limited.

Adlerian Counselling

Founders and Developers Alfred Adler (1870–1937) was the founder of the Adlerian approach to counselling, also known as *individual psychology* (to emphasize the holistic and indivisible nature of people). He was a contemporary of Sigmund Freud and even a member of his Vienna Psychoanalytic Society. However, Adler differed from Freud about the importance of biological drives as the primary motivating force of life and stressed the importance of subjective feelings and social interests. His theory is more hopeful. Individual psychology waned in popularity after his death but was revitalized by Rudolph Dreikurs, Manford Sonstegard, Oscar Christensen, Raymond Corsini, Donald Dinkmeyer, and Thomas Sweeney, among others.

View of Human Nature A central idea for Adler in regard to human nature is that people are primarily motivated by *social interest*—that is, a feeling of being connected to society as a part of the social whole, an active interest in and empathy with others, as well as a need and willingness to contribute to the general social good (Mosak & Maniacci, 2008). Those with social interest take responsibility for themselves and others and are cooperative and positive in regard to their mental health. "Those who are failures, including neurotics, psychotics, and criminally oriented individuals are failures because they are lacking in social interest" (Daugherty, Murphy, & Paugh, 2001, p. 466).

Adler's theory holds that conscious aspects of behaviour, rather than the unconscious, are central to the development of personality. A major Adlerian tenet is that people strive to become successful (i.e., the best they can be), a process he called *striving for perfection* or completeness (Adler, 1964). There is also a tendency for each person initially to feel inferior to others. If this feeling is not overcome, the person develops an *inferiority complex*. Such a complex, if not changed, becomes the basis by which one's personality is defined. In contrast, a person who overcompensates for feelings of inferiority develops a *superiority complex*, something Adler also described as a *neurotic fiction* that is unproductive.

Adler believed that people are as influenced by future (teleological) goals as by past causes. His theory also places considerable emphasis on *birth order*; those who share ordinal birth positions (e.g., firstborns) may have more in common with one another than siblings from the same family (Dreikurs, 1950). Five ordinal positions are emphasized in Adlerian literature on the family constellation: firstborns, secondborns, middle children, youngest children, and the only child (Dreikurs, 1967; Dreikurs & Soltz, 1964; Sweeney, 1998).

In addition to birth order, the family environment is important to a person's development, particularly in the first five years of life. Adlerian theory stresses that each person creates a style of life by age five, primarily through interacting with other family members. A negative family atmosphere might be authoritarian, rejecting, suppressive, materialistic, overprotective, or pitying (Dreikurs & Soltz, 1964), whereas a positive family atmosphere might be democratic, accepting, open, and social. Nevertheless, perception of the family atmosphere, rather than any events themselves, is crucial to the development of a style of life (Adler, 1964). Individuals behave as if the world were a certain way and are guided by their *fictions*—that is, their subjective evaluations of themselves and their environments.

Overall, Adlerians believe there are three main life tasks: society, work, and sexuality. As mentioned previously, Adlerian theory places strong emphasis on developing social interest and contributing to society. The theory holds that work is essential for human survival and that we must learn to be interdependent. Furthermore, a person must define his or her sexuality in regard to self and others, in a spirit of cooperation rather than competition. Adler also mentions two other challenges of life, although he does not fully develop them: spirituality and coping with self (Dreikurs & Mosak, 1966). According to Adlerian theory, it is crucial to emphasize that, when facing any life task, *courage* (a willingness to take risks without knowing what the consequences may be) is required.

Role of the Counsellor Adlerian counsellors function primarily as diagnosticians, teachers, and models in the egalitarian relationships they establish with their clients. They try to assess why clients are oriented to a certain way of thinking and behaving. The counsellor makes an assessment by gathering information on the family constellation and a client's earliest memories. The counsellor then shares impressions, opinions, and feelings with the client and concentrates on promoting the therapeutic relationship. The client is encouraged to examine and change a faulty lifestyle by developing social interest (Adler, 1927; 1931).

Adlerians are frequently active in sharing hunches or guesses with clients and are often directive when assigning clients homework, such as to act "as if" the client were the person he or she wants to be. Adlerian counsellors employ a variety of techniques, some of which are borrowed from other approaches.

Goals The goals of Adlerian counselling revolve around helping people develop healthy, holistic lifestyles. This may mean educating or re-educating clients about what such lifestyles are as well as helping them overcome feelings of inferiority. One of the major goals of Adlerian counselling is to help clients overcome a *faulty style of life*; that is, a life that is self-centred and based on mistaken goals and incorrect assumptions associated with feelings of inferiority. These feelings might stem from being born with a physical or mental defect, being pampered by parents, or being neglected. The feelings must be corrected and inappropriate forms of behaviour must be stopped. To do so, the counsellor assumes the role of teacher and interpreter of events. Adlerian counselling deals with the whole person (Kern & Watts, 1993). The client is ultimately in charge of deciding whether to pursue social or self-interests.

Techniques The establishment of a counselling relationship is crucial if the goals of Adlerian counselling are to be achieved. Certain techniques help enhance this process. Adlerian counsellors try to develop a warm, supportive, empathic, friendly, and equalitarian relationship with clients. Counselling is seen as a collaborative effort (Adler, 1956). Counsellors actively listen and respond in much the same way as do person-centred counsellors (James & Gilliland, 2003).

After a relationship has been established, the counsellor concentrates on an analysis of the client's lifestyle, including examination of the family constellation, early memories, dreams, and priorities. As previously noted, the family constellation and the atmosphere in which children grow greatly influence both self-perception and the perceptions of others. No two children are born into the same environment, but a child's ordinal position and assessment of the family atmosphere have a major impact on development and behaviour. Often a client is able to gain insight by recalling early memories, especially events before the age of 10. Adler (1931) contended that a person remembers childhood events that are consistent with his or her present view of self, others, and the world in general. Adlerian counsellors look both for themes and specific details within these early recollections (Slavik, 1991; Statton & Wilborn, 1991; Watkins, 1985). Figures from the past are treated as prototypes rather than specific individuals. Recent and past dreams are also a part of life-style analysis. Adlerian theory holds that dreams are a possible rehearsal for future courses of action. Recurrent dreams are especially important. A look at the client's priorities is helpful in understanding his or her style of life. A client may persist in one predominant life-style, such as always trying to please, unless challenged to change.

Counsellors next try to help clients develop insight, especially by asking open-ended questions and making interpretations. Open-ended questions allow clients to explore patterns in their lives that have gone unnoticed. Interpretation often takes the form of intuitive guesses. The ability to empathize is especially important in this process, for the counsellor must be able to feel what it is like to be the client before zeroing in on the reasons for the client's present behaviours. At other times, interpretations are based on the counsellor's general knowledge of ordinal position and family constellation.

To accomplish behavioural change, the counsellor uses specific techniques:

- *Confrontation.* The counsellor challenges clients to consider their own private logic. When clients examine this logic, they often realize they can change it and their behaviour.

- *Asking "the question."* The counsellor asks, "What would be different if you were well?" Clients are often asked this question during the initial interview, but it is appropriate at any time.

- *Encouragement.* Encouragement implies faith in a person (Dinkmeyer & Losoncy, 1980; Dreikurs & Soltz, 1964). Counsellors encourage their clients to feel good about themselves and others (Adler, 1931). They state their belief that behaviour change is possible for clients. Encouragement is the key to making productive life-style choices in learning and living.

- *Acting "as if."* Clients are instructed to act "as if" they are the persons they want to be; for instance, the ideal persons they see in their dreams (Gold, 1979). Adler originally got the idea of acting as if from Hans Vaihinger (1911), who wrote that people create the worlds they live in by the assumptions they make about the world.

- *Spitting in the client's soup.* A counsellor points out certain behaviours to clients and thus ruins the payoff for the behaviour. For example, a mother who always acts superior to her daughter by showing her up may continue to do so after the behaviour has been pointed out, but the reward for doing so is now gone.

- *Catching oneself.* Clients learn to become aware of self-destructive behaviours or thoughts. At first, the counsellor may help in the process, but eventually this responsibility is taken over by clients.

- *Task setting.* Clients initially set short-range, attainable goals and eventually work up to long-term, realistic objectives. Once clients make behavioural changes and realize some control over their lives, counselling ends.

- *Push button.* Clients are encouraged to realize they have choices about what stimuli in their lives they pay attention to. They are taught to create the feelings they want by concentrating on their thoughts. The technique is like pushing a button in that clients can choose to remember negative or positive experiences (Mosak & Maniacci, 2008).

Strengths and Contributions The Adlerian approach to counselling has a number of unique contributions and emphases:

- The approach fosters an egalitarian atmosphere through the positive techniques that counsellors promote. Rapport and commitment are enhanced by its processes, and the chances for change are increased. Counsellor encouragement and support are valued commodities. Adlerian counsellors approach their clients with an educational orientation and take an optimistic outlook on life.

- The approach is versatile over the lifespan. "Adlerian theorists have developed counselling models for working with children, adolescents, parents, entire families, teacher groups, and other segments of society" (Purkey & Schmidt, 1987, p. 115). Play therapy for children aged four to nine seems to be especially effective.

- The approach is useful in the treatment of a variety of disorders, including conduct disorders, antisocial disorders, anxiety disorders of childhood and adolescence, some affective disorders, and personality disorders (Seligman, 1997).

- The approach has contributed to other helping theories and to the public's knowledge and understanding of human interactions. Many of Adler's ideas have been integrated into other counselling approaches.

- The approach can be employed selectively in different cultural contexts (Brown, 1997). For instance, the concept of "encouragement" is appropriately emphasized in working with groups that have traditionally emphasized collaboration, such as Hispanics and Asian Americans, whereas the concept of "sibling rivalry" may be highlighted with European North Americans, who traditionally stress competition.

Limitations Adlerian theory is limited in the following ways:

- The approach lacks a firm, supportive research base. Relatively few empirical studies clearly outline Adlerian counselling's effectiveness.

- The approach is vague in regard to some of its terms and concepts.

- The approach may be too optimistic about human nature, especially social cooperation and interest. Some critics consider his view neglectful of other life dimensions, such as the power and place of the unconscious.

- The approach's basic principles, such as a democratic family structure, may not fit well in working with clients whose cultural context stresses the idea of a lineal social relationship, such as with traditional Arab Americans (Brown, 1997).

- The approach, which relies heavily on verbal erudition, logic, and insight, may be limited in its applicability to clients who are not intellectually bright (James & Gilliland, 2003).

Case Example: What Would *You* Do?

Ansley had always been verbally aggressive. She had a sharp tongue and an exceptional vocabulary. She could put other girls in their place quickly. Thus, she was both admired and hated.

On the suggestion of a friend, Ansley saw an Adlerian counsellor. She liked the social emphasis that she learned so she decided to change her ways. Ansley thought the quickest way to become the person she wanted to be was to act "as if."

1. Was Ansley naive to think that acting "as if" would help her become her ideal?

2. From an Adlerian perspective, what else would you suggest she do or try?

JUNGIAN THEORY

Several influential concepts derived from Jung's theory, including synchronicity, archetypes, collective unconscious, introversion, and extraversion. He believed that the main purpose of counselling was to help people *individuate*, which is the process of becoming whole by becoming increasingly conscious of unconscious images. Much of this process occurred through dream analysis.

Jungian Counselling

Founders and Developers Carl Jung (1875–1961) was a close colleague of Freud, but as he became disillusioned with Freud's theory, his ideas evolved into his own brand, which he called *analytical psychology* to differentiate it from psychoanalysis (James & Gilliland, n.d.). Jung was born in a small Swiss village to a well-educated family that included religious leaders. As a child, he learned to read several modern and ancient languages, including Sanskrit, the language of Hindu holy books. Carl didn't care much for school, but he was harassed by peers, and he soon developed a tendency to faint when he felt pressured. In adulthood, he studied medicine and specialized in psychiatry. After

World War II, he travelled widely and visited tribal peoples in Africa, America, and India. He retired in 1946 (Boeree, 2006).

View of Human Nature Jungians maintain a positive view of human nature, believing that people are predisposed to make a positive difference in the world (James & Gilliland, n.d.). Jungian theory emphasized unconscious determinants of personality, as did Freud's, but the unconscious to Jung had two components: the personal and the collective. The *personal unconscious* is analogous to Freud's concept of the unconscious mind. The *collective unconscious* is an ancestral warehouse of archetypes, myths, and symbols that are inborn and represent universal ways of seeing the world (Enns, 1994). *Archetypes* are the images of universal experiences contained in the collective unconscious. Some examples include the mother archetype, the father, the family, the child, the hero, the maiden, the wise old man, the trickster, the warrior, and the goddess.

Jung devoted special attention to archetypes that were important in shaping personality, including (a) the *persona*, which is the mask that one wears in public (the façade); (b) the *shadow*, or negative aspects of one's personality; (c) the *anima*, or the feminine side of the male psyche; and (d) the *animus*, or the masculine side of the female psyche (Enns, 1994). Jung believed that our unconscious can be accessed through dreams, free association, and active imagination, and that through exploration of all three vehicles, one can learn to understand his or her archetypes.

Jung distinguished between the causality and the finality of dreams. *Causality* answered the question, "What *caused* the person to have this particular dream?" *Finality* answered the question, "What is the *purpose* of this dream?" He believed that the meaning of a dream was specific to the person having the dream, in contrast to Freud's fixed interpretation of dreams (Koppel, 1999).

Jung was the first theorist to describe the introverted and extraverted personality types. The *introvert* derived and replenished energy by focusing inward, thereby becoming contemplative and aloof to varying degrees, while the *extravert* derived and replenished energy by focusing outward, thereby becoming outgoing, talkative, and friendly to varying extents.

Jung also wrote about synchronicity. *Synchronicity* occurs when two related events that are not linked causally occur at about the same time (Boeree, 2006). For example, a man dreams that his mother dies and the next day, it happens. An example that many of us have had is calling a friend at the exact moment the friend is phoning us.

Role of the Counsellor The counsellor's role in Jungian work is to help clients uncover their archetypes and other important symbols through dream work, free association, and using active imagination to make the unconscious conscious. By becoming aware of all aspects of self, including the shadow, clients learn to integrate and accept these aspects.

Goals Jungian therapy is intended to bring conscious and unconscious aspects of one's psyche into balance, thereby facilitating the process of individuation. Psychological symptoms occur when the "psyche is fragmented, unbalanced, and ill-adapted to reality" (Toub, 2010, p. 1).

Techniques Jungian therapists use three *techniques* to help bring forward images from the unconscious mind: (a) explication, (b) amplification, and (c) active imagination (Adams, n.d.). Often these three techniques are used while doing dream work, but they can be used for unconscious material revealed through other means. *Explication* is the interpretative process of understanding the meaning behind uncovered unconscious material. Generally Jung assumed that images meant nothing more than what they apparently meant, so a vine in a dream is a vine (and not a penis, as Freud might have interpreted). *Amplification* is the second interpretative process of looking beyond the uncovered unconscious material by comparing it to similar objects, images, myths, fairy tales, folktales, art, literature, and culture (Adams, n.d.). For example, a vine might be interpreted in relation to Aesop's fable *The Fox and the Grapes* and other typical (or "archetypal") images. Lastly, *active imagination* is a technique for experiencing the unconscious by deliberately bringing images forward and then engaging in conversation with these images. For example, one could relax comfortably before re-imagining a recent dream. Once the image of the dream is clear, you could pose a question to a figure in the dream (a person, let's say) and "compel the figure to give you an answer" (Adams, n.d.).

Hill (2002) described four *stages* of analytical treatment, which include the following:

1. *Confession.* Jung believed that "the beginning of all analytical treatment was to be found in the religious prototype of the confessional" (p. 439).

2. *Explanation.* After admitting to problems and releasing emotions associated with them, the next stage involved consciousness raising, which would allow new possibilities for the future (e.g., the more you know about yourself, the more you can move in a different direction).

3. *Education.* Jung appreciated Adler's focus on education, and Jung believed that clients must be educated and encouraged toward new behaviours.

4. *Transformation.* The final stage occurred as the therapeutic relationship began acting as a change agent for both the client and the therapist. Jung believed the therapist could help the client improve no further than the limit imposed by his or her own development (i.e., individuation).

Strengths and Contributions Jung's theory includes mystical and spiritual components and, consequently, it has become popular with Christian writers and clergy (Erickson, 1987; Hunt-Meeks, 1983; Koppel, 1999). The Jungian approach will likely appeal to therapists and clients who value dream interpretation and use of the imagination as central to the counselling process. Furthermore, his theory was first to suggest a commonly accepted personality difference—that between introversion and extraversion.

Based on his theory, one of the most popular tests of personality preferences emerged—the Myers Briggs Type Indicator (MBTI) (Myers, 1962; 1980). The test is commonly used in helping people and couples understand their personality strengths and weaknesses better, and it is used extensively in career counselling. The MBTI is described in detail in Chapter 16.

Limitations Most psychologists and personality theorists have a great deal of trouble with Jung's theory. Beyond its rooting in *teleology* (the idea that we have free will, in contrast to *mechanism*, which means that the past determines the present), Jung went a step further by introducing the mystical idea of synchronicity and the interconnectedness of the universe that it implies (Boeree, 2006). For that matter, the idea of archetypes residing within us from birth is also considered unscientific. In effect, what makes Jung's theory attractive to spiritual healers, ministers, and priests makes his theory unattractive to scientist-practitioners, which includes most psychologists.

Another limitation is that Jungian archetypes are often described in a sexist manner and do not attend sufficiently to social and cultural factors (Enns, 1994). The mythopoetic men's movement, for example, suggests that women in the mother and feminist archetypes are to blame for men's figurative emasculation. Consequently, leaders in the movement suggest that men need to re-empower themselves by embracing the warrior archetype, one that if embellished will likely have a reverse effect on creating an egalitarian world for women (Enns, 1994). Lastly, Jungian analysis often extends over several years (New York Association for Analytical Psychology, 2008), making it unavailable and unaffordable for many clients.

Case Example: What Would *You* Do?

Matthew, aged 19, comes to see you because he is having a recurring nightmare that is worrying him. In the dream, Matthew is Superman. The dream always begins with Matthew flying and feeling invincible. Once he is expected to help someone in distress, however, he soon begins to lose his powers: He becomes unable to fly and his mind fills with self-doubt. Sometimes he ends up getting picked up by a motorist in the dream and Matthew tells you that the driver always has a deeply concerned look in her face. For whatever reason, he is always picked up by a woman. You also find out in the session that Matthew is struggling with his university classes and that he has suffered a recent relationship breakup.

1. The archetype of Superman is not uncommon, but what is your interpretation for why he keeps losing his ability to fly?

2. What significance do you think it has that Matthew only gets picked up by a concerned woman in his dreams? What questions could you ask Matthew that might help substantiate whatever interpretations you or he has made?

SUMMARY AND CONCLUSION

This chapter covered the nature and importance of theory in counselling. In addition, it focused on the practice of theory in counselling today, especially different forms of eclecticism. Three orientations to counselling—psychoanalytic, Adlerian, and Jungian—were also described and discussed. Most of the psychoanalytic theories have fallen in popularity as today's emphasis in counselling practice is now on approaches that are brief and empirically validated. Jung's theory has come to be viewed disfavourably by many psychologists because of its metaphysical and spiritual aspects, while Adlerian counselling may be increasing in popularity due to its brief focus, its psycheducational aspects, and its present and future orientation.

There is evidence that psychologists choose a theoretical orientation that fits their personality type. This is also true for the approaches discussed in the next few chapters.

Your Personal Reflections

1. Consider occasions when you received coaching or instruction on how to kick a ball or draw a figure so that you could improve as an athlete or an artist. How do you think that experience relates to a good counselling theory?

2. Sometimes classic psychoanalysis is characterized this way—too much superego, you're a cabbage; too much id, you're a savage. How does such a characterization do justice or injustice to achieving a healthy ego? What does it say about the therapeutic challenge of implementing the psychoanalytic approach in counselling?

Classroom Activities

1. Talk with another classmate about what counselling would be like without theories. Then talk with your class as a whole about counselling as an atheoretical profession and the advantages and disadvantages of such an approach.

2. Compare and contrast the strengths and limitations of psychoanalysis. How would you explain its benefits and drawbacks to a person unfamiliar with it?

3. Adler emphasized courage (a willingness to take risks without knowing what the consequences may be) as one part of his theory. Talk to another classmate about when you have had courage and what a difference it has made in your life.

4. Which psychoanalytic or psychodynamic theory described in this chapter appeals to you the most? Divide into subgroups within your class with individuals who also find that theory appealing and talk about the way it resonates in your mind as well as its strengths and weaknesses.

5. Have a discussion with classmates about recent dreams you have had. Does it make sense to interpret the dream as though it has universal meaning (Freud's view) or is it better interpreted as particular in meaning to you alone (Jung's view)?

Chapter 10

Behavioural and Cognitive Theories of Counselling

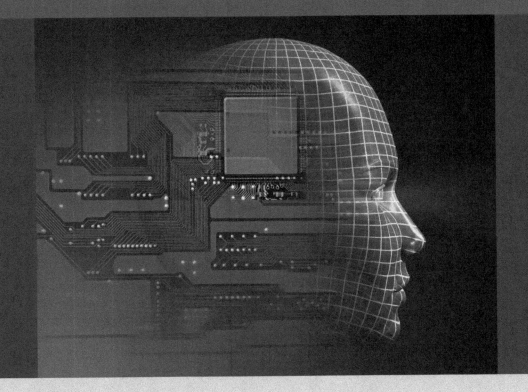

PRACTICE REFLECTION

While watching a large bird-eating tarantula in a pet shop in West Edmonton Mall recently, I was reminded of several clients I have had over the years with arachnophobia. I learned that the best way to treat this condition is to begin with systematic desensitization (SD) (which I usually combine with hypnotic suggestion) before beginning *in vivo* desensitization (ID), which is doing desensitization in real life. To overcome most fears, particularly phobias, one needs to face the fear at some point, and this is usually best done with a coach (perhaps you or a psychological assistant).

For a spider phobia, after a few sessions of SD, I ask the client to buy a pet tarantula (they usually don't forget to buy the small cage as well!). It is important to inform the client that, although tarantulas do have venom, they are not inclined to bite a human (and will not when treated and held properly, which I teach them later) and if they do bite, it is no worse than a wasp sting.

Before buying the tarantula, just as the clients and I have together created the imaginal hierarchy for use in SD, we do the same for creating the real life hierarchy. The ID may begin with watching the spider and feeding it live food, such as a few crickets every few days. Next, it may involve touching the top of the spider and eventually its hairy legs. Then I ask them to bring their pet spider with them to our next session. There I teach them how to pick it up properly, which ensures their safety and the safety of their pet. Next, I ask that they spend time in an open room with the spider and, after getting comfortable with this, to close the door.

Over time, the goal is to help the clients become comfortable having the spider on the palm of their hand and allow them to move from there. This is not nearly as morbid as it sounds, by the way, but it is essential that clients become desensitized to the spider. I would like to say that I then teach them to feed it carrot sticks while holding it, but tarantulas don't eat carrot sticks and, besides that, the work is done. By learning to treat the spider as a pet, the fear is counter-conditioned and becomes neutralized.

For many mental health professionals, the psychoanalytical and psychodynamic approaches were unscientific. They lacked the appearance of having face validity, which is whether something seems valid by looking at it from a common-sense perspective or from its appearance (i.e., from the surface, or "face"). It didn't help either when well-known psychologist Hans J. Eysenck's (1952) paper was published, indicating that psychotherapy was essentially not effective—about two thirds of neurotic clients improved with or without psychological help! Much research since has shown that therapy or counselling is effective in helping to ameliorate problems, but at the time this was a serious accusation. These, among several other factors, led to the emergence and growing popularity of the second movement, or force, in psychology: behaviourism.

This chapter covers behavioural and cognitive theories of counselling. Behavioural counselling will be treated as an entity in and of itself, even though those who prefer a more cognitive approach and professionals who are more action-oriented are also included in this method. Under cognitive counselling, rational emotive behavioural therapy (REBT), a theory that started out much more cognitive than it is today, will be described, along with reality therapy (RT), Aaron Beck's cognitive therapy (CT),and Donald Meichenbaum's stress inoculation training (SIT). Sometimes these theories are described as cognitive-behavioural. The recent additions to cognitive-behaviour counselling will also be described, including mindfulness-based stress reduction (MBSR), mindfulness-based cognitive therapy (MBCT), dialectical behaviour therapy (DBT), and acceptance and commitment therapy (ACT).

In all of these theories, and as in the previous chapter, a uniformed descriptive method will be used. Specifically, the sections describing these theories will focus on founders and developers, the view of human nature, the role of the counsellor, goals, techniques, strengths and contributions, and limitations.

BEHAVIOURAL COUNSELLING

BEHAVIOURAL THEORIES OF COUNSELLING FOCUS ON A BROAD RANGE OF CLIENT BEHAVIOURS. Often, a person has difficulties because of a deficit or an excess of behaviour. Counsellors who take a behavioural approach seek to help clients learn new, appropriate ways of acting, or to help them modify or eliminate excessive actions. In such cases, adaptive behaviours replace those that were maladaptive, and the counsellor functions as a learning specialist for the client (Fall, Holden, & Marquis, 2010).

Behavioural counselling approaches are especially popular in institutional settings, such as hospitals, mental health clinics, schools, and community counselling centres. They are the approaches of choice in working with clients who have specific problems such as eating disorders, substance abuse, and psychosexual dysfunction. Behavioural approaches are also useful in addressing difficulties associated with anxiety, stress, assertiveness, parenting, and social interaction (Cormier & Hackney, 2008; Seligman, 1997; 2006).

Behavioural Therapy

Founders and Developers B. F. (Burrhus Frederick) Skinner (1904–1990) is the person most responsible for the popularization of behavioural treatment methods. Applied behaviour analysis is "a direct extension of Skinner's (1953) radical behaviorism" (Wilson, 2008, p. 224), which is based on operant conditioning. Other notables in the behavioural therapy camp are historical figures such as Ivan Pavlov, John B. Watson, and Mary Cover Jones. Contemporary figures, such as Albert Bandura, John Krumboltz, Neil Jacobson, Steven Hayes, and Marsha Linehan, have also greatly added to this approach to working with clients.

View of Human Nature Behaviourists, as a group, share the following ideas about human nature (Rimm & Cunningham, 1985; Seligman, 2006):

- a concentration on behavioural processes—that is, processes closely associated with overt behaviour (except for cognitive-behaviourists)
- a focus on the here and now as opposed to the then and there of behaviour
- an assumption that all behaviour is learned, whether it be adaptive or maladaptive
- a belief that learning can be effective in changing maladaptive behaviour
- a focus on setting up well-defined therapy goals with clients
- a rejection of the idea that the human personality is composed of traits

In addition, behaviourists stress the importance of obtaining empirical evidence and scientific support for any techniques they use. Some behaviourists who embrace the social-cognitive form of learning stress that people acquire new knowledge and behaviour by observing other people and events without engaging in the behaviour themselves and without any direct consequences to themselves (i.e., modelling). This type of learning does not require active participation.

Role of the Counsellor A counsellor may take one of several roles, depending on his or her behavioural orientation and the client's goal(s). Generally, however, a behavioural counsellor is active in counselling sessions. As a result, the client learns, unlearns, or relearns specific ways of behaving. In the process, the counsellor functions as a consultant, teacher, adviser, reinforcer, and facilitator (James & Gilliland, 2003). He or she may even instruct or supervise support people in the client's environment who are assisting in the change process. An effective behavioural counsellor operates from a broad perspective and involves the client in every phase of counselling.

Goals The goals of behaviourists are similar to those of many other counsellors. Basically, behavioural counsellors want to help clients make good adjustments to life circumstances and achieve personal and professional objectives. Thus, the focus is on modifying or eliminating the maladaptive behaviours that clients display while helping them acquire healthy, constructive ways of acting. Just to eliminate a behaviour is not enough; unproductive actions must be replaced with productive ways of responding. A major step in the behavioural approach is for counsellors and clients to reach mutually agreed-upon goals.

Techniques Behavioural counsellors have at their disposal some of the best-researched and most effective counselling techniques available.

General Behavioural Techniques General techniques are applicable in all behavioural theories, although a given technique may be more applicable to a particular approach at a given time or in a specific circumstance. Some of the most general behavioural techniques are briefly explained here.

- *Use of reinforcers.* Reinforcers are those events that, when they follow a behaviour, increase the probability of the behaviour repeating. A reinforcer may be either positive or negative.
- *Schedules of reinforcement.* When a behaviour is first being learned, it should be reinforced every time it occurs—in other words, by continuous reinforcement. After a behaviour is established, however, it should be reinforced less frequently—in other words, by intermittent reinforcement. Schedules of reinforcement operate according to either the number of responses (*ratio*) or the length of time (*interval*) between reinforcers. Both ratio and interval schedules are either fixed or variable.
- *Shaping.* Behaviour learned gradually in steps through successive approximation is known as shaping. When clients are learning new skills, counsellors may help break down behaviour into manageable units.

- *Generalization.* Generalization involves the display of behaviours in environments outside of where they were originally learned (e.g., at home, at work). It indicates that transference into another setting has occurred.

- *Maintenance.* Maintenance is defined as being consistent in performing the actions desired without depending on anyone else for support. In maintenance, an emphasis is placed on increasing a client's self-control and self-management. One way this may be done is through self-monitoring, when clients learn to modify their own behaviours. It involves two self-monitoring related processes: self-observation and self-recording (Goldiamond, 1976). *Self-observation* requires that a person notice particular behaviours he or she does; *self-recording* focuses on recording these behaviours.

- *Extinction.* Extinction is the elimination of a behaviour because of a withdrawal of its reinforcement. Few individuals will continue doing something that is not rewarding.

- *Punishment.* Punishment involves presenting an aversive stimulus to a situation to suppress or eliminate a behaviour.

Specific Behavioural Techniques Specific behavioural techniques are refined behavioural methods that combine general techniques in precise ways. They are found in different behavioural approaches.

- *Behavioural rehearsal.* Behavioural rehearsal consists of practising a desired behaviour until it is performed the way a client wishes (Lazarus, 1985).

- *Environmental planning.* Environmental planning involves a client's setting up part of the environment to promote or limit certain behaviours.

- *Systematic desensitization.* Systematic desensitization is designed to help clients overcome anxiety in particular situations. A client is asked to describe the situation that causes anxiety and then to rank this situation and related events on a hierarchical scale (see Table 10.1), from aspects that cause no concern (0) to those that are most troublesome (100). To help the client avoid anxiety and face the situation, the counsellor teaches him or her to relax physically or mentally. The hierarchy is then reviewed, starting with low-anxiety items. When the client's anxiety begins to mount, the client is helped to relax again and the procedures then start anew until the client is able to be calm even when thinking about or imagining the event that used to create the most anxiety.

- *Assertiveness training.* The major tenet of assertiveness training is that a person should be free to express thoughts and feelings appropriately without undue anxiety (Alberti & Emmons, 2001). The technique consists of counter-conditioning anxiety and reinforcing assertiveness. A client is taught that everyone has the right (not the obligation) of self-expression. The client then learns the differences among aggressive, passive, and assertive actions.

- *Contingency contracts.* Contingency contracts spell out the behaviours to be performed, changed, or discontinued; the rewards associated with the achievement of these goals; and the conditions under which rewards are to be received (Corey, 2005).

Table 10.1 Joe's Anxiety Hierarchy

Amount of Anxiety (%)	Event
90	Marriage relationship
85	In-law relationship
80	Relating to my newborn child
75	Relating to my dad
70	Relating to my mother
65	General family relations and responsibilities
60	Being a project manager at work
50	Work in general
40	Coming to counselling
35	Personal finances
20	Having fun (being spontaneous)
10	Going to sleep

- *Implosion and flooding.* Implosive therapy is an advanced technique that involves desensitizing a client to a situation by having him or her imagine an anxiety-producing situation that may have dire consequences. The client is not taught to relax first (as in systematic desensitization). Flooding is less traumatic, as the imagined anxiety-producing scene does not have dire consequences.

- *Time-out.* Time-out is a mild aversive technique in which a client is separated from the opportunity to receive positive reinforcement. It is most effective when employed for short periods of time, such as five minutes.

- *Overcorrection.* Overcorrection is a technique in which a client first restores the environment to its natural state and then makes it "better than normal."

- *Covert sensitization.* Covert sensitization is a technique in which undesired behaviour is eliminated by associating it with unpleasantness.

Strengths and Contributions Among the unique and strong aspects of the behavioural approach are the following:

- The approach deals directly with symptoms. Because most clients seek help for specific problems, counsellors who work directly with symptoms are often able to assist clients immediately.

- The approach focuses on the here and now. A client does not have to examine the past to obtain help in the present. A behavioural approach saves both time and money.

- The approach offers numerous techniques for counsellors to use.

- The approach is based on learning theory, which is a well-formulated way of documenting how new behaviours are acquired (Bandura, 1977; 2004; Lipnevich & Smith, 2009; Thyer, 2008; Wong, 2008).

- The approach is buttressed by the Association for Behavioural and Cognitive Therapies (ABCT), which promotes the practice of behavioural counselling.

- The approach is supported by exceptionally good research on how behavioural techniques affect the process of counselling (Melnyk, 2009).

- The approach is objective in defining and dealing with problems and demystifies the process of counselling.

Limitations The behavioural approach has several limitations, among which are the following:

- The approach does not deal with the total person, just explicit behaviour. Critics contend that many behaviourists have taken the person out of personality.

- The approach is sometimes applied mechanically.

- The approach is best demonstrated under controlled conditions that may be difficult to replicate in normal counselling situations.

- The approach ignores the client's past history and unconscious forces.

- The approach does not consider developmental stages.

- The approach programs the client toward minimum or tolerable levels of behaving, reinforces conformity, stifles creativity, and ignores client needs for self-fulfillment, self-actualization, and feelings of self-worth (James & Gilliland, 2003).

Case Example: What Would *You* Do?

Betty came to see me because she was having trouble controlling her three-year-old son, Tyson. Tyson was rambunctious and difficult to control. Whenever Betty went shopping, Tyson would throw temper tantrums and draw much attention from other shoppers with his screaming. This would continue until she bought him what he wanted. She was exasperated.

1. What would you recommend Betty do when Tyson begins a tantrum?

2. Would spanking Tyson be helpful in correcting his behaviour? Why or why not?

COGNITIVE AND COGNITIVE-BEHAVIOURAL COUNSELLING

Cognitions are thoughts, beliefs, and internal images that people have about events in their lives (Holden, 1993; 2001). Cognitive counselling theories focus on mental processes and their influences on mental health and behaviour. A common premise of all cognitive approaches is that how people think largely determines how they feel and behave (Beck & Weishaar, 2008). As a rule, cognitive theories are successful with clients who have the following characteristics (Cormier & Hackney, 2008):

- They are average to above-average in intelligence.
- They have moderate to high levels of functional distress.
- They are able to identify thoughts and feelings.
- They are not psychotic or disabled by present problems.
- They are willing and able to complete systematic homework assignments.
- They possess a repertoire of behavioural skills and responses.
- They process information on visual and auditory levels.
- They frequently have inhibited mental functioning, such as depression.

Three theories that have a cognitive base—rational emotive behavioural therapy (REBT), reality therapy (RT), and cognitive therapy (CT)—are discussed here under the cognitive umbrella. In practice, these theories are cognitive-behavioural in nature because they emphasize both cognitions and behaviours. They are humanistic as well.

Rational Emotive Behaviourial Therapy (REBT)

Founders and Developers The founder of rational emotive behavioural therapy (REBT) is Albert Ellis (1913–2007). His theory has similarities to Aaron Beck's cognitive therapy (which was formulated independently at about the same time) and David Burns's new mood therapy. An interesting variation on REBT is rational behaviour therapy (RBT), which was developed by Maxie Maultsby and is more behavioural.

View of Human Nature Ellis (2008) believed that people have both self-interest and social interest. However, REBT also assumes that people are "inherently rational and irrational, sensible and crazy" (Weinrach, 1980, p. 154). According to Ellis (2008), this latter duality is biologically inherent and perpetuated unless a new way of thinking is learned (Dryden, 1994). *Irrational thinking*, or as Ellis defined it, *irrational Beliefs* (iBs), may include the invention of upsetting and disturbing thoughts.

Although Ellis did not deal with the developmental stages of individuals, he thought that children are more vulnerable to outside influences and irrational thinking than adults are. By nature, he believed human beings are gullible, highly suggestible, and easily disturbed. Overall, people have within themselves the means to control their thoughts, feelings, and actions, but they must first realize what they are telling themselves (*self-talk*) to gain command of their lives (Ellis, 1962; Weinrach, et al., 2001). This is a matter of personal, conscious awareness. The unconscious mind is not included in Ellis's conception of human nature. Furthermore, Ellis believed it is a mistake for people to evaluate or rate themselves beyond the idea that everyone is a fallible human being.

Role of the Counsellor In the REBT approach, counsellors are active and direct. They are instructors who teach and correct the client's cognitions. "Countering a deeply ingrained belief requires more than logic. It requires consistent repetition" (Krumboltz,

1992). Therefore, counsellors must listen carefully for illogical or faulty statements from their clients and must challenge beliefs. Ellis (1980) and Walen, DiGuiseppe, and Dryden (1992) identified several characteristics desirable for REBT counsellors. They need to be bright, knowledgeable, empathetic, respectful, genuine, concrete, persistent, scientific, interested in helping others, and users themselves of REBT.

Goals The primary goals of REBT focus on helping people realize that they can live more rational and productive lives. REBT helps clients stop making demands and becoming upset through "catastrophizing." Clients in REBT may express some negative feelings, but a major goal is to help them avoid having more of an emotional response to an event than is warranted (Weinrach et al., 2001).

Another goal of REBT is to help people change self-defeating habits of thought or behaviour. One way this is accomplished is through teaching clients the A-B-C-D-E model of REBT (See Table 10.2 for an example of the A-B-C-D-E model):

A signifies the activating experience;

B represents how the person thinks about the experience;

C is the emotional reaction to *B*.

D is disputing irrational thoughts, usually with the help of a REBT counsellor, and replacing them with

E, the effective thoughts and hopefully new personal philosophy that will help clients achieve great life satisfaction (Ellis, 2008).

Table 10.2 Example of the A-B-C-D-E Model

1. *A* (relationship breakup) → *C* (emotional devastation)

2. The *C* is moderated by *B* ("I cannot live without him/her. I will never fall in love again. I will become forever lonely and desperate")

3. *D*
   (a) Question: What evidence is there you cannot live without him/her? Answer: None, I can live without any particular person, albeit unhappily at the moment. My existence is not contingent on being in a relationship.
   (b) Question: What proof do you have that you will never fall in love again? Answer: None. I cannot predict the future. If I learn about what went wrong in this relationship, I increase the likelihood of making a better partner choice next time.
   (c) Question: What connection is there between losing this partner and becoming forever lonely? Answer: There is no connection really—it is just my feelings speaking. I have plenty of friends and family members, and they are still there for me. It is likely just a matter of time before I meet someone again who rocks my world.
   (d) Question: What truth is there in the idea that you need to be desperate because of this breakup? Answer: None—again, it is just my feelings speaking. Rationally, I could survive on a deserted island by myself if I was stranded. I would be frustrated, lonely, and unhappy, but even that would not mean I need to be *desperate*.

4. *E* (the edge is taken off your feeling of devastation. Instead of devastated, you now feel sad, hurt, angry, and filled with grief—all considered rational emotions given what you have experienced).

Through this process, REBT helps people learn how to recognize an *emotional anatomy*—that is, to learn how feelings are attached to thoughts. Thoughts about experiences may be characterized in four ways: positive, negative, neutral, or mixed.

REBT also encourages clients to be more tolerant of themselves and others and urges them to achieve personal goals. These goals are accomplished by having people learn to think rationally to change self-defeating behaviour and by helping them learn new ways of acting.

Case Example: What Would *You* Do?

Delores went wild one night at a sorority party and became noticeably drunk. The president of the sorority, Kissa, approached her, took the beer from her hand, and told her she had had too much to drink and that she would not be allowed to have another drink that night. Being a follower of the REBT philosophy, Delores knew she could think one of four ways. The easiest was negative:

"Kissa should have minded her own business and not taken my drink or scolded me!"

1. What might Delores have said to herself that was positive?

2. What mixed message could she have given herself?

3. How would those messages have affected her feelings?

Techniques REBT encompasses a number of diverse techniques. Two primary ones are teaching and disputing. Teaching involves having clients learn the basic ideas of REBT and understand how thoughts are linked with emotions and behaviours. This procedure is didactic and directive and is generally known as rational emotive education (REE).

Disputing thoughts and beliefs takes one of three forms: cognitive, imaginal, and behavioural. The process is most effective when all three forms are used (Walen et al., 1992). *Cognitive disputation* involves the use of direct questions, logical reasoning, and persuasion. *Imaginal disputation* uses a client's ability to imagine and employs a technique known as rational emotive imagery (REI) (Maultsby, 1984). *Behavioural disputation* involves behaving in a way that is the opposite of the client's usual way, including role-playing and the completion of a homework assignment in which the client actually does activities previously thought impossible to do. Sometimes behavioural disputation may take the form of bibliotherapy, in which clients read self-help books such as *A Guide to Rational Living* or *Staying Rational in an Irrational World.*

Two other powerful REBT techniques are confrontation and encouragement. REBT counsellors explicitly encourage clients to abandon thought processes that are not working and try REBT. Counsellors will also challenge a client who claims to be thinking rationally but in truth is not.

Strengths and Contributions REBT has a number of unique dimensions and special emphases.

- The approach is clear, easily learned, and effective. Most clients have few problems in understanding the principles or terminology of REBT.

- The approach can easily be combined with other behavioural techniques to help clients more fully experience what they are learning.

- The approach is relatively short in term and clients may continue to use the approach on a self-help basis.

- The approach has generated a great deal of literature and research for clients and counsellors. Few other theories have developed as much bibliotherapeutic material.

- The approach has continued to evolve over the years as techniques have been refined.

- The approach has been found effective in treating major mental health disorders such as depression and anxiety (Puterbaugh, 2006).

Limitations The limitations of the REBT approach are few but significant.

- The approach cannot be used effectively with individuals who have mental problems or limitations, such as schizophrenics and those with severe thought disorders.

- The approach may be too closely associated with its founder, Albert Ellis. Many individuals have difficulty separating the theory from Ellis's eccentricities.

- The approach is direct, and the potential for the counsellor to be overzealous and not as therapeutic as would be ideal is a real possibility (James & Gilliland, 2003).

- The approach's emphasis on changing thinking may not be the simplest way of helping clients change their emotions.

- REBT de-emphasizes the importance of the working alliance. Consequently, some clients will terminate counselling before they might potentially benefit from it (James & Gilliland, 2003).

Reality Therapy (RT)

Founders and Developers William Glasser (1925–) developed reality therapy in the mid-1960s. Robert Wubbolding advanced this approach through both his explanation of it and his research into it.

View of Human Nature Reality therapy does not include a comprehensive explanation of human development, as Freud's system does, yet it offers practitioners a focused view of some important aspects of human life and human nature. A major tenet of reality therapy is its focus on consciousness: Human beings operate on a conscious level; they are not driven by unconscious forces or instincts (Glasser, 1965; 1988; 2005).

A second belief about human nature is that everyone has a health/growth force (Glasser & Wubbolding, 1995) that is manifest on two levels: the physical and the psychological. Physically, there is the need to obtain life-sustaining necessities such as food, water, and shelter and to use them. According to Glasser, human behaviour was once controlled by the physical need for survival (e.g., behaviours such as breathing, digesting, and sweating). He associates these behaviours with physical, or old-brain, needs because they are automatically controlled by the body. In modern times, most important behaviour is associated with psychological, or new-brain, needs. The four primary psychological needs include the following:

1. *Love and belonging*—the need for friends, family, and love
2. *Power*—the need for self-esteem, recognition, and competition
3. *Freedom*—the need to make choices and decisions
4. *Fun*—the need for play, laughter, learning, and recreation

Associated with meeting these psychological needs is the need for *identity*—that is, the development of a psychologically healthy sense of self. Identity needs are met by being accepted as a person by others.

Reality therapy proposes that human learning is a life-long process based on choice. If individuals do not learn something early in life, such as how to relate to others, they can choose to learn it later. In the process they may change their identity and the way they behave (Glasser, 2000; 2005; Glasser & Wubbolding, 1995).

Role of the Counsellor The counsellor serves primarily as a teacher and model, accepting the client in a warm, involved way and creating an environment in which counselling can take place. The counsellor immediately seeks to build a relationship with the client by developing trust through friendliness, firmness, and fairness (Wubbolding, 1998). Counsellors use *-ing* verbs, such as *angering* or *bullying*, to describe client thoughts and actions. Thus, there is an emphasis on choice—on what the client chooses to do. Counsellor–client interaction focuses on behaviours that the client would like to change and ways to go about making these desires a reality. It emphasizes positive, constructive actions (Glasser, 1988; 2005). Special attention is paid to metaphors and themes clients verbalize.

Goals The primary goal of reality therapy is to help clients become psychologically strong and rational and realize they have choices in the ways they treat themselves and others. Related to this first goal is a second one: to help clients clarify what they want in life. It is vital for persons to be aware of life goals if they are to act responsibly. In assessing goals, reality therapists help their clients examine personal assets as well as environmental supports and hindrances. It is the client's responsibility to choose behaviours that fulfill personal needs. A third goal of reality therapy is to help the client formulate a realistic plan to achieve personal needs and wishes.

Another goal of reality therapy is to have the counsellor become involved with the client in a meaningful relationship (Glasser, 1980; 1981; 2000). This relationship is based on understanding, acceptance, empathy, and the counsellor's willingness to express faith in the client's ability to change. A fifth goal of reality therapy is to focus on behaviour and the present. Glasser (1988) believes that behaviour (i.e., thought and action) is interrelated with feeling and physiology. Thus, a change in behaviour also brings about other positive changes.

Finally, reality therapy aims to eliminate punishment and excuses from the client's life. Often, a client uses the excuse that he or she cannot carry out a plan because of punishment for failure by either the counsellor or people in the outside environment. Reality therapy helps the client formulate a new plan if the old one does not work.

Techniques Basically, reality therapy uses action-oriented techniques that help clients realize that they have choices in how they respond to events and people and that others do not control them any more than they control others (Glasser, 1998; Onedera & Greenwalt, 2007). Reality therapy eschews external control psychology and what Glasser (2000) calls its seven deadly habits (i.e., "criticizing, blaming, complaining, nagging, threatening, punishing, and bribing") (p. 79). Some of reality therapy's more effective and active techniques are teaching, employing humour, confronting, role-playing, offering feedback, formulating specific plans, and composing contracts.

Reality therapy uses the WDEP system as a way of helping counsellors and clients make progress and employ techniques. In this system, the *W* stands for *wants*; at the beginning of the counselling process, counsellors find out what clients want and what they have been doing (Wubbolding, 1988; 1991). Counsellors in turn share their wants for and perceptions of clients' situations. The *D* in WDEP involves clients further exploring the *direction* of their lives. Effective and ineffective self-talk is discussed and even confronted. Basic steps strategically incorporated in these two stages include establishing a relationship and focusing on present behaviour.

The *E* in the WDEP procedure stands for *evaluation* and is the cornerstone of reality therapy. Clients are helped to evaluate their behaviours and to determine how responsible their personal behaviours are. Behaviours that do not contribute to helping clients meet their needs often alienate them from the self and from significant others. If clients recognize a behaviour as unproductive, they may be motivated to change. If there is no recognition, the therapeutic process may break down. It is therefore crucial that clients, not the counsellor, do the evaluation. The use of humour, role-playing, and offering feedback can help at this juncture.

After evaluation, the final letter of the WDEP system, *P*, for *plan*, comes into focus. A client concentrates on making a plan for changing behaviours. The plan stresses actions that the client will take, not behaviours that he or she will eliminate. The best plans are simple, attainable, measurable, immediate, and consistent (Wubbolding, 1998). They are controlled by clients and are sometimes committed to the form of a written contract in which responsible alternatives are spelled out. Clients are then requested to make a commitment to the plan of action.

Strengths and Contributions Reality therapy has a number of strengths and has made contributions to counselling as follows:

- The approach is versatile and can be applied to many different populations. It is especially appropriate in the treatment of conduct disorders, substance abuse disorders, impulse control disorders, personality disorders, and antisocial behaviour. It can be employed in individual counselling with children, adolescents, adults, and the aged and in group, marriage, and family counselling.

- The approach is concrete. Both counsellor and client are able to assess how much progress is being made and in what areas, especially if a goal-specific contract is drawn up.

- The approach emphasizes short-term treatment. Reality therapy is usually limited to relatively few sessions that focus on present behaviours.

- The approach has national training centres and is taught internationally.

- The approach promotes responsibility and freedom in individuals without blame or criticism or an attempt to restructure the entire personality.

- The approach has successfully challenged the medical model of client treatment. Its rationale and positive emphasis are refreshing alternatives to pathology-centred models (James & Gilliland, 2003).

- The approach addresses conflict resolution.

- The approach stresses the present because current behaviour is most amenable to client control. Like behaviourists, Gestaltists, and rational emotive behaviour therapists, reality therapists are not interested in the past (Wubbolding, 2000).

Limitations Reality therapy also has limitations, among which are the following:

- The approach emphasizes the here and now of behaviour so much that it sometimes ignores other concepts, such as the unconscious and personal history.

- The approach holds that all forms of mental illness are attempts to deal with external events (Glasser, 1984). Consequently, clients are viewed as causing their own mental disorder through irresponsibility (James & Gilliland, 2003).

- The approach has few theoretical constructs, although it is now tied to choice theory, which means that it is becoming more sophisticated.

- The approach does not deal with the full complexity of human life, preferring to ignore developmental stages.

- The approach is susceptible to becoming overly moralistic.

- The approach is dependent on establishing a good counsellor–client relationship.

- The approach depends on verbal interaction and two-way communication. It has limitations in helping clients who, for any reason, cannot adequately express their needs, options, and plans (James & Gilliland, 2003).
- The approach keeps changing its focus (Corey, 2005).
- The approach reflects little appreciation for multicultural differences (James & Gilliland, 2003).

Cognitive Therapy (CT)

Founder and Developer Aaron Beck (1921–), a psychiatrist, is credited as the founder of cognitive therapy (CT). His initial work began about the same time as that of Ellis. Like Ellis, he was initially trained to be psychoanalytic and formulated his ideas about CT only after conducting research into the effectiveness of using psychoanalytic theories in the treatment of depression, which he found inadequate.

View of Human Nature Beck proposes that perception and experience are "active processes that involve both inspective and introspective data" (Tursi & Cochran, 2006, p. 388). Furthermore, how a person "apprises a situation is generally evident in his cognitions (thoughts and visual images)" (p. 388). Therefore, dysfunctional behaviour is caused by dysfunctional thinking. If beliefs do not change, there is no improvement in a person's behaviours or symptoms. If beliefs change, symptoms and behaviours change.

Role of the Counsellor The CT counsellor is active in sessions. He or she works with the client to make covert thoughts more overt. This process is especially important in examining cognitions that have become automatic, such as "Everyone thinks I'm boring."

Goals The goals of CT centre around examining and modifying unexamined and negative thoughts. CT counsellors especially hone in on excessive cognitive distortions, such as all-or-nothing thinking, negative prediction, overgeneralization, labelling of oneself, self-criticism, and personalization (i.e., taking an event unrelated to the individual and making it meaningful; "It always rains when I want to play tennis").

Simultaneously, counsellors work with clients on overcoming their lack of motivation, which is often linked with the tendency that clients have to view problems as insurmountable.

Techniques There are a number of techniques associated with CT.

- challenging the way individuals process information
- countering mistaken belief systems (i.e., faulty reasoning)
- doing self-monitoring exercises designed to stop negative "automatic thoughts"
- improving communication skills
- increasing positive self-statements and exercises
- doing homework, including disputing irrational thoughts

Table 10.3 provides an example of cognitive therapy in practice.

Table 10.3 An Example of Cognitive Therapy

Client:	I have never amounted to anything—I am a worthless person.
Counsellor:	You told me earlier that you have kept your full-time job for the past four years. The idea that you have never amounted to anything is an example of a cognitive distortion. Do you remember what this one is called?
Client:	It is an overgeneralization, I know. But I hate my job.
Counsellor:	I know, but this is something you can change once you are no longer depressed. How does being unhappy about your job suggest that you are a worthless person?
Client:	Well, I just don't feel I am worthwhile—my job sucks and so do I.
Counsellor:	Does not feeling worthwhile *mean* you are not worthwhile?
Client:	No, I guess not.
Counsellor:	You don't sound convinced.
Client:	You're right. I am trying not to feel this way, but I don't seem able to stop it.
Counsellor:	And your feelings are not something you have control over. Your thoughts, however, are something you can learn to have more control over with practice. How would you feel about using the triple column technique every time you *feel* that you are lacking in some way?
Client:	How does that work again?
Counsellor:	In the left column, write down the thoughts that accompany your negative feelings. In the second column, write down whichever cognitive distortions you are using. Then in the third column, write out healthier thoughts that you hope will become automatic at some point. Here is an example:

Automatic Thought(s)	Distortion(s)	Rational Response(s)
I am *not* a worthwhile person.	1. All-or-nothing thinking 2. Disqualifying the positive 3. Emotional reasoning 4. Labelling	Hating my job has nothing to do with my self-worth. My self-worth cannot be rated simply according to my success or failure at something, or whether I like something or not. One's worth cannot be reduced to all or nothing categories. Furthermore, I am not paying attention to the fact that I am actually very good at doing my job—evaluations have stated this every year. I need to stop labelling myself as one thing or another thing—I am a mixture of many qualities. My feelings will never be a reflection of my worth.

Client:	Thank you for the example. I will do this and bring back my completed triple columns next week. I will also spend time focusing every day on reflecting on the content in the third column. Thank you!
Counsellor:	Great—I will see you again next Thursday.

Strengths and Contributions Among the strengths of CT are the following:

- CT has been adapted to treat a wide range of disorders, including depression and anxiety (Puterbaugh, 2006).

- CT has spawned, in conjunction with cognitive-behavioural therapy, *dialectical behaviour therapy*, a psychosocial treatment for individuals who are at risk for self-harm, such as people diagnosed with borderline personality disorder (BPD). The objective is to help clients be more mindful and accepting of things that cannot be easily changed and live lives worth living (Day, 2008).

- CT is applicable in a number of cultural settings. For instance, Beck's model of cognitive therapy was introduced in China in 1989 and a variation of it has been popular there since (Chang, Tong, Shi, & Zeng, 2005).

- CT is a well-researched, evidence-based therapy that has proven effective for clients from multiple backgrounds.

- CT has spawned a number of useful and important clinical instruments, including the Beck Anxiety Inventory, the Beck Hopelessness Scale, and the Beck Depression Scale (Beck & Weishaar, 2008).

- CT has a number of training centres around the United States and Europe, including the Beck Institute in Bala Cynwyd, Pennsylvania (Beck & Weishaar, 2008).

Limitations The CT approach has several limitations, among which are the following:

- CT is structured and requires clients to be active, which often means completing homework assignments.

- CT is not an appropriate therapy for people seeking a more unstructured, insight-oriented approach that does not require their strong participation (Seligman, 2006).

- CT is primarily cognitive in nature and not usually the best approach for people who are intellectually limited or who are unmotivated to change.

- CT is demanding. Clinicians as well as clients must be active and innovative. The approach is more complex than it would appear on the surface.

- CT is harshly criticized by some feminist therapists and multicultural counsellors for its worldview, which is patriarchal and Euro-American in focus (James & Gilliland, 2003).

Stress Inoculation Training

Founder and Developer Donald Meichenbaum originated Stress Inoculation Training (SIT) in 1976 (Meichenbaum, 2007). He began his university career at the University of Waterloo in 1966 and retired in 1998. He continues to be an active and distinguished professor emeritus. He also helped open the Melissa Institute for Violence

Prevention and Treatment of Victims of Violence in Miami, Florida, and currently serves as its research director (see www.melissainstitute.org).

View of Human Nature The theory underlying SIT is the transactional view of stress and coping upheld by Lazarus and Folkman (1984). This view maintains that people experience stress when they perceive that the demands of a situation outweigh their perceived coping abilities to manage it. Consequently, stress "lies in the eyes of the beholder" (Meichenbaum, 2007, p. 500). SIT also adheres to a constructive narrative perspective, meaning that people create narratives (i.e., stories) about themselves, others, the world, and their future. Both theories emphasize the role of subjective cognitions in creating stressful reactions.

Role of the Counsellor SIT counsellors help clients become aware of behaviours that maintain and increase the clients' distress. They help clients develop a more adaptive narrative (a new life story) and to engage in constructive problem-solving activities. This also means teaching clients skills in emotional regulation, coping, and cognitive restructuring.

Goals The goal of SIT is to strengthen clients' coping skills so that they can deal more effectively with life stressors. It is also focused on helping clients develop a healthier narrative to enhance various aspects of their lives and to move from a "survivor" to a "thriver" mentality.

Techniques Meichenbaum (2007) considers SIT to be a flexible and individually tailored form of cognitive-behaviour therapy. It neither advocates a set of "canned" interventions, nor does it act as a panacea. It is often used as a supplement along with other interventions. There are three interrelated phases of treatment: (a) the conceptual educational phase, (b) the skills acquisition and consolidation phase, and (c) the application and follow-through phase.

- *Skill acquisition and consolidation phase.* A working alliance is first created with the client. Through a Socratic dialogue (questioning stance), clients learn about the nature and impact of their stress and their coping resources. Several techniques are used to help clients reconceptualize their stressful experiences and their reactions so that they begin to become and feel empowered and resourceful.

- *Skills acquisition and consolidation phase.* Here the counsellor helps clients acquire coping skills and consolidate those they already possess. They are first taught in the clinical setting and then practised in real life.

- *Application and follow-through phase.* Clients apply their newly learned coping skills in a graduated way, increasing the demands as they progress. This is where they become *inoculated* from their stresses at increasing intensity. The techniques commonly used include many of the behavioural methods described earlier in the chapter: imagery and behavioural rehearsal, modelling, role-playing, and shaping.

A central feature of SIT is the teaching of relapse prevention procedures. Acting like a trainer, the counsellor explores with clients a variety of potential high-risk stressful situations. The client is coached collaboratively in rehearsing and practising coping skills that could be used in such situations (Meichenbaum, 2007).

Strengths and Contributions SIT has been found useful with acute time-limited stressors (e.g., preparing for exams, dental work), invasive medical examinations (e.g., biopsies, cardiac catheterization), traumatic events (e.g., terrorist attacks, sexual assaults, natural disasters), grief caused by major losses (e.g., death of a loved one, unemployment), chronic intermittent stressors (e.g., competitions), episodic physical disorders (e.g., migraine headaches), occupational stressors (e.g., military combat), and chronic stressors (e.g., severe medical or psychiatric illnesses, marital or familial discord, poverty) (Meichenbaum, 1996a; 2007; Sheehy & Horan, 2004). A meta-analysis has shown SIT's effectiveness with children and adolescents (Maag & Kotlash, 1994). It has demonstrated effectiveness in reducing anxiety (Saunders, Driskell, Johnston, & Salas, 1966) and Meichenbaum (1996b) and is effective with post-traumatic stress disorder and with anger control and aggressive behaviours (Meichenbaum, 2001).

Limitations There are currently no limitations reported in the published literature regarding SIT. The reader should not assume there are none, however—it is more likely that researchers have simply focused their efforts elsewhere.

RECENT APPROACHES IN COGNITIVE-BEHAVIOURAL COUNSELLING

A so-called "new wave" of behavioural approaches (Cirarrochi & Robb, 2005) has emerged over the past few years. Instead of challenging dysfunctional thoughts, the emphasis in these new approaches is to become mindful of their content and in some cases to learn to accept them. *Mindfulness* is defined as "the awareness that emerges through paying attention on purpose, in the present moment, and nonjudgmentally to the unfolding of experience" (Kabat-Zinn, 2003, p. 145).

These "new wave" approaches—which some argue are merely additions to earlier ones and are not as new wave as some would like to believe (Leahy, 2008; Salzinger, 2008)—include the following: (a) mindfulness-based stress reduction (MBSR), (b) mindfulness-based cognitive therapy (MBCT); (c) dialectical behaviour therapy (DBT), and (d) acceptance and commitment therapy (ACT). These approaches have received a substantial amount of empirical support (Cirarrochi & Robb, 2005a). However, the Canadian Psychiatric Association and the Canadian Network for Mood and Anxiety Treatments recently partnered to create evidence-based clinical guidelines for the treatment of depressive disorders and concluded that ACT, motivational interviewing (not reviewed here), MBCT, and psychodynamic therapies do not have sufficient evidence as acute treatments (Parikh et al., 2009).

Lau and colleagues (2006) developed a measure of mindfulness that they call the Toronto Mindfulness Scale (TMS). The TMS has good psychometric properties and is predictive of treatment outcome.

Although each of the approaches described here focuses on developing mindfulness skills, the methods for teaching it vary. While MBSR and MBCT incorporate regular meditation practices to teach mindfulness skills, DBT teaches psychological and behavioural versions of meditation and ACT teaches non-meditative aspects of mindfulness (Burke, 2010).

Mindfulness-Based Stress Reduction

Founder and Developer Jon Kabat-Zinn (1984; 1990) is the originator of mindfulness-based stress reduction (MBSR). While MBSR is not specifically designed to produce relaxation, it often creates it. Its primary goal is to bring out a state of nonjudgmental awareness of body and mind without having any expectation of producing a result (Allen, Blashki, & Gullone, 2006).

View of Human Nature The idea and practice of mindfulness is rooted in many contemplative, cultural, and philosophical traditions. Buddhism, for example, provides many instructions on mindfulness practices (Allen et al., 2006). Mindfulness has been adopted by many individuals and counsellors of varied philosophies, religions, and cultures; one cannot say that it purports any particular view of human nature. It is accepted as a means by which one can create feelings of personal well-being, however.

Role of the Counsellor counsellor teaching MBSR will lead a group of up to 30 participants for eight to ten group sessions (Bohlmeijera, Prengera, Taala, & Cuijpersb, 2010). The central purpose of each session is to teach mindfulness.

Goals The "primary goal [of MBSR] is the integration of mindfulness into everyday life as a support in dealing with the individual's unique stressful life situations" (Patel, Carmody, & Simpson, 2007, p. 376). MBSR is designed to help people learn to become mindful and present of their psychological states. In so doing, it is intended to help individuals regulate their emotions and reduce the impact of negative emotions (Goldin & Gross, 2010). Furthermore, mindfulness is intended to help people become more aware of automatic and destructive responses so that they can make conscious choices (Learning Strategies Development, 2006).

Techniques There are a variety of techniques used in MBSR, and they all focus on meditative activities (Allen et al., 2006). Techniques may include (a) mindfulness of movement, (b) brief periods of "mindful meditation" throughout the day, and (c) the concept of everyday mindfulness (i.e., trying to be aware of the present as much as possible). Clients might also be taught body scans and yoga as ways of becoming more mindful.

Bishop (2002) described sitting mediation as a way of illustrating MBSR. It involves the following components:

1. *Posture*. Maintain an upright sitting posture in a chair or cross-legged on the floor.

2. *Attend to breathing*. Sustain attention to each breath.

3. *Acknowledge and accept thoughts*. Participants acknowledge and accept whatever thoughts and feelings arise without making judgments. They then relinquish these as they return their focus to breathing.

The format is skill-based and psychoeducational. Clients are taught about stress and emotions and much time is devoted to experiential exercises. A substantial amount of time is spent in discussion of various mindfulness techniques. Clients are expected to practise the techniques outside the sessions, and they are typically given audio recordings to guide them through the exercises (Bishop, 2002).

Strengths and Contributions MBSR has been found useful in the following ways:

- MBSR has been used in hospital clinics and community settings for 25 years. It has been found helpful in reducing anxiety, stress, affective disorders, and disordered eating (Allen et al., 2006).

- In a meta-analytic study, MBSR was shown to be effective in reducing stress levels in healthy people (Chiesa & Serretti, 2009).

- It may help improve cancer patients' adjustment to their disease (Ledesma & Kumano, 2009) and have long-term benefits for women with fibromyalgia (Grossman, Tiefenthaler-Gilmer, Raysz, & Kesper, 2007).

- To date, there have not been any negative side effects documented for MBSR (Praissman, 2008).

- Overall, research provides support for its use with children and adolescents, although more rigorous studies are needed to confirm this (Burke, 2010). A recent meta-analysis revealed that MBSR has small effects on depression, anxiety, and psychological distress for people experiencing physical disorders (Bohlmeijera et al., 2010).

Limitations The following limitations to MBSR have been found:

- In their review of controlled research, Toneatto and Nguyen (2007) concluded that "MBSR does not have a reliable effect on depression and anxiety" (p. 260).

- Further studies are needed to verify its effectiveness, particularly as compared to other cognitive-behavioural treatments (Allen et al., 2006).

- Furthermore, Allen et al. (2006) mention other limitations:

  (a) *The time investment*. The minimum amount of time needed to gain certain benefits is unknown, and practitioners vary widely in their offerings.

  (b) *Possible worsening of psychiatric symptoms*. Empirical evidence regarding meditation in general (not on MBSR specifically) has found that some mediators experience distracting thoughts, uncomfortable emotions, altered reality testing, feelings of depersonalization, psychotic symptoms in those already predisposed and in some without psychiatric histories, and worsening of depression. Shapiro (1992) found that 7.4% of 27 long-term meditators experienced several unpleasant reactions.

(c) *Group delivery.* Most psychiatrists and many other mental health professionals are accustomed to seeing clients individually. Consequently, counselling groups may not be part of their repertoire.

(d) *Not a panacea.* Mindfulness "requires sustained effort, [it] can have associated discomfort, and [it] is not without potential for adverse consequences" (Allen et al., 2006, p. 292).

Mindfulness-Based Cognitive Therapy

Founder and Developer Major depression is often a chronic relapsing condition, with between 50% and 80% of sufferers experiencing more than one bout in their lifetime (Williams et al., 2010). Mindfulness-based cognitive therapy (MBCT) was developed by Segal, Williams, and Teasdale (2002) with the intent of preventing relapses into depression. MBCT is derived from mindfulness-based stress reduction and cognitive-behavioural therapy (Allen, Bromley, Kuyken, & Sonnerberg, 2009; Evans et al., 2008). MBCT is taught as eight two-hour group classes with eight to twelve participants per group (Allen et al., 2009).

View of Human Nature The theory underlying MBCT is that people become episodically depressed because they have learned to strongly associate negative cognitions with low mood states. Once a low mood develops, the person becomes unable to break free of the "closed circuit of self-devaluative thinking" (Allen et al., 2009, p. 423). It is also hypothesized that the mindfulness training aspect of MBCT enables depressed individuals to reflect on past crises in a detailed yet detached way, fostering more positive associations that help prevent relapse (Hargus, Crane, Barnhofer, & Williams, 2010).

Role of the Counsellor The counsellor's role is to train clients in mindfulness practices and cognitive-behavioural techniques in a psychoeducational group format.

Goals The goal of MBCT is to reduce the risk of relapse into depression by teaching individuals to become aware of factors that lead to it (Oberman, 2009). The intent of MBCT is for people to learn to become more aware of bodily sensations, thoughts, and feelings that are associated with depressive relapse and to learn to reconstruct these experiences (Allen et al., 2009).

Techniques According to Crane (2009), four strategies are used in MBCT.

1. *Encourage clients to eliminate ruminative thinking.* This helps clients become aware of their negative thinking patterns.

2. *Increase clients' awareness of their relapse potential.* Clients are taught to avoid *mindlessness* (i.e., being on "automatic pilot"). This requires that clients learn to acknowledge their habitual thought patterns and to learn to think and act in different ways.

3. *Change clients' mindsets.* Clients move from self-sabotaging ways of thinking to establishing and working toward goals, thereby shifting their mindsets.

4. *Encourage clients to engage in new experiences in a mindful way.* Clients are taught to become involved in life while continuing to observe what is happening.

Crane (2009) describes how to conduct a MBCT group in her book. One activity intended to teach mindfulness is to have the clients eat a raisin. Before doing so, however, they are instructed to observe, touch, and smell it before eating it. Another technique is the body scan, during which clients are guided through relaxation while they attend to movements from their toes to their heads. During walking meditation, clients are asked to focus on the sensation of each footstep rather than on their destination.

Strengths and Contributions   MBCT has been found useful in the following ways:

- Outcome research has shown that, when compared to typical treatments for depression, MBCT boasts half the relapse rate over a 60-week follow-up period with clients who have experienced three or more previous major depressive episodes (Allen et al., 2009). MBCT has also been shown helpful in reducing suicidal thoughts and behaviours (Williams & Swales, 2004).

- Clients who have experienced MBCT report that it has given them a sense of greater control over depression and greater acceptance of their depression-related feelings and thoughts (Allen et al., 2009). Clients also value the development of mindfulness skills (Mason & Hargreaves, 2001).

- Hick and Chan (2010) reported that theirs was the first review of using MBCT in social work practice. They concluded that social workers should use MBCT with clients to help decrease depressive relapses.

- Ree and Craigie (2007) suggested that MBCT may be helpful for a range of psychological conditions.

- MBCT may be effective as an adjunct to pharmacotherapy for people experiencing panic disorder (Kim et al., 2009; 2010) and generalized anxiety disorder (Kim et al., 2009).

- There is research suggesting that MBCT-C (a modified 12-session program) holds promise in helping children with attention and behaviour problems (Semple, Lee, Rosa, & Miller, 2010).

Limitations   The following limitations to MBCT have been found:

- It is not understood how MBCT actually works to prevent relapse (Allen et al., 2009).

- Depressed individuals are prone to self-devaluation and some participants in the study by Allen et al. (2009) reported that they believed they had failed at learning mindfulness practices properly.

Dialectical Behaviour Therapy (DBT)

Founder and Developer   DBT was developed by Marsha M. Linehan and her colleagues in the early 1990s. Linehan worked with chronically suicidal self-injurious women and found they did not respond to conventional behavioural methods. Most of her clients would have met the criteria for borderline personality disorder (BPD). Her belief was that their central problem was emotion dysregulation, which would lead to such issues as mood swings and anger problems (Koons, 2008).

View of Human Nature   Linehan theorized that those with BPD had a biological predisposition to emotion dysregulation, but this was compounded when these individuals had a history of ongoing and persistent invalidation. Her theory is thus known as a biosocial theory (Koons, 2008).

The theory is deterministic in that its roots and methods are anchored in behaviourism, Zen principles, and dialectics. "Zen emphasizes the wisdom inherent in each individual" (Koons, 2008, p. 113). DBT incorporates core mindfulness skills that derive from Zen. The idea of mindfulness is for the individual to focus all attention on one thing at a time with a nonjudgmental, accepting stance (Koons, 2008).

Dialectics advances the idea that "truth is found in the struggle of opposites" (Koons, 2008, p. 114). A dialectical truth moves from a thesis to an antithesis to a synthesis. For example, if a client's practice is to yell at people when she gets upset (thesis) but she stops doing this, she will likely experience greater stress. Greater stress, in turn, may mean that she takes more tranquilizers to cope (antithesis). Eventually, she could be taught to cope with the stress by talking assertively to people instead of yelling at them (synthesis).

Role of the Counsellor   The DBT counsellor is active in sessions. He or she works with the five functions of DBT delivered in four modes across four stages. The functions include (a) enhancing capabilities, (b) increasing motivation, (c) enhancing generalization outside of counselling sessions, (d) structuring the environment, and (e) enhancing the counsellor's ability and motivation to be effective. The four modes include (a) working within a dyadic relationship between counsellor and client; (b) skills training aimed at teaching clients mindfulness, distress tolerance, emotional regulation, and interpersonal effectiveness; (c) skills generalization; and (d) use of a consultation team to support the counsellors themselves and thereby reduce the likelihood of burnout. Finally, the four stages of DBT include (a) eliminating the most disabling and dangerous behaviours, (b) shifting client from desperation to experiencing emotions, (c) dealing with problems in living, and (d) helping the client experience freedom and joy (Lynch, Trost, Salsman, & Linehan, 2007).

Goals The main goal of DBT is to balance acceptance and change, a middle position common to Zen practice. Furthermore, the counsellor helps the client to develop synthesis with the dialectical tensions that arise when a thesis leads to an antithesis (Koons, 2008).

Techniques An enormous number of techniques have come to be associated with DBT; here only the two core strategies will be mentioned.

- *Problem solving*. These strategies mostly emerge from behavioural and cognitive therapies. It begins with behavioural assessment of the problem by looking at the antecedents and consequences of behaviours. After a thorough assessment, interventions are decided and implemented.

- *Validation*. The counsellor validates the client's thoughts, feelings, and behaviours throughout treatment. This fits with a biosocial perspective in that the client's experience is understandable given all the factors that affect him or her.

Strengths and Contributions DBT has been found useful in the following ways:

- Lynch et al. (2007, p. 201) claim that the "literature quickly reveals that DBT is the only treatment for BPD [borderline personality disorder] considered well established or efficacious and specific."

- Research on DBT has shown it to be an empirically supported treatment for BPD (Lynch et al., 2007).

- DBT has demonstrated effectiveness to some extent with a wide range of psychological disorders (Dimeff & Koerner, 2007).

- With adaptations, it also has demonstrated some degree of effectiveness with adolescent problems (Katz, Fott, & Postl, 2009).

Limitations Two limitations cited in the literature include the following:

- The benefits of DBT for suicidal adolescents remains unknown despite encouraging results found in preliminary studies (Katz et al., 2009).

- When compared to three other methods of psychotherapy to help BPD clients, Zanarini (2009) concludes that DBT has not shown itself to be superior.

Acceptance and Commitment Therapy

Founder and Developer Acceptance and commitment therapy (ACT, pronounced as the word "act") was developed by Steven C. Hayes during the 1990s, together with Strasahl and Wilson (Hayes, Strosahl, & Wilson, 1999). ACT was designed to be an approach that integrates acceptance and mindfulness with commitment and behaviour change strategies (Pull, 2009).

View of Human Nature Philosophically, ACT is rooted in functional contextualism, and is theoretically rooted in relational frame theory. *Functional textualism* views events as though they are actions that shift in response to a specific context. It does not concern itself with the logic or evidence for a particular thought but focuses on its context (Ruiz, 2010). Functional textualists are interested in how thoughts predict and influence behaviour.

Relational frame theory (RFT) concerns itself with "how language influences cognition, emotion, and behavior" (Arch & Craske, 2008, p. 264). It is a learned ability to relate arbitrary events into something the mind perceives as meaningful, as well as to change the functions of events based on their relationship to one another (Arch & Craske, 2008). Here is an example: You are electrically shocked by person A (a person of small stature) but you later find out that person B (larger stature) was watching. According to RFT, you will have a greater emotional response when in the presence of person B (Arch & Craske, 2008). In this way, RFT argues that language becomes associated with psychopathology. ACT hypothesizes that psychological disorders develop when people try to avoid events, such as thoughts, feelings, memories, and body sensations, that are experienced as aversive (Ruiz, 2010).

Role of the Counsellor ACT counsellors are active in sessions. They work to accomplish two tasks: (a) to promote values clarification and to act in accordance with these values (i.e., *commit* to values-based action), and (b) to promote diffusion between the valued endpoint (i.e., goal attainment) and the private fear residing within the person (Ruiz, 2010).

Goals The primary goal of ACT is to help people become more flexible so that they overcome their avoidance behaviour. The way this is achieved is for clients to become able to experience the present moment more fully and consciously (i.e., mindfulness) and to either change or continue behaviour that serves a purpose they value. Instead of fearing the event the client avoids, the client is taught to *accept* it rather than trying to control it. The goal is not to directly reduce discomfort but instead to act despite its presence. The intent is to live in the moment while accepting whatever one is experiencing, whether it is good or bad.

Techniques There are a number of techniques associated with ACT.

- ACT makes use of metaphors, paradoxes, and experiential exercises (Ruiz, 2010) to obtain its objectives. The goal is not to reduce or extinguish the discomfort but to help clients learn to experience their privately feared events while achieving their valued goals.

- Counsellors make use of six core processes in ACT (Baruch, Kanter, Busch, & Juskiewicz, 2009):

  1. *Acceptance*—encouraging clients to accept privately feared events.

  2. *Cognitive defusion*—targeting problems with *fusion*, which are attempts to decrease the control that thoughts have without changing their content (i.e.,

accepting threatening thoughts). The intent in defusion is to learn to distance oneself "from the literal meaning and content of language" (Arch & Craske, 2008, p. 265). For example, trying to stop feeling anxious may actually contribute to the problem and not the solution (Hofmann & Asmundson, 2008)

3. *Self-as-context*—defusing the effect that one's own use of words have on promoting avoidant behaviour (e.g., accepting the thought of "I can't do it" while doing it anyway).

4. *Contact with the present moment*—increasing clients' awareness of their current experience (e.g., thoughts, feelings, sensations).

5. *Values*—helping clients to identify and clarify their values so they have a clear rationale for why they need to accept the feared events that try and hold them back from achieving their valued goals.

6. *Committed action*—learn to become congruent with stated values and actual behaviour (i.e., clients doing what they say is important to them).

Strengths and Contributions   The following strengths are evident in the ACT approach:

■ The most recent review of ACT finds that it is an efficacious treatment for a wide range of problems, particularly where avoidance is a dynamic. Several of these studies demonstrated these results after very few sessions (Ruiz, 2010).

■ ACT has received some empirical support for helping people experiencing psychotic symptoms, depression, anxiety, epilepsy, substance abuse, chronic skin picking, hair pulling, obsessive-compulsive disorder, and diabetic management (Baruch et al., 2009).

■ Hofmann and Asmundson (2008) state that learning to regulate emotional states is important in facilitating social adjustment and overall well-being.

Limitations   The ACT approach has several limitations, among which are the following:

■ The research base supporting ACT has been criticized for not fulfilling the criteria of what constitutes an empirically-validated treatment (Ost, 2008).

■ Pull (2009) concluded that there is a need for better controlled studies to verify whether ACT is as or more effective than traditional CBT. A more recent meta-analytic review found that ACT was more effective than waiting-list and no-treatment conditions but that it was not more effective than traditional, established CBT treatments (Powers, Zum Vorde Sive Vording, & Emmelkamp, 2009). Levin and Hayes (2009) re-analyzed Powers et al.'s (2009) database, however, and concluded that ACT is, in fact, better than traditional treatments. Ruiz (2010) concluded that the comparison of ACT's and CBT's efficacy is just beginning.

■ Hofmann (2008) wonders if ACT is even a new approach at all as it has many similarities with Morita therapy, which was developed 80 years ago.

SUMMARY AND CONCLUSION

This chapter covered behavioural counselling, four cognitive-behavioural theories—rational emotive behavioural therapy (REBT), reality therapy (RT), cognitive therapy (CT), and stress inoculation training (SIT)—and four recent cognitive-behavioural approaches—mindfulness-based stress reduction (MBSR), mindfulness-based cognitive therapy (MBCT), dialectical behaviour therapy (DBT), and acceptance and commitment therapy (ACT).

All of these approaches are widely used and in demand because of the premises on which they are based and their effectiveness in practice. The fact that none of them are extensive in regard to time commitment is a positive factor influencing their popularity.

Your Personal Reflections

1. Refer back to the section called "Schedules of Reinforcement" found earlier in the chapter. Now think of times when you have been on the various schedules described there. Which did you prefer? Why?

2. When have you made a new plan when your old plan did not work? When have you abandoned your plan altogether? What made the difference?

3. Which of the mindfulness approaches have the greatest appeal to you? Why? How could you incorporate this approach into your life right now?

Classroom Activities

1. What theories of counselling covered in this chapter and the preceding one most appeal to you? Can you imagine integrating them in such a way that you could develop a healthy eclectic approach? Discuss your ideas with a fellow classmate. Be as specific as possible.

2. Think about the approaches generated by Albert Ellis and Aaron Beck. Which would you prefer if you were a client? Name some specific reasons.

3. What do you see as the main advantages of a behavioural counselling approach? Where would you use or not use behavioural counselling?

4. Cognitive-behavioural approaches to counselling have been found, for the most part, to be very effective. What aspects of this approach make it so potent?

5. Get together with one other student in the class. Role-play as though one of you is a reality therapist and the other the client. As client, talk about a problem you are currently having that has to do with school or your academic performance. After explaining the problem for a few minutes, both of you together should look at what psychological need is being thwarted as a result of the problem. (The psychological needs are love and belonging, power, freedom, and/or fun.) Look at the various options for resolving or minimizing the impact of the problem by focusing on changing behaviour, *not* by changing cognitions (thoughts) or feelings. Finally, discuss the natural consequences that would likely result if the client were to follow the various options.

6. Engage in a class discussion focused on the four recent additions to cognitive-behaviour therapy (i.e., MBSR, MBCT, DBT, and ACT). Is mindfulness complementary or contradictory to traditional forms of cognitive-behaviour therapy? Why or why not? When students in the class are having problems with anxiety or depression to varying degrees, which would they find more helpful—an approach based on disputing the irrationality or illogical aspects underlying the negative thoughts or an approach based on developing an awareness and acceptance of these thoughts? Why or why not?

Chapter 11
Humanistic Theories of Counselling

PRACTICE REFLECTION

Making important life decisions is required of all of us, and we are the ones who must live with the consequences. When Daniel, aged 32, came into my office, I saw a defeated person who had no sense of direction. After a deep sigh, Daniel began, "I am confused about everything in my life right now. I've worked at Wendy's since I dropped out of school after Grade 10, and although I was told I would likely be a manager within five years, I am still flipping burgers. I don't think I would make a good manager anyway, because I am shy and I don't have any confidence. I also want to get married but there is no woman that shows interest in me."

"Daniel," I replied, "You sound really disappointed that your life is not what you expected it to be by now." "Yes, I am disappointed, but actually, I think my problem is that I never knew what I wanted."

"Do you mean that you never had a plan for what you consider important in life?" I asked. "Correct," Daniel said, "I never gave it much thought." "It sounds like that has now changed for you—you are now looking for a sense of direction." "Yes, and the sooner the better—I have witnessed most of my good friends get married and have children. I want this too." I replied, "I understand this, Daniel. You feel stuck and you want to begin moving forward. Tell me about your pursuit to find a life partner." "That's a big problem. I haven't actually ever had a date in my life. I try to get the courage to ask a woman out, and inevitably I seize at the last minute," Daniel lamented. I said, "Your shyness has been to your detriment. Nonetheless, you are now ready to do something about this and not let shyness stand in the way of your happiness."

"Exactly! But what do I do?" "Let me throw it back at you, Daniel—what are *you* prepared to do?" "Well, I have thought about calling a dating service, although I don't know if I can afford this on my meager salary," Daniel pondered. I said, "If the service was too expensive, what other alternatives can you think of that you would be willing to explore?"

The session continued in a similar manner and by the end of it, Daniel had decided to force himself to join a singles club that he knew was inexpensive. Over a few other sessions, he began to focus on career planning. It was my pleasure to see Daniel take responsibility for his life and pursue goals that were important to him. He came back to see me several months later and he had started dating a woman who was very gregarious—pretty much the opposite of Daniel in this regard. Through her social network, Daniel began to develop better social skills, which in turn increased his confidence. I was glad that he was putting his commitments into action.

While the behavioural, psychoanalytic and psychodynamic approaches were dominating the first half of the 20th century, some theorists were becoming disgruntled with the negative and deterministic view that these theories held toward people. Such a view was surely not helped by world events such as World War II and the Holocaust, and the famous Milgram experiment that shed doubt as to whether we could be anything more than sheep (under the right behavioural circumstances) or better than the depravity of our own unconscious minds (our "ids" running wild). Do we not have free will and, consequently, do we have not some responsibility for our own behaviour?

The stage was set for a new movement in psychology, the third force, and the name for it was "humanism," suggesting in name alone a greater concern for the person and his or her ability to move in a self-chosen direction, a direction propelled by a desire to become a "better" person. This new ideology appeared to spring up everywhere, from the flower children of San Francisco and Vancouver to the growing discontent of young people everywhere with government and its power over one's destiny. From humanistic philosophy emerged the most nondirective form of counselling that was yet to hit the therapeutic scene: "person-centred counselling."

HUMANISTIC THEORIES

THE TERM HUMANISTIC, AS A DESCRIPTOR OF COUNSELLING, FOCUSES ON THE POTENTIAL OF individuals to actively choose and purposefully decide about matters related to themselves and their environments. Professionals who embrace humanistic counselling approaches help people increase self-understanding through experiencing their feelings. The term is broad and encompasses counselling theories that are focused on people as decision makers and initiators of their own growth and development. Three of these theories are covered here: person-centred, existential, and Gestalt.

Person-Centred Counselling

Founders and Developers Carl Rogers (1902–1987) is the person most identified with person-centred counselling. Indeed, it was Rogers who first formulated the theory in the form of nondirective psychotherapy in his 1942 book, *Counseling and Psychotherapy*. The theory later evolved into client-centred and person-centred counselling with multiple applications to groups, families, and communities as well as individuals.

View of Human Nature Implicit in person-centred counselling is a particular view of human nature: People are essentially good (Rogers, 1961). Humans are characteristically "positive, forward-moving, constructive, realistic, and trustworthy" (Rogers, 1957, p. 199). Each person is aware, inner-directed, and moving toward self-actualization from infancy on.

According to Rogers, self-actualization is the most prevalent and motivating drive of existence and encompasses actions that influence the total person. "The organism has one basic tendency and striving, to actualize, maintain, and enhance the experiencing organism" (Rogers, 1951, p. 487). Person-centred theorists believe that each person is capable of finding a personal meaning and purpose in life. "Dysfunctionality is really a failure to learn and change" (Bohart, 1995, p. 94).

Rogers views the individual from a *phenomenological perspective*: What is important is the person's perception of reality rather than an event itself (Rogers, 1955). This way of seeing the person is similar to Adler's. The concept of self is another idea that Rogers and Adler share. But for Rogers the concept is so central to his theory that his ideas are often referred to as *self theory*. The self is an outgrowth of what a person experiences, and an awareness of self helps a person differentiate him- or herself from others (Nye, 2000).

For a healthy self to emerge, a person needs *positive regard*—love, warmth, care, respect, and acceptance. But in childhood, as well as later in life, a person often receives *conditional regard* from parents and others. Feelings of worth develop if the person behaves in certain ways because conditional acceptance teaches the person to feel valued only when conforming to others' wishes. Thus, a person may have to deny or distort a perception when someone on whom the person depends for approval sees a situation differently. An individual who is caught in such a dilemma becomes aware of incongruities between self-perception and experience. If a person does not do as others wish, he or she will not be accepted and valued. Yet if a person conforms, he or she opens up a gap between the *ideal self* (what the person is striving to become) and the *real self* (what the person is). The further the ideal self is from the real self, the more alienated and maladjusted a person becomes.

Role of the Counsellor   The counsellor's role is a holistic one. He or she sets up and promotes a climate in which the client is free and encouraged to explore all aspects of self (Rogers, 1951; 1980). This atmosphere focuses on the counsellor–client relationship, which Rogers describes as one with a special "I-Thou" personal quality. The counsellor is aware of the client's verbal and nonverbal language, and the counsellor reflects back what he or she is hearing or observing (Braaten, 1986). Neither the client nor the counsellor knows what direction the sessions will take or what goals will emerge in the process. The client is a person in process who is "entitled to direct his or her own therapy" (Moon, 2007, p. 277). Thus, the counsellor trusts the client to develop an agenda on which he or she wishes to work. The counsellor's job is to work as a facilitator rather than a director. In the person-centred approach, the counsellor is the process expert and expert learner (of the client). Patience is essential (Miller, 1996).

Goals   The goals of person-centred counselling focus on the client as a person, not on his or her problem. Rogers (1977) emphasizes that people need to be assisted in learning how to cope with situations. One of the main ways to accomplish this is by helping a client become a fully functioning person who has no need to apply defense mechanisms to everyday experiences. Such an individual becomes increasingly willing to change and grow. He or she is more open to experience, more trusting of self-perception, and engaged in self-exploration and evaluation (Rogers, 1961). Furthermore, a fully functioning person develops a greater acceptance of self and others and becomes a better decision maker in the here and now. Ultimately, a client is helped to identify, use, and integrate his or her own resources and potential (Boy & Pine, 1983; Miller, 1996).

Techniques   For person-centred therapists, the quality of the counselling relationship is much more important than techniques (Glauser & Bozarth, 2001). Rogers (1957) believed there are three necessary and sufficient (i.e., core) conditions of counselling:

1. Empathy
2. Unconditional positive regard (acceptance, prizing)
3. Congruence (genuineness, openness, authenticity, transparency)

Empathy may be subjective, interpersonal, or objective (Clark, 2004; Rogers, 1964). Often it is a combination of all three. In therapeutic situations, empathy is primarily the counsellor's ability to feel with clients and convey this understanding back to them. This may be done in multiple ways, but essentially empathy is an attempt to think with, rather than for or about, the client and to grasp the client's communications, intentions, and meanings (Brammer et al., 1993; Clark, 2007; Moon, 2007). Rogers (1975) noted, "The research keeps piling up and it points strongly to the conclusion that a high degree of empathy in a relationship is possibly the most potent and certainly one of the most potent factors in bringing about change and learning" (p. 3). Unconditional *positive regard*, also known as acceptance, is a deep and genuine caring for the client as a person—that is, prizing the person just for being (Rogers, 1961; 1980). *Congruence* is the condition of being transparent in the therapeutic relationship by giving up roles and façades (Rogers, 1980). It is the "counselor's readiness for setting aside concerns and personal preoccupations and for being available and open in relationship with the client" (Moon, 2007, p. 278).

Since 1980, person-centred counsellors have tried a number of other procedures for working with clients, such as limited self-disclosure of feelings, thoughts, and values (Corey, 2005). Clients, however, grow by experiencing themselves and others in relationships (Cormier & Cormier, 1998). Therefore, Rogers (1967) believed that "significant positive personality change" could not occur except in relationships (p. 73).

Methods that help promote the counsellor–client relationship include, but are not limited to, active and passive listening, accurate reflection of thoughts and feelings, clarification, summarization, confrontation, and general or open-ended leads. Questions are avoided whenever possible (Tursi & Cochran, 2006).

Strengths and Contributions   Person-centred counselling's unique aspects include the following:

- The approach revolutionized the counselling profession by linking counselling with psychotherapy and demystifying it by making audiotapes of actual sessions and publishing actual transcripts of counselling sessions (Goodyear, 1987; Sommers-Flanagan, 2007).

- The person-centred approach to counselling is applicable to a wide range of human problems, including institutional changes, labour–management relationships, leadership development, career decision making, and international diplomacy. For instance, Cornelius-White (2005) has found the person-centred approach can be effective in promoting multicultural counselling. Likewise, Lemoire and Chen (2005) have argued that "the person-centred approach seems to have the potential to create the necessary conditions that counteract stigmatization, allowing adolescents who are associated with a stigmatized sexual minority group to cope with their sexual identity in a manner that is more constructive for them" (p. 146).

- The approach has generated extensive research (Tursi & Cochran, 2006). It initially set the standard for doing research on counselling variables, especially those that Rogers (1957) deemed "necessary and sufficient" to bring about therapeutic change.

- The approach is effective in a number of settings. Person-centred counselling helps improve psychological adjustment, learning, and frustration tolerance and decrease defensiveness. It is appropriate in treating mild to moderate anxiety states, adjustment disorders, and conditions not attributable to mental disorders, such as uncomplicated bereavement or interpersonal relations (Seligman, 1997).

■ The person-centred approach may be especially helpful in working with clients who have experienced tragedies since it allows them "to struggle through emotions and actually become less affected in time by fully realizing feelings related to the trage- dies" (Tursi & Cochran, 2006, p. 395).

■ The approach focuses on the open and accepting relationship established by counsel- lors and clients and the short-term nature of the helping process.

■ The basics of the approach take a relatively short time to learn. With its emphasis on mastering listening skills, person-centred counselling is a foundation for training many paraprofessional helpers. Furthermore, it is the basis for several new and emerging approaches to treatment, and it is frequently combined with other theoreti- cal orientations to counselling, such as cognitive and behavioural (Prochaska & Nor- cross, 2007; Seligman, 2006).

■ The approach has a positive view of human nature and it continues to evolve.

Limitations The limitations of person-centred theory are also noteworthy.

■ The approach may be too simplistic, optimistic, leisurely, and unfocused for clients in crisis or who need more structure and direction (Seligman, 2006; Tursi & Coch- ran, 2006).

■ The approach depends on bright, insightful, hard-working clients for best results. It has limited applicability and is seldom employed with severely disabled individuals or young children (Thompson & Henderson, 2007).

■ The approach ignores diagnosis, the unconscious, developmental theories, and innately generated sexual and aggressive drives. Many critics think it is overly optimistic.

■ The approach deals only with surface issues and does not challenge the client to explore deeper areas. Because person-centred counselling is short term, it may not make a permanent impact on the person.

■ The approach is more attitudinal than technique-based. It is void of specific tech- niques to bring about client change (Moon, 2007).

Existential Counselling

Founders and Developers Rollo May (1909–1994) and Viktor Frankl (1905–1997) are two of the most influential professionals in the field of existential counselling. May dealt extensively with anxiety, especially in regard to his life and death struggle with tuberculosis, whereas Frankl, who was interred in Nazi concentration camps during World War II, focused on the meaning of life even under the most horrendous death camp conditions.

View of Human Nature "The existential approach disclaims the deterministic view of human nature and emphasizes the freedom that human beings have to choose what to make of their circumstances" (Fernando, 2007, p. 226). As a group, existentialists believe that people form their lives by the choices they make. Even in the worst situations, such as the Nazi death camps, there is an opportunity to make important life-and-death decisions, including whether to struggle to stay alive (Frankl, 1969). Existentialists focus on this free will of choice and the action that goes with it. They view people as the authors of their lives. They contend that people are responsible for any decision they make in life and that some choices are healthier and more meaningful than others.

According to Frankl (1962), the "meaning of life always changes but it never ceases to be" (p. 113). His theory, known as logotherapy, states that meaning goes beyond self-actualization and exists at three levels: (a) ultimate meanings (e.g., there is an order to the universe); (b) meaning of the moment; and (c) common, day-to-day meaning (Das, 1998). We can discover life's meaning in three ways:

1. *By doing a deed*—that is, by achieving or accomplishing something
2. *By experiencing a value*—such as a work of nature, culture, or love
3. *By suffering*—that is, by finding a proper attitude toward unalterable fate

Existentialists believe that psychopathology is a failure to make meaningful choices and maximize one's potential (Schneider & Krug, 2010). Choices may be avoided and potentials not realized because of the anxiety that is involved in action. Anxiety is often associated with paralysis, but May (1977) argues that normal anxiety may be healthy and motivational and can help people change.

Role of the Counsellor There are no uniform roles that existential counsellors follow. Every client is considered unique. Therefore, counsellors are sensitive to all aspects of their clients' character, "such as voice, posture, facial expression, even dress and apparently accidental movements of the body" (May, 1939, p. 101). Basically, counsellors concentrate on being authentic with their clients and entering into deep and personal relationships with them. "The counselor strives to be with the client in the here-and-now, and to understand and experience the ongoing emotional and mental state of the client. In order to do this, the counselor needs to express his or her own feelings" (Fernando, 2007, p. 231). Therefore, it is not unusual for an existential counsellor to share personal experiences with a client to deepen the relationship and help the client realize a shared humanness and struggle. Schneider and Krug (2010) suggest that existential counsellors focus on person-to-person relationships that emphasize mutuality, wholeness, and growth. Counsellors who practise from Frankl's logotherapy perspective are Socratic in engaging their clients in dialogue (Alex Vesley, June 19, 2007, personal communication).

However, all existential counsellors serve as a model of how to achieve individual potential and make decisions. They concentrate on helping the client experience subjective feelings, gain clearer self-understanding, and move toward the establishment of a new way of being in the world. The focus is living productively in the present, not recovering a personal past. They also "focus on ultimate human concerns (death, freedom, isolation, and meaninglessness)" (May & Yalom, 2000, p. 289).

Goals The goals of existentialists include helping clients realize the importance of meaning, responsibility, awareness, freedom, and potential. Existentialists hope that during the course of counselling, clients will take more responsibility for their lives. "The aim of therapy is that the patient experience his existence as real" (May, Angel, & Ellenberger, 1958, p. 85). In the process, the client is freed from being an observer of events and becomes a shaper of meaningful personal activity and an embracer of personal values that lead to a meaningful lifestyle.

Techniques "Existential theory does not limit the counselor to specific techniques and interventions" (Fernando, 2007, p. 230). The existential approach has fewer techniques available than almost any other model of counselling. Yet this apparent weakness (i.e., a lack of therapeutic tricks and psychological jargon) is paradoxically a strength because it allows existential counsellors to borrow ideas as well as use a wide range of personal and professional skills. "Approaching human beings merely in terms of techniques necessarily implies manipulating them," and manipulation is opposed to what existentialists espouse (Frankl, 1967, p. 139). Thus, existentialists are free to use techniques as widely diversified as desensitization and free association or to disassociate themselves from these practices entirely (Corey, 2005).

The most effective and powerful technique existential counsellors have is the relationship with the client. Ideally, the counsellor transcends his or her own needs and focuses on the client. In the process, the counsellor is open and self-revealing in an attempt to help the client become more in touch with personal feelings and experiences. The emphasis in the relationship is on authenticity, honesty, and spontaneity (Mendelowitz & Schneider, 2008).

Existential counsellors also make use of confrontation. Clients are confronted with the idea that everyone is responsible for his or her own life. Existential counsellors borrow some techniques from other models of counselling, such as the employment of awareness exercises, imagery, paradox, deflection, and goal-setting activities.

Strengths and Contributions The existential approach to counselling has a number of strengths.

- The approach emphasizes the uniqueness of each individual and the importance of meaningfulness in their lives. It is a very humanistic way of working with others (Alex Vesley, June 19, 2007, personal communication).

- The approach recognizes that anxiety is not necessarily a negative condition. Anxiety is a part of human life and can motivate some individuals to make healthy and productive decisions (Fernando, 2007).

- The approach gives counsellors access to a tremendous amount of philosophy and literature that is both informative and enlightening about human nature (Mendelowitz & Schneider, 2008).

- The approach stresses continued human growth and development and offers hope to clients through directed readings and therapeutic encounters with the counsellor.

- The approach is effective in multicultural counselling situations because its global view of human existence allows counsellors to focus on the person of the client in an "I-Thou" manner without regard to ethnic or social background (Epp, 1998; Jackson, 1987).

- The approach helps connect individuals to universal problems faced by humankind, such as the search for peace and the absence of caring (Baldwin, 1989).

- The approach may be combined with other perspectives and methods (such as those based on learning principles and behaviourism) to treat extremely difficult problems, such as addiction (Fernando, 2007).

- The approach stresses the importance of the therapeutic relationship, the therapist's and the client's personal styles, and the establishment of a healing environment—all considered the most important considerations in counselling outcome research (Schneider & Krug, 2010).

- A considerable amount of empirical support has shown existential counselling to be effective (Schneider & Krug, 2010).

Limitations Professionals who embrace different and more structured approaches have noted several limitations in the existential approach.

- The approach has not produced a fully developed model of counselling. Professionals who stress developmental stages of counselling are particularly vehement in this criticism.

- The approach lacks educational and training programs. Each practitioner and counselling experience is unique (Walsh & McElwain, 2002). Although uniqueness is valued, it prohibits the systematic teaching of theory.

- For counsellors who rely on a set of techniques in order to practise, existential counselling will be particularly limited (Vontress, 2008).

- Existential counselling requires that counsellors have developed wisdom and deep understanding regarding their own existential questions. Younger counsellors without much life experience will struggle substantially in trying to offer this approach to clients (van Deurzen, 2002).

- The approach is difficult to implement beyond an individual level because of its subjective nature. Existentialism lacks the type of methodology and validation processes prevalent in most other approaches. In short, it lacks the uniformity that beginning counsellors can readily understand.

- The approach is closer to existential philosophy than to other theories of counselling. This distinction limits its usefulness in some cases.

Ned was an existentialist who believed in nothingness. He did not think there was any meaning or logic to life and that those who took the opposite position were naive. His strong stance at times alienated him from others, but generally Ned was respected for his philosophical reasoning.

One day, seeking support for his views, Ned called a local private practice group and made an appointment to see Jim, a counsellor who had a reputation for being an existentialist. Ned expected Jim to discuss philosophy with him and to support his nihilism. Instead, Jim told Ned that he found great meaning every day in all that he did. Ned was surprised.

1. How could Ned have been so inaccurate in his assessment of Jim?

2. How could the gulf between Ned and Jim be broached constructively?

Gestalt Therapy

Gestalt therapy is associated with Gestalt psychology, a school of thought that stresses perception of completeness and wholeness. The term *gestalt* means whole figure. Gestalt psychology and therapy arose as a reaction to the reductionist emphasis in other schools of psychology and counselling, such as psychoanalysis and behaviourism. Thus, Gestalt therapy emphasizes how people function in their totality. There are currently thousands of counsellors around the world who have received extensive training and supervision in Gestalt therapy (Yontef & Fairfield, 2008).

Founders and Developers Frederick (Fritz) Perls (1893–1970) is credited with establishing Gestalt therapy and popularizing it both through his flamboyant personality and his writings. Laura Perls (his wife) and Paul Goodman helped Perls develop and refine his original ideas. A number of other theorists, particularly Joen Fagan and Irma Lee Shepherd (1970), developed the model further.

View of Human Nature Gestaltists believe that human beings work for wholeness and completeness in life. Each person has a self-actualizing tendency that emerges through personal interaction with the environment and the beginning of self-awareness. Self-actualization is centred in the present. The Gestalt view of human nature places trust on the inner wisdom of people, much as person-centred counselling does. Each person seeks to live integratively and productively, striving to coordinate the various parts of the person into a healthy, unified whole. From a Gestalt perspective, persons are more than a sum of their parts (Perls, 1969).

The Gestalt view is antideterministic: Each person is able to change and become responsible (Hatcher & Himelsteint, 1997). Gestalt therapists believe that people are constantly developing, and they accomplish this by continuing to explore, adapt, and self-reflect (Parlett & Denham, 2007).

Individuals are actors in the events around them, not just reactors to events. Overall, the Gestalt point of view takes a position that is existential, experiential, and phenomenological: The now is what really matters (Yontef, 2007). One discovers different aspects of oneself through experience, not talk, and a person's own assessment and interpretation of his or her life at a given moment in time are what is most important.

According to Gestalt therapy, many troubled individuals have an overdependency on intellectual experience (Simkin, 1975). Such an emphasis diminishes the importance of emotions and the senses, limiting a person's ability to respond to various situations. Another common problem is the inability to identify and resolve unfinished business—that is, earlier thoughts, feelings, and reactions that still affect personal functioning and interfere with living life in the present. The most typical unfinished business in life is not forgiving one's parents for their mistakes. Gestaltists do not attribute either of these difficulties to any unconscious forces within. Rather, the focus is on awareness, "the ability of the client to be in full mental and sensory" contact of "experiencing the now" (James & Gilliland, 2003, p. 49). Every person operates on some conscious level, from being very aware to being very unaware. Healthy individuals are those who are most aware.

According to Gestaltists, a person may experience difficulty in several ways. First, he or she may lose contact with the environment and the resources in it. Second, the person may become overinvolved with the environment and out of touch with the self. Third, he or she may fail to put aside unfinished business. Fourth, he or she may become fragmented or scattered in many directions. Fifth, the person may experience conflict between the *top dog* (what one thinks one should do) and the *underdog* (what one wants to do). Finally, the person may have difficulty handling the dichotomies of life, such as love/hate, masculinity/femininity, and pleasure/pain.

Role of the Counsellor The role of the Gestalt counsellor is to create an atmosphere that promotes a client's exploration of what is needed to grow. The counsellor provides such an atmosphere by being intensely and personally involved with clients and being honest. "Gestalt therapy is permission to be exuberant, to have grandness, to play with the nicest possibilities for ourselves within our short lives" (Zinker, 2009, p. 123). Involvement occurs in the now, which is a continuing process (Perls, 1969). The now often involves having the counsellor help a client focus on blocking energy and using that energy in positive and adaptive ways (Zinker, 1978). The now also entails the counsellor's helping the client recognize patterns in his or her life (Fagan, 1970).

Goals The goals of Gestalt therapy are well defined. They include an emphasis on the here and now and a recognition of the immediacy of experience (Bankart, 1997). Further goals include a focus on both nonverbal and verbal expression, and a focus on the concept that life includes making choices (Fagan & Shepherd, 1970). The Gestalt approach concentrates on helping a client resolve the past to become integrated. This goal includes the completion of mentally growing up. It emphasizes the coalescence of the emotional, cognitive, and behavioural aspects of the person. A primary focus is the acceptance of polarities within the person (Gelso & Carter, 1985).

As a group, Gestalt therapists emphasize action, pushing their clients to experience feelings and behaviours. They also stress the meaning of the word *now*. Perls (1969) developed a formula that expresses the word's essence: "Now = experience = awareness = reality. The past is no more and the future not yet. Only the now exists" (p. 14).

Techniques Some of the most innovative counselling techniques ever developed are found in Gestalt therapy (Harman, 1997). These techniques take two forms: exercises and experiments. *Exercises* are ready-made techniques, such as the enactment of fantasies, role-playing, and psychodrama (Coven, 1977). They are employed to evoke a certain response from the client, such as anger or exploration. *Experiments*, on the other hand, are activities that grow out of the interaction between counsellor and client. They are not planned, and what is learned is often a surprise to both the client and the counsellor. Many of the techniques of Gestalt therapy take the form of unplanned experiments (Zinker, 2009). The concentration here, however, is on exercise-oriented counselling techniques.

One common exercise is dream work. Perls described dreams as messages that represent a person's place at a certain time (Bernard, 1986). Unlike psychoanalysts, Gestalt counsellors do not interpret. Rather, clients present dreams and are then directed to experience what it is like to be each part of the dream—a type of dramatized free association. In this way, a client can get more in touch with the multiple aspects of the self.

Another effective technique is the empty chair (see Figure 11.1). In this procedure, clients talk to the various parts of their personality, such as the part that is dominant and the part that is passive. An empty chair is the focus. A client may simply talk to the chair as a representative of one part of the self, or the client may switch from chair to chair and have each chair represent a different part. In this dialogue, both rational and irrational parts of the client come into focus; the client not only sees these sides but also becomes able to deal with the dichotomies within the self. This method is not recommended for those who are severely emotionally disturbed (Bernard, 1986).

One of the most powerful Gestalt exercises is confrontation. Counsellors point out to clients incongruent behaviours and feelings, such as a client's smiling when admitting to nervousness. Truly nervous people do not smile. Confrontation involves asking clients *what* and *how* questions. *Why* questions are avoided because they lead to intellectualization.

Some other powerful Gestalt exercises that are individual-oriented are often used in groups (Harman, 1997).

- *Making the rounds.* This exercise is employed when the counsellor feels that a particular theme or feeling expressed by a client should be faced by every person in the group. The client may say, for instance, "I can't stand anyone." The client is then instructed to say this sentence to each person in the group, adding some remarks about each group member. The rounds exercise is flexible and may include nonverbal and positive feelings, too. By participating in it, clients become more aware of inner feelings.

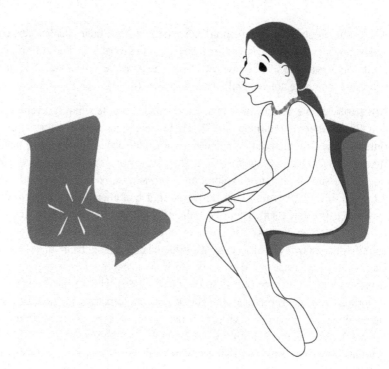

Figure 11.1 The empty chair

- *I take responsibility.* In this exercise, clients make statements about perceptions and close each statement with the phrase "and I take responsibility for it." The exercise helps clients integrate and own perceptions and behaviours.

- *Exaggeration.* Clients accentuate unwitting movement or gestures. In doing so, the inner meaning of these behaviours becomes more apparent.

- *May I feed you a sentence?* The counsellor, who is aware that implicit attitudes or messages are implied in what the client is saying, asks whether the client will say a certain sentence (provided by the counsellor) that makes the client's thoughts explicit. If the counsellor is correct about the underlying message, the client will gain insight as the sentence is repeated.

Strengths and Contributions Gestalt therapy strengths and contributions include the following:

- The approach emphasizes helping people incorporate and accept all aspects of life. An individual cannot be understood outside the context of a whole person who is choosing to act on the environment in the present (Passons, 1975).

- The approach helps a client focus on resolving areas of unfinished business. When a client is able to make these resolutions, life can be lived productively.

- The approach places primary emphasis on doing rather than talking. Activity helps individuals experience what the process of change is about and make more rapid progress.

- The approach is flexible and not limited to a few techniques. Any activity that helps clients become more integrative can be employed in Gestalt therapy.

- The approach is appropriate for certain affective disorders, anxiety states, somatoform disorders, adjustment disorders, and DSM-IV-TR diagnoses such as occupational problems and interpersonal problems (Seligman, 1997). In short, Gestalt therapy is versatile.

Limitations Gestalt therapy also has some limitations.

- The approach lacks a strong theoretical base. Some critics view Gestalt counselling as all experience and technique—that is, as too gimmicky (Corey, 2005). They maintain that it is antitheoretical.

- The approach deals strictly with the now and how of experience (Perls, 1969). This two-pronged principle does not allow for passive insight and change, which some clients are more likely to use.

- The approach eschews diagnosis and testing.

- The approach is too concerned with individual development and is criticized for its self-centredness. The focus is entirely on feeling and personal discovery.

SUMMARY

There are three distinct theories in the humanistic orientations: person-centred, existential, and Gestalt. Each of these theories, while helping and empowering clients to make choices and be in touch with their feelings, differs significantly from the others. Therefore, the humanistic orientation to counselling is more diverse than the psychoanalytic and Adlerian approaches described in the previous chapter.

Although person-centred counselling is considered very nondirective, this is certainly not true of other humanistic approaches. While existential counselling is highly variable in the extent to which it is nondirective or directive with a particular client, Gestalt therapists are highly directive, pushing clients to grow through the many techniques that Perls and his followers developed.

Your Personal Reflections

1. What do you find most appealing about the person-centred approach? Why? What do you find least appealing? Why?

2. What is something in your life that is greater than the sum of its parts?

3. What techniques in Gestalt therapy would you consider using after you become a counsellor? Why those ones and not others?

Classroom Activities

1. Do you think cognitive-behavioural theories are more powerful and useful than humanistic counselling? Why or why not?

2. In pairs, have a discussion about which humanistic approach you would prefer if you were a client. Explain why you would prefer that approach.

3. In pairs, practise one of the skills often used in person-centred counselling: showing empathy. Decide on who is counsellor and who is client. As client, say anything that comes to mind in one or two sentences. As counsellor, paraphrase what was said to you by the client. For example, client says, "I fight this class really interesting." Counsellor might reply, "You are enjoying this counselling course." As client, give the counsellor feedback as to whether they have paraphrased you correctly or if he or she missed something. Then say another sentence or two and continue in this fashion. Switch roles halfway.

4. In pairs, one of you role-plays a Gestalt therapist while the other is the client. You will need three chairs for this role-play. As therapist, ask your client to describe briefly a mild jealousy that he or she has experienced (the more recent the better). The therapist now asks the client to pretend that the person who did something that led to the client's jealousy is sitting in the empty chair. Now ask the client to talk to the chair as though that person were sitting in it and to tell him or her whatever the client thinks ought to be said. The goal is for the client to own his or her feelings and to discharge them in the safety of the empty chair technique.

Chapter 12
Postmodern Theories of Counselling and Crisis Counselling

PRACTICE REFLECTION

I felt intimidated when I first met Arthur several years ago. He relayed to me the story of how he had murdered his girlfriend 18 years earlier. Now living in a halfway house on day parole, he had failed at his first hearing to get full parole. Arthur felt that he was fully rehabilitated and that he was no longer a risk to anyone. After expressing his anger with how his hearing proceeded, he said that he did not understand how his use of language had been used against him. He asked if I would review the complete tape of his hearing, which he had a copy of, and then provide him feedback as to how his words may have been misconstrued. I agreed and I later listened carefully to the tape.

He was asked many questions at the hearing and I heard his responses as often having a defensive tone and a holier-than-thou quality. Arthur tried very hard to tell the parole board about his reform, but near the end of the hearing, he was told that he continued to be rigid and inflexible in his thinking. The parole board stated that it was these two qualities that had precipitated the escalation that led to the murder. If I had been on the board myself, I would have concurred after listening to the tape.

As I provided this feedback to Arthur at the next session, I could see that he was becoming defensive and rigid in my office! Although he had asked for my feedback, he clearly did not want to hear it. I stopped momentarily and said, "You asked for my feedback but I see you becoming agitated with it. Do you think this may have happened during the hearing itself?" Arthur replied, "Well, yes, it did. Every time I am asked to recount the story of what happened 18 years ago, I become anxious and defensive. I want to hear your feedback, but I can't help reliving some of how I felt at these hearings. I attended several hearings before this one in order to get day parole, and most of my sessions with my parole officer feel the same way."

I then switched to a postmodern stance and began asking Arthur questions such as, "How would you like to feel, think, and act differently the next time you attend a hearing? What would you need to do to create this? Tell me about times in the past where you have felt composed and non-defensive when being asked to tell your side of the story about something. Let's embellish that feeling of being in control by having you describe more about how you managed to stay so calm despite the accusations being made against you."

At the end of the session, I noticed that Arthur no longer looked defensive or rigid. He was smiling and presenting a more confident demeanour than I had seen in our two previous sessions. I have no idea what happened after he left my office, but I was struck by the change as he began to see that he could act differently if he worked at it.

During the 1980s, psychologists and researchers in Canada and the United States were again becoming disgruntled with the available theories and therapies. There were several reasons for this. Academics, for example, were becoming increasingly aware that the positivist paradigm (the view that there is a singular truth that can be found through quantitative research) was limited. Many people did not "fit" the findings gleaned from quantitative research, particularly those from other cultures and societies, past and present. For every "truth" there were innumerable exceptions.

Furthermore, in counselling practice, research revealed that most multicultural clients visited counsellors only once and did not return for further sessions. Given that we have Canadian policies that address respect for diversity (recall Chapters 4 and 5), such findings are disturbing. Did this suggest that our counselling practices themselves were unintentionally discriminatory toward minority groups?

As mentioned in Chapter 9, Pedersen (1999) argued that we have now entered the fourth movement in psychology, the movement of multiculturalism and postmodern thinking (the idea that there are multiple truths,) with a concomitant appreciation for the naturalistic paradigm (the view that there are multiple truths that can be described through qualitative studies). As postmodern thought emerged, so did philosophies and therapies based on it. Such approaches appeared to be more respectful of the plurality of our diverse clientele. In actuality, all approaches can be adapted to become respectful of individual and cultural differences, and the fourth wave has seen many successful attempts.

The fact that the postmodern therapies were designed to be brief was highly advantageous to their growing popularity given that we are in an age where people and institutions are demanding quick and effective mental health services. The skills employed in these approaches are vital for counsellors working in managed care settings (such as in firms offering counselling through Employee and Family Assistance Programs—EAFP firms) and for counsellors in public settings who are expected to do more in less time (Presbury, Echterling, & McKee, 2002).

The most popular postmodern approaches include narrative counselling, solution-focused counselling, and collaborative counselling. These counselling approaches are characterized by both their foci and their time-limited emphasis. The techniques used are concrete and goal-oriented. In addition, counsellors are active in helping foster change and in bringing it about. The emphasis in brief counselling is to identify solutions and resources rather than to focus on etiology, pathology, or dysfunction. Therefore, the number of sessions conducted is limited to increase client focus and motivation. This chapter ends with an overview of crisis counselling, which is also time-limited and highly focused in its purpose.

POSTMODERN APPROACHES

WHAT IF YOU WOKE UP ONE MORNING AND DISCOVERED THAT THE REALITY YOU HAD BEEN living in until now had disappeared while you were sleeping? What would happen to you? How would you go about defining the world in which you live? What would matter, what would make sense, and what would be the point of it all?

Interestingly, something similar happened in the field of psychology, and this fourth wave has been aptly called postmodernism. It has shaken up the foundation upon which the scientific method is based. Research has traditionally sought to find the "truth" about people—a singular truth that applies to every one of us. The new postmodern paradigm suggests that there are multiple truths and, consequently, reality becomes whatever you make or perceive it to be. All points of view are accepted, and in its purest form, postmodernism can be *nihilistic*, meaning that nothing is accepted as truth, and values themselves become baseless constructs.

However, few postmodernists would take such an extreme stance. Few people, for example, deny the physical reality that surrounds us or the reality of life and death. In the field of counselling, the postmodern paradigm is focused on social constructionism. *Social constructionism* is the view that human meaning is created through language and interactions with others (Gergen, 1985; 2009). In any socially constructed group (e.g., a society, a culture, an organization), past and present, the view of reality that is most believed or acted upon is call the *meta-narrative*, while those that are less "privileged" are viewed as *subjugated knowledges*.

Some of the basic tenets underlying postmodern thought have implications for counselling practice. Some of these understandings that the counsellor brings to the postmodern counselling session include the following:

1. *Accept that no one has privileged knowledge.* Consequently, the counsellor does not take the expert role. Clients are experts of their own knowledge, regardless of whether it is shared by others.

2. *Be aware of the counsellor's position of power.* Counsellors are often held in high regard by clients, and clients desire help. These dynamics alone create a power differential. Counsellors must be aware of how their own position of gender, race, and so on influences their view of reality and their view of how to be helpful to others.

3. *Recognize that psychology itself is a set of power practices and narratives.* In its search for a singular truth, most research in psychology has privileged one narrative over another. Counsellors must be careful not to impose a narrative from psychological research or psychological "wisdom" onto their clients.

4. *Assume a "not-knowing" position.* No one can understand other people without finding out from them firsthand. If counsellors want to take their clients in a certain direction, they must decide that direction collaboratively.

5. *Remember that clients already hold knowledge about how to be successful.* Whatever the goal, clients are believed to already have the knowledge within them regarding how to improve their lives. Counsellors are primarily there to help clients unlock their own personal wisdom and experience. This may mean re-activating old narratives that were helpful or creating new ones.

6. *Know that the focus on some themes means de-emphasizing other possibilities.* Just as every story emphasizes some themes over other themes, whatever direction people take in life is about emphasizing one path over other possible paths for a period of time. Clients need to take ownership over whatever path they choose to take right now.

7. *Avoid all interpretations and reframes of client's thoughts, feelings, and actions.* In so doing, counsellors avoid privileging their own knowledge over that of their clients.

Although postmodern approaches to counselling have become immensely popular, the practitioner should be aware that there is a risk with postmodern thought: One may forget the positive contributions that modernist theories had in developing the counselling profession. As previous chapters revealed, these contributions are notable.

While postmodernism has itself added significantly to new understandings of how to help people, the approach can be captivating and charming to unsuspecting clients. As Ellerman (2010) cautions, postmodern counsellors can be unwittingly dangerous as their education, values, and ethics give way to a view of truth that is obsolete and/or irrelevant. Although the postmodern approaches described here are generally referred to as "therapies" in the literature, this chapter refers to them as counselling approaches instead, which seems more in keeping with their philosophical stance, which is opposed to viewing the counsellor as the expert.

Narrative Counselling

Founders and Developers Michael White and David Epston (1990), practitioners from Australia and New Zealand, respectively, created narrative counselling, a postmodern and social constructionist approach. Other prominent practitioners and theorists in the field include Michael Durrant and Gerald Monk.

David Epston was born in Canada and began his career by pursuing an MA in anthropology. He switched to social work in the 1970s and emigrated to New Zealand. In 1996, he was awarded an honorary doctorate in literature by John F. Kennedy University in California.

Michael White was a practising social worker and family counsellor. The prevailing social mileau of the 1960s taught him to appreciate dominant discourse and its power over people (Duvall & Young, 2009). After developing narrative counselling, he trained thousands of practitioners to work with individuals, couples, families, groups, and communities. He was also known for his work with children, Aboriginal people, schizophrenia, anorexia/bulimia, men's violence, and trauma. He died unexpectedly at the age of 59 on April 4, 2008, from a heart attack while offering training in San Diego.

One of his final publications (White, 2009) reviewed how couples could overcome their conflicts through narrative counselling. Recent articles by others have shown narrative counselling's application with children (Young, 2008), career counselling (Locke & Gibbons, 2008), coaching (Law, 2008), gay men (McLean & Marini, 2008), and the ethical dilemmas that may arise in its use (Miller & Forrest, 2009).

View of Human Nature Narrative counsellors emphasize "that meaning or knowledge is constructed through social interaction" (Worden, 2003, p. 8). There is no absolute reality except as a social product. People are seen as internalizing and judging themselves through creating stories of their lives. Many of these stories highlight negative qualities about individuals or situations and are troublesome or depressing. Through treatment, clients can re-author their lives and change their outlooks in a positive way.

Role of the Counsellor The narrative approach to change sees counsellors as collaborators and masters of asking questions (Walsh & Keenan, 1997). Like counsellors in other traditions, those who take a narrative orientation engage their clients and use basic relationship skills such as attending, paraphrasing, clarifying, summarizing, and checking to make sure they hear the client's story or problem correctly (Monk, 1998). They assume that symptoms do not serve a function and are, in fact, oppressive. Therefore, an effort is made by the counsellor to address and eliminate problems as rapidly as possible. Overall, the counsellor uses *narrative reasoning*, which is characterized by stories, meaningfulness, and liveliness, in an effort to help clients redefine their lives and relationships through new narratives.

Goals "Within a narrative frame, human problems are viewed as arising from and being maintained by oppressive stories which dominate the person's life" (Carr, 1998, p. 486).

According to the narrative viewpoint, "people live their lives by stories" (Kurtz & Tandy, 1995, p. 177). Therefore, the emphasis in this approach is shifted to a narrative way of conceptualizing and interpreting the world. Clients who undergo narrative counselling learn to value their own life experiences and stories if they are successful. They also learn how to construct new stories and meaning in their lives and, in the process, create new realities for themselves.

Techniques The narrative approach emphasizes developing unique and alternative stories of one's life in the hope that a client will come up with novel options and strategies for living. Several techniques are used to help accomplish this.

1. *Working collaboratively.* In working collaboratively with the client, the counsellor takes the stance of privileging clients' language, questioning them about multiple viewpoints rather than searching for objective facts, honouring listening over questioning, and remaining open to authoring new possibilities.

2. *Externalizing the problem.* The problem that is brought to counselling is externalized (Strong, 2008). In externalization, the problem *is* the problem. In other words, the intent is to help clients see themselves as separate from their problems. The problem is objectified so that the resources of a client can be focused on how a situation such as chaos or a feeling such as depression can be dealt with. A narrative counsellor may say something like, "When depression *visits* you, what do you feel? What thoughts come along with it? When depression leaves, in what ways do you feel different?"

3. *Searching for unique outcomes.* This involves helping clients find times in their lives when they were not affected by their problems (i.e., looking for unique times when the problem didn't exist). The client is then asked to describe these valued experiences.

4. *Focusing on the unique outcomes.* The client is asked to focus on these valued experiences. The counsellor assists this process by asking questions that help them look deeper at the events, sequences, and plots that surround the experience and their meanings.

5. *Linking and extending the outcomes.* The preferred experiences are extended into the future by focusing on the preferred self-narrative—the story (i.e., narrative) that the person wants to embrace.

6. *Inviting witnesses.* Invite outsiders, usually close significant others, to witness this preferred self-narrative.

7. *Encouraging remembering practices.* Have the client imagine and focus on the supportive people in their lives who have been part of their preferred self-narratives.

8. *Using positive written materials.* Counsellors ask their clients to bring to sessions certificates and awards, letters of reference, journal entries, and other written documents that speak to their preferred self-narrative. These are used to reinforce and celebrate the person's desired life.

9. *Helping others.* Counsellors also encourage clients to write what they have learned in counselling for other clients with similar problems. They may arrange for new clients to meet with them for what will hopefully become a mutually beneficial mentoring process (points 1 and 3 through 9 were adapted from Carr's 1998 article).

Other ways narrative counsellors work are through *raising dilemmas*, so that a client examines possible aspects of a problem before the need arises, and *predicting setbacks*, so the client will think about what to do in the face of adversity. *Re-authoring* lives is one of the main foci for the treatment, though. By refining one's life and relationships through a new narrative, change becomes possible (White, 1995). In changing their stories, clients perceive the world differently and are freed up to think and behave differently.

Counsellors send letters to families about their clients' progress. They also hold formal celebrations at the termination of treatment and give out certificates of accomplishment when clients overcome an externalized problem such as apathy or depression.

Strengths and Contributions The narrative approach has contributed a number of unique qualities to counselling. Among them are the following:

- Blame is alleviated and dialogue is generated as everyone works to solve a common problem (Walsh & Keenan, 1997).
- Clients create a new story and new possibilities for action.
- Exceptions to problems are highlighted, as in solution-focused counselling.
- Clients are prepared ahead of time for setbacks or dilemmas through counsellor questions.

Limitations Narrative counselling is not without its limitations, however:

- This approach is quite cerebral and does not work well with clients who are not intellectually astute.
- There are no norms regarding who clients should become.
- The history of a difficulty is not dealt with.
- The leading proponents of narrative counselling have been overly harsh toward other forms of counselling, thereby calling into question whether the approach really does value diverse narratives equally (Doan, 1998).
- There remains a lack of clinical and empirical studies validating its claims, particularly rigorously controlled quantitative studies (Etchison & Kleist, 2000).

It is a common practice for narrative counsellors to write letters to their clients with words of encouragement, expressing sentiment regarding the changes they see occurring, reinforcing the preferred self-narrative, externalizing the problem, and/or focusing on other therapeutic endeavours.

1. In Canada, lawyers can often bill at about twice the rate as psychologists in private practice. They also bill for time spent on the telephone, for letters they write, and for other time spent on the client file. Should narrative counsellors, whether they are psychologists, social workers, or certified counsellors, also bill for their letter-writing time? Why or why not?

2. What do you see as some of the advantages of providing therapeutic letters?

3. What do you see as some of the drawbacks of this practice?

Solution-Focused Counselling

Founders and Developers Solution-focused counselling, also commonly known as solution-focused brief counselling (SFBT), is a midwestern phenomenon, having originated in the late 1970s with Steve de Shazer and his collaborator and wife, Insoo Kim Berg, along with a team of colleagues in Milwaukee (McCollum, 2007; Trepper, Dolan, McCollum, & Nelson, 2006). Other prominent practitioners and theorists connected with solution-focused counselling are Bill O'Hanlon and Michele Weiner-Davis.

SFBT has been used with reported success with many clinical problems, including substance abuse, sexual abuse, sexual dysfunction, depression, domestic violence, and even pet-assisted counselling (McCollum, 2007). It has also been used by business consultants and by educators (McCollum, 2007). It has become "one of the popular and widely used psychotherapy approaches in the world" (Trepper et al., 2006, p. 134).

Steve and his colleagues observed that the typical client attended approximately six sessions (Gingerich, 2006). This led them to question their therapeutic approaches, which were based on longer-term counselling, and client experience, which was to receive services for a shorter duration. Together, de Shazer and his colleagues reversed the traditional interview process by focusing their clients on solutions and away from the problems that brought them into counselling (Trepper et al., 2006).

View of Human Nature Solution-focused counselling does not have a comprehensive view regarding human nature but focuses on client health and strength (Fernando, 2007). It traces its roots, as do some of the other theories in this chapter, to the work of Milton Erickson (1954), particularly Erickson's idea that people have within themselves the resources and abilities to solve their own problems even if they do not have a causal understanding of them. Erickson also "believed that a small change in one's behaviour is often all that is necessary to lead to more profound changes in a problem context" (Lawson, 1994, p. 244).

In addition to its Ericksonian heritage, solution-focused counselling sees people as being *constructivist* in nature, meaning that reality is a reflection of observation and experience. Finally, solution-focused counselling is based on the assumption that people really want to change and that change is inevitable.

Role of the Counsellor The solution-focused counsellor's first role is to determine how active and committed a client is to the process of change. Clients usually fall into three categories:

1. *Visitors*, who are not involved in the problem and are not a part of the solution

2. *Complainants*, who complain about situations but can be observant and describe problems even if they are not invested in resolving them

3. *Customers*, who are not only able to describe problems and how they are involved in them, but are willing to work on finding solutions (Fleming & Rickord, 1997)

In addition to determining commitment, solution-focused counsellors act as facilitators of change to help clients "access the resources and strengths they already have but are not aware of or are not utilizing" (Cleveland & Lindsey, 1995, p. 145). They encourage, challenge, and set up expectations for change. They do not blame or ask "why." They are not particularly interested in how a problem arose. Rather, they are concerned with working together with the client to arrive at a solution to the problem. Basically, they allow the client to be the expert on his or her life (Helwig, 2002).

Goals A major goal of solution-focused counselling is to help clients tap inner resources and to notice *exceptions* to the times when they are distressed. The goal is then to direct them toward solutions to situations that already exist in these exceptions (West, Bubenzer, Smith, & Hamm, 1997). Thus, the focus of sessions and homework is on positives and possibilities either now or in the future (Walter & Peller, 1992).

Techniques Solution-focused counselling is a collaborative process between the counsellor and client. Nonetheless, solution-focused counsellors are known for inventing or describing several of their own techniques.

1. *Introductory questions.* These questions help introduce the client to the idea of focusing on solutions instead of on problems. For example, the counsellor might ask, "What will be the first sign to you that you are improving as a result of coming here? How would others see that you are getting better?" (James & Gilliland, 2003).

2. *Looking for exceptions.* The counsellor asks the client to describe times when the problem was either less evident or didn't exist at all in their lives. Following this lead, the counsellor then poses questions to help the client *indwell* (focus deeply and for a sustained period) on their past success (with the implied suggestion that what once was can be again).

3. *The miracle question.* The *miracle question* basically focuses on a hypothetical situation in which a problem has disappeared. One form of it goes as follows: "Let's

suppose tonight while you were sleeping a miracle happened that solved all the problems that brought you here. How would you know it? What would be different?" (deShazer, 1991).

4. *Scaling questions.* In *scaling*, the client is asked to use a scale from 1 (low) to 10 (high) to evaluate how severe a problem is. Scaling helps clients understand both where they are in regard to a problem and where they need to move in order to realistically achieve their goals.

5. *Externalizing the problem.* This is the same technique used in narrative counselling where the problem resides outside clients and they develop a "relationship" of sorts with it.

6. *Compliments and cheerleading.* Paying the client many compliments, both verbally and in writing, and acting as a cheerleader when they attain some success is common in SFBT. Compliments are usually given right before clients are given tasks or assignments.

7. *Clues.* These are intended to alert clients to the idea that some behaviours they are doing now are likely to continue and they should not worry about them.

8. *Skeleton keys.* These are procedures that have worked before and that have universal applications in regard to unlocking a variety of problems.

9. *Not-knowing stance.* The counsellor acts in a manner that suggests he or she is not knowledgeable about the client's problem or its resolution.

10. *Reframing.* Reframing problems is a technique used in SFBT to encourage resolution.

Taylor (2005) offered a "map" (Table 12.1) to act as a helpful resource for those learning to offer SFBT. He suggested placing the map on an overhead, using it as a handout, or pasting it onto a fridge magnet:

Table 12.1 Five Key Shifts in Language

What I *don't* want	→	What I *do* want
When things go *wrong*	→	When things go *right*
Forces *beyond* my control	→	Forces *within* my control
I'm *stuck*	→	I'm *progressing*
More *troubles* to come	→	Positive *possibilities*

Taylor (2005, p. 29) suggested that these shifts in language can be facilitated by trainees by using his five lines of inquiry: (a) What is the goal? (b) When do little pieces of that happen? (c) How do you do that? (d) What good things result from that? and (e) What's next?

Strengths and Contributions Unique strengths of solution-focused family counselling include the following:

- The approach emphasizes brevity and empowerment of client families (Fleming & Rickord, 1997).
- The approach displays flexibility and excellent research in support of its effectiveness.
- The approach reveals a positive nature to working with a variety of clients.
- The approach focuses on change and its premise emphasizes small changes in behaviour.
- The approach can be combined with other counselling approaches, such as existentialism (Fernando, 2007).
- The short-term nature of the approach has been welcomed by clients, social workers, and managed care companies (Kim, 2008).
- Clients are not expected to attend a certain number of sessions. Instead, clients choose for themselves how long they wish to continue receiving SFBT (Corcoran & Pillai, 2009).

Limitations Solution-focused counselling also has limitations. These include the following:

- The approach pays almost no attention to client history.
- The approach has a lack of focus on insight.
- The approach uses teams, at least by some practitioners, which makes the cost of this treatment high.
- Some criticize the approach for being simplistic (Kim, 2008).
- Few controlled outcome studies have been done (Corcoran & Pillai, 2009; Gingerich, 2006), although those that have been conducted suggest that SFBT is effective when compared to no-treatment control groups (Kim, 2008; Trepper et al., 2006).
- Because of its emphasis on compliments and cheerleading, it can easily come across to clients as overly optimistic and "Pollyanna-ish" (i.e., naive optimism).

Case Example: What Would *You* Do?

Saul read and studied solution-focused counselling. He even took advanced continuing education seminars in it. He liked its philosophy and, most important, he liked the empowerment it gave clients and its overall effectiveness.

One day a family came to see Saul because of a daughter who was constantly running away. When Saul asked about exceptions to her behaviour, everyone agreed there were none. Saul was shocked.

1. How could Saul counsel therapeutically besides continuing to probe and ask for exceptions? (Hint: Think about the miracle question or scaling.)

2. Without knowing the reasons the daughter runs away, how could a solution-focused counsellor help her?

Collaborative Language Systems (Collaborative Counselling)

Founders and Developers Long-time collaborators Harold "Harry" Goolishian and Harlene Anderson, together with others at the Houston-Galveston Institute, developed the collaborative language systems approach in the 1980s and early 1990s (McDaniel & Gergen, 1993). Tom Strong (personal communication, March 7, 2010), a Canadian researcher with strong links to collaborative language systems, stated that Anderson now prefers to refer to collaborative language systems as simply collaborative counselling. Here it will be referred to as *collaborative counselling*.

Goolishian was especially interested in how language creates meaning, a central tenet in this postmodern approach. "Harry saw therapy as collaborative storytelling and himself as a therapeutic conversationalist, helping people develop new meanings and new stories about their lives by facilitating open dialogue" (McDaniel & Gergen, 1993, p. 292).

View of Human Nature Comparable to the other two postmodern approaches, collaborative counselling perceives clients as having the resources to solve their own problems (Cox & Anderson, 2003). A common expression used by collaborative counsellors is "the client is the expert" (Anderson & Goolishian, 1992). Although postmodernists do not believe in one truth regarding social reality, Cox and Anderson (2003, p. 113) stated that "most clients strive for healthy relationships and successful lives," which implies a positive view of human nature and a striving to become better individuals.

Role of the Counsellor The counsellor pays attention to the particular words that clients use and then intentionally uses their language in working with them. Anderson (1995) believes this facilitates a cooperative spirit with clients and reduces resistance to change. She views the counsellor role as that of consultant. One of her trainees commented that, without knowing her, it would be impossible to know which one was the counsellor (Anderson, 1995). Counsellors are expected to be transparent with information and to share their personal biases with the client (Cheong & Murphy, 2007). For this to occur, counsellors need to know themselves well. The counsellor, however, maintains a not-knowing stance (same as in SFBT) and the client determines the direction of counselling. Generally, counsellors using CLS share little about themselves unless asked specific questions by the client, a stance that is more passive and muted compared to the other two postmodern approaches (Cheong & Murphy, 2007).

Goals The goal of collaborative counselling is to help clients develop a greater degree of *self-agency*, which is the ability to move in whatever direction one desires. Talking creates meaning, and this in turn leads to change. The *self* is continually being constructed. The belief in collaborative counselling is that language creates knowledge and knowledge is not cumulative (Anderson, 1995).

Techniques Collaborative counsellors use some of the same methods used by other postmodern counsellors, including the following:

1. *Not-knowing stance.* As mentioned earlier, the counsellor responds as being there to learn from the client without making presuppositions.

2. *Problem organized system.* Those who communicate with each other concerning the problem should be included in the treatment (Blanton, 2002).

3. *Respectful listening.* This involves listening in an active, responsive way so that clients feel that what they have to say is worth listening to (Anderson, 1995).

4. *Conditional questioning.* Questions and comments reflect a tentativeness, such as "I wonder what this might mean to you," or "Are you trying to say that you do not know the next step?"

5. *Collaborative conversations* or *shared inquiry.* The counsellor and client work together in an egalitarian fashion toward learning about and working at understanding what the other person means (Blanton, 2002). As the dialogue unfolds, both client and counsellor may change as a result (Anderson, 1995).

6. *Possibility conversations.* Not all conversations facilitate change. Those that do create the environment for new meanings, new understandings, and new possibilities to unfold (Blanton, 2002).

7. *Dissolving.* As the client develops self-agency, the problem is said to dissolve.

Strengths and Contributions Some noted strengths of collaborative counselling include the following:

- The collaborative nature creates a less hierarchical, more respectful, and more egalitarian approach than is typical of most counselling approaches (Anderson, 1995).

- The approach is usually said to be brief (Anderson, 1995).

- It may be particularly well suited for those who are integrating spirituality into family counselling (Blanton, 2002).

- The approach is customized to fit each client. This is both a strength and a weakness (it cannot be standardized to allow for typical outcome research) (T. Strong, personal communication, March 7, 2010).

Limitations

- Collaborative counselling is the newest of the postmodern therapies and relies extensively on techniques used by other approaches.

- A psychinfo search did not reveal *any* controlled outcome studies. Consequently, the scientific merit of the approach and its effectiveness is currently unknown.

CRISIS COUNSELLING APPROACHES

A crisis is "a perception or experiencing of an event or situation as an intolerable difficulty that exceeds the person's current resources and coping mechanisms" (James, 2008, p. 3). *Crisis counselling* is the employment of a variety of direct and action-oriented approaches to help individuals find resources within themselves and/or deal externally with crisis. In all forms of crisis counselling, quick and efficient services are provided in specialized ways.

The Canadian Psychological Association has a section called *Traumatic Stress* (www.cpa.ca/aboutcpa/cpasections/traumaticstress) for psychologists and others interested in this subject. An excellent resource is provided in both English and French by Dr. Alain Brunet at McGill University through a website called i-TRAUMA (www.info-trauma.org/splash.html). Links are provided for those who have experienced trauma, for those wanting more information about trauma, and for who want to take specialized training in this field. In the case of a national emergency or disaster, the Office of Emergency Response Services is responsible for supporting emergency services throughout Canada (Public Health Agency of Canada, 2010).

Research in suicide prevention dominates the bulk of published literature in crisis intervention. Recent Canadian research in suicide intervention has also focused on the themes expressed when callers phone a suicide line (Barber, Blackman, Talbot, & Saebel, 2004), suicide agreements and contracts (Page & King, 2008), prevention efforts with suicidal adolescents (Stewart, Manion, & Davidson, 2002), Aboriginal youth (White, 2007) and adults (Cutcliffe, 2005), the elderly (Heisel, 2006), and prisoners (Daigle, 2007).

A recent review published in the *Canadian Journal of Psychiatry* reported that there are two suicide prevention strategies that are commonly employed: (a) reducing risk factors for suicide, and (b) looking for people who are at risk for suicide and referring them to treatment. The first strategy has been met with mixed results with the best outcomes following reductions in the availability of lethal methods (e.g., gun control) and educating general medical practitioners about depression management. The latter strategy includes suicide prevention programs, and these have generally been viewed as underevaluated. Furthermore, the studies that have been done suggest these programs have little effect (Isaac et al., 2009).

The United Nations recommends gatekeeper training as the most effective strategy to reduce suicidal behaviour. *Gatekeepers* are those who have contact with suicidal individuals and know how to identity them, including both helping professionals and laypeople with formal training in the issue. Isaac et al.'s (2009) review suggests that gatekeeper training is successful in improving attitudes, knowledge, and skills of the trainees. Large-scale studies with military personnel and physicians are showing encouraging results regarding a reduction in suicidal ideation, suicide attempts, and suicidal deaths by those who are identified as suicidal.

Crisis Counselling

Founders and Developers   Erich Lindemann (1944; 1956) and Gerald Caplan (1964) are considered two of the most prominent pioneers in the field of crisis counselling. Lindemann helped professionals recognize normal grief due to loss and the stages that individuals go through in resolving grief. Caplan expanded Lindemann's concepts to the total field of traumatic events. He viewed crisis as a state resulting from impediments to life's goals that are both situational and developmental.

View of Human Nature   Loss is an inevitable part of life. Developmentally and situationally, healthy people grow and move on, leaving some things behind, whether intentionally, by accident, or because of growth. In leaving, there may be grieving, which is a natural reaction to loss. The extent of the grief and its depth are associated with the value of what has been lost and how. In some cases, the pain may be small because the person was not attached to or invested in the object left behind, or the person had adequate time to prepare. In other cases, an individual may feel overwhelmed because of the value the person, possession, or position had in his or her life or because of the sudden and/or traumatic way the loss occurred. In such cases, there is a crisis.

People can have a variety of crises. Four of the most common types include the following:

1. *Developmental*, which takes place in the normal flow of human growth and development under circumstances that are considered normal (e.g., birth of a child, retirement).

2. *Situational*, in which uncommon and extraordinary events occur that an individual has no way of predicting or controlling (e.g., automobile accident, kidnapping, loss of job).

3. *Existential*, which includes "inner conflicts and anxieties that accompany important human issues of purpose, responsibility, independence, freedom, and commitment"

(James, 2008, p. 13) (e.g., realizing at age 50 that one has wasted one's life and cannot relive past years).

4. *Ecosystemic*, in which "some natural or human-caused disaster overtakes a person or a . . . group of people who find themselves, through no fault or action of their own, inundated in the aftermath of an event that may adversely affect virtually every member of the environment in which they live" (James, 2008, p. 14) (e.g., a hurricane, a blizzard, an act of terrorism).

Goals Many crises, but not all, are time-limited and last somewhere between six and eight weeks. Goals within crisis counselling revolve around getting immediate help in a variety of forms (e.g., psychological, financial, legal) for those who are suffering. "What occurs during the immediate aftermath of the crisis event determines whether or not the crisis will become a disease reservoir that will be transformed into a chronic and long-term state" (James, 2008, p. 5). Initially, counsellors use basic crisis theory to help "people in crisis recognize and correct temporary affective, behavioural, and cognitive distortions brought on by traumatic events" (p. 11). This service is different from brief counselling approaches that try to help individuals find remediation for more ongoing problems. Long-term adjustment and health may require considerable follow-up on the part of the crisis counsellor or another helping specialist.

Role of the Counsellor Counsellors who work in crises need to be mature individuals with a variety of life experiences with which they have successfully dealt. They need to have a good command of basic helping skills, high energy, and quick mental reflexes, and yet be poised, calm, creative, and flexible in the midst of highly charged situations.

Counsellors are often direct and active in crisis situations. The role is quite different from that of ordinary counselling.

Techniques Techniques used in crisis counselling vary according to the type of crisis, as mentioned earlier, and the potential for harm. Expert consensus dictates that there are five essential aspects of crisis intervention: (a) establish safety, (b) enhance calming, (c) build self-and-other efficacy, (d) reconnect to social networks, and (e) instill hope (Hobfoll et al., 2007). According to James (2008), what a crisis worker does and when he or she does it is dependent on assessing the individuals experiencing crisis in a continuous and fluid manner (see Figure 12.1).

After assessment, there are three essential listening activities that need to be implemented:

1. *Defining the problem*, especially from the client's viewpoint
2. *Ensuring client safety*, which means minimizing physical and psychological danger to the client or others
3. *Providing support*, which means communicating to the client genuine and unconditional caring

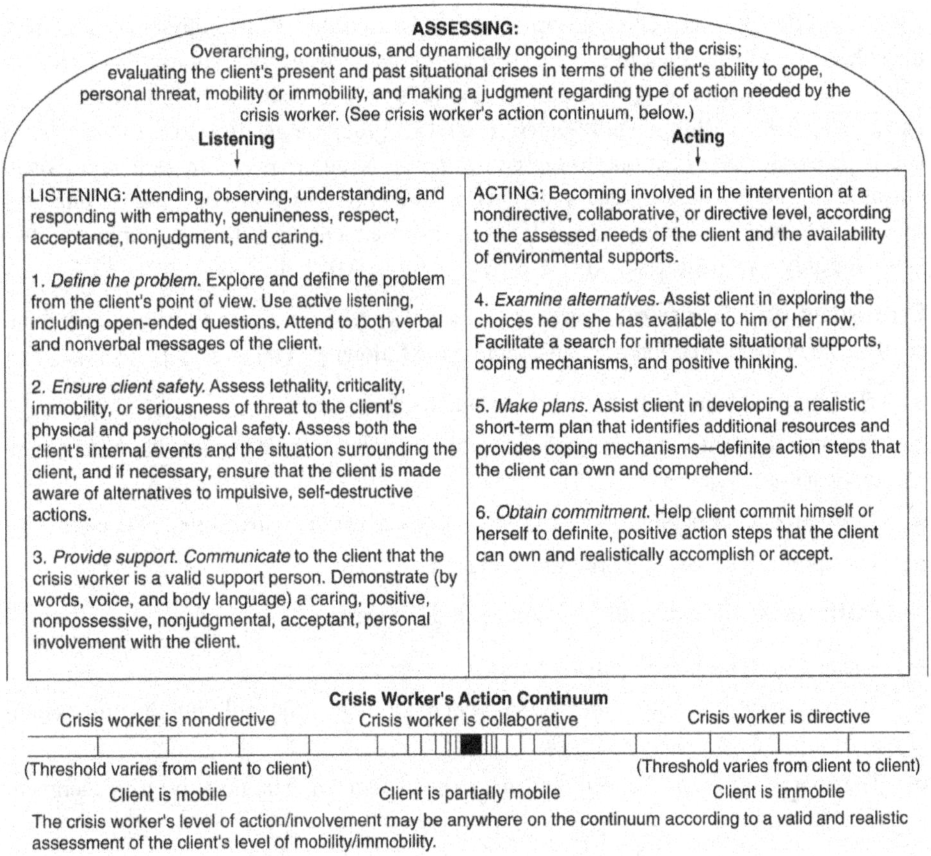

Figure 12.1 The six-step model of crisis intervention

Source: From *Crisis Intervention Strategies* (6th ed.) by R. K. James. Copyright © by Thomson Brooks/Cole Publishing Company. Reprinted by permission of Wadsworth Publishing Company.

After listening skills come *acting strategies,* which include:

1. *Examining alternatives* (i.e., recognizing alternatives that are available and realizing that some choices are better than others)

2. *Making plans,* where clients feel a sense of control and autonomy in the process so they do not become dependent

3. *Obtaining commitment* from the client to take actions that have been planned

Where possible, counsellors should follow up with clients to make sure they have been able to complete their plan and to further assess whether they have had delayed reactions to the crisis they have experienced, such as post-traumatic stress disorder.

Critical incident stress debriefing (CISD) and one-on-one crisis counselling are two of the most common approaches that make use of the techniques just described (Jordan,

2002). In CISD, a seven-stage group approach is used that helps individuals deal with their thoughts and feelings in a controlled environment using two counsellors (Roberts, 2000). This approach evolves through an emphasis on introduction, facts, thoughts, reactions, symptoms, teaching, and re-entry. The CISD group ranges from one to three hours and is generally "provided one to ten days after an acute crisis and three to four weeks after the disaster in mass disasters" (Roberts, 2000, p. 86). One-to-one counselling uses some of the same techniques as in CISD but the treatment lasts from 15 minutes to two hours for only one to three sessions (Everly, Lating, & Mitchell, 2000).

Strengths and Contributions As a specialty, crisis counselling is unique and has contributed to the profession of counselling in the following ways:

- The approach benefits from its brevity and its directness.
- The approach uses modest goals and objectives because of the sudden and/or traumatic nature of crises.
- The approach relies on its intensity, which is greater than regular forms of counselling.
- The approach utilizes a more transitional nature.

Limitations Crisis counselling is limited in these ways:

- The approach deals with situations of an immediate nature.
- The approach does not go into the same depth in regard to resolution that most counselling approaches do.
- The approach is more time-limited and trauma-oriented than most forms of therapeutic interventions.
- There is no current evidence-based consensus on what constitutes crisis intervention (Hobfoll et al., 2007)
- Research regarding the efficacy of CISD has resulted in equivocal findings (Pender & Prtichard, 2009) and the debate regarding its use is currently at a standstill (Robinson, 2008).

SUMMARY AND CONCLUSION

This chapter reviewed the three major theories and approaches to postmodern counselling, including narrative counselling, solution-focused brief counselling, and collaborative counselling. Each approach is based on the central tenet that in psychology there are numerous truths and that knowledge is situational and therefore changeable, not only for people in general but also for any particular individual. Postmodern thinking has become a counter force to the positivist paradigm that promulgates the idea that there is a singular truth that can be discovered through quantitative studies with replicable findings. Postmodern counselling approaches have grown in popularity, a popularity that may be being won more because of the briefness purported by each theory's advocates than because of a paradigm shift.

The chapter concluded with crisis counselling, included here because these approaches are also brief, sometimes concluding after as little as 15 minutes.

Your Personal Reflections

1. Think about something that has upset you recently. Instead of replaying this in your mind, think about an earlier time that you handled a similar situation better than the more recent one. What did you do differently that time? How did you feel differently?

2. If a client is deeply depressed, a narrative counsellor would likely first listen to his or her story before moving into exceptions to the problem, while a solution-focused counsellor would move immediately to solutions. Which approach would *you* prefer if you were depressed? Aside from which one you would prefer, which approach do you actually think would be most helpful to you? Why?

3. Do you agree with the idea that language that creates knowledge? Why or why not? Can you think of exceptions?

4. Crisis counselling has shown itself to be very helpful. If you were the first at the scene of a motor vehicle accident with some occupants experiencing minor injuries, what would you want to say to the occupants that could be beneficial to them?

Classroom Activities

1. In pairs, tell another student about the story of a time when you were struggling with a difficult school assignment and felt stressed. Then share a time when you had another difficult school assignment but managed your reaction to the work better. Your partner then asks you questions aimed at helping you explore this narrative deeper. What was different when you were not feeling as stressed?

2. Write a short paragraph about a negative quality or characteristic you have that expresses itself periodically. Then write another paragraph describing the way you would like this quality or characteristic to look. Then in pairs, read your two paragraphs and afterward your partner should ask you about how you would act differently if you embraced this new aspect of self.

3. At home, assemble a number of old magazines. Create a collage by cutting out pictures and photographs that address some aspect of what you would like in your future. You could focus your collage on work/career, health goals or appearance, relationships, and so on. Then paste these images onto a large piece of cardboard and bring it to class. In small groups, tell a story about how you want to see your life in the future.

4. The class is divided into two. One side of the class takes the view that anxiety is created from within the individual, while the other side argues that anxiety (or another common human problem) is externalized, something that comes to the individual when certain conditions exist. Allow the two sides of the class to debate their perspectives. At the end of the debate, have a class discussion about the pros and cons of externalizing the problem.

5. In pairs, one of you take the role of counsellor and the other the role of client. Collaborate on a topic of the "client's" that will become the focus, but something not too personal (perhaps involving school or work). As counsellor, ask the miracle question as follows:

   a) What is the first thing you notice that tells you things are different?
   b) How will that make a difference?
   c) What else? And what else?
   d) What will you be doing differently than now?
   e) How will you be feeling differently compared to now?
   f) What differences will other people who know you be able to see?

6. How does crisis counselling differ from other mainstream counselling approaches covered in this and the preceding chapter? How is it the same?

Chapter 13

Groups in Counselling

PRACTICE REFLECTION

I led a group for depressed men and women a few years ago. After the group had already met for several sessions, participants became freer to express what was really bothering them. In other words, a relationship based on trust had developed. George spoke up and said that he was gay and that he felt unsupported in Calgary. Consequently, he did not believe he could be happy until he moved to either Vancouver or Toronto, where there are much larger and more visible gay communities.

While I was thinking about what to say to him, another participant, Esther, spoke up and said, "George, your depression is more about not taking necessary steps to help keep you from experiencing seasonal affective disorder (SAD). I know because I suffer from it too. I don't think you need to move at all. You have some family here and a few friends. Personally, I think you would be depressed right now regardless of where you live. The problem is inside you, not outside. Besides, why don't you first consider making more supportive friends?"

Counsellors are taught not to give advice, but group participants often offer it to one another. Sometimes advice falls on deaf ears, but other times the effect can be quite dramatic, particularly when the person providing the advice is highly respected. George respected Esther for several reasons, but partly because she also experienced SAD.

The next week, George looked brighter and happier. After a feeling check-in with all of the group members (i.e., each participant provides a word for how they feel at the beginning of the group), George began, "After you suggested I make more friends last week, Ester, I decided that perhaps you were right. I placed a note on my neighbour's door—she lives next to me in our condo complex—and invited her to join me for coffee sometime. She e-mailed me the next day to say she would like that. It turned out she had recently moved to Calgary from Toronto and had few friends here. She relished the idea of making more friends, particularly a gay guy, because she had several gay friends back home and enjoyed hanging out with them without the sexual complications that sometimes arise with her straight male friends. Truthfully, she is a very attractive woman, but more than that, she is so outgoing, upbeat, and active that she has already inspired me to start doing more things. I think I might be making a new friend!"

It was encouraging to hear George saying something positive for a change. All the group had heard for several weeks was one complaint after another. Finally, George was showing some improvement. It is so hard for depressed people to begin taking action, especially doing something that they find challenging, and many people find meeting new people an enormous undertaking at the best of times.

If I had asked George to do the same thing, I doubt it would have been as impactful. Everyone in a group knows I have a vested interest in running the group, whether it be for monetary gain or training purposes. Esther, however, was there for the same reason George was—simply to get better. Anything she said was a gift without any anticipated reward. I continue to ask myself, "How can I get this group working in such a way that they all create a powerful healing bond?"

Working in groups is a counselling activity that is often effective in helping individuals resolve personal and interpersonal concerns. Organized groups make use of people's natural tendency to gather and share thoughts and feelings as well as work and play cooperatively. "Groups are valuable because they allow members to experience a sense of belonging, to share common problems, to observe behaviours and consequences of behaviours in others, and to find support during self-exploration and change" (Nims, 1998, p. 134). By participating in a group, people develop social relationships and emotional bonds and often become enlightened (Posthuma, 2002).

This chapter examines the following aspects of groups: their history; their place in counselling, including the types of groups most often used; their theoretical basis; issues and stages in groups; and qualities of effective group leaders. Both national and local organizations have been established for professionals engaged primarily in leading groups. One of the most comprehensive (and the one to which most professional counsellors belong) in the United States is the Association for Specialists in Group Work (ASGW; www.asgw.org), a national division of the American Counseling Association (ACA). This organization, which has a diverse membership, was chartered by the ACA in 1974 (Carroll & Levo, 1985). It has been a leader in the field of group work in establishing best practice guidelines, training standards, and principles for diversity-competent group workers. ASGW also publishes a quarterly periodical, the Journal for Specialists in Group Work. *The founding conference for the Canadian Group Psychotherapy Association occurred in Banff, Alberta, in October 1980 and today is a major force nationally in the field of group psychotherapy.*

A BRIEF HISTORY OF GROUPS

GROUPS HAVE A LONG AND DISTINGUISHED HISTORY IN THE SERVICE OF COUNSELLING. Joseph Hersey Pratt, a Boston physician, is generally credited with starting the first psychotherapy/counselling group in 1905. Pratt's group members were tubercular outpatients at Massachusetts General Hospital who found the time they regularly spent together informative, supportive, and therapeutic. Although this group was successful, the spread of groups to other settings and the development of different types of groups was uneven and sporadic until the 1970s. The following people were pioneers in the group movement along with Pratt:

- Jacob L. Moreno, who introduced the term "group psychotherapy" into the counselling literature in the 1920s

- Kurt Lewin, whose field theory concepts in the 1930s and 1940s became the basis for the Tavistock small study groups in Great Britain and the T-group movement in the United States

- Fritz Perls, whose Gestalt approach to groups attracted new interest in the field by stressing the importance of awareness and obtaining congruence within oneself

- W. Edwards Deming, who conceptualized and implemented the idea of quality work groups to improve the processes and products people produce and to build morale among workers in businesses

- William Schutz and Jack Gibb, who emphasized a humanistic aspect to T-groups that focused on personal growth as a legitimate goal

- Carl Rogers, who devised the basic encounter group in the 1960s that became the model for growth-oriented group approaches

- John Salvendy and others affiliated with the Ontario Group Psychotherapy Association (OGPA) (Salvendy, 1999) led the development of a national organization in Canada. Salvendy organized their conference in 1976 in Toronto and, with Irving Yalom as the keynote speaker, the conference attracted over 300 registrants. This led to a great deal of enthusiasm to establish a national organization, later resulting in creation of the Canadian Group Psychotherapy Association (Salvendy, 1999).

Besides influential individuals, a number of types of groups, some of which have just been mentioned, developed before groups were classified as they are today. Chronologically, psychodrama was the first, followed by T-groups, encounter groups, group marathons, and self-help/support groups. We will briefly look at each type of group because each has had an influence on groups today.

Psychodrama

Jacob L. Moreno, a Viennese psychiatrist, is credited as the originator of psychodrama. This type of group experience, employed for decades with mental patients at Saint Elizabeth's Hospital in Washington, DC, was initially used with ordinary citizens in Vienna, Austria (Moreno's original home), at the beginning of the 20th century. In psychodrama, members enact unrehearsed role-plays, with the group leader serving as the director. Other group members are actors in the protagonist's play, give feedback to the protagonist as members of the audience, or do both (Blatner, 2000). This type of group is popular with behaviourists, Gestaltists, and affective-oriented group leaders who have adapted it as a way of helping clients experience the emotional qualities of an event.

T-Groups

The first T-group (the *T* stands for training) was conducted at the National Training Laboratories (NTL) in Bethel, Maine, in 1946. These groups appeared at a time when neither group counselling nor group psychotherapy had evolved. In fact, they may be considered the beginning of modern group work (Ward, 2002). Kurt Lewin's ideas about group dynamics formed the basis for the original groups. Since that time, T-groups have evolved from a focus on task accomplishment to a primary emphasis on interpersonal relationships. Although it is difficult to classify T-groups in just one way, members of such groups are likely to learn from the experience how one's behaviour in a group influences others' behaviour and vice versa. In this respect, T-groups are similar to some forms of family counselling in which the emphasis is on both how the system operates and how an individual within the system functions.

Encounter Groups

Encounter groups emerged from T-groups in an attempt to focus on the growth of individual group members rather than the group itself. They were intended for "normally functioning" people who wanted to grow, change, and develop (Lieberman, 1991). These groups took many forms in their heyday (the 1970s), from the minimally structured groups of Carl Rogers (1970) to the highly structured, open-ended groups of William Schutz (1971). Regardless of the structure, the primary emphasis of such groups was on individual expression and recognition of affect.

Group Marathons

A group marathon is an extended, one-session group experience that breaks down defensive barriers that individuals may otherwise use. It usually lasts for a minimum of 24 hours. Frederick Stoller and George Bach pioneered the concept in the 1960s. Group marathons have been used successfully in working with substance abusers in rehabilitation programs and well-functioning individuals in other group counselling settings. Often labour and peace negotiations are held in a group marathon setting to achieve breakthroughs.

Self-Help/Support Groups

Self-help groups and mutual help groups are synonymous (Klaw & Humphreys, 2004, p. 630). They take two forms: those that are organized by an established, professional helping organization or individual (support groups) and those that originate spontaneously and stress their autonomy and internal group resources (self-help groups in the truest sense). Self-help groups usually develop spontaneously, centre on a single topic, and are led by a layperson with little formal group training but with experience in the stressful event that brought the group together (Riordan & Beggs, 1987). For example, residents in a neighbourhood may meet to help each other make repairs and clean up after a natural disaster, or they may assemble to focus government attention on an issue, such as toxic waste, that directly affects the quality of their lives. Self-help groups can be either short or long term, but they basically work to help their members gain greater control of their lives. Over 10 million people are involved in approximately 500 000 such groups in the United States, and the number continues to increase.

Support groups, as noted, are similar to self-help groups in their focus on a particular concern or problem, but are established by professional helping organizations or individuals (such as Alcoholics Anonymous, Lamplighters, or Weight Watchers) (Gladding, 2008). Some support groups charge fees; others do not. The involvement of laypeople as group leaders varies. Like self-help groups, support groups centre around topics that are physical, emotional, or social (L'Abate & Thaxton, 1981).

Self-help and support groups partly fill the needs of populations that can best be served through groups and that might otherwise not receive services. They meet in churches, recreation centres, schools, and other community buildings as well as in mental health facilities.

Lieberman (1994) sees self-help and support groups as healthy for the general public, and Corey (2008) thinks such groups are complementary to other mental health services. Like other group experiences, however, "cohesion is always a vital characteristic for success," and proper guidelines must be set up to ensure the group will be a positive, not a destructive, event (Riordan & Beggs, 1987, p. 428).

MISPERCEPTIONS AND REALITIES ABOUT GROUPS

Because the history of groups is uneven, certain misperceptions about groups have sprung up. Some of the reasons for these misperceptions occurred in the 1960s when groups were unregulated and yet a popular part of the culture, with the *New York Times* even declaring 1968 as the "Year of the Group." It was during this time that a number of inappropriate behaviours happened in groups, with the stories generated from the actions taking on a life of their own after being passed on by word of mouth. It is the remnants of these stories that make some people skeptical about groups or keep them from joining groups (Gladding, 2008). The majority of misperceptions involve counselling and psychotherapy groups (as opposed to psychoeducational and task/work groups). Some prevalent myths about groups are as follows (Childers & Couch, 1989):

- They are artificial and unreal.
- They are second-rate structures for dealing with problems.
- They force people to lose their identity by tearing down psychological defenses.
- They require people to become emotional and spill their guts.
- They are touchy-feely, confrontational, and hostile; they brainwash participants.

The reality is that none of these myths are true, at least in well-run groups. Indeed, the opposite is normally true. Therefore, it is important that individuals who are unsure about groups ask questions before they consider becoming members. Doubts and misperceptions they may have can be addressed and their anxiety may be lessened, and they may be able to benefit significantly within a group environment.

THE PLACE OF GROUPS IN COUNSELLING

A group is defined as two or more people interacting together to achieve a goal for their mutual benefit. Everyone typically spends some time in group activities each day (for example, with schoolmates or business associates). Gregariousness is part of human nature, and many personal and professional skills are learned through group interactions. It is only natural, then, for counsellors to make use of this primary way of human interaction.

Most counsellors have to make major decisions about when, where, and with whom to use groups. In some situations groups are not appropriate ways of helping. For instance, a counsellor employed by a company would be unwise to use groups to counsel employees with personal problems who are unequal in rank and seniority in the corporate network. Likewise, a school counsellor would be foolish to use a group setting as a way of working with children who are behaviourally disruptive. But a group may be ideal for helping people who are not too disruptive or unequal in status and who have common concerns. In such cases, counsellors generally schedule a regular time for people to meet in a quiet, uninterrupted setting and to interact together.

Groups differ in purpose, composition, and length. Basically, however, they all involve work, which Gazda (1989) describes as "the dynamic interaction between collections of individuals for prevention or remediation of difficulties or for the enhancement of personal growth/enrichment" (p. 297). Hence, the term "group work" is often used to describe what goes on within groups. The ASGW (2000) defines group work as

> a broad professional practice involving the application of knowledge and skill in group facilitation to assist an independent collection of people to reach their mutual goals, which may be intrapersonal, interpersonal, or work related. The goals of the group may include the accomplishment of tasks related to work, education, personal development, personal and interpersonal problem solving, or remediation of mental and emotional disorders. (pp. 329–330)

Groups have a number of general advantages in helping individuals. Yalom (2005) has characterized these positive forces as therapeutic factors. For counselling and psychotherapy groups, these factors include the following:

- *Instillation of hope* (i.e., assurance that treatment will work)
- *Universality* (i.e., the realization that one is not alone, unique, or abnormal)
- *Imparting of information* (i.e., instruction about mental health, mental illness, and how to deal with life problems)
- *Altruism* (i.e., sharing experiences and thoughts with others, helping them by giving of oneself, working for the common good)
- *Corrective recapitulation of the primary family group* (i.e., reliving early family conflicts and resolving them)
- *Development of socializing techniques* (i.e., interacting with others and learning social skills as well as more about oneself in social situations)
- *Imitative behaviour* (i.e., modelling positive actions of other group members)
- *Interpersonal learning* (i.e., gaining insight and correctively working through past experiences)
- *Group cohesiveness* (i.e., bonding with other members of the group)
- *Catharsis* (i.e., experiencing and expressing feelings)

- *Existential factors* (i.e., accepting responsibility for one's life in basic isolation from others, recognizing one's own mortality and the capriciousness of existence)

The group may also serve as a catalyst to help persons realize a want or a need for individual counselling or the accomplishment of a personal goal.

Case Example: What Would *You* Do?

Gerard moved to a large city where he did not know anyone. He worked in isolation at his job in computer programming. Therefore, when he saw that a local church was starting a series of small-group studies, he decided to join. He found his particular group, which focused on social issues, to be stimulating and he looked forward to the weekly meetings. The group even worked with the city to improve a neighbourhood project. Members actively talked to one another in between meetings. After about a month, Gerard reported to his friends back home that he was now feeling better and more a part of his new environment.

1. Although this group was not one devoted to counselling, how do you think it helped Gerard?

2. Which of Yalom's factors may have been important in the process?

BENEFITS AND DRAWBACKS OF GROUPS

Groups have specific advantages that can be beneficial in helping individuals with a variety of problems and concerns. Literally hundreds of studies describe group approaches and statistically support the effectiveness of various forms of groups. Documentation of group experiences is occurring at such a fast rate, however, that it is difficult to stay abreast of the latest developments. Some researchers in the field regularly write comprehensive reviews on select group activities that help practitioners become better informed. Some recent findings about groups reveal the following:

- Group counselling can be used to help Grade 9 and 10 students learn social problem-solving behaviours that help them in career decision preparation (Hutchinson, Freeman, & Quick, 1996).

- Groups can promote career development in general (Pyle, 2000) and can be used effectively in vocational planning with some underserved populations, such as battered and abused women (Peterson & Priour, 2000).

- Group treatment, under the right conditions, can help adult women improve their functioning and general subjective well-being (Marotta & Asner, 1999).

- Group counselling and psychoeducational programs can help persons who have sustained heart attacks deal better with stressors in their lives (Livneh & Sherwood-Hawes, 1993).

- Group intervention with adolescent offenders can help them increase their maturational processes, especially the ability to work in a sustained way and to achieve a sense of relationship with others (Viney, Henry, & Campbell, 2001).

- Group counselling that occurs in college and university counselling centres is effica- cious (McEneaney & Gross, 2009; Perusse, Goodnough, & Lee, 2009; Whiston & Quinby, 2009), despite the finding that most school counsellors are not sufficiently trained in offering group work (Steen, Bauman, & Smith, 2008).

- Group psychotherapy is an established treatment approach that has gained in popu- larity over the past decade (Hopper, Kaklauskas, & Green, 2008).

Yet groups are not a panacea for all people and problems. They have definite limita- tions and disadvantages. For example, some client concerns and personalities are not well-suited for groups. Likewise, the problems of some individuals may not be dealt with in enough depth within groups. In addition, group pressure may force a client to take action, such as self-disclosure, before being ready. Groups may also lapse into a group- think mentality, in which stereotypical, defensive, and stale thought processes become the norm and creativity and problem solving are squelched. Another drawback to groups is that individuals may try to use them for escape or selfish purposes and disrupt the group process. Furthermore, groups may not reflect the social milieu in which individual mem- bers normally operate. Therefore, what is learned from the group experience may not be relevant. Finally, if groups do not work through their conflicts or developmental stages successfully, they may become regressive and engage in nonproductive and even destruc- tive behaviours such as scapegoating, group narcissism, and projection (McClure, 1994).

TYPES OF GROUPS

Groups come in many forms. "There seems to be a group experience tailored to suit the interests and needs of virtually anyone who seeks psychotherapy, personal growth, or simply support and companionship from others" (Lynn & Frauman, 1985, p. 423). There are a number of group models appropriate for a wide variety of situations.

Recognized training in group work is available through the Canadian Group Psycho- therapy Association through their regional training programs in Toronto, Winnipeg, and Calgary. Their national conference is another rich opportunity to learn more about offer- ing group counselling (Canadian Group Psychotherapy Association, n.d. -a).

Lively debate persists about how groups should be categorized, especially in regard to goals and process (Waldo & Bauman, 1998). Nonetheless, the following types of groups have training standards developed by the ASGW (2000).

Psychoeducational Groups

Psychoeducational groups, sometimes known as guidance groups or educational groups, are preventive and instructional (Brown, 1998; Pence, Paymar, Ritmeester, & Shepard, 1998). Their purpose is to teach group participants how to deal with a potential threat (such as AIDS), a developmental life event (such as growing older), or an immediate life crisis (such as the death of a loved one). These types of groups are often found in educational settings such as schools but are increasingly being used in other settings such as hospitals, mental health centres, social service agencies, and universities (Jones & Robinson, 2000).

One of the most important parts of the process in such groups revolves around group discussions of how members will personalize the information presented in the group context (Ohlsen, 1977). In school settings, instructional materials such as unfinished stories, puppet plays, films, audio interviews, and guest speakers are employed in psychoeducational groups. In adult settings, other age-appropriate means using written materials or guest lecturers are used.

An example of a psychoeducational group is the promotion of student development on college and university campuses. During the traditional college-age years, "students grow and change in complexity along a variety of dimensions" (Taub, 1998, p. 197). Their development can be enhanced through psychoeducational groups that address issues important to them such as control of anger, dating relationships, and study skills. These groups are relatively brief in duration and meet for only a limited time, yet they prepare those who attend more adequately for the issues that are covered.

Counselling Groups

Counselling groups, sometimes known as interpersonal problem-solving groups, seek "to help group participants to resolve the usual, yet often difficult, problems of living through interpersonal support and problem solving. An additional goal is to help participants develop their existing interpersonal problem-solving competencies so they may be better able to handle future problems. Non-severe career, educational, personal, social, and developmental concerns are frequently addressed" (ASGW, 1992, p. 143).

Distinguishing between group counselling and a psychoeducational group is sometimes difficult to do. Generally, group counselling is more direct than a psychoeducational group in attempting to modify attitudes and behaviours. For instance, group counselling stresses the affective involvement of participants, whereas a psychoeducational group concentrates more on the cognitive understanding of its members. A second difference is that group counselling is conducted in a small, intimate setting, whereas a psychoeducational group is more applicable to room-size environments (Gazda, Ginter, & Horne, 2001).

At times, a counselling group and a psychoeducational group may overlap (Taub, 1998; Waldo & Bauman, 1998). An example of a brief but effective group counselling approach that overlaps in some aspects with a psychoeducational group is a structured group for high school seniors making the transition to university and to military service (Goodnough & Ripley, 1997). These groups are held for soon-to-be high school graduates. They give the students an opportunity to deal with the complex set of emotions they are experiencing while providing them with information that will assist them in gaining a helpful cognitive perspective on what they are about to do. In group counselling such as this, participants get "airtime" (an opportunity to speak) to discuss their own concerns. The interaction of group members and the personalizing of the information are greater than in a psychoeducational group.

Psychotherapy Groups

Psychotherapy groups, sometimes known as personality reconstruction groups, are set up to help individual group members remediate in-depth psychological problems. "Because the depth and extent of the psychological disturbance is significant, the goal is to aid each individual to reconstruct major personality dimensions" (ASGW, 1992, p. 13).

Sometimes there is overlap in group counselling and group psychotherapy, but the emphasis on major reconstruction of personality dimensions usually distinguishes the two. Group psychotherapy often takes place in inpatient facilities, such as psychiatric hospitals or other mental health facilities that are residential in nature, because it may be necessary to keep close control over the people involved. Certain types of individuals are poor candidates for outpatient, intensive group psychotherapy. Among them are depressives, incessant talkers, paranoids, schizoid and sociopathic personalities, suicidals, and extreme narcissists (Yalom, 2005). It may be easier to identify group psychotherapy candidates who should be excluded than choose those who should be included. Regardless, group psychotherapy is a form of treatment and has provided much of the rationale for group counselling.

Task/Work Groups

Task/work groups help members apply the principles and processes of group dynamics to improve practices and accomplish identified work goals. "The task/work group specialist is able to assist groups such as task forces, committees, planning groups, community organizations, discussion groups, study circles, learning groups, and other similar groups to correct or develop their functioning" (ASGW, 1992, p. 13).

Like other types of groups, task/work groups run best when the following factors are in place:

- the purpose of the group is clear to all participants
- process (dynamics) and content (information) are balanced
- time is taken for culture-building and learning about each other
- conflict is addressed
- feedback between members is exchanged
- leaders pay attention to the "here and now"
- time is taken by leaders and members to reflect on what is happening (Hulse-Killacky, Killacky, & Donigian, 2001)

The classic example of a task/work group is a team. In athletics, arts, and employment settings, teams are often formed to accomplish objectives that would be impossible for an individual to achieve alone. The quality circle, an employee-run group of workers who meet weekly to examine the processes they are using in their jobs and to devise ways to improve them, is a business example of a task/work group (Johnson & Johnson, 2006).

However, counsellors often work in teams to resolve internal and external situations as well as to plan and implement ideas, so these groups have broad applicability.

Another type of task/work group that counsellors may employ is focus groups (Kress & Shoffner, 2007). These groups "can be defined broadly as a technique wherein eight to twelve individuals discuss a particular topic of interest for one or two hours under the direction of a group moderator" (p. 190). The moderator promotes interaction by asking group members open-ended questions and ideally elicits "a synergistic effect that cannot be obtained through individual interviews" (p. 192). Themes are delineated in the process, and the group facilitator may gain valuable information about group members' preferences as well as be able to describe, evaluate, and assess programs such as mental health services.

Case Example: What Would *You* Do?

Thomas was in charge of his office's innovation team. The purpose of the team was to think of ideas that would help streamline work and promote a more cooperative spirit. The task was challenging and, after a few good ideas, nothing new came out of the weekly meetings of the team. Therefore, Thomas decided to hold a team retreat away from the office to help his members focus more and come up with new ideas.

When the team met for the morning in a lovely setting, Thomas made sure that everyone was warmly welcomed and had refreshments. Then he divided team members into groups of three and assigned each a task.

1. What do you think of Thomas's plan?

2. Are there other ways the group could have tackled the task at hand? What might they be?

3. Do you think that having the group work together as a whole would be more productive than having small groups concentrate on a particular task? Why or why not?

THEORETICAL APPROACHES IN CONDUCTING GROUPS

Theoretical approaches to counselling in groups vary as much as individual counselling approaches. In many cases, the theories are the same. For instance, within group work there are approaches based on psychoanalytic, Gestalt, person-centred, rational emotive behaviour, cognitive, and behavioural theories. Because the basic positions of these theories are examined elsewhere in this text, they will not be reviewed here. Yet the implementation of any theoretical approach differs when employed with a group because of group dynamics (the interaction of members within the group).

In an evaluation of seven major theoretical approaches to groups, Ward (1982) analyzed the degree to which each approach paid attention to the individual, interpersonal, and group levels of the process. For instance, psychoanalytic, Gestalt, and behavioural approaches were strong in focusing on the individual but weak on interpersonal and group-level components of the group process. However, the person-centred approach was strong on the individual level and medium on the interpersonal and group level. Ward pointed out the limiting aspects of each approach and the importance of considering other factors, such as the group task and membership maturity, in conducting comprehensive group assignments.

Similarly, Frey (1972) outlined how eight approaches to group work can be conceptualized on a continuum from insight to action and rational to affective, whereas Hansen et al. (1980) conceptualized group approaches on a continuum from process to outcome and leader-centred to member-centred. Group leaders and potential group members must know how theories differ in order to make wise choices. Overall, multiple theoretical models provide richness and diversity for conducting groups.

Three factors, in addition to the ones already mentioned, are useful for group leaders to consider when deciding on what theoretical approach to take.

1. Do I need a theoretical base for conducting the group?
2. What uses will the theory best serve?
3. What criteria will be employed in the selection process?

A theory is a lot like a map. In a group, it provides direction and guidance in examining basic assumptions about human beings. It is also useful in determining goals for the group, clarifying one's role and functions as a leader, and explaining the group interactions. Finally, a theory can help in evaluating the outcomes of the group. Trying to lead a group without an explicit theoretical rationale is similar to attempting to fly an airplane without a map and knowledge of instruments. Either procedure is foolish, dangerous, and likely to lead to injury.

A good theory also serves practical functions (Gladding, 2008). For example, it gives meaning to and a framework for experiences and facts that occur within a setting. Good theory helps make logical sense out of what is happening and leads to productive research. With so many theories from which to choose, the potential group leader is wise to be careful in selecting an approach.

Ford and Urban (1998) believe counsellors should consider four main factors when selecting a theory: personal experience, consensus of experts, prestige, and a verified body of knowledge. All these criteria contain liabilities and advantages. Therefore, it is crucial for beginning counsellors to listen to others and read the professional literature critically to evaluate the theories that are most verifiable and that fit in with their personality styles.

STAGES IN GROUPS

Groups, like other living systems, go through stages. If an individual or group leader is not aware of these stages, the changes that occur within the group may appear confusing rather than meaningful and the benefits may be few. Leaders can maximize learning by either setting up conditions that facilitate the development of the group or "using developmentally based interventions, at both individual and group levels" (Saidla, 1990, p. 15). In either case, group members and leaders benefit.

There is debate in the professional literature about what and when groups go through stages. Developmental stages have been identified in various types of groups, such as learning groups and training groups, yet much of the debate about stages centres around group counselling. Group counselling is most often broken into four or five stages, but some models depict as few as three stages and others as many as six. Tuckman's stage model is considered mainstream.

Tuckman (1965) was one of the first theorists to design a stage process for group counselling. He believed there were four stages of group development: forming, storming, norming, and performing. This concept was later expanded to include a fifth stage: adjourning (Tuckman & Jensen, 1977) or mourning/termination (Waldo, 1985). In each stage certain tasks are performed. For example, in the *forming* stage, the foundation is usually laid for what is to come and who will be considered in or out of group deliberations. In this stage (the group's infancy), members express anxiety and dependency and talk about non-problematic issues. One way to ease the transition into the group at this stage is to structure it so that members are relaxed and sure of what is expected of them. For example, before the first meeting, members may be told they will be expected to spend three minutes telling others who they are (McCoy, 1994).

In the second stage, *storming*, considerable turmoil and conflict usually occur, as they do in adolescence. Conflict within the group at this and other times "forces group members to make some basic decisions about the degree of independence and interdependence in their relationship with one another" (Rybak & Brown, 1997, p. 31). Group members seek to establish themselves in the hierarchy of the group and deal successfully with issues concerning anxiety, power, and future expectations. Sometimes the group leader is attacked at this stage.

The third stage, *norming*, is similar to young adulthood, in which "having survived the storm the group often generates enthusiasm and cohesion. Goals and ways of working together are decided on" (Saidla, 1990, p. 16). This stage is sometimes combined with the storming stage, but whether it is combined or not, it is followed by *performing/working*, which parallels adulthood in a developmental sense. In the performing stage, group members become involved with each other and their individual and collective goals. This is the time when the group, if it works well, is productive.

Finally, in the *mourning/termination* stage, the group comes to an end, and members say goodbye to one another and the group experience. In termination, members feel either fulfilled or bitter. Sometimes there is a celebration experience at this point of the group; at a minimum, a closure ceremony almost always takes place.

Table 13.1 offers a brief breakdown and summary of the characteristics of each of the five stages discussed here.

Table 13.1 Characteristics of the Five Group Stages

Forming	Storming	Norming	Performing/Working	Mourning/Termination
Characterized by initial caution associated with any new experience; attempt to avoid being rejected by others.	**Characterized** by a time of conflict and anxiety; group moves from primary to secondary tension; attempt to balance between too much and too little tension.	**Characterized** by a feeling of "We-ness" that comes when individuals feel that they belong to the group; often enthusiasm and cooperation at this time.	**Characterized** by a focus on the achievement of individual and group goals and the movement of the group into a more unified and productive system.	**Characterized** by participants coming to know themselves on a deeper level; primary activities in termination—reflect on past experiences, process memories, evaluate what was learned, acknowledge ambivalent feelings, engage in cognitive decision making.
Peer relationships: group members tend to be superficial and centre conversion around historical or future events that do not have a direct impact on the group.	**Peer relationships:** group members tend to be more anxious in their interactions with one another; concern for power is prevalent.	**Peer relationships:** identification with others in the group; hope, cooperation, collaboration, cohesion.	**Peer relationships:** genuine concern on a deep, personal level by members for one another; greater willingness to self-disclose on the part of members; increased awareness in the group about individual participants and the world of each person.	**Peer relationships:** feelings of empathy, compassion, and care abound; participants relate to one another on a deep and sometimes emotional level; feelings of warmth and sorrow often occur simultaneously.
Task processing: dealing with apprehension; reviewing members' goals and contracts; specifying more clearly or reiterating group rules; setting limits; promoting positive interchange among members so they will want to continue.	**Task processing:** concentration on direct objectives diminishes; a healthy "pause" takes place; scapegoating may occur.	**Task processing:** members must agree on the establishment of norms from which to operate the group; groups accept both prescriptive and proscriptive norms; importance of commitment is stressed during this time.	**Task processing:** major emphasis on productivity whether the results are tangibly visible or not; maintenance of interpersonal relationships must be attended to and balanced with productivity.	**Task processing:** major emphasis on promoting a successful end to the group and relationships in the group; consolidation of gains; finding of meaning in group, making decisions for new ways of behaving; preparing for a new beginning after group ends.
Useful procedures: joining, linking, cutting off, drawing out and clarifying purpose.	**Useful procedures:** levelling, feedback, informal and formal feedback.	**Useful procedures:** supporting, empathizing, facilitating, self-disclosure.	**Useful procedures:** modelling, exercises, group observing group, brainstorming, nominal-group technique, synectics, written projections, group processing, teaching skills.	**Useful procedures:** summarization, rounds, dyads, written reactions, rating sheets, homework, time limits, capping skills, and modelling.

Overall, the developmental stages of a group are not always easily differentiated at any one point in time. "A group does not necessarily move step by step through life stages, but may move backward and forward as a part of its general development" (Hansen et al., 1980, p. 476). The question of what stage a group is in and where it is heading can best be answered through retrospection or insightful perception.

ISSUES IN GROUPS

Conducting successful groups entails a number of issues. Some deal with procedures for running groups; others deal with training and ethics. Before a group is set up, the leader of the group needs to have a clear idea of why the group is being established and what its intermediate as well as ultimate goals are. It is only from such a process that a successful group will emerge.

Selection and Preparation of Group Members

Screening and preparation are essential for conducting a successful group (Couch, 1995) because the maturity, readiness, and composition of membership plays a major role in whether the group will be a success (Riva, Lippert, & Tackett, 2000). Some individuals who wish to be members of groups are not appropriate candidates for them. If such persons are allowed to join a group, they may end up being difficult group members (e.g., by monopolizing or manipulating) and cause the group leader considerable trouble (Kottler, 1994b). They may also join with others who are at an equally low level of functioning and contribute to the regression of the group. When this happens, members become psychologically damaged, and the group is unable to accomplish its goals (McClure, 1990).

Screening and preparation are usually accomplished through pre-group interviews and training, which take place between the group leader and prospective members. During a *pre-group interview* group members should be selected whose needs and goals are compatible with the established goals of the group. These are members who will not impede the group process, and whose well-being will not be jeopardized by the group experience. Research indicates that *pre-group training*, in which members learn more about a group and what is expected of them, provides important information for participants and gives them a chance to lower their anxiety (Sklare, Petrosko, & Howell, 1993).

In following ethical guidelines and best practices for group counsellors (ASGW, 1998), certain individuals may need to be screened out or may elect to screen themselves out of the group. Screening is a two-way process. Potential group members may not be appropriate for a certain group at a particular time with a designated leader. They should be advised of their options if they are not selected for a group, such as joining another group or waiting for a group to form that is better able to address their situation. In selecting group members, a group leader should heed Gazda's (1989) advice that individuals in the group be able to identify with other group members at least on some issues. In essence, the screening interview "lays the foundation upon which the group process will rest" (McCoy, 1994, p. 18).

Before the group begins, group members and leaders need to be informed as much as possible about *group process* (how group member interactions influence the development of the group). For instance, in *homogeneous groups* (in which members are more alike than unalike), there is usually less conflict and risk taking, more cohesion and support, and better attendance. In contrast, in *heterogeneous groups* (in which members are more unalike than alike), there is more conflict initially and greater risk taking, but support and cohesion may lag and members may drop out (Merta, 1995). It is the process of the group, not the content, focus, or purpose, that will eventually determine whether a group succeeds. In successful groups, the process is balanced with content (Donigian & Malnati, 1997; Kraus & Hulse-Killacky, 1996) (see Figure 13.1). "When either the content or the process of . . . groups becomes disproportionate, the group may experience difficulty accomplishing work" (Nelligan, 1994, p. 8). Veterans of group experiences usually need minimal information about how a group will be conducted, whereas novice participants may require extensive preparation. Members who are informed about the procedures and focus of a group before they begin will do better in the group once it starts.

In joining a group, it is important to check first with the group organizer and become clear about what possibilities and outcomes are expected in a group experience. Corey

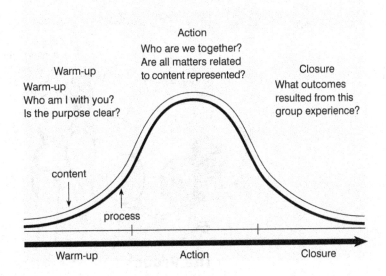

Figure 13.1 Balanced process and content

Source: From "Leadership in Groups: Balancing Process and Content," presentation at the annual convention of the American Counseling Association, April 1994, Minneapolis, MN. Reprinted with permission of Diane Hulse-Killacky, University of New Orleans.

(2008) lists issues that potential participants should clarify before they enroll in a group. The following are among the most important:

- a clear statement of the group's purpose

- a description of the group format, ground rules, and basic procedures

- a statement about the educational and training qualifications of the group leader(s)

- a pre-group interview to determine whether the potential group leader and members are suited for the group at the time

- a disclosure about the risks involved in being in a group and the members' rights and responsibilities

- a discussion about the limitations of confidentiality and the roles group leaders and participants are expected to play within the group setting

Regardless of the perceived need for information, research supports the idea that "providing a set of expectations for participants prior to their initiation into a group improves the possibility of members having a successful group . . . experience" (Sklare, Keener, & Mas, 1990, p. 145). Specifically, group leaders can facilitate "here and now group counselling . . . by discouraging 'you' and 'we' language, questioning, speaking in the third person, seeking approval, rescuing, and analyzing. Group leaders must model the behaviours they wish others to emulate, such as using 'I messages,'" as the cartoon in Figure 13.2 shows (Kraus, 1994).

Figure 13.2 The use of "I" in the group.

Source: © 1994 by Kurt Kraus. Used with permission.

Finally, group leaders must know how to handle challenges to their leadership and resistance from individual group members or from the group as a whole.

Group Size and Duration

A group's size is determined by its purpose and preference. Large groups are less likely to spotlight the needs of individual members. Therefore, outside of group guidance there is an optimal number of people who should be involved. A generally agreed-on number is six to eight group members, although Gazda (1989) notes that if groups run as long as six months, up to 10 people may productively be included. Group size and duration affect each other. Corey (2008) states, "For ongoing groups with adults, about eight members with one leader seems to be a good size. Groups with children may be as small as three or four. In general, the group should have enough people to afford ample interaction so it doesn't drag and yet be small enough to give everyone a chance to participate frequently without . . . losing the sense of 'group'" (p. 72).

Open Versus Closed Groups

Open-ended groups admit new members after they have started; *closed-ended groups* do not. Lynn and Frauman (1985) point out that open-ended groups are able to replace lost members rather quickly and maintain an optimal size. Many long-term outpatient groups are open-ended. Closed-ended groups, although not as flexible in size, promote more cohesiveness among group members and may be productive in helping members achieve stated goals.

Confidentiality

Groups function best when members feel a sense of *confidentiality*—that is, what has been said within the group setting will not be revealed outside. To promote a sense of confidentiality and build trust, a group leader must be active. In the prescreening interview, the subject of confidentiality should be raised. The importance of confidentiality needs to be stressed during the first meeting of the group and on a regular basis thereafter (Corey et al., 2007).

Furthermore, it is the group leader's role to protect his or her members by clearly defining what confidentiality is and the importance and difficulty of enforcing it. Whenever any question arises about the betrayal of confidentiality within a group, it should be dealt with immediately. Otherwise, the problem grows and the cohesiveness of the group breaks down. Olsen (1971) points out that counsellors must realize they can only guarantee their own adherence to the principles of confidentiality. Still, they must strive to ensure the rights of all group members.

Physical Structure

The setting in which a group is conducted is either an asset or a liability. Terres and Larrabee (1985) emphasize the need for a physical structure (a room or a setting) that ensures the safety and growth of group members. Groups in schools and community agencies need to be conducted in places that promote the well-being of the group. The furnishings of the space (attractive) and the way the group is assembled (preferably in a circle) can facilitate the functioning of the group.

Co-Leaders

It is not necessary for groups to have *co-leaders* (two leaders), but such an arrangement can be beneficial to the group and the leaders, especially if the group is large (over 10 members). With co-leaders, one leader can work with the group while the other monitors the group process. A co-leader arrangement may also be beneficial when an inexperienced leader and experienced leader are working together. In such a setup, the inexperienced leader can learn from the experienced one. Many group specialists advocate that an inexperienced leader co-lead a group first before attempting the process alone (Ritter, 1982).

Dinkmeyer and Muro (1979) suggest that successful, experienced co-leaders (a) possess a similar philosophical and operational style, (b) have similar experience and competence, (c) establish a model relationship for effective human interaction, (d) be aware of splitting and member loyalty ties to one leader or the other and help the group deal with this, and (e) agree on counselling goals and the processes to achieve them so that power struggles are avoided.

Pietrofesa, Hoffman, and Splete (1984) recommend that co-leaders sit opposite each other in a group so that leader responsibility and observation are maximized. They point out that it is not necessary for group co-leaders to be of the opposite sex; skills, not gender, matter most.

Self-Disclosure

Shertzer and Stone (1981) define *self-disclosure* as "here and now feelings, attitudes, and beliefs" (p. 206). The process of self-disclosure is dependent on the trust that group members have for one another (Bunch, Lund, & Wiggins, 1983). If there is high trust, greater self-disclosure will ensue. An interesting aspect of this phenomenon is that self-disclosure builds on itself. During the first stages of the group, it may have to be encouraged. Morran (1982) suggests that leaders, in the beginning sessions of a group, use self-disclosure often to serve as a model for others and promote the process. As Stockton, Barr, and Klein (1981) document, group members who make few verbal self-disclosures are more likely than others to drop out of a group.

Feedback

Feedback is a multidimensional process that consists of group members' responding to the verbal messages and nonverbal behaviours of one another. It is one of the most important and abused parts of any group experience. When feedback is given honestly and with care, group members can gauge the impact of their actions on others and attempt new behaviours.

Corey (2008) distinguishes between group feedback given at the end of a session and that given at the termination of a group. During the latter process, Corey encourages group members to be clear, concise, and concrete with one another. Group members should give themselves feedback about how they have changed during the group experience. After processing feedback information, group members should record some of the things said during final feedback sessions so they will not forget and can make use of the experience in evaluating progress toward their goals.

To promote helpful feedback, Pietrofesa et al. (1984) list criteria for feedback evaluation. Here are some important recommendations:

- Feedback should be beneficial to the receiver and not serve the needs of the giver.
- Feedback is more effective when it is based on describable behaviour.
- In the early stages of group development, positive feedback is more beneficial and more readily accepted than negative feedback.
- Feedback is most effective when it immediately follows a stimulus behaviour and is validated by others.
- Feedback is of greater benefit when the receiver is open and trusts the giver (p. 376).

Follow-Up

Follow-up is used in a group to keep in touch with members after the group has terminated to determine how well they are progressing on personal or group goals. Group leaders often fail to conduct proper follow-up. This failure is especially prevalent in short-term counselling groups or groups led by an outside leader (Gazda, 1989). ASGW's *Best Practice Guidelines* (1998) (which clarify the application of the ACA's Code of Ethics to the field of group work) states that group workers should provide for follow-up after the termination of a group as appropriate to assess outcomes or when requested by a group member(s). Follow-up helps group members and leaders assess what they gained in the group experience and allows the leader to refer a group member for help, if appropriate (Gladding, 2008). Follow-up sessions maximize the effects of a group experience and encourage members to keep pursuing original goals (Jacobs, Harvill, & Masson, 2006).

Corey (2008) suggests that a follow-up session for a short-term group be conducted about three months after termination. He points out that the process of mutual feedback and support from other group members at this time can be very valuable. If group members are aware during the termination stage of their group that they will meet again for a follow-up, they are more likely than not to continue pursuing their goals. In addition to a whole-group follow-up, individual follow-up between leaders and group members is important, even if these sessions are conducted by phone.

QUALITIES OF EFFECTIVE GROUP LEADERS

There are distinguishing qualities of effective and ineffective group leaders. For instance, group leaders who are authoritarian, aggressive, confrontational, or emotionally removed from the group are ineffective and produce *group casualties* (members who drop out or are worse after the group experience) (Yalom & Lieberman, 1971). However, the following four leadership qualities have a positive effect on the outcome of groups if they are not used excessively (Yalom, 2005):

1. *Caring*—the more, the better
2. *Meaning attribution*—includes clarifying, explaining, and providing a cognitive framework for change
3. *Emotional stimulation*—involves activity, challenging, risk taking, self-disclosure
4. *Executive function*—entails developing norms, structuring, and suggesting procedures

It is vital that group leaders find a position between the two extremes of emotional stimulation and executive function for the group's well-being. Leaders should not allow members to experience so much emotion that they are unable to process the material being discovered in the group, nor should they structure the situation so rigidly that no emotion is expressed.

Kottler (1994a) states that effective leaders understand the forces operating within a group, recognize whether these forces are therapeutic, and, if they are not, take steps to better manage the group with the assistance of its members. His assessment of leadership complements that of Yalom (2005) and Osborne (1982), who believe that good group leaders behave with intentionality because they are able to anticipate where the group process is moving and recognize group needs. An example of this phenomenon is the ability of group leaders to treat the group homogeneously when there is a need to manage group tensions and protect members and to emphasize heterogeneous qualities when the group has become too comfortable and is not working.

In addition, Corey (2008) maintains that effective group leaders are committed to self-improvement to become effective as human beings. He lists a number of personal qualities that are related to effective group leadership. Among them are presence, personal power, courage, willingness to confront oneself, sincerity, authenticity, enthusiasm, sense of identity, and inventiveness/creativity.

A final quality of effective group leaders is that they are well educated in group theory, practice, and techniques. For instance, in group counselling and psychotherapy, "the group leader's task is to translate symptoms into interpersonal issues" (Pistole, 1997a, p. 7). By so doing, the leader helps participants in groups learn how to develop distortion-free and gratifying relationships. Regardless of the type of group, leaders employ a number of techniques, such as active listening, clarifying, summarizing, questioning, supporting, empathizing, evaluating, giving feedback, modelling, blocking, and terminating.

Case Example: What Would *You* Do?

Lydia was a caring and energetic counsellor. She loved what she did and had much success working with individuals.

One day Lydia's supervisor, Susan, asked her to lead a group of clients who were all experiencing trauma of various kinds. Lydia wanted to be helpful, but she had never experienced trauma and was not sure what to do. When she expressed her reservations to Susan, Susan's reply was this: "Use the skills you already have as a counsellor of individuals. The group will work well if you do."

1. Is Susan's advice to Lydia very helpful?

2. What other skills and abilities might Lydia need in order to lead the group she has been assigned?

THE FUTURE OF GROUP WORK

The future of group work is filled with possibilities and headed in many directions. One focus of group work is the development of new ways of working in groups that are theory driven. For example, solution-focused counselling and brief therapy groups appear to be gaining in popularity and have been found through research to be effective (LaFountain, Garner, & Eliason, 1996; Shapiro, Peltz, & Bernadett-Shapiro, 1998). These groups differ from problem-solving groups in their "focus on beliefs about change, beliefs about complaints, and creating solutions" (LaFountain et al., 1996, p. 256).

Groups are also becoming more preventive. Life-skill training in groups is one example of the prevention emphasis. Four areas of this approach are (a) interpersonal communication and human relations, (b) problem solving and decision making, (c) physical fitness and health maintenance, and (d) development of identity and purpose of life. Another preventive development is how group leaders today infuse a "social justice consciousness" (Singh & Salazar, 2010, p. 93) into their work—a topic significant enough to command two consecutive special issues in the *The Journal for Specialists in Group Work* (Singh & Salazar, 2010

Overall, the future of group work seems robust and headed toward more diversity in both its theory and practice (DeLucia-Waack, 1996). Men as a group have underutilized counselling services, including participation in groups (Cochran, 2005). Nahon and

Lander (2008) provided suggestions on how to increase men's enrollment and participation in groups dealing with relationship dissolution at an Ottawa hospital-based program.

Multicultural issues, especially in regard to awareness of others, self, training, and research, are receiving more attention (Merta, 1995). This is prudent and timely, given that counsellors offering groups are expected to be multiculturally competent (Anderson, 2007). For example, Conyne (1998) has developed a set of "multicultural sensitizers" that can be used along with Hanson's (1972) original group process observation guidelines to help students and other trainees become more aware of multicultural issues in group work. Likewise, guidelines for groups that focus on working with specific cultural minorities have been devised. For instance, ways of working with African American women in groups have been formulated and published (Pack-Brown, Whittington-Clark, & Parker, 1998). More such developments should occur in the 21st century.

SUMMARY AND CONCLUSION

Groups are an exciting, necessary, and effective way to help people. They can take an educational, preventive, or remedial form. The ASGW has formulated standards for psychoeducational groups, counselling groups, psychotherapy groups, and task groups. National training standards in Canada are currently being developed by the Canadian Group Psychotherapy Association (n.d., -b). The theories and some of the techniques used in groups are often the same as those employed in working with individuals. There are differences in application, however.

To be maximally effective, group leaders must be competent in dealing with individual as well as group issues. Learning how to do this is a developmental process. Effective group leaders know what type of groups they are leading and share this information with potential members. Leaders follow ethical, legal, and procedural guidelines of professional organizations. They are concerned with the general well-being of their groups and the people in them. They anticipate problems before they occur and take proactive steps to correct them. They systematically follow up with group members after the group has terminated, and they keep up with the professional literature about groups and are constantly striving to improve their personal and professional levels of functioning.

Overall, groups are a stage-based and expanding way of working with people to achieve individual and collective goals. Professional counsellors must acquire group skills if they are to be well-rounded and versatile.

Your Personal Reflections

1. What self-help groups have you been a part of or watched develop? Do you think most self-help groups are successful? Why or why not?

2. There are a number of horrific examples of dysfunctional groups, many of which ended in loss of life (e.g., Jim Jones and the People's Temple group). On the other hand, there

are a number of exemplary groups that have made a difference in the lives of others and society (e.g., our governments' response to the earthquake in Haiti that occurred on January 12, 2010). Make a list of groups you are aware of and, on a scale of 1 (being lowest) to 10 (being highest), rate them in regard to their functionality.

3. Not being selected for a group may be painful for many people. How might you tell someone he or she was not chosen for a particular group in a diplomatic but truthful way?

Classroom Activities

1. Reflect on the types of groups mentioned in this chapter. Discuss those groups you are most knowledgeable about and comfortable with now. Anticipate the types of groups you might lead in the future.

2. Divide into pairs and discuss the problems and potentials you see in leading a group. Pretend you have been asked to lead a group of your own choosing. What feelings do you have about this upcoming event? How do you see yourself behaving and thinking during each stage of the process?

3. Examine copies of professional counselling journals from the past five years. Report to the class on articles about groups that you are particularly interested in. Compare your findings with those of other class members.

4. Imagine you are a counsellor without any group skills. How do you see yourself functioning in the following settings: a school, an employee assistance program, a private practice? Discuss with the class your thoughts about counsellor engagement in various types of groups.

5. Select a topic that is interesting to a wide variety of individuals (e.g., proper diet or dealing with anger), and present a psychoeducational group lesson to your classmates based on information you have researched. Process this experience directly with the class as soon as you complete it. How difficult or easy was the project?

Chapter 14
Consultation

PRACTICE REFLECTION

One of the most important areas of consultation I do (and one for which I feel most honoured) concerns transsexual adults. Although so many of these people are economically and socially disadvantaged, some have professional jobs, which often means it would not be easy to simply relocate at the time they intend to begin transitioning. For example, male-to-female transsexual individuals will begin developing breasts when they commence female hormone therapy, and for at least a year they will need to dress in feminine attire 24 hours a day. For female-to-male transsexual individuals, their voice will deepen when they begin male hormone therapy and several of their body characteristics will change (e.g., facial hair growth, greater muscularity). These changes and requirements are obvious to employers.

I have worked with several transsexual clients where I have acted as a consultant to their employer (after receiving signed consent). In a larger firm, this has meant first contacting human resources (HR) and informing the appropriate person. From there, a meeting is arranged with this HR person and the manager(s) of my client. This meeting may be the first time the manager becomes aware of my client's issue and the intent to begin transitioning. I begin by providing handouts about transsexuality and then lead a discussion so that "knee jerk" reactions and questions can be addressed. After about an hour, my client is invited to join the group, where we begin planning how and when this person will disclose to their colleagues, the timing of the transition process, and dealing with other employer/employee concerns, such as when he or she will begin using the washroom of the opposite gender.

This approach has proven to be highly successful. In follow-up discussion with my clients, each has been treated with respect, and none have felt that the employer was attempting to create a case for discharge. Quite the contrary has occurred. For example, the president of one company, a deeply religious man, found compassion and became a staunch supporter of his employee.

Consultation directed at helping a client is immensely rewarding, whether it be with an employer, a psychiatrist, a family physician, or any other person. As you will learn in this chapter, this too is only one kind of consultation activity.

Although counsellors in a variety of work settings provide "some consulting services as part of their professional responsibilities, the formal literature on consultation as a function of counselors did not emerge until the late 1960s and early 1970s" (Randolph & Graun, 1988, p. 182). Initially, consultant was defined as an expert with special knowledge to share with the consultee. Therefore, certain theoretical approaches to counselling (such as Adlerian, cognitive, and behavioural) were considered to be best suited for this activity because of their emphases on teaching and pragmatic application. Affective theories were considered to be less desirable because of their focus on close personal relationships and their generally less precise structure. However, as time has shown, consultation can be premised on a variety of theoretical concepts depending on the need of the client or the group.

Regardless of the orientation, consultation is a function expected of all counsellors and one that is receiving increased attention. Sometimes counsellors who function in this capacity are referred to as counsellor–consultants (Randolph & Graun, 1988); at other times, only the word consultant is used. "First and foremost, [consultation is] a human relationship" process (Dougherty, 2005, p. v). It requires a personal touch as well as professional input if it is to be effective. It also requires an acute sensitivity to cultural nuances and multicultural issues (Jackson & Hayes, 1993).

CONSULTATION: DEFINING A MULTIFACETED ACTIVITY

MANY ATTEMPTS HAVE BEEN MADE THROUGH THE YEARS TO DEFINE CONSULTATION, although there is still no universal agreement on the definition. As early as 1970, Caplan defined it as "a process between two professional persons, the consultant, who is a specialist, and the consultee, who invokes the consultant's help in regard to current work problems" (p. 19). Brosseau (1973), working then in Edmonton with both the Separate School District and the University of Alberta, defined consulting as "the procedure by which a consultee seeks help in dealing with a client from a third party, a consultant who is the expert" (p. 259). In relation to elementary school counselling, Brosseau focuses on the counsellor as the consultant, while clearly there are times when the counsellor becomes the consultee, looking for expert help from a specialist.

In the late 1970s, two special issues of the *Personnel and Guidance Journal* (February and March 1978) were published dealing with consultation, followed seven years later by a special issue of *The Counseling Psychologist* (July 1985) devoted exclusively to the same topic. Eight years later, two issues of the *Journal for Counseling and Development* (July/August and November/December 1993) addressed the subject of consultation again in multiple ways. All five publications, and others like them, brought consultation to the forefront of counselling and helped professionals delineate common aspects of the consultation process as follows:

- it is problem-solving focused
- it is tripartite in nature
- it emphasizes improvement (Dougherty, 2005)

In spite of all the attention it has received, consultation is not well conceptualized by many counsellors, who often do not understand its exact nature (Drapela, 1983). Consequently, some counsellors misinterpret the concept, feel uncomfortable about engaging in consultative activities, or both (Goodyear, 1976). Brown (1983) relates the story of a man whose image of a consultant was "someone who blows in, blows off, and blows out" (p. 124). As inaccurate as this idea is, it may reflect the impreciseness implied by the term.

Consultation has "proliferated wildly" since the early 1970s. However, the "theory and research lag far behind" actual practice (Gallessich, 1985, p. 336). The reasons for this lag include the following:

- There is an atheoretical attitude toward consultation that inhibits its development. Consultation originated in many different settings with various groups and has multiple forms, thereby making it hard to organize (Gallessich, 1982). In addition, many counselling consultants do not conceptualize or practise consultation as a specialized professional process.

- Consultation is not the primary activity of all professionals or of any professional group. It lacks "the organizational support, leadership, and resources necessary for theory-building and research" (Gallessich, 1985, p. 342).

- Consultation practices have changed rapidly. Unlike most other forms of helping, consultation reacts quickly to social, political, or technical changes. For example, the humanistic consultation practices of the late 1960s were not widely employed in the more conservative 1980s.

Other factors inhibiting the growth and development of consultation involve difficulties in (a) defining variables and obtaining permission to do specialized research in organizational settings and (b) understanding the changing nature of goals in the consultation process. In other words, initial goals may change.

Some debate still persists about the exact definition of *consultation* (Kurpius & Fuqua, 1993). One of the best definitions is by Kurpius (1978), who defines it as "a voluntary relationship between a professional helper and help-needing individual, group, or social unit in which the consultant is providing help to the client(s) in defining and solving a work-related problem or potential problem with a client or client system." Regardless of its definition, a recent meta-analysis including 1643 studies of consultation outcomes found consultation to be an effective intervention (Gibson & Chard, 1994).

In general, consulting approaches have the following characteristics in common (Gallessich, 1985; Kurpius & Fuqua, 1993; Newman, 1993):

- Consultation is content-based (supported by a recognized body of knowledge).

- Consultation is goal-oriented; it has an objective, often a work-related one.

- Consultation is governed by variable roles and relationship rules.

- Consultation is process-oriented; it involves gathering data, recommending solutions, and offering support.

- Consultation is triadic.

- Consultation is based on ideologies, value systems, and ethics.

Kurpius (1986a; 1988) also stresses that consultation is systems-oriented. It aims to help change aspects of the system, such as its structure or people and to change the system itself. Forces within systems either facilitate or inhibit their receptivity to the consultation process (Kurpius, Fuqua, & Rozecki, 1993) (see Figure 14.1).

Because of its importance to the overall role of counsellors, "a generic consultation course is required in many counsellor training programs, and consultation experiences have been included in the Council for Accreditation of Counseling and Related Programs (CACREP) . . . standards for accreditation of such programs" (Randolph & Graun, 1988, p. 182).

Accreditation of doctoral programs in counselling psychology in Canada shows that they require training in consultation (Canadian Psychological Association, 2009). This is

	System Is Closed to Change	System Is Open to Change
Equilibrium	1. Do Not Accept Contract—Little Chance for Helping	2. Accept Contract but Inform Members That Change May Be Slower
Disequilibrium	3. Accept Contract but Expect High Conflict and Slow Change	4. Best Chance for Successful Helping

Figure 14.1 System openness and balance of forces

Source: Reprinted from "The Consulting Process: A Multidimensional Approach," by D. J. Kurpius, D. R. Fuqua, and T. Rozecki, 1993, *Journal of Counseling and Development, 71*, p. 602. © 1993 by ACA. Reprinted with permission. No further reproduction authorized without written permission of the American Counseling Association.

important, as ethical violations can occur in consultative activities (Thomas, 2010) as is true in all areas of psychological practice in the 21st century.

CONSULTATION VERSUS COUNSELLING

Schmidt and Osborne (1981) found that in actual practice most counsellors they surveyed did not distinguish between consultation and counselling activities. These researchers concluded "the ultimate goals of both are so similar that it is difficult to differentiate between the two when studying them as general processes" (p. 170). Indeed, many of the principles and processes are similar. For example, consultation and counselling may be offered on a primary (preventive) level, and both are interpersonal processes. Yet there are distinctions.

One of the differences between consultation and counselling is that "the content of the consulting interview, unlike counseling, is a unit external to the counseltee" (Stum, 1982, p. 297). Most consultation takes place in a natural setting (often the consultee's work environment), whereas most counselling occurs at a designated centre where a counsellor is employed (Kurpius, 1986b).

A further distinction between counselling and consultation is that consultation services are usually sought when a "system is in decline or crisis" (Nelson & Shifron, 1985, p. 301). Some people do not seek counselling until they are under stress or in distress; others seek counselling for primary prevention reasons or in anticipation of situational or developmental concerns.

Skill in communication is another area in which there are contrasts between these two activities. Communication skills employed in consultation do not differ much from those used in counselling (Kurpius, 1988; Schmidt, 2007). Both counsellors and consultants listen, attend, question, clarify, confront, and summarize. But consultants initially focus more on content than feeling because the process concentrates primarily on problems and issues.

Another difference between consultation and counselling is in the role of practitioners. Professionals who operate from either position try to initiate change in the people with whom they work. Yet consultants play more of a catalyst role because they do not have "direct control over the consultee or the consultee's client" (Kurpius, 1986a, p. 58).

Finally, even though the goals of counselling and consulting are similar ("to help individuals become more efficient, effective, independent, and resourceful in their abilities to solve the problems that they face"), consultation activities work indirectly rather than directly (Nelson & Shifron, 1985, p. 298). Often consultants teach consultees a skill that can be applied to a third party, whereas counselling skills are usually focused on and directly applicable to a specific individual, group, or system.

Case Example: What Would *You* Do?

Katie has been a counsellor for a number of years. She finds the work highly rewarding. However, she wants to do more on a global society level. A friend, Shawn, suggested she become a consultant. Katie is not sure if such work will really make a difference.

1. From what you have read so far, how do you think consultants make a difference?

2. Do you think their impact is as great as a counsellor's?

3. How might you combine counselling and consultation?

FIVE CONCEPTUAL MODELS

Many different models of consultation exist, but only a few of them are comprehensive and useful in counselling. Five of the most comprehensive models of consultation elaborated on by a number of experts (Hoffman et al., 2006; Keys, Bemak, Carpenter, & King-Sears, 1998; Kurpius, 1978; Kurpius & Brubaker, 1976; Schein, 1978) follow:

1. *Expert or provision model.* In the expert model, consultants provide a direct service to consultees who do not have the time, inclination, or perceived skills to deal with a particular problem area. This model of consultation was the first to be developed (Kurpius & Robinson, 1978). It was used extensively in the 1940s and early 1950s. The advantage of the model is that experts can handle difficult problems and leave consultees free to manage their other duties without work conflicts. The major disadvantage is that consultants are blamed if a particular problem does not get better.

2. *Doctor-patient or prescription model.* In the prescription model, consultants advise consultees about what is wrong with the targeted third party and what should be done about it. A good way to conceptualize this method is to compare it with the

traditional medical model in which patients' problems are diagnosed and a prescription to rectify their situations is given. This model is usually implemented when consultees lack confidence in their own intervention strategies. It does not require consultants to bring about a change or a cure, as the provision model does.

3. *Mediation model.* Consultants act as coordinators in the mediation model. Their main function is to unify the services of a variety of people who are trying to solve a problem (Baker & Gerler, 2008). They accomplish this goal by (a) coordinating the services already being provided or (b) creating an alternative plan of services that represents a mutually acceptable synthesis of several solutions. A consultant might work this way in a school system in which a child with a disability is receiving a variety of different services that are disruptive to both the child and the school. Through mediation, services are offered in a systematic way, and less disruption results.

4. *Process consultation or collaboration model.* Consultants are facilitators of the problem-solving process in the collaboration model. Their main task is to get consultees actively involved in finding solutions to the present difficulties they have with clients. Thus, in a school situation, consultees (i.e., parents, educators, youth, counsellors, and community agency professionals) would define their problems clearly, analyze them thoroughly, design workable solutions, and then implement and evaluate their own plans of action. This approach does not assume that any one person has sufficient knowledge to develop and implement solutions and that the group assembled must work as an interdependent team (Keys et al., 1998).

5. *Feminist or multicultural model.* In this model, consultation is both non-hierarchical and open to extra-personal and outside factors. The consultant acts as an agent of social change and is an advocate for both the consultee and the system. Consequently, the authors maintain that the approach is culturally responsive and empowering to consultees (Hoffman et al., 2006). Given that Canada is a pluralistic society, the multicultural model holds promise. Gutow, Rynkewitz, and Reicher (2009) maintain that the role of the school psychologist in Canada has already evolved from that of a gatekeeper for special education services to that of a change agent within schools. Recent research from a cultural consultation service developed in Montreal indicated that cultural misunderstandings resulted in incomplete assessments, incorrect diagnoses, inadequate or inappropriate treatments, and poor working alliances with mental health practitioners (Kirmayer, Groleau, Guzder, Blake, & Jarvis, 2003). Another recent study revealed the importance of multicultural competence in providing psychiatric consultation services to the Inuit people of Northern Canada (Kassam, 2006).

Setting up an atmosphere in which effective consultation takes place is a major task for consultants. It requires the use of a number of interpersonal counselling skills, such as empathy, active listening, and structuring (Baker & Gerler, 2008). In addition, counsellors who work as consultants must be highly intelligent and analytical thinkers who are able to generate enthusiasm, optimism, and self-confidence in others. They must also be able to integrate and use affective, behavioural, and cognitive dimensions of problem solving.

LEVELS OF CONSULTATION

Consultation services may be delivered on several levels. Three of the most common ways to implement the process involve working at the individual, group, and organizational/community levels (Kurpius, 1988).

Individual Consultation

Kisch (1977) has discussed aspects of one-to-one consultation. He employs a *role-reversal process*, in which a client role-plays either an active or passive consultant while the counsellor role-plays the client. The client sits in different chairs when playing the separate roles. When passive, the client gives only familiar, safe, nonthreatening advice in response to the presented problem, and there is no confrontation. When active, the client reflects "thoughts, feelings, and strategies that are assertive, confrontive, and may be novel and frightening" (p. 494). In each case, counsellors ask clients about the payoffs and risks of the client- and consultant-initiated ideas for change.

Another form of individual consultation involves teaching self-management skills. Kahn (1976) points out that externally maintained treatment modalities are not very effective. To replace them, he proposes a four-part interdependent component model with the following requirements:

- *Self-monitoring*—persons observe their own behaviour
- *Self-measurement*—persons validate the degree to which the problem exists
- *Self-mediation*—persons develop and implement strategies of change
- *Self-maintenance*—persons continually monitor and measure the desired effects of the self-management process

Kahn gives examples of excessive and deficit behaviours that can be managed through this model, including cigarette smoking, obesity, assertiveness, and depression. He points out that when individuals learn the steps of self-management, they can take preventive and remedial actions on their own.

Kurpius (1986a) emphasizes that "mutual trust and respect are essential" on an individual consultation level (p. 61). For example, Fogle (1979) suggests that teaching individuals a constructive negative-thinking process can sometimes alleviate anxiety, restore motivation, promote risk-taking behaviours, and shift attention to the present. In this process, clients are instructed to think negatively about future-oriented events and make contingency plans if the worst possible situation occurs. They are instructed to follow the instructions of the consultant only if they believe what is being suggested will work.

Overall, at the individual consultation level, a consultant is often required to model a skill or prescribe a solution. Working on an individual level is appropriate if the consultee clearly has an individual problem, a systems intervention is inappropriate or impossible, or individual change would be more beneficial and efficient (Fuqua & Newman, 1985). One recent form of individual consultation that has become increasingly popular, especially in business, is executive coaching (Sears, Rudisill, & Mason-Sears, 2006).

Group Consultation

Group consultation is employed when several individuals share a similar problem (e.g., in a work setting). Kurpius (1986a) states that in work situations in which group consultation is employed, the group may be focused on either problem solving or persons. In problem-solving groups, the consultant acts as a catalyst and facilitator. In person-focused groups, the consultant may help group members build teams to understand and resolve person problems (Sears et al., 2006).

The *C group* was one of the first effective collaborative consultation models (Dinkmeyer, 1971; 1973b; Dinkmeyer & Carlson, 1973; 2006). All aspects of the approach begin with a *C*: collaboration, consultation, clarification, confrontation, concern, confidentiality, and commitment. Its primary purpose is to present new knowledge about human behaviour to members of the group. It encourages group members to work together as equals (collaboration); to give and receive input from each other (consultation); to understand the relationship among beliefs, feelings, and actions (clarification); to share openly with each other (confrontation); to empathize with one another (concern); to keep information within the group (confidentiality); and to make plans for specific changes (commitment). Although the C group has the potential to influence parent–child interactions dramatically, the group is always composed of adults because its Adlerian orientation assumes that adults control parent–child interactions for better or worse. Furthermore, it is never used for counselling purposes, only for sharing information and mutual support.

Voight, Lawler, and Fulkerson (1980) have developed a program that assists women who are making midlife decisions. It has some parallels to C groups because it is directed toward promoting self-help and providing information in a group setting. The program makes use of women's existing social networks to help them become psychologically stronger and more informed about community resources and opportunities. A lasting advantage is that participants not only become better educated and self-directed, but also continue to live in an environment where they can receive support and input from others who have gone through the same experience. Similarly, a self-help centre for adolescents has been designed to function as a form of group consultation (O'Brien & Lewis, 1975). At the centre, which was originally set up for substance abusers, clients are empowered with information and methods of helping themselves and each other.

Organization/Community Consultation

Because organization and community consultations are much larger in scope than individual or group consultations, consultants must possess sophisticated knowledge of systems to operate effectively at this level (Levinson, 2009). Unlike individual or group consultants, organization or community consultants are external to the project, although most of their activities involve individuals or groups (Sears et al., 2006). For example, counsellors may function as political consultants because they are "in a pivotal position to effectively communicate the concerns of people they serve to policy makers at local, state, and national levels of government" (Solomon, 1982, p. 580). Such activities involve lobbying with individual representatives as well as testifying before and making recommendations to special committees.

Conyne (1975) mentions other ways of consulting at a community or organizational level. He emphasizes the individual within the environment, stressing *environmental mapping*. In other words, he believes that when counsellors find individuals who exist in less-than-optimal mental health settings, they can work as change agents to improve the situation of the target population. Focusing on social action and social justice improves clients' conditions and their mental health while sometimes lessening their need for counselling (Lee, 2006a; Lee & Walz, 1998).

Barrow and Prosen (1981) also address the importance of working as consultants on environmental factors, but they advocate a global change process. In addition to helping clients find coping techniques to deal with stress, counsellors must help clients change stress-producing environments. This process is best achieved by working to change the structure of the system rather than the person within it. Aplin (1985) formulated a model that depicts the content and process areas that a consultant should be aware of when working on an organizational or community basis (see Figure 14.2).

Case Example: What Would *You* Do?

Rebecca was called in as a consultant to help the executive director of a mental health centre, Roy, become more efficient in his job. As she worked with him, she realized he did not follow through on the recommendations she made. Instead, he told her one thing and then did another. Roy rationalized this behaviour to himself by telling himself that he knew more about the organization than Rebecca ever would.

As time went by, it became obvious that Roy was not changing and that morale was slipping among centre employees. Roy was stuck in his ways, Rebecca was frustrated, and the efficiency of the centre was deteriorating rapidly.

1. What do you think should be the next action taken by Rebecca? Why?

2. In such a scenario, it would not be uncommon for employees working for Roy to complain to you, the consultant. How would you handle their complaints without alienating Roy, your *employer*?

Figure 14.2 Aplin's model

Source: From "Business Realities and Organizational Consultation," by J. C. Aplin, 1978, *Counseling Psychologist*, *13*, p. 400, copyright © 1978 by Sage Publications, Inc. Reprinted by permission of Sage Publications, Inc.

STAGES AND ATTITUDES IN CONSULTATION

Developmental stages are an important part of many consultation activities (Wallace & Hall, 1996). Two well-known theories propose distinct consultation stages. The first is Splete's (1982a) nine-stage process based on the premise that clients collaborate with consultants to work on predetermined concerns. The order of the stages in this approach is as follows:

1. *Pre-contract*. The consultant clarifies personal skill and areas of expertise that can be used in the consultation process.

2. *Contract and exploration of relationship*. The consultant discusses a more formal arrangement between himself or herself and the consultee. The consultee's readiness and the consultant's ability to respond must be determined.

3. *Contracting.* A mutual agreement is set up that defines what services are to be offered and how.

4. *Problem identification.* Both the consultant and consultee determine and define the precise problem to be worked on and the desired outcome.

5. *Problem analysis.* The focus is on reviewing pertinent information and generating possible solutions.

6. *Feedback and planning.* Here the alternative solutions generated in stage 5 are evaluated and the probabilities of success are determined. One or more solution plans are then systematically implemented.

7. *Implementation of the plan.* The consultee carries out the proposed plan with the consultant's support.

8. *Evaluation of the plan.* Both the consultant and consultee determine how well the plan worked in relationship to the desired outcome.

9. *Conclusion and termination of relationship.* Both parties in the process review what has happened and plan for any follow-up, either independently or with the consultant.

Although Splete's plan is detailed and useful, it does not elaborate on counsellor skills contained within the process. A second model that does has been proposed by Dustin and Ehly (1984). It outlines a five-stage process of consultation along with counsellor techniques and behaviours that accompany each stage. The model assumes that the consultant is working in a school setting with either a parent or teacher, but it has potential usefulness outside the school environment—for example, in business, government, corrections, and rehabilitation. Its stages are as follows:

1. *Phasing in.* The focus is on relationship building and can be compared with Splete's (1982a) pre-contract stage. The consultant uses skills such as active listening, self-disclosure, and empathy and promotes a sense of trust.

2. *Problem identification.* Comparable to stages 2 through 4 in the Splete model, this step focuses on determining whether a suspected third-party problem really exists. Consultants employ focusing skills as well as other counselling techniques, such as paraphrasing, restatement, genuineness, and goal setting.

3. *Implementation.* Similar to stages 5 through 7 of Splete's scheme, this stage defines strategies and sets up a timeframe. Feedback is an important part of this process. Flexibility, dealing with resistance and negative feelings, and patience are other counsellor skills involved.

4. *Follow-up and evaluation.* This stage merges with stage 3 at times, but its focus is distinct. It concentrates on the results gained from the consultation process, especially if the consultee is satisfied with the outcome of changes. Counsellor skills include risk taking, openness, and persistence. These skills are especially important if the consultee is dissatisfied or frustrated.

5. *Termination.* The consultant helps bring closure to previous activities. Relationship skills such as empathy and genuineness are again employed. Giving and asking for feedback time are important. It is vital that the consultant and consultee evaluate what was most profitable for each and what aspects of the procedure were less effective.

Splete (1982a) also lists four attitude areas that are important for consultants. First, they must display an attitude of professionalism; they must take responsibility for helping their clients deal with immediate and long-term problems. Second, consultants must show maturity; they have to be willing to stand up for their own views, take risks, and deal with hostility or rejection. Third, consultants need to demonstrate open-mindedness and not close off ideas and input into the problem-solving process too soon. Finally, they need to believe in the importance of individuals and place people above technology.

SPECIFIC AREAS OF CONSULTATION

Consultation often takes place in schools and community agencies, but the process may occur in almost any environment. In this section, some of the work conducted in schools and agencies will be examined as examples of the kinds of consultation programs that can be set up.

School Consultation

Kahnweiler (1979) has traced the concept of school counsellors as consultants from its beginnings in the United States in the late 1950s. As he points out, the accompanying literature has evolved in theory and practice. The development of school consultation has been summarized by Bundy and Poppen (1986), who surveyed articles from *Elementary School Guidance and Counseling* and *The School Counselor* over 28 years and found that consultation was effective in prevention and intervention in schools. Consultation by school counsellors also enhances overall school achievement, improves student self-concept, reduces stress in certain populations, leads to better classroom management skills, and facilitates the moral growth of students (Carlson & Dinkmeyer, 2001; Cecil & Cobia, 1990; Conoley & Conoley, 1992; Kampwirth, 2006). As a process, "consultation is an efficient method of impacting the well-being and personal development of many more students than can be seen directly by a counsellor" (Otwell & Mullis, 1997, p. 25).

Generally, school counsellors are in the perfect position to act as consultants and change agents (Baker & Gerler, 2008; Podemski & Childers, 1980). On most school organizational charts, the counsellor is positioned as a staff authority rather than a line authority. Persons in staff authority positions are expected to have specialized knowledge, such as familiarity with the multiple levels of laws that may be applicable (McCarthy & Sorenson, 1993). Therefore, they can act in an advisory and supportive way for others. By functioning in this manner, school counsellors help bring about environmental and systemic changes (Schmidt, 2007). They advise persons in positions of power about what conditions need modifying and then support efforts to make improvements.

Umansky and Holloway (1984) view the many aspects of consultation as a way of serving students and the larger population of the school community without increasing expenditures. They advocate four approaches to consultation in the schools: Adlerian, behavioural, mental health, and organizational development.

The *Adlerian-based approach* is a psychological education model that assumes that individuals, groups, and communities lack information. The consultant teaches within the organizational structure of the school and emphasizes ways to promote positive behaviour in children (Carlson, Watts, & Maniacci, 2006).

The *behavioural approach*, also geared to teaching, concentrates on instructing consultees how to use behavioural principles in working with students and how to collect empirical data to validate each intervention strategy (Kampwirth, 2006).

The *mental health approach* is based on the broader community mental health approach developed by Caplan (1970). Psychodynamic theory underlies mental health consultation. The goal of this approach is to help teachers and other powerful personnel in the school gain new insight into themselves and their students.

Finally, the *organizational development approach* emphasizes the context in which problems arise. Thus, if students and teachers have problems, the climate of the school becomes the focus of concern. To be most helpful, the consultant has to work on changing the school's atmosphere and structure (Baker & Gerler, 2008). Sometimes the task requires the support of administrators who may not favour such an objective. In other cases, it involves asking school counsellors to set up an environment in which other school personnel, mainly teachers, feel "that it is natural to consult and work with counsellors" (Edgemon, Remley, & Snoddy, 1985, p. 298).

Consultation with teachers is an effective way to provide services for them and for the school in general. In this systemic process, school counsellors can use a developmental counselling and therapy-based model to access how teachers are conceptualizing students' behaviours. Furthermore, they can respond to the stress teachers may feel in connection with certain behaviours. Just as importantly, if not more so, through their consultation efforts, they may indirectly effect change in classroom systems (Clemens, 2007; Kampwirth, 2006).

Offering consultation for curriculum developers and community organizations is yet another way school counsellors can provide services. This broader type of consultation takes time and effort but is worth it. Theoretical bases for this group consultation process include those that are person-centred, Adlerian, and behavioural.

School counsellors can also work from a parent–counsellor consulting model, which aims to solve student problems (behavioural, attitudinal, or social) and educate parents on how to help their children with particular situations (Campbell, 1993a; Ritchie & Partin, 1994). In offering consultation services to parents, counsellors may face resistance, such as

- excuses ("I can't come during the day"),
- negative mindsets ("My child is doing well; why bother me?"), and
- denial ("There is nothing wrong with my child's relationship to the school").

To overcome resistance, school counsellors can be empathetic, arrange for parental observations of a child, help the parent refocus or reframe situations, and share parables (i.e., stories of similar situations).

One aspect of school consultation (which can be used in agency consultation, too) is the use of peers. A peer consultant group can "provide appropriate supervision and feedback for school counsellors" (Logan, 1997, p. 4) while increasing self-confidence, self-direction, and independence for counsellors. Peer consultation also is time-efficient. It can be organized to provide "(a) case consultation; (b) solution-focused problem solving; (c) peer support; (d) constructive feedback without concern for evaluation or necessity for change unless the member chooses to do so; and (e) access to needed materials and resources" (p. 4). In the Structured Peer Consultation Model for School Counsellors (SPCM-SC), a total of nine 90-minute sessions are held every other week in which counsellors "use their basic helping skills" to help one another progress in their growth as professionals (Benshoff & Paisley, 1996, p. 314). Such a model makes use of talent within a group of similarly employed counsellors and can be as useful and productive as more formalized supervision sessions.

A final model for school consultation is to have an outside professional, a collaborative consultant, work with the school community in an action research approach (Lusky & Hayes, 2001). Such an approach is global in scope and premised on the fact that many school counsellors cannot for various reasons provide overall consultation services for their schools. However, they can participate with others in the school environment in such research and evaluation and can help implement outcomes that are generated from the process. This type of collaborative consultation involves five major phases: planning, analyzing, designing, implementing, and evaluating. At the genesis of this process an outside consultant meets with the school program stakeholders, including the superintendent and school board, in order to get a "buy in" for the consultation intervention that re-examines current practices within a school and future goals. School personnel, parents, and students help shape and own the process by contributing ideas, giving feedback along the way, and working in teams with the consultant. Such a procedure, when successful, takes time and effort but is focused at the uniqueness of the school and results in a school climate that is ready and willing to implement needed changes on a continuous basis.

School consultation in Canada began in 1960, and compared to the United States, there are some differences. In Canada, school consultation is less clearly conceptualized. Furthermore, the research literature in the United States is voluminous compared to that in Canada, even when allowing for proportional differences (Sladeczek & Heath, 1997).

Also, compared to the United States, the behavioural approach to consultation has not been widely studied in Canada (Sladeczek, Madden, Illsley, Finn, & August, 2006). In their study, Sladeczek et al. (2006) surveyed both school psychologists and parents. The psychologists rated the behavioural approach as the preferred intervention for academic, behavioural, and social-emotional problems. Parents also rated the approach as highly acceptable for use with their children.

Agency Consultation

According to Werner (1978), agency consultation in the United States resulted from the passage of the *Community Mental Health Centers Act* of 1963. Implicit within the act is the philosophy that mental health should be viewed from a local community perspective with an emphasis on prevention.

Caplan (1964) sets forth a three-level definition of *prevention*. The first level consists of *primary prevention*, a reduction in the incidence of mental disorders. This goal is achieved within the general population "by actively changing environments and settings and by teaching life skills" (Goodyear, 1976, p. 513). One of the primary activities at this level of intervention is consultation. Waxer and White (1973) discussed research focused on providing primary prevention at a central Canadian university.

Secondary prevention, a reduction in the duration of mental disorders, is the next focus. This goal is achieved by working with individuals to forestall or alleviate problem areas and attempting early detection and reversal of acute psychological crises. Finally, *tertiary prevention* is a reduction in the impairment that may result from psychological disorders. One way to conceptualize this level of prevention is as treatment. The more successful primary and secondary prevention are, the less need there is for tertiary prevention.

Examples abound of primary prevention in agency settings. Werner (1978) and Caplan and Caplan (1993) propose six levels of community mental health consultation.

1. *Client-centred case consultation.* The goal is to enable the consultee to deal more effectively with the current situation and similar situations in the future.

2. *Consultee-centred case consultation.* The goal is collaboratively to identify consultee difficulties in working with certain types of clients and to help the consultee develop the skills to deal effectively with this and similar situations in the future.

3. *Program-centred administrative consultation.* The goal is to help the consultee deal more effectively with specific parts of a mental health program and to improve his or her abilities to function with similar program problems in the future.

4. *Consultee-centred administrative consultation.* The goal is to identify consultee problems generated by implementing a mental health program and to develop collaboratively the consultee's skills in dealing with similar problems.

5. *Community-centred ad hoc consultation.* The goal is to enable an ad hoc consultee to deal more effectively with community problems encountered while developing a temporary program of mental health services.

6. *Consultee-centred ad hoc consultation.* The goal is to identify collaboratively the ad hoc consultee's problems generated in providing temporary mental health services and to take steps to help the consultee develop skills in dealing with these problems.

Aplin (1985) points out that consultants who work with agencies such as public corporations, governments, or universities must be aware of trends that affect the process of consultation itself. He lists five trends that have continued to influence agency consultation:

1. Downsizing of organizations
2. Creation of semi-autonomous work units brought about by mergers
3. Rebirth of commitment leadership by managers
4. Process-based technologies (such as robotics and computers) in manufacturing
5. Egalitarian social and organizational values

Because of the rapid changes in agencies, consultation skills are in great demand, but "the key to successfully implementing systems change programs is to increase the basic skills the consultant brings to the change process." Alpin (1985) stresses that the demands on consultants "will grow in direct proportion to growth in organizational complexity and turbulence associated with underlying social and economic change" (p. 401).

Case Example: What Would *You* Do?

I recently had a 16-year-old client, Robert, who concerned me a great deal. Another psychologist referred him to me as he had cut himself several times in the past, at one point was highly suicidal, and was now talking about how he always wanted to be a female. I first consulted with the parents to get their perspective on what was occurring with their son. They did not feel the gender question was significant, but instead saw Robert as highly imaginative, prone to suggestion, and "quirky."

The referring psychologist also wondered if Robert had Asperger's Disorder, a disorder marked by social impairment and odd mannerisms or stereotyped and repetitive behaviours. I wondered this myself as I watched Robert, who had some atypical facial expressions and moved his hands in odd ways. He also reported several strange sensations and mental experiences; for example, his mind would automatically create female avatars shortly before he fell asleep. Furthermore, Robert did not want to ever have gender reassignment surgery or to cross-dress. I referred him to an early intervention psychosis program, knowing that they would assess him more thoroughly and place him in a special program if needed.

1. If Robert was diagnosed as having schizophrenia in its early stages (or, in fact, before it had had a chance to develop), what level of intervention would the clinic be providing if its program successfully prevented a psychotic breakdown?

2. If you were Robert's counsellor, how might you be helpful, regardless of whether he is schizophrenic or not?

TRAINING IN CONSULTATION

Since the late 1970s, a number of models for training individuals in consultation skills have been proposed and developed (Brown, 1993; Brown, Pryzwansky, & Schulte, 2005; Conoley, 1981; Kampwirth, 2006; Sears et al., 2006). Most models are competency-based and emphasize various modes of training consultants, such as didactic, laboratory, field placement, and supervision (Gallessich, 1974).

Stum's (1982) Directed Individual Response Educational Consulting Technique (DIRECT) is an excellent example of a model that has attempted to synthesize previous knowledge and help students learn what they are supposed to do in a consulting interview and how they are supposed to do it. Stum views consulting as a systematic process with sequential steps. The model is structured so that beginning students can conceptualize the consultation process developmentally. It includes the following steps: (a) establish the consulting relationship, (b) identify and clarify the problem situation, (c) determine the desired outcome, (d) develop ideas and strategies, (e) develop a plan, (f) specify the plan, and (g) confirm the consulting relationship. The DIRECT model also specifies four sequential leads for each of the seven developmental steps. Based on systematic human relations training, these leads provide guidelines for the consultant and consultee to enter, initiate, educate, and evaluate each step in the consulting process. Cue words are provided for the consultant trainee at each step and level of the process. An evaluation chart, the Technique and Relationship Evaluation Chart (TREC), is available to assess the degree of competency achieved by the consultant trainee (see Figure 14.3).

Brown (1985; 1993) also proposes developmental stages for training human services consultants. He stresses didactic, laboratory, and field placement competencies that must be mastered. In addition, he elaborates on problems (e.g., resistance) and strategies to overcome these problems (e.g., ways to select proper interventions). His model requires instructors to help trainees master consultation skills by analyzing case histories, modelling cognitive strategies by talking through cases, and employing a Socratic method of inquiry. Brown emphasizes that the well-trained consultant should master conceptual and relationship skills at five discernable stages of consultation: (a) relationship or entry, (b) assessment or problem identification, (c) goal setting, (d) choosing and implementing change strategies, and (e) evaluation and termination.

Gallessich (1985) advocates that future consultation models and training be based on one of three models, which are not mutually exclusive:

1. *Scientific/technological consultation.* In this model, which focuses on knowledge deficits, the consultant's primary role is that of an expert on information and technique.

2. *Human-development consultation.* The consultant's primary role, according to this model, is to be an educator and facilitator in affective and cognitive processes that influence professional and personal relationships in an organization.

3. *Social/political consultation.* In this model, the consultant takes a partisan role to help change organizations so that they conform to particular values, such as democracy. Methods of training consultants in this model are still being developed.

Step A—Establish Consulting Format

Behaviour	Lead
Level 1 The consultant listens, observes, repeats, and paraphrases. Attending and responding promotes understanding.	"You're saying that _____ ." "The problem seems to be _____ ." "So, the situation is _____ ."
Level 2 The consultant uses the term *consult* or *collaborate* in regard to working together. Explaining the use of a systematic process sets the tone for the interview.	"We can consult together about _____ ." "In our work, we'll use a problem-solving process."
Level 3 The consultant briefly explains the initial steps in the problem-resolution process. This is the first "teaching" of the model and further establishes the direction for the consulting interview.	"We'll go through several steps working together." "First, in clarifying the problem, we'll be _____ ." "Later on, we'll be trying to set some goals in regard to _____ ."
Level 4 The consultant "checks-in" regarding this step and then suggests moving ahead to the next step.	"Can we work together along these lines?" "Let's go ahead and clarify the problem further."

Step B—Identify-Clarify the Problem

Behaviour	Lead
Level 1 The consultant clarifies the history, environment, causes and effects of the problem-situation.	"Tell me more about the background of _____ ." "What do you see as the effects of _____ ." "So, your position in this is that of _____ ."
Level 2 The consultant summarizes the major factors presented in the problem-situation. A dominant "theme" is stated.	"The major factor seems to be _____ ." "Then to summarize, _____ ."

Figure 14.3 DIRECT chart

Source: Reprinted from "DIRECT—A Consultation Skills Training Model," by D. Stum, 1982, *Personnel and Guidance Journal, 60,* p. 300. © 1982 by ACA. Reprinted with permission. No further reproduction authorized without written permission of the American Counseling Association.

In addition to training consultants, Zins (1993) emphasizes the need to educate consultees in skills such as problem solving, communication, and intervention techniques before the actual consultation process. If consultees have these skills, they can make better use of consultation services in specific environments.

SUMMARY AND CONCLUSION

Consultation is a systematic concept with a set of skills (Parsons, 1996). Although it is growing in importance, it is still in the process of being defined. Several definitions of consultation emphasize that it is primarily an indirect service; usually triadic; voluntary; and based on roles, rules, values, and goals. Consultation and counselling have distinct differences, such as the directness of the activity, the setting in which it is conducted, and the way communications are focused. Counsellors are in an ideal position to function as human service consultants, but they must receive specialized training to do so.

The five models of comprehensive consultation found in the literature (i.e., expert [provision], doctor-patient [prescription], mediation, process/collaboration, and feminist or multicultural) emphasize the multidimensional aspects of consultation. There are distinct consultation levels (individual, group, and organizational) and definite stages that the process goes through (e.g., phasing in, identifying problems, implementing, following up, terminating). Important skills and attitudes make up the complete process. Consultation is implemented in schools and agencies, and training models are being used to teach consultation skills. The concept and implementation of counsellor as consultant are ideas that are still developing.

Your Personal Reflections

1. Why do you think it might be important to be a practising counsellor first if an individual aspires to be a consultant to counsellors? What would be the drawback of this lack of experience?

2. Of the five models of consultation presented, which do you like the most or feel most drawn toward? Try to assess your reason for being attracted to a particular model, drawing on events or experiences you have had.

3. Bruce Springsteen has a lyric that says, "You can't go the distance with too much resistance." Obviously, as discussed in the chapter, there is resistance in consultation settings. What are some things you could say to address excuses, negative mindsets, and denial?

Classroom Activities

1. How do you distinguish consultation from counselling? Discuss your ideas with a fellow classmate and then with the class as a whole.

2. Which of the four comprehensive models of consultation do you think is most appropriate for clients you plan to work with in the future? Why? Which of these models do you consider least appropriate for your future work? Discuss your opinions with another classmate and then with the class as a whole.

3. Which stage in the consultation process do you think is most important? Which one do you think is most difficult? Are they the same? With three other classmates, discuss what skills you possess that will enable you to be an effective consultant. Identify skills you must refine or develop within yourself to work in this capacity.

4. What theoretical approach do you find most attractive as a basis for consultation services? Divide the class into groups based on similar orientations. After each group has had an opportunity to discuss its ideas, share them with fellow classmates.

5. Do you think there are other proactive activities counsellors can engage in that cannot be classified as a part of counselling or consultation? What specific behaviours would you place in this category? Discuss your ideas in groups of four and then with the class as a whole.

Chapter 15
Evaluation and Research

PRACTICE REFLECTION

When I worked at a community college, I was head of the counselling centre for a total of seven years. Postsecondary schools went through some difficult financial times during some of those years, as is often the case during government cutbacks and economic recessions. There was even talk of having our department outsourced during the really lean years, and that was a threat I needed to deal with through much of my time as head.

How do you convince administrators that what you do makes a difference, and that the difference you make is more than an outsource could provide? The answer lies partly in how one works within the political structure (I attempted to make us as valuable to the institution as possible by connecting all of my department's objectives to institutional ones), but ultimately, our main work was counselling students, an activity that is confidential and done behind closed doors. Who was going to see what we did?

Evaluation was the key. We began by having students—our clients—complete a quantitative evaluation during a few weeks of the academic year. I could then say that, on average, we received 4.5 out of 5, which meant that most students met their counselling goals and that they appreciated us as helpers. As that information was sent to administration, it occurred to us that the impact was favourable, and yet still they had no idea what we actually did behind the closed doors of our offices.

It was time to educate administration and others who were curious. During the spring term when our centre was a little quieter, we each wrote two or three case summaries regarding students we had counselled. Each about one page, they contained a brief background history, a statement of the presenting issue, the treatment approach taken, the number of sessions, and a synopsis of the outcome. Despite how selective these were, they were informative—finally administrators understood what we did. It made sense to them. In the year I left, as part of the college's expansion project, one of the largest new counselling centres in the province was being built.

Evaluation, especially in this case qualitative evaluation, had made a significant impact. We were helping students succeed. Who would not want to invest in that?

Evaluation and research are essential parts of counselling and counselling-related activities (LaFountain & Bartos, 2002). It is not enough for counsellors to be warm, caring, and empathetic persons trained in the theories, methods, and techniques of counselling. Rather, counsellors must be evaluators and researchers too, for it is through evaluation and research that they come to understand and improve their practices (Hadley & Mitchell, 1995; May, 1996). Counsellors who lack research and evaluation abilities place themselves and the counselling profession in jeopardy, along with with the general public, third-party payers, and specific clients who rightfully demand accountability. A failure to evaluate and research counselling methods also puts counsellors in danger of being unethical because they cannot prove that the counselling services they offer have a reasonable promise of success, as required by the ethical codes of the professional counselling associations (Heppner, Wampold, & Kivlighan, 2008; Sexton & Whiston, 1996).

Thus, evaluation and research are ways counsellors can ensure quality client care and positive outcomes (Herman, 1993). These counselling procedures also help counsellors pause and examine their practices. At such times, counsellors may "think differently about, and even behave differently in counseling," thereby improving themselves and the profession (Watkins & Schneider, 1991, p. 288).

Being an evaluator, a researcher, and a consumer of evaluations and research demands time and a thorough understanding of the commonly used methods in these domains (Sexton, 1996). This chapter explores the processes of evaluation and research in counselling, with the assumption that counsellors can cultivate skills in these areas.

THE NATURE OF EVALUATION AND RESEARCH

EVALUATION AND RESEARCH ARE DIFFERENT, YET THEY HAVE MUCH IN COMMON. WHEELER and Loesch (1981) note that the two terms have often been paired conceptually and are frequently used interchangeably. Krauskopf (1982) asserts that there is "essentially no difference between the two. The same empirical attitude is there, and the same tools are needed" (p. 71). However, Burck and Peterson (1975) make a distinction between the concepts. According to these authors, *evaluation* "is more mission-oriented, may be less subject to control, is more concerned with providing information for decision makers, tends to be less rigorous or sophisticated, and is concerned primarily with explaining events and their relationship to established goals and objectives" (p. 564). For example, in counsellor preparation programs, students may prepare a portfolio as an end-of-term project on which they will be evaluated (i.e., receive a grade). Based on their grade, faculty and students decide how much progress has been made and whether to continue their course of study. Whether academic or clinical, "quality services, careful evaluation, and good communication of evaluation" are the three main components of a solid counselling program (Ohlsen, 1983, p. 357). If evaluation is not conducted or positive results are not disseminated, a counselling program will most likely suffer.

Research, however, is "more theory-oriented and discipline-bound, exerts greater control over the activity, produces more results that may not be immediately applicable, is more sophisticated in terms of complexity and exactness of design, involves the use of judgment on the part of the researcher, and is more concerned with explaining and predicting phenomena" (Burck & Peterson, 1975, p. 564). For example, counsellors may conduct research to assess which of several theoretical techniques has the most positive results when applied to a client population suffering from the same disorder. In such a setting, variables such as age, gender, and cultural background are controlled as tightly as possible so that the researcher can be accurate in gaining a clear picture of what works and on whom so that the results can be reported and the findings translated appropriately. In counselling research, most counsellors are *applied researchers*: They use knowledge from research studies in their own work settings.

In the following sections, we will explore how evaluation and research are commonly employed in the practical world of professional counselling.

EVALUATION

Evaluation usually involves gathering meaningful information on various aspects of a counselling program to guide decisions about the allocation of resources and ensure maximum program effectiveness (Gay, Mills, & Airasian, 2006; Wheeler & Loesch, 1981). Evaluation has a quality of immediate utility. In clinical settings, it gives counsellors direct feedback on the services they provide and insight into what new services they need to offer. It also enables clients to have systematic, positive input into a counselling program. Some type of evaluation should be provided for every counselling program regardless of the setting (Hosie, 1994; Oetting, 1976).

Incorrect Evaluation Methods

Although many solid models of evaluation are available, there are a number of incorrect evaluation procedures used by the uninformed (Daniels, Mines, & Gressard, 1981). These ill-conceived methods, which produce invalid and unreliable results, have some or all of the following defects (Burck & Peterson, 1975):

- They restrict opinion sampling.
- They make comparisons between nonequivalent groups.
- They promote services rather than evaluate.
- They try to assess a program without any clear goals.

Steps in Evaluation

Program evaluation should be systematic and follow a sequential step-by-step process. The steps may vary in different evaluations, but a procedure laid out by Burck and Peterson (1975) for implementing an evaluation program is a solid one to follow.

According to these authors, the first step in formulating an evaluation program involves a *needs assessment*. If counsellors are to be accountable, they must first identify problems or concerns within their programs. A *need* is "a condition among members of a specific group . . . that reflects an actual lack of something or an awareness (perception) that something is lacking" (Collison, 1982, p. 115). Needs are assumed to exist based on a number of factors, such as institutional or personal philosophy, government mandate, available resources, history or tradition, and expert opinion. "Needs assessment techniques include clearly identifying the target of the survey, specifying a method of contact, and resolving measurement-related issues" (Cook, 1989, p. 463).

The second step in evaluation is "stating goals and performance objectives." Here, both *terminal program outcomes* (those that are most immediately recognizable) and *ultimate program outcomes* (those that are most enduring) are described in terms of measurable performance objectives. There are normally "several performance objectives for each goal statement" (Burck & Peterson, 1975, p. 567).

The third step in evaluation is designing a program. When a program is developed to meet stated objectives, activities that focus on the stated goals can be precisely designed. The fourth step is revising and improving a program. Specific activities and the adequacy of communication patterns are both evaluated at this point.

The fifth and final step is "noting and reporting program outcome" (Burck & Peterson, 1975, p. 567). This task is performed primarily by disseminating the findings of the program evaluation to the general public. Such consumer information is vital for potential clients if they are to make informed decisions, and counsellors in clinical programs need this kind of feedback to improve their skills and services.

Edward was in a new position as director of student life at his college. The former director had been terminated because he was not providing services students wanted. Edward did not want to make that mistake and he sincerely wished to do a good job, so he decided to do a needs evaluation. His plan was to have students vote on a list of activities offered to students at a large nearby university. Even though he was working at a small, liberal arts college, he thought programs that were popular could be added to the student life curriculum if there was a demand for them. He also imagined he might eliminate some less popular programs at his college in the process and use that money for implementing other activities.

1. What is solid about Edward's plan?

2. What are its flaws?

3. How could Edward's needs evaluation be improved?

Evaluators must get others involved in the evaluation process for the results of the study to have any direct impact on a program. Individuals who have an investment in conducting a needs assessment are more likely to help counsellors meet identified needs and establish program goals than people who are not involved.

Selecting an Evaluation Model

Because evaluation is a continual part of their profession, counsellors must prepare accordingly (Wheeler & Loesch, 1981). Part of this preparation includes setting aside time to conduct evaluations. Equally important is educating oneself and others about the different models of evaluation available. House (1978) offers a list of evaluation models and the critical dimensions of each (see Table 15.1). The models are systems analysis, behavioural objectives, decision making, goal free, art criticism, accreditation, adversary, and transaction.

Daniels and colleagues (1981) studied the dimensions along which these major evaluation models are judged and have offered some practical ways of comparing them to determine the most appropriate model for a specific situation. They note that both internal and external restrictions "define the limits to which each model may be effectively applied" (p. 580). They provide a framework to help counsellors judge which model to employ in given situations (see Figure 15.1).

Questions raised before an evaluation (i.e., *a priori* questions) are more likely to be answered satisfactorily than those brought up after an evaluation is complete (*ex post facto* questions). In some cases, such as investigations into clients' perspectives on suicidal behaviour, researchers have little choice but to ask survivors of suicide attempts to give them insights into their thoughts after they have displayed their behaviours (Paulson & Worth, 2002).

Table 15.1 Comparison of Major Evaluation Models

Type of Model	Major Audiences	Outcome	Consensual Assumptions	Methodology	Typical Questions
Systems analysis	Economists, managers	Program efficiency	Goals, known cause and effects, quantified variables	PPBS, cost-benefit analysis	Are the expected effects achieved? What are the most efficient programs?
Behavioral objectives	Managers, psychologists	Productivity, accountability	Prespecified objectives, quantified variables	Behavioral objectives, achievement tests	Are the students achieving the objectives? Is the teacher producing?
Decision making	Administrators	Effectiveness, quality control	General goals, evaluation criteria	Surveys, questionnaires, interviews, natural variation	Is the program effective? What parts are effective?
Goal free	Consumers	Consumer choices, social utility	Consequences, evaluation criteria	Bias control, logical analysis	What are all of the effects of the program?
Art criticism	Connoisseurs, consumers	Improved standards	Critics, standards of criticism	Critical review	Would a critic approve this program?
Accreditation	Professional peers, public	Professional acceptance	Panel of peers, procedures and criteria for evaluation	Review by panel, self-study	How would professionals rate this program?
Adversary	Jury, public	Resolution	Procedures, judges	Quasi-legal procedures	What are the arguments for and against the program?
Transaction	Client practitioners	Understanding	Negotiations, activities	Case studies, interviews, observations	What does the program look like to different people?

Source: Reprinted from "A Meta-model for Evaluating Counseling Programs," by M. H. Daniels, R. Mines, and C. Gressard, 1981 (adapted from House, 1978), *Personnel and Guidance Journal, 59*, p. 579. © 1981 by ACA. Reprinted with permission. No further reproduction authorized without written permission of the American Counseling Association.

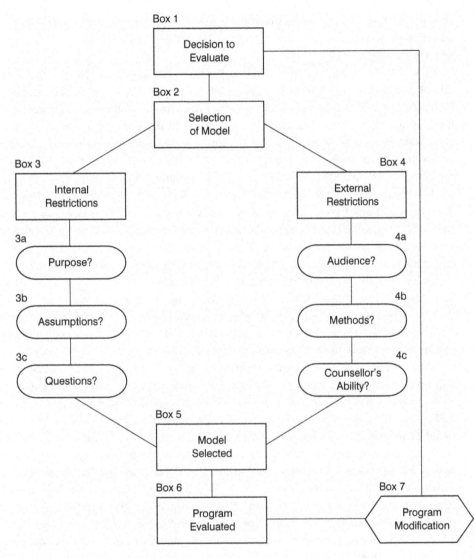

Figure 15.1 An evaluation framework

A methodological approach to research where questioning of the underlying structures of a phenomenon as experienced by participants is studied is called *concept mapping* (Kunkel & Newsom, 1996). Regardless, evaluators must ask themselves at the outset what they wish to evaluate and how they are going to do it (Davidson, 1986). Three models incorporate these concerns: the program plus personnel equal results model

(P + P = R) (Gysbers & Henderson, 2006b); the planning, programming, budgeting system (PPBS); and the context-input-process-product (CIPP) model (Humes, 1972; Stufflebeam et al., 1971).

The *P + P = R evaluation* is one that Gysbers and Henderson (2006b) devised for school counsellors, and a school example will be given here; however, this evaluation model can be modified to work in a number of institutional environments. According to Gysbers and Henderson, counsellors in schools are increasingly being asked to demonstrate that their work contributes to student success, particularly student academic achievement, as a result of the passage of the *No Child Left Behind Act* (PL 107–110) in the United States in 2001 (McGannon, Carey, & Dimmitt, 2005). School counsellors can do this through using three kinds of *evaluation* to demonstrate how the counselling program they administer contributes to overall student success. *Personnel evaluation* is the first kind of measure and describes the way counsellors in a school are supervised and evaluated. *Program evaluation* is the second kind of assessment. It benchmarks the status of a particular program against established program standards to ascertain the degree to which the program is being implemented. Finally, there is *results evaluation,* which focuses on the impact that the activities and services of a program are having on students, the school, and the community. Although each type of evaluation is important, it is crucial that all of the evaluations relate to and interact with each other. Personnel evaluation plus program evaluation equals results evaluation.

The *PPBS model* emphasizes planning programs with specifically stated goals, objectives, and evaluation criteria. The situation, population, and treatment involved are all major concerns of this model. Humes (1972) points out that information derived from a PPBS model is *criterion referenced* (related directly to the dimension being measured) rather than *normative referenced* (related to other members of a group, as is the case when standardized tests are used). Therefore, if proper planning and programming are carried out, the evaluator is able to demonstrate that effective counselling is an important variable in a client's progress. Moreover, when budgeting decisions are being made, the impact of counselling and its cost-effectiveness can be clearly shown and program strengths and weaknesses can be documented. Counselling services administrators are in a better position at such times to justify requests for funds for developing and delivering services not currently being provided. This aspect of program analysis is vital.

The *CIPP model* presents four types of evaluation. In the first, *context evaluation,* a comparison is made between what the program sets out to do and what it actually accomplishes. In the second, *input evaluation,* information is gathered about what resources are needed and which are available to meet program objectives. This part of the evaluation demonstrates cost-effectiveness and points out the need for additional resources as well. The third type of evaluation, *process evaluation,* focuses on the strengths and weaknesses of the program's design. If there are weaknesses, such as the design of communication flow, corrective measures may be taken. The fourth type of evaluation, *product evaluation,* focuses on the final results of the entire program. At this stage evaluators ask how effective the program really is. Plans can be made to continue, reuse, expand, or eliminate the program. Regardless of the type of evaluation used, most evaluation processes employ research in reaching their conclusions.

SOME IMPORTANT AND RECENT CANADIAN EVALUATION STUDIES

Research studies (including evaluation) are often expensive to conduct. Two of the major funding bodies in Canada at the federal level are the Social Sciences and Humanities Research Council (SSHRC) and the Canadian Institutes of Health Research (CIHR). In response to recent funding cuts to research in the CIHR category, Clark, MacGrath, and MacDonald (2007) sent a letter requesting participation in a 15-minute interview to all 308 Members of Parliament (MPs) in June, 2006. They interviewed 101 MPs or senior aides (about one third were senior aides). All 101 rated health care as the highest priority facing Canada; however, this did not mean that they believed health research was a priority to Canadian voters. Also, 32% knew nothing about the role of CIHR. Consequently, increasing MPs' knowledge of the importance of research was deemed a priority.

Most Canadians are familiar with the Big Brothers Big Sisters (BBBS) community match program. The BBBS program matches children from single-parent families with a same-sex adult mentor who commits to spending regular time with the child. While children growing up in single-parent families are more likely to experience emotional and behavioural problems, most will mature into well-adjusted adults (De Wit et al., 2007). De Wit et al.'s (2007) two-year pilot evaluation of the BBBS program revealed that having a big brother or sister in the community was effective in reducing emotional problems and social anxiety while also improving social skills. However, compared to children in the waiting list control condition (WLCC), there was little difference. The authors concluded that one reason for this finding is that the WLCC children may have had adult mentors outside of the BBBS matching program while they waited for the study to conclude.

A few other examples of recent Canadian evaluation research are as follows:

1. *Do anti-bullying programs in schools work?* Despite the large sums of money being spent on these programs worldwide, a recent study has shown that many of the anti-bullying program evaluations lack rigour and are therefore unable to identify cause-effect relationships (Ryan & Smith, 2009).

2. *Do graduated driver licensing (GDL) programs reduce collisions and fatalities in beginning drivers?* A meta-analysis revealed strong evidence supporting the effectiveness of GDL programs, although longer evaluation periods (two years rather than one) are recommended (Vanlaar et al., 2009).

3. *Can a program successfully reduce recidivism in sexual offenders?* A carefully-conducted evaluation of a program started 15 years ago in Ontario has provided evidence that recidivism has been reduced by 83%, with a 73% reduction in all types of violent re-offending (Wilson, Cortoni, & McWhinnie, 2009).

What is still lacking that has import to counselling professionals is outcome measurement of programs and services to diverse populations (Arthur & Lalande, 2009). In relation to the whole of Canada, the Aboriginal population is growing faster than the total population, and the number of citizens and residents belonging to "visible minority groups has also increased dramatically" (Arthur & Lalande, 2009, p. 2).

COUNSELLORS AND RESEARCH

The profession of counselling has had "a long and ambivalent relationship" with research (Sprinthall, 1981, p. 465). The word *research* has a certain mystique about it (Leedy & Ormrod 2001). It suggests an activity that is exclusive, elusive, and removed from everyday life. Some counsellors are drawn to research because of its mystique and their own general interests in investigation. However, "research typically evokes emotional reactions of fear, anxiety, and even disdain" among other counsellors (Fall & VanZandt, 1997, p. 2). These counsellors feel that the majority of research studies are poorly related to their practical needs. Furthermore, they perceive research as cold and impersonal (Krauskopf, 1982).

Some practitioners find that the demands of daily work with clients leaves them little time to be investigative, let alone keep up with the latest findings and outcome studies (Sexton, 1993). Therefore, most counsellors do not engage in research activities, and there appears to be a serious gap in the integration of research into the practice of counselling (Sexton & Whiston, 1996). Indeed, a number of counsellor practitioners have even "shown evidence of hostility and resentment toward researchers" and research (Robinson, 1994, p. 339).

Counsellors' negative feelings about research and their reluctance to spend time and energy on it are related to a number of factors. Chief among them are

- a lack of knowledge about research methods
- an absence of clear goals and objectives for the programs in which they work
- a lack of awareness of the importance of research in planning effective treatment procedures
- a fear of finding negative results
- a discouragement from peers or supervisors
- a lack of financial support
- low aptitudes and limited abilities for conducting investigative studies (Heppner & Anderson, 1985; Sexton, 1993)

In addition, some counselling theories de-emphasize the importance of empirical investigations.

Yet, despite the strain between some counsellors and research, there are similarities between the activities of counselling practice and outcome research. Both involve a six-stage process (Whiston, 1996) (see Table 15.2).

Table 15.2 Analogous Stages of Counselling Practice and the Research Process

Stages in Counseling	Stages in Outcome Research
1. Identification of problems or difficulties	1. Identification of research question(s)
2. Formulation of goals	2. Formulation of research design
3. Determine interventions	3. Determine methods for ensuring treatment integrity and measures of outcome
4. Implementation of counseling	
5. Appraisal and evaluation of progress	4. Data collection
6. Termination	5. Data analysis
	6. Interpretation and conclusions

Source: Reprinted from "Accountability through Action Research: Research Methods for Practitioners," by S. C. Whiston, 1996, *Journal of Counseling and Development, 74*, p. 617. © 1996 by ACA. Reprinted with permission. No further reproduction authorized without written permission of the American Counseling Association.

For instance, the first stage in both processes involves identification. In counselling, the identification is of a client's problem or difficulty, whereas in research the focus is on identifying a question or questions to investigate. Similarly, in step 2, there is an analogy in formulating treatment goals and formulating a research design. Then a determining stage follows, in which counselling interventions are selected; in research, methods for ensuring treatment integrity are chosen. In the fourth stage, action occurs in the form of either implementing counselling or collecting data, followed by an appraisal and evaluation of progress in counselling or data analysis in research. Finally, both processes end with either the completion of counselling or the interpretation and conclusions from research.

RESEARCH

There are many definitions of research, but Barkley (1982) gives one of the best: "*Research* is the systematic collection, organization, and interpretation of observations in order to answer questions as unambiguously as possible" (p. 329). The challenge of research is to answer questions that do not yield truths easily. The quality of research depends on the degree to which resistance can be overcome and ways can be devised to answer questions with maximum confidence by minimizing contaminating influences.

Steps in the Research Process

Good research is scientific in the broadest definition of the word. As alluded to before, it begins with systematic observations that concentrate on a particular population, variable, or question (Gay et al., 2006; Heppner et al., 2008). Such complete and systematic observation attempts to explain relations among variables and why certain events happen. Explanation leads to understanding and eventually to some degree of prediction and control.

Some guidelines for conducting research investigations are available. Campbell and Katona (1953), for instance, developed a flowchart to indicate the sequence of steps involved in carrying out surveys. More recently, Ary (1996) devised an eight-step process for conducting research. It is ideally suited for clinical work but is also applicable to other areas of counselling research.

1. *Statement of the problem.* This statement must be clear and concise. If there is confusion at this step, the investigative endeavour will probably produce little of value. An example of a clear problem statement is "The purpose of this research is to test the hypothesis that eye contact between counsellor and client is related to the effectiveness of the counselling process."

2. *Identification of information needed to solve the problem.* This step may include a variety of information derived from sources such as psychological or educational tests or systematic observations, including experiments. Some data that investigators need may be impossible to collect. They must then decide whether to modify the problem statement or end the research.

3. *Selection or development of measures for gathering data.* Common measures for gathering data are surveys, tests, and observational report sheets. If researchers cannot find an existing appropriate measure, they must develop one and test its reliability and validity.

4. *Identification of the target population and sampling procedures.* If a group is small enough, an entire population may be studied. Otherwise, a sample is selected by careful standard sampling procedures.

5. *Design of the procedure for data collection.* This step involves determining how, when, where, and by whom information will be collected.

6. *Collection of data.* A systematic procedure is implemented to obtain the desired information. Usually this process involves careful monitoring and a substantial investment of time.

7. *Analysis of data.* Select procedures are employed at this step to organize the data in a meaningful fashion and to determine whether they provide an answer to the problem being investigated.

8. *Preparation of a report.* Research results should be made available to others in some meaningful form, such as a journal article or a professional presentation.

The Relevance of Research

One primary question raised by readers of counselling research focuses on the relevance of a study's results for practitioners. Much research does not produce results relevant to practical issues and is not useful (Goldman, 1976; 1977; 1978; 1979; 1986; 1992). Many research efforts lack vision, concentrating instead on small details. Researchers who conduct their work in such a way have too readily accepted the experimental research designs of the physical and biological sciences and, in the process, have failed to develop research methods appropriate for counselling. What they pass on as research is often sterile and trivial.

The argument for research relevancy centres on the fact that not all knowledge is equally useful for counsellors (Krumboltz & Mitchell, 1979). Therefore, the limited funds and energy should be directed toward studies that are likely to make a difference in the way counsellors function. One way to define relevance in research is to emphasize studies that focus on the reasons individuals seek counselling, such as their goals, intentions, and purposes (Howard, 1985). Another important way to assess relevance is to determine "how closely the research approximates what is done in the counselling office" (Gelso, 1985, p. 552). Such research is called *experience-near research*. Because it is applicable to counsellors, it is likely to be read and used.

Action research is a form of experience-near research. It focuses on resolving practical problems that counsellors routinely encounter, such as how to help manage a child with learning disabilities or evaluate the effects of a self-esteem program on a group of children (Gillies, 1993). Action research includes studies aimed at diagnostic action, participant action, empirical action, and experimental action. Some of this research is likely to be less controlled and not as easily generalized as more rigorous research. To help solve the problem of relevancy in research, Gelso (1985) suggests reading all research studies with certain questions in mind, such as "How was this research conducted?" and "How will it influence the way I practise counselling?"

Choosing a Research Method

Despite problems inherent in counselling research, counsellors regularly employ a number of investigative methodologies. Kaplan (1964) defines a *method* as a procedure that is applicable to many disciplines. In contrast, a *technique* is a discipline-specific procedure. Most counselling research uses procedures, such as controlled observations, that are common to other disciplines. Therefore, the term *method* rather than *technique* is appropriate when referring to ways of doing counselling research. None of these methods is considered "best to test the counselling process" (Hill, 1982, p. 16). Rather, different research methods address different research questions (Watkins & Schneider, 1991). Ultimately, research methods provide answers to research questions by controlling select variables that have an impact on the counselling process (Kerlinger & Lee, 2000).

All research methods have what Gelso (1979) describes as *bubbles*, or flaws. Gelso says that selecting research methods is like putting a sticker on a car windshield. Bubbles always appear; even though you might try to eliminate as many bubbles as possible, some remain. The only way to eliminate the bubbles totally is to remove the sticker. In research, the only way to avoid all flaws is to not do research. Yet as imperfect as research methods are, they are necessary for professional edification and development. The alternative is to remain uninformed about the effects of counselling and forego the development of newer methods and techniques.

Emphases of Research

Counselling research has several different emphases. Four of the most prominent can be represented as contrasts:

1. Laboratory versus field research
2. Basic versus applied research
3. Process versus outcome research
4. Quantitative (group) versus qualitative (individual) research

Each of these emphases is concerned with the contrast between two investigative dimensions. The various dimensions are not mutually exclusive; many research studies, such as those that quantitatively report the outcome of counselling techniques in a laboratory setting, include more than one of them (Creswell, 2002).

The first emphasis is on laboratory research versus field research. *Laboratory research* concentrates on conducting the investigation within a confined environment, such as a counselling lab, where as many extraneous variables as possible may be controlled (Dobson & Campbell, 1986). Under such conditions, some researchers think they can obtain the most reliable information. Indeed, researcher John Gottman found that his "love lab" yielded extremely pertinent information about the quality of couple relationships. Practitioners of *field research*, however, see most laboratory investigations as artificial and believe that counselling theories and techniques are best observed and recorded in actual counselling situations, such as counselling centres and clinics. They argue that these settings are realistic and that the results are likely to be applicable to other practitioners.

The second emphasis is basic research versus applied research. *Basic research* is oriented to theory, and those who practise it are "interested in investigating some puzzle or problem that is suggested by theory" (Forsyth & Strong, 1986, p. 113). An example is research that focuses on the number of times Rogerian-based counsellors use reflective versus confrontive clinical methods. In contrast, *applied research* focuses on examining

Figure 15.2 Relation of basic research, applied research, and practice

Source: From "Counseling Research as an Applied Science," by T. J. Tracey, 1991, in C. E. Watkins, Jr., and L. J. Schneider (Eds.), *Research in Counseling* (p. 27), Hillsdale, NJ: Erlbaum. © 1991 by Lawrence Erlbaum Associates, Inc. Used with permission.

practical problems and applying their findings to existing problems. An example of applied research is a program evaluation in which information about services at a counselling centre is collected from recipients and analyzed as to its efficiency, effectiveness, and impact on the community served (Astramovich & Coker, 2007). Tracey (1991) offers one way of distinguishing basic and applied research (see Figure 15.2).

The third emphasis is process research versus outcome research. According to Hill (1991), *process research* focuses on what "happens in counseling and therapy sessions" (p. 85). She states that identifying the changes in counselling "can be quite overwhelming and frustrating" (Hill, 1982, p. 7). It demands a concentrated amount of time and energy focused on a few variables, such as the reactions of the counsellor to the client. The burnout rate among process-oriented researchers is high. Yet such research is indispensable in enlightening counsellors about the dynamics of the counselling relationship itself. An example of process research is the work of Allen Ivey (1980) in assessing the importance of counsellor skills in select stages of counselling. *Outcome research*, however, is "the experimental investigation of the impact of counselling on clients" (Lambert, Masters, & Ogles, 1991, p. 51). It is "typified by measurement before and after treatment on specified dependent variables" (Hill, 1982, p. 7). An example of outcome research would be the effect of person-centred counselling with depressed persons. Outcome research emphasizes results rather than the factors producing them.

The fourth emphasis is quantitative research versus qualitative research (i.e., naturalistic inquiry). *Quantitative research* is deductive and objective, usually involving numbers and subordinating subjective understanding to clarity, precision, and reproducibility of objective phenomena. A quantitative approach is based on a positive-reductive conceptual system that "values objectivity, linearity, cause and effect, repeatability and reproductivity, predictability, and the quantification of data" (Merchant & Dupuy, 1996, p. 538). Two basic quantitative research designs are the experiment and the survey (Rosenthal, 2001). An example of quantitative research that also yielded practical outcomes in regard to what counsellors actually do is a survey of the nationwide Practice Research Network (PRN) that investigated the daily practice of mental health workers (Smith, Sexton, & Bradley, 2005).

In contrast, *qualitative research* is inductive, naturalistic, cybernetic, and phenomenological. A brief definition of these terms follows. *Inductive* refers to the notion that, in qualitative research, one does not pursue evidence that supports or fails to support previously established hypotheses (a deductive process). Instead, one learns from others without having pre-determined hypotheses by making sense of the data (usually transcripts from interviews or from observations) that emerges (an inductive process). *Naturalistic* means that qualitative research occurs in a real-life setting and not in an experiment, which by definition is a controlled setting where variables are manipulated. *Cybernetic* in this context is about reviewing the communication that occurs in qualitative research and then pursuing feedback from participants to check accuracy. *Phenomenology* is about understanding a phenomenon from a subjective point of view (as opposed to the "objective" striving for a singular truth through quantitative research). The notion in qualitative research is that one person's truth is as valid as another person's—consequently, there is an acceptance and appreciation of "multiple" truths.

Qualitative research places primary emphasis on understanding the unique frameworks within which people make sense of themselves and their environments. It is useful in situations where theory and research are lacking (Merriam, 2002). It focuses on understanding a complex social situation without previously defined parameters (Creswell, 2002; Jencius & Rotter, 1998). Furthermore, "qualitative research examines what people are doing and how they interpret what is occurring rather than pursuing patterns of cause and effect in a controlled setting" (Merchant & Dupuy, 1996, p. 537). In many ways qualitative research is especially appropriate for counselling "because the centrality of interpersonal relations defines its [counselling's] domain" (Berrios & Lucca, 2006, p. 175). Overall, "qualitative research in counseling requires a dual commitment both to service delivery and to a scientific investigation of that delivery" (p. 181).

Frequently used qualitative methods are field research, case studies, narratives, in-depth interviews, and life histories. Mark Savickas (2005) has proven to be a master of qualitative research in using the narrative counselling method for helping clients fit work into their lives, rather than fit themselves to jobs. His approach looks at a client's life as a novel being written. It emphasizes recurring themes that reveal how the client uses work to advance his or her life projects.

Thus, the emphasis of these two approaches differs because of the purposes of each and the different assumptions each makes about the goals of research (May, 1996; Merchant & Dupuy, 1996). Neither quantitative nor qualitative research is superior to the other, per se. Rather, the use of each depends on what question is being asked and for what reason. The major strength of quantitative research is its emphasis on analyzing large amounts of data in a clear, mathematical fashion. The major strength of qualitative research is the way it picks up subtle, individually focused, developmental, and experientially reported aspects of counselling (Creswell, 2002; Denzin & Lincoln, 2000; Mertens, 1998).

Counselling is moving toward espousing research that is both qualitative (versus quantitative) and field-oriented (versus laboratory) (Goldman, 1992; Watkins & Schneider, 1991). Clients are seen as active rather than passive in the counselling process (Gelso, 1985; Howard, 1985). Overall, a more holistic emphasis in counselling research is being proposed (Froehle, 1985).

Major Research Methods

The research methods that counsellors choose are determined by the questions they are trying to answer, their special interests, and the amount of time and resources they have available for the study (Heppner et al., 2008). Methods should be the slaves of research, not the masters (Smith, 1981). No method is suitable for all research attempts. Indeed, as Ohlsen (1983) states, "developing and clarifying a research question is a slow, painstaking process" (p. 361). A *research question* provides the context in which one begins to consider a method. In most cases, a research question is about the state of affairs in the field of counselling (LaFountain & Bartos, 2002). Once a question has been decided, a quantitative or qualitative method may be chosen.

Methods and ways of obtaining data may differ for research conducted in personal, group, or couple/family counselling. A research strategy, which is "the guiding or underlying force that directs" a research project, is intended to place the investigator "in the most advantageous position" possible (Husband & Foster, 1987, p. 53). The primary research method can be chosen from among those that present data from historical, descriptive, or experimental points of view (Galfo & Miller, 1976; Vacc & Loesch, 2001). The procedures used in these methods are not mutually exclusive. For example, Tracey (1983) reports that *N of 1 research*, which focuses on the study of a single qualitative entity (such as a person), may be employed in historical studies, case studies, and intensive design studies. Such research may be either associational or experimental. The fact that this and other research methods are so flexible gives investigators more latitude in planning their strategies and carrying out their studies.

Historical Methods Historical research has been largely neglected in counselling (Goldman, 1977). The reasons are numerous, but among the most salient is the association of historical research with psychohistory (Frey, 1978). Psychohistory has been closely linked to the theory of psychoanalysis, and its usefulness as a way of understanding people and events has been questioned (Thoresen, 1978). Yet as Frey (1978) reports, psychohistory as practised by Erik Erikson (1958) and the Wellfleet group (whose members included Kenneth Keniston and Robert Coles) involves the following two aspects:

1. Experiencing and reporting events and procedures from earlier times that have influenced the development of the profession

2. Embellishing current theories and generating new research hypotheses

For the most part, counselling journals limit their dealings with historical research to printing obituaries of prominent counsellors and featuring interviews with pioneers in the profession (Heppner, 1990a; b). Although the methods used in historical research are usually less rigorous and more qualitative than those employed in other research, they produce interesting and enlightening results. They have an important place in the understanding of people, as exemplified in Gordon Allport's idiographic studies of traits and personality. This approach to research is clearly open to further development.

Descriptive Methods Descriptive research concentrates on depicting present factors in a profession. It has three subcategories: surveys, case studies, and comparative studies.

Surveys Surveys are one of the most popular and widely used methods for gathering information about the occurrence of behaviours and describing the characteristics of those that are not well understood (Fong, 1992; Heppner et al., 2008). Surveys are similar to other methods of research: They begin with the formation of a research question, then the generation of hypotheses, the selection of a research design, and the collection and analysis of data (Kerlinger & Lee, 2000). Survey data can be collected in four traditional ways: personal interviews, mailed questionnaires, telephone interviews, and non-reactive measures such as existing records or archives (Hackett, 1981; Marken, 1981; Moser & Kalton, 1972). Increasing numbers of researchers are currently relying on the internet to host their surveys (Hine, 2008; Markham & Baym, 2009). Data are gathered in either a structured or non-structured way with either a *cross-section* of people (many people at one point in time) or *longitudinally* (the same people at two or more points in time).

If conducted properly, survey research can provide counsellors with a great deal of information about how clients perceive them and their programs. Surveys can also offer information about clients' needs (Heppner et al., 2008; Hosie, 1994). Nevertheless, four major problems often plague survey research.

- Survey instruments may be poorly constructed.
- They may not generate a very high rate of return.
- The sample surveyed is sometimes non-random and unrepresentative of the population (Hackett, 1981; Marken, 1981). In either of these cases, the results are essentially useless because the design and methodology of the survey research lack rigour (Fong, 1992).
- Participants may not feel deeply committed to providing honest, thorough answers on surveys.

For all of the reasons stated above, the quality of responses may be deficient in several respects in survey research. Web-based survey research has received significant criticism, despite its popularity (Hagger-Johnson, 2003; Tuten, Urban, & Bosnjak, 2002). A final problem of survey research (or almost any research, for that matter) is that it can be expensive (Robinson, 1994).

Just as counselling can have an enormous impact in people's lives, research can also have a longstanding effect, regardless of how well it is conducted. The social impact of survey research is apparent in the work of Kinsey on the sexual practices of men, for example. Kinsey, Pomeroy, and Martin (1948) reported their shocking findings in 1948: They found that, based on interviews with 5300 American men, about 37% had engaged in homosexual behaviour to the point of orgasm at least once in their lives, while about 10% had engaged in mostly homosexual activity for at least three years between ages 16 and 55.

Equally shocking is how poorly, by today's standards, the study was conducted. As Michaels (1996) indicated, the Kinsey et al. (1948) study was fraught with methodological problems that overinflated the estimate of homosexual behaviour. A few of these problems included that (a) the sample was not randomly selected; (b) men were included from prisons, reform schools, and gay social networks; and (c) those willing to be interviewed were likely men who were more sexually active and comfortable with their sexuality in the first place. Survey research can certainly draw attention to a social condition, but it can also overinflate, underinflate, or misrepresent a social condition, depending on the extent of sample and design flaws.

Well-conducted research can have an enormous impact. For example, the national American survey of counsellor education programs that was originally started by Joe Hollis (see Hollis, 2000; the book of results is now in its 12th edition) is an example of the usefulness of this method for counselling. Every few years, Hollis, and now the National Board of Certified Counselors, gathers information for a published directory of counsellor education programs. This survey is quantitative in emphasis and yields relevant data about American trends in counselling. *Cognica*, the quarterly newsletter of the Canadian Counselling and Psychotherapy Association (2009), is dedicated to keeping its members informed about current trends in Canadian counselling.

Case Studies A *case study* is an attempt to understand one unit, such as a person, group, or program, through an intense and systematic investigation of that unit longitudinally. Almost any phenomenon can be examined by means of the case study method (Leedy & Ormrod, 2001). Some case studies rely on self-report methods that are not very reliable; others involve naturalistic inquiry in which the study extends over a period of time (Smith, 1981). The difficulties involved in naturalistic research are many and include issues such as what constitutes good research, the high cost of labour, the problems of establishing causality, and restrictions on generalizing results. In addition, they often demonstrate problems of observed bias and the *halo effect* (a favourable observation generalized to a person or situation as a whole) (Goldman, 1977). To help minimize such problems, Anton (1978) and Huber (1980) describe several intensive experimental designs suitable for case studies. Counsellors with limited time and resources may find them useful in tracing changes over time. These designs will be discussed in a later section on experimental methods.

Comparative Studies Comparative research studies (also called *correlational studies*) form a link between historical/case study methods and experimental and quasi-experimental designs. They make directional and quantitative comparisons between sets of data. Such studies are non-manipulative (Cozby, 2001). They simply note similarities in variations among factors with no effort to discern cause-and-effect relationships. An example of such a study is the relationship of scores on a test of religiosity, with scores on instruments measuring various aspects of mental health (Gladding, Lewis, & Adkins, 1981). A major finding of this study was that people who scored high on the religiosity test also scored high on the mental health instruments. The results do not suggest that religiosity causes a person to have better mental health; rather, they simply compare the direction of the scores. Any study that compares measures in this manner is an example of comparative research.

Experimental Methods *Experimental research* methods are employed to describe, compare, and analyze data under controlled conditions (Galfo & Miller, 1976; Heppner et al., 2008; McLeod, 1995). Experimental methods used in counselling research have their origin in the natural sciences. The purpose of using these methods is to determine the effect of one variable on another by controlling for other factors that might explain the effect. In other words, researchers who use this method are seeking to determine causation. To do this, they define independent and dependent variables. The *independent variable* is the one manipulated by the researcher, such as treatment. The *dependent variable* is the one in which the potential effect is recorded, such as the client's behaviour. The researcher assumes that if the effect of other factors is eliminated, then any change in the dependent variable will be a result of the independent variable. Examples of independent variables in counselling might be the age, gender, personal attractiveness, or physical appearance of the counsellor. Examples of dependent variables are a client's reactions to these counsellor traits, such as degree of relaxation, cooperation, and overall responsiveness in the counselling setting. The reactions could be measured by a variety of procedures, including an analysis of an audio- or videotape or a post-counselling interview or questionnaire.

Cohen (1990) recommends two general principles for those who are conducting research with independent and dependent variables: Less is more, and simple is better. The fewer variables there are to keep track of and the more clearly they can be reported (e.g., through graphs), the easier it is for researchers and consumers to understand the significance of counselling research studies.

It is imperative in conducting experimental research that the counsellor be sure to control for *contaminating variables* (variables that invalidate a study, such as one group of clients that is healthier than another). One of the most common ways of controlling for potentially contaminating variables is by establishing equivalent experimental and control groups. When the independent variable is manipulated for the experimental group while being held constant for the control group, the effect of the independent variable can be determined by comparing the post-experimental data for the two groups. Campbell and Stanley (1963) describe in detail the problems involved in experimental and quasi-experimental research; their work is recommended to readers who wish to pursue the issue further.

Traditional experimental research has involved group comparison studies. Since the 1970s, *single-subject research*, commonly known as N of 1 (i.e., $n = 1$) research, has become increasingly accepted in the field of counselling but is underutilized by counsellors (Sharpley, 2007). "Essentially, an $n = 1$ research study is one in which the data from a single participant (rather than a group) are the focus of the research design" (p. 350). There are a number of advantages to single-case research designs.

- They are theory free, thus allowing counsellors of any persuasion to use them.
- They are flexible and appropriate for use in practice settings.
- They may improve counselling effectiveness.
- They do not require the use of statistical methods.
- They produce scientifically effective evidence that leads to professional credibility.
- They are "consistent with CACREP standards that call for increased emphasis on research, accountability, and diverse research methodologies in the scientist-practitioner model of counsellor preparation" (Lundervold & Belwood, 2000, p. 100).

Miller (1985, p. 491) summarizes six major advantages that single-subject research has over traditional group studies. (His study is derived from Hill, Carter, & O'Farrell [1983] and Sue [1978b].)

1. It allows a more adequate description of what happens between a counsellor and client.
2. Positive and negative outcomes can be understood in terms of process data.
3. Outcome measures can be tailored to the client's specific problems.
4. It allows for the study of a rare or unusual phenomenon.
5. It is flexible enough to allow for novel procedures in diagnosis and treatment.
6. It can be used in evaluating the effectiveness of an intervention strategy on a single client.

A potential problem in single-subject studies is "when they are used following a period of standard treatment that has not worked." Some general improvement may occur that has nothing to do with the treatment being used but is a *regression toward the mean* (i.e., "the tendency of an extreme value when it is remeasured to be closer to the mean"; Aldridge, 1994, p. 337). To overcome this problem, especially if medication is involved, the researcher may allow for a *washout period*—a time when no treatment occurs and there is an opportunity for previous effects (such as medication) to leave the body by natural means.

Three intense experimental designs that focus on individuals are simple time series, reversal design, and multiple baseline design.

Simple Time Series A simple time series, the most common intense experimental design method, is referred to as an *AB design* (Sharpley, 2007). First, a baseline (A) is established by having the client observe and record the occurrence of the targeted behaviour every day. Then an intervention strategy (B) is introduced. The client continues to record the targeted behaviour in the same way as before. The manifestation of the targeted behaviour is compared during these two periods and trends are noted. By graphing results, counsellors can determine what, if any, effect the intervention strategy had.

Reversal Design   A reversal design is more complex than a simple time series. It involves a reversal—an *ABAB design*. The first part is executed as it is in the simple time series, but the intervention strategy (B) is discontinued after a time, and a second baseline and intervention follow. "If the second intervention period produces proportionately the same results as the first intervention period, then it can be safely assumed that it is the strategy itself that is causing the changes in the level of interactions made" (Huber, 1980, p. 212).

Multiple Baseline Design   The most complex of these experimental designs, the multiple baseline design, permits greater generalization of the results. There are three types of multiple baseline research designs: across individuals, across situations, and across behaviours (Schmidt, 1974). Each emphasizes a different focus. The common trait of all three is that intervention is initially employed with a select individual, situation, or behaviour while the researcher continues to gather baseline data on other persons, situations, or behaviours. When intervention strategies are extended to the baseline populations, counsellors are able to see more clearly the power of the intervention. As with other designs, it is important to graph the results.

Overall, there are five steps in intensive experimental designs on individuals:

1. Identify an observable problem that can be monitored for change.
2. Gather baseline data.
3. Decide on the intervention to be studied.
4. Carry out the intervention strategy through one of the three research designs.
5. Evaluate the changes, if any, in the targeted behaviour.

Case Example: What Would *You* Do?

Shannon was fascinated by the idea of doing single-subject research. She thought it would be easier and simpler than any type of quantitative method. She had experienced a serious eating disorder (anorexia) and was still in recovery. Shannon wondered if she could systematically study her own recovery while she experienced it. To her advantage, she was sensitive, perceptive, smart, and passionate about the topic. She also had had excellent writing skills, a talent that she might use later to write fiction stories as an extra source of income.

Delighted to hear that there was a methodology she could use (i.e., autoethnography), she decided to take this on for her master's thesis.

1. Despite autoethnography being a valid research method, do you think it is unethical in Shannon's case to become her own participant, and in fact her *only* participant? Why or why not?

2. Aside from ethical considerations, would it be wise for Shannon to take it on the project this way? What are the pluses and minuses for her personally?

3. How might her thesis be useful to other people suffering from anorexia?

Guidelines for Using Research

Counsellors who use research as a base for their practices can follow certain guidelines. They include recognizing the flaws and strengths of research methods, taking care to define terms carefully, and not overgeneralizing beyond the scope of particular findings. Such procedures help consumers evaluate studies as objectively as possible so that they can employ the results more skillfully and ethically.

Several writers have been concerned about the fair assessment of gender differences (McHugh, Koeske, & Frieze, 1986; Wakefield, 1992). Altmaier, Greiner, and Griffin-Pierson (1988, p. 346) offer some of the most salient advice on this issue.

- Readers should note the values on which particular research studies are based.

- Counsellors should look for findings that are in accord with their experiences and findings that converge across settings and studies.

- Consumers of research should not overlook topics of importance to women, such as childbearing.

- The assumption should not be made that differences between men and women fall along one continuum in a bipolar fashion.

- The magnitude of effects should be considered in reading research about gender differences. In other words, the reader should note how much variance in the observed behaviour is accounted for by the significance of gender difference.

In the final analysis, counsellors who use research should do so in relation to the skills they acquired in their graduate and continuing education programs. Clinicians must study research methodology well so that their practices reflect only the best professional knowledge available.

STATISTICS

Statistics and statistical testing first became prominent in the early 1900s (Thompson, 2002). They have been the lifeblood and bane of helping professionals such as counsellors ever since. Whether counsellors are drawn to do statistically significant research or not, all counsellors should be aware of several research tools, such as libraries and their resources, computers and their software, techniques of measurement, and statistics. Statistics are not a fixed part of evaluation and research, and using statistics is not what "makes" or "breaks" a good study (Leedy & Ormrod, 2001). Rather, statistics are simply a means for researchers to use in analyzing and interpreting findings and communicating those findings to others (Wilson & Yager, 1981). As Barkley (1982) emphasizes, "it is possible to be a good researcher and know nothing about sophisticated statistical techniques. It is also possible to know a great deal about statistics and be a mediocre or poor researcher" (p. 327). The distinction between research and statistics is important.

Statistical Concepts

There are some statistical concepts that every counsellor must know in order to read and evaluate research reports intelligently. One is *measures of the central tendency*—that is, the median, the mean, and the mode. All these measures encompass different meanings of the term "average" (LaFountain & Bartos, 2002). The *median* is the midpoint of a distribution of scores ranked highest to lowest. The *mean* is the arithmetic average of scores. The *mode* is the score or measure that occurs most often in a distribution. In a true normally distributed population (which can be graphed as a *bell-shaped* or *normal curve*), the median, mean, and mode are the same. In actuality, however, this situation rarely occurs.

Two other important statistical concepts are standard deviation and sampling procedure. A *standard deviation* is "a measure of the dispersion of scores about their mean" (Marken, 1981, p. 42). It indicates how much response variability is reflected in a set of scores; that is, it is a measure of how homogeneous a group is. "The larger the standard deviation, the greater the variability among the individuals" (Thorndike, 1997, p. 41). *Sampling* is important because it determines how applicable research findings are. If a sample does not adequately represent the population on which it is based, the results cannot be considered applicable to the population. When samples are chosen in a representative, random way, results can be generalized to the population with confidence.

Statistical Methods

Descriptive, correlational, and inferential statistics are the three most widely used statistical methods in research (Mertens, 1998).

- *Descriptive statistics* literally describe characteristics of a sample. These devices, which are used to organize and summarize data, are also used in analyzing single-subject research and simply describing populations (Miller, 1985). Mean and standard deviation are examples of descriptive statistics.

- *Correlational statistics* describe the strength and connection of relationships—for example, the strength of a relationship between one's attitude toward drugs and one actually using drugs (Creswell, 2002).

- *Inferential statistics* allow for group comparisons or make predictions about an entire population from a given sample. They determine whether research results are due to chance or the treatment of variables in a study (Cozby, 2001).

A number of statistical tests have been devised to measure the probability of change occurring by chance in an experimental research design. Two broad categories of tests are used for this purpose: parametric and nonparametric.

- *Parametric tests* are usually more powerful. Parametric tests are used when it is thought that the population being described has evenly distributed characteristics that could be represented by a bell-shaped curve. Examples of parametric tests are the Pearson product moment correlation and *t* tests.

- *Nonparametric tests* are used when no normal curve distribution can be assumed but sharp dichotomies can. Nonparametric tests require larger sample sizes to yield a level of significance similar to parametric tests. Examples of nonparametric tests are the Spearman rank-order correlation and chi-square (Leedy & Ormrod, 2001).

In addition, statistics can be used to compare research findings across studies. One prominent approach is through an empirical method known as *meta-analysis* (Glass, 1976; Willson, 1981). Before the conceptualization of meta-analysis, researchers were forced to compare studies through narrative methods that were often filled with errors. With meta-analysis, large amounts of data can be compared and contrasted (Baker, Swisher, Nadenichek, & Popowicz, 1984).

Statistics are invaluable to the counsellor who wants to understand, organize, communicate, and evaluate data (Remer, 1981). Consumers of research should expect that authors of research reports will provide them with indices of practical and clinical significance of their works (e.g., effect size) for "statistical significance is not sufficiently useful to be invoked as the sole criterion for evaluating the noteworthiness of counseling research" (Thompson, 2002, p. 66).

SUMMARY AND CONCLUSION

This chapter focused on the relationship between evaluation and research. Although the terms are sometimes defined identically, each has an individual purpose. Evaluation aims at helping counsellors decide how programs are meeting the goals and objectives of staff and clients. A major first step in conducting an evaluation is to do a needs assessment. Several excellent models are available for counsellors to use in completing this task.

Research scares many counsellors. Yet this fear may diminish as counsellors become more aware that there are many ways to conduct investigative studies. Three main research methods are historical, descriptive, and experimental. For years, experimental research has been valued most highly, but this emphasis is changing. Case studies and intensive experimental designs are gaining popularity. In addition, the difference between understanding research methods and statistical concepts is growing; that is, people are realizing that the two approaches are not the same. Both are important, but it is possible for researchers to be stronger in one area than the other.

Counsellors must constantly strive to update their research and evaluation skills and stay current. The lifespan of knowledge is brief, and counsellors who do not exercise their minds and find areas of needed change will become statistics instead of an influence.

Your Personal Reflections

1. What do you think about the differences between evaluation and research? How are they complementary?

2. Does knowing how counselling and research are similar in the stages they go through make you feel any differently about research? If so, how?

3. From what you know about counselling now, what questions are you most interested in finding out answers to? Do you think your questions might best be answered through qualitative or quantitative research methods?

4. Once counsellors are employed, they often do not avail themselves of the applied research that continues to be published, even when it is in their specialty area(s). Consequently, many times research does *not* inform practice, as it ideally should. What do you think contributes to this? What could improve this situation?

Classroom Activities

1. In small groups, visit a mental health agency or school and find out what procedures are used to evaluate services and personnel. Read the institution's annual reports, and assess how uniformly an evaluative method is employed in describing the institution's activities. Report your field study findings to the class. Discuss what recommendations you would make to the agency or school.

2. As a class, gather examples of needs assessments from schools and agencies. Evaluate the instruments according to the step-by-step procedure outlined in this chapter. What are the strengths and weaknesses of these assessments? What improvements would you make if you were put in charge of the procedure? Have select members of the class role-play the steps they would take when conducting a needs assessment at a particular site.

3. As a class, choose two three-person teams to debate the pros and cons of this statement: Counselling research must be relevant. What definition of relevant does each side advocate? How does an interpretation of the term influence the type of research recommended? After the debate, discuss the merits of doing basic and applied research.

4. One of the complexities of making sense of research findings is noting that often researchers find what they are looking for. Those in favour of an outcome find it, and those against it do not. Have a class discussion about what factors may be operating in quantitative research, qualitative research, or both that may explain this frequent occurrence.

5. Which of the three major types of research (historical, descriptive, or experimental) would you be most comfortable conducting? Divide the class according to research interests and, in groups, discuss the reasons behind your choice. After your group agrees on a combined rationale for choosing a particular research approach, report your ideas to the class as a whole.

6. What are your feelings about statistics? In triads, discuss how feelings can either promote or interfere with learning statistical procedures. Practise taking a thinking approach to learning statistics. Does thinking rather than feeling affect your attitude and approach to learning these procedures? Discuss your impressions with the class. Does your class believe there are any counselling approaches that would be useful in helping a person overcome anxiety related to learning statistics? Which ones?

Chapter 16

Testing, Assessment, and Diagnosis in Counselling

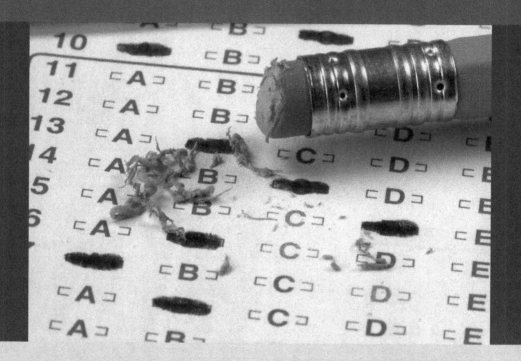

PRACTICE REFLECTION

I remember a young Arab woman who came to see me, frustrated that she was having to work so hard at college to pass her courses. She also had a career choice that would require transfer to university to complete a degree. I found out that she worked hard at her studies but had trouble getting the grades she wanted. It struck me that, given the amount of time she was devoting to her studies, she should be getting satisfactory marks.

I decided that as part of my assessment, I would have her take the General Aptitude Test Battery (GATB), a test that purportedly measures one's *aptitude*, which is one's ability to learn new skills or acquire knowledge. At the next appointment, we planned to go over the results. A few days later, she returned. It was one of those days where I was behind schedule, which meant I only had a few minutes to review her test before bringing her into the session. My jaw fell as I reviewed her exceptionally low scores. The GATB provides an estimate of IQ, and her score would have placed her in the mildly retarded range!

I decided to keep her waiting a bit longer. While I wondered what I would tell her, I pulled up her transcript on my computer. Although her marks were not exceptional, they were mostly Bs and Cs—an overall grade point average close to a B-. I knew that grades measured over an extended period (i.e., several semesters) were a better measure of one's likelihood of academic success than a test administered over less than two hours. I brought her into my office and said, "I'm afraid the test results are invalid for some reason. I think it is because the test does not take multicultural differences into account. Either way, we need to discard the results and focus instead on how you have been doing in your courses up to this point." She was disappointed she could not get the results back, but she was satisfied with my answer.

I did wonder many times afterward about why she scored so low on the test. Perhaps it was because the test was not culture free, or maybe she was lower functioning, or both. Either way, I have learned through experience that when in doubt, do not let test results label people as deficient who are proving otherwise through their grades. The only purpose that would serve is to diminish their self-esteem and sense of self-determination.

Did she succeed at university? I don't know, but I believe that with enough perseverance and moxie, someone functioning at the lower end of intelligence can still earn a postsecondary credential—maybe not with As, but all one needs in most programs to graduate is a C average. I really hope she was one of them.

Testing, assessment, and diagnosis "are integral components of the counseling process that are used in all stages of counseling from referral to follow-up" (Hohenshil, 1996, p. 65). According to Hood and Johnson (2007), "During the early days, counseling and testing were virtually synonymous. Many of the counseling centers established during the 1930s and 1940s were called Counseling and Testing Centers" (p. 3). Today, virtually all counsellors are involved in testing, assessment, and diagnosis. The amount they do of each is dependent on their theoretical backgrounds, education, values, and settings. Therefore, it is essential for counsellors to understand the procedures connected with each process.

Counsellors interested in activities that require the use of measurement and associated procedures need to consult with the ethical guidelines governing their practice to ensure they are using tests appropriately and competently. Standardized testing is most often used by clinical psychologists, school psychologists, and neuropsychologists in Canada, and they often belong to the appropriate section of the Canadian Psychological Association (clinical psychology, clinical neuropsychology,

*and psychologists in education, respectively. See www.cpa.ca/aboutcpa/cpasections).
Most standardized tests require specialized training, and this training is often available to counsellors with various backgrounds.*

*This chapter examines the nature of tests, assessment, and diagnosis and how
each activity fits into the counselling profession. It covers basic concepts associated with testing, such as validity, reliability, and standardization. In addition, it
reviews some of the major tests that counsellors use and are expected to understand. Finally, it examines the nature of assessment and diagnosis and their
usefulness.*

TESTS AND TEST SCORES

ANASTASI (1982) DEFINES A PSYCHOLOGICAL TEST (OR TEST, FOR SHORT) AS "ESSENTIALLY
an objective and standardized measure of behavior" (p. 22). Most often test results are
reported as test scores, statistics that have meaning only in relation to a person. A score is
a reflection of a particular behaviour at a moment in time. Test scores are important in
counselling despite their limitations, for they provide information that might not be
obtained in any other way and do so with comparatively small investments of time and
effort. Although tests and test scores have been criticized for a number of reasons, testing
is an indispensable part of an evaluation process. How tests and test scores are used
depends on the user (Anastasi & Urbina, 1997; Urbina, 2005). As Loesch (1977)
observes, "we usually don't have a choice about whether we will be involved with testing"
(p. 74). There is a choice, however, about whether counsellors will be informed and
responsible.

To understand a test, counsellors must know the following:

- the characteristics of its standardization sample
- the types and degree of its reliability and validity
- the reliability and validity of comparable tests
- the scoring procedures
- the method of administration
- the limitations
- the strengths (Kaplan & Saccuzzo, 2005)

Much of this information is contained in the test manuals that accompany standardized tests, but acquiring a thorough knowledge of a particular test takes years of study
and practice. Because it is important that counsellors use tests to the fullest extent possible, they are wise to "prepare local experience tables" so they can give test takers more
specific information about what their scores mean in relation to a particular community
or situation (Goldman, 1994a, p. 216).

Today in the United States, approximately 10 million "counselees each year complete 'tests,' 'inventories,' and other 'assessments' and that estimate does not include school achievement tests or college entrance exams" (Prediger, 1994, p. 228). Although Canadian statistics are unavailable, there is no reason to believe that testing is less popular here.

Some counselling professionals specialize in the administration and interpretation of tests. Those employed as testing and appraisal specialists are known as *psychometrists* and their discipline of comparing the test scores of a person to a norm-referenced group is known as *psychometrics* (Gladding, 2006). (The opposite of psychometrics is *edumetrics*, based on a constructivist trend in education, where client achievement is compared to the client's previous and best results [Tymofievich & Leroux, 2000].) Regardless, most professionals who administer and interpret tests do not do so on a full-time basis. Usually they are counsellors and other helping professionals who are sometimes surprisingly uncomfortable with testing instruments and the negative connotation of the word *test*. A test is often linked to "a heavy emphasis on objectivity" (Loesch, 1977, p. 74), and the process of testing can be mechanical, creating psychological distance between the examiner and the client. To overcome such barriers, counsellors who test need to be well trained in good test practice and the use of the most frequently given tests, as well as other standardized instruments.

Many periodicals review standardized tests, including *Measurement and Evaluation in Counseling and Development*, the *Journal of Counseling Psychology*, the *Journal of Counseling and Development*, the *Journal of Personality Assessment*, and the *Review of Educational Research*. Don Saklofske, an international expert in intelligence testing, is a Canadian researcher at the University of Calgary who also serves as editor of the *Journal of Psychoeducational Assessment* and co-editor of the *Canadian Journal of School Psychology*, both of which review tests.

A number of authoritative reference books on tests are also available. O. K. Buros originated a series of reference books on personality tests, vocational tests, and other similar instruments. His most well-known reference was entitled *Tests in Print*. It continues to be updated periodically by the institute he established, the Buros Institute of Mental Measurements, and is now in its 7th edition. Buros also edited eight editions of the *Mental Measurements Yearbook*, which is considered his best work in this area and will be in its 18th edition in spring 2010 (www.unl.edu/buros/bimm/html/catalog.html).

PROBLEMS AND POTENTIAL OF USING TESTS

There are similarities between the tests administered by counsellors and those used by psychologists (Bubenzer, Zimpfer, & Mahrle, 1990). However, the ways in which tests are given is more crucial for their success in serving the welfare of clients and the general public than the professional identity of who administers them (Harris, 1994).

Tests may be used alone or as part of a group (a *test battery*). Cronbach (1979) asserts that test batteries have little value unless competent, well-educated counsellors are available to interpret them. The same is true for individual tests. Many of the problems associated with testing are usually the result of the way instruments are employed and interpreted rather than problems with the tests themselves (Hood & Johnson, 2007).

Shertzer and Stone (1980) maintain that opponents of tests generally object to them for the following reasons:

- Testing encourages client dependency on both the counsellor and an external source of information for problem resolution.

- Test data prejudice the counsellor's picture of an individual.

- Test data are invalid and unreliable enough so that their value is severely limited (p. 311).

Other critics conclude that tests are culturally biased and discriminatory, measure irrelevant skills, obscure talent, are used mechanically, invade privacy, can be faked, and foster undesirable competition (Hood & Johnson, 2007; Shertzer & Linden, 1979; Talbutt, 1983). "Over-reliance on test results, especially in isolation from other information about an individual, is one of the most serious test misuse problems" (Elmore et al., 1993, p. 76). Another criticism is that tests are regressive and used for predictability rather than screening or self-exploration (Goldman, 1994b).

The use of tests with minorities has been an especially controversial area and one in which abuse has occurred (Suzuki & Kugler, 1995; Suzuki, Meller, & Ponterotto, 2001). Assessment instruments must take into consideration the influences and experiences of persons from diverse cultural and ethnic backgrounds if they are going to have any meaning. Oakland (1982) points out that testing can be a dehumanizing experience, and minority culture students may spend years in ineffective or inappropriate programs as a result of test scores. To avoid cultural bias, the Canadian Psychological Association (CPA) published a document entitled *Guidelines for Non-Discriminatory Practice* (www.cpa.ca/membership/membershipbenefitsandservices/cpapublications; CPA, 2001). Ethical guidelines for test use are also contained in the CPA document entitled *Recommendations by the Canadian Psychological Association for Improving the North American Safeguards That Help Protect the Public against Test Misuse* (Simner, 1994). These standards, as well as those drawn up by other professional associations, should be consulted when trying to prevent test abuse with minority populations (Hansen, 1994). In assessing bias it should be recognized that prejudicial acts may result from omission as well as acts of commission (Chernin, Holden, & Chandler, 1997).

Success or failure with tests is related to the sensitivity, ability, and knowledge of the counsellors who select, administer, and interpret them. "Counselors have a general obligation to take an empirical approach to their instruments, especially those for which there are not complete norms and substantial validation" (Carlson, 1989, p. 489). If they do not consider multiple criteria in the selection process, counsellors are likely to make mistakes that are costly to clients and themselves. To avoid these situations, some counsellors include clients in the process of test selection.

Psychological tests provide useful information for diagnostic, predictive, and treatment purposes. Several, including the following examples, have been recently tested in Canada:

- The Brief Core Schema Scales has proven helpful in developing preventative interventions for young people at risk of experiencing psychosis (Addington & Tran, 2009).

- The Youth Psychopathic Traits Inventory was found useful as a measure of psychopathic traits in young people (Campbell, Doucette, & French, 2009).

- The Strengths and Difficulties Questionnaire, used for mental-health screening, has been found useful with looked-after children (e.g., foster children) (Marquis & Flynn, 2009).

- The Interpersonal Reactivity Index, a measure of both cognitive and emotional empathy, has been found useful in assessing empathy expressed in romantic relationships (Peloquin & Lafontaine, 2010).

- Actuarial measures have been found more useful in predicting the likelihood that sexual offenders will reoffend compared to professional judgments (Hanson & Morton-Bourgon, 2009).

Other measures are developed so that countries can make international comparisons. For example, the International Society for the Prevention of Child Abuse and Neglect recently took the lead in bringing together child abuse experts from around the world to create three new instruments designed to look at child victimization (i.e., child abuse). The final version of these instruments allows comparisons to be made across time and across nations, including both western and non-western countries (Runyan, Dunne, & Zolotor, 2009).

Furthermore, Learner (1981) and Oakland (1982) report that the general public's attitude toward testing is positive, even among minority cultures, perhaps because people believe that tests serve many useful purposes. From the public's perspective, the primary function of tests is to help clients make better decisions about their futures. Tests may also do the following:

- help clients gain self-understanding
- help counsellors decide if clients' needs are within their range of expertise
- help counsellors better understand clients
- help counsellors determine which counselling methods might be most appropriately employed
- help counsellors predict the future performance of clients in select areas, such as mechanics, art, or graduate school
- help counsellors stimulate new interests within their clients
- help counsellors evaluate the outcome of their counselling efforts (Shertzer & Stone, 1980)

QUALITIES OF GOOD TESTS

All tests are not created equal, but those that do the job best have certain qualities in common. Among the most important are validity, reliability, standardization, and norms, which facilitate the interpretation of scores (Aiken & Groth-Marnat, 2006; Hogan, 2007).

Validity

Validity is unquestionably the most important test quality. It is "the degree to which a test measures what it is supposed to measure and consequently permits appropriate interpretation of scores" (Gay et al., 2006, p. 134). If a test does not fulfill this function, it is basically useless. The validity of a test is determined by comparing its results with measures of a separate and independent criterion. Thus, if a test purports to measure an individual's probability of succeeding in a professional field such as medicine, law, or counselling, the test scores are correlated with measures of success, such as grades and ratings of instructors, once the tested individual completes his or her education. Examples of such tests would be the MCAT, the LSAT, the GRE, and the Miller's Analogies Test (MAT), all of which are used as screening devices in admitting students to professional and graduate programs of study. If scores on the testing instrument correlate highly and positively with these independent measures of success, then the instrument is said to possess a high degree of validity.

There are four types of validity: content, construct, criterion, and consequential (Anastasi & Urbina, 1997; Kaplan & Saccuzzo, 2005; Tymofievich & Leroux, 2000; Urbina, 2005). *Content validity*, sometimes referred to as *face validity*, is an indication of the degree to which a test appears to measure what it is supposed to measure (Aiken & Groth-Marnat, 2006). More important, content validity is concerned with whether the test includes a fair sample of the universe of factors it is supposed to assess. As a general rule, content validity is associated with achievement, aptitude, and ability tests.

Construct validity is the most important type of validity "because it asks the fundamental validity question: What is the test really measuring?" (Gay et al., 2006, p. 137). Simply defined, construct validity is "the degree to which a test measures an intended hypothetical construct" (p. 137) such as empathy or intelligence. Much depends on the test maker's definition of the construct, but generally construct validity is applied to personality and interest inventories.

Criterion validity refers to the comparison of test scores with a person's actual performance of a certain skill across time and situations. For example, a test that measures a person's fine-motor skills may be validated against that person's ability to type. When the criterion is available at the time of testing, then the concurrent validity of the test is being measured. When the criterion is not available until after the test is administered, then the predictive validity of the test is being measured (Aiken & Groth-Marnat, 2006). Two well-known criterion-based instruments are frequently used in counselling environments: the Minnesota Multiphasic Personality Inventory-2 (MMPI-2), a test with concurrent validity (Butcher, Williams, & Fowler, 2001), and the revised Strong Interest Inventory (SII), a test with predictive validity (Osborne, Brown, Niles, & Miner, 1997).

Finally, the newest type of validity is *consequential validity*, the social implications or consequences of test use and interpretation (Tymofievich & Leroux, 2000). Test score interpretations have both long-term and short-term effects on clients. Counsellors must consider the client's perspective and position in using tests of any sort regardless of his or her age. Tests are just one technique in counsellors' repertoires and, in interpreting results, counsellors should not be too dogmatic or authoritarian (Meier & Davis, 2008).

Overall, validity appears strong for most standardized tests. In a comprehensive review of the research literature based on more than 125 meta-analyses of psychological test validities, Meyer et al. (2001) found evidence that psychological tests are comparable with the validity of most medical tests and have "strong and compelling" validity for use in counselling practice, especially if multi-method assessment procedures are used.

Reliability

"In everyday English, reliability means dependability or trustworthiness. The term means the same thing when describing measurement (Gay et al., 2006, p. 139). Thus, reliability is a measure of the degree to which a test produces consistency of test scores when people are retested with the same or an equivalent instrument (Anastasi & Urbina, 1997; Hogan, 2007; Urbina, 2005). Although reliability is related to validity, a test score may be reliable but not valid. There are three traditional ways of determining reliability:

1. *Test-retest*, in which the same test is given again after a period of time;
2. *Parallel-form* or *alternate-form*, in which two equivalent forms of the same test are administered; and

3. *Internal consistency analysis*, in which the scores of two arbitrarily selected halves of a test are compared.

Standardization and Norms

Standardization refers to the uniform conditions under which a test is administered and scored (Aiken & Groth-Marnat, 2006). Standardization makes possible the comparison of an individual's successive scores over time as well as the comparison of scores of different individuals. Norms, or average performance scores for specified groups, make possible meaningful comparisons among people in regard to what can be expected (Kaplan & Saccuzzo, 2005). Test norms have their limitations and may be misused. For example, a major criticism of some tests is that their norms were established on members of the majority population; therefore, they may discriminate against cultural minorities and people who are disadvantaged and disabled. Counsellors must carefully examine the norming procedures of tests, and they should also establish their own local norms. In this way prejudice and the inappropriate use of tests can be minimized.

CLASSIFICATION OF TESTS

There are many classifications of tests. Shertzer and Stone (1981) list seven:

1. *Standardized versus non-standardized*—tests that are administered and scored according to specific directions (e.g., the Self-Directed Search) as opposed to those that are not (e.g., an experimental projective test)

2. *Individual versus group*—tests that are designed to be given to one person at a time (e.g., the Kaufman Assessment Battery for Children [Kamphaus, Beres, Kaufman, & Kaufman, 1996]) as opposed to those that are given to groups (e.g., Minnesota School Attitude Survey [Callis, 1985])

3. *Speed versus power*—tests that must be completed within a specified period of time (e.g., most achievement tests) as opposed to those that allow for the demonstration of knowledge within generous time boundaries (e.g., many individually administered intelligence tests)

4. *Performance versus paper and pencil*—tests that require the manipulation of objects (e.g., the Object Assembly subtest of the Wechsler Intelligence Scale for Children-IV [WISC-IV]) as opposed to those in which subjects mark answers or give written responses (e.g., the Adjective Check List)

5. *Objective versus subjective*—tests that require the scorer not to make a judgment (e.g., short answer, true–false, matching, multiple-choice [Aiken & Groth-Marnat, 2006]) as opposed to those that require the scorer to exercise a judgment (e.g., the Vocabulary subtest of the Wechsler Adult Intelligence Scale-III [WAIS-III; Wechsler, 1997])

6. *Maximum versus typical performance*—tests that require the examinees to do their best (e.g., tests of intelligence and special abilities) as opposed to those that measure what a person is most likely to do or usually does (e.g., tests that indicate interests or attitudes)

7. *Norm versus criterion based*—tests that compare an individual's score with scores within a group (e.g., intelligence or achievement test) as opposed to those that measure a person's score compared to a desirable level or standard (e.g., a reading test; Aiken & Groth-Marnat, 2006; Hogan, 2007)

Another way that tests may be classified, and one that is even more important for counsellors, is "by the purpose for which they are designed or by the aspects of behavior they sample" (Shertzer & Stone, 1981, p. 242). In this classification Shertzer and Stone (1981) list six categories of tests: mental ability, aptitude, achievement, interests, career development, and personality. Yet another system of classification includes the following categories: educational, vocational, or personal aspects of counselling (Elmore & Roberge, 1982). A third classification scheme, originated by Sylvania (1956), groups tests according to their frequency of use: intelligence/scholastic aptitude, vocational (and other aptitude), and achievement/diagnostic. All these classification systems have their merits and limitations. Counsellors are usually involved in dealing with four distinct but sometimes overlapping categories of tests: intelligence/aptitude, interest/career, personality, and achievement.

Case Example: What Would *You* Do?

Carl had a difficult time finding tests that he wanted to use. He realized he could alphabetize them, but he wanted a better system, so Carl decided to use colour codes like those found in doctors' offices. He colour-coded all intelligence tests with a green tag, all personality tests with a blue tag, and so on. He then put the colour-coded tests in order of most used to least used. After testing clients, Carl added a colour or colours to their files, with some being only one hue and some being many.

1. What do you think of Carl's system?

2. How would you go about coding test instruments that you might use?

Intelligence/Aptitude

Among the most controversial but popular types of tests are those that attempt to measure general intelligence and special aptitude. *Intelligence* is defined in many different ways, and there is no absolute meaning associated with the word (Gardner, 1993). Indeed, Anastasi (1982) reports that most intelligence tests "are usually overloaded with certain functions, such as verbal ability, and completely omit others" (p. 228). She notes that many intelligence tests are "validated against measures of academic achievement" and "are often designated as tests of scholastic aptitude" (Anastasi, 1982, p. 228). In line with her observation is Aiken and Groth-Marnat's (2006) definition of an intelligence test as an instrument designed to measure an individual's aptitude for scholastic work or other kinds of occupations requiring reasoning and verbal ability. Many intelligence tests are used primarily as screening devices in counselling and are followed by more specialized aptitude tests that assess aptitude in particular areas, such as music or mechanics.

Shavinina (2008) criticizes intelligence tests, particularly regarding their use in assessing for giftedness, because (a) they measure a person's learning but not their ability to learn; (b) they do not measure creative, practical, emotional, and social forms of giftedness; (c) they reveal more about having better educational and socialization opportunities (middle and upper social classes) than about real intellectual abilities; and (d) they overemphasize mental speed and psychomotor speed. On the other hand, Gottfredson and Saklofske (2009) promote their use because of their ever-increasing sophistication with resulting increased ability to measure "intelligence" with greater "sensitivity, precision, and economy of time" (p. 193).

Most modern intelligence tests are descendants of the original scales developed in France by Alfred Binet in the early 1900s. The Stanford-Binet Intelligence Scale, a revision of the Binet-Simon scales, was prepared by L. M. Terman and published in 1916; it is the grandparent of American intelligence tests. The test is individually administered and has traditionally been used more with children than adults. In 2000, it underwent a fifth revision (SB5) and now has a more modern look as well as appropriateness for adults and those who are less verbally fluent.

Another popular series of individually administered intelligence tests are those originated by David Wechsler. They are the Wechsler Preschool and Primary Scale of Intelligence-IV (WPPSI-IV), designed for ages 2.6 years to 7 years, 3 months; the Wechsler Intelligence Scale for Children-Fourth Edition (WISC-IV), designed for ages 6 years through 16 years, 11 months; and the Wechsler Adult Intelligence Scale-Fourth Edition (WAIS-IV), designed for ages 16 years to 90 years (Hartman, 2009). The WAIS-IV was normed on 2200 Americans and 688 Canadians (Weiss, Saklofske, Coalson, & Engi Raiford, 2010). Pearson offers both a WAIS-IV Canadian Report Writer and a WAIS-IV Canadian Scoring Assistant (Pearson Education, 2010).

The Wechsler intelligence tests provide a verbal IQ, performance IQ, and full-scale IQ score. Extensive research has been done on all the Wechsler scales, and they are often the instruments of choice in the evaluation of intelligence (Piotrowski & Keller, 1989; Thorndike, 2005).

There are a number of other widely respected, individually administered intelligence tests. Among them are the Bayley Scales of Infant Development, the Vineland Social Maturity Scale, the Kaufman Assessment Battery for Children (K-ABC), the McCarthy Scales of Children's Abilities, the Peabody Picture Vocabulary Test (PPVT-IV), and the Kaufman Adolescent and Adult Intelligence Test (KAIT).

Also available are numerous intelligence scales intended to be administered to groups. These instruments were first developed during World War I when the United

States Army created its Alpha and Beta intelligence tests, the best-known forerunners of today's group intelligence instruments. These tests were initially employed to screen army inductees and classify them for training according to ability level. Among the most widely used and respected group intelligence tests are the Otis-Lennon School Ability Test, the Cognitive Abilities Test, and the Test of Cognitive Skills. The Montreal Cognitive Assessment is a recent test developed in Canada for use in identifying mild cognitive impairments in elderly persons (Koski, Xie, & Finch, 2009).

Aptitude tests are similar in many ways to intelligence tests, but they are designed to tap a narrower range of ability. Aiken and Groth-Marnat (2006) define an *aptitude* as a capability for a task or type of skill and an *aptitude test* as one that measures a person's ability to profit from further training or experience in an occupation or skill. Aptitude tests are usually divided into two categories: (a) multi-aptitude batteries, which test a number of skills by administering a variety of tests, and (b) component ability tests, which assess a single ability or skill, such as music or mechanical ability (Bradley, 1984). Some of the best-known multi-aptitude batteries are the Scholastic Aptitude Test (SAT), the American College Testing (ACT) Assessment, the Miller Analogies Test (MAT), the Differential Aptitude Test (DAT), and the Armed Services Vocational Aptitude Battery (ASVAB; Anastasi & Urbina, 1997; Hood & Johnson, 2007; Urbina, 2005).

Another aptitude test that has been used in both the United States and Canada is the General Aptitude Test Battery (GATB) (Baydoun & Neuman, 1992; Pettersen & Turcotte, 1996), a test mentioned at the beginning of the chapter in the Practice Reflection. Before 1980 in the United States, the test was used mostly for vocational counselling, but in the early 1980s, it was used as a means of selecting qualified workers (Baydoun & Neuman, 1992). In July 1986, the U.S. Department of Labor urged that use of the test be halted. Several reasons were provided, including the finding that minority groups generally scored lower on the test (Baydoun & Neuman, 1992). Bias against minority groups was also found in a Canadian study looking at recruitment for police constables (Hausdorf, LeBlanc, & Chawla, 2002).

Interest/Career

Although there is an expected relationship between ability and an interest in exercising that ability, tests that best measure interests are those designed specifically for the purpose. Aiken and Groth-Marnat (2006) define *interest inventory* as a test or checklist that assesses a person's preferences for activities and topics. Responses derived from such tests are compared with the scores of others at a similar developmental level (e.g., in an educational setting) or with people already working in a particular area (e.g., in a vocational setting). Anastasi (1982) notes that "the study of interests has probably received its strongest impetus from educational and career counseling" because a person's achievement in a learning situation or a career is greatly influenced by his or her interests

(p. 534). Indeed, "interest inventory interpretation is one of the most frequently used interventions in career counseling" (Savickas, 1998, p. 307).

Instruments that measure career interests began in a systematic and standardized way with the 1927 publication of the Strong Vocational Interest Blank (SVIB). The test has been revised and expanded half a dozen times since its inception, with the latest edition of this instrument, the Strong Interest Inventory (SII), encompassing 207 occupations. The test's founder, E. K. Strong, Jr., devised only 10 occupational scales for the original test (Donnay, 1997). SII test results are explained in three forms: general occupational themes, basic interest scales, and occcupational scales. Thus, they help clients examine themselves in both a general and a specific way. Another attractive feature of the instrument is its link to John Holland's theory of career development, which proposes six major types of people and environments: realistic (R), investigative (I), artistic (A), social (S), enterprising (E), and conventional (C) (RIASEC) (Holland, 1997). The closer the correlation between people and environment types, the more satisfying the relationship (Spokane & Catalano, 2000).

Overall, the SII offers a breadth and depth in the measurement of occupational interests that are unmatched by any other single instrument. The accompanying user's guide suggests ways of employing the test with adults, cross-cultural groups, and special populations (Drummond & Jones, 2006). In addition, strong theoretical underpinnings, empirical construction, and a long history are major benefits of this inventory. One study (Hansen & Dik, 2005) of 148 women and 93 men found that, 12 years later, the SII had provided excellent to moderate predictions between freshmen scores and current occupation (61% for women, 54% for men). Also, the SII has been shown to have robust results with people of different ethnicities (Fouad & Mohler, 2004). Another study, based on 1403 women and 469 men, found that the basic interest scales are excellent predictors of university majors for both genders (Gasser, Larson, & Borgen, 2007).

Another popular career inventory, also based on Holland's six personality/ environmental types, is the Self-Directed Search (SDS) (Holland, 1994). This instrument is self-administered, self-scored, and sometimes self-interpreted. It comprises 228 items divided into three sets: activities, competencies, and occupations (Krieshok, 1987). After scoring, clients examine a three-letter *Occupational Code Finder* (a booklet that accompanies the SDS), comparing it with career codes found in the *Dictionary of Occupational Titles* (DOT). The inventory has four versions, including Form E, which is designed for poor readers. Test takers from ages 15 to 70 report that the SDS is enjoyable and useful.

In Canada, instead of using the American DOT to find occupations from the SDS, we use the National Occupational Classification (NOC), a system that organizes over 30 000 job titles in Canada (Human Resources and Skills Development Canada, [HRSDC] 2009). To make the best use of the SII and the SDS, it is a good idea to refer to a copy of the *Directory of Holland Codes for the NOC Career Handbook*, also produced by HRSDC. (For information on attaining a copy, go to http://openlibrary.org/b/OL20675884M/Directory_of_Holland_codes_for_the_NOC_career_handbook).

A third popular interest/career inventory is the Kuder Occupational Interest Survey (KOIS), which was first published in 1939 and continues to evolve (Kuder, 1939; 1977). The latest revision of the KOIS was in 1991 (Betsworth & Fouad, 1997). There are six forms of this activity preference, item-type, untimed instrument, but each form has a forced-choice, triad-response format (Zytowski, 1992). Some forms of the test are computer scored, while others are self-scored. Clients respond to each triad by selecting the most and least preferred activity. Scores on the Kuder correlate highly with commonly expressed interests of select career groups and university majors (Zytowski & Holmberg, 1988). The test's 10 broad career areas include the following (Zytowski, 1992, pp. 245–246):

1. *Social services*—"preference of helping people"—comparable to the Holland "social" scale

2. *Persuasive*—"preference for meeting and dealing with people and promoting projects or selling things and ideas"—comparable to the Holland "enterprising" scale

3. *Clerical*—"preference for tasks that require precision and accuracy"—comparable to the Holland "conventional" scale

4. *Computational*—"preference for working with numbers"—comparable also to the Holland "conventional" scale

5. *Musical*—"preference for going to concerts, playing musical instruments, singing, and reading about music and musicians"—comparable to the Holland "artistic" scale

6. *Artistic*—"preference for creative work involving attractive design, colour, form, and materials"—comparable to the Holland "artistic" scale

7. *Literary*—"preference for reading and writing"—comparable to the Holland "artistic" scale

8. *Mechanical*—"preference for working with machines and tools"—comparable to the Holland "realistic" scale

9. *Outdoor*—"preference for activities that keep you outside most of the time, and usually deal with animals and plants"—comparable to the Holland "realistic" scale

10. *Scientific*—"preference for discovering new facts and solving problems"—comparable to the Holland "investigative" scale

Vocational interests may be "the most stable of all psychological constructs" (Hansen, 2005, p. 284). A recently published follow-up study of both junior and senior high school students, first tested in 1975 with the KOIS, found that interests were moderately stable for individuals 30 years later (Rottinghaus, Coon, Gaffey, & Zytowski, 2007).

A fourth instrument, primarily career-focused, is the Career Beliefs Inventory (CBI) (Krumboltz, 1991). "The CBI is an instrument which, when used sensitively by a qualified professional, can help people identify the beliefs that might be blocking them" (Krumboltz, 1992, p. 1). It is most usefully employed at the beginning of a career-counselling session. It makes possible the exploration of deep-seated attitudes and assumptions.

Other well-known interest/career tests include the California Occupational Preference System, the Jackson Vocational Interest Survey, the Ohio Vocational Interest Survey, the Unisex Edition of the ACT Interest Inventory, and the Vocational Preference Inventory.

A recently-published public domain inventory (i.e., no cost) is called the Oregon Vocational Interest Scales (ORVIS; Pozzebon, Visser, Ashton, Lee, & Goldberg, 2010). Eight scales comprise the ORVIS: leadership, organization, altruism, creativity, analysis, producing, advertising, and erudition. The scales have good internal consistency and construct validity (Pozzebon et al., 2010).

For students who are not university bound, Bradley (1984) reports three interest inventories designed to "measure interests in occupations that do not require college training" (p. 7). These include (a) the Minnesota Vocational Interest Inventory, (b) the Career Assessment Inventory, and (c) the Career Guidance Inventory in Trades, Services, and Technologies. Interest tests designed for more specialized use are the Bem Sex-Role Inventory, the Jenkins Activity Survey, the Personal Orientation Inventory, the Survey of Values, and the Survey of School Attitudes.

In selecting appropriate interest/career instruments, "you [must] know what you are looking for and . . . what you are getting" (Westbrook, 1988, p. 186). Two excellent resource books describe career decision-making and assessment measures are *Handbook of Vocational Psychology* (Walsh & Savickas, 2005) and *A Counselor's Guide to Career Assessment Instruments* (Kapes & Whitfield, 2001). The latter text reviews 52 major career assessment instruments and annotates 250 others, and describes their intended populations.

Personality

Personality can be defined in many ways; what is considered normal in one culture may be perceived as abnormal in another. Nevertheless, there are a number of personality theories that examine the biological, social, and environmental aspects of human beings. The most popular 20th-century theorist of personality assessment was Henry A. Murray. He was especially cognizant of needs (or environmental forces/presses) and how they determine behaviour (Drummond & Jones, 2006).

A *personality test* may be defined as any of several methods of analyzing personality, such as checklists, personality inventories, and projective techniques (Aiken & Groth-Marnat, 2006). Such tests may be divided into two main categories: objective and projective. Some of the best-known objective tests are the Minnesota Multiphasic Personality Inventory-2 (MMPI-2), the Myers-Briggs Type Indicator (MBTI), and the Edwards Personal Preference Schedule (EPPS). These tests yield scores that are independent of any opinion or judgment of the scorer, as are all objective tests. Projective tests include the Rorschach, the Thematic Apperception Test (TAT), and the House-Tree-Person (HTP) Test. These types of tests yield measures that, in varying degrees, depend on the judgments and interpretations of administrators/scorers.

The prototype of the personality test was a self-report inventory known as the Personal Data Sheet, developed during World War I by R. S. Woodworth (Kaplan & Saccuzzo, 2005). The first significant projective test was the Rorschach Inkblot Test, published in 1921 (Erdberg, 1996). Because objectively scored personality tests are more widely used in counselling, we will begin our discussion with a review of them.

The Minnesota Multiphasic Personality Inventory-2 (MMPI-2) is the most widely used psychological test in the world (Butcher, 1994; Holden & Troister, 2009). It is a revision of the original MMPI. Instead of being normed on a limited population, however, this version uses a geographically and ethnically diverse reference group representative of the population of the United States. The re-standardized MMPI-2 is also on tape for individuals who are blind, illiterate, semiliterate, or disabled (Drummond & Jones, 2006). It has several forms, including one for adolescents (the MMPI-A), but the most popular form consists of 567 affirmative statements that clients respond to in one of three ways: true, false, or cannot say. There are 10 clinical scales on the MMPI-2 (see Table 16.1)

Table 16.1 Clinical Scales on the Minnesota Multiphasic Personality Inventory–2

Scale	Item Total	Item Content
Hypochondriasis (Hs)	(32)	Undue concern with physical health
Depression (D)	(57)	Depression, denial of happiness and personal worth, lack of interest, withdrawal
Hysteria (Hy)	(60)	Specific somatic complaints, denial of psychological or emotional problems, discomfort in social situations
Psychopathic deviate (Pd)	(50)	Antisocial acting-out impulses, constricted social conformity
Masculinity-femininity (Mf)	(56)	Identification with culturally conventional masculine and feminine choices, aesthetic interests, activity-passivity
Paranoia (Pa)	(40)	Delusions of persecution and ideas of reference, interpersonal sensitivity, suspiciousness, moral self-righteousness
Psychasthenia (Pt)	(48)	General dissatisfaction with life, difficulty with concentration, indecisiveness, self-doubt, obsessional aspects
Schizophrenia (Sc)	(78)	Feeling of being different, feelings of isolation, bizarre thought processes, poor family relationships, sexual identity concerns, tendency to withdraw
Hypomania (Ma)	(46)	Elevated energy level, flight of ideas, elevated mood, increased motor activity, expansiveness, grandiosity
Social introversion-extroversion	(69)	Introversion-extroversion; social insecurity

Source: From *Appraisal Procedures for Counsellors and Other Helping Professionals* (2nd ed., p. 181), by R.J. Drummond, Upper Saddle River, NJ: Prentice Hall. © 1992. Reprinted by permission of Prentice Hall, Inc., Upper Saddle River, NJ.

and three major validity scales: Lie (L), Infrequency (F), and Correction (K). In addition, there is a "?" scale, which is a compilation of unanswered questions throughout the test. In addition to distinguishing individuals who are experiencing psychiatric problems, the MMPI-2 is able to discern important characteristics such as anger, alienation, Type A behaviour, and even marital distress. Extensive training and experience are necessary for counsellors to use this instrument accurately and appropriately. Overall, uses of the MMPI-2 are still being refined (Austin, 1994).

Besides the MMPI-2, counsellors and psychologists also have two other highly popular self-report instruments to choose from when looking at abnormal personality: the Millon Clinical Multiaxial Inventory-III (MCMI-III) and the Personality Assessment Inventory (PAI) (Wise, Streiner, & Walfish, 2010). The MCMI-III is used to purportedly diagnose personality disorders while the PAI is used frequently in forensic and medical settings (Wise et al., 2010). The PAI is the only instrument that also provides norms for university students (Wise et al., 2010). Interestingly, compared to the MCMI-III and the PAI, the MMPI-2 has the weakest reliability coefficients of the three tests, despite its popularity (Wise et al., 2010).

The Myers-Briggs Type Indicator (MBTI) is a test that reflects Carl Jung's theory of personality type (Myers, 1962; 1980). The inventory "has been widely used in various contexts including career counseling, marital and family therapy, and team building" (Vacha-Haase & Thompson, 2002, p. 173). The MBTI contains 166 two-choice items concerning preferences or inclinations in feelings and behaviours (Aiken & Groth-Marnat, 2006). It yields four indexes: extroversion versus introversion (EI), sensing versus intuition (SN), thinking versus feeling (TF), and judgment versus perception (JP). The MBTI consists of four bipolar scales:

1. *Extroversion or introversion (EI)*—whether perception and judgment are directed to the outer (E) or inner (I) world

2. *Sensing or intuitive (SN)*—which kind of perception is preferred when one needs to perceive

3. *Thinking or feeling (TF)*—which kind of judgment is trusted when a decision needs to be made

4. *Judgment or perception (JP)*—whether to deal with the world in the judgment attitude (using thinking or feeling) or in the perceptual attitude (using sensing or intuition)

Combinations of these four indexes result in 16 possible personality types. A clear understanding of personality type provides counsellors with constructive information on how clients perceive and interact with their environments (Lynch, 1985). Research indicates that different MBTI types appear to be attracted to certain occupations and lifestyles (Healy & Woodward, 1998). For example, 76% of tested counselling students score high on the intuitive/feeling scales of the MBTI and are described as insightful, enthusiastic, and able to handle challenging situations with personal warmth (Myers, 1980). Alternative tests to the MBTI that also yield Jungian psychological-type preferences include the

Keirsey Temperament Sorter (Keirsey & Bates, 1984) and the Personal Preferences Self-Description Questionnaire (PPSDQ; Thompson, 1996).

On the other hand, a recent study found that the MBTI did not offer much additional power in predicting the major of undecided university students when used in conjunction with the SII (Pulver & Kelly, 2008). Furthermore, the MBTI has been repeatedly criticized for its (a) dichotomous scoring (e.g., a zero preference score still results in a preference), (b) forced-choice response format (an item must be chosen out of two or three alternatives), and (c) differential gender weighting (different weightings are used for men and women on the TF scales) (Vacha-Haase & Thompson, 2002). The study by Vacha-Haase and Thompson (2002) found that results using the PPSDQ (Thompson, 1996) were as good as or superior to those using the MMBI.

The Edwards Personal Preference Schedule (EPPS) is based on the need-press theory of personality developed by Henry Murray (1938). It consists of 225 forced-choice questions that examine the strength of 15 individual needs in relation to a person's other needs (Anastasi & Urbina, 1997; Urbina, 2005). The scores are plotted on a percentile chart based on group norms for university students or adults in general. Other objectively scored, self-report personality tests are the California Psychological Inventory (CPI), the Guilford-Zimmerman Temperament Survey, the Mooney Problem Check List, the Sixteen Personality Factor Questionnaire (16 PF), and the State-Trait Anxiety Inventory (STAI).

Projective personality tests are much less structured and far more difficult to score, but they are harder for the client to fake. Advocates claim that these tests measure deeper aspects of a client's personality than do other instruments. Some researchers and clinicians, such as Exner (2003), have tried to standardize the methods by which projectives are administered and scored. There are still those who, armed with anecdotal evidence, argue for the usefulness of the Rorschach Inkblot Test, for example, in clinical practice (Bram, 2010).

Although there has been success for some instruments, the scoring of many other projectives, such as the Thematic Apperception Test, is questionable. In addition to the tests already mentioned in this section, projective tests include the Holtzman Inkblot Technique, the Bender Gestalt, the Draw-a-Person Test, the Children's Apperception Test, and the Rotter Incomplete Sentences Blank.

Achievement

An *achievement test* is a measure of an individual's degree of accomplishment or learning in a subject or task (Aiken & Groth-Marnat, 2006). Achievement tests are much more direct as measurement instruments compared with any other type of test. Their results give clients a good idea of what they have learned in a certain area relative to what others have learned. The tests give clients the type of information they need to make sound educational and career decisions (Bradley, 1984). If a client has aptitudes, interests, or personality dispositions suitable for select career areas but has little knowledge or skill, he or she can take positive steps to correct these deficiencies.

Achievement tests may be either teacher-made or standardized. The advantages of teacher-made tests are that they measure specific units of study emphasized in an educational setting, are easy to keep up-to-date, and reflect current emphases and information. Standardized tests measure more general educational objectives, are usually more carefully constructed, and give the test taker a good idea about how he or she compares with a wider sample of others in a particular subject. Teacher-made and standardized tests complement each other, and both may be used profitably in the helping process.

Various achievement tests are employed for distinct purposes. In a school setting, a combination of teacher-made and standardized tests are linked to age and grade levels. General achievement batteries used in elementary and secondary schools measure basic skills. They include the TerraNova Tests, the Iowa Tests of Basic Skills, the SRA Achievement Series, the Metropolitan Achievement Tests, the Wide Range Achievement Test, and the Stanford Achievement Test (Anastasi & Urbina, 1997; Urbina, 2005). School counsellors must become especially knowledgeable about these instruments to converse intelligently and efficiently with teachers, parents, administrators, students, and educational specialists.

Instruments are also available that measure adult achievement, such as the Adult Basic Learning Examination and the Tests of General Education Development (GED). Professionally oriented achievement tests include the National Teacher Examination, Law School Admissions Test, and the National Counsellor Examination (NCE). These latter tests help protect the public and the professions they represent by ensuring that individuals who pass them have achieved a minimum level of informational competence.

ADMINISTRATION AND INTERPRETATION OF TESTS

A major criticism of test use in counselling focuses on administration and interpretation. The process of administering a test is described in the manual that accompanies each one, and most tests specify uniform procedures to be followed at each step, from preparing the room to giving instructions. Some tests have specialized instructions, and counsellors must follow these procedures if they expect to obtain valid test results.

One question usually not addressed in manuals is whether a test taker should be involved in selecting the test and, if so, how much he or she should be involved. In some cases, such as the administration of achievement tests in elementary schools, it is inappropriate for test takers to be involved in test selection, but on other occasions participation is beneficial. Goldman (1971) lists several advantages of involving test takers in test selection. Among the reasons are the following:

- the willingness of the tested population to accept test results
- the promotion of independence

- the value of the decision-making experience that might generalize to other decision-making opportunities
- the opportunity for diagnosis based on the test taker's reactions to various tests
- the selection of tests that best fit the needs of the tested population

After tests are selected, administered, and scored, counsellors need to interpret the results for the tested population in an understandable way (Tymofievich & Leroux, 2000). Four basic interpretations can be helpful to test takers, depending on the test (Goldman, 1971; Hanna, 1988):

1. *Descriptive interpretation*, which provides information on the current status of the test taker

2. *Genetic interpretation*, which focuses on how the tested person got to be the way he or she is now

3. *Predictive interpretation*, which concentrates on forecasting the future

4. *Evaluative interpretation*, which includes recommendations by the test interpreter

Unfortunately, some counsellors fail to learn how to administer or interpret tests. "Misuse occurs in all three basic testing areas, employment, educational, and clinical" (Azar, 1994, p. 16). Misuse can result from administering and interpreting a good test in the wrong way or giving it to the wrong person for the wrong reason. In any case, when tests are misused, clients may not understand the meaning of "the numbers, charts, graphs or diagrams presented to them" (Miller, 1982, p. 87) and may leave counselling as uninformed and unenlightened as when they began.

By maintaining conditions of standardization when tests are administered; by knowing the strengths and limitations of the norms, reliability, and validity of particular instruments; and by translating raw test data into meaningful descriptions of current or predicted behaviour, counsellors assure that tests are used to promote the welfare of their clients. (Harris, 1994, p. 10)

Several ways have been suggested to correct deficiencies associated with test interpretation. For example, besides making sure that those who give tests are well educated and sensitive, Hanna (1988, p. 477) recommends using a person's *percentile rank* ("the percentage of persons in a reference group who scored lower than the person") as one way to provide descriptive interpretation clearly and concisely (see Figure 16.1).

Another way of rectifying deficiencies in interpretive skills depends on counsellor–client preparation for the process of interpretation. First, counsellors should be educated

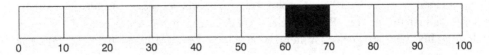

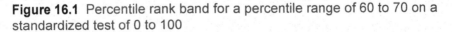

Figure 16.1 Percentile rank band for a percentile range of 60 to 70 on a standardized test of 0 to 100

in test theory and construction. Counsellors cannot explain test results unless they are well-informed about the instruments with which they are dealing.

Second, Tyler (1984) points out that scores are only clues and should be seen as such. Scores must be considered in light of what else is known about a client. The total combination of information can form the basis for a more meaningful and productive dialogue between counsellor and client. Goldman (1971) points out that if a test is given on an individual basis, counsellors notice many things about clients that otherwise would be missed. This extra information, when combined with the test scores, often allows for a more complete assessment of the client.

Third, Tinsley and Bradley (1986), Miller (1982), and Strahan and Kelly (1994) advocate concrete ways of dealing with test results. Tinsley and Bradley believe that, before meeting with a client, the counsellor must be prepared to make a clear and accurate interpretation of test results. They advise against interpreting "off the cuff." A reasonable plan is to begin the interpretation with concrete information, such as interest or achievement scores, and then move to abstract information, such as personality or ability results. If the interpretation of information is to be meaningful, the emotional needs of the client must be considered and the information must be fresh in the counsellor's mind. One way to achieve both goals is to *interpret test results on an as-needed basis*—that is, interpret the scores the client needs to know only at a point in time (Goldman, 1971). There is less information to deal with when this approach is followed, and both counsellor and client are likely to remember results better. The major disadvantage of this approach is that it may become fragmented.

Tinsley and Bradley (1986) propose that when interpretation occurs, a client should be prepared through the establishment of rapport between counsellor and client. Test information can then be delivered in a way that focuses on what the client wants to know. Client feedback is promoted and dialogue is encouraged.

Miller (1982) makes similar remarks in his five-point plan for interpreting test results to clients. First, he has his client remember feelings on the test day and give impressions of the test or tests. He then reviews with the client the purpose of testing and how test scores are presented (e.g., by percentiles). Next, he and the client actually examine the test results together and discuss what the scores mean. Meaning is elicited by asking the client open-ended questions. The client can then integrate scores with other aspects of self-knowledge. The final stage involves incorporating all knowledge into a client-originated plan for continuing self-study. Counsellors can help clients formulate a plan, but the plan itself should come from the client.

A final way of making test results concrete is to present them in simple graph displays (Strahan & Kelly, 1994). Graphical data help clients see test results in a simple, clear, and interesting way. For example, if the data from the RIASEC code of the Strong Interest Inventory are graphed from greatest to least degree of liking, the results of a particular profile might look like the graph depicted in Figure 16.2.

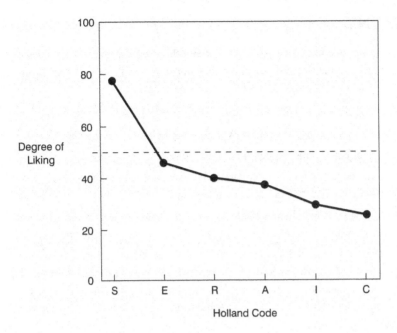

Figure 16.2 A simple graph display

Source: Reprinted from "Showing Clients What Their Profiles Mean," by R. F. Strahan and A. E. Kelly, 1994, *Journal of Counseling and Development, 72,* p. 330. © 1994 by ACA. Reprinted with permission. No further reproduction authorized without written permission of the American Counseling Association.

Overall, test interpretation may be the most sensitive part of any assessment process. "When done properly . . . test results may enhance the counselling process and facilitate client change. Research has shown that many clients benefit from receiving feedback about their test results" (Hanson & Claiborn, 2006, p. 349).

Case Example: Inez Attempts Interpretation

The first time Inez attempted to give her client, Harry, feedback on tests he had taken, she stumbled. She was used to being reflective and she was very dedicated to empowering her clients. Therefore, she first gave Harry his test results and asked him to give her feedback on what they meant. Needless to say, Harry, who was unsophisticated in test interpretation, had real questions about aspects of some of the instruments used, such as whether the lie scale meant he was not telling the truth or what exactly was indicated when his score on the masculine/feminine scale was high. To her credit, Inez became more direct and interactive with Harry.

1. What does Harry's experience tell you about your role as an interpreter of tests?

2. What is your style in conveying information, and does it need to be modified if you are going to give clients feedback about their test results?

ASSESSMENT

In addition to and supplementing testing is *assessment*, the procedures and processes of collecting information and measures of human behaviour outside of test data. According to Cormier and Cormier (1998, p. 151), assessment has six purposes:

1. To obtain information on a client's presenting problem and on other related problems

2. To identify the controlling or contributing variables associated with the problem

3. To determine the client's goals/expectations for counselling outcomes

4. To gather baseline data that will be compared to subsequent data to assess and evaluate client progress and the effects of treatment strategies

5. To educate and motivate the client by sharing the counsellor's view of the situation, increasing client receptivity to treatment, and contributing to therapeutic change

6. To use the information obtained from the client to plan effective treatment inventions and strategies. The information obtained during the assessment process should help to answer this well-thought-out question: "*What* treatment, by *whom*, is most effective for *this* individual with *that* specific problem and under *which* set of circumstances?" (Paul, 1967, p. 111)

Assessment can be obtained "through a variety of formal and informal techniques including standardized tests, diagnostic interviews, projective personality measures, questionnaires, mental status examinations, checklists, behavioral observation, and reports by significant others (medical, educational, social, legal, etc.)" (Hohenshil, 1996, p. 65). Usually it involves a combination of procedures and not just one method (Hood & Johnson, 2007; Wall & Walz, 2004). The word *assessment* emphasizes the humanness of counselling. Included in "humanness" is a total picture of the person being evaluated. According to Anastasi (1992b), "the term assessment is being used increasingly to refer to the intensive study of an individual, leading to recommendations for action in solving a particular problem" (p. 611).

As stated previously, the goal of the assessment process is a comprehensive evaluation of individuals, usually in the present. Often it includes a formulation of a treatment plan that will result in positive and predictable outcomes (Groth-Marnat, 1997; Kaplan & Saccuzzo, 2005). To help counsellors formulate such treatment plans, commercial as well as local treatment planners are available. For instance, Jongsma and Peterson (1995) have produced a manual that includes definitions of problematic behaviours along with long- and short-term goals. In addition, therapeutic interventions as well as bibliotherapy suggestions are given.

One way of conducting assessment is through the use of biographical and behavioural measures. Numerous *structured clinical interviews* are available for collecting this type of information. "In general, a structured clinical interview consists of a list of relevant behaviors, symptoms, and events to be addressed during an interview, guidelines for conducting the interview, and procedures for recording and analyzing the data" (Vacc &

Juhnke, 1997, p. 471). The questions are asked in an ordered sequence; from the results of the interview, an assessment is made that is either diagnostic (specifically related to the *Diagnostic and Statistical Manual* [DSM]) or descriptive (indicating the degree of psychopathology that is present or giving a non-DSM dysfunctional descriptor).

Although not a formal psychometric instrument, the *mental status examination* (MSE) is being "increasingly used by counsellors in work settings requiring assessment, diagnosis, and treatment of mental disorders" (Polanski & Hinkle, 2000, p. 357). The MSE is organized under the following categories:

- appearance (i.e., physical characteristics of client), attitude (i.e., client's approach to the interview and interaction with examiner), and activity (i.e., physical or motor movement)

- mood (i.e., predominant internal feeling state) and affect (i.e., outward expression of a client's emotional state)

- speech and language (i.e., the ability to express oneself and to comprehend word meaning)

- thought process (i.e., the organization, flow, and production of thought), thought content, and perception (i.e., delusions, hallucinations, anxiety symptoms, phobias)

- cognition (i.e., ability to think, use logic, intellect, reasoning, and memory)

- insight and judgment (i.e., awareness of one's own personality traits and behaviours, insight, and the ability to consider long-term effects and possible outcomes)

The MSE "provides counselors with a format for organizing objective (observations of clients) and subjective (data provided by clients)" (Polanski & Hinkle, 2000, p. 357). It is included in many managed care treatment plans as well as plans used in mental health centres and psychiatric hospitals. There are even computer-assisted MSE programs to aid counsellors in report writing.

Overall, assessment (whether one uses the MSE or not) is crucial because it allows counsellors not only to determine what a client's problem is but to learn the client's orientation to problem solving. Such a procedure helps counsellors and clients avoid blaming and work collaboratively in finding solutions that bring about positive change rather than repeating past patterns. Assessment then makes sense to the degree that it contributes to learning and to formulating interventions in counselling that work (Egan, 2007). In clinical settings, assessment is a continuous process because once initial difficulties are resolved, new ones sometimes arise or come more into focus.

DIAGNOSIS

"*Diagnosis* . . . is the meaning or interpretation that is derived from assessment information and is usually translated in the form of some type of classification system" (Hohenshil, 1993, p. 7). Thus, a diagnosis is a description of a person's condition and not a judgment of a person's worth (Rueth et al., 1998). For instance, the fourth edition text-revised version of the DSM, the DSM-IV-TR (American Psychiatric Association, 2000), which provides the standard nomenclature for describing most symptomatology and dysfunctionality in the United States and Canada, recommends referring to clients as

> people with particular types of mental disorders, such as "a person with schizophrenia" or "a person with mental retardation," rather than using terms like the "mentally retarded" or the "schizophrenics." . . . Using labeling in this way emphasizes that the mental disorder is only one characteristic of the individual, not a descriptor of the whole person. (Hohenshil, 1996, p. 65)

"All clients experiencing symptoms of illness also possess basic strengths and complex coping skills" (Harris et al., 2007, p. 5). Therefore, a diagnosis is a measure in time and not a fixed entity.

Like test interpretation, some diagnostic categories are appropriately shared with clients. However, most diagnoses from the DSM categories are withheld from clients because they may prove frightening or misleading (Moursund & Kenny, 2002). In addition, negative diagnoses may set up self-fulfilling prophesies for clients where they begin to behave as they were diagnosed. Instead, diagnoses may be used to guide the counsellor in formulating a treatment plan for helping.

When used appropriately, diagnoses do the following:

- describe a person's current functioning
- provide a common language for clinicians to use in discussing the client
- lead to a consistent and continual type of care
- help direct and focus treatment planning
- help counsellors fit clients into their scope of treatment (Rueth et al., 1998)

Diagnoses are important for at least two other reasons. First, some insurance companies will reimburse for counselling services only if clients are diagnosed. Second, to work with psychiatrists, psychologists, and some medical specialists, as well as managed care specialists and some governmental agencies, counsellors must be able to speak about, understand, or report a client diagnosis (Hamann, 1994; Hinkle, 1999).

To make proper diagnoses, counsellors must receive extensive training and supervision. They should know diagnostic categories, particularly those in the DSM-IV-TR. They should also realize that diagnostic decisions are an evolving process and not a static event (Hohenshil, 1996). "Diagnosis and treatment planning are now such standard components of counseling practice" that a failure to diagnose on some level or a lack of professional diagnostic training may be construed as unethical (Sommers-Flanagan & Sommers-Flanagan, 1998, p. 189).

In making a diagnosis, a counsellor must observe a client for signs of symptoms, listen for complaints, and look for functional disturbances (Lopez et al., 2006). In doing so, a counsellor must take into account cultural, developmental, socioeconomic, and spiritual aspects of a client's life as well as coping mechanisms, stressors, and learned behaviour (Rueth et al., 1998). Sometimes a behaviour in a client's life is merely a symptom of a situational problem in living, whereas at other times it is due to the manifestation of a severe disorder. Therefore, difficulties are best represented as occurring on a continuum and counsellors must be careful to neither overdiagnose nor underdiagnose. After all, a diagnosis is only as helpful as it is reliable and valid (Sherry, Lyddon, & Henson, 2007). "When a formal diagnosis is made, certain symptoms must exist; [and] they must be severe enough to interfere significantly with the client's life" (Hohenshil, 1996, p. 65). In some cases, a *dual diagnosis* will be made, which basically means that an individual is perceived to be carrying both a substance abuse and mental health diagnosis.

To properly diagnose, a counsellor is wise to delay the decision initially so that there will be time to assess as many factors as possible in the client's life (Hill & Ridley, 2001). Sound clinical judgment and decision making take time and reflection. As a group, accurate clinicians arrive at their final diagnoses later than those who are less accurate (Elstein, Shulman, & Sprafka, 1978).

Finally, in making a diagnosis, a counsellor should consider alternative conceptualizations of behaviour, including developmental meaning (Ivey et al., 2005), a continuum of personality dimensions (Oldham & Morris, 1995), and levels of well-being (i.e., whether a person is "flourishing" or "languishing"; Keyes & Lopez, 2002). Substitutes for the DSM have not been widely accepted at this point in time but they hold promise, especially those that expand the DSM to include

- re-anchoring Axis V so that good health and optimal functioning could be included, as well as impaired functioning (Lopez et al., 2006),

- creating Axis VI to include personal strengths and facilitators of growth, so that a more comprehensive picture of a client could be created (Lopez et al., 2006), and

- developing a system of new diagnostic classification based on psychological strengths, such as the VIA Classification of Strengths system (Peterson & Seligman, 2004), which is the antithesis of the DSM-IV-TR.

SUMMARY AND CONCLUSION

This chapter covered the intricacies of testing, assessment, and diagnosis in counselling, with a particular emphasis on the qualities of useful test instruments and the types of tests counsellors use. Testing is almost as old as the profession of counselling itself, but the popularity of test use in counselling has varied over the years. Nevertheless, testing will most likely remain an essential part of counselling. Therefore, counsellors must be well versed in the types of tests available and their appropriate use in counselling. With this knowledge they can attain greater professional competence and help clients live healthier, more productive lives. Being well-informed involves an awareness of the validity, reliability, standardization, and norms of the instruments used. A test that is reliable but not valid is inappropriate. Similarly, an instrument that discriminates against cultural minorities because it has been normed only on the majority population has no value; in fact, it can be quite harmful.

Counsellors usually encounter four main types of tests: intelligence/aptitude tests, interest/career tests, personality tests, and achievement tests. A wide variety of instruments is available in each category. Counsellors who work with tests must constantly examine current research results to ensure that various instruments are appropriate. They also need to consult with clients to be certain that the tests give clients the type of information they want.

Finally, counsellors must be sensitively involved with the interpretation of test data. From the interpretation of tests and analysis of other data, such as behaviours and verbal complaints, counsellors make assessments and diagnoses. It is on their assessments and diagnoses that counsellors base treatment plans. Such plans should help their clients change unwanted, destructive, or unproductive behaviours, thoughts, or feelings. Therefore, to be accountable and competent, counsellors must master all three processes so that they provide the best services possible to benefit their clients.

Your Personal Reflections

1. What tests or assessment instruments have you taken in your life? What do you remember about taking them? What do you remember about the results you were given? How could the feedback have been improved?

2. When have you questioned the reliability of a test score? How do you think that outside variables, such as your general health at a particular time, influence test results? If you question the reliability of test results, what are some things you can do?

3. To be nationally certified as a counsellor in Canada by the Canadian Counselling and Psychotherapy Association (go to www.ccacc.ca/en/memberbenefits/certification for details) and to receive the protected title *Canadian Certified Counsellor (CCC)*, a counsellor must have a completed master's degree in counselling that includes a practicum. Furthermore, continuing education is a requirement, as well as adhering to a formal code of ethics and advising and disciplining members regarding professional conduct. What do you think would be the most difficult part of fulfilling these requirements? What informs you that you would be nonetheless up for the challenge?

Classroom Activities

1. Look online for educational and psychological tests from major test publishers. Examine the variety of tests available and the information the publisher gives you about each. Try

to group these tests under the four categories outlined in this chapter. What tests are easy to classify? Which ones are most difficult? Report your results to the class.

2. In pairs, do an in-depth report on one of the tests mentioned in this chapter or one recommended by your instructor. Be sure to notice the validity, reliability, standardization, and norms of the instrument. When you report your results to the class, explain when you think the instrument could be appropriately used in counselling.

3. Some counsellors do not think that tests should be used in counselling. Divide the class into two debate teams. One side should take the position that counselling and testing are not compatible (see Goldman, 1972b; 1994a). The other side should advocate the use of tests in counselling (see Tinsley & Bradley, 1986). Discuss your conclusions.

4. In triads, discuss times when you have had a test interpreted for you. What did you think when the test interpreter explained your results? What do you remember most from the experience (e.g., the data, your feelings, your behaviour)? How does this experience still affect your reaction to tests, test interpretations, and the assessment process?

5. In groups of four, discuss the ethical and legal considerations of diagnosis. What issues does your group think are most sensitive? Consult the ethical codes and guidelines of professional associations on diagnosis. Share your group's findings and opinions with the whole class.

Chapter 17

Career Counselling Over the Life Span

PRACTICE REFLECTION

Jeff, a 20-year-old international student from Hong Kong, came to see me for help with career planning. As is often the case, career counselling cannot be done within a vacuum—people live in psycho-socio-cultural milieus that bring up issues for them. Consequently, career work often entails personal counselling.

In Jeff's case, he wanted to pursue a career in social sciences and not in commerce, as his father wanted for him. Jeff's dad, Ernie, still lived in Hong Kong, and Jeff and his younger brother lived with their aunt in Calgary. I began by having Jeff complete two tests that are commonly used in career planning: the Strong Interest

Inventory (SII) and the Myers Briggs Type Indicator (MBTI). The SII has been researched more than any other psychological test in existence. The test has strong psychometric properties, including well-substantiated validity and reliability. The MBTI, on the other hand, is weak psychometrically but it is useful nonetheless in ascertaining personality preferences. Such personality preferences may or may not find expression in one's work.

On the SII, Jeff fit the ASI Holland occupational code, which meant his highest career interests were in artistic, social, and investigative occupations. True to this code, he had high scores in occupations such as social worker, lawyer, and music teacher. Social work was particularly appealing to Jeff and this was the occupation he wished to pursue. On the MBTI, Jeff's preferences suggested he was most closely aligned with the INFJ personality type, a type noted for being reflective and drawn toward human service occupations.

As luck would have it, Ernie was travelling to Calgary in a few weeks for business reasons. I suggested that Jeff ask him if the three of us could meet for lunch somewhere on the weekend he would be here. I was aware that in Chinese families, the father is the head of the household and the one who must give consent regarding a change in plans for a family member. This is generally truer for those living in mainland China compared to Hong Kong, which is more westernized, so I first asked if this was true in Jeff's case. This was confirmed.

Jeff set up the meeting and I met the two of them on a Sunday. Ernie was a proud man of affluence, and he immediately respected the fact that I left my usual hours to meet at a convenient time for him. I went over the test results with Ernie and provided information about the sessions I had had with Jeff (I already had written permission from Jeff to do this). I asked Ernie to take this into consideration regarding his son's future. At the end of our lunch, Ernie was willing to give Jeff permission to change his career plans and to pursue his first love of social work.

I never saw Jeff again as there was no need. I wonder now as I write this about what happened in his life. Did he complete his degree? Is he practising in Calgary or elsewhere? As is so often the case, we, as counsellors, do not know a client's future. All we can hope is that we made a positive difference.

The counselling profession began charting its course when Frank Parsons (1909) outlined a process for choosing a career and initiated the vocational guidance movement. According to Parsons, it is better to choose a vocation than merely hunt for a job. Since his ideas first came into prominence, a voluminous amount of research and theory has been generated in the field of career development and counselling.

Choosing a career is more than simply deciding what one will do to earn a living. Occupations influence a person's whole way of life, including physical and mental health. "There are interconnections between work roles and other life roles" (Imbimbo, 1994, p. 50). Thus, income, stress, social identity, meaning, education, clothes, hobbies, interests, friends, lifestyle, place of residence, and even personality characteristics are tied to one's work life (Herr, Cramer, & Niles, 2004). Qualitative research indicates that individuals who appear most happy in their work are committed to following their interests, exhibit a breadth of personal competencies and strengths, and function in work environments that are characterized by freedom, challenge, meaning, and a positive social atmosphere (Henderson, 2000).

Yet despite the evidence of the importance of one's work, systematically exploring and choosing careers often does not happen. Particularly in Canada, there is a general lack of knowledge concerning the value and impact of career development services (Lalande & Magnusson, 2007), which is unfortunate given that meta-analytic studies have shown the effectiveness of career counselling (Flynn, 1994). Shields (2006), in her analysis of Statistics Canada data, found that while most Canadian workers were satisfied with their jobs in 2002, one in twelve (about 8%) was not. Just over 6% of workers were "not too satisfied" while another 2% were "not at all satisfied."

The process of selecting a career is unique to each individual. It is influenced by a variety of factors. For instance, personality styles, developmental stages, and life roles come into play (Drummond & Ryan, 1995). Happenstance and serendipity (Guindon & Hanna, 2002), family background (Chope, 2006), gender (Hotchkiss & Borow, 1996), giftedness (Maxwell, 2007), and age (Canaff, 1997) may also influence the selection of a career. In addition, the global economy at the time one decides on a career is a factor (Borgen, 1997). In the industrial age, punctuality, obedience, and rote work performance were the skills needed to be successful; in the present technological–service economy, emphasis is on "competitive teamwork, customer satisfaction, continual learning, and innovation" (Staley & Carey, 1997, p. 379).

Because an enormous amount of literature on careers is available, this chapter can provide only an overview of the area. It will concentrate on career development and counselling from a holistic, lifespan perspective (as first proposed by Norman Gysbers). In the process, theories and tasks appropriate for working with a variety of clients will be examined.

THE IMPORTANCE OF CAREER COUNSELLING

DESPITE ITS LONG HISTORY AND THE FORMULATION OF MANY MODELS, CAREER COUNSELLING has not enjoyed the same degree of prestige as have other forms of counselling or psychotherapy. This is unfortunate for both the counselling profession and the many people who need these services. Surveys of high school juniors and seniors and university undergraduates show that one of the counselling services they most prefer is career counselling. Brown (1985) also posits that career counselling may be a viable intervention for some clients who have emotional problems related to non-supportive, stress-producing environments. The contribution of career counselling to personal growth and development is well documented (Imbimbo, 1994; Krumboltz, 1994). In fact, Herr and colleagues (2004) contend that a variety of life difficulties and mental problems ensue when one's career or work life is unsatisfactory.

Crites (1981, pp. 14–15) lists important aspects of career counselling, which include the following:

1. *"The need for career counseling is greater than the need for psychotherapy."* Career counselling deals with the inner and outer world of individuals, whereas most other counselling approaches deal only with internal events.

2. *"Career counseling can be therapeutic."* A positive correlation exists between career and personal adjustment (Crites, 1969; Hinkelman & Luzzo, 2007; Krumboltz, 1994; Super, 1957). Clients who successfully cope with career decisions may gain skill and confidence in the ability to tackle other problem areas. They may invest more energy into resolving non-career problems because they have clarified career objectives. Although Brown (1985) provides a set of assessment strategies that are useful in determining whether a client needs personal or career counselling first, Krumboltz (1994) asserts that career and personal counselling are inextricably intertwined and often must be treated together. Indeed, research data refute the perspective "that career help seekers are different from non-career help seekers" (Dollarhide, 1997, p. 180). For example, people who lose jobs and fear they will never find other positions have both a career problem and a personal anxiety problem. It is imperative to treat such people in a holistic manner by offering information on the intellectual aspects of finding a career and working with them to overcome their emotional concerns about seeking a new job or direction in life.

3. *"Career counseling is more difficult than psychotherapy."* Crites states that to be an effective career counsellor a person must deal with both personal and work variables and know how the two interact. "Being knowledgeable and proficient in career counselling requires that counsellors draw from a variety of both personality and career development theories and techniques and that they continuously be able to gather and provide current information about the world of work" (Imbimbo, 1994, p. 51). The same is not equally true for counselling, which often focuses on the inner world of the client.

THE CHANGING WORLD OF WORK

The days where one chooses a career and sticks with it until retirement are over for most people (Bujold & Fournier, 2008; Metz & Guichard, 2009; Tucker, 2002). The notion of permanent work continues to become a thing of the past while the proportion of part-time work is increasing in most modern societies (Bujold & Fournier, 2008). Nonstandard work and precariousness leads many workers to experience burnout, financial stress, and loss of meaning (Tucker, 2002).

Amundson (2006), a well-known Canadian researcher in career planning and development, summarized the following dramatic changes that have occurred in the workforce:

1. Increased competition and pressure to produce
2. Less predictable career paths and search strategies for finding work
3. Increased organizational change caused by mergers, joint ventures, and other alliances
4. More opportunity to work in other countries
5. Increased number of temporary and contract positions
6. Increased need to consider self-employment
7. Increased need for technological skills and skilled-trade workers
8. More diversity in the workforce
9. Greater work complexity
10. Increased need for having strong interpersonal skills
11. Increased need for continuous learning and innovation
12. Fewer opportunities to be upwardly mobile in an organization
13. Greater income incongruencies between workers and managers
14. Increased need for both partners in a relationship to have careers outside the home

The career landscape in Canada and abroad has changed, and along with many choices comes greater need for careful planning and soul-searching. As mentioned in Hansen and Amundson (2009), Amundson believes that besides relying on Rogers's core conditions (i.e., genuineness, unconditional positive regard, and empathic understanding), career counsellors will also need to embrace creativity and flexibility—essential attributes when helping today's Canadians navigate an uncertain and unpredictable future. Career counselling, then, is arguably more important than ever.

CAREER COUNSELLING ASSOCIATIONS AND CREDENTIALS IN CANADA

The career development chapter is a subgroup of the Canadian Counselling and Psychotherapy Association (www.ccacc.ca/en/chapters/details/?ID=9) that is primarily devoted to career development and career counselling. Psychologists who work in the career area may also belong to the organizational psychology section of the Canadian Psychological Association (www.cpa.ca/aboutcpa/cpasections/industrialorganizationalpsychology).

There are many organizations in Canada, especially regionally, that assist Canadians and permanent residents with career planning. For those needing help with career planning and learning about career prospects across Canada, an excellent resource called *Job Futures: Welcome to Canada's Career and Education Planning Tool* is available from Service Canada (2007) at their website. Another excellent resource for career planning is hosted by the University of Waterloo (n.d.; http://emanual.uwaterloo.ca/login_new.aspx).

Also at the national level, there is the Canadian Career Development Foundation (2006), a charitable group committed to improving career services for Canadians of all ages. The foundation has developed a document called the *Canadian Standards and Guidelines for Career Development Practitioner*s, serving as a benchmark for Canada and other countries. Certification as a career practitioner is available in Québec, Alberta, and British Columbia (http://ccdf.ca/ccdf2/cms/displaySubSection.asp?lang=en&id=14&section=leadership for details).

The Canadian Career Information Association (2005) is a national organization concerned with developing career information resources. In 1975, Employment and Immigration Canada initiated the National Consultation on Career Development (Conference Board of Canada, 2010), a yearly conference that attracts career professionals from across the nation.

Two Canadian journals that publish career development and career counselling manuscripts are the *Canadian Journal of Career Development* (www.contactpoint.ca/cjcd) and the *Canadian Journal of Counselling and Psychotherapy* (http://cjc-rcc.ucalgary.ca/cjc/index.php/rcc). There are also several American and international journals that publish in this area.

Canada continues to play a significant role in career development and career counselling throughout the world. For example, Bryan Hiebert, professor emeritus from the University of Calgary, is current president of the International Association for Educational and Vocational Guidance, while Roberta Neault, a psychologist in British Columbia, is editor of the *Journal of Employment Counseling*.

THE SCOPE OF CAREER COUNSELLING AND CAREERS

Career counselling is a hybrid discipline, often misunderstood and not always fully appreciated by many helping professionals, businesspeople, the public, or the government (Hoyt, 2005). Bédard and Spain (1999) define *career counselling* as

> primarily a means of helping people who need assistance in their career path. Because of its humanist thrust, it aims for the acquisition of skills that enable each individual to realize their unique potential. Its scope extends beyond the simple choice of a career and the unique moment of that type of decision to span the full duration of [individuals' lives and their] career as a whole. In this light, career counselling becomes a stimulus, is future-oriented, fits into a developmental perspective, focuses on prevention and constitutes a process. (p. 101)

Throughout its history, career counselling has been known by a number of different names, including *vocational guidance, occupational counselling,* and *vocational counselling.* Crites (1981) emphasizes that the word *career* is more modern and inclusive than the word *vocation. Career* is also broader than the term *occupation,* which Herr et al. (2004) define as a group of similar jobs found in different industries or organizations. A *job* is merely an activity undertaken for economic returns (Fox, 1994).

Career counsellors clearly must consider many factors when helping persons make career decisions. Among these factors are avocational interests, age or stage in life, maturity, gender, familial obligations, and civic roles. Some of these factors are represented in various ways. For example, the integration and interaction of work and leisure in one's career over the lifespan, according to McDaniels (1984), is expressed in the formula $C = W + L$, where C equals *career,* W equals *work,* and L equals *leisure* (Gale, 1998, p. 206).

All theories of counselling are potentially applicable and useful in working with individuals on career choices, but people gain understanding and insight about themselves and how they fit into the world of work through educational means as well as counselling relationships. Well-informed persons may need fewer counselling services than others and respond more positively to this form of helping.

CAREER INFORMATION

The National Career Development Association (formerly the NVGA) has defined *career information* as "information related to the world of work that can be useful in the process of career development, including educational, occupational, and psychosocial information related to working, e.g., availability of training, the nature of work, and status of workers in different occupations" (Sears, 1982, p. 139). A more modern term for career information is *career data,* meaning "a collection of facts about occupational and educational opportunities" (Niles & Harris-Bowlsbey, 2005, p. 176). Data become information only when they are "understood by clients and used to inform decision making, that is, to assist them to choose one alternative over another" (p. 177).

As has been discussed in previous chapters, the word *guidance* is usually reserved for activities that are primarily educational. *Career guidance* involves all activities that seek to disseminate information about present or future vocations in such a way that individuals become more knowledgeable and aware about who they are in relation to the world of work. Guidance activities can take the form of

- career fairs (inviting practitioners in a number of fields to explain their jobs),
- library assignments,
- outside interviews,
- computer-assisted information experiences,
- career shadowing (following someone around on his or her daily work routine),

- didactic lectures, and

- experiential exercises such as role-playing.

Career guidance and the dissemination of career information is traditionally pictured as a school activity. But this process is often conducted outside a classroom environment—for example, at governmental agencies, industries, libraries, and homes, or with a private practitioner (Harris-Bowlsbey, 1992). According to C. H. Patterson, career guidance is "for people who are pretty normal and have no emotional problems that would interfere with developing a rational approach to making a vocational or career choice" (Freeman, 1990, p. 292). As mentioned in Chapter 16, Human Resources and Skills Development Canada (2009) classifies all occupations in Canada using the National Occupational Classification (NOC) system, and Service Canada (2007) provides occupational information regarding many occupational titles. Furthermore, regional career centres in Canada also provide ample information regarding careers and career forecasts pertaining to particular geographic areas (e.g., see http://alis.alberta.ca). Overall, the ways of becoming informed about careers are extensive.

Not all ways of learning are as effective as others are, however, and people who fail to personalize career information to specific situations often have difficulty making vocational decisions. The result may be *unrealistic aspirations*, or goals beyond a person's capabilities (Salomone & McKenna, 1982). Therefore, it is vital to provide qualitative and quantitative information to individuals who are deciding about careers, including the nature of the career decision process, such as mentioning that "career decidedness develops over time" (Krieshok, 1998, p. 212) and "the decision-making process is complex, not simple" (p. 214). Knowledge of career information and the processes associated with it does not guarantee self-exploration in career development, but good career decisions cannot be made without these data. A lack of enough information or up-to-date information is one reason that individuals fail to make decisions or make unwise choices.

Case Example: What Would *You* Do?

On a good day, Mugsy Bogues stood 5 foot 3 inches tall and weighed 136 pounds. Yet he went on to play college basketball and then to play 14 years in the National Basketball Association (NBA). He was an exceptional passer, a ball stealer, and one of the fastest men on the court. He came from an impoverished background and yet managed to attain fame and fortune at the end of the 20th century.

1. How does a case like Mugsy Bogues's reflect on the value of career counselling? (Almost no career counsellor would have advised him in high school or college to try to play professional basketball!)

2. If Mugsy grew up playing hockey, what indicators would be necessary before a career counsellor should suggest he consider trying out to become a professional in the National Hockey League?

A number of *computer-based career planning systems* (CBCPS) and computer-assisted career guidance systems (CACGS) offer career information and help individuals sort through their values and interests or find job information. One of the advantages of computer-based and computer-assisted career planning and guidance systems is their accessibility: They are available in many settings to diverse people across cultures and the lifespan (Harris-Bowlsbey, 1992; Niles & Harris-Bowlsbey, 2005; Sampson & Bloom, 2001). Some of the top programs include SIGI-Plus (System of Interactive Guidance and Information, with "Plus" indicating a refinement of the system), DISCOVER, and the Kuder Career Planning System (Maples & Luzzo, 2005). Two other CBCPSs that are often used in Canada include Career Cruising (www.careercruising.com) and CHOICES (www.bridges.com/us/prodnserv/choicescd_hs/index.html).

SIGI-Plus (www.valparint.com/sigi.htm; Katz, 1975; 1993) is comprised of five components, with a focal point on

1. self-assessment (values),
2. identification of occupational alternatives (locate),
3. review of occupational information (compare),
4. review of information on preparation programs (planning), and
5. making tentative occupational choices (strategy).

By using SIGI-Plus, searchers are able to clarify their values, locate and identify occupational options, compare choices, learn planning skills, and develop rational career decision-making skills.

DISCOVER (www.act.org; ACT, 1998) contains nine modules:

1. Beginning the career journey
2. Learning about the world of work
3. Learning about yourself
4. Finding occupations
5. Learning about occupations
6. Making educational choices
7. Planning next steps
8. Planning your career
9. Making transitions

Most users of DISCOVER proceed through the modules in a sequential order, but the modules may be accessed on demand depending on need.

The Kuder Career Planning System (www.kuder.com) offers a comprehensive solution for career planners at all stages of career development. It includes, among other tools, the Kuder Online Career Portfolio and Research-Based Assessments. The Online Career Portfolio facilitates lifelong career planning that allows individuals to store personal and academic information, search and save educational and occupational data, build resumes, and access assessment progress and results from any internet connection. The Research-Based Assessments, which are available in English or Spanish, help system users discover their interests, skills, and work values and how these characteristics relate to the world of work.

Ways of enhancing computer-based career planning systems and computer-assisted career guidance systems are constantly being implemented, including interactive programs (Niles & Harris-Bowlsby, 2005; Zunker, 2006). No matter how sophisticated the programs, however, it is wise to have trained career counsellors available to assist those individuals who may make use of this technology but still have questions about its applicability to their lives (Walker-Staggs, 2000).

In addition to these instruments, career choices curriculums developed by the National Occupational Information Coordinating Committee (NOICC) can be used in educational settings such as high schools to provide career information relevant to students in English, math, and social science classes.

Furthermore, some self-help books, such as Bolles and Nelson's (2007) *What Color Is Your Parachute?* and Kay's (2006) *Life's a Bitch and Then You Change Careers: 9 Steps to Get Out of Your Funk and on to Your Future*, are still available in print. These books outline practical steps that most individuals, from late adolescence on, can follow to define personal values and successfully complete career-seeking tasks such as writing a résumé. These texts also provide a wealth of information on how to locate positions of specific interest.

CAREER DEVELOPMENT THEORIES AND COUNSELLING

Career development theories try to explain why individuals choose careers. They also deal with the career adjustments people make over time. Modern theories, which are broad and comprehensive in regard to individual and occupational development, began appearing in the literature in the 1950s (Gysbers, Heppner, & Johnstone, 2003). The theories described here (i.e., trait-and-factor, developmental, and social-cognitive) and the counselling procedures that go with them are among the most prominent and widely used in the field of career counselling.

Trait-and-Factor Theory

The origin of trait-and-factor theory can be traced back to Frank Parsons. It stresses that the traits of clients should first be assessed and then systematically matched with factors inherent in various occupations. Its most widespread influence occurred during the Great Depression when E. G. Williamson (1939) championed its use. It was out of favour during the 1950s and 1960s but has resurfaced in a more modern form, which is best characterized as "structural" and is reflected in the work of researchers such as John Holland (1997). The trait-and-factor approach has always stressed the uniqueness of individuals. Original advocates of the theory assumed that a person's abilities and traits could be measured objectively and quantified. Personal motivation was considered relatively stable. Thus, satisfaction in a particular occupation depended on a proper fit between one's abilities and the job requirements.

In its modern form, trait-and-factor theory stresses the interpersonal nature of careers and associated lifestyles as well as the performance requirements of a work position. Holland (1997) identifies six categories in which personality types and occupational environments can be classified: realistic, investigative, artistic, social, enterprising, and conventional (RIASEC) (see Figure 17.1). According to prestige levels, investigative (I) occupations rank highest, followed by enterprising (E), artistic (A), and social (S) occupations, which have roughly the same level of prestige. The lowest levels of prestige are realistic (R) and conventional (C) occupations (Gottfredson, 1981).

Khan, Alvi, and Kirkwood (1990) conducted a confirmatory factor analysis with 155 Canadian high school students who completed the Self-Directed Search. The researchers concluded that Holland's model did explain the relationships between the six types comprising the RIASEC model, thus providing evidence that the Holland model is applicable to Canadian high school students.

In an analysis of census data using the Holland codes, Reardon, Bullock, and Meyer (2007) confirmed that the distribution across Holland's types is asymmetrical. They found that from 1960 to 2000, "the Realistic area had the largest number of individuals employed and that the Artistic area had the fewest number employed" (p. 266). The gap

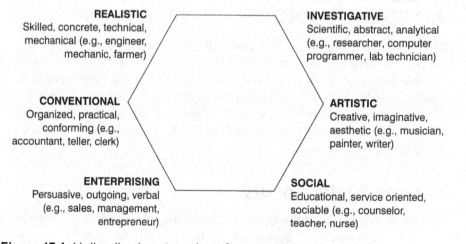

Figure 17.1 Holland's six categories of personality and occupation

between the number of people employed in the realistic and enterprising areas shrunk during the five decades; in 2000, there were approximately equal numbers of people employed in both areas. Interestingly, the people employed in the investigative area more than doubled during this time, whereas the other four areas remained relatively stable. Regardless of age, between 75% and 85% of male workers were employed in the realistic and enterprising areas; women were more varied and were concentrated in conventional, realistic, social, and, more recently, enterprising areas.

Personal satisfaction in a work setting depends on a number of factors, but among the most important are the degree of congruence between personality type, work environment, and social class (Gade, Fuqua, & Hurlburt, 1988; Holland & Gottfredson, 1976; Savickas, 1989; Trusty, Robinson, Plata, & Ng, 2000). Also, as a general rule with notable exceptions, "women value language-related tasks more, and men value mathematics-related tasks more" (Trusty et al., 2000, p. 470). Some non-psychological factors, such as economic or cultural influences, account for why many professional and nonprofessional workers accept and keep their jobs (Brown, 2007; Salomone & Sheehan, 1985).

Nevertheless, as Holland emphasizes, it is vital for people to have adequate knowledge of themselves and occupational requirements to make informed career decisions. According to Holland, a three-letter code represents a client's overall personality, which can be matched with a type of work environment. Three-letter codes tend to remain relatively stable over the lifespan beginning as early as high school (Miller, 2002). A profile of SAE would suggest a person is most similar to a social type, then an artistic type, and finally an enterprising type. However, it is the interaction of letter codes that influences the makeup of the person and his or her fit in an occupational environment. Miller (1998) suggests that, instead of using the three highest scores on Holland's hexagon for such a purpose, the top two, middle two, and lowest two scores should be paired and presented to give the client a fuller picture of his or her personality profile and similarity to others in a given career. Given the first criteria, Donald Super's profile would be S/I/R, whereas John Holland's would be A/E/IRS. The second criteria would yield a profile for Super of SI/RA/EC, with Holland's profile being AE/IR/SC (Weinrach, 1996).

Trait-and-factor career counselling is sometimes inappropriately caricatured as "three interviews and a cloud of dust." The first interview session is spent getting to know a client's background and assigning tests. The client then takes a battery of tests and returns for the second interview to have the counsellor interpret the results of the tests. In the third session, the client reviews career choices in light of the data presented and is sent out by the counsellor to find further information on specific careers. Williamson (1972) originally implemented this theory to help clients learn self-management skills. But as Crites (1969; 1981) notes, trait-and-factor career counsellors may ignore the psychological realities of decision making and fail to promote self-help skills in their clients. Such counsellors may overemphasize test information, which clients either forget or distort.

Hannah had loved tools from the time she was a little girl. Now in Grade 11, she wondered whether she should go to a liberal arts college or a trade school. She saw advantages to both. Her dad was a carpenter and her mother a teacher. They told her they would help her regardless of what she decided to do. Her Holland profile was a bit unusual: SR/CA/IE. She was ambivalent.

1. What advice might you give to Hannah about her upcoming decision if you were a trait-and-factor career counsellor?

2. Given Canadian society today, what advantages and disadvantages would Hannah face in attempting to find work as a carpenter?

3. Is it ever appropriate to reject a career choice because of the possibility or likelihood of facing stigma or possible discrimination in securing employment and/or once hired? Why or why not?

Developmental Theories

Two of the most widely known career theories are those associated with Donald Super and Eli Ginzberg, both based on personal development. The original developmental theory proposed by Ginzberg and associates (Ginzberg, Ginsburg, Axelrad, & Herma, 1951) has had considerable influence and has been revised (Ginzberg, 1972). However, Super's theory is examined in detail here because more extensive work has been done with it and it has overshadowed other developmental approaches to career counselling.

Compared with other theoretical propositions, developmental theories are generally more inclusive, more concerned with longitudinal expression of career behaviour, and more inclined to highlight the importance of self-concept. Super (1957; 1990) believed that making a career choice is "linked with implementing one's vocational self-concept" (Hinkelman & Luzzo, 2007, p. 143). People's views of themselves are reflected in what they do. He suggested that vocational development unfolds in five stages, each of which contains a developmental task to be completed (see Table 17.1). The first stage is growth (from birth to age 14). During this stage, with its substages of fantasy (ages 4–10), interest (ages 11–12), and capacity (ages 13–14), children form a mental picture of themselves in relation to others. Support affirming the multiple dimensions of this stage in Super's theory has been substantiated (Palladino Schultheiss, Palma, & Manzi, 2005). During the process of growth, children become oriented to the world of work in many ways (e.g., exploration, information, interests, and so on).

The second stage, exploration (ages 14–24), has three substages: tentative (ages 14–17), transition (ages 18–21), and trial (ages 22–24). The major task of this stage is a general exploration of the world of work and the specification of a career preference.

Table 17.1 Super's Stages

Growth	Exploration	Establishment	Maintenance	Decline
Birth to Age 14	**Ages 14 to 24**	**Ages 24 to 44**	**Ages 44 to 64**	**Ages 64 and Beyond**
Self-concept develops through identification with key figures in family and school; needs and fantasy are dominant early in this stage; interest and capacity become more important with increasing social participation and reality testing; learn behaviours associated with self-help, social interaction, self-direction, industrialness, goal setting, persistence.	Self-examination, role try-outs, and occupational exploration take place in school, leisure activities, and part-time work.	Having found an appropriate field, an effort is made to establish a permanent place in it. Thereafter changes that occur are changes of position, job, or employer, not of occupation.	Having made a place in the world of work, the concern is how to hold on to it. Little new ground is broken, continuation of established pattern. Concerned about maintaining present status while being forced by competition from younger workers in the advancement stage.	As physical and mental powers decline, work activity changes and in due course ceases. New roles must be developed: first, selective participant and then observer. Individual must find other sources of satisfaction to replace those lost through retirement.

Substages

Growth

Fantasy (4–10) Needs are dominant; role-playing in fantasy is important.

Interest (11–12) Likes are the major determinant of aspirations and activities.

Capacity (13–14) Abilities are given more weight and job requirements (including training) are considered.

Substages

Exploration

Tentative (15–17) Needs, interests, capacities, values and opportunities are all considered; tentative choices are made and tried out in fantasy, discussion, courses, work, and so on. Possible appropriate fields and levels of work are identified.

Substages

Establishment

Trial-Commitment and Stabilization (25–30) Settling down. Securing a permanent place in the chosen occupation. May prove unsatisfactory resulting in one or two changes before the life work is found or before it becomes clear that the life work will be a succession of unrelated jobs.

Advancement (31–44) Effort is put forth to stabilize, to make a secure place in the world of work. For most persons these are the creative years. Seniority is acquired; clientele are developed; superior performance is demonstrated; qualifications are improved.

Substages

Decline

Deceleration (65–70) The pace of work slackens, duties are shifted, or the nature of work is changed to suit declining capacities. Many find part-time jobs to replace their full-time occupations.

Retirement (71 on) Variation on complete cessation of work or shift to part-time, volunteer, or leisure activities.

(Continued on next page)

Table 17.1 Super's Stages *(Continued)*

Growth	Exploration	Establishment	Maintenance	Decline
Tasks	**Task—Crystallizing a Vocational Preference**	**Tasks**	**Tasks**	**Tasks**
Developing a picture of the kind of person one is.	*Transition* (18–21) Reality considerations are given more weight as the person enters the labour market or professional training and attempts to implement a self-concept. Generalized choice is converted to specific choice.	Finding opportunity to do desired work.	Accepting one's limitations.	Developing non-occupational roles.
Developing an orientation to the world of work and an understanding of the meaning of work.		Learning to relate to others.	Identifying new problems to work on.	Finding a good retirement spot.
		Consolidation and advancement.	Developing new skills.	Doing things one has always wanted to do.
		Making occupational position secure.	Focusing on essential activities.	Reducing working hours.
		Settling down in a permanent position.	Preservation of achieved status and gains.	
	Task—Specifying a Vocational Preference			
	Trial-Little Commitment (22–24) A seemingly appropriate occupation having been found, a first job is located and is tried out as a potential life work. Commitment is still provisional, and if the job is not appropriate, the person may reinstitute the process of crystallizing, specifying, and implementing a preference. Implementing a vocational preference. Developing a realistic self-concept. Learning more about more opportunities.			

Source: From Edwin L. Herr, Stanley H. Cramer, and Spencer Niles, *Career Guidance and Counselling Through the Life Span: Systematic Approaches*, 6/e. Published by Allyn and Bacon, Boston, MA. Copyright © 2004 by Pearson Education. Reprinted by permission of the publisher.

The third stage is known as establishment (ages 24–44). Its two substages, trial (ages 24–30) and advancement (ages 31–44), constitute the major task of becoming established in a preferred and appropriate field of work. Once established, persons can concentrate on advancement until they tire of their job or reach the top of the profession.

The fourth stage, maintenance (ages 44–64), has the major task of preserving what one has already achieved. The final stage, decline (age 65 to death), is a time for disengagement from work and alignment with other sources of satisfaction. It has two substages: deceleration (ages 65–70) and retirement (age 71 to death).

The major contributions of developmental career counselling are its emphases on the importance of the lifespan in career decision making and on career decisions that are influenced by other processes and events in a person's life. This "life pattern paradigm for career counseling encourages counsellors to consider a client's aptitudes and interests in a matrix of life experiences, not just in comparison to some normative group" (Savickas, 1989, p. 127).

The developmental approach can be conceptualized as career-pattern counselling (Super, 1954a). Although this method has been criticized for its historical and descriptive emphases, these features, along with the conceptual depth of the theory, have also been considered strengths (Herr, 1997). Overall, developmental career counselling as conceptualized by Super has a number of applications. "For example, it has been used as the framework for career development programs for children and adolescents" (Brown, 2007, p. 54). In addition, the comprehensive *rainbow theory* that Super conceptualized toward the end of his life continues to attract research interest (Super, 1990; Super, Thompson, & Lindeman, 1988) (see Figure 17.2). Finally, the theory has been used not only as the basis for career counselling but also for attempts at understanding the development of career maturity. One of the drawbacks to Super's approach, however, is its lack of applicability to groups other than those with a Eurocentric background, such as Asian Canadians who subscribe to more collaborative social values.

Social Cognitive Career Theory

Social cognitive career theory (SCCT) was first published in 1994 and has had a tremendous impact on research regarding career choice. It stems from the initial work of Albert Bandura and his emphasis on the "triadic reciprocal model of causality, which assumes that personal attributes, the environment, and overt behavior" operate with each other in an interlocking, bidirectional way (Niles & Harris-Bowlsbey, 2005, p. 87). The most important part of this triad is self-efficacy; that is, "a person's beliefs regarding her or his ability to successfully perform a particular task" (Maples & Luzzo, 2005, p. 275).

Among other central propositions of SCCT are the following:

1. The interaction between people and their environments is highly dynamic (i.e., they influence each other).

2. Career-related behaviour is influenced by four aspects of the person: behaviour, self-efficacy, outcome expectations, and goals, in addition to genetically determined characteristics.

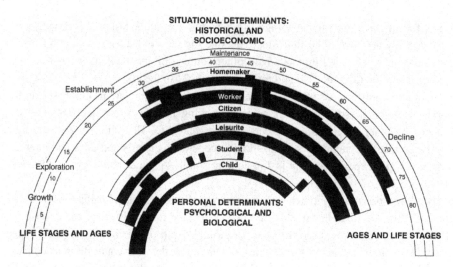

Figure 17.2 Super's rainbow theory: Six life roles in schematic life space

Source: From "A Life-Span, Life-Space Approach to Career Development," by D. E. Super, 1980, *Journal of Vocational Behavior*, 16, pp. 282–298. Copyright 1980 by Academic Press. Reprinted by permission.

3. Self-efficacy beliefs and expectations of outcomes interact directly to influence interest development.

4. In addition to expectations of outcome, factors such as "gender, race, physical health, disabilities, and environmental variables influence self-efficacy development."

5. Actual career choice and implementation are influenced by a number of direct and indirect variables other than self-efficacy, expectations, and goals (e.g., discrimination, economic variables, and chance happenings).

6. All things being equal, people with the highest levels of ability and the strongest self-efficacy beliefs perform at the highest level. (Brown, 2007, p. 69)

One other important assumption of SCCT is that "self-efficacy and interests are linked" and interests "can be developed or strengthened using modeling, encouragement, and most powerfully, by performance enactment. Therefore, groups of clients, such as women [and minorities] who may have little opportunity to engage in certain activities because of sex-typing [or discrimination], can benefit from the application of this theory" (Brown, 2007, p. 70).

Social cognitive career theory can be used in a number of settings. For instance, it can be used with rural Appalachian youth to help them develop, change, and go after career interests (Ali & Saunders, 2006). It can also be used with first-generation university students who need information that will counteract incorrect beliefs they may have (Gibbons & Shoffner, 2004). Overall, SCCT-based interventions can be used with diverse groups. "An additional strength of SCCT is that it addresses both intra-individual and contextual variables in career development" (Niles & Harris-Bowlsbey, 2005, p. 91).

Krumboltz (1979; 1996) has formulated an equally comprehensive but less developmental social-cognitive approach to career development. He takes the position that four factors influence a person's career choice:

- genetic endowment
- conditions and events in the environment
- learning experiences
- task-approach skills (e.g., values, work habits)

According to Krumboltz, career decisions are controlled by both internal and external processes. There is continuous learning, which results in what Krumboltz labels

- *self-observation generalizations*, an overt or covert self-statement of evaluation that may or may not be true;
- *task-approach skills*, an effort by people to project their self-observation generalizations into the future in order to predict future events; and
- *actions*, or implementations of behaviours, such as applying for a job.

Overall, a strength of Krumboltz's theory is that it views people as having some control over events they find reinforcing. Whereas individuals and the world change, persons can learn to take advantage of learning opportunities and make career decisions accordingly. "In summary, Krumboltz outlines a dynamic approach to career counseling that can be applied to males and females, as well as to racial and ethnic minorities who have individualistic perspectives" (Brown, 2007, p. 68).

CAREER COUNSELLING WITH DIVERSE POPULATIONS

Career counselling and education are conducted with a wide variety of individuals in diverse settings. Brown (1985) observes that career counselling typically is offered in university counselling centres, rehabilitation facilities, employment offices, and public schools. He thinks it could be applied with great advantage in many other places as well, including mental health centres and private practice offices. Jesser (1983) agrees, asserting that there is a need to provide career information and counselling to potential users, such as people who are unemployed, learning disabled, in prison, and those released from mental hospitals who seek to re-enter the job market. Reimbursement is a drawback to offering career counselling outside its traditional populations and settings. Career concerns are not covered in the DSM-IV-TR, and most health-care coverage excludes this service from reimbursement.

This lack of coverage is unfortunate because many people have difficulties making career decisions. These difficulties are related to three factors present both prior to and during the decision-making process. These factors are

- lack of readiness,

- lack of information, and

- inconsistent information.

A taxonomy of career decision-making difficulties that is inclusive of these factors and more has been formulated (Gati & Saka, 2001). Although the taxonomy (and diagram) was initially meant for school counsellors working with adolescents, it has applicability across the lifespan (see Figure 17.3).

Because the concept of careers encompasses the lifespan, counsellors who specialize in this area find themselves working with a full age range of clients, from young children to octogenarians. Consequently, many different approaches and techniques have been developed for working effectively with select groups.

Career Counselling with Children

The process of career development begins in the preschool years and becomes more direct in elementary school. A recent Canadian study revealed that children as young as age 11 "perceive themselves to be ready, willing, and able to seriously consider their future career plans" (Bardick, Bernes, Magnusson, & Witko, 2006, p. 267). Herr and colleagues (2004) cite numerous studies to show that during the first six years of school, many children develop a relatively stable self-perception and make a tentative commitment to a vocation. These processes are observed whether career counselling and guidance activities are offered or not. Nevertheless, it is beneficial for children, especially those who live in areas with limited employment opportunities, to have a broad, systematic program of career counselling and guidance in the schools. Such a program should

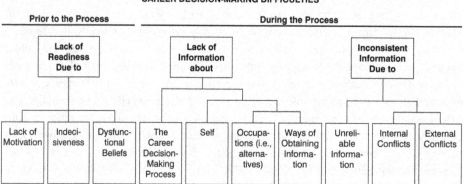

Figure 17.3 A taxonomy of career decision-making difficulties

Source: Reprinted from "High School Students' Career-Related Decision-Making Difficulties," by I. Gati and N. Saka, 2001, *Journal of Counseling and Development, 79*, p. 333. © 2001 by ACA. Reprinted with permission. No further reproduction without written permission of the American Counseling Association.

focus on awareness rather than firm decision making. It should provide as many experiential activities as possible and should help children realize that they have career choices. As children progress in the elementary school grades, they should receive more detailed information about careers and become acquainted with career opportunities that might transcend socioeconomic levels and gender (Bobo, Hildreth, & Durodoye, 1998).

Jesser (1983) suggests that levels of career awareness in elementary schoolchildren may be raised through activities such as field trips to local industries, bakeries, manufacturing plants, or banks. For example, "because pizza is an immediate attention getter with elementary school children, a field trip to a pizza restaurant can provide an entertaining learning experience" (Beale & Nugent, 1996, p. 294) (see Figure 17.4). When such trips are carefully preplanned, implemented, and followed up with appropriate classroom learning exercises (e.g., class discussions), children become aware of a wider spectrum of related occupations, the value of work, and the importance of teams in carrying out tasks.

Other ways of expanding children's awareness of careers are through "inviting parents into the elementary classroom and encouraging parents to invite students into their work environments" (Wahl & Blackhurst, 2000, p. 372). Such a process capitalizes on parents' influence as role models and may be especially helpful for children whose parents are unemployed or underemployed. To break down children's stereotypes connected with careers, persons who hold nontraditional occupations may be invited to speak. Reading stories about or seeing videos about people and their typical activities at work may likewise be helpful. For example, the *Children's Dictionary of Occupations* (Paramore, Hopke, & Drier, 1999) and other publications like it that contain student activity packages are excellent sources of accurate information.

Splete (1982b) outlines a comprehensive program for working with children that includes parent education and classroom discussions jointly planned by the teacher and counsellor. He emphasizes that there are three key career development areas at the elementary school level: self-awareness (i.e., uniqueness), career awareness and exploration, and decision making. Well-designed career guidance and counselling programs that are implemented at an early age and coordinated with programs across all levels of the educational system can go a long way toward dispelling irrational and decision-hindering career development myths, such as "a career decision is an event that should occur at a specific point in time" (Lewis & Gilhousen, 1981, p. 297).

Career Counselling with Adolescents

The majority of junior high school students in a southern Alberta sample stated their desire to continue education beyond high school (Bardick et al., 2006). Furthermore, most view career planning as important (Bardick, Bernes, Magnusson, & Witko, 2004). However, southern Alberta junior high school students are most likely to rely on parents and friends for help rather than teachers or counsellors (Bardick et al., 2004).

Activity Sheet #5
Pizza Connection Word Scramble

See how many of these words you can unscramble. The words are from your field trip to a pizza restaurant.

1. risdhawshe _____

2. eanmarg _____

3. norew _____

4. tinjoar _____

5. oshetss _____

6. tisasrwe _____

7. fhec _____

8. tawire _____

9. ihcsrea _____

10. uertntraas _____

11. ezpaziri _____

12. psbuoerns _____

Answers: (1) dishwasher; (2) manager; (3) owner; (4) janitor; (5) hostess; (6) waitress; (7) chef; (8) waiter; (9) cashier; (10) restaurant; (11) pizzeria; and (12) busperson.

Figure 17.4 Pizza connection word scramble

Source: Reprinted from "The Pizza Connection: Enhancing Career Awareness," by A. V. Beale and D. G. Nugent, 1996, *Elementary School Guidance and Counseling, 30*, p. 301. © 1996 by ACA. Reprinted with permission. No further reproduction authorized without written permission of the American Counseling Association.

Borgen and Hiebert (2006) stated that the self-professed needs of Canadian youth have been studied for more than 20 years. Concerns about the future, including that of career, are rated among their top worries. About 75% of high school students expect to attend post-secondary education after high school.

Cole (1982) stresses that in middle school, career guidance activities should include the exploration of work opportunities and students' evaluation of their own strengths and weaknesses in regard to possible future careers. Assets that students should become aware of and begin to evaluate include talents and skills, general intelligence, motivation level, friends, family, life experience, appearance, and health (Campbell, 1974). "Applied arts curriculum such as industrial arts (applied technology), home economics (family life education) and computer literacy classes . . . offer ideal opportunities for integrated career education. Libraries and/or career centers may have special middle level computerized *career information delivery systems (CIDS)* for student use" (NOICC, 1994, p. 9). The four components common to most CIDS are "assessment, occupational search, occupational information, and educational information" (Gysbers et al., 2003, p. 135). Overall, "career exploration is an important complement to the intellectual and social development" of middle school students (Craig, Contreras, & Peterson, 2000, p. 24).

At the senior high school level, career guidance and counselling activities are related to students' maturity. The greatest challenge and need for career development programs occur on this level, especially in the area of acquiring basic skills (Bynner, 1997). In general, career counselling at the high school level has three emphases: stimulating career development, providing treatment, and aiding placement. More specifically, counsellors provide students with reassurance, information, emotional support, reality testing, planning strategies, attitude clarification, and work experiences, depending on a student's needs and level of functioning (Herr et al., 2004).

Several techniques have proven quite effective in helping adolescents crystallize ideas about careers. Some are mainly cognitive, whereas others are more experiential and comprehensive. Among the cognitive techniques is the use of guided fantasies, such as imagining a typical day in the future, an awards ceremony, a mid-career change, or retirement (Morgan & Skovholt, 1977). Another cognitive technique involves providing fundamental information about career entry and development. For example, a career day or a career fair "featuring employers and professionals from a variety of occupations allows students to make a realistic comparison of each occupation's primary duties, day-to-day activities, and training needs" (Wahl & Blackhurst, 2000, p. 372). Completing an occupational family tree (Figure 17.5) to find out how present interests compare with the careers of family members is a final cognitive approach that may be useful (Dickson & Parmerlee, 1980).

More experiential and comprehensive techniques include offering youth apprenticeships. Apprenticeships are a popular approach that provides work-based learning for adolescents. Apprenticeships also help students who are not university-bound make a smooth transition from high school to the primary work environment. Although apprenticeships hold much promise, they pose several challenges for career counsellors, such as

(a) helping clients learn adaptive skills that will enable them to change with change, (b) helping clients find ways to acquire the kinds of work [identified in government reports], and (c) helping clients to develop a personally meaningful set of work values that will enable them to humanize the workplace for themselves and thus receive the personal satisfaction that comes from true work. (Hoyt, 1994, p. 222)

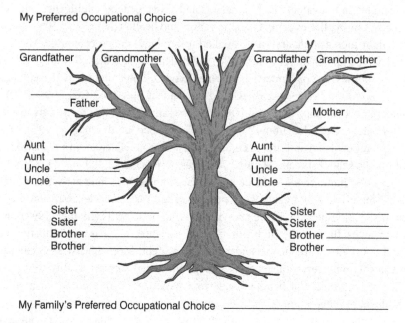

My Preferred Occupational Choice _____

Grandfather | Grandmother

Grandfather Grandmother

Father

Mother

Aunt _____
Aunt _____
Uncle _____
Uncle _____

Aunt _____
Aunt _____
Uncle _____
Uncle _____

Sister _____
Sister _____
Brother _____
Brother _____

Sister _____
Sister _____
Brother _____
Brother _____

My Family's Preferred Occupational Choice _____

Figure 17.5 Occupational family tree

Source: Reprinted from "The Occupational Family Tree: A Career Counseling Technique," by G. L. Dickson and J. R. Parmerlee, 1980, *School Counselor, 28*, p. 101. © 1980 by ACA. Reprinted with permission. No further reproduction without written permission of the American Counseling Association.

In addition to helping youth in school, career counsellors must make special efforts to help high school students who leave school before graduation (Rumberger, 1987). These young people are at risk of unemployment or underemployment for the rest of their lives. Educational and experiential programs, such as Mann's (1986) four Cs (cash, care, computers, and coalitions), can help at-risk students become involved in career exploration and development. According to Bloch (1988; 1989), successful educational counselling programs for students at risk of dropping out follow six guidelines:

1. They make a connection between a student's present and future status (i.e., cash— students are paid for attending).

2. They individualize programs and communicate caring.

3. They form successful coalitions with community institutions and businesses.

4. They integrate sequencing of career development activities.

5. They offer age- and stage-appropriate career development activities.

6. They use a wide variety of media and career development resources, including computers.

Career Counselling with University Students

"Committing to a career choice is one of the main psychosocial tasks that college students face" (Osborn, Howard, & Leierer, 2007, p. 365). Approximately half of all university students experience career-related problems (Herr et al., 2004). Part of the reason is that, despite appearances, "most college students are rarely the informed consumers that they are assumed to be" (Laker, 2002, p. 61). Therefore, university students need and value career counselling services, such as undergraduate career exploration courses (Osborn et al., 2007). Even students who have already decided on their university majors and careers seek such services both to validate their choices and to seek additional information.

In responding to student needs, comprehensive career guidance and counselling programs in institutions of higher education attempt to provide a number of services. Among these services are the following:

- helping with the selection of a major field of study
- offering self-assessment and self-analysis through psychological testing
- helping students understand the world of work
- facilitating access to employment opportunities through career fairs, internships, and campus interviews
- teaching decision-making skills
- meeting the needs of special populations (Herr et al., 2004)

Besides being offered these options, students need "life-career developmental counseling," too (Engels, Jacobs, & Kern, 2000). This broader approach seeks to help people plan for future careers while "balancing and integrating life–work roles and responsibilities" in an appropriate way; for example, being a worker and a family member, parent, and citizen (p. 192). Anticipating problems related to work, intimate relationships, and responsibilities is an important career-related counselling service for university students. Otherwise, *work-family conflicts* (WFC) arise and negatively affect a person's behaviour, emotions, and health (Frone, 2003).

A way that university students can avoid problems and create *realistic job previews* (RJPs) of a specific job is to contact and interview people with knowledge about the careers they are considering. RJPs ultimately benefit potential job seekers in an occupation by both decreasing employee turnover and by increasing employee satisfaction (Laker, 2002). Students should supplement these types of interviews by completing computer-based career planning systems (CBCPSs) such as DISCOVER; the completion of such systems is active, immediate, and empowering, and is rewarded with a printed result that promotes self-efficacy and the likelihood that individuals will complete other career-exploratory behaviours (Maples & Luzzo, 2005).

Career Counselling with Adults

Career interest patterns tend to be more stable after university than during. Nevertheless, many adults continue to need career counselling (Swanson & Hansen, 1988). Indeed, adults experience cyclical periods of stability and transition throughout their lives, and career change is a developmental as well as situational expectation at this stage of life (Borgen, 1997; Kerka, 1991). Developmentally, some adults have a midlife career change that occurs as they enter their forties and what Erik Erikson described as a stage of generativity versus stagnation. At this time, adults may change careers as they become more introspective and seek to put more meaning in their lives. Situationally, adults may seek career changes after a trauma such as a death, layoff, or divorce (Marino, 1996).

Adults may have particularly difficult times with their careers and career decisions when they find "themselves unhappy in their work yet feel appropriately ambivalent about switching directions" (Lowman, 1993, p. 549). In such situations they may create illogical or troublesome career beliefs that become self-fulfilling and self-defeating (Krumboltz, 1992). An example of such a belief is "I'll never find a job I really like." It is crucial in such cases to help people change their ways of thinking and become more realistic.

There are two dominant ways of working with adults in career counselling: the differential approach and the developmental approach. The *differential approach* stresses that "the typology of persons and environments is more useful than any life stage strategies for coping with career problems" (Holland & Gottfredson, 1976, p. 23). It avoids age-related stereotypes, gender and minority group issues, and the scientific and practical difficulties of dealing with lifespan problems. "At any age, the level and quality of a person's vocational coping is a function of the interaction of personality type and type of environment plus the consistency and differentiation of each" (Holland & Gottfredson, 1976, p. 23).

According to this view, a career counsellor who is aware of typological formulations such as Holland's can predict the characteristic ways a given person may cope with career problems. For example, a person with a well-defined social/artistic personality (typical of many individuals employed as counsellors) would be expected to have high educational and vocational aspirations, to have good decision-making ability, to have a strong and lifelong interest in learning, to have moderate personal competency, and to have a marked interest in creative and high-level performance rather than in leadership (Holland, 1997). A person with such a profile would also have a tendency to remould or leave an environment in the face of adversity. A major advantage of working from this approach is the ease with which it explains career shifts at any age. People who shift careers, at any point in life, seek to find more consistency between personality and environment.

The *developmental approach* examines a greater number of individual and environmental variables. "The experiences people have with events, situations and other people play a large part in determining their identities (i.e., what they believe and value, how they respond to others, and what their own self images are)" (Gladstein & Apfel, 1987, p. 181). Developmental lifespan career theory proposes that adults are always in the process of evaluating themselves in regard to how they are affected by outside influences (e.g., spouse, family, friends) and how they impact these variables. Okun (1984) and Gladstein and Apfel (1987) believe the interplay of other people and events strongly influences career decisions in adulthood.

Gladstein and Apfel's (1987) approach to adult career counselling focuses on a combination of six elements: developmental, comprehensive, self-in-group, longitudinal, mutual commitment, and multi-methodological. These elements work together in the process of change at this stage of life. This model, which has been implemented on a practical level at the University of Rochester Adult Counseling Center, considers the person's total identity over time. In a related model, Chusmir (1990) stresses the interaction of multiple factors in the process that men undergo when choosing *nontraditional careers* (careers in which people of one gender are not usually employed) (see Figure 17.6). Whether or not careers are nontraditional, the fact is that many forces enter into career decisions.

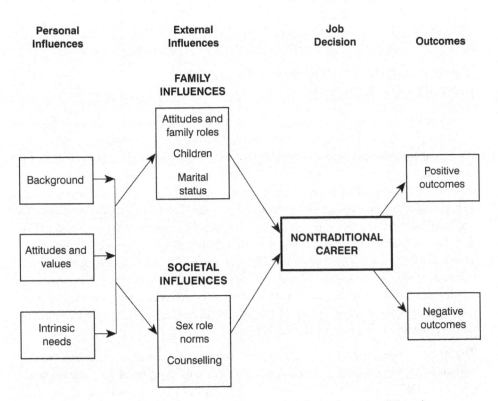

Figure 17.6 Factors contributing to men's adoption of nontraditional careers

Source: Reprinted from "Men Who Make Nontraditional Career Choices," by L. H. Chusmir, 1990, *Journal of Counseling and Development, 69*, p. 21. © 1990 by ACA. Reprinted with permission. No further reproduction authorized without written permission of the American Counseling Association.

Dick Doss had struggled with holding a job for years. He moved from one position to another as a cook, a sanitation engineer, a security officer, and a landscaper. Not being satisfied with any of his work, at 29 he went to see Susan, a career counsellor.

Susan gave Dick several inventories, including those on O*Net. She noted from Dick's results that he had a predominant artistic and social theme, which was just the opposite of the realistic and conventional jobs he had been dissatisfied with. Susan then explored with Dick what he could do at various levels of education with this predominant theme, and through the use of the National Occupational Classification system and other regional resources, what job growth was expected in each area.

Dick decided to enroll in a local community college to further his education so that he could pursue a career in the entertainment industry. He was pleased. He said to Susan at the end of his work with her, "This type of career just feels right for me."

1. What advantages and disadvantages of a career in the entertainment industry would you want Dick to be aware of?

2. What would you suggest that Dick do so that he becomes aware of what the industry is like in Canada?

Career Counselling with Women and Ethnic Minorities

"Many of the assumptions inherent in traditional theories of career development fall short in their application to women and ethnic minorities" (Luzzo & McWhirter, 2001, p. 61). Women and ethnic minorities historically have received less adequate career counselling than Caucasian males have and have faced more barriers in pursuit of their careers (Brown, 2002). The reason has often involved stereotypical beliefs and practices connected with these two groups (Herr, Cramer, & Niles, 2004). For example, society has generally assumed that women will have discontinuous career patterns to accommodate their families' needs. Likewise, ethnic minorities have often been viewed as interested in only a limited number of occupations. The growing social activism among women and ethnic minority groups, combined with a growing body of research, is helping challenge constraining negative forces and create models of career counselling for these populations (Peterson & Gonzalez, 2000). That is why, among other reasons, career counsellors should promote social justice in the workplace.

Women Gender-based career patterns for women have changed for several reasons. For one thing, women compose almost half (47%) of the Canadian labour force (Statistics Canada, 2006). Furthermore, "children are being exposed to greater and more varied career choices. Additionally, women have moved into careers previously reserved for men, thereby creating a broader range in the role models they provide girls" (Bobo et al.,

1998, pp. 40–41). On the other hand, as of 2003, women continued to earn 71% of what their male counterparts made (Statistics Canada, 2006).

Since 1970, there has been a dramatic rise in research on and interest in the career development of women (Luzzo & McWhirter, 2001; Whitmarsh, Brown, Cooper, Hawkins-Rodgers, & Wentworth, 2007). "Research on women's career development has identified both internal and external barriers associated with women's career development, documenting that the process of career decision making and maintaining a career are more complex and restricted for women than for men" (Sullivan & Mahalik, 2000, p. 54). Unfortunately, most theories of career development cannot be appropriately applied to women because they were formulated for men or are incomplete (Cook et al., 2002; Gottfredson, 2005; Jackson & Scharman, 2002).

Therefore, in working with women, counsellors need to realize they are often entering new territory and must watch out for and resist *occupational sex-role stereotyping*, even at the elementary school level (McMahon & Patton, 1997). Common stereotypes include viewing women as primarily mothers (nurturing) with children (dependent) who are iron maidens (hard-driving) and sex objects (Gysbers et al., 2003), or mistakenly assuming that, as a group, females prefer social, artistic, and conventional occupations as opposed to realistic, investigative, and enterprising occupations (Tomlinson & Evans-Hughes, 1991).

In addition, there is the *"glass ceiling" phenomenon* in which women are seen as able to rise only so far in a corporation because they are not viewed as being able to perform top-level executive duties. When these myths are accepted, girls and women are not challenged to explore their abilities and possibilities and as a result some women fail to develop their abilities or gifts to the fullest. Consequently, they never work, they develop a low or moderate commitment to work, or they focus on "safe," traditional, female-dominated occupations such as teaching, clerical work, nursing, or social services (Betz & Fitzgerald, 1987; Brown, 2002; Walsh & Osipow, 1994).

Other barriers outside of these myths must be considered in career counselling for women. For instance, a company culture may revolve around the expectation of working far more hours than may be described in a job, attendance at certain events, or being "one of the guys." Thus, women must overcome these realities, as well as the myths that surround them, in order to achieve career goals (Luzzo & McWhirter, 2001). Counsellors may advise them that they may more readily find a job that is not in a female-dominated occupational field by socially contacting men rather than women (Mencken & Winfield, 2000). Overcoming barriers and misperceptions and finding balance is an essential part of the counselling process.

To understand how women may combine a career and a family, Jackson and Scharman (2002) studied a national sample of "26 women identified as having creatively constructed their careers to maximize time with their families" (p. 181). Eight different themes emerged as to how these women managed to construct family-friendly careers. Their strategies ranged from "peaceful trade-offs" to "partner career flexibility." However, "each participant found satisfying solutions to combining career and family that did not require an either/or choice" (p. 184). Overall, these women demonstrated remarkable self-efficacy (i.e., confidence in themselves to cope with or manage complex or difficult situations). This ability is becoming an increasingly important factor in the career development of women. Career self-efficacy can be increased through working with women in groups to address factors that compose it, such as performance accomplishments, vicarious experiences, emotional arousal, and verbal persuasion (Sullivan & Mahalik, 2000).

Another helpful career counselling strategy in working with women, especially if they are depressed and indecisive about a career, is to offer "*career plus life counseling*, meaning that in counseling they [the women] focus on personal and relationship issues in addition to explicit career issues" (Lucas, Skokowski, & Ancis, 2000, p. 325). An ecological perspective, where career counsellors work with women on career development issues in the context and complexity of the environment in which they live, is increasingly gaining recognition as a way of helping women become more empowered and shape their futures (Cook et al., 2002).

An area that warrants counsellors' attention in career counselling with women in the future is demographics and trends. The labour market has shifted from goods-producing to service-producing industries (Van Buren, Kelly, & Hall, 1993). Service jobs are those such as sales clerk and computer operator. When young women take these jobs when they are qualified to pursue higher paying, nontraditional careers in skilled trades, they become more subjected to economic forces (such as poverty, social welfare, and dependence on men) that are not in their or society's best interest. Therefore, there is "an urgent need for career counseling interventions" offered through live or video modelling "that will persuade young women to consider the economic benefits of nontraditional career choices" or choices that are in line with their real interests (Van Buren et al., 1993, p. 101). Interestingly, more women are beginning to pursue their career interests and in recent years have been turning to enterprising occupations where they may earn more and be more in charge of their lives (Reardon et al., 2007).

Emerging from a conference held in 1986, the First Ministers of Canada directed that a Collaborative Action Working Group on Counselling be created. The working group had representatives from Newfoundland, Nova Scotia, New Brunswick, and British Columbia, along with two government departments, Employment and Immigration Canada and Status of Women Canada (Ward & Bezanson, 1991). They came up with nine guidelines for career counselling with girls and women, with the intent that associations or jurisdictions would adopt these, at least as a starting point in preparing their own policies and training strategies:

1. Counsellors must be aware that theories of career counselling may not apply the same way to women as to men.

2. Counsellors do not place their own limitations on the career directions or decisions of women.

3. Counsellors use gender-inclusive language.

4. Counsellors are knowledgeable about support services for women and refer as appropriate.

5. Counsellors continue to learn through careers about the social, biological, and psychological influences on female development, and specifically about their career development.

6. Counsellors are aware of the impact of stereotyping, prejudice, and discrimination that adversely affect many women's sense of self.

7. Counsellors continually review their own values, beliefs, and attitudes that affect their female clients. They also engage in gender-fair practices.

8. Counsellors maintain a social justice agenda to help eliminate gender bias within institutions and individuals.

9. Where possible, counsellors will honour a client's preference for an opposite- or same-gender counsellor.

A consistent finding is that women tend to enter occupations defined as social or conventional in the Holland model (Lalande, Crozier, & Davy, 2000). Relative to men, women's career planning involves greater consideration of home and family, and Lalande et al. (2000) recommend that having their partner or family join them in career counselling may be advantageous.

Ethnic Minorities   "Career counseling must incorporate different variables and different processes to be effective for clients from different cultural contexts" (Fouad & Byars-Winston, 2005, p. 223). Yet cultural minorities are so diverse that it is almost impossible to focus on all the factors that career counsellors must deal with in working with them individually or collectively.

In 2006, visible minorities comprised 16.2% (about 5 million) of Canada's population (Statistics Canada, 2008). According to a 2003 Statistics Canada survey, 36.0% of visible minorities reported that they had felt or experienced discrimination, and in 64% of these cases, it occurred in the workplace (Human Resources and Skills Development Canada [HRDC], 2006). In 2002, Aboriginal men and women earned 85.4 cents and 87.3 cents for every dollar earned by the average Canadian man and woman, respectively (HRDC, 2006). Aboriginal men and women also had much higher rates of unemployment—19.1% compared to 7.1% (HRDC, 2006).

In 2008, Canadian-born employees between 25 and 54 years of age earned an average of $23.72 per hour, while immigrant workers earned an average of $21.44 per hour. The gap was widest between Canadian-born workers and immigrants holding university degrees. Forty-two percent of immigrant workers aged 25 to 54 had higher educational levels than what their jobs required, compared to 28% of Canadian-born workers. Another indicator of economic disparity is that the proportion of immigrants earning less than $10 an hour in 2008 was 1.8 times higher compared to Canadian-born workers. On the positive side, however, immigrants who came to Canada more than 10 years ago had employment indicators, including salary, more closely resembling those of Canadian-born workers (Statistics Canada, 2009).

Not surprisingly, then, ethnic minorities have difficulty obtaining meaningful employment because of employers' discrimination practices, lack of marketable skills, and limited access to informal networks that lead to good jobs (Leong, 1995). Having poorly developed English or French language skills is also often a barrier. Consequently, many racial/ethnic minorities are "concentrated in lower level positions and unskilled occupations" (Fouad & Byars-Winston, 2005, p. 223). In addition, the interest patterns of ethnic minorities (as a group) in the United States have tended not to necessarily fall within Holland's (1997) circular RIASEC ordering in the same way as that of Caucasian Americans, thus presenting challenges for many career counsellors (Osipow & Fitzgerald, 1996).

Counsellors must remember that ethnic minorities have special needs in regard to establishing themselves in careers. Thus, counsellors need to be sensitive to such issues and at the same time help individuals overcome artificial and real barriers that prohibit them from maximizing their potential. For example, employment has a major affect on the psychological well-being and adaptation of immigrants and refugees in Canada (Arthur, Merali, & Djuraskovic, 2009). They often face at least two paradoxes in finding work: (a) although they seek Canadian experience to improve their employability, they are barred from many jobs that would provide this experience; and (b) although they are often rejected for senior-level positions because of language barriers and lack of Canadian experience, they are seen as overqualified for lower-level positions (Arthur et al., 2009). Furthermore, the academic and employment credentials they bring from their country of origin may not be accepted or may be devalued when they immigrate to Canada, thus creating further employment barriers. Underemployment continues to be one of their overriding issues (Arthur et al., 2009).

First Nations people also have special needs when it comes to career planning activities. When counselling First Nations people, the major goal is "interconnectedness rather than autonomy" (Neumann, McCormick, Amundson, & McLean, 2000, p. 174), thus respecting their integral view regarding the importance of family and community. Other aspects of respecting their culture are found in McCormick, Neumann, Amundson, and McLean's (1999) *First Nations Career/Life Planning Model*. Compared to non-Native students, Native students are less confident in their vocational abilities and in their ability to secure gainful employment (Krebs, Hurburt, & Schwartz, 1988). As noted earlier, their salaries are often lower when compared to the "average Canadian."

Career Counselling with Gay, Lesbian, Bisexual, and Transgender (GLBT) Individuals

Special diverse groups not often considered in career counselling are GLBT individuals. These people face unique concerns as well as many that are common to other groups. Of special concern to many GLBT individuals is whether to be overt or covert in disclosing their sexual orientation or gender identity at work (Chojnacki & Gelberg, 1994). Persons with minority sexual orientations and gender expressions face personal and professional developmental concerns, including discrimination, if they openly acknowledge their beliefs and practices (Degges-White & Shoffner, 2002). This may be especially true if gay members of this population are in male-dominated occupations, which tend to be more homophobic than other occupational groups (Jome, Surething, & Taylor, 2005).

Whether one can disclose their GLBT status is partly dependent on the degree to which their work environment is heterosexist. Chojnacki and Gelberg (1994) proposed four levels of work environment heterosexism that affect gay, lesbian, and bisexual (GLB) individuals at work: (a) *Level 1* (overt discrimination)—both formal and informal policies discriminate against people based on sexual orientation (e.g., the Canadian military before the ban on gay and lesbian individuals was lifted); (b) *Level 2* (covert discrimination)—although there is no formal antidiscrimination policy, informal discrimination occurs in the work place; (c) *Level 3* (tolerance)—there is a formal antidiscrimination policy regarding sexual orientation; and (d) *Level 4* (affirmation)—in addition to a formal antidiscrimination policy, there is an extension of insurance for partners, employee sensitivity training on diversity, and support systems for GLB individuals.

Helping GLBT individuals assess the type of work environment heterosexism they will likely encounter in a career choice or in a specific work setting is an important aspect of providing effective career counselling. Often this information can be gleaned from people working in the field (perhaps especially from other GLBT individuals), and from the human resources departments of larger organizations.

Before a counsellor works with GLBT individuals, Alderson (2004) recommends they answer the following seven questions:

1. Would you continue to seek the services of a physician or dentist who was an openly GLBT individual?

2. How would you feel if your son or daughter announced that he or she identified as GLBT?

3. How would you feel about sharing a hotel room with a GLBT person of your gender?

4. Would you allow yourself to become close friends with someone who is a GLBT person?

5. Would you invite open GLBT individuals to your wedding, and encourage them to dance with their partners?

6. Do you believe that GLBT people are equal to heterosexual individuals in every respect?

7. If you were (or are) a GLBT individual, how open would you feel (or do you feel) about it where you live and where you work?

If you feel some hesitancy or reluctance in answering the first six questions, you have some work to do before you are ready to work effectively with GLBT individuals. Largely out of necessity, GLBT clients become very sensitive to the views that others hold of them. Often this is communicated very subtly, and it is through this subtleness that GLBT people become adept at discerning who they can trust (Alderson, 2009).

Consequently, career counsellors must assess both their and the surrounding community's stereotyping of GLBT persons. In such an assessment, they must gauge personal, professional, and environmental bias toward people who are not heterosexual. In addition, they need to use gender-free language and to become familiar with support networks that are within their communities for members of these groups. Furthermore, they need to become informed about overt and covert discrimination in the workplace, such as blackmail, ostracism, harassment, exclusion, and termination. The *"lavender ceiling"* also needs to be discussed with those identifying as GLBT. This barrier to advancement in a career is the equivalent to the glass ceiling for women, where a career plateaus early due to discreet prejudice by upper management against persons because of beliefs about them related to their sexuality (Friskopp & Silverstein, 1995; Zunker, 2006).

SUMMARY AND CONCLUSION

This chapter covered information on various aspects of career counselling, including its importance and associations within counselling, such as the career development chapter of the Canadian Counselling and Psychotherapy Association. Major theories of career counselling—trait-and-factor, developmental, and social-cognitive—were reviewed. Career counselling with particular populations, especially individuals at different developmental ages and stages in life, women, ethnic minorities, and GLBT individuals, were examined.

Overall, multiple factors including inner needs and drives and external circumstances such as the economy, gender, educational attainment, ethnicity, and the social milieu combine to influence career decisions. Developments around the world, especially in technology, are impacting the field of careers as well. "The information age continues to alter the number of job openings as well as the way in which a wide variety of jobs are done" (Walls & Fullmer, 1996, p. 154). As advancing technology creates new or modifies old kinds of jobs, previously valued skills and entire occupations may diminish or vanish. Therefore, career counselling is becoming ever more important, and counsellors who are going to be relevant to their clients must be knowledgeable about procedures and practices in this field across the lifespan.

Among the many functions that career and employment counsellors perform are

- administering and interpreting tests and inventories,
- conducting personal counselling sessions,

- developing individualized career plans,
- helping clients integrate vocational and avocational life roles,
- facilitating decision-making skills, and
- providing support for persons experiencing job stress, job loss, or career transition.

Your Personal Reflections

1. How did you become interested in the career you are pursuing? Did you receive any career counselling? If so, was it helpful? If not, what use might you have made of career counselling?

2. How does Super's developmental career theory fit with your own experience? Do you see any patterns in your own professional development over time?

3. Think about careers that you aspired to during childhood (before the age of 12). List as many as you can think of, but at least five. How similar are they to each other according to John Holland's code? How similar are they to the profession of counselling?

4. From all you have read in this chapter, as well as your own observations, why is it important to have different theories and approaches for career counselling with women? Do you think some theories and approaches apply equally to both sexes?

Classroom Activities

1. Think back to your childhood and the careers you were aware of at that time. How do your early career dreams (before age 12) relate to your present professional aspirations? With the class, discuss your memories and how they influenced or continue to influence you.

2. With another classmate, discuss your opinions about the importance of leisure in regard to choosing a career. How would you evaluate leisure in importance compared to other variables (e.g., age or stage in life, maturity, gender, familial obligations) that impact career decision making? Share your ideas with the whole class.

3. Read about and evaluate a technique that could be used in career information guidance with an age group that you are interested in. Share your information with the class in an oral report.

4. Evaluate Super's theory of career choice in relation to an individual you know who is established in a career. Interview the person, if possible. Discuss with your classmates how Super's theory was or was not verified by the information you obtained.

5. Which particular age or category group covered in this chapter appeals to you most in regard to career counselling? Divide the class according to preferences. Focus on areas you consider most crucial for your age or category group in regard to career decision making. Report your results back to the whole class.

Chapter 18
Marriage, Couple, and Family Counselling

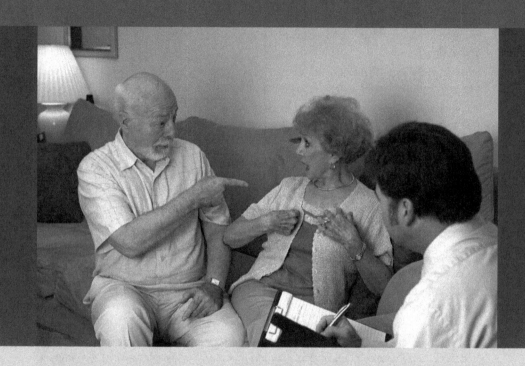

PRACTICE REFLECTION

I worked at an employee and family assistance (EAFP) program for several years during a time when I did not want the responsibility of a part-time private practice. I never knew who was coming in next or for what reason.

As Sean and Olivia walked in my office, Olivia began to cry. Crying soon after entering or after beginning to speak is common in counselling practice. There is a wonderful catharsis that occurs when people realize they are taking a step toward getting help. Other times, their tears reflect the anguish they have felt and their inability to resolve their problems on their own.

I learned that Sean didn't mind mixing a little pleasure with business. He had had a two-year affair with Jennifer, a woman who worked with him. Olivia had met Jennifer at company Christmas parties, and she felt deeply betrayed that Sean would allow this to happen. She had found out about three weeks before they had arranged the appointment with me, and she continued to distrust him and felt unable to forgive him. Besides this, Sean had lost interest in his wife sexually.

Week after week, I worked at helping Olivia put this behind her as I was reassured that Sean was acting in a faithful and committed manner. I also tried to re-establish the loving connection that the two of them had enjoyed for years. Unfortunately, Sean continued to report that he felt little to no passion for Olivia.

After several weeks, the couple stopped coming to see me. I was disappointed that I had not been of greater help to them. As I often do, I reflected numerous times on what I could have done differently. Nonetheless, I had other clients to attend to and I soon forgot about Sean and Olivia.

Months later, I came across Sean and Olivia's file and noticed they had had sessions with a different psychologist. In an EAFP firm and in other organizations where a client may see more than one therapist, files are kept in a central location where everyone has access. I was curious.

After opening the file, my curiosity soon turned to outrage. It turned out that Sean had continued the affair with Jennifer throughout the time I saw the two of them. The new therapist was again attempting what I had worked on—helping Olivia forgive and helping Sean become a faithful spouse.

I sat down for a moment, nearly frothing at the mouth. Here I had given this couple all that I had and experienced my own sense of failure when I could not help Sean re-develop passion for Olivia. Many marriage therapists will not see their clients alone for a session, but since this experience, I always make it a point to meet alone with each for either half of the first session or for a full session before I begin marriage or couples counselling.

I have a very strong value about honouring relationships, given whatever rules have been established. In my work with couples, I also need to honour *my* values. Ethically, we are expected to refer when a client's values or needs are beyond what we can provide for or beyond what we value. What values are sacrosanct to you?

Marital relations and family life are rooted in antiquity. Whether arranged by a family or the couple themselves, men and women have paired together in unions sanctioned by religion and society for economic, societal, and procreation reasons for millennia. The terms marriage, couple, *and* family *have distinct connotations in different societies. Marriage is generally seen as a socially or religiously sanctioned union between a man and a woman for economic and/or procreational reasons. However, the introduction of same-sex marriages may be altering that definition for some people. Marriage might also be sought to solidify a relationship based on love and commitment.*

The term couple *is more informal and broader than the term* marriage. *It simply denotes two people in a relationship together. They may be married or not, intimate or not. Nevertheless, they are seen as linked together in one or more ways. A family, on the other hand, consists of "those persons who are biologically and/or psychologically related . . . [through] historical, emotional, or economic bonds . . . and who perceive themselves as a part of a household" (Gladding, 2007, p. 6). These definitions of marriage, couple, and family allow for maximum flexibility and can encompass a wide variety of forms.*

Marriage, couple, and family counselling is a popular pursuit of counsellors. There are at least three reasons why.

First is the realization that people are directly affected by how their families function (Goldenberg & Goldenberg, 2002). For instance, chaotic families frequently produce offspring who have difficulty relating to others because of a lack of order or even knowledge of what to do, whereas enmeshed families have children who often have difficulty leaving home because they are overdependent on parents or other family members.

A second reason couple and family counselling is attractive is a financial consideration. Problems can often be addressed more economically when a couple or family is seen together.

Finally, the encompassing nature of marriage, couple, and family counselling work makes it intrinsically appealing. There are multiple factors to be aware of and to address. Counsellors who are engaged in helping marital units, couples, and families must constantly be active mentally and even sometimes physically. The process itself can be exciting as well as rewarding when change takes place. Marriage, couple, and family counselling attracts many clinicians who wish to work on complex, multifaceted levels in the most effective way possible.

This chapter examines the genesis and development of marriage, couple, and family counselling along with an overview of marriage, couple, and family counselling organizations and research. It also describes the family life cycle and addresses how family counselling differs from individual and group counselling. The process of marriage, couple, and family counselling from beginning to termination is also looked at.

THE CHANGING FORMS OF FAMILY LIFE

THE CANADIAN FAMILY IS CHANGING. FEWER FAMILIES NOW HAVE CHILDREN LIVING AT home, and the size of the average Canadian family has shifted from 4.3 persons in 1921 to 3.7 in 1971 and 2.5 in 2006 (Human Resources and Skills Development Canada (HRSDC), 2010). The number of common-law families increased by 8.5% between 1981 and 2006, with Québec having the highest percentage of common-law families in the nation (HRSDC, 2010). Furthermore, the proportion of single-parent families has also increased steadily over the past 25 years (HRSDC, 2010).

The strong interest in marriage, couple, and family counselling today is partly due to the rapid change in Canadian family life since World War II. Before the war, two types of families, which still exist, dominated our cultural life:

■ the nuclear family, a core unit of husband, wife, and their children

■ the multigenerational family, households that include at least three generations, such as a child/children, parent(s), and grandparent(s). This type of family sometimes includes unmarried relatives such as aunts and uncles.

After the war, a rising divorce rate made two more family types prevalent:

■ the single-parent family, which includes one parent, either biological or adoptive, who is solely responsible for the care of self and a child/children

■ the remarried (i.e., blended, step) family, a household created when two people marry and at least one of them has been previously married and has a child/children

In addition, changes in societal norms and demographics since the 1950s have fostered the development and recognition of several other family forms besides those already mentioned, specifically,

■ the dual-career family, where both marital partners are engaged in work that is developmental in sequence and to which they have a high commitment

■ the childless family, which consists of couples who consciously decide not to have children or who remain childless as a result of chance or biological factors

■ the aging family, where the head or heads of the household are aged 65 or above

■ the gay/lesbian family, which is made up of same-sex couples with or without a child/children from either a previous union or as a result of artificial insemination or adoption

■ the multicultural family, where individuals from two different cultures unite and form a household that may or may not have children

Couples and families in the 21st century are quite varied. Those who choose to enter such relationships face a host of economic, social, and developmental challenges that demand their attention daily. They also find a number of rewards in such unions, including physical, financial, and psychological support. The drawbacks and impacts of marriage, couple, and family life are great and sometimes complicated. Professional counsellors who work with the married, couples, and families must be attuned to a host of difficulties as well as possibilities. They must be ready to deal with extremely intricate and unsettling developmental or situational changes (Napier, 1988).

THE BEGINNINGS OF MARRIAGE, COUPLE, AND FAMILY COUNSELLING

The profession of marriage, couple, and family counselling is relatively new (Framo, 1996). Its substantial beginnings can be traced to the 1940s and early 1950s, but its real growth occurred in the late 1970s and the 1980s (Nichols, 1993). It is interesting to note that the rise in popularity of marriage, couple, and family counselling closely followed dramatic changes in the form, composition, structure, and emphasis of the Canadian family noted earlier (Markowitz, 1994). In this section, trends and personalities that influenced the development of the field will be noted, including some contemporary leaders.

Trends

At the end of World War II, Canada and the United States experienced an unsettling readjustment from war to peace that manifested in three trends that had an impact on the family, other than a rise in different types of family forms (Walsh, 1993). One was a sharp rise in the divorce rate, which took place almost simultaneously with the baby boom beginning in 1946. Whereas divorce had been fairly uncommon up to that point, it rose dramatically thereafter and did not level out until the 1990s. The impact of this phenomenon was unsettling.

Although the divorce rates in Canada have increased since divorce laws were introduced in 1968 (Ottawa Divorce.com, 2007), they have actually been decreasing since the 1990s (Institute of Marriage and Family Canada, 2009). Our all-time high was in 1987, when 50.6% of marriages were expected to end in divorce. Today, the projected figure is that 37.7% of Canadian marriages will not last 30 years (Ottawa Divorce.com, 2007).

A second trend that influenced the rise of marriage, couple, and family counselling was the changing role of women. After World War II, more women sought employment outside the home. Many women became the breadwinners of their families as well as the bread makers. The women's rights movement of the 1960s fostered the development of new opportunities for women. Thus, traditions and expectations fell and/or were expanded for women. The results were unsettling, as any major social change is, and both men and women in families and marriages needed help in making adequate adjustments. In 2006, a representative study of 2088 women (aged 18+) found that approximately 60% of Canadian women were either married or living common-law, while the remaining 40% were single (20%), divorced (16%), or widowed (4%) (MasterCard Worldwide, 2006). Statistics Canada revealed that in 2006, about 48.5% of the Canadian adult population was married (Divorce Magazine.com, 2010). "This is the first known time in Canadian history that the percentage [of married adults] was under half" (Divorce Magazine.com, 2010, p. 1).

The expansion of the lifespan is the third event that had an impact on family life and made marriage, couple, and family counselling more relevant to the Canadian public. As of 2007, the average life expectancy in Canada was 80.7 years (78.3 for men, 83.0 for women) (Statistics Canada, 2010). Even a decade earlier, life expectancy in Canada was lower, at 78.4 years (Statistics Canada, 2010).

Due to increased longevity, couples found themselves living with the same partners longer than at any previous time in history (Maples & Abney, 2006). Many were not sure exactly how to relate to their spouses, partners, or children over time because there were few previous models.

Thus, the need to work with families, couples, and individuals who were affected by these changes brought researchers, practitioners, and theorists together. They set the stage for an entirely new way of conceptualizing and working with married people, couples, and families.

Family Therapy Pioneers and Contemporary Leaders

A number of helping specialists advanced the field of marriage, couple, and family counselling after World War II and up to the present—more than can be mentioned here. Some, like Nathan Ackerman and Virginia Satir, did it using the persuasive nature of their personalities. Others, such as Salvador Minuchin and John Gottman, became important and notable because of the research they conducted.

The work of Nathan Ackerman (1958), a New York City psychoanalyst, was especially critical in focusing the attention of a well-established form of therapy, psychoanalysis, on families. Before Ackerman, psychoanalysts had purposely excluded family members from the treatment of individual clients for fear that family involvement would be disruptive. Ackerman applied psychoanalytic practices to the treatment of families and made family therapy respected in the profession of psychiatry.

Two other pioneers that emerged on a national level about the time of Ackerman were experiential in nature: Virginia Satir and Carl Whitaker. Both of these individuals had engaging personalities and a presence that commanded attention. Satir was an especially clear writer and presenter, whereas Whitaker was a maverick whose unorthodox style and creativity, such as falling asleep during a session and having a dream, provoked considerable thought and discussion in the marriage and family field and in the couples and families with whom he worked.

Jay Haley was probably the dominant figure of the early family therapists, however. Haley culled ideas from Milton Erickson, blended them with his own thoughts, and through persistence kept early family counsellors in touch with each other and with developing ideas in the field. Haley also had a major role in developing strategic family therapy and in influencing structural family therapy.

Other pioneers worked in teams to conduct exploratory studies in the area of family dynamics and in the etiology of schizophrenia. Among the teams were the Gregory Bateson group (Bateson, Jackson, Haley, & Weakland, 1956) in Palo Alto, California, and the

Murray Bowen and Lyman Wynne groups (Bowen, 1960; Wynne, Ryckoff, Day, & Hirsch, 1958) at the National Institute of Mental Health (NIMH). They observed how couples and families functioned when a family member was diagnosed as schizophrenic. The Bateson group came up with a number of interesting concepts, such as the double bind, where a person receives two contradictory messages at the same time and, unable to follow both, develops physical and psychological symptoms as a way to lessen tension and escape. Bowen went on to develop his own systemic form of treatment based on multigenerational considerations and originated a now widely popular clinical tool called the genogram (a three-generational visual representation of a family tree depicted in geometric figures, lines, and words).

The group movement, especially in the 1960s, also had an impact on the emergence of couple and family counselling. Some practitioners, such as John Bell (e.g., Bell, 1975, 1976), even started treating families as a group and began the practice of couple/family group counselling (Ohlsen, 1979; 1982). Foreign-born therapists have had a major influence on marriage, couple, and family therapy since the 1960s. These include Salvador Minuchin, the originator of structural family therapy; Mara Selvini Palazzoli, a creator of a form of strategic family therapy known as the Milan approach; and, more recently, Michael White and David Epston, the founders of narrative therapy.

Most recently there has been an influx in the field led by Steve deShazer and Bill O'Hanlon, who developed brief therapeutic therapies that emphasize solutions and possibilities. In addition, Monica McGoldrick (McGoldrick, Giordano, & Pearce, 1996) has emphasized the importance of multicultural factors and cultural background in treating couples and families. Included in the idea of culture today are inherited cultures (e.g., ethnicity, nationality, religion, groupings such as baby boomers) and acquired cultures (learned habits, such as those of being a counsellor) (Markowitz, 1994). Betty Carter and a host of others have focused on awakening gender-sensitive issues in the marriage, couple, and family counselling field, such as the overriding importance of power structures. Finally, exemplary researchers such as John Gottman and Neil Jacobson have helped practitioners better understand the dynamics within marriages, couples, and families, especially factors related to domestic violence and higher functioning marital relationships (Peterson, 2002).

SYSTEMS THEORY

Systems theory has had a significant impact in counselling practice, particularly as it relates to marriage, couple, and family counselling. For example, Qualls and Anderson (2009) noted that systems theory constitutes the theoretical foundation for family therapy, and many marriage and couple counsellors use systems theory as their theoretical base. *Systems theory* is a generic term for conceptualizing a group of related elements (e.g., people) that interact as a whole entity (e.g., a family or a group). As a concept, systems theory "is more of a way of thinking than a coherent, standardized theory" (Worden,

2003, p. 8). The originator of general systems theory was Ludwig von Bertalanffy (1968), a biologist. According to the theory, any living organism is composed of interacting components mutually affecting one another. Three basic assumptions distinguish systems theory from other counselling approaches:

1. Causality is interpersonal,

2. "Psychosocial systems are best understood as repeated patterns of interpersonal interaction," and

3. "Symptomatic behaviors must . . . be understood from an interactional viewpoint" (Sexton, 1994, p. 250).

Thus, the focus in general systems theory is on how the interaction of parts influences the operation of the system as a whole.

Circular causality is one of the main concepts introduced by this theory—the idea that events are related through a series of interacting feedback loops. Scapegoating (in which one person is singled out as the cause of a problem) and linear causality (in which one action is seen as the cause of another) are eliminated.

There are a number of approaches to counselling that are based on systems theory. One is Bowen systems theory, which was developed to help persons differentiate themselves from their families of origin. Structural family therapy is a second theory and one that focuses on creating healthy boundaries. A third approach, strategic therapy, originated from the work of Milton Erickson and has a variety of forms, which can be employed in a variety of ways. These approaches, and emotion-focused marriage, couple, and family therapy, will be described near the end of the chapter.

ASSOCIATIONS, EDUCATION, AND RESEARCH

Associations

In Canada, accredited marriage and family counsellors (often called therapists) belong to the largest and oldest professional association in the United States—the American Association for Marriage and Family Therapy (AAMFT). The AAMFT was established in 1942. While there are over 90 AAMFT-recognized schools in the United States, there are only six in Canada, located in British Columbia, Alberta, Manitoba, Saskatchewan, Ontario, and Québec. As of 2004, there were 1406 AAMFT members practising in Canada (Beaton, Dienhart, Schmidt, & Turner, 2009). The Registry of Marriage and Family Therapists in Canada (www.marriageandfamily.ca) maintains a list of all AAMFT members (Beaton et al., 2009).

Québec is the only province that currently licenses Canadian couple/marital and family therapists (CMFTs), although other provincial CMFT associations are lobbying to do the same (Beaton et al., 2009). Consequently, most CMFT counsellors are licensed psychologists or social workers. There is also a section in the Canadian Psychological Association devoted to family interventions and research, known simply as the *Family* section (see www.cpa.ca/aboutcpa/cpasections/familypsychology).

In the United States, there are three other professional associations that attract marriage, couple, and family clinicians.

- The International Association of Marriage and Family Counselors (IAMFC), a division of the American Counseling Association (ACA), was chartered in 1986.

- Division 43 (Family Psychology), a division of the American Psychological Association (APA), was formed in 1984 and is comprised of psychologists who work with couples and families.

- The American Family Therapy Association (AFTA) was formed in 1977 and is identified as an academy of advanced professionals interested in the exchange of ideas (Gladding, 2007).

Education

Both the AAMFT and the IAMFC have established guidelines for training professionals in working with couples and families. AAMFT standards are drawn up and administered by the Commission on Accreditation for Marriage and Family Therapy Education (CAMFTE); those for IAMFC are handled through the Council for Accreditation of Counseling and Related Educational Programs (CACREP). A minimum of a master's degree is required to become a marriage, couple, and family counsellor/therapist for Canadians wishing or needing to belong to the AAMFT, although debate persists over the exact content and sequencing of courses (see Table 18.1).

Research

Regardless of professional affiliation and curriculum background, professionals are attracted to marriage, couple, and family counselling largely due to a societal need for the specialty and its growing research base. Gurman and Kniskern (1981) reported that approximately 50% of all problems brought to counsellors are related to marriage and family issues. Unemployment, poor school performance, spouse abuse, depression, rebellion, and self-concept issues are just a few of the many situations that can be dealt with from this perspective. Individual development dovetails with family and career issues (Okun, 1984). Each one impacts the resolution of the other in a systemic manner. Bratcher (1982) comments on the interrelatedness of career and family development, recommending the use of family systems theory for experienced counsellors working with individuals seeking career counselling.

Table 18.1 Example of Coursework Areas Required for a Master's Degree in AAMFT-Accredited and CACREP-Accredited Programs

CACREP Curriculum	AAMFT Curriculum
Human Growth and Development	Introduction Family/Child Dev.
Social and Cultural Foundations	Marital and Family Systems
Helping Relationships	Intro. Family/Child Development
Groups	Dysfunctions in Marriage/Family
Lifestyle and Career Development	Advanced Child Development
Appraisal/Assessment	Assessment in Marital/Family
Research and Evaluation	Research Methods Child/Family
Professional Orientation	Professional Issues Family
Theoretical Foundation MFT	Theories of MFT
Techniques/Treatment MFT	Marriage/Family Pre-Practicum
Clinical Practicum/Internship	Clinical Practicum
Substance Abuse Treatment	Human Sexual Behaviour
Human Sexuality	Thesis
Electives	Electives

Source: From "The Training of Marriage and Family Counselors/Therapists: A 'Systemic' Controversy among Disciplines," by Michael Baltimore, 1993, *Alabama Counseling Association Journal, 19*, p. 40. Copyright 1993, Alabama Counseling Association. Reprinted with permission.

Note: Accreditation of master's programs in Canada is offered through the Canadian Counselling and Psychotherapy Association (see www.ccacc.ca/en/accreditation), while accreditation of doctoral programs is offered through the Canadian Psychological Association (see www.ccacc.ca/en/accreditation).

Research studies summarized by Doherty and Simmons (1996), Gurman and Kniskern (1981), Haber (1983), Pinsof and Wynne (1995), and Wohlman and Stricker (1983) report a number of interesting findings.

- First, family counselling interventions are at least as effective as individual interventions for most client complaints and lead to significantly greater durability of change.

- Second, some forms of family counselling (e.g., using structural-strategic family therapy with substance abusers) are more effective in treating problems than other counselling approaches.

- Third, the presence of both parents, especially noncompliant fathers, in family counselling situations greatly improves the chances for success. Similarly, the effectiveness of marriage counselling when both partners meet conjointly with the counsellor is nearly twice that of counsellors working with just one spouse.

- Fourth, when marriage and family counselling services are not offered to couples conjointly or to families systemically, the results of the intervention may be negative and problems may worsen.

- Finally, there is high client satisfaction from those who receive marital, couple, and family counselling services, with over 97% rating the services they received from good to excellent. Overall, the basic argument for employing marriage and family counselling is its proven efficiency. This form of treatment is logical, fast, satisfactory, and economical.

Case Example: What Would *You* Do?

Shasta grew up in a single-parent family that was often strapped for money. Therefore Shasta learned to hoard food and to hide any valuables she might obtain. Later, she married Marcus, who was financially quite successful. Still, she hoarded and hid items around the house to the point that it caused tension in the relationship.

Shasta finally realized she needed help and sought out a marriage and family counsellor.

1. Do you think such a counsellor could help her resolve her problem? If so, how? If not, why not?

2. Would it make more sense for Shasta to see an individual counsellor? Why or why not?

FAMILY LIFE AND THE FAMILY LIFE CYCLE

Family life and the growth and developments that take place within it are at the heart of marriage, couple, and family counselling. The *family life cycle* is the name given to the stages a family goes through as it evolves over the years. These stages sometimes parallel and complement those in the individual life cycle, but often they are unique because of the number of people involved and the diversity of tasks to be accomplished. Becvar and Becvar (2006) outline a nine-stage cycle that begins with the unattached adult and continues through retirement (see Table 18.2).

The Becvar and Becvar (2006) model applies only to those belonging to the dominant white heterosexual community. Collectivist values may conflict with goals inherent in some of these stages for those from other cultures. Furthermore, gay and lesbian families experience a different life cycle (Goldberg, 2010).

Some families and family members are more "on time" in achieving stage-critical tasks that go with the family life cycle and their own personal cycle of growth. In such cases, a better sense of well-being is achieved (Carter & McGoldrick, 1999). Regardless of timing, all families have to deal with *family cohesion* (emotional bonding) and *family adaptability* (ability to be flexible and change). These two dimensions each have four levels, represented by Olson (1986) in the circumplex model of marital and family systems (see Figure 18.1). "The two dimensions are curvilinear in that families that apparently are very high or very low on both dimensions seem dysfunctional, whereas families that are balanced seem to function more adequately" (Maynard & Olson, 1987, p. 502).

Table 18.2 Stages of the Family Life Cycle

Stage	Emotion	Stage-Critical Tasks
1. Unattached adult	Accepting parent-offspring separation	a. Differentiation from family of origin b. Development of peer relations c. Initiation of career
2. Newly married	Commitment to the marriage	a. Formation of marital system b. Making room for spouse with family and friends c. Adjusting career demands
3. Childbearing	Accepting new members into the system	a. Adjusting marriage to make room for child b. Taking on parenting roles c. Making room for grandparents
4. Preschool-age child	Accepting the new personality	a. Adjusting family to the needs of specific child(ren) b. Coping with energy drain and lack of privacy c. Taking time out to be a couple
5. School-age child	Allowing child to establish relationships outside the family	a. Extending family/society interactions b. Encouraging the child's educational progress c. Dealing with increased activities and time demands
6. Teenage child	Increasing flexibility of family boundaries to allow independence	a. Shifting the balance in the parent-child relationship b. Refocusing on mid-life career and marital issues c. Dealing with increasing concerns for older generation
7. Launching centre	Accepting exits from and entries into the family	a. Releasing adult children into work, college, marriage b. Maintaining supportive home base c. Accepting occasional returns of adult children
8. Middle-age adult	Letting go of children and facing each other	a. Rebuilding the marriage b. Welcoming children's spouses, grandchildren into family c. Dealing with aging of one's own parents
9. Retirement	Accepting retirement and old age	a. Maintaining individual and couple functioning b. Supporting middle generation c. Coping with death of parents, spouse d. Closing or adapting family home

Source: From *Family Therapy: A Systematic Integration* (pp. 128–129), by Dorothy Stroh Becvar and Raphael J. Becvar.
© 1993 by Allyn & Bacon. All rights reserved. Reprinted with permission.

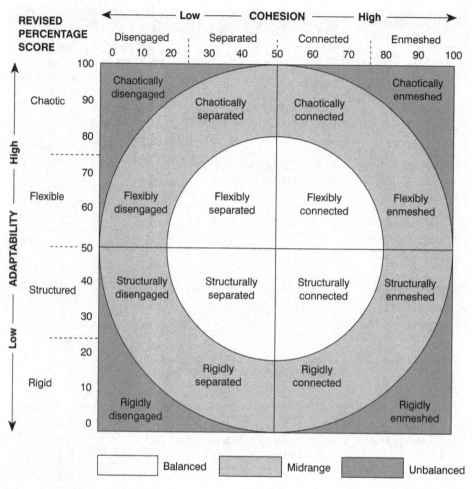

Figure 18.1 The circumplex model

Source: From Prepare/Enrich, Inc., David H. Olson, president, Minneapolis, MN. © 1979 (rev. 1986). Reprinted with permission.

Families that are most successful, functional, happy, and strong are not only balanced but committed, appreciate each other, spend time together, have good communication patterns, have a high degree of religious/spiritual orientation, and are able to deal with crisis in a positive manner (Stinnett, 1998; Stinnett & DeFrain, 1985).

According to Wilcoxon (1985), marriage, couple, and family counsellors need to be aware of the different stages within the family while staying attuned to the developmental tasks of individual members. When counsellors are sensitive to individual family members and the family as a whole, they are able to realize that some individual manifestations, such as depression (Lopez, 1986), career indecisiveness (Kinnier, Brigman, & Noble, 1990), and substance abuse (West, Hosie, & Zarski, 1987), are related to family structure and functioning. Consequently, they are able to be more inclusive in their treatment plans.

When evaluating family patterns and the mental health of everyone involved, it is crucial that an assessment be based on the form and developmental stage of the family constellation. To facilitate this process, Carter and McGoldrick (1999) propose sets of developmental tasks for traditional and nontraditional families, such as those headed by single parents or blended families. It is important to note that nontraditional families are not pathological because of their differences; they are merely on a different schedule of growth and development.

Bowen (1978) suggests terms such as *enmeshment* and *triangulation* to describe family dysfunctionality regardless of the family form. (*Enmeshment* refers to family environments in which members are overly dependent on each other or are undifferentiated. *Triangulation* describes family fusion situations in which the other members of the triangle pull a person in two different directions.) Counsellors who effectively work with couples and families have guidelines for determining how, where, when, or whether to intervene in the family process. They do not fail to act (e.g., neglect to engage everyone in the therapeutic process), nor do they overreact (perhaps place too much emphasis on verbal expression) (Gladding, 2007).

MARRIAGE/FAMILY COUNSELLING VERSUS INDIVIDUAL/GROUP COUNSELLING

There are similarities and differences in the approaches to marriage or family counselling and individual or group counselling (Gladding, 2007; Hines, 1988; Trotzer, 1988). A major similarity centres on theories. Some theories used in individual or group counselling (e.g., person-centred, Adlerian, reality therapy, behavioural) are used with couples and families (Horne, 2000). Other approaches (e.g., structural, strategic, solution-focused family therapy) are unique to marriage, couple, and family counselling and are systemic in nature. Counsellors must learn about these additional theories as well as new applications of previous theories to become skilled at working with couples or families.

Marriage, couple, or family counselling and individual counselling share a number of assumptions. For instance, both recognize the importance the family plays in the individual's life, both focus on problem behaviours and conflicts between the individual and the environment, and both are developmental. A difference is that individual counselling usually treats the person outside his or her family, whereas marriage, couple, or family counselling generally includes the involvement of others, usually family members. Further, marriage, couple, and family counselling works at resolving issues within the family as a way of helping individual members better cope with the environment (Nichols & Schwartz, 2006).

Marriage, couple, and family counselling sessions are similar to group counselling sessions in organization, basic dynamics, and stage development. Furthermore, both types of counselling have an interpersonal emphasis. However, the family is not like a typical group, although knowledge of the group process may be useful. For example, family members are not equal in status and power. In addition, families may perpetuate myths, whereas groups are initially more objective in dealing with events. More emotional baggage is carried among family members than members of another type of group because the arrangement in a family is not limited in time and is related to sex roles and affective bonds that have a long history (Becvar, 1982). Although the family may be a group, it is not well suited to work that takes place only through group theory.

Finally, the emphasis of marriage, couple, and family counselling is generally on dynamics as opposed to linear causality, as is the case in much individual and some group counselling. In other words, the dynamics behind marriage, couple, and family counselling generally differ from the other two types of counselling. In making the transition from an individual perspective to a family orientation, Resnikoff (1981) stresses specific questions that counsellors should ask themselves in order to understand family functioning and dynamics. By asking the right questions, the counsellor becomes more attuned to the family as a client and how best to work with it.

- What is the outward appearance of the family?
- What repetitive, nonproductive sequences are noticeable; that is, what is the family's dance?
- What is the basic feeling state in the family, and who carries it?
- What individual roles reinforce family resistance, and what are the most prevalent family defenses?
- How are family members differentiated from one another, and what are the subgroup boundaries?
- What part of the life cycle is the family experiencing, and what are its problem-solving methods?

Counsellors working with couples, whether married or not, also ask many of these questions.

OVERVIEW OF MARRIAGE, COUPLE, AND FAMILY COUNSELLING

Marriage and Couple Counselling

Early pioneers in marriage and couple counselling focused on the marriage or couple relationship, rather than just the individuals involved. The new emphasis meant that three entities were considered in such relationships: two individuals and one couple. Thus, from its beginning, marriage and couple counsellors set a precedent for seeing couples together in conjoint sessions, a practice that continues today.

Couples seek marriage or relationship counselling for a wide variety of reasons, including finances, children, fidelity, communication, and compatibility (Long & Young, 2007). Almost any situation can serve as the impetus to seek help. Regardless of who initiates the request, it is highly recommended that the counsellor see both members of the couple from the beginning if at all possible. Whitaker (1977) notes that if a counsellor is not able to structure the situation in this way, he or she may not help the couple and may in fact do harm. Furthermore, if one member of a couple tries to change without the other's knowledge or support, conflict is bound to ensue.

Trying to treat one spouse or partner alone for even one or two sessions increases the other's resistance to counselling and his or her anxiety. However, this effect may be mediated if the counsellor then meets with the non-attending spouse for one or two sessions to equalize "the playing field." In this instance, the next session would then require that both partners attend.

In some instances, it might be advisable to meet each partner for an individual session or each individually for half of the first session. For example, if one or the other partner has been having an affair, he or she might not disclose their intent of continuing this in front of the spouse. If the therapist knows this information, it may help establish appropriate interventions.

Wilcoxon and Fenell (1983) have developed a therapist-initiated letter explaining the process of marriage therapy to an absent partner, which outlines the perils of treating just one partner. It is sent by counsellors through the attending person in counselling to the non-attender to help him or her see the possibilities that can accrue when working with both members of the couple (see Figure 18.2).

If both partners decide to enter marriage and couple counselling, the counsellor may take a variety of approaches. Five of the main approaches are psychoanalytic, cognitive-behavioural, Bowen systems, structural-strategic, and rational emotive behaviour therapy (Jacobson & Gurman, 2003). All of these theoretical perspectives have their strengths, but the overall theoretical basis for most marriage and couples counselling is not as strong as it is for family counselling. There are several reasons for this phenomenon, but the main reason is that, historically, many marriage and couples counsellors were primarily practitioners, not researchers or writers. As practitioners, they did not have the time or interest in defining and publishing unique theoretical approaches to working with couples. Instead, they borrowed and modified existing individual and family theories. Moreover, until recently, marriage and couples counselling has been viewed as a subspecialty within family counselling. However, marriage and couples counselling is now becoming a stronger discipline and specific work is under way to delineate special ways of working in this area (Jacobson & Gurman, 2003).

Family Counselling

Families enter counselling for a number of reasons. Usually, there is an *identified patient* (IP)—an individual who is seen as the cause of trouble within the family structure—whom family members use as their ticket of entry. Most family counselling practitioners do not view one member of a family as the problem but instead work with the whole family system. Occasionally, family therapy is done from an individual perspective but with the hope that changes in the person will have a ripple effect and positively impact a family (Nichols, 1988).

(Date)

Mr. John Jones
111 Smith Street
Anytown, USA 00000

Dear Mr. Jones,

As you may know, your wife, Jill, has requested therapy services for difficulties related to your marriage. However, she has stated that you do not wish to participate in marital therapy sessions.

As a professional marriage therapist, I have an obligation to inform each of you of the possible outcome of marital therapy services to only one spouse. The available research indicates that one-spouse marital therapy has resulted in reported increases in marital stress and dissatisfaction for both spouses in the marriage. On the other hand, many couples have reported that marital therapy which includes both spouses has been helpful in reducing marital stress and enhancing marital satisfaction.

These findings reflect general tendencies in marital research and are not absolute in nature. However, it is important for you and Jill to be informed of potential consequences which might occur through marital therapy in which only your spouse attends. Knowing this information, you may choose a course of action which best suits your intentions.

After careful consideration of this information, I ask that you and Jill discuss your options regarding future therapy services. In this way, all parties will have a clear understanding of another's intentions regarding your relationship.

As a homework assignment for Jill, I have asked that each of you read this letter and sign in the spaces provided below to verify your understanding of the potential consequences to your relationship by continuing one-spouse marital therapy. If you are interested in joining Jill for marital therapy, in addition to your signature below, please contact my office to indicate your intentions. If not, simply sign below and have Jill return the letter at our next therapy session. I appreciate your cooperation in this matter.

Sincerely,

Therapist X
_____

We verify by our signatures below that we have discussed and understand the potential implications of continued marital therapy with only one spouse in attendance.

_____   _____
Attending Spouse   Date

_____   _____
Non-Attending Spouse   Date

Figure 18.2 Letter to engage a non-attending spouse

Source: From "Engaging the Non-Attending Spouse in Marital Therapy through the Use of a Therapist-Initiated Written Communication," by A. Wilcoxon and D. Fennel, pp. 199–203. Reprinted from Vol. 9, No. 2 of the *Journal of Marital and Family Therapy*. © 1983 by American Association for Marriage and Family Therapy. Reprinted with permission.

Family counselling has expanded rapidly since the mid-1970s and encompasses many aspects of couples counselling. Although a few family counsellors, such as behaviourist, narrative, or solution-focused therapists, are linearly based and work on a cause-and-effect or a constructivist perspective, most are not. Rather, the majority of counsellors in the field operate from a general systems framework and conceptualize the family as an open system that evolves over the family life cycle in a sociocultural context. Functional families follow rules and are flexible in meeting the demands of family members and outside agencies. Family systems counsellors stress the idea of circular causality. They also emphasize the following concepts:

- *Non-summativity*. The family is greater than the sum of its parts. It is necessary to examine the patterns within a family rather than the actions of any specific member alone.

- *Equifinality*. The same origin may lead to different outcomes, and the same outcome may result from different origins. Thus, the family that experiences a natural disaster may become stronger or weaker as a result. Likewise, healthy families may have quite dissimilar backgrounds. Therefore, treatment focuses on interactional family patterns rather than particular conditions or events.

- *Communication*. All behaviour is seen as communicative. It is important to attend to the two functions of interpersonal messages: *content* (factual information) and *relationship* (how the message is to be understood). The *what* of a message is conveyed by *how* it is delivered.

- *Family rules*. A family's functioning is based on explicit and implicit rules. Family rules provide expectations about roles and actions that govern family life. Most families operate on a small set of predictable rules, a pattern known as the *redundancy principle*. To help families change dysfunctional ways of working, family counsellors have to help them define or expand the rules under which they operate.

- *Morphogenesis*. The ability of the family to modify its functioning to meet the changing demands of internal and external factors is known as morphogenesis. Morphogenesis usually requires a *second-order change* (the ability to make an entirely new response) rather than a *first-order change* (continuing to do more of the same things that have worked previously) (Watzlawick et al., 1974). Instead of just talking, family members may need to try new ways of behaving.

- *Homeostasis*. Like biological organisms, families have a tendency to remain in a steady, stable state of equilibrium unless otherwise forced to change. When a family member unbalances the family through his or her actions, other members quickly try to rectify the situation through negative feedback. The model of functioning can be compared to a furnace, which comes on when a house falls below a set temperature and cuts off once the temperature is reached. Sometimes homeostasis can be advantageous in helping a family achieve life-cycle goals, but often it prevents the family from moving on to another stage in its development.

Counsellors who operate from a family systems approach work according to the concepts just listed. For instance, if family rules are covert and cause confusion, the counsellor helps the family make these regulations overt and clear. All members of the family are engaged in the process so that communication channels are opened. Often, a genogram is constructed to help family members and the counsellor detect intergenerational patterns of family functioning that have an impact on the present (McGoldrick, Gerson, & Petry, 2008).

For a genogram, three generations of the family should be drawn. Names, dates of birth, marriage, separation, and divorce should be indicated, along with basic information such as current age and occupation. A genogram can also be used in a multicultural context to assess the worldview and cultural factors that often influence family members' behaviours (Thomas, 1998). Overall, "the genogram appears to provide an effective and personally meaningful strategy to facilitate systems thinking," especially by new client families and counsellors who are just beginning to work with families (Pistole, 1997b, p. 339).

THE PROCESS OF MARRIAGE, COUPLE, AND FAMILY COUNSELLING

The process of marriage, couple, and family counselling is based on several premises. One is that the individuals conducting the counselling are psychologically healthy and understand their own families of origin well. When such is the case, counsellors are able to clearly focus on their client families and not contaminate sessions with material from their own family life that they have not resolved.

A second premise of working with families is that counsellors will not overemphasize or underemphasize possible aspects or interventions in the therapeutic process (Gladding, 2007). In other words, counsellors will balance what they do. Such a process means not being overly concerned about making family members happy but at the same time engaging members in a personable way.

A third component of conducting marriage, couple, and family counselling is for the counsellor to win the *battle for structure* (i.e., establish the parameters under which counselling is conducted) while letting the family win the *battle for initiative* (i.e., motivation to make needed changes) (Napier & Whitaker, 1978). The battle for structure is won when counsellors inform clients about ways they will work with them, including important but mundane facts about how often they will meet, for how long, and who is to be involved. A good part of structure can be included in a disclosure statement that the counsellor has the couple or family read and sign. Initiative in the therapeutic process must come from couples and families themselves; however, once counsellors listen and outline what they see as possibilities, couple or family members often pull together toward common goals.

Fourth, marriage, couple, and family counsellors need to be able to see the couple or family difficulties in the context in which they are occurring. Thus, the counsellor needs to be developmentally sophisticated on multiple levels of life and have some life experiences, including resolving toxic or adversarial conditions in less-than-ideal conditions. Such skills and insights bring to counsellors an understanding of how couples and families become either more together or further apart when faced with different life stages, cultural norms, or situational circumstances.

Pre-Session Planning

Before a couple or family is seen for counselling, several matters should be addressed. One is the expectation(s) the caller has for an initial session or for treatment in general. The person who calls gives a rationale for seeking therapy that may or may not be the reason anyone else in the couple or family relationship has for wanting or not wanting counselling. Nevertheless, the counsellor must listen carefully and obtain essential clinical information, such as a concise description of the problem, and factual information, such as the caller's name, address, and phone number. In gathering this information, the counsellor should listen for what is conveyed as well as what is not said. In doing so, the counsellor can begin to hypothesize about issues that are prevalent in certain family life stages and cultural traditions as they may relate to the caller's family. For example, a family with adolescents may expect to have boundary problems; however, the way they are handled in a traditional Italian family versus a traditional British family may be quite different. Regardless, by the end of the initial phone call, an appointment should be scheduled.

Initial Session(s)

Research indicates that the first few sessions are the most critical in regard to whether counsellors have success therapeutically with couples and families (Odell & Quinn, 1998). Therefore, getting off to a good start is essential. One way a good beginning can be fostered is for the counsellor to establish rapport with each person attending and the couple or family unit as a whole. This type of bonding where trust, a working relationship, and a shared agenda evolve is known as the *working alliance* (this was explained in Chapter 6). It can be created through a number of means, such as

- *maintenance*—where the counsellor confirms or supports a couple's or family member's position;
- *tracking*—where a counsellor, through a series of clarifying questions, tracks or follows a sequence of events; and
- *mimesis*—where a counsellor adopts a couple's or family's style or tempo of communication, such as being jovial with a light-hearted couple or family or serious with a couple or family that is somber.

In establishing a working alliance, it is important for the counsellor to engage the couple or family and its members enough to gain a perspective on how individuals view the presenting problem, person, or situation. This perspective is called a *frame*. The counsellor may challenge the frame of a couple or of family members to gain a clearer perspective of what is happening in the relationship or to give the couple or family another option of how they can perceive their situation (i.e., reframe).

In the initial session or sessions, the counsellor is also an observer. He or she looks for a phenomenon called the *couple* or *family dance*, which is the way a couple or family typically interacts on either a verbal or nonverbal level (Napier & Whitaker, 1978). If the counsellor misses this interaction at first, he or she need not worry, for the pattern will repeat itself. It is important in observing the family dance to see whether some member or members of the family are being *scapegoated* (i.e., blamed for the family's problems). For instance, a family may accuse its teenage son of being a lazy troublemaker because the adolescent sleeps late whenever possible and gets into mischief when he is out on the town with his friends. Although it may be true that the son has some problems, it is more likely that he is not the main cause of the family's problems. Thus, again, the counsellor will need to probe and even challenge the family members' perceptions of where difficulties are located.

One way of broadly defining or clarifying what is happening in the couple or family is to ask *circular questions*—that is, questions that focus attention on couple or family connections and highlight differences among members. For instance, in a family, the father might be asked how his daughter responds when verbally attacked by his wife and how other members of the family react as well, including himself. Such a strategy helps counsellors and the families they work with see more of the dynamics involved in family life and may take pressure off the person who has been seen as the problem. This type of questioning may also help the counsellor and family see if *triangulation* is taking place (i.e., the drawing in of a third person or party into a dyadic conflict, such as the mother enlisting the father's support whenever she has an argument with the daughter).

Case Example: What Would *You* Do?

Cleo had worked at family services for some time, but the call she received from a distraught mother at 2 a.m. confirmed the importance of listening to details. Helena, the mother, was sobbing; she told Cleo that she would like to make an appointment for her family because of abuses occurring within it. Cleo carefully probed and found out there was no immediate danger, but still something felt wrong. She took the names and addresses of family members and their relationship to one another as well as other details. Finally, she said to Helena: "I can see your family in my office at 9 a.m. tomorrow morning," to which Helena responded: "I hope you can straighten them out for me."

Cleo then realized what was happening. Helena was not planning to come to the session but instead was going to send her family to the therapist to be "fixed."

1. What would be your response to Helena at this point? What would you hope to accomplish by responding to her in this way?

2. What difficulties might arise if the referring members of a family did not come to a session?

In addition to these aspects of engaging the couple or family, it is crucial that the counsellor develop the capacity to draw some initial conclusions in regard to the way the couple or family behaves (e.g., in a family, who talks to whom and who sits next to whom). In this way the counsellor can gauge the dimensions of boundaries (i.e., those that allow closeness and care-giving versus ones that may be intrusive, such as a parent speaking for a child who is capable of speaking for him- or herself) (Worden, 2003). Intimacy and power can also be determined in this way. Essentially, through observation and engagement of the couple or family in conversation, the counsellor becomes attuned to the dynamics within the couple or family, which in the long run are usually as important as, if not more important than, the content of conversations that occur within the counselling process.

Overall, a first session(s) usually is one in which a counsellor evaluates how the couple or family is functioning and what may need to be done to help the relationship run more smoothly. Tentative goals are set, too, and a return appointment is made.

The Middle Phase of Marriage, Couple, and Family Counselling

The middle phase of marriage, couple, and family counselling consists of those sessions between the initial session(s) and termination. This part of treatment is where the couple or family will most likely make needed changes in themselves, if they change at all.

During this time, couples or families and the counsellor explore new behaviours and take chances. Couples and families that are not sure if they wish to change will often only make superficial alterations in what they do. This type of change is known as a *first-order change*. An example is parents setting a curfew back by an hour without any real discussion about it or the importance of a teenage daughter accepting responsibility for her actions. *Second-order change*, where structured rules are altered, is quite different and is the type of change that is hoped for in a couple or family undergoing therapy. An example of second-order change is a rigid, authoritarian family becoming more democratic by adopting new rules regarding family interactions after everyone has had a chance to make suggestions and give input in regard to them (Watzlawick et al., 1974).

In fostering change within the couple or family, the counsellor stays active mentally, verbally, and behaviourally (Friedlander, Wildman, Heatherington, & Skowron, 1994). The counsellor also makes sure the couple or family goes beyond merely understanding what they need to do because cognitive knowledge alone seldom produces change. In addition, during the middle phase of counselling, the counsellor links the couple or family with appropriate outside agencies, if possible. For example, in working with a family that has one or more members who are alcohol abusers, the counsellor makes sure they find out information about Alcoholics Anonymous (AA) (an organization of individuals who help one another stay sober), Al-Anon (a self-help organization for adult relatives and friends of people with drinking problems), and/or Alateen (a similar program to Al-Anon but for younger people, usually aged 12 to 19).

Throughout the middle phase of treatment, there is a continuous focus on the process of what is happening within the couple or family. In many cases, couples and families make the easiest changes first. Consequently, counsellors must press the couple or family for greater change if treatment is going to have any significance for them. The press is manifested in concentrating on cognitions, as well as their affective responses and behaviours (Worden, 2003). Sometimes this action is done in a straightforward manner; at other times it is accomplished through injecting humour into the therapeutic process, a right that a counsellor has to earn through first showing care and developing trust. An example of using humour in treatment to promote change can be seen in the following mother and daughter interaction:

Mother to daughter:	I will just die if she repeats that behaviour again.
Daughter to mother:	You will not. You're just trying to make me feel guilty.
Counsellor:	Sounds like this plan has worked before.
Daughter:	It has. But she never dies and I just get mad and frustrated.
Mother:	I tell you, if you do it one more time, I will die!
Counsellor to mother:	So your daughter is pretty powerful. She can end your life with an action?
Mother (dramatically):	Yes.
Counsellor to daughter:	And you have said before that you love your mother.
Daughter:	I do. But I'm tired of her reactions to what I do. They are just so overdone.
Counsellor to daughter:	But your mother says you are powerful and could kill her. Since you love her, I know you wouldn't do that. However, since you have so much power I wonder if you would ever consider paralyzing one of her arms with a lesser behaviour?
Mother:	What?!
Daughter (laughing):	Well, it might get her to stop harping at me and give us a chance to talk.
Counsellor to both:	Maybe that chance is now and no one has to suffer physically if we do it right.

The counsellor in this case addressed a pressing issue of power and drama in a serious but somewhat humorous way that got the attention of the two individuals most involved in the struggle, broke a dysfunctional pattern, and set up an opportunity for real dialogue and new interactions to emerge.

In addition to the previous ways of working, the counsellor must look for evidence of stability of change such as a couple or family accommodating more to one another through subtle as well as obvious means. For instance, seating patterns, the names family members call each other, or even the tone individuals use when addressing one another are all signs that somewhat permanent change has occurred in the couple or family if they differ greatly from where they were when the therapeutic process began. In the case of a couple or family that is changing, the tone of addressing one another might go from harsh to inviting.

In the middle phase of marriage, couple, and family counselling, it is crucial that the counsellor not get ahead of the couple or family members. Should that happen, therapeutic progress will end because the couple or family will not be invested. Therefore, staying on task and on target requires the counsellor to keep balanced and push only so far. A way to help couples and families stay engaged and make progress is to give them *homework* (i.e., tasks to complete outside of the counselling sessions such as setting aside time for a conversation) and *psychoeducational assignments* (i.e., reading a book or viewing a video) to complete together so that they are literally learning more and interacting together. For example, the family might watch some episodes from the 1960s comedy television show *The Addams Family*. They could then come back and talk about how they are like and unlike in regard to the macabre family they viewed. Such a way of working gives family members even more in common than would otherwise be the case, may draw them closer psychologically, and helps them clarify who they are and what they do.

Termination

Termination can be considered to be a misnomer in couple or family counselling since "from a family systems perspective, the therapist–family therapeutic system has reached an end point, but the family system certainly continues" (Worden, 2003, p. 187). Regardless, termination (including follow-up) is the final phase of treatment in working with couples and families.

The couple or family, the counsellor, or both may initiate termination. There is no one person who should start the process or one single way that termination should be conducted. However, termination should not be sudden and should not be seen as the highlight of counselling (Gladding, 2007). Rather, termination is designed to provide a counsellor and a couple or family with closure. It should be a means to assess whether couple or family goals have been reached.

Thus, in beginning termination, the counsellor and couple or family should ask themselves why they are entering this phase. One reason may be that enough progress has been made that the couple or family is now able to function on its own better than ever before. Likewise, everyone involved may agree that the couple or family has accomplished what it set out to do and that to continue would not be a wise investment in time or effort.

Whatever the reason for terminating, the counsellor should make sure that the work the couple or family has done is summarized and celebrated (if appropriate) so that the couple or family leaves counselling more aware and feeling stronger in realizing what they accomplished. In addition to summarization, another aspect of termination is deciding on *long-term goals*, such as creating a calm household where members are open to one another. This projective process gives couple and family members something to think about and plan out (sometimes with the counsellor's input). A part of many termination sessions involves *predicting setbacks* so that couples and families do not become too upset when they fail to achieve their goals as planned.

A final part of termination is *follow-up* (i.e., checking up on the couple or family following treatment after a period of time). Follow-up conveys care and lets couples and families know that they can return to counselling to finish anything they began there or to work on other issues. Client couples and families often do better when they have follow-up because they become aware that their progress is being monitored both within and outside the context in which they live.

A SELECTION OF POPULAR APPROACHES TO MARRIAGE, COUPLE, AND FAMILY COUNSELLING

The approaches described here will follow the same format used in earlier chapters to describe individual approaches to counselling: (a) their founders and developers, (b) the view of human nature, (c) the role of the counsellor, (d) goals, (e) techniques, (f) strengths and contributions, and (g) limitations. Also be aware that many counsellors who work with individuals will still operate from a systems perspective or will use an emotion-focused approach. Although the postmodern approaches (i.e., narrative, solution-focused, and collaborative) are often used in marriage, couple, and family counselling (MCFC) in Canada (Beaton et al., 2009), they were described earlier in Chapter 12 regarding individual approaches. The behavioural and cognitive-behavioural approaches are also very popular in MCFC and have the largest research base supporting their use (Sanderson et al., 2009). These approaches were discussed in Chapter 10.

Bowen Systems Theory

Founders and Developers One of the earliest systems approaches to working with clients, especially in regard to family members, was created by Murray Bowen (1913–1990). According to Bowen, who had personal difficulty with his own family of origin, individuals who do not examine and rectify patterns passed down from previous generations are likely to repeat them in their own families (Kerr, 1988). Therefore, it is important to examine the past so as to be informed in the present. Michael Kerr is the successor to Bowen at the Georgetown Family Center. Edwin Friedman also made major contributions to Bowen's systems work.

View of Human Nature Bowen believed that there is chronic anxiety in all life that is both emotional and physical. Some individuals are more affected than others by this anxiety "because of the way previous generations in their families have channeled the transmission" of it to them (Friedman, 1991, p. 139). If anxiety remains low, few problems exist for people or families. However, if anxiety becomes high, people are much more "prone to illness" and may become chronically dysfunctional (Greene, Hamilton, & Rolling, 1986, p. 189). Thus, the focus of Bowen systems theory is on *differentiation*, or distinguishing one's thoughts from one's emotions and oneself from others (Kerr & Bowen, 1988; Kim-Appel, Appel, Newman, & Parr, 2007).

For example, people marry at the same level of emotional maturity, with those who are less mature being prone to have a more difficult time in their marriage relationships than those who are more mature. When a great deal of friction exists in a marriage, less mature partners tend to display a high degree of *fusion* (undifferentiated emotional togetherness) or *cutoff* (physical or psychological avoidance) because they have not separated themselves from their families of origin in a healthy way, nor have they formed a stable self-concept. When they are stressed as persons within the marriage, these individuals tend to *triangulate* (focus on a third party) (Papero, 1996). The third party might be the marriage itself, a child, an institution (such as a church or school), or even a somatic complaint. Regardless, it leads to unproductive couple interactions.

Role of the Counsellor The role of the counsellor is to coach and teach the client to be more cognitive in his or her dealings with others. At its best, the process of counselling is "just like a Socratic dialogue, with the teacher or 'coach' calmly asking questions, until the student learns to think for him- or herself" (Wylie, 1991, p. 27). The counsellor may construct a multigenerational genogram with the client to aid in this process (see Figure 18.3).

Goals If counselling is successful, clients will understand and modify the coping strategies and patterns of coping with stress that have been passed on from generation to generation. They will display a non-anxious presence in their daily lives and will be able to separate their thoughts from their feelings and themselves from others.

Techniques Techniques in this approach focus on ways to create an individuated person with a healthy self-concept who can interact with others and not experience undue anxiety every time the relationship becomes stressful. Ways of achieving this goal include assessment of self and family in a number of ways. One of them is through the construction of a multigenerational *genogram*, which is a visual representation of a person's family tree depicted in geometric figures, lines, and words (Sherman, 1993). "Genograms include information related to a family and its members' relationships with each other over at least three generations. A genogram helps people gather information, hypothesize, and track relationship changes in the context of historic and contemporary events" (Gladding, 2007, pp. 143, 145).

Another technique is to focus on cognitive processes, such as asking *content-based questions* of one's family (Bowen, 1976). The objective is to understand what happened in one's family without any emotional overlay. A client may also *go home again* and visit with his or her family in order to get to know them better. Such a procedure promotes *person-to-person relationships* on a dyadic level and the *asking of questions* about pivotal events that had an impact on the family, such as deaths, births, and marriages. Asking questions is an especially important tool in Bowen's work.

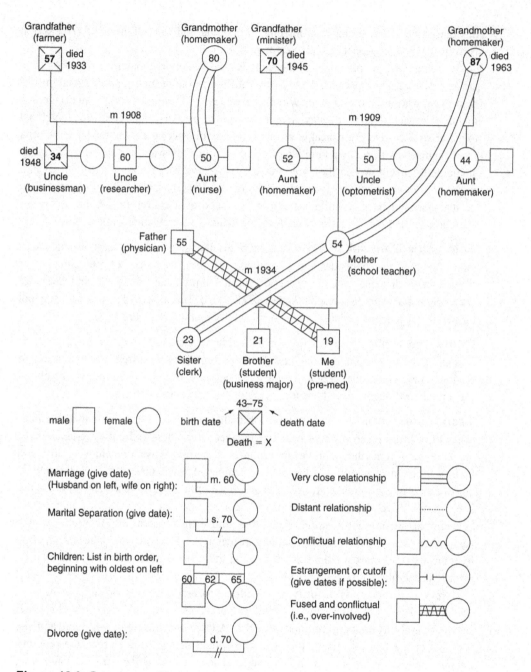

Figure 18.3 Genogram: Three generations of the Smith family (as of 1965)

Source: *Community and Agency Counseling*, by Samuel T. Gladding (p. 132). © 1997 by Prentice-Hall, Inc. Reprinted by permission of Pearson Education, Inc., Upper Saddle River, NJ.

In addition, there is a focus on *detriangulation*, which involves "the process of being in contact and emotionally separate" with others (Kerr, 1988, p. 55). Detriangulation operates on two levels. One is to resolve anxiety over family situations and not project feelings onto others. The second is to avoid becoming a target or scapegoat for people who may be overcome with anxiety. Finally, there is the *differentiation of self*, which is the ability of a person to distinguish between subjective feelings and objective thinking. Becoming differentiated involves most, if not all, of the techniques previously mentioned plus some confrontation between the client and counsellor.

Strengths and Contributions There are a number of unique aspects surrounding Bowen systems theory.

- The approach focuses on multigenerational family history and the importance of noticing and dealing with past patterns in order to avoid repeating these behaviours in interpersonal relationships.

- The approach uses the genogram to plot historical links, which is a specific tool that was originated with the Bowen approach. Today this instrument is borrowed by many other approaches.

- The cognitive emphasis of this approach and its focus on differentiation of self and detriangulation are unique.

Limitations Bowen systems theory is limited in these ways:

- The approach is extensive and complex. The theory is inseparable from the therapy and the intertwine makes the approach more involved than many other therapeutic approaches.

- Clients who benefit most from Bowen work are those who are severely dysfunctional or have a low differentiation of self.

- This approach may require considerable investment on multiple levels, which some clients may not be willing or able to do.

Structural Family Counselling

Founders and Developers Salvador Minuchin (1921–) is the founder of structural family counselling. Minuchin formulated the theory while serving as director of the Philadelphia Child Guidance Clinic in the 1960s. Braulio Montalvo and Jay Haley are also notable contributors to this approach.

View of Human Nature Every family has a structure, according to Minuchin (1974). A structure is the informal way a family organizes itself and interacts. Structure influences people in families for better or worse. If there is a hierarchical structure, people relate well to each other. However, if there is no such structure or little structure, developmental or situational events increase family stress, rigidity, chaos, and dysfunctionality, throwing the family into crisis. In such circumstances, *coalitions* (i.e., alliances between specific members against a third member) or *cross-generational alliances* (alliances between family members of two different generations) arise. Neither works well in the healthy growth of individuals or a family.

Role of the Counsellor Structural family counselling practitioners are both observers and experts in making interventions to modify and change the underlying structure of a family. They advocate for structural changes in the organization of the family unit, with particular attention on changing interactional patterns in subsystems of the family, such as in the marital dyad. They also work at establishing clear boundaries among family members (Minuchin, Montalvo, Guerney, Rosman, & Schumer, 1967).

In working with families, structural family counsellors join with the family in a position of leadership. They map in their minds the structure of a family, determining how it is stuck in a dysfunctional pattern, and how to help it change.

Goals In structural family therapy, action is emphasized over insight in order to alter and reorganize a family into a more functional and productive unit. Dated and outgrown rules are replaced with ones that are more related to the family's current realities. Distinctions and differentiation between subsystems are stressed with a special focus on parents being in charge of their children. If all works well, the cultural context of a family is changed.

Techniques Structuralists employ a number of techniques aimed at getting a family to change the way it operates (Minuchin & Fishman, 1981). One primary technique is to work with *family interaction*. When family members repeat nonproductive sequences of behaviour or demonstrate a disengaged or enmeshed position in the family structure, the counsellor will rearrange the physical environment so they have to act in a different way. The technique may be as simple as having people face each other when they talk.

Structural family counsellors also use *reframing*, a technique that involves helping the family see its problem from a different and more positive perspective. For example, if a child is misbehaving, the behaviour may be labelled "naughty" instead of "crazy." As a consequence, the child and his or her actions will be viewed as less pathological.

Other structural techniques include the following:

- *Punctuation*—"the selective description of a transaction" (Colapinto, 2000, p. 158); for instance, declaring a person competent at a specific moment in time

- *Unbalancing*—a procedure wherein the counsellor supports an individual or subsystem against the rest of the family (e.g., a daughter who is lobbying against her parents for a later curfew)

- *Enactment*—a process that consists of a family bringing its problematic behaviours, such as making decisions, into treatment sessions and demonstrating them. In the process, the counsellor challenges existing patterns and rules as the family gains heightened awareness of the way each member functions.

- *Boundary making*—the process of creating lines that separate people or subsystems from each other psychologically in order to maximize individual and group development and functioning

- *Intensity*—the structural method of changing maladaptive transactions by using strong affect, repeated intervention, or prolonged pressure in order to help an individual or family reach a goal by doing something differently (Minuchin & Fishman, 1981)

- *Restructuring*—changing the structure of a family by altering existing hierarchies or interaction patterns so that problems are not maintained (e.g., uniformly refusing to obey a certain request or to act in a specific way)

- *Adding cognitive constructions*—the verbal component of what is a primarily action-oriented approach that includes advice, information, pragmatic fictions (i.e., pronouncements that help people change), and *paradox* (a confusing message, such as "don't change," meant to frustrate and motivate an individual or group to seek alternative actions)

Strengths and Contributions Structural family therapy is unique in its contribution to counselling in the following ways:

- The approach is quite versatile; it is appropriate for low socioeconomic-level families as well as high-income families (Minuchin, Colapinto, & Minuchin, 1999).

- The approach is effective, having been used in treating juvenile delinquents, alcoholics, and anorexics (Fishman, 1988).

- The approach is culturally sensitive and appropriate for use in multicultural settings.

- The approach is clear in its definition of terms and procedures and is easily applicable.

- The approach emphasizes symptom removal and a reorganization of the family in a pragmatic way.

Limitations The structural approach's main limitations include the following:

- Critics have charged that structural work is not complex enough, may be sexist at times, and focuses too much on the present.

- The accusation that structural therapy has been influenced by strategic family therapy and the charge that it is difficult to distinguish it from strategic therapy at times is problematic.

- Since the counsellor is in charge of the process of change, families may not become empowered enough, which may limit their overall adjustment and change in the future (Friesen, 1985).

Strategic (Brief) Counselling

Founders and Developers John Weakland, Paul Watzlawick, Jay Haley, Cloe Madanes, and the Milan Group (Selvini-Palazzoli, Boscolo, Cecchin, & Prata, 1978) are prominent leaders in the strategic school of counselling. This school and the individuals who are proponents of it are subdivided into several branches—the Mental Research Institute (California), the Milan Systemic theory approach (Italy), and the Family Therapy Institute (Washington, DC). Nevertheless, there are some common threads that weave the strategic counselling approach together so that it is recognizable as an entity with a number of subgroup emphases.

View of Human Nature Strategic theory is based on the belief that when dysfunctional symptoms occur, they are an attempt to help people adapt. This approach sees problems as occurring within a developmental framework of the family life cycle. For instance, marital difficulties are generated by the system the couple is in. Consequently, the symptoms that emerge help maintain the marital system in which they operate (Todd, 1986).

As a group, strategic counsellors focus on several dimensions of family life that are developmentally significant, such as

- *family rules*—the overt and covert rules families use to govern themselves,
- *family homeostasis*—the tendency of families to remain in their same pattern of functioning unless challenged to do otherwise,
- *quid pro quo*—the responsiveness of family members to treat each other in the ways they are treated (i.e., something for something), and
- *circular causality*—the idea that events are interconnected and that factors behind a behaviour are multiple.

Role of the Counsellor Strategic counsellors take a systemic view of problem behaviours and focus on the process rather than on the content of dysfunctional interactions. The job of a strategic counsellor is to get people to try new behaviours because their old behaviours are not working. Usually, a specific behaviour is targeted for change. If this behaviour can be modified, a *spillover effect* is hypothesized; that is, the results will help individuals make other behaviour changes as well.

Thus, strategic counsellors strive to resolve presenting problems and pay little attention to instilling insight. To bring about change, counsellors are active, direct, and goal-oriented as well as problem-focused, pragmatic, and brief (Snider, 1992; Todd, 1986). They usually limit the number of times they see families to 10 visits or less.

Goals The idea behind the strategic approach is to resolve, remove, or ameliorate a problematic behaviour brought to counselling. In the process, new functional behaviours are generated that will help individuals, couples, and families achieve a specific goal. By limiting the number of sessions available for treatment, strategic counsellors hope to increase the motivation and determination of the client to be successful. Another goal of the approach is for the persons involved in the process to learn new skills for resolving future conflicts.

Techniques As a group, strategic family counsellors are quite innovative. Each intervention is tailored to the specifics of persons and problems. This customization makes strategic counselling one of the most technique-driven approaches to helping in systems theory. Strategic family counsellors are non-blaming, avoid pathological labels, accept the presenting problems of families, and view symptoms as serving the positive purpose of communication.

Relabelling (giving a new perspective to a behaviour) is frequently used. (For example, in regard to asking for a second helping of pie several times, Johnny's behaviour might be relabelled "assertive" rather than "rude.") *Paradoxing* (insisting on just the opposite of what one wants) and *prescribing the symptom* (having the couple or family display voluntarily what they had previously manifested involuntarily, such as fighting) are employed, too. In addition, the counsellor may use *pretend* to have the client make changes or carry out homework assignments that would not be completed otherwise (Madanes, 1984; Minuchin, 1974).

Individuals or families are sometimes asked to go through *ordeals*, such as travelling or suffering, during the treatment process. The idea is that, if people have to make sacrifices to get better, the long-term improvements of treatment are enhanced. A major aspect of strategic family counselling is the assignment of original *homework* tasks (often given in the form of prescriptions or directives) that are to be completed between sessions.

Strengths and Contributions Like other approaches, strategic counsellors have unique aspects to what they do and how. Among the most prominent of these emphases are the following:

- Many of these therapists work in teams.
- The nature of the approach is pragmatic and flexible.
- The focus of practitioners is on innovation and creativity, which is in the lineage of Milton Erickson, who was especially good at devising novel ways to help his clients.
- The emphasis of the approach is to change the perceptions of people as a way of fostering new behaviours.
- A deliberate attempt is made to work on one problem at a time and limit the number of sessions clients can be seen so that the focus and motivation for doing things differently is enhanced.
- The approach may be modified and carried over into settings such as schools, where it may be systemically applied to serve a total population, as well as individuals and families (Nelson, 2006).

Limitations The limitations of the strategic approach are few in number but significant.

- First, some of its underlying foundation and techniques overlap with other system and brief therapy theories. Therefore, there is sometimes confusion as to whether a counsellor is using the strategic approach or another approach, such as the structural.

- Second, some of the stands taken by leading strategic practitioners are controversial, such as Jay Haley's view that schizophrenia is not biologically based.

- Finally, the emphasis within strategic camps on the expertise and power of the counsellor may mean that clients do not attain as much independence or ability as they might otherwise.

Emotion-Focused Couples and Family Therapy (EFCFT)

Founders and Developers EFCFT was developed in the early 1980s by Canadian researchers Sue Johnson and Les Greenberg. It is a short-term approach, lasting eight to twenty sessions, on average. Research has shown it to be effective, with 90% of couples showing significant improvement. Johnson and Greenberg's research and training centre, located in Ottawa, is called the International Centre for Excellence in Emotionally Focused Therapy (ICEEFT, 2007).

View of Human Nature EFCFT counsellors believe that "relationships are at the core of human experience" (ICEEFT, 2007, para. 2). If a nurturant social environment exists, people will maximize their potential.

Role of the Counsellor The EFCFT counsellor focuses on creating a stronger and healthier emotional bond between partners in a couple and/or between family members. Often anger is a secondary emotion, masking the primary emotion(s) of fear, shame, sadness, abandonment, invalidation, violation, and so on. The counsellor's goal is to help clients identify their primary emotions and express them to others (Greenberg & Goldman, 2008).

Goals ICEEFT seeks to create a shift in how couples or family members relate to one another. Another goal is to enhance the emotional bond between the individuals involved. The expression of underlying feelings is believed to be important to the change process that occurs in EFCFT (Greenberg, Paul, & Conry, 1988). Another goal may be to help partners or family members forgive one another for perceived or actual wrongdoings (Greenberg, Warwar, & Malcolm, 2010).

Techniques Johnson and Greenberg (Greenberg & Goldman, 2008) recently expanded their five-stage framework to include 14 steps for counsellors offering EFCFT:

I. Validate and establish the working alliance.
   1. Show empathy and validation to the clients.
   2. Determine and assess the conflicts between them.

II. De-escalate the negative cycle that has developed.
   3. Identify the negative cycle, each person's role in it, and then externalize the problem.
   4. Identify the attachment- and/or identity-related emotions that reside in each person's position.
   5. Identify each person's weak areas and sensitivities and their origins.
   6. Reframe the problem in terms of unmet attachment and identity needs.
III. Access underlying feelings.
   7. Identify or delve into the unexpressed or unacknowledged feelings of each person and have him or her relay this to the others present.
   8. If blocks in accessing these feelings occur, help each person overcome them so these emotions can be accurately expressed.
   9. Help each person identify needs and aspects of self that have been disowned, and then bring these into the interactions with the others present.
IV. Restructure the negative communications.
   10. Help the clients accept each other's experience and aspects of disowned self.
   11. Facilitate the expression of feelings, wants, and needs to create genuine, authentic interaction and engagement.
   12. Promote each person's ability to self-soothe and work at transforming unhelpful emotions to facilitate self-change and lasting couples/familial change.
V. Consolidate and integrate the changes.
   13. Facilitate the new ways of relating to one another and help remediate unhelpful interactions.
   14. Foster the consolidation of new narratives and new ways of seeing each other.

Strengths and Contributions The following are some of the strengths of this approach:

- The approach is based on empirical research and on Bowlby's well-known attachment theory.
- It has been validated through 20 years of empirical research.
- It has been successfully applied to many different types of problems and populations.
- The strategies and interventions are clearly articulated (ICEEFT, 2007).

Limitations The following limitations apply to EFCFT:

- Although Johnson (2003) claimed that EFCFT is the *most* effective form of couples therapy based on her perusal of the research, Sparks and Duncan (2010) critique this claim. They suggest that it is fraught with difficulty for the founder of a therapy to become the primary auditor of its effectiveness.

- The studies exploring EFCFT have in some cases been done on less distressed samples than those using behavioural family therapy (Wright, Sabourin, Mondor, McDuff, & Mamodhoussen, 2007).

- EFCFT is contraindicated where violence is present in the relationship or family unit (ICEEFT, 2007).

- The approach might not be valued in cultures where strong display of emotions is discouraged or frowned upon.

EFFECTIVENESS AND LIMITATIONS OF MARRIAGE, COUPLE, AND FAMILY COUNSELLING

Rather than learn what approach to use with each disorder, Sparks and Duncan (2010) recommend that today's marriage, couple, and family (MCF) counsellor learn to deliver an approach that is a good fit and that is beneficial in the moment. Rather than being driven by theory and ideology, the future of MCF counselling will likely give way to practices that are *evidence-based*—techniques that have demonstrated their effectiveness through rigorous empirical outcome studies (Carr, 2009). An important issue in the MCF field today is increasing sensitivity to diversity (Carr, 2009).

Indications

Cross-cultural research has indicated that the three most common issues that clients bring to MCF counsellors in Canada and the United States are couple/marital issues, depression, and anxiety (Beaton et al., 2009). Family therapy is considered the appropriate choice of treatment for familial conflict, pre- and post-divorce adjustment, parental remarriage, and coping with the illness or death of a family member. For children and adolescents, it is appropriate for psychological problems (depression, anxiety) and behavioural problems (substance abuse, delinquency) (Lambert & Williams, 2009).

Effectiveness

Family As one would expect, Manassis (2005) indicated that the effectiveness of family therapy varies greatly by disorder. It has been found useful with the conditions mentioned above, as well as reducing the incidence of relapse with schizophrenia and with anorexia nervosa. Behavioural management training for parents with children having school problems has shown favourable results with lasting effects up to 14 years (Miller & McLeod, 2001). Carr (2009) stated that family counselling is effective with academic problems, with adolescents associating with negative influence peers, and possibly even in the treatment of bipolar disorder. It has *not* been found very effective in treating autism or

ADHD, however (Manassis, 2005). Similar to individual counselling, the most evaluated interventions are those belonging to the behavioural and cognitive-behavioural approaches (Qualls & Anderson, 2009; Sanderson et al., 2009).

Family therapy has been attempted through use of video-conferencing, whereby the family members stay in their own home. The handful of studies currently available suggest promising results. It may be as effective as face-to-face therapy (Gilkey, Carey, & Wade, 2009). However, some families may be uncomfortable with technology and counsellors need to discourage distractions (e.g., phones, televisions, some members entering and leaving the room) (Gilkey et al., 2009).

Couples The current push in many treatment modalities is toward evidence-based practices, and this is also true for marriage and couple (MC) therapy (Wright et al., 2007). Sparks and Duncan (2010) noted that between 40 and 50% of couples attain complete recovery status with MC therapy. Meta-analytic studies have generally shown that MC counselling does effectively reduce relationship distress (Wright et al., 2007). Couples counselling where one partner is depressed has also proven helpful, in addition to adult substance misuse (Carr, 2009). In comparison to family therapy, the statistical effect sizes are generally higher for marriage and couples counselling (Sparks & Duncan, 2010).

Limitations

A criticism of family approaches is that they lack a uniform theory and consistency in their intervention methods (Chan, 2003). Surprisingly, despite the recommendation by many theorists—including Ackerman, Minuchin, and Satir—that children be included in family therapy, in actuality most family therapists do not do so (Miller & McLeod, 2001).

Perhaps the greatest limitation of supporting the inclusion of children in family therapy is the lack of empirical evidence to support its efficacy (Miller & McLeod, 2001). Regarding MC counselling, most longitudinal follow-up studies show that many couples experience limited recovery, and some decline in relationship functioning occurs over time (Wright et al., 2007). Furthermore, relapses are common (Wright et al., 2007).

SUMMARY AND CONCLUSION

Canadian families have changed over the years from a few dominant forms to a great many varieties. These changes were brought about by a number of forces within society, such as the women's movement, global and regional wars, and federal legislation. With these changes has come a greater need for working with married and unmarried couples as well as families. The professions of marriage, couple, and family counselling have grown rapidly since the 1950s for a number of reasons, including theory development and proven research effectiveness. It has also prospered because it has had strong advocates and has generated a number of unique and effective approaches for a variety of couple and family forms.

Professionals who enter the marriage, couple, and family counselling field in Canada align with either the American Association for Marriage and Family Therapy (AAMFT) and/or their own professional association. Regardless of affiliation, those who work with couples and families need to know the life cycle of families in order to assess whether a marriage or family problem is developmental or situational. Marriage, couple, and family counsellors also need to be aware of systems theories and the ways that couples and families work systemically.

The field of marriage counselling is sometimes incorporated into family counselling models, but professionals in this specialty need to be aware of the theories and processes that are used in each area. They must also realize how individual or group theories may complement or detract from work with families. Furthermore, marriage, couple, and family counsellors need to be well-schooled in the stages that family counselling entails— preplanning, initial session(s), the middle phase, and termination—and the general techniques and emphasis within each.

The common approaches to marriage, couple, and family counselling include Bowen systems theory, structural family therapy, and strategic therapy; approaches originating in Canada include emotion-focused marriage, couple, and family counselling.

Overall, working with couples and families is a dynamic and exciting way of helping people. Because of its complexity and the intricacies of the process, it is not for everyone, but it is an entity that many counsellors seem to enjoy and from which many people in society benefit.

Your Personal Reflections

1. What type of family did you grow up in? What were its strengths? What were its weaknesses? What type of family listed in this chapter would you prefer, if you could choose? Why?

2. Who were you closest to in your family of origin? Who were you most distant from? What factors or events brought you together? What factors or events distanced you from one another?

3. Most people today carry cell phones. What do you notice about their ring tones? Are some more appealing than others? Could the same kind of linkage be made in regard to the tones family members use with each other? How would you react if your ring tone always conveyed a harsh sound?

4. Every family has a "family dance," a sequence of actions within the family that repeat when certain situations arise, such as yelling and then withdrawing from each other during stress. What was one of the dances your family of origin engaged in when you were growing up? Was your family ever able to structure it differently (i.e., create a new pattern)?

5. Which approach to marriage, couple, or family counselling are you most attracted to? What most attracts you to that approach? Likewise, what approach are you least attracted to, and why?

Classroom Activities

1. What family forms (e.g., nuclear, dual-career, blended, multicultural, etc.) are you most familiar with? How do you think this knowledge could help or hinder you in working with couples and families?

2. Determine where you are in your own family life cycles. If the life cycle does not fit for you, explain why you think this is the case. Talk with a classmate about what changes you anticipate making in the next few years because of life-cycle demands.

3. What are the advantages and disadvantages of working with individuals with family concerns on a one-to-one basis rather than a family counselling basis? Do you think it is possible to work effectively with only one member of a couple or family? Divide the class into two teams and debate the issue.

4. Which processes in marriage, couple, and family counselling do you prefer or believe you might be best at accomplishing? What are the reasons behind your decision? Form groups with classmates who share your view and present your rationale to other class members.

5. Research the contributions of a pioneer in marriage, couple, and family counselling. What legacy did the person leave? Are there processes or techniques this individual advocated that are still used with couples and families today?

6. In pairs, reflect on a time when you were angry. According to emotion-focused theory, anger is a secondary emotion. Share with your dyad partner the primary emotion(s) that was occurring at the time. Then discuss whether sharing this primary emotion(s) with someone else, such as a counsellor but particularly with the person who precipitated your anger (if it was triggered by someone else), would have been a helpful practice for you in this instance.

Chapter 19
Counselling Children, Adolescents, and Young Adults

PRACTICE REFLECTION

I have a 22-year-old client at the moment who I will call Derrick. Sadly, Derrick has little self-esteem when it comes to most aspects of his life. His girlfriend broke up with him a few months ago, telling him that he was not "masculine enough." If by this she meant that he does not fit the traditional male gender role of rough, rugged, and ready, she would be correct. Instead, Derrick is an intellectually gifted young man who is particularly sensitive, gentle, and unassuming.

My main approach to help Derrick has been to use cognitive-behaviour therapy (CBT). Derrick continues to have automatic thoughts that tell him he is worthless, unattractive, unlovable, and lacking in every life area. In effect, he believes he is not smart enough and not good enough. Derrick's father is aggressive, perfectionistic, judgmental, and harsh toward his sons when they don't live up to his expectations. Regardless of Derrick's early years, when using CBT one adopts the view that problems are only maintained in the present because of irrational and self-perpetuating automatic thoughts.

In CBT, there are many techniques that can be used, but in general they involve questioning the irrationality embedded in these automatic thoughts and collaboratively coming up with rational alternatives. Once these rational responses are uncovered, it is important that clients learn to indoctrinate themselves through various means into actually believing them. After all, there is a difference between knowing something (e.g., learning about the Bible) and actually believing it (e.g., having deeply rooted Christian beliefs).

In Derrick's case, I have had him make use of a triple column by writing down his automatic thoughts (first column below) as they occur, questioning these thoughts (see sample questions below), and then writing down a rational response (third column below). The questioning aspect means subjecting the automatic thoughts to a Socratic-like challenge:

1. What proof do I have that this is true?
2. Do I have any evidence that indicates it is not true?
3. Are there any competing "truths"? Is another belief just as valid?
4. Does everyone think this way? Why not?

   Below is the chart that Derrick uses:

Maladaptive Thought or Belief	Questioning It	Healthier Thought or Belief

Progress is slower than I wish, but I do not set the timing of when someone will internalize healthier beliefs. A counsellor is a facilitator of change but not the one who ultimately must internalize the sought-after change.

The Diagnostic and Statistical Manual of Mental Disorders *(DSM)—the book physicians and psychologists use in Canada and the United States to provide diagnoses—contains a section called "Disorders Usually First Diagnosed in Infancy, Childhood, or Adolescence." Many of the problems that adults face begin in the formative years of life. Working with children and youth requires that a counsellor be aware of what normal development (and, alternatively, abnormal development) looks like at various ages, and knowing what treatments are likely to be impactful when behaviour runs amuck.*

This chapter will begin with reviewing some of the important considerations in counselling children and youth, particularly from a Canadian perspective. Then it will move into looking at the role of the school counsellor both in grade schools (elementary, middle, and secondary) and in postsecondary institutions. Some children are developmentally ready to begin school, eager and able, whereas others are disadvantaged because of physical, mental, cultural, or socioeconomic factors. Yet a third group carries the burden of traumas, such as various forms of abuse, through no fault of their own (Fontes, 2002; Richardson & Norman, 1997).

Like children in other countries, Canadian schoolchildren face a barrage of complex events and processes that have temporary and permanent impacts on them. Alcohol and other drug abuse, changing family patterns, poor self-esteem, hopelessness, AIDS, racial and ethnic tensions, crime and violence, teenage pregnancy, sexism, and the explosion of knowledge have negative influence on these children regardless of their age or environment (Keys & Bemak, 1997; McGowan, 1995).

Counselling interventions can make a difference, whether offered outside or within school settings. More than 30 years of research have concluded that, in school environments, "counseling interventions have a substantial impact on students' educational and personal development" (Borders & Drury, 1992, p. 495). Meta-analysis studies have shown that, overall, counselling interventions generally have a moderate but clear effect on altering problematic child and adolescent behaviours (Prout, 2007).

GENERAL CONSIDERATIONS

PROUT (2007) CITED SEVERAL STUDIES SUGGESTING THAT ANYWHERE FROM 10 TO 22% OF youth experience some form of emotional, behavioural, or developmental problem. The most current research suggests a prevalence rate of about 20%; however, about 10% have a problem that substantially affects their functioning. Some problems, such as antisocial/delinquent behaviours and substance abuse, are currently on the increase. Clearly, many youth are in need of counselling services. A national report to the federal Minister of Health in 2007 indicated that mental health was one of the three top priorities for Canadian children and youth (Kutcher & McLuckie, 2009). However, the gravest concern mentioned by school counsellors at the 2010 Canadian Association of Counselling and Psychotherapy Conference was that counselling services are often targeted for cutbacks when provincial and territorial budgets are tight while concurrently the demand for school counselling has increased (J. Graham-Migel, personal communication, May 12, 2010). Little seems to have changed since Paterson and Janzen (1993) provided their report regarding school counselling in Canada. Furthermore, there continues to be no national Canadian standard for school counselling; consequently, many school counsellors have little more than a Bachelor of Education degree in their chosen field (e.g., math, English, social studies).

In counselling children and adolescents, it is important to remember that they are not "little adults." Consideration must be given to factors like (a) their developmental stage, (b) their environment, (c) their reasons for beginning counselling, and (d) other relevant considerations that will likely necessitate a different and perhaps creative approach to working with them successfully (Prout, 2007). For example, most children and adolescents (herein referred to as "youth") do not initiate a request for counselling. Instead, a caregiver or concerned adult makes the referral. Consequently, youth may have (a) little interest in pursuing counselling (if any at all), (b) an uncooperative spirit, (c) little insight into their problem, and (d) no idea what counselling is or how it is supposed to be helpful (Prout, 2007).

Unlike most adults, the personality of youth is still forming. Their defense mechanisms are less entrenched as well. Consequently, counselling youth has the potential to be helpful in changing both personality and their response to stress (Prout, 2007). On the flip side, adolescents are more likely than adults to be "impatient, intolerant, and uncommunicative" (Prout, 2007, p. 12) when entering a counselling relationship. In light of all these concerns, the youth counsellor will likely need to spend more time creating a positive working alliance than is required for most adult clients. To be successful in this, it helps if the counsellor can relate to youth in developmentally appropriate ways, knowing their common concerns, their slang, and their culture (Prout, 2007). Following the creation of a working alliance, the counsellor will likely find greatest success with an approach that is "here and now" focused instead of psychoanalytic or psychodynamic (Weiner, 1992).

Regarding developmental stage, a youth counsellor needs to have awareness of what is considered normal or typical development and what is considered abnormal, atypical, or unhealthy development. Consequently, the counsellor needs to have a good understanding of the developmental stage theories, including those of Freud, Piaget, Kohlberg, and Erikson (Prout, 2007). As these theories are covered in every developmental text, they will not be elaborated here. Nonetheless, a few examples will make the point.

- *Freud's theory.* Working with a 10-year-old girl who is sexually interested and preoccupied is atypical. Girls and boys of this age are in the latency period, where sexual interests are very low. A girl or boy experiencing this has likely been sexualized, either without coercion (e.g., perhaps the parents talk a lot about sex openly with their child or the child is exposed to erotica) or with coercion (e.g., sexual abuse).

- *Piaget's theory.* Working with a child in the pre-operational, operational, or formal operational phase will require different interventions based on his or her cognitive ability and limitations. Children who are eight years old are not going to articulate a well-reasoned opinion on why the famous Milgram study is unethical by today's standards, for example.

- *Kohlberg's theory.* A 13-year-old boy at a lower stage of moral development may be inclined toward delinquency. Interventions aimed at fostering moral development may be instrumental in helping to prevent childhood deviance.

- *Erikson's theory.* A nine-year-old girl who suffers guilt when she does well at school has perhaps not successfully worked through the initiative versus guilt stage. As this is usually accomplished during the pre-school years through the positive influence of primary caregivers, a youth counsellor should be interested in knowing the extent of family dysfunction.

Normal adolescent development is characterized by a period of storm and stress, meaning that teens often experience distressing and unpredictable thoughts, feelings, and behaviours. Weiner (1992) warns that counsellors of adolescents must be careful not to pathologize behaviours in teens that might seem bizarre. On the other hand, the discerning counsellor must also be capable of recognizing thoughts, emotions, and behaviours that are abnormal and fall in the range of psychotic as some clinicians believe that early intervention is helpful (Addington, Addington, Jones, & Ko, 2001).

Current research from British Columbia found that the percentage of youth having sexual intercourse decreased between 1992 and 2003 (males down from 33.9% to 23.3%; females down from 28.6% to 24.3%) (Saewyc, Taylor, Homma, & Ogilvie, 2008). National research reveals that Canadian adolescents find oral sex to be a good alternative to vaginal sex (Dalton & Galambos, 2009). There is also evidence that the sexual health of Canadians teens and young adults is better than in previous generations and that they are using condoms more consistently, although sexually transmitted diseases are still a problem, particularly with youth living in poverty, those living in rural areas, and Aboriginal youth (Maticka-Tyndale, 2008).

Copeland (1974) provides several characteristics of adolescent thought and behaviour that are common and therefore not usually indicative of pathology.

1. *Self-preoccupation.* The adolescent may appear quite narcissistic as they learn to focus on themselves.

2. *Fantasy preoccupation.* Fantasy is often used as a means of controlling the strong drives and feelings that teens experience.

3. *Self-expression preoccupation.* This often reflects the adolescent's quest to develop a unique sense of identity.

4. *Theories, ideas, and philosophical preoccupation.* Along with formal operational thoughts comes a desire to understand the world with greater complexity than in the past. The search, however, is still often for "absolute truths" and "ultimate reality."

5. *Sexuality preoccupation.* Most teens are very interested in sexuality, not surprising given the surge in sex hormones released following puberty. They may also become preoccupied with their dress and their appearance.

6. *Asceticism and/or hedonism preoccupation.* The intensity of an adolescent's drive requires a response, and the choice is often whether to deny gratification out of guilt or pursue it wholeheartedly.

7. *Conformity*. Most adolescents (at least those from an individualistic culture) shift their focus from their parents to their peers, and their need to conform also shifts to their peer group. Consequently, their dress and other interests may be in sharp contrast to that of their parents.

A Brief History of Youth Counselling

Most view Sigmund Freud's conceptualization of "Little Hans" and his phobia as the first attempt to treat and conceptualize a childhood disorder. Not surprisingly, then, the first movement in youth treatment became the psychoanalytic approach, and Freud's daughter Anna and Melanie Klein fostered the expansion of this approach with children (Prout, 2007). Psychoanalytic treatment remained popular through the 1940s and into the 1950s.

In 1947, Virginia Axline had her book on play therapy published. This was a non-directive approach to play therapy and effectively became a child version of Rogers's person-centred counselling.

The next movement was behavioural and, in the 1960s, it became the most frequently used approach with youth. Today, the recent movement involves approaches that are evidence-based (Prout, 2007). As the behavioural and cognitive-behavioural approaches have the largest research base, most evidence-based treatments have remained cognitive-behavioural, although there is growing evidence that interpersonal therapy with adolescents is effacious with depression (Lee, 2007).

Evidence-Based Treatments with Youth

The *Journal of Clinical Child and Adolescent Psychology* (formerly the *Journal of Clinical Child Psychology*) has served as the flagship journal for Section 1 of Division 12 (Clinical Psychology) of the American Psychological Association (Silverman & Hinshaw, 2008). This journal has published two issues—one in 1998 (see Lonigan, Elbert, & Johnson, 1998) and one in 2008 (see Silverman & Hinshaw, 2008)—devoted to evidence-based treatments for youth. For a treatment to be considered evidence-based, it needs to be considered both efficacious and effective.

Efficacy means that the treatment has been shown in experimental studies to reduce symptoms and impairment when the study has used random assignment, control groups, and manualized procedures. Such studies are high in internal validity. *Effectiveness* means that the treatment has been shown in real-life settings to reduce symptoms and impairment. These studies typically occur in mental health clinics and private practice settings and have high external validity (Silverman & Hinshaw, 2008).

Specifically, articles were published in these two issues that provide empirical support for the treatment of "autism, depression, phobic and anxiety, disruptive behavior disorders (including oppositional defiant and conduct disorder), and ADHD [attention-deficit hyperactivity disorder]" (Silverman & Hinshaw, 2008, p. 4). Lee (2007) from the

University of Ottawa has developed a course that focuses on evidence-based approaches for children and their families. Thomas, Solorzano, and Cobb (2007) provided a list of considerations for counselling ethnic-minority youth. While play therapy may be effective with children facing medical procedures, it lacks empirical support for other childhood problems or disorders (Phillips, 2010).

Counsellors are well advised to do a literature search for the evidence-based treatments that might exist for a certain problem before deciding on a treatment plan. Such treatments often represent the quickest and most effective methods available; they are also one's best defense against a possible misconduct allegation.

Common Disorders in Youth

Sadly, research reveals that the number and intensity of childhood behaviour problems is slowly increasing while children's ability to cope is concomitantly decreasing (Miller & McLeod, 2001). The "psychosocial adjustment of children is directly related to parenting style and communication" (Miller & McLeod, 2001, p. 377). Working successfully with children often means working with the parents as well.

Although many people guess that ADHD is the most common problem that children present to counsellors, in actuality the most common presenting problems are anxiety and depression (Miller & McLeod, 2001). The lifetime rate for anxiety disorders beginning in childhood is between 10 and 22%. Depression has a lifetime prevalence rate of between 2 and 17%, and depression is being diagnosed at increasing frequencies with children (Miller & McLeod, 2001). Depression left untreated may lead to suicide.

Following motor vehicle accidents, which claim the highest number of young lives in Canada, suicide is the second leading cause of death for youth aged 10 to 24. Each year, 294 youths in Canada die from suicide and, unfortunately, many more attempt it. Aboriginal teens and gay and lesbian youth are at particularly high risk (Canadian Children's Rights Council, 1998–2010).

Addiction is also a problem for some youth. A Canadian study of 19 018 students in 2002 and 29 243 students in 2004 in Grades 7 to 9 revealed that alcohol was the most prevalent substance used by youth, compared to tobacco and marijuana (Leatherdale, Hammond, & Ahmed, 2008). It was rare to find youth who had smoked marijuana or tobacco without having used alcohol at some point. The researchers concluded that alcohol, tobacco, and marijuana are used by a substantial number of youth, despite laws forbidding their use. Furthermore, their results were consistent with previous studies from Canada and the United States. Parental rejection is positively associated with drug usage while parental warmth is negatively correlated with it (Pires & Jenkins, 2007).

Violent behaviour by youth has also increasingly become a concern. Violent crime rates for youth were higher in 1998 compared to 1988 (Willoughby & Perry, 2002), and while most youth become less aggressive over time, one sixth of boys (mostly from disadvantaged backgrounds) in a study of 10 658 Canadian children became increasingly physically aggressive over a six-year period (Cote, Vaillancourt, LeBlanc, Nagin, & Tremblay, 2006). Aboriginal youth in Canada are overrepresented in the youth correctional system, and they are generally given longer sentences than non-Aboriginal youth (Latimer & Foss, 2005). Bullying behaviour has also become of enormous interest to researchers around the world, those in Canada included (Pepler, Jiang, Craig, & Connolly, 2008).

Youth in care (e.g., foster homes, residential treatment centres) often have families of origin where there is abuse, neglect, or domestic violence (Marquis & Flynn, 2009). They are at increased risk of developing mental health problems, including (a) poor interpersonal skills, (b) problems in mood regulation, (c) anxiety, (d) low self-esteem, and (e) aggressiveness (Marquis & Flynn, 2009). Again, in Canada Aboriginal youth are grossly overrepresented in youth care facilities, comprising approximately 35% of the in-care youth population (Filbert & Flynn, 2010). A promising approach in child and youth care work is providing services within the home to troubled youth and their families (Phelan, 2003).

COUNSELLING IN CANADIAN SCHOOLS

Historically, professional school counsellors have been asked to perform multiple duties as part of their daily work. Some school counsellors have struggled to prove their worth to superintendents, principals, teachers, students, and parents who sometimes have misunderstood what they do (Guerra, 1998). As mentioned earlier, Canadian school counsellors do not have a national set of standards and many are practising without adequate counselling credentials.

The Canadian Education Association (2010) is Canada's oldest national education association, first established in 1891. It wasn't until 1981, however, that it became federally incorporated. It is a bilingual, nonprofit organization dedicated to linking researchers, teachers, government, and education leaders and students.

Canadian school counsellors can voluntarily join the School Counsellors Chapter of the Canadian Counselling and Psychotherapy Association (www.ccpa-accp.ca/en/chapters/details/?ID=8). Two other national organizations that are open to some school counsellors are the Canadian Professional Counsellor's Association (n.d.) and the Canadian Psychological Association. In some jurisdictions, registered social workers might also be employed as school counsellors.

According to the Counsellors Network (2008), British Columbia, Alberta, Saskatchewan, Manitoba, Ontario, Québec, Prince Edward Island, Nova Scotia, and Newfoundland and Labrador each have a provincial school counsellors association. *Canadian School Counselling* (www.msca.mb.ca/csc.shtml) is a peer-reviewed scholarly journal written for school counsellors, psychologists, mental health practitioners, clinicians, and those who work with students in Kindergarten to Grade 12. The *Canadian Journal of Counselling and Psychotherapy* (http://cjc.synergiesprairies.ca/cjc/index.php/rcc) is also of interest to many school counsellors.

SCHOOL COUNSELLORS AT VARIOUS LEVELS

Within the field of school counselling, the professional literature focuses on three distinct school-age populations: elementary school children (Grades K–5), middle school children (Grades 6–8), and secondary school children (Grades 9–12). Each of these populations has particular concerns and universal needs.

Table 19.1 Appropriate and Inappropriate Counselling Responsibilities

Inappropriate (noncounseling) activities:	Appropriate (counseling) responsibilities:
Registering and scheduling all new students	Designing individual student academic programs
Administering cognitive, aptitude, and achievement tests	Interpreting cognitive, aptitude and achievement tests
Signing excuses for students who are tardy or absent	Counseling students with excessive tardiness or absenteeism
Performing disciplinary actions	Counseling students with disciplinary problems
Sending home students who are not appropriately dressed	Counseling students about appropriate school dress
Teaching classes when teachers are absent	Collaborating with teachers to present guidance curriculum lessons
Computing grade-point averages	Analyzing grade-point averages in relationship to achievement
Maintaining student records	Interpreting student records
Supervising study halls	Providing teachers with suggestions for better study hall management
Clerical record keeping	Ensuring student records are maintained in accordance with [board and provincial] regulations
Assisting with duties in the principal's office	Assisting the school principal with identifying and resolving student issues, needs, and problems
Working with one student at a time in a therapeutic, clinical mode	Collaborating with teachers to present proactive, prevention-based guidance curriculum lessons

Source: American School Counselor Association (2002). *Executive Summary, ASCA National Model.* Alexandria, VA: Author. p. 4.

ELEMENTARY SCHOOL COUNSELLING AND GUIDANCE

Elementary school counselling and guidance is a relatively recent development. The first book on this subject was published in the 1950s, and the discipline was virtually nonexistent before 1965 (Dinkmeyer, 1973a; 1989). In fact, fewer than 10 universities offered coursework in elementary school counselling in 1964 (Muro, 1981).

The development of elementary school counselling was slow for three reasons (Peters, 1980; Schmidt, 2007). First, many people believed that elementary school teachers should serve as counsellors for their students because they work with them all day and are in an ideal position to identify specific problems. Second, counselling at the time was primarily concerned with vocational development, which is not a major focus for elementary school children. Finally, many people did not recognize a need for counselling at the elementary school level. Psychologists and social workers were employed by some secondary schools to diagnose emotional and learning problems in older children and offer advice in difficult family situations, but full-time counselling at the elementary level was not considered.

Emphases and Roles

Elementary school counsellors are a vanguard in the mental health movement in educational settings (Gysbers & Henderson, 2006b). No other profession has ever been organized to work with individuals from a purely preventive and developmental perspective. Elementary school counsellors regularly

- implement effective classroom guidance,
- provide individual and small-group counselling,
- assist students in identifying their skills and abilities,
- work with special populations,
- develop students' career awareness,
- coordinate school, community, and business resources,
- consult with teachers and other professionals,
- communicate and exchange information with parents/guardians, and
- participate in school improvement and interdisciplinary teams (Campbell & Dahir, 1997).

Case Example: What Would *You* Do?

Pat was an elementary school counsellor. One day his principal, Daniel, came by to see him and announced he was considering retirement. During the conversation, Daniel mentioned that he thought Pat would make a great principal. To get Pat ready for taking on such a responsibility and to make him an attractive candidate, Daniel suggested shifting some of his administrative duties to Pat. "It won't take much time," he said, "and it is important. Besides, you'll make a lot more money."

1. Put yourself in Pat's shoes. How would you respond and why?

2. What are the different skill sets required of counsellors compared to administrators?

3. What are the ethical complications of acting in two different capacities?

In an important article on the effectiveness of elementary school counselling, Gerler (1985) reviewed research reports published in *Elementary School Guidance and Counseling* from 1974 to 1984. He focused on studies designed to help children from behavioural, affective, social, and mental image/sensory awareness perspectives. Gerler found strong evidence that elementary school counselling programs "can positively influence the affective, behavioral, and interpersonal domains of children's lives and, as a result, can affect children's achievement positively" (p. 45). In another article, Keat (1990) detailed how elementary school counsellors can use a multimodal approach called HELPING (an acronym for Health, Emotions, Learning, Personal relationships, Imagery, Need to know, and Guidance of actions, behaviours, and consequences) to help children grow and develop.

The fact that elementary school counsellors can and do make a difference in the lives of the children they serve is a strong rationale for keeping and increasing their services. It is easier to handle difficulties during the younger years than at later times (Bailey, Deery, Gehrke, Perry, & Whitledge, 1989; Campbell & Dahir, 1997). Elementary school counsellors who have vision (for example, that children can be problem solvers) and follow through can transform the culture of a school (Littrell & Peterson, 2001).

Activities

Elementary school counsellors engage in a number of activities. Some of these are prescribed by law, such as the reporting of child abuse. Most activities of elementary school counsellors are not so legally mandated, however, and include a plethora of preventive and remedial activities. Prevention is preferred because of its psychological payoff in time invested and results.

Prevention Elementary school counselling programs strive to create a positive school environment for students. They emphasize the four Cs: counselling services, coordination of activities, consultation with others, and curriculum development. The last activity, curriculum development, is both developmental and educational. It focuses on formulating "guidance classes [on] life skills and in preventing . . . difficulties" that might otherwise occur (Bailey et al., 1989, p. 9).

At their best, classroom guidance lessons are proactive and focus on prevention (e.g., school violence) as well as promotion (e.g., a positive body image). As an example of proactive classroom guidance, Magnuson (1996) developed a lesson for Grade 4 students that compared the web that Charlotte, the spider, spins for physical nutrition in the book *Charlotte's Web* (White, 1952) with the webs that human beings spin for personal nurturing. Just as Charlotte needed a variety of insects to stay healthy, the lesson stressed that people need to attract a variety of friends and support to live life to the fullest. The lesson ended with children not only discussing the parallels between Charlotte and themselves but also drawing a "personal web" filled with significant and important persons in their lives.

A first priority for elementary school counsellors is making themselves known and establishing links with others. "School personnel are not usually viewed by young children as the first source of help" (Bachman, 1975, p. 108). Therefore, elementary school counsellors need to publicize who they are, what they do, and how and when they can help. This process is usually handled best through orientation programs, classroom visits, or both. The important point is to let children, parents, teachers, and administrators know what counselling and guidance services are available and how they are a vital part of the total school environment.

For instance, in situations in which very young children (three- to five-year-olds) are part of the school environment, elementary school counsellors can make themselves known by offering special assistance to these children and their families, such as monitoring developmental aspects of the children's lives (Hohenshil & Hohenshil, 1989). Many children in this age range face detrimental conditions including poverty, family/community violence, and neglect (Carnegie Task Force on Meeting the Needs of Young Children, 1994). The efforts of elementary school counsellors with these children may include offering prosocial classroom guidance lessons centred around socialization skills (Morganett, 1994; Paisley & Hubbard, 1994). Furthermore, elementary school counsellors can consult with teachers and other mental health professionals to be sure that efforts at helping these young children are maximized.

It is especially important to work with parents and the community when children, regardless of age, are at risk for developing either low self-concepts or antisocial attitudes (Capuzzi, 2008). Having lunch with parents where they work, even at odd hours, is one way for counsellors to reach out and support families in the education of their children (Evans & Hines, 1997). Family counselling interventions by school counsellors is another way to focus on three primary subsystems: the family, the school, and the subsystem formed by the family and school interactions (Lewis, 1996). Elementary school counsellors (and for that matter middle and secondary school counsellors) must avoid assuming that most student problems are a result of dysfunctional families and instead focus on constructively addressing all three subsystems as needed.

Another way of combatting potential destructiveness is known as *multiple concurrent actions*. In this approach, counsellors access more than one set of services within the community at a time—for example, social services and learning disabilities specialists. This type of coordinated action between school and community agencies is collaborative and integrative, and it requires energy and commitment on the part of the counsellor (Keys et al., 1998).

While publicizing their services and establishing relationships with others in the community, elementary school counsellors must be active in their schools in a variety of ways, especially in guidance activities. Myrick (2003) recommends a proactive, developmental, comprehensive approach to guidance programs: two to three large classroom meetings each week and twice as many small-group sessions. These activities focus on structured learning, such as understanding oneself, decision making, problem solving, establishing healthy girl—boy relations, and how to get along with teachers and make friends (Coppock, 1993;

Snyder & Daly, 1993). Classroom guidance should also address conflict resolution and peer mediation, in which students learn peaceful and constructive ways of settling differences and preventing violence (Carruthers, Sweeney, Kmitta, & Harris, 1996).

Other preventive services offered by elementary school counsellors include setting up peer mediation programs and consultation/education activities. *Peer mediators/counsellors* are specially selected and trained students who serve the school and the counsellor in positive and unique ways. They may help students get to know one another, create an atmosphere of sharing and acceptance, provide opportunities for other students to resolve personal difficulties, and enhance the problem-solving skills of the students (Garner, Martin, & Martin, 1989).

The effectiveness of peer mediation on the elementary school level can be seen in preventing and reducing schoolwide violence. For example, Schellenberg, Parks-Savage, and Rehfuss (2007) found in a three-year longitudinal study that a schoolwide peer mediation program reduced out-of-school suspensions and resulted in "significant mediator knowledge gains pertaining to conflict, conflict resolution, and mediation" (p. 475). Peer counsellors have been utilized in Canada at every school level, from elementary grades through university (Altmann, Nysetvold, & Downe, 1986; Carr, 1988; Gougeon, 1989; Henriksen, 1991; Kingsland & Carr, 1986; Lawson, 1989).

By implementing consultation and education sessions for teachers, administrators, and parents, counsellors address common concerns and teach new ways of handling old problems by getting many people committed to working in a cooperative manner (Dougherty, 1986). For example, helping establish culturally compatible classrooms in which student diversity is recognized, appreciated, and used is a service elementary school counsellors can provide constituents (Herring & White, 1995; Lee, 2001). Promoting communication skills between teachers and students is another crucial cooperative service elementary school counsellors can set up (Hawes, 1989). Yet a third cooperative service that elementary school counsellors can provide is a class on parenting skills that emphasizes effective communication procedures and behaviour management (Ritchie & Partin, 1994).

Skilled elementary school counsellors can even use their counselling role in a preventive way. For instance, by meeting regularly in individual sessions with *at-risk children* (those most likely to develop problems because of their backgrounds or present behaviours), counsellors can assess how well these children are functioning and what interventions, if any, might be helpful to them or to significant others (Webb, 1992). *Bullying* behaviour may be one place where preventive interventions can also take place. Although bullying is usually thought of "as one person threatening or actually physically assaulting another person for no apparent reason," it can include "name-calling, teasing, writing hurtful statements, intentional exclusion, stealing, and defacing personal property" (Beale & Scott, 2001, p. 300). Regardless, bullying behaviour can be addressed in a preventive fashion through the use of peer-performed psychoeducational drama that "allows students to indirectly experience many of the negative consequences of bullying in an impersonal, non-threatening way" (p. 302). Providing positive adult role models for children to emulate may be helpful as a preventive measure along with systemically addressing negative influences such as parental physical discipline, negative peer models, lack of adult supervision, and neighbourhood safety concerns (Espelage, Bosworth, & Simon, 2000).

Besides obvious problems such as bullying, preventive counselling services are also needed for less obvious groups and behaviours. For example, gifted and talented students may need special help from a prevention perspective. Although this subgroup of students usually appears to function well, in reality these individuals may have some concerns, such as underachieving, overextending, and handling stress (Greene, 2006). Helping them learn to manage stress, plan ahead, and not be overcritical of themselves or their abilities are just some of the ways elementary school counsellors can help these talented students stay balanced and develop healthy self-concepts.

In working with children and the topic of divorce, elementary school counsellors can do much good at the preventive level (Crosbie-Burnett & Newcomer, 1989) by addressing divorce as a topic in classroom guidance classes. Such classes should be informationally humane in intent and aimed at alleviating much of the negative stereotyping and myths that surround divorce. As well, elementary school counsellors can use small groups to concentrate on specific children's needs regarding divorce, thereby preventing further problems. Groups for children experiencing divorce have been found effective in reducing dysfunctional behaviours, especially if both the custodial and noncustodial parents are involved (Frieman, 1994).

Small-group counselling programs at the elementary level can help students increase learning behaviours and narrow the gap between poor students, ethnic minorities, and students who have material and psychological advantages (Steen & Kaffenberger, 2007). Integrating academic interventions and group counselling improves students' behaviours (e.g., asking questions, completing assignments, and staying on task) related to school achievement. At the same time, it can address personal and social concerns such as "changing families, friendships, and/or anger management" (p. 516).

Remediation   *Remediation* is the act of trying to make a situation right. The word implies that something is wrong and that it will take work to implement correction. In elementary school counselling, a number of activities come under the remediation heading. One example is children's self-esteem.

Children's self-esteem is related to their *self-concept*, how they "perceive themselves in a variety of areas, academically, physically, socially, and so forth" (McWhirter, McWhirter, McWhirter, & McWhirter, 1994, p. 190). *Self-esteem* results from the comparison of oneself to others in a peer group. Although it may be situational or characterological, self-esteem is basically how well individuals like what they see—how people evaluate themselves (Street & Isaacs, 1998). It is always evolving (Duys & Hobson, 2004). To enhance self-esteem is an arduous process. For such a task, counsellors need an understanding of developmental theory, such as that of Robert Kegan. Such a theory can help them conceptualize the evolution of self-esteem, especially since Kegan incorporates cognitive, moral, and psychosocial development into his assumptions about the evolution of self-esteem. Pragmatically, counsellors must focus on helping low self-esteem children, who are at risk for failure, improve in the following areas: critical school academic competencies, self-concept, communication skills, coping ability, and control. McWhirter et al. (1994) call these the "Five Cs of Competency" (p. 188). Counsellors can enhance self-esteem in these areas by skill building, such as improving social skills, problem-solving skills, and coping skills (Street & Isaacs, 1998). In working in remediation, elementary school counsellors must rely on their individual and group counselling skills as well as their social action abilities when making environmental changes and modifications.

One way of determining what needs to be remediated and at what level is to use a needs assessment. *Needs assessments* are structured surveys that focus on the systematic appraisal of the types, depths, and scope of problems in particular populations (Cook, 1989; Rossi & Freeman, 1999). Needs assessments may be purchased commercially, borrowed and modified from others, or originated by an institution's staff. In school settings, counsellors can gain a great deal of useful information if they regularly take the time to survey students, teachers, parents, and support personnel. This knowledge helps them address specific problems. Typically, concerns uncovered through needs assessments fall into four main areas: school, family relations, relationships with others, and the self (Dinkmeyer & Caldwell, 1970). The Self-Assessment Towards Academic Success (Alderson, 2004) is an excellent example of a needs assessment (see Figure 19.1).

In remediation sessions, young children often respond best to counselling strategies built around techniques that require active participation. Play therapy, bibliotherapy, and the use of games are three strategic interventions that help counsellors establish rapport with young children and facilitate their self-understanding.

Play therapy is a specialized way of working with children that requires skill and training. As mentioned previously, play therapy lacks carefully controlled empirical studies that meet the minimum standard for an evidence-based treatment (Phillips, 2010).

Bibliotherapy can also be used in counselling and guidance activities with elementary school children (Borders & Paisley, 1992; Gladding & Gladding, 1991). Bibliotherapy is "the use of books [or media] as aids to help children gain insight into their problems and find appropriate solutions" (Hollander, 1989, pp. 184–185). For example, books and videos that emphasize diversity, such as *Babe, Pocahontas, The Lion King,* or *The Little Mermaid,* may be used to promote acceptance and tolerance (Richardson & Norman, 1997). These counselling tools are especially helpful if counsellors summarize stories for children, openly discuss characters' feelings, explore consequences of a character's action, and sometimes draw conclusions (Schrank, 1982).

School counsellors who work directly with children who have been abused may also choose to use bibliotherapy because of the way media promote nonthreatening relationships. A number of books can be used therapeutically with children who have been sexually abused. Two of the best are *I Can't Talk About It,* a book about how a young girl deals with her father touching her private parts, and *My Body Is Private,* a book about a young girl's awareness of her body and her discussion with her mother about keeping one's body private.

Self-Assessment Towards Academic Success

There are many reasons why students do not do as well in school as they had hoped. Place a checkmark in the second column for those factors that you anticipate or know are a problem for you:

Time Management Concerns
Poor time management skills
Procrastination
Too many other commitments

    ____   (a) part-time or full-time job
    ____   (b) family responsibilities
    ____   (c) other

Insufficient time spent with assignments
Academic Concerns
Insufficient academic background (i.e., you were not adequately prepared)
Inappropriate course selection (i.e., you took courses that you did not want, need or like)
Difficulties in the area of:

    ____   (a) reading skills
    ____   (b) writing skills
    ____   (c) math skills
    ____   (d) memorization
    ____   (e) exam anxiety
    ____   (f) note-taking
    ____   (g) inefficient study strategies
    ____   (h) concentration

Other Concerns
Career uncertainty
Financial difficulties
Lack of motivation, boredom, or apathy
Low energy level
Difficulties in the area of:

    ____   (a) regular exercise
    ____   (b) healthy diet
    ____   (c) sleep
    ____   (d) social/recreational activities
    ____   (e) excessive use of drugs/alcohol
    ____   (f) problem behaviours

Lack of readiness or desire to be a student
Lack of commitment to school
Lack of assertiveness
Experienced a recent crisis
Emotional difficulties (i.e., depression, anxiety)
Difficulties with relationships
Self-defeating attitudes/beliefs (i.e., you view things negatively, especially yourself and your own capabilities)
Physical Illness
Home problems
Learning disability
Other problem not covered by this inventory (specify):

Figure 19.1 Alderson's Self-Assessment Towards Academic Success

Adapted from Alderson, K. (2004). *Grade power: The complete guide to improving your grades through self-hypnosis.* Toronto, ON: Insomniac Press.

Games are a third way to work with elementary school children in counselling. They "offer a safe, relatively non-threatening connection to children's problems" (Friedberg, 1996, p. 17). They are also familiar to children and valued by them. What's more, games are considered fun and enhance the counselling relationship. For example, playing with a Nerf ball may relax a nervous child and lead to the child revealing some troublesome behaviours.

A number of games have been professionally developed to deal with such common elementary school child problems as assertiveness, anger, self-control, anxiety, and depression (Berg, 1986; 1989; 1990a; 1990b; 1990c; Erford, 2008). In addition, counsellors can make up games, the best of which are simple, flexible, and connected with the difficulties the child is experiencing (Friedberg, 1996).

MIDDLE SCHOOL COUNSELLING AND GUIDANCE

Emphasis on middle school counselling and guidance is an even more recent phenomenon than elementary school counselling. It came into prominence in the 1970s as a hybrid way to offer services for students who did not fit the emphases given by either elementary school or high school counsellors (Cole, 1988; Stamm & Nissman, 1979). The idea of a special curriculum and environment for preadolescents and early adolescents was first implemented in the 1960s as a junior high concept—an attempt to group younger adolescents (ages 12–14 and Grades 7–9) from older adolescents.

Middle schools typically enroll children between the ages of 11 and 14 and encompass Grades 6 through 9. "In addition to experiencing the normal problems that exist in the family, school, and community, middle school boys and girls adjust to changes in the body, pressure from peers, demands by the school for excellence, conflicting attitudes of parents, and other problems with establishing self-identity" (Matthews & Burnett, 1989, p. 122). There is little homogeneity about them, and their most common characteristic is unlikeness.

According to Dougherty (1986), we know less about this age group than any other. Part of the reason is that few middle school counsellors conduct research or publish their findings about this population (St. Clair, 1989). We do know that children in this age group deal with several developmental issues, such as developing increased emotional awareness, working through identity questions, recognizing their social boundaries, and owning up to responsibilities (Shelton & Allen, 2006). They also deal with students who are at risk of assaulting other children and adults and/or who have already done so (Fortin, Carney, Rundle, Mackie, & Roberts, 2007). Middle school counsellors are expected to demonstrate that their interventions work, and Studer, Oberman, and Womack (2007) provided methods for creating instruments that are effective in providing program and intervention evaluation.

The Gesell Institute of Child Development and other child study centres offer a description of cognitive, physical, and emotional factors that can be expected during this time (Johnson & Kottman, 1992); however, too few counsellors avail themselves of this data. On a general level, however, most middle school counsellors are aware of the major physical, intellectual, and social developmental tasks that middle school children must accomplish. Thornburg (1986) outlines them as follows:

■ becoming aware of increased physical changes

■ organizing knowledge and concepts into problem-solving strategies

■ making the transition from concrete to abstract symbols

■ learning new social and sex roles

■ identifying with stereotypical role models

■ developing friendships

■ gaining a sense of independence

■ developing a sense of responsibility (pp. 170–171)

Case Example: What Would *You* Do?

Marge wanted to know she was making a difference in the lives of middle schoolers as their counsellor. Therefore, she thought she would set up a research study. She was not sure where to begin, but she thought a "before and after" design would be helpful.

She distributed a survey at the beginning of the school year asking students to check off problems or concerns they had. At the end of the year she did the same thing and compared results. To her surprise and delight, some problems were checked fewer times. To her dismay, some were checked more often.

1. What did Marge do right in regard to her research with middle schoolers?

2. What did she do wrong?

3. What could she do, if anything, to fix the flaws in her approach?

Elkind (1986) notes that, in addition to developmental tasks, middle graders also must deal successfully with three basic stress situations. A *Type A* stress situation is one that is foreseeable and avoidable, such as not walking in a dangerous area at night. A *Type B* situation is neither foreseeable nor avoidable, such as an unexpected death. A *Type C* situation is foreseeable but not avoidable, such as going to the dentist.

Overall, middle school children tend to experience more anxiety than either elementary or high school students. Therefore, they are at risk for not achieving or successfully resolving developmental tasks (Matthews & Burnett, 1989; Schmidt, 2007). Middle school counsellors can be most helpful during times of stress because they can provide opportunities for children to experience themselves and their worlds in different and creative ways (Schmidt, 2004). Counsellors can also help middle schoolers foster a sense of uniqueness as well as identify with universal common concerns. In such a process, counsellors help middle schoolers overcome their restlessness and moodiness and counter influences by peers and the popular culture that suggest violence or other destructive behaviours are an acceptable solution to complex, perplexing problems (Peterson & O'Neal, 1998).

Emphases and Roles

Schools often neglect the physical and social development of the child while stimulating intellectual growth (Thornburg, 1986). Middle school counselling and guidance, like elementary school counselling and guidance, seeks to correct this imbalance by focusing on the child's total development. The emphasis is holistic: Counsellors stress not only growth and development but also the process of transition involved in leaving childhood and entering adolescence (Cobia & Henderson, 2007; Schmidt, 2007). Their activities include

- working with students individually and in groups;
- working with teachers and administrators;
- working in the community with education agencies, social services, and businesses; and
- partnering with parents to address unique needs of specific children (Campbell & Dahir, 1997).

These roles may be fulfilled more easily if counsellors develop capacities and programs in certain ways. The necessary capacities, according to Thornburg (1986), include general information about developmental characteristics of middle schoolers and specific tasks students are expected to achieve. In addition, middle school counsellors must understand the specific child with whom they are interacting and his or her perspective on a problem. Finally, middle school counsellors need to know how to help students make decisions so that they can help themselves in the future.

The ideal role of middle school counsellors includes providing individual counselling, group experiences, peer support systems, teacher consultation, student assessment, parent consultation, and evaluation of guidance services (Bonebrake & Borgers, 1984; Schmidt, 2007). In a survey of Kansas principals and counsellors, Bonebrake and Borgers (1984) found that participants agreed on not only the ideal role of the middle school counsellor but also a counsellor's lowest priorities: serving as principal, supervising lunchroom discipline, and teaching non-guidance classes. This survey is encouraging because it shows the close agreement between principals and counsellors concerning ideal roles. After all, principals usually "determine the role and function of counselors within the school" (Ribak-Rosenthal, 1994, p. 158).

Outside the school, various groups have different perceptions and priorities about the purpose of middle school counsellors. To ease the tension that may arise from such evaluations, Bonebrake and Borgers (1984) recommend that counsellors document their functions and run "a visible, well-defined, and carefully evaluated program" (p. 198). Middle school counsellors also need to be in constant communication with their various publics about what they do and when. Publicity as well as delivery of services is as crucial at this level as it is in elementary schools (Ribak-Rosenthal, 1994).

Activities

Working with middle school children requires both a preventive and a remedial approach. It is similar to dealing with elementary school children except that counsellors must penetrate more barriers if they are to be truly helpful in a holistic way.

Prevention Bullying is a major problem in American schools (Pergolizzi et al., 2009) and middle school counsellors are expected to design, assist, and/or administer prevention programs. One popular anti-bullying program is called the Olweus Bullying Prevention Program, although its effectiveness has recently been challenged (Bauer, Lozano, & Rivara, 2007). Other examples of such programs include dating violence and/or sexual harassment prevention programs (Ting, 2009; Weist et al., 2009), substance use prevention programs (Ringwalt et al., 2003), and gang prevention programs (Lim, 2010). One of the most promising prevention programs for middle schoolers is the Succeeding in School approach (Gerler & Anderson, 1986). Composed of 10 50-minute classroom guidance units, this program is geared toward helping children become comfortable with themselves, their teachers, and their schools (Gerler, 1987). Furthermore, the approach is "designed to help students focus on behaviors, attitudes, and human relations skills that lead to improved academic success" (Baker & Gerler, 2008, p. 22). Each lesson plan focuses on a prosocial aspect of personal and institutional living, such as identifying with successful people, being comfortable in school, cooperating with peers and teachers, and recognizing the bright side of life events (Baker & Gerler, 2008; Gerler, Drew, & Mohr, 1990). Succeeding in School is now online and can be accessed through http://genesislight.com/succeedinginschool. Its interactive program activities allow students to complete pre- and post-program measures of school success online.

A complement to the Succeeding in School program is Rosemarie Smead's (1995) group counselling activities for children and adolescents. These activities develop skills for living. Because her exercises for small groups can be used in various ways, middle school counsellors have flexibility in helping students deal with sensitive areas such as anger, grief, stress, divorce, assertiveness, and friendship. As Akos, Hamm, Mack, and Dunaway (2007) have pointed out, group work is particularly appropriate for working with middle schoolers because they "naturally coalesce into peer groups" (p. 53).

In addition to classroom guidance and group work, middle school counsellors (like elementary school counsellors) can use individual counselling, peer counselling, and consultation activities to foster problem prevention (Thompson & Henderson, 2007). One theoretical approach that helps in this process is developmental counselling and therapy (DCT) (Ivey et al., 2005). DCT incorporates developmental concepts from individual theories such as those by Kohlberg, Gilligan, Kegan, and Erikson along with family theories and multicultural theories (Myers, Shoffner, & Briggs, 2002). It provides a systematic way for counsellors to relate to middle schoolers in their preferred developmental orientation—sensorimotor, concrete, formal operations, and dialetic/systemic. Most middle schoolers will relate on the first two levels, with the third occasionally coming into play.

Another preventive type of program is *peer mentoring*. In this arrangement, an older child, such as a Grade 8 student, is paired with a younger student, such as a Grade 6 child. The older student both accepts and teaches the younger student through a cooperative learning arrangement. Noll (1997) reports that, in a cross-age mentoring program she set up to help younger students with learning disabilities acquire social skills, the arrangement worked well. The younger students made significant gains in their social development, and the older students achieved an increase in their "ability to relate better to parents, an increase in self-esteem, better conflict resolution skills, and enhanced organization skills" (p. 241).

Middle school counsellors may also set up teacher-advisor programs (TAPs), which are based on the ideas that "guidance is everybody's responsibility, that there are not enough trained counselors to handle all of a school's guidance needs, and that teacher-based guidance is an important supplement to school counseling" (Galassi & Gulledge, 1997, p. 56). Through such programs, teachers become more involved with counsellors and with the nonacademic lives of their students. The beneficiaries of these programs are middle schoolers and the schools in which they study.

Remediation One of the best ways to work remedially with middle school students is to combine remediation with a preventive approach. According to Stamm and Nissman (1979), the activities of middle school counsellors are best viewed as services that revolve around "a Human Development Center (HDC) that deals with sensitive human beings (students, teachers, parents, and the community as a whole)" (p. 52). They recommend developing a rapport with these persons and coordinating middle school counselling and guidance services with others to provide the most productive program possible. Stamm and Nissman outline eight service areas that they believe are vital to a comprehensive middle school counselling and guidance program. Their model is based on service clusters.

Each service cluster is linked with the others. However, middle school counsellors cannot perform all the recommended functions alone, so they must delegate responsibility and solicit the help of other school personnel, parents, and community volunteers. A counsellor's job, then, entails coordinating service activities as well as delivering direct services when able.

The *communication service cluster* is primarily concerned with public relations. It is the counsellor's outreach arm and is critical for informing the general public about what the school counselling program is doing. *Curriculum service*, however, concentrates on facilitating course placements and academic adjustment. Middle school counsellors need to help teachers "psychologize" the curriculum so that students can deal with significant issues in their lives, such as peer relationships and values (Beane, 1986). If the curriculum is not relevant to children at this age, they often divert their energy to nonproductive activities. The *assessment service cluster* provides testing and evaluation services and is often linked to the *career resource cluster*, which focuses on the student's future goals and vocation.

The *counselling service cluster* and the *crisis centre cluster* are also closely connected. Counselling services are provided on an individual, peer, and group level and are offered during off-school and in-school hours. Sometimes counselling activities are aimed at *self-counselling*, which is "when people (including middle graders) think the ideas that they believe, then react to those ideas with logical emotional reactions and logical physical behaviors" (Maultsby, 1986, p. 207). Rational self-counselling is one research-based way to help students help themselves deal effectively with their emotions. At other times, peer facilitators help middle schoolers make friends and learn about their environments and schoolwork (Bowman, 1986; Sprinthall, Hall, & Gerler, 1992).

In the Stamm and Nissman model, someone is designated as a *crisis person* during the school day. This individual deals with emergencies and, with the help of the counsellor, finds an appropriate way to assist the child who is experiencing sudden distress. On an individual level, a crisis and the resulting distress may be connected with loss or internal or external pressures that result in a child acting out or withdrawing. On a group level, a crisis and the resulting distress may involve "cases of trauma that affect large numbers of students, such as homicide, suicide, accidental death, or severe accident" (Lockhart & Keys, 1998, p. 4). (It is vital that elementary and secondary school counsellors have both a crisis plan and a crisis person or, better yet, a crisis team, in their school counselling programs.)

The *community contact cluster* focuses on working with parents and other interested people to open the lines of communication between the school and other agencies. The *professional growth cluster* provides programs for school staff and paraprofessionals. This last task is critical to the counsellor's success. If the total school environment is to be positively affected, middle school counsellors must help "teachers develop skills related to enhancing the students' self-concept and self-esteem" (Beane, 1986, p. 192).

SECONDARY SCHOOL COUNSELLING AND GUIDANCE

"There are few situations in life more difficult to cope with than an adolescent son or daughter during their attempt to liberate themselves" (Freud, 1958, p. 278). Liberation variables among adolescents include "relating to parents with new independence, relating to friends with new intimacy, and relating to oneself with new understanding" (Coll, Thobro, & Hass, 2004, p. 41). Although most adolescents make it through this period of their lives by addressing these variables and the tasks that go with them in a healthy way, some experience great difficulty. Secondary school counsellors must deal with this thorny population and the problems unique to it. They may take some comfort in the fact that some problems in adolescence are more cyclical than others. For example, "delinquent behaviours are rare in early adolescence, almost universal by midadolescence (ages 15 to 17), and decrease thereafter" (McCarthy, Brack, Lambert, Brack, & Orr, 1996, p. 277). However, many other concerns connected with this population are situational and unpredictable.

Secondary school counselling and guidance began in the early 1900s, when its primary emphasis was on guidance activities that would help build better citizens (Gysbers & Guidance Program Field Writers, 1990). Frank Parsons influenced the early growth of the profession, although John Brewer really pushed for the establishment of secondary school guidance in the 1930s (Aubrey, 1979). Brewer believed that both guidance and education meant assisting young people in living. His ideas did not gain wide acceptance at the time, but under the name *life skills training* they have become increasingly popular (Gazda, 1989).

Emphases and Roles

Counsellors in high school environments concentrate on the following tasks:

- providing direct counselling services individually, in groups, and to the school as a whole
- providing educational and support services to parents
- offering consultation and in-service programs to teachers and staff
- delivering classroom guidance
- facilitating referrals to outside agencies
- networking to postsecondary schools and businesses
- advising academically (Campbell & Dahir, 1997)

Aubrey (1979) argues that a real conflict exists for secondary school counsellors, who are faced with two needs: (a) engaging in student counselling and (b) doing academic and administrative tasks, such as scheduling, which school administrative personnel often require. He contends that school counsellors, especially at the high school level, frequently get bogged down in nonprofessional activities. Brown (1989) states that dysfunctional counsellors are frequently misunderstood or misdirected by their principals, are poorly educated, lack a plan of action, are not engaged in public relations, and violate ethical standards. To combat attempts to cast them into inappropriate roles, secondary school counsellors need to develop and publicize what they do and how they do it, not only to students but to teachers, principals, and administrators as well (Guerra, 1998).

An important function for any school counsellor is the constant remodelling of the counselling program (Gysbers & Henderson, 2006b). A systematic plan is crucial to this process. It includes not only implementation of services but also evaluation of these activities. Some stress can be expected in setting up and restructuring guidance and counselling activities within the school, but a great deal of satisfaction also results. Secondary school counsellors must be in constant touch with their constituents if they are to keep their services and roles appropriate and current.

Activities

The activities of secondary school counsellors can be divided into several areas. In addition to evaluating their own activities, they are involved in prevention, remediation and intervention, and cooperation and facilitation. These categories are not mutually exclusive, and there are a multitude of concerns under each heading.

Prevention Secondary school counsellors, like elementary and middle school counsellors, stress preventive services. These efforts "need to be comprehensive, multifaceted, and integrated" (Keys & Bemak, 1997, p. 257) because adolescent problems outside the classroom and school problems are interrelated (McCarthy et al., 1996). Therefore, to address one situation and neglect the other usually will not work.

Sprinthall (1984) notes that primary prevention in the secondary school creates "classroom educative experiences that affect students' intellectual and personal development simultaneously" (p. 494). Through primary prevention, students become more self-reliant and less dominated by their peer group. They also become less egocentric, more attuned to principles as guidelines in making decisions, and more empathic. Relationships between the teacher and counsellor and the student and counsellor are enhanced in this process.

There are a multitude of ways to build primary prevention programs. One way for secondary school counsellors to practise prevention is for them to become familiar with current popular songs (Ostlund & Kinnier, 1997). By listening attentively to the lyrics of these songs, secondary school counsellors become "more knowledgeable about adolescent subcultures and may be better able to help many teenagers cope with typical adolescent problems" (pp. 87–88).

A second way for counsellors to practise prevention is to run groups, particularly thematic groups, which "bring together students experiencing similar problems and allow counselors to make effective use of their time and skills" (Zinck & Littrell, 2000, p. 51). Research indicates that group counselling has been especially effective in addressing and/or preventing adolescent problems in a number of areas. For instance, a 10-week group for at-risk adolescent girls was found to foster effective, positive, and lasting change (Zinck & Littrell, 2000).

Another way for counsellors to be proactive in secondary school environments is occasionally to teach prevention-based curriculum offerings in classes. Anxieties about school and tests, study skills, interpersonal relationships, self-control, and career planning may be dealt with in this way. Such an approach has two major advantages: Less time needs to be devoted to remediation and intervention activities, and the counsellor maintains a positive high profile with teachers and students. As an adjunct or an integrated part of curriculum offerings, counsellors can have class members participate in an interactive bibliotherapy process in which they read either fiction or nonfiction books on specific subjects and discuss their reactions with the counsellor. (This process may be individualized in personal counselling, too.) Books dealing with illness and death, family relations, self-destructive behaviours, identity, abuse, race and prejudice, and sex and sexuality are readily available. Christenbury, Beale, and Patch (1996) suggest several of them. Other works are easily attainable through *Books for You* (Christenbury, 1995).

Case Example: What Would *You* Do?

Leslie realized that students in her high school listened to music all day. They not only listened, but also talked about lyrics, and occasionally a student would saunter down the hall singing. Therefore, Leslie decided to use music and lyrics in her guidance lessons and to promote interpersonal skills.

She created the "Song Olympics," in which students had to either fill in original lyrics or make up

prosocial lyrics. Everyone was enthused, but the activity soon became very competitive.

1. How might Leslie modify the activity to make it more of a learning experience for everyone?

2. What other interests are typical of high school students? How might their interests be useful for counsellors?

Four examples of problem areas in which prevention can make a major difference are substance abuse, adolescent suicide/homicide, prevention of HIV infection/AIDS, and abusive relationships. Programs for preventing substance abuse work best when they are started early in students' lives, based on social influence models, tailored to the age and stage of different student groups, and "involve students, parents, teachers, and community members in the planning process" (Mohai, 1991). A specific effective model is one in which counsellors work with potentially susceptible at-risk students in a multidimensional way (Gloria & Kurpius Robinson, 2000). In general, multidimensional approaches increase self-esteem, reduce negative peer influence, and provide drug information.

Student assistance programs (SAPs) set up by counsellors in schools are also effective (Moore & Forster, 1993). SAP teams are composed of school personnel from a variety of backgrounds and function in ways similar to multidisciplinary special education teams in schools. They may be specific or general in nature but are aimed at being informative and helping students to cope with their problems (Rainey, Hensley, & Crutchfield, 1997).

Suicide and homicide prevention programs follow broad-based approaches that stress the seriousness of such violence and alternatives. Suicide is the second leading cause of death among Canadian youth aged 15 to 19 (Everall, Altrows, & Paulson, 2006). Although more girls attempt suicide than boys, boys are more successful in carrying it out.

Because antisocial behaviours like suicide and homicide are multi-determined phenomena, a variety of interventions are needed to prevent them (Dykeman, Daehlin, Doyle, & Flamer, 1996). Some ways to prevent suicide and homicide are to help students, parents, and school personnel become aware of their danger signs and alert counsellors and other mental health helpers to the professional and legal standards that deal with breaking confidentiality (Peach & Reddick, 1991; Remley & Sparkman, 1993; Sheeley & Herlihy, 1989). Involving school peers, families, and significant others in the community is also vital (Cashwell & Vacc, 1996; Ritchie, 1989). It is important that suicide and homicide prevention programs in schools be proactive rather than reactive, as well as systematically designed. One approach to such aggression is a concept known as *wrap-around programs* (Cautilli & Skinner, 1996). These programs have multiple services provided by a team of many mental health professionals, including counsellors, who work together to provide direct assistance to the youth at risk of violence as well as his or her family, and to community and school personnel who come in contact with the youth.

A common factor among suicidal and homicidal youth is feelings of depression and anger. Therefore, preventive programs, such as support or psychoeducational groups, that deal with improving self-esteem, social competence, and coping with loss and rejection are important. Such programs help youth use their intelligence wisely in a wide range of situations and assist them in developing *resilience*—"an adaptive process whereby the individual willingly makes use of internal and external resources to overcome adversity or threats to development" (Everall et al., 2006). Likewise, programs aimed at preventing copycat and cluster suicides and at providing community awareness are vital (Popenhagen & Qualley, 1998). Individual identification of youth at risk for either suicide or homicide is crucial, too. Youth intervention programs tailored to the needs and circumstances of potential suicide victims and homicide perpetrators are essential. A plan of action for dealing with suicide and homicide potential should be as broad-based as possible (Capuzzi, 1994).

When working to prevent HIV/AIDS, counsellors may or may not persuade students to change their sexual activity. But they can help them avoid contracting AIDS and other sexually transmitted diseases by employing both an informational and skills-based intervention system (Stevens-Smith & Remley, 1994). For instance, the school counsellor can make sure students know how HIV is spread and what behaviours, such as sharing intravenous needles and unprotected casual sex, put them into greatest danger (Keeling, 1993). In addition, counsellors can offer students opportunities for interpersonal skill building by simulating situations that are potentially hazardous. They can also support teenagers who decide to try new and positive behaviours such as changing their habits or environments. Support groups, workshops for parents and administrators, and peer education programs can also be used. Peer education is one of the strongest means of dissuading adolescents from engaging in destructive behaviours and helping them focus on productive action (Wittmer & Adorno, 2000).

Finally, interpersonal violence (i.e., abusive relationships) can be prevented through school counsellor interventions (Becky & Farren, 1997; Bemak & Keys, 2000). In such programs, counsellors work with students in groups to emphasize to them that slapping, pushing, and emotionally threatening language are not a normal or necessary part of interpersonal relationships. Furthermore, they focus on teaching students violence-prevention strategies such as anger management, assertiveness, and responsible verbal and nonverbal communication. "Dating Safely" is one model available in a programmed format that is easy to follow.

Overall, as these examples show, school counsellors are in a strong position because of their skills, training, and knowledge "to be leaders in the development of . . . school- and community-based intervention" programs (Stevens-Smith & Remley, 1994, p. 182). They can help students master *coping skills*—that is, "an ability to adapt to stress and adversity" (Compass, Connor-Smith, Saltzman, Thomsen, & Wadsworth, 2001, p. 87). This mastery can take place through active or passive means, such as through consequential thinking or simply observing (Balkin & Roland, 2007).

Remediation Secondary school counsellors initiate remediation and intervention programs to help students with specific problems that are not amenable to prevention techniques. Some common mental disorders of childhood and adolescence manifest clearly at this time, such as problems centring around adjustment, behaviour, anxiety, substance abuse, and eating (Geroski et al., 1997). The identification, assessment, referral, and in some cases treatment of these disorders found in the *Diagnostic and Statistical Manual of Mental Disorders*, fourth edition (DSM-IV-TR) are among the most valuable services a secondary school counsellor, or any school counsellor, can render (often in consultation with other mental health providers). Because of time and resources, secondary school counsellors usually do not deal directly in treating severe mental disorders but rather focus on other specific problematic behaviours that occur in their settings.

Canadian children whose parents eventually divorce tend to develop mental health problems, such as depression and antisocial behaviour (Statistics Canada, 2005). Nearly one in two divorces in Canada involves dependent children (Statistics Canada, 2005). Secondary school counsellors can help children, parents, and teachers adjust to divorce through both direct and indirect services (Cook & McBride, 1982). Interventions that directly address the problems of divorce include individual and group counselling services in schools for affected children. Structured, short-term group work can make a positive impact in helping secondary school students sort out and resolve their feelings about the divorce experience (Morganett, 1995). More indirect services can also be implemented, such as consulting with teachers and parents about the children's feelings. Teachers and parents need information about what to expect from children of divorce and what useful interventions they might employ in the process of helping.

Teenage parenting is filled with emotional issues for both society and teens. When parenting results from an out-of-wedlock pregnancy, feelings run high. The challenge for school counsellors is to develop outreach strategies for working with members of this population. In addition, counsellors must address personal and career concerns of young parents and make necessary referrals. Usually the process is accomplished best through collaborative efforts between school counsellors and community mental health workers (Kiselica & Pfaller, 1993). One essential task is to prevent teenage parents from having a second child. Another crucial aspect is keeping unwed mothers (and fathers) in school and increasing their success in academic, personal, and interpersonal arenas (DeRidder, 1993).

Cooperation and Facilitation Cooperation and facilitation involve the counsellor in a variety of community and school activities beyond that of caregiver. Counsellors who are not aware of or involved in community and school groups are not as effective as they could otherwise be (Bradley, 1978). Part of a counsellor's responsibility is becoming involved with others in ways outside of direct counselling services (Lee & Walz, 1998). Thus, secondary school counsellors often have to take the initiative in working with teachers and other school personnel. By becoming more involved with teachers, administrators, and sponsors of extracurricular activities, counsellors integrate their views into the total life of schools and "help create the kind of school environments that stimulate growth and learning" (Glosoff & Koprowicz, 1990, p. 10).

In a very practical article on the role of the school counsellor as service coordinator, DeVoe and McClam (1982) stress the importance of counsellors' being accountable for performing three roles. The first role is *information retriever*. Here, the counsellor either collects information or works with other professionals to collect information about particularly complex situations, such as the abused and drug-dependent pregnant teenager. The second role is related to s*ervice coordination*. The counsellor determines whether he or she has the expertise to meet particular students' needs. If the counsellor does not have the expertise, an appropriate referral is made. The third role is *information administrator*. The counsellor coordinates a plan in which individuals or agencies in nonschool counselling settings deliver student services. This activity involves planning and implementing continuous communication among service providers.

A less involved but important way that counsellors can cooperate with others in the school and community is through participation in *individualized education programs* (IEPs)—that is, educational programs tailored to the specialized needs of certain children (Humes, 1980). Counsellors engage in either direct interventions or support services with students for whom IEPs are drawn up. Regardless of special considerations, counsellors can work closely with other school and community personnel to ensure that atypical students receive appropriate educational and support services. Thus, fewer students drop out of school or are lost to the communities in which they live (Kushman, Sieber, & Heariold-Kinney, 2000).

POSTSECONDARY SCHOOL COUNSELLING IN CANADA

Postsecondary counselling involves understanding how postsecondary students of all ages learn, grow, and develop. Note that in the remainder of this chapter, we are referring to young adults, and not to the significant numbers of adults of all ages who return to school for career transitioning or as part-time students interested in lifelong learning.

Professionals in postsecondary counselling can use a number of theoretical models as guides in working with students experiencing predictable developmental situations. From an ideological viewpoint, three traditions dominate: *in loco parentis*, student services, and student development (Rodgers, 1989). *In loco parentis* gives faculty and staff the parental role of teaching moral values. The *student services* model emphasizes students as consumers and mandates services that facilitate development. This approach stresses a cafeteria-style manner of program offerings that students select according to what they think they need. *Student development* focuses on creating research-based environments that "help college students learn and develop" (Rodgers, 1989, p. 120). Student development is proactive because it makes opportunities available for special groups of students.

Within student development, at least four kinds of developmental theories guide professionals' activities: psychosocial, cognitive-structural, person–environment interaction, and typological. *Psychosocial theories* are embodied most thoroughly in the writings of Arthur Chickering (e.g., Chickering & Reisser, 1993). He contends that there are seven specific developmental tasks of postsecondary students: competence, autonomy, managing emotions, identity, purpose, integrity, and relationships. These tasks are in line with Erik Erikson's (1968) ideas about the developmental processes of young adults.

A major strength of Chickering is that he elaborates and specifies Erikson's concepts in such a way that college counsellors and student-life professionals can plan and evaluate their practices and programs around three key issues: career development, intimacy, and formulation of an adult philosophy of life. For example, first-year students and seniors differ in their specific levels of development, with first-year students being more preoccupied than seniors with establishing competence, managing emotions, and developing autonomy. Seniors, however, concentrate more on issues such as establishing identity, freeing interpersonal relationships, developing purpose, and establishing integrity (Rodgers, 1989).

Cognitive-structural theories focus on how individuals develop a sense of meaning in the world. They deal with perception and evaluation and are best described in the moral and intellectual models of Perry (1970) and Kohlberg (1984). These models are process-oriented, hierarchical, and sequential. For example, Perry's model assumes growth from "simple dualism (positions 1 and 2) through multiplicity (positions 3 and 4) and relativism (positions 5 and 6) to commitment within a relativistic framework (positions 7 through 9)." Kohlberg's model "outlines three levels of moral development: the preconventional, the conventional, and the postconventional" (Delve, Mintz, & Stewart, 1990, p. 8). According to these theories, each new stage contains the previous one and is a building block for the next one. Cognitive discomfort is the impetus for change. Explicit in this approach is the idea that "people need the opportunity to learn how to think and act responsibly in order to control their own behavior in a democratic society" (Herman, 1997, p. 147).

The *person–environment interaction model* "refers to various conceptualizations of the college student and the college environment and the degree of congruence that occurs when they interact" (Rodgers, 1989, p. 121). Congruence is believed to lead to "satisfaction, stability, and perhaps, development" (Rodgers, 1980, p. 77). The theories in this model stress that development is a holistic process that involves all parts of the person with the environment in an interacting way. It is similar to the psychosocial approach in assuming that development in one area of life can facilitate growth in another. For example, when students participate and take leadership positions in student organizations, their life management skills develop more positively than those of students who are more passive (Cooper, Healy, & Simpson, 1994). Likewise, students who volunteer in community service initiatives (also known as "service learning") become more informed about environmental needs, less egocentric, and more empathetic (Delve, Mintz, & Stewart, 1990). Unlike psychosocial theories, person–environment theories "are not developmental per se" (Rodgers, 1980, p. 77). In many ways, they are rooted in Kurt Lewin's (1936) formula: $B = f(P, E)$, where behaviour (B) is a function (f) of person (P) and environment (E).

Typological theories focus on individual differences, such as temperament, personality type, and patterns of socialization. These differences are assumed to persist over time, and most often individuals are combinations of types. Patterns of personality influence individuals to vary in their developmental growth patterns and are related to their motivation, effort, and achievement. This approach is exemplified in the writings of John Holland (1997), which study how personalities fit with work environments.

Professional Preparation

Proper preparation is one of the difficulties in the field of postsecondary counselling. Because there is such diversity in the functions of student-life professionals, no single professional preparation program can meet the needs of all graduate students. Those who enter this specialty "do not need the same kind of graduate work" (Sandeen, 1988, p. 21). Many if not most postsecondary counsellors have a background in counselling psychology at either the master's or doctoral level. Consequently, many choose to become licensed psychologists in their jurisdiction while others may become Canadian Certified Counsellors through the Canadian Counselling and Psychotherapy Association (see www.ccacc.ca/en/memberbenefits/certification).

Emphases and Roles

The emphases and roles of postsecondary counsellors vary from campus to campus depending on the types of students particular institutions attract and the support for services that are funded. The work of postsecondary counsellors is influenced by the models under which they operate, too. Traditionally, there have been four main models of counselling services that postsecondary counselling centres have followed (Westbrook et al., 1993).

1. *Counselling as psychotherapy*. This model emphasizes long-term counselling with a small percentage of students. The counsellor deals with personality change and refers other vocational and educational concerns to student academic advisers. The premise behind this approach is that "identity development is a core therapeutic issue in counseling traditional-age college students" (Hinkel & Luzzo, 2007, p. 144).

2. *Counselling as vocational guidance.* This model emphasizes helping students productively relate academic and career matters. The counsellor deals with academic or vocationally undecided students and refers those with personal or emotional problems to other agencies.

3. *Counselling as traditionally defined.* This model emphasizes a broad range of counselling services, including short- or long-term relationships and those that deal with personal, academic, and career concerns (Hinkelman & Luzzo, 2007). The counsellor's role is diverse.

4. *Counselling as consultation.* This model emphasizes working with the various organizations and personnel who have a direct impact on student mental health. The counsellor offers indirect services to students through strategic interventions.

A fifth model, *counselling as global* (i.e., an interactive, interdependent, community system), has been advocated (Pace et al., 1996). This model is dynamic and fluid. It proposes that the counselling centre staff work interactively with other members of a postsecondary community to create a mentally healthy environment and to use personnel and other resources available on campus. The idea is an evolution of the "Cube" concept (Morrill, Oetting, & Hurst, 1974, p. 355) and this model focuses on three main areas as places for counsellors to intervene: target (individual, primary group, associational group, and institution or community), purposes (remedial, preventive, or developmental), and methods (direct, consultation and training, or media). The global model changes the role of the counsellor and the focus of the college counselling centre by having centre staff be more flexible and interactive. In reality, most postsecondary counselling centres offer a variety of services to help their diverse client populations and to meet local campus needs.

Case Example: What Would *You* Do?

Debra worked long and hard to become the director of a college counselling centre. She loved working with students and she quickly assembled a fine staff. There was just one problem: Debra was not sure what services would be most in demand. However, her intuition told her she could not go wrong by offering counselling as traditionally defined, so that is how the centre operated.

1. What other types of services should Debra have considered when deciding what the counselling centre would offer?

2. What model do you think would work best at your institution? Why?

Activities

The activities of postsecondary counsellors are similar to those of other student-life professionals in being comprehensive and varied. Some services of these two groups even overlap. Lewing and Cowger (1982) identify nine counselling functions that generally dictate the agendas of postsecondary counsellors:

1. Academic and educational counselling

2. Vocational counselling

3. Personal counselling

4. Testing

5. Supervision and training

6. Research

7. Teaching

8. Professional development

9. Administration

In truth, three of these activities—personal, vocational, and educational counselling—account for more than 50% of postsecondary counsellors' time. Most of the counselling theories covered in this book are implemented in college counselling centres. For instance, Thurman (1983) found that rational emotive behaviour therapy, including the use of rational emotive imagery, can be effective in reducing *Type A behaviour* (time-urgent, competitive, and hostile) among postsecondary students and help them become healthier achievers.

Likewise, Watkins (1983) found a person-centred approach to be most effective in helping students evaluate present and future plans and deciding whether to stay in school. Even systems theory, most often used in marriage and family counselling, has proven effective in helping students understand family dynamics and patterns of interaction and how family patterns continue to influence important decisions about education (Openlander & Searight, 1983).

Similarly, brief therapy, a form of systems theory, has been employed in postsecondary counselling centres to help expand the "therapeutic framework to include nonfamilial members [who] can affect therapeutic progress" for better or worse (Terry, 1989, p. 352). In this treatment, conflictual non-family members in a campus community are brought together to form meaningful relationships and make changes in problematic situations. The idea behind the treatment is that students on campus can help each other problem-solve and make their environments healthier through the resolution of problem behaviours. In the process, blaming and scapegoating cease.

A difficulty postsecondary counsellors have faced in offering services is that of dealing effectively with mandated referrals, which are accepted by over 88% of campus counselling centres (Kiracofe & Wells, 2007). These cases are challenging because judicial boards and administrators who make referrals are more concerned with external behavioural changes than with anything else. To further aggravate the situation, there is virtually no theoretical literature for dealing with students who come involuntarily. Kiracofe and Wells suggest a readiness for change strategy be used with mandated clients based on Prochaska's (1999) readiness model (see Figure 19.2).

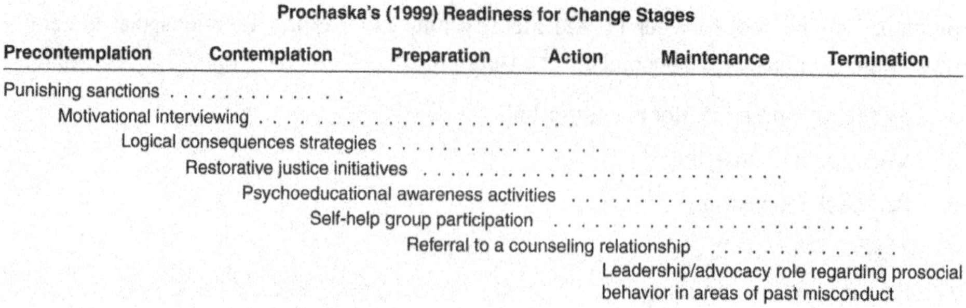

Precontemplation	Contemplation	Preparation	Action	Maintenance	Termination

Punishing sanctions . . . .
    Motivational interviewing . . . .
        Logical consequences strategies . . . .
           Restorative justice initiatives . . . .
              Psychoeducational awareness activities . . . .
                Self-help group participation . . . .
                  Referral to a counseling relationship . . . .
                     Leadership/advocacy role regarding prosocial
                     behavior in areas of past misconduct

Figure 19.2 Continuum of strategies for judicial action based on students' readiness for change

Source: "Mandated Disciplinary Counseling on Campus," by N. M. Kiracofe and L. Wells, 2007, *Journal of Counselling ad Development*, 85, p. 265. Reprinted with permission. No further reproduction authorized without written permission of the American Counseling Asociation.

Students at the pre-contemplative stage have no motivation to change and may respond best to punishment and sanctions. However, students who can be brought along through motivational interviews and psychoeducational awareness activities may commit to changes and actions that enhance their lives. Therefore, clients to postsecondary counselling centres should be accepted only when there is an indication that they are in the preparation and action stages of readiness.

Another challenge that postsecondary counsellors face is a constantly changing student culture (Bishop, 1992). For example, "with approximately 24% of college students [in the United States] having a body modification . . . tattoos and body piercings may represent an emerging cultural norm" (Roberti & Storch, 2005, p. 15). Behaviours among postsecondary students change with each generation (see Table 19.2). The culture of the current student population is not the same as its predecessors. Indeed, postsecondary counselling centre directors in recent years in both Canada and the United States have reported their perception of a continually increasing level of pathology among student clientele (Cairns, Massfeller, & Deeth, 2010).

A three-year study from a large Canadian university recently reported finding that the most common reasons that students ($N = 2943$) seek counselling, in rank order, are for problems with (a) relationships, (b) anxiety and stress, (c) depression and grief, (d) academic concerns, and (e) career guidance (Cairns, Massfeller, & Deeth, 2010). The first three reasons are also common reasons that adults who are not students seek professional help from counsellors.

When services are varied and numerous at the professional level, everyone benefits. The College Adjustment Scales are a means of screening postsecondary students for common developmental and psychological problems (Anton & Reed, 1991). These nine scales measure psychological distress in the following areas: anxiety, depression, suicidal ideation, substance abuse, self-esteem problems, interpersonal problems, family problems, academic problems, and career problems. It is an important assessment instrument for postsecondary counselling centres to use in deciding what services and programs they will emphasize.

Table 19.2 A Taxonomy of Client Problems Seen in Postsecondary Counselling Centres

Personal and Social Adjustment

Relationship Difficulties

- Anger/irritability/impulse control
- Breakup of a relationship
- Dating concerns
- Death of a significant other
- Problems making friends/loneliness
- Family/parents/siblings
- Romantic partner/spouse

Self-Esteem

- Self-image
- Shyness
- Self-confidence/assertiveness
- Fear of failure

Existential Concerns

- Meaning of life
- Role of religion
- Value conflicts

Depression

- Suicidal feelings or thoughts
- Feelings of hopelessness
- Grief over loss

Sexual Abuse and Harassment

- Abuse
- Harassment

Academic and Career Concerns

Academic Concerns

- School performance
- Procrastination
- Poor study skills
- Grades

Career Concerns

- Career uncertainty
- Career path unclear
- Lack of knowledge about interests/abilities

Stress and Psychosomatic Symptoms

Stress

- Headaches/stomachaches
- Insomnia
- Post-traumatic stress disorder

Anxiety

- Problems concentrating
- Performance anxiety
- Nervousness
- Irrational fears/phobias
- Panic attacks

Distressing Symptoms

- Substance abuse
- Drugs/alcohol

Sexual Dysfunction

- Arousal problems
- Impotency

Eating Disorders

- Anorexia
- Bulimia
- Body image problems

Unusual Behaviour

- Confused thinking
- Hallucinations
- Social isolate
- Paranoid ideation
- Borderline personality

Source: Appendix A from Bishop, J. B., Gallagher, R. P., & Cohen, D. (2000), College students' problems: Status, trends, and research. In D.C. Davis and K. M. Humphrey (Eds.), *College Counseling: Issues for a New Millennium* (pp. 109–110). Alexandria, VA: American Counseling Association. Reprinted with permission. No further reproduction authorized without written permission of the American Counseling Association.

Peer counsellors are also an effective way of reaching students beyond the traditional postsecondary counselling centre. As a rule, students turn first to friends for help, then to close relatives, before finally turning to faculty and counselling services.

Sometimes peer counsellors take the role of resident assistants (RAs). In this arrangement, RAs are assigned to live in selected residence halls. Their services, which include dealing with remedial, preventive, and developmental issues, are given high exposure (Schuh, Shipton, & Edman, 1986). RAs provide crisis intervention, short-term counselling, conflict mediation, and referral services (Blimling & Miltenberger, 1981). They help students to keep favourable attitudes toward counselling and counselling-related services and, at the same time, to become more aware of opportunities offered by postsecondary counselling centres (Johnson, Nelson, & Wooden, 1985). In addition, RAs sponsor programs for residents on mental and physical health topics, bringing in faculty and staff from across the campus to give presentations. RAs usually receive ongoing professional training and supervision from the campus counselling centre. This arrangement benefits the RAs, the students in the residence halls, and the campus as a whole because of its integrative and preventive focus.

Postsecondary counsellors can also offer services and programs in conjunction with other student-life professionals. Four of the most needed services relate to alcohol, sexual abuse and violence, eating disorders, and depression.

"Alcohol use is a serious problem on college campuses" (Laux, Salyers, & Kotova, 2005, p. 41). Nearly 90% of students drink alcohol at some time during an academic year, and approximately 20% qualify as heavy drinkers, averaging one ounce of alcohol per day per month (Steenbarger, 1998). Thus, it is not surprising that alcohol-related problems, including the abuse of alcohol and its concomitant disorders, are prevalent (Kadison & DiGeronimo, 2004).

Binge drinking (having five or more drinks at a time for men and four or more drinks for women) appears to be increasing, and one in three university students drinks primarily to get drunk (Commission on Substance Abuse at Colleges and Universities, 1994). In addition, irresponsible drinking may lead to violence in the form of date rape, unsafe sex, academic difficulties, and suicide. Riots on or near postsecondary campuses may occur when postsecondary administrators ban alcohol at certain campus events or areas (Lively, 1998).

Thus, alcohol abuse is likely to bring students in contact with counsellors and other student-life professionals (Gill-Wigal, Heaton, Burke, & Gleason, 1988; Kadison & DiGeronimo, 2004). Systematic steps are usually implemented to help students get through the denial they may have connected with alcohol abuse because, before effective treatment can take place, students need to realize their need for help in correcting out-of-control behaviour. Intervention is sometimes done individually, but often it involves a group and usually a wide variety of treatments, including insight and behavioural change.

Many students who abuse alcohol have grown up in dysfunctional families. They frequently experience problems related to growing up in such environments (e.g., workaholism, depression, dependency, antisocial tendencies, food addictions). Specific interventions counsellors use with these students include helping them define more clearly the roles they played in their family-life dramas and then helping them break nonproductive patterns of interaction (Crawford & Phyfer, 1988). One way counsellors can break nonproductive patterns is to respond to these students in functionally healthy ways that contrast with the behaviours they have experienced before. Peer counselling may also be helpful to an extent in this process.

Sexual assault and violence, including incest and rape, are matters that many students, primarily women, must deal with during their postsecondary experience. The dynamics surrounding sexual crimes have similarities and differences. A common denominator in many cases is alcohol abuse: Most campus rapes are alcohol-related, as are assaults (National Centre on Addiction and Substance Abuse at Columbia University, 2007). There are at least two stages in the recovery process: the acute, which is characterized by disorganization, and long-term reorganization, which includes dealing with the pain of trauma and rebuilding one's life through support (Burgess & Holstrom, 1974; Scrignar, 1997).

Case Example: What Would *You* Do?

Al had heard stories from his relatives about how much fun he would have in university. Most of the stories revolved around alcohol-related incidents. Thus, Al was determined to make sure he had access to beer, and before too long he had found the right connections.

Instead of applying himself to his studies, Al focused on his suds. He played "thumper" and other drinking games almost nightly. However, one night he was stopped by the campus police while driving in a less than sober state. When he was mandated to go to the campus counselling centre, Al did so reluctantly. His first words to Charlotte, his counsellor, were "Can't a guy have a little fun without everyone getting upset with him? Geeee!"

1. Put yourself in Charlotte's position. How would you reply to engage Al and yet let him know that he has a problem that needs to be worked on?

2. What strategies might you suggest to help Al reduce his alcohol consumption?

Eating disorders, especially bulimia and anorexia nervosa, are a third area in which postsecondary counsellors can team up with other student-life professionals, such as health educators, in offering services. There is a great need to address eating disorders in universities, although many students with such disorders do not believe their behaviours warrant therapy (Meyer, 2005). Research indicates these disorders occur along a continuum of degree. People who are caught up in them usually have maladaptive cognitions or faulty information concerning weight control techniques (Tylka & Subich, 2002). Regardless, it is estimated that up to 65% of women in their first year of postsecondary education display "some behavioral and psychological characteristics of disturbed eating" (Meyer & Russell, 1998, p. 166). To address these needs, eating disorders must "be considered within a developmental framework" (Sharkin, 1997, p. 275). Programs that emphasize the characteristics of eating disorders as well as highlight ways of combatting such tendencies before they become full blown can do much to educate those most likely to experience them. Furthermore, such programming can give participants sources to which they can turn if they or someone they know becomes caught up in a bulimic cycle. One key factor in education and prevention is the use of adaptive coping strategies (VanBoven & Espelage, 2006).

A fourth area of concern for postsecondary counsellors is depression (Kadison & DiGeronimo, 2004). "It is estimated that college students are twice as likely to have clinical depression and dysthymia as are people of similar ages and backgrounds in the workforce" (Dixon & Reid, 2000, p. 343). Depression and depressive symptoms are devastating in a postsecondary environment because they often interfere with learning and lead to a lack of success. Counsellors can treat depression through cognitive approaches, such as Beck's thought modification process; through behavioural approaches, such as helping clients engage in activities where they have success; and cognitive-behavioural approaches such as rational emotive behaviour therapy. It appears that depression is modified through positive life experiences (Dixon & Reid, 2000), so working with others in the postsecondary environment to assist depressed postsecondary students in finding successful experiences may be good, not only as therapeutic practice, but also for the postsecondary school itself in retaining students and creating a more socially hospitable atmosphere.

In addressing issues pertinent to postsecondary students, counsellors, in cooperation with student-life professionals, can take preventive action on tertiary, secondary, and primary levels. *Tertiary prevention* "is akin to remediation and includes direct services to victims" (Roark, 1987, p. 369). It includes encouraging the reporting of aggression and helping the victim use available resources. *Secondary prevention* is geared toward problems, such as date rape, already in existence on campus and is aimed at raising consciousness among potential victims and perpetrators and setting policies to stop known abuses. *Primary prevention* focuses on stopping problems from ever developing. It involves modifying the physical environment as well as addressing causes and providing training to create awareness and to change values. For example, to help students manage stress, a program referred to by the acronym BRIMS (breathing, relaxing, imagery, message, and signs) might be offered (Carrese, 1998). This program is a type of cognitive self-hypnosis that helps students relax both physically and mentally while giving themselves positive messages and physical signs that help them recall constructive ways of feeling and viewing a situation. In the process, students "transform negative thoughts into constructive energy, allowing control over situations that produce unnecessary anxiety" (p. 140).

COUNSELLING NONTRADITIONAL STUDENTS

In addition to working with mainstream groups, postsecondary counsellors address the needs of nontraditional students. These may be older students, first-generation postsecondary students, minority culture students, or even student athletes. A common characteristic of nontraditional students is financial independence (51%), followed by part-time attendance (48%), and delayed enrollment (46%) (Evelyn, 2002).

Older Students

As a group, older nontraditional students are highly motivated, prefer interactive learning, have family and financial concerns, view education as an investment, and have multiple commitments and responsibilities that are not related to school (Richter-Antion, 1986). Within this large group there are two basic subgroups: students aged 25–50 and those aged 50–80.

The first subgroup is usually motivated to return to school because of changing job or career requirements or opportunities that include family life transitions (e.g., marriage, divorce) (Aslanian & Brickell, 1980; Chao & Good, 2004). Building up self-esteem and providing academic and social support are particularly important for these younger nontraditional students. The latter subgroup, often called senior students, come to campus for many purposes, which include obtaining degrees and finding personal enrichment. When working with senior students, postsecondary counsellors must take several factors into consideration, such as modifications to the environment (perhaps brighter lighting or warmer room temperatures), the clients' developmental stage (e.g., dealing with issues of generativity or integration), the pace of the counselling sessions (slower may be better), potentially difficult areas (such as transference), and the use of counselling techniques (e.g., bibliotherapy, journal writing) (Huskey, 1994). With an increase in the number of older people in society at large, the numbers of senior students will most likely continue to grow.

Regardless of how fast that population grows, the overall number of nontraditional students will also increase because of business downsizing, the rapid advance of technology, and increased opportunities for professional development. Community and technical colleges and public universities are most likely to enroll the majority of these nontraditional students. As is the case with traditional students, more females than males will enroll, there will be an increase in the number of part-time students, and more cultural and racial minorities will seek a postsecondary education (Hodgkinson, Outtz, & Obarakpor, 1992). All these events will test the limits of counselling.

Part-Time Students

Part-time undergraduates, especially exclusively part-time students, comprise almost 40% of students in higher education. As a group, they are at a distinct disadvantage relative to those who are enrolled full time because

- they come from minority and low-income family backgrounds;
- they are not as well-prepared for higher education as their full-time peers;
- they are highly concentrated in two-year colleges and non-degree/certificate programs; and
- many of them work full-time while enrolled and are not enrolled continuously.

Thus, part-time enrollment is negatively associated with persistence and degree completion six years after beginning postsecondary education, even after controlling for a wide range of factors related to these outcomes (Chen, 2007).

To help part-time students, postsecondary counsellors must make special efforts to stay in contact with or reconnect with students as they transition in and out of classes. If part-time students know there is someone to whom they can talk or find information from, they are more likely to persevere in their studies. Providing special programming for these students on overcoming barriers to part-time enrollment may also be helpful, especially if it is kept brief and factual.

First-Generation Students

A third group of nontraditional students is first generation postsecondary students—that is, students who are the first in their family to enter postsecondary education. The individuals in this category come from a wide variety of backgrounds, including second-generation immigrants and upwardly mobile poor (Hodgkinson et al., 1992). "Family support for education is the key difference between first generation and second generation students. Family support is also a fundamental variable in the decision to attend college and in the successful completion of college" (Fallon, 1997, p. 385).

Thus, first-generation postsecondary students have numerous needs. They must master knowledge of the postsecondary environment, including its specific vocabulary; for example, credit hours, GPA, and dean (Fallon, 1997). They must also become committed to the role of being a student, decipher the value systems of second-generation postsecondary students, and learn to understand student-life services and study skills. Language barriers and social or cultural customs must also be addressed.

Minority Culture Students

Minority culture students face a number of challenges different from other students, such as "a lack of support and an unwelcoming academic climate" (Ancis, Sedlacek, & Mohr, 2000, p. 180). In many cases, minority students fall into categories besides being minorities, such as being first-generation students, older students, or student athletes. They also may be more interdependent and relational-oriented than majority students (Berkel & Constantine, 2005).

A recent analysis was based on the longitudinal Youth in Transition Survey (Thiessen, 2009). Computer-assisted telephone interviews were conducted with 23 592 Canadian youth (response rate: 80.9%) in 2000. A follow-up occurred two years later (response rate: 83.9%). Those who were Japanese, Chinese, or Korean were combined into an "East Asian" category, while all other Asian respondents were collapsed into a category called "other Asian." Thiessen (2009) found that East Asian Canadians were the most likely to enroll in a university program. Immigrant "other Asians" were the least likely to attend postsecondary school, followed by First Nations youth. The third least likely group to attend postsecondary were Canadian-born African and Latino Canadians.

In helping minority culture students adjust to postsecondary schools and/or do well overall, postsecondary counsellors can offer them encouragement and social support, as well as provide them tangible means by which to foster ethnic pride. Small- or large-group events that promote and enhance ethnic identity and self-concept may also prove useful and positive, as does mentoring. For example, "research indicates that Latino students who have a mentor who takes personal and academic interest in their educational experiences are more likely to succeed" (Gloria & Rodriguez, 2000, p. 151). Overall, helping that promotes and protects "strong ethnic identity" fosters "minority students' self-esteem and allows them to feel more integrated with the college environment" (Jourdan, 2006, p. 328).

In addition to offering minority students encouragement, specialized attention, and customized events, counsellors need to understand the campus environments in which they work and the perception of it by minority groups. Racism and stereotyping are frequently a part of the climate (Vereen et al., 2006). Therefore, counselling that effectively responds to these degrading influences needs to be fostered and self-efficacy promoted. For instance, counsellors who understand culturally specific humour can empower minority students to address issues they may face in a productive manner through seeing the absurdity of situations and laughing instead of feeling hopeless and becoming angry (Vereen et al., 2006).

To make an even wider impact and bring about needed changes, counsellors can work on campus-wide programming that impacts all aspects of the campus (i.e., faculty, staff, and students). Such programming can take the form of presentations to specific groups (e.g., academic classes, residence hall groups) or it can be in the form of sponsoring or cosponsoring campus wellness fairs or student services expos (Marks & McLaughlin, 2005). By being proactive in such venues, postsecondary counsellors can challenge biases and promote understanding and appreciation of others (Ancis et al., 2000).

Case Example: What Would *You* Do?

Patricia was raised in a first-generation Guatemalan household. Her parents spoke broken English and worked in minimum-wage jobs, but they had great ambition for their daughter. Patricia was ambitious as well, and at the end of high school she was offered a scholarship to a predominantly white university, where at first glance she looked like everyone else.

However, near the end of her second year, Patricia was feeling isolated and alone. Her parents did not understand what she was feeling and her fellow students did not relate well to a Latina.

When she sought counselling, Patricia's counsellor, Ibby, suggested that Patricia's family come with her to the next session so that they could discuss the situation together. In the meantime, she referred Patricia to the dean of Student Services to see if she could get more involved with an activity on campus.

1. What do you think of the counsellor's strategy in addressing Patricia's situation?

2. What might you do?

Student Athletes

A fifth group of nontraditional students consists of student athletes. These students are less likely than others to seek help through counselling (Watson, 2005). Yet many of them have "problems in relating to the university system and the larger society" (Engstrom & Sedlacek, 1991, p. 189). They are often seen by others as problem students who have trouble relating either socially or academically (Burke, 1993). In addition, many are from minority cultural groups and are the first from their families to attend postsecondary school (Kirk & Kirk, 1993). A sports-oriented environment may foster dependence on a coach or a team.

Therefore, these students may become isolated and alienated from the mainstream of postsecondary life and find stress as well as challenges in their dual roles of being students and athletes (Watson, 2005). Teaching time management and social skills are areas where counsellors can help.

In addition, when student athletes lose their athletic identity through loss of eligibility or because of injury, they need assistance in making an integrative transition back to postsecondary life (Wooten, 1994). Counsellors can work with student athletes on both an emotional and cognitive basis by helping them identify and express their feelings and confront and correct irrational thoughts. Student athletes also need help in learning to see themselves beyond the postsecondary years, most likely as nonprofessional athletes. Therefore, career counselling and life-planning skills are important services to provide.

SUMMARY AND CONCLUSION

Many of the problems that adults face begin in childhood or adolescence. Working with children and youth requires that a counsellor be aware of what normal development (and, alternatively, abnormal development) looks like at various ages.

Elementary school counsellors focus on offering preventive services and increasing student awareness of individual needs and ways of meeting them in a healthy, prosocial manner. Much work at this level is the result of emphasizing curriculum issues (i.e., classroom guidance), conducting small groups, and providing consultation to others. Middle school counsellors are more focused on helping students make the smoothest possible transition from childhood to adolescence.

Secondary school counselling has traditionally emphasized individual counselling services with high-risk and high-achieving individuals. Secondary school counsellors today are more involved in making an impact on the whole-school environment and in implementing both prevention and remediation programs. They assist students in making a transition from a school environment into the world of work or further study. Resolving developmental and situational factors associated with this transition are equally important to them.

Overall, school counsellors have multiple tasks and responsibilities. There is a new awareness that passive or poorly educated school counsellors have not and will not work for the good of children and society (Cecil & Cobia, 1990; Guerra, 1998; House & Hayes, 2002).

Postsecondary counselling emphasizes the total growth and maturation of students in postsecondary environments. It is focused on helping students to become more self-aware and to use their abilities fully. In postsecondary counselling centres, emphasis is increasingly placed on global outreach and interaction and a proactive stance in the delivery of services (Bishop, 1990; Marks & McLaughlin, 2005; Pace et al., 1996). These services include consultation, career counselling, crisis management, retention, personalization and humanization of the campus environment, establishment of self-help programs, and cooperation with other campus units (Stone & Archer, 1990).

Overall, Canadian students face a barrage of complex events and processes that have temporary and permanent impacts on them. Counselling interventions can make a difference, whether offered outside or within school settings. Meta-analysis studies have shown that overall, counselling interventions generally have a moderate but clear effect on altering problematic child and adolescent behaviours (Prout, 2007).

Your Personal Reflections

1. What do you remember most about the school counsellors you had growing up? What duties did they perform? Was there a difference in their focus at various levels?

2. As you read in this chapter, elementary school counsellors work hard at providing preventive mental health services. How do you think they might present their work to the public, especially since many individuals are skeptical of prevention programs?

3. Think of your middle school experience and what you learned from peers. How do you think a peer mentor could have helped you (assuming you did not have one)? How do you think being a peer mentor is helpful (whether you were one or not)?

4. There are a number of developmental theories that postsecondary student workers use as the basis for their interactions with postsecondary students. Which of the four theories covered in this chapter appeals to you most? Why?

5. Which problems for postsecondary students listed in Table 19.2 surprised you? Which would you expect to occur? What does this tell you about your awareness of the difficulties students encounter and seek help for?

6. What did you lose when you went to postsecondary school? How did that loss affect you? What did you gain when you went to postsecondary school? How did that gain impact your life?

Classroom Activities

1. In groups of three, talk about your perceptions of and experiences with counsellors in your elementary, middle, and high schools. How did they exemplify the roles outlined in this chapter? What were the best things they did for you or your school? What could they have done differently to improve their services?

2. Reflect on your life as a middle school student. What were your greatest concerns then, and how did you handle them? With another classmate, share your reflections (to the point you feel comfortable doing so). What counsellor-related activities do you think might have been helpful to you then?

3. What do you think are the greatest concerns of high school students today? Write down your top five ideas. Share them with other classmates in groups of three, and then compare your rank-ordered group list with the class as a whole. How much agreement exists among the class? As a class, discuss ways of addressing one of these problems.

4. Pretend you are an elementary school counsellor. Design a guidance lesson on the topic of your choice. Then either tell or show the class how you would carry out your plan. What is your rationale for choosing your topic? How might children in your class eventually benefit from the experience?

5. Check your postsecondary school library to see which of the journals mentioned in this chapter it subscribes to. Examine recent issues of the journals and find an article that interests you. Summarize the contents of this article for your classmates in an oral report.

6. Invite a resident assistant at your postsecondary school to discuss his or her job with the class. How does the actual job compare with your idea of what it could be? What parts of the position do you find appealing or not appealing?

7. Postsecondary students are bright and articulate. What theories do you imagine might be effective with this population that would not be as useful with a less educated group?

8. What concerns or problems on your school campus do you think counsellors should address? Pretend you have been asked to set up programs to take care of these situations. What are some steps you might take to be effective?

Chapter 20
Mental Health Counselling: Abuse, Addictions, and Disabilities

PRACTICE REFLECTION

It is commonly accepted that most heavy drinkers minimize the amount they actually consume. "I had a couple after work" generally translates into maybe five or six. I have worked with a couple off and on for years, sometimes together and sometimes individually. As a result, we have a solid real and trusting relationship—one aspect of having a strong working alliance—and they open up to me about nearly everything. James e-mailed me and said his wife, Tamara, has been on his back about his drinking. She tells him he drinks too much and spends too much time away from home.

I met with the two of them to find out their perspectives. As expected, both had a different rendition as to how much James actually drinks. Tamara focused on the many times over the 20-plus years of their marriage that he had been seriously inebriated, while James preferred to look at the occasions where he had maintained control over his drinking. Nevertheless, he did see that he was not always in control and he did want to do something about it.

In a situation like this one, the counsellor attempts to understand the depth of the problem, asking questions such as, "Tell me about your drinking style—how often, how much, et cetera." "How often do you drink only the amount that you intend to drink, and what is occurring when you are unable to stop at this amount?" "What is the most you drink on one occasion, and how often does this happen?" "How do you feel the next day after such an occasion of drinking?" "Describe for me the intensity of your cravings to drink." "What happens to you when you are unable to drink for any reason?" Some individuals have become highly dependent on alcohol and may need to abstain completely to live successfully, while others may be able to re-train their drinking patterns and perceptions of drinking through cognitive-behavioural or other therapies.

The three of us tentatively concluded that James may be able to re-train himself to drink less and have more control. I created a consumption log for him that he was to complete daily. A smaller version is reprinted below:

Consumption Log
(Remember the goal is moderation—one or two drinks a day of red wine or dark beer is healthy, more is not. Allow yourself three or four drinks on two occasions per week—not more than that.)
Level of Emotion (rate on a 0 to 10 scale): 0 = no emotion, 5 = moderate emotion, 10 = extreme emotion
Feeling of Intoxication (rate on a 0 to 10 scale): 0 = no intoxication, 5 = moderate intoxication, 10 = extreme intoxication

Date	Trigger or Upcoming Situation in Which You Will Drink	Level of Emotion	Your Plan for Not Drinking Excessively	Number of Drinks	Feeling of Intoxication	Behaviour Following Drinking
Sunday						
Monday						
Tuesday						
Wednesday						
Thursday						
Friday						
Saturday						

As Tamara had begun to act like a "parent" in transactional analysis terms and James as the "child," it was important to bring their relationship back to "adult–adult." I asked James to complete the consumption log alone each day and to e-mail it back to me each week. In that way, he reported only to me regarding his actual drinking, but when the three of us met together, it gave Tamara a chance to provide a qualitative description of how she felt James was doing with his consumption and his behaviour following drinking (which was also a concern to her).

After several sessions, James was complying with his consumption goals (stated in the log chart) about 95% of the time. The three of us agreed that further treatment was no longer needed; Tamara was willing to accept the odd "slip," as his overall consumption and behaviour while drinking had improved significantly and sufficiently.

Working in a mental health or community counselling setting, including private practice, is a goal for many counsellors. Those who choose such settings usually do so for various reasons. Among the factors that these environments provide are opportunities to work with the public and governmental organizations in the promotion of wellness, the prevention and treatment of mental illnesses, and sometimes the opportunity to be an independent contractor or consultant. The chance to make a difference in any of these ways is exciting and stimulating for many clinicians. As mental health counselling is provided by many different specialists, such as psychiatrists, psychologists, social workers, Certified Canadian Counsellors, and psychiatric nurses, practitioners are regulated by their governing bodies.

This chapter begins by reviewing the advantages and limitations of working as a mental health counsellor, including private practice. It highlights the work emphasis in these areas and what clinicians in each specialty actually do. In examining these areas, particular attention will be focused on prevention and the promotion of positive health, as well as the treatment of disorders.

Next, the chapter moves into a looking at counsellors who work with abused, addicted, or disabled clients. Counsellors who specialize in these areas of treatment focus on a number of areas, including the promotion of healthy lifestyles, the identification and elimination of stressors, the modification of toxic environments, and the preservation or restoration of physical and mental health. Specific ways in which clients are served depend on the counsellors' skills and the needs of client populations.

MENTAL HEALTH COUNSELLING

"MENTAL ILLNESS IS THE MOST PERVASIVE HEALTH PROBLEM IN CANADA" (GOODMAN, 2010, para. 13). In fact, most Canadians are affected directly or indirectly by mental illness, and 20% of Canadians will personally experience a mental disorder during their lifetime (Health Canada, 2006b). Furthermore, "most mental illness begins during adolescence and young adulthood" (Health Canada, 2006b, para. 2).

A representative Canadian study found that the average consumer of psychological services is female, middle-aged, and separated, divorced, or widowed. The most likely consumers are those with higher education and income, while those with the greatest mental health needs are least likely to utilize psychological services (Hunsley, Lee, & Aubry, 1999).

The World Health Organization (WHO; 2005–2010) defines mental health as

> the ability to think and learn, and the ability to understand and live with one's emotions and the reactions of others. It is a state of balance within a person and between a person and the environment. Physical, psychological, social, cultural, spiritual and other interrelated factors participate in producing this balance. The inseparable links between mental and physical health have been demonstrated. (para. 1)

The problem of mental health is so extensive that WHO has identified it as a global priority (WHO, 2005–2010). Although services for the mentally ill are paid for by the universal medicare system in Canada, it does not cover the cost of those working in community agencies or in private practice. If a person decides to avail themselves of practitioners working in these settings, he or she will need to pay out of pocket (the exception being some nonprofit community agencies, which provide services at no cost). Extended health care plans in Canada, however, provide some reimbursement coverage for licensed psychologists and in some cases for other mental health professionals.

Mental health counselling has been defined in many ways during its relatively brief history. Initially, it was described as a specialized form of counselling performed in non-educational, community-based, or mental health settings (Seiler & Messina, 1979). Over the years, however, different views of mental health counselling have evolved, including those that are developmental (Ivey, 1989); relationship-focused (Ginter, 1989); and slanted toward treatment, advocacy, or personal and environmental coping (Hershenson, Power, & Seligman, 1989). "It shares a border with professional counselling in its conceptual and philosophical perspective that is more educational-developmental-preventive than clinical remedial" (Pistole & Roberts, 2002, p. 15).

MENTAL HEALTH COUNSELLING AS A SPECIALTY

It is clear that "mental health counseling is interdisciplinary in its history, practice settings, skills/knowledge, and roles performed" (Spruill & Fong, 1990, p. 19). This interdisciplinary nature is an asset in generating new ideas and energy. At the same time, it is a drawback in helping those who identify as mental health counsellors distinguish themselves from some closely related mental health practitioners (Wilcoxon & Puleo, 1992).

Regardless, many practitioners in the counselling profession use the term *mental health counsellor* to describe themselves. As a group, mental health counsellors work in a variety of settings, including mental health centres, community agencies, hospitals, employee assistance programs (EAPs), health and wellness promotion programs (HWPs), geriatric centres, crisis control agencies, and child guidance clinics. Some are private practitioners, too. They counsel a diverse group of clients, including rape victims, depressive's families, potential suicide victims, and those with diagnosable disorders. In addition, they consult, educate, and at times perform administrative duties (Hosie, West, & Mackey, 1988; West, Hosie, & Mackey, 1987). They often work closely with other helping professionals, such as psychiatrists, psychologists, clinical social workers, psychiatric nurses, and other counselling specialists, to become part of a team effort (Hansen, 1998). Thus, it is crucial that mental health counsellors know psychopathology as defined by the *Diagnostic and Statistical Manual* (DSM-IV-TR) classifications so they can converse intelligently with other health professionals and skillfully treat dysfunctional clients (Hinkle, 1994; Vacc, Loesch, & Guilbert, 1997).

Mental health counsellors have basic counselling skills as well as specialty skills related to the needs and interests of particular populations or problems. Major duties of counsellors in mental health are assessing and analyzing background and current information on clients, diagnosing mental and emotional conditions, exploring possible solutions, and developing treatment plans. Preventive mental health activities and recognition of the relationship between physical and mental health have become prominent also.

As a group, mental health counsellors are interested in professional development related to applied areas of counselling, such as marriage and family counselling, substance abuse and chemical dependency, third-party reimbursement, and small-group counselling (Wilcoxon & Puleo, 1992). Such interest is understandable in light of the fact that most mental health counsellors are practitioners and earn a living by offering services for remuneration.

Theories and Functions

Mental health counsellors are diverse in the ways they use theories and techniques in their practices, in part because they work in such varied settings and have a wide range of functions. One theoretical position, existential theory, has been advocated as "congruent with the essential principles of mental health counseling" (Bauman & Waldo, 1998, p. 27), but a large number of theories have been used in the field. The selection of theories by mental health counsellors depends on their clients' needs. Generally, the literature about mental health counselling focuses on two major issues that have theoretical implications: prevention and promotion of mental health and treatment of disorders and dysfunctions. Both topics are likely to continue attracting attention because they are considered primary roles of mental health counsellors.

Primary Prevention and the Promotion of Mental Health A primary philosophical emphasis throughout the history of mental health counselling has been on prevention and promotion of mental health services. "Many mental health counselors are actively involved in primary prevention types of programs through the schools, colleges, churches, community health centers, and public and private agencies" where they are employed (Weikel & Palmo, 1989, p. 15). Primary prevention is characterized by its "before the fact quality"; it is intentional and "group- or mass-, rather than individually, oriented" (Baker & Shaw, 1987, p. 2). It may be directly or indirectly implemented, but it is based on a sound theoretical foundation (Cowen, 1982). For example, the establishment of over 1200 suicide and emotional help lines worldwide and on the internet to deal with the warning signs of suicide is a primary prevention approach (Befrienders International, 2007). When successful, primary prevention ultimately results in healthier and better-adjusted individuals and communities.

Hall and Torres (2002) recommend two primary prevention models appropriate for community-wide implementation with adolescents. They are Bloom's (1996) *configural model of prevention* and Albee's *incidence formula* (Albee & Gullotta, 1997).

Bloom's model focuses on three dimensions. First, counsellors need to work to increase individual strengths and decrease individual limitations. Second, they must increase social support (e.g., through parents and peers) and decrease social stress. Finally, environmental variables, such as poverty, natural disasters, and community programming for youth, must be addressed.

Albee's model is global in scope and emphasizes that counsellors must decrease the negative effects of biology and stress while simultaneously increasing the positive effects of adolescents' coping skills, self-esteem, and support systems. Both models require a willingness by the counsellor to network with other agencies and individuals. He or she must invest considerable time and energy in program construction that may not have an immediate payoff.

Case Example: What Would *You* Do?

Ned was much more interested in doing preventive work than in doing treatment. However, it was not easy for him to support himself because there were few positions for prevention specialists. Therefore, he had to string together a series of grants that periodically either ran out or required renewal.

One day, exhausted from his work, Ned came to the office to find a grant agent there questioning his facts and figures. At first Ned was intimi dated.

Then he thought: "I have a network of professionals who know my work and can vouch for my statistics." They did exactly that and Ned actually received a larger grant from the foundation that had questioned him.

1. What other strategies could Ned have used in this case?

2. Why do you think prevention is so difficult to fund at times?

One place where primary prevention is emphasized is in the area of suicide. Suicide is the fifth leading cause of death among Canadians (Paulson & Worth, 2002). When assessing clients for suicide, mental health counsellors need to be mindful that there are various factors that influence the rates and lethality of suicide attempts. For instance, "three times as many females as males attempt suicide but about three times as many males as females are successful" (McWhirter, McWhirter, McWhirter, & McWhirter, 2004, p. 197). Tragically, the likelihood of suicide for gay and lesbian youth is two to three times higher than for heterosexual youth. In addition, different ethnic groups are more at risk for suicide behaviour than others. In Canada, suicide rates are between five and seven times higher for First Nations youth than for non-Aboriginal youth, and even more frightening is that the rate for Inuit youth is 11 times the national average (Health Canada, 2006a).

In addition to these gender, sexual-orientation, and multicultural variables, clinicians need to use assessment instruments to evaluate suicidal ideation more accurately. One global scale they may use is the SAD PERSONS scale (Patterson, Dohn, Bird, & Patterson, 1983) for adults or the Adapted-SAD PERSONS scale (A-SPS) for children (Juhnke, 1996) to determine which individuals are most likely to be at high risk. The letters in this scale stand for the following:

*S*ex (male)
*A*ge (older clients)
*D*epression
*P*revious attempt
*E*thanol (alcohol) abuse
*R*ational thinking loss
*S*ocial support system lacking (lonely, isolated)
*O*rganized plan
*N*o spouse
*S*ickness (particularly chronic or terminal illness)

It is the combination of these factors in an interactive process that is likely to yield information pertinent for the mental health counsellor to use in prevention.

Another form of primary prevention is emphasizing healthy development—that is, positive coping and growth skills so that individuals are able to deal effectively with crises (Hershenson, 1982; 1992). "Insofar as counseling derives from a model based on healthy development, it can reasonably hope to achieve its purpose of promoting healthy development in its clients" (Hershenson, 1982, p. 409). Erik Erikson (1963) and Abraham Maslow (1962) offer basic premises from which mental health counsellors can work. The writings of these theorists were based on observations about human development and emphasized the promotion of healthy growth and development. The integration of these two systems of thought yields six personal development trends: survival, growth, communication, recognition, mastery, and understanding. The first two trends focus on the self, the middle two on interpersonal functions, and the final two on the accomplishment of tasks. Mental health counselling is geared toward the improvement of the self in interpersonal relationships and task performances.

In an important article on healthy personal development, Heath (1980) outlined a comprehensive model of healthy maturation. He pointed out that research demonstrates that an adolescent's psychological maturity is a major predictor of adult mental health and vocational adaptation and that degree of adult maturity is related to marital sexual adjustment and vocational adaptation. Heath then proposed practical general principles that counsellors can apply in promoting client development. Four are listed here (Heath, 1980, p. 395):

1. *"Encourage the anticipatory rehearsal of new adaptations,"* such as those that deal with jobs and intimate relationships.

2. *"Require constant externalization of what is learned and its correction by action."* In essence, Heath believes practice makes perfect in the accomplishment of all human tasks. Learning is accomplished through feedback.

3. *"Allow a person to experience the consequences of his or her decisions and acts."* Heath agrees with Alfred Adler on this idea. He notes that inappropriate or excessive rewards may have an unhealthy effect on a person's development.

4. *"Appreciate and affirm strengths."* Reinforcement, according to behaviourist principles, is crucial to new learning. Heath agrees and says that the acknowledgment and acceptance of people's strengths can bolster self-confidence and help them take the risks necessary for new learning.

Focusing on environment is another preventive emphasis of mental health counsellors, whether it is conducted globally or more individually. Huber (1983) sums up the research in this growing area of interest, noting that environments have personalities just as people do. Some environments are controlling and rigid, whereas others are more flexible and supportive. To make effective use of this *social-ecological perspective*, mental health counsellors should do the following:

- Identify the problem as one essentially connected with a particular setting. Some environments elicit or encourage specific behaviours that may not be healthy.

- Gain the agreement of clients and significant others that the environment is the client. It is much easier for most people to see a difficulty as simply a matter related to the individual.

- Assess the dynamic variables within an environment. Moos (1973) developed a number of ways to evaluate environments. Counsellors can work with clients to determine how environments function in favour of or counter to the clients' needs.

- Institute social change and social justice initiatives where needed. Counsellors can help clients with specific methods for improving the present environment.

- Evaluate the outcome. There is no one way to do this, but the more clearly the client states his or her criteria for the ideal environment, the better the evaluation possibility.

Related to the social-ecological perspective is *ecosystemic thinking*, "thinking that recognizes the indivisible interconnectedness of individual, family, and sociocultural context" (Sherrard & Amatea, 1994, p. 5). In this view, mental health counselling is enlarged to consider the cultural contexts in which people relate and communicate. The meaning that individuals give to their interpersonal and environmental interactions becomes a consideration in counselling (Conyne & Cook, 2004).

Marriage is a situation that illustrates the importance of both personal and environmental factors in individuals' well-being (Gladding, 2007). A study conducted by Wiggins, Moody, and Lederer (1983) on marital satisfaction found that the most significant predictor of such satisfaction was the compatibility of couples' tested personality typologies. They concluded that individuals express "satisfaction with and seek interaction in environments that meet their psychological needs" (p. 177). In interracial marriages, which are increasing worldwide, mental health counsellors can be therapeutic in helping couples identify and address predictable stressors in their lives. Such stressors may manifest in the form of prejudice or identity issues regarding the marriage relationship and biracial children, among others. In these matters, mental health counsellors help couples find support within each other, within groups in their communities, or in special programs such as marriage enrichment (Solsberry, 1994).

Case Example: What Would *You* Do?

Eileen grew up in a small town in northern Ontario where people were friendly and the pace was slow. However, when she married George, she left the town and moved to a larger city where no one spoke to strangers and the pace was very fast. Eileen hated it, but she loved George and wanted to adjust to her new environment if at all possible.

Because she had never finished college, Eileen enrolled in a nearby community college. Besides being stimulated by the environment, she found a support group of young women in the same situation she was in. The support group expanded to not only meeting on campus but to holding social events with spouses and partners. At the end of the first year, Eileen realized she actually liked her new surroundings.

1. Although Eileen may not have intentionally worked to shape her environment, ecologically minded counsellors do. What are some ways you can shape your environment to make it and you healthier?

2. From an ecological perspective, what other steps could Eileen take to increase her social network?

An overall emphasis in mental health prevention is on *positive wellness* (health-related activities that are both preventive and remedial and have a therapeutic value to individuals who practice them consistently). Such activities include eating natural foods, taking vitamins, going to health spas, meditating, participating in regular exercise, and exploring a variety of humanistic and transpersonal approaches to helping (O'Donnell, 1988). "For the person to be a whole, healthy, functioning organism, one must evaluate the physical, psychological, intellectual, social, emotional, and environmental processes" (Carlson & Ardell, 1988, p. 383). Signs of the holistic movement toward health and well-being are apparent everywhere; for instance, the spring 2007 issue of the *Journal of Humanistic Counseling, Development and Education* was devoted completely to wellness and ways of promoting health. Americans and Canadians of all ages have become more aware of positive and negative habits with an increased emphasis on increasing the former and decreasing the latter.

Research backs up the basis for this movement toward health and well-being and in some ways leads it. In an extensive review of the literature on the effectiveness of physical fitness on measures of personality, Doan and Scherman (1987) found strong support for the idea that regular exercise can have a beneficial effect on people's physical and psychological health. Their review supports counsellors who prescribe health habits to accompany regular counselling practices. Their findings have had more recent support from the review of research in this field by Penedo and Dahn (2005).

Other strategies for working from a wellness perspective include

- having counsellors dwell on positive, life-enhancing things the individual can do;
- altering traditional screening to include more emphasis on overall health;
- conducting more research; and
- highlighting the physical dimension of clients' lives as one aspect of what Lazarus (1989) calls *multimodal therapy* (BASIC I.D.: behaviour, affect, sensation, imagery, cognition, interpersonal relationships, and drugs/biology).

Secondary and Tertiary Prevention

In addition to primary prevention, mental health counsellors concentrate on *secondary prevention* (controlling mental health problems that have already surfaced but are not severe) and *tertiary prevention* (controlling serious mental health problems to keep them from becoming chronic or life-threatening). In such cases (in contrast to primary prevention), mental health counsellors assess client functioning and then, if appropriate, use theories and techniques developed by major theorists such as Rogers, Ellis, Skinner, and Glasser to treat symptoms and core conditions.

Mental health counsellors who work in treatment face a number of challenges, such as responding adequately to the number of people who need and seek mental health services. Gadit (2007) of Memorial University stated in the *Journal of Medicine* that "mental illness has reached an alarming proportion over the globe and has become a vitally important issue for the nations in terms of morbidity, mortality and huge economic burden" (para. 2). That is compounded by the fact that there is a worldwide shortage of mental health workers, both in developed and developing countries (Gadit, 2007). The number of children with serious mental health issues has continued to grow dramatically, concurrent with the growth of social problems like poverty, homelessness, and substance abuse (Collins & Collins, 1994).

Another challenge for clinicians in mental health counselling is the trend in in-patient psychiatric hospitals to shorten the length of stays for severely disturbed clients. These shortened stays mean more disturbed individuals are either not receiving the treatment they need or are being seen in outpatient facilities where counsellors may have less experience working with people who have severe mental health problems.

Some of the areas mental health counsellors focus on in treatment are general and specific lifespan disorders such as mild depression (Kolenc, Hartley, & Murdock, 1990), smoking cessation (Pinto & Morrell, 1988), obsessive-compulsive behaviour (Dattilio, 1993), and eating disorders such as bulimia (Latner & Wilson, 2000). They may also be expected to assess and treat disorders using the DSM-IV-TR. Some deal with severe mental disorders; others specialize in working with either less severely disturbed persons or specific populations and the disorders that impact these groups most. In order to get a feel for what treatment is like in working with difficult mental disorders such as schizophrenia, novice counsellors and those who do not work in this field may view such films as *Sybil*, *Three Faces of Eve*, and *A Beautiful Mind*.

Depression and anxiety are "the most common clinical symptoms associated with presentation for counseling services" (Hinkle, 1999, p. 475). Regarding one-year prevalence, 12.2% of Canadians reported having anxiety disorders while 4.1 to 4.6% reported an episode of major depression (Health Canada, 2002). In 2008, 6.8% of Canadians aged 12 and older reported they had received a diagnosis of a mood disorder (depression, bipolar, or mania), up from 5.3% in 2003 (Statistics Canada, 2009) (Note: These findings were based on the 2008 Canadian Community Health Survey, which did not include residents of Indian reserves, health care institutions, some remote areas, and full-time RCMP). Depression "may be the most common disorder of mental health workers themselves . . . with research suggesting that from one third to more than 60% of mental health professionals" reported "a significant episode of depression within the previous year" (p. 116).

Regardless of the exact figures and populations affected, depression and anxiety are common in society for a number of reasons, many of which are featured nightly on the evening news or on talk radio. Like anxiety, there are various forms of depression. The good news is that there are a number of treatments for both depression and anxiety, such as problem-solving therapy, solution-focused therapy, narrative therapy, and cognitive-behavioural counselling. All seem to work well in the treatment (i.e., recovery) and prevention of these maladies (Dixon, 2000; Gladding, 2005; Paradise & Kirby, 2005).

In addition to treating depression and anxiety disorders, mental health counsellors, like many counsellors in other settings, are called upon to work with individuals who suffer hopelessness and suicidal ideology. There are several models for working with suicidal clients but two that are prominent are the crisis intervention model and the continuing-therapy model (Paulson & Worth, 2002). "Both models stress the significance of a positive therapeutic relationship and the understanding and validation of client's feelings" (p. 87). They also emphasize the importance of helping suicidal clients to develop self-awareness and construct a new identity. All of these factors have been found through research to be essential components in overcoming suicidal thoughts and behaviours. Whereas both approaches work, the continuing-therapy model is more advantageous because it provides a lengthier time frame for client–counsellor interactions.

In addition to these two models, counsellors can also help suicidal clients create meaning through the use of an existential-constructivist framework (Rogers, 2001). As opposed to the more pragmatic and technological characteristics of much therapeutic work with suicidal clients, this theoretical approach delves into an "increased understanding of suicidal individuals from a phenomenological meaning perspective" (p. 16). It requires the counsellor and client to commit to long-term therapeutic work and to deal with the community and others as well as intrapersonal thoughts and feelings.

COMMUNITY AGENCY COUNSELLING

Community agency counselling is defined more by the setting in which a counsellor works than anything else. As a group, counsellors working in a community agency are generalists who identify more with the profession of counselling as a whole than with any counselling specialty, process, or orientation. Community agency counsellors are found in almost all non-school settings (Hershenson & Berger, 2001).

One place where community agency counsellors are being hired in increasing numbers is *employee assistance programs* (EAPs) (Gladding & Newsome, 2004). These programs are found in many businesses and institutions across Canada. Their purpose is to work with employees in preventive and remedial ways in order to help them avoid or work through problems that might detrimentally affect their on-the-job behaviour. To be effective, EAP counsellors set up programs that deal with a variety of subjects that employees have an interest in, such as wellness or retirement. They invite outside experts to make presentations at convenient times and arrange for follow-up material or input if needed. EAP counsellors also offer short-term counselling services to employees who may be experiencing difficulties. These services are usually time-limited; for example, three sessions. However, as experts in community resources, EAP counsellors are able to make referrals to mental health professionals who can offer employees more expertise. As an overall rule, large companies and institutions will offer EAP services on their premises (i.e., in-house) whereas smaller operations will usually rely on EAP counsellors who serve a number of companies and institutions (i.e., outsource).

Another place where community agency counsellors may be employed is with crisis-oriented organizations, such as the Red Cross or local emergency telephone and walk-in counselling centres. In crisis situations, respondents must take care of a multitude of needs ranging from physical to mental health. Thus, local communities, and even international groups, hire counsellors and other mental health professionals who can offer needed counselling and supportive services to victims of disasters, whether natural or human-made (Gladding, 2002). Individuals who work in these situations may have jobs that differ from the norm in regard to hours and activities. They also have above-average excitement and challenges in the work they perform.

Finally, community agency counsellors are also found in settings where many other helping specialists work. For example, they may be employed in substance abuse centres, hospices, child guidance clinics, wellness centres, colleges, hospitals, and private practices.

PRIVATE PRACTICE AS A SPECIALTY

Private practice counsellors have less of a formalized history than either mental health or community counsellors but such professionals have existed since the beginning of counselling. Private practitioners aspire to work for themselves in an individual or group practice unaffiliated with an agency. They are like physicians in working on a fee-for-service basis.

Private practice remains popular, perhaps especially with psychologists, where charging services to a third party is common. When many students first enroll in a counselling program, they aspire to set up a private practice; indeed, doctoral graduates of counselling programs indicate that private practice is their preferred venue of service delivery (Zimpfer, 1996; Zimpfer & DeTrude, 1990). Often counsellors conceptualize that a private practice setting will give them more control over their lives and be more financially rewarding. Indeed, a private practice can be a wonderful experience. However, it usually takes a great deal of work to begin such a practice unless a professional buys, or is invited into, an already established practice.

Difficulties Setting Up a Private Practice

To be successful as a private practitioner, a counsellor needs a number of abilities beyond clinical expertise. Among the most salient of these abilities, he or she

- must be able to balance business skills with those of counselling, or find a competent business manager
- must build up support networks in a way not as necessary in agency work, where one is often surrounded by colleagues who can supply needed information on treatment or referrals to appropriate specialists
- must overcome or avoid the use of restrictive covenants or noncompetitive agreements that some agencies put in their contracts with counsellors that prohibit them from setting up a private practice within a certain geographical area or within a certain time period after leaving the agency (Wyatt, Daniels, & White, 2000)
- must invest time and hard work in "pull marketing" relationships (i.e., making oneself attractive by generating referrals through offering needed services to others in groups [such as singles, the divorced, or the widowed]) and meeting other community professionals regularly in order to learn about them and to introduce oneself (Crodzki, 2002)
- must be willing to donate services and participate in endeavours for the public good in order to build up a reputation and a practice, for as Allen Ivey remarked, "There is just a very small window for private practitioners to make big money" (Littrell, 2001, p. 117).

Cecily could hardly wait to finish her master's training in counselling psychology at McGill. She had always dreamed of being independent. As soon as she completed her degree, she moved back to Alberta and threw a party where she announced that within the next few months she would start her new life as a private practitioner.

After the announcement, Cecily realized she could not become a private practitioner until she was licensed, which required completing a one-year internship and jumping several other hurdles. She also realized she had no specialty and therefore she doubted that people would line up to see her. Finally, she confessed that she did not have a clue as to how to go about setting up a business, which a private practice is. Putting away her dreams of practicing independently, Cecily went to work for a mental health agency.

1. Have you ever had dreams like Cecily's? If so, what do you think you will have to do to make them come true? If not, what do you think of Cecily's decision to work for a mental health agency?

2. Alberta is one of the few provinces that allows psychologists to become registered with only a master's credential—most require a doctoral degree. Given that Alberta has licensed psychologists at both the master's and doctoral levels, what advice would you give to someone who wanted to have a full-time private practice?

Advantages of Setting Up a Private Practice

There are opportunities for counsellors to enter private practice and succeed. Among the advantages private practitioners have are the following:

- *Confidentiality.* In many, if not most, grade schools, postsecondary institutions, community agencies, and hospital settings, client files are kept in a central filing station. This means that anyone in the office has access to these files. Greater confidentiality can be assured when files are kept by a private practitioner only.

- *Reputation enhancement.* Counsellors in private practice have a greater chance of becoming known in their communities as professionals who provide quality service. Consequently, they have better opportunities to build excellent reputations.

- *Autonomy.* Private practitioners set their own office hours, and they can come and go as they please.

- *Specialization.* Being in private practice allows counsellors to become specialists, especially if they live in large urban areas where there are abundant numbers of clients with specific problems.

Overall, whereas private practice has some drawbacks, it will continue to be a setting in which many counsellors elect to work.

COUNSELLING THE ABUSED CLIENT

Abuse is the misuse or maltreatment of people, places, or things. It can be active or passive in nature, but the end result is usually damaging to whoever is involved. People abuse for a number of reasons; however, that does not diminish the results of their actions or neglect. The two primary areas of abuse most prevalently seen in counselling are interpersonal abuse (e.g., abuse of children, spouse, or siblings) and intrapersonal abuse (e.g., substance abuse, gambling, and workaholism).

Interpersonal Abuse

Since the 1980s, the federal government has gathered national-level information on family violence in Canada. Examples of ground-breaking studies and surveys include the 1984 *Badgley Report on Child Sexual Abuse*, the 1993 *Violence Against Women Survey*, the 1993 *Canadian Panel on Violence Against Women*, and the 1996 *Royal Commission on Aboriginal Peoples*. National surveys, such as the *General Social Survey* (GSS), the *Canadian Incidence Study of Reported Child Abuse and Neglect*, and the *Uniform Crime Reporting Survey*, provide valuable information on victimization and crime trends related to many forms of family violence. The results of national surveys and research have made it clear that family violence is not just an individual, private or family matter; it is a pervasive and complex societal problem in Canada. (Department of Justice Canada, 2009, p. 9)

Interpersonal abuse involves violent or neglectful actions against others, especially those within one's family (i.e., siblings, spouse/partner, children). It can take more subtle forms, such as emotional abuse, or it can be blatant, such as physical abuse.

Emotional Abuse Of all the types of abuse, *emotional abuse* is probably the most common. It is more subtle at times than other forms of abuse, although it can be blatant. It is not confined to an age, stage, or gender. Therefore, emotional abuse is prevalent across the lifespan and various family forms. In reality, though, emotional abuse is more prevalent in partners, regardless of their sexual orientation or marital status.

Berg-Cross (2002) suggests that there are 12 signs of emotional abuse between partners:

- healousy
- controlling behaviour
- unrealistic expectations
- isolation
- blaming for problems and for feelings
- hypersensitivity
- verbal abuse
- rigid sex roles

- sudden changes in personality and mood
- threats of violence
- breaking or striking objects
- use of force during arguments

Child Abuse Child abuse (which involves acts of commission) and child neglect (which involves acts of omission) are major concerns in Canadian family life. The 2003 *Canadian Incidence Study of Reported Child Abuse and Neglect* (CIS) is the second nation-wide study to examine the incidence of reported child abuse. Led by researchers Trocmé et al. (2005), the CIS-2003 tracked 14 200 child abuse investigations across Canada in the fall of 2003. The CIS focuses on physical abuse, sexual abuse, neglect, and emotional maltreatment.

The data from Québec were collected in a different manner than from the rest of Canada, but the combined total of child abuse investigations in 2003 was estimated at 235 315. Nearly half of these investigations were substantiated, leading to a national incidence rate of 18.67 cases of substantiated maltreatment per 1000 children.

Child neglect is the most prevalent form of child abuse in Canada with nearly a third (30%) of substantiated cases falling into this category (rate = 6.38 cases per 1000). Being exposed to domestic violence is the second most common form (rate = 6.17 per 1000), followed closely by physical abuse (rate = 5.31 per 1000). Emotional abuse ranks in third place with 15% of child abuse cases (rate = 3.23 per 1000); lastly, sexual abuse represents 3% of all cases (rate = 0.62 per 1000) (Trocmé et al., 2005). Despite the finding that sexual abuse only accounts for 3% of child maltreatment cases, these cases still represent 61% of all sexual assault victims reported to police in Canada (Department of Justice Canada, 2009). This is striking, given that minors only comprise 21% of the Canadian population (Department of Justice Canada, 2009).

Physical harm was found in 10% of substantiated cases, and a third of these were serious enough to require medical treatment. Emotional harm was noted in 20% of cases, while treatment was warranted in 14% of the substantiated cases. Children of Aboriginal heritage accounted for 15% of the substantiated cases (First Nations Status children = 10%; Métis children = 2%; First Nations non-Status children = 2%; Inuit children = 1%).

> While girls made up 49% of victims, girls made up a larger proportion of victims in cases of sexual abuse (63%) and emotional maltreatment (54%), whereas boys were more often victims in cases of physical abuse (54%), neglect (52%), and exposure to domestic violence (52%). (Trocmé et al., 2005, p. 6)

The CIS study was repeated in 2008. Results from the study were expected to be released to the public in October 2010 (Canadian Child Welfare Research Portal, 2009).

The effects of child abuse, especially emotional and psychological abuse, include aggression, delinquency, and suicide, as well as cognitive, emotional, academic, and psychological impairment in children (Gibb & Abela, 2008; McWey, 2004; Yates & Wekerle,

2009). Child abuse may also have a powerful influence on adult behaviour that is lifelong (Elam & Kleist, 1999). Adults who were abused as children appear to be less satisfied with their lives and prone to suffer from a number of disorders, including those that are behavioural, cognitive, and affective, such as depression and low self-esteem (May, 2005). Furthermore, data from the 1999 Canadian General Social Survey (9170 women; 7823 men) found that being a victim of childhood sexual abuse consistently predicted intimate partner violence in adulthood for both women and men, although the relationship was somewhat weaker for men (Daigneault, Hebert, & McDuff, 2009). However, research has shown that there is not a *causal* relationship between abuse and adult symptoms (Mullen et al., 1995).

Child physical abuse resides on a continuum from physical contact that is mild to that which is severe (Kemp, 1998). Severe physical child abuse is manifested in everything from skin injuries to death. In between are physical traumas such as broken bones, soft-tissue swelling, and bleeding. In addition to physical marks, psychological consequences result from physical abuse that range from fearfulness of others to post-traumatic stress responses. Many children who are physically abused become distrustful of others, delinquent, and even depressed. In addition, a number of these children have difficulty forming close, lasting relationships with peers, let alone adults. Finally, physical child abuse can lead to serious cognitive problems including cognitive impairment, poor school performance, and later substance abuse (Skowron & Platt, 2005).

One of the most insidious forms of child abuse is *childhood sexual abuse* (CSA). This type of abuse includes unwanted touching (i.e., fondling), sexual remarks, voyeurism, intercourse, oral sex, and pornography (Cobia, Sobansky, & Ingram, 2004; Elam & Kleist, 1999). Sexual abuse is tragically an all-too-common occurrence. Its long-term effects are usually damaging regardless of whether the sexually abused person is male or female, heterosexual or homosexual (Hunter, 2006). When sexual abuse occurs in childhood it often leads to distress, acute trauma, and even post-traumatic stress disorder (PTSD).

"It is generally believed that sexual abuse of all children is significantly underreported, with sexual abuse of boys being reported least" (Tomes, 1996, p. 55). In sexual abuse situations, "most abuse of boys is done by perpetrators outside the family; girls' abuse is predominantly intrafamilial" (Hutchins, 1995, p. 21). Almost one in three girls is sexually abused by age 18 (Crespi & Howe, 2000) and 12% to 18% of boys are sexually abused during childhood or adolescence (Cobia et al., 2004; Tomes, 1996).

It is difficult to detect and determine sexual abuse in families because in many cases all involved deny such actions and do not report them. Most victims (between 60% and 80%), for example, do not disclose their abuse until adulthood, and some never do (Alaggia, 2010; Gordon & Connolly, 2010). A qualitative national sample of 1621 young people from across Canada revealed that youth who have been abused or who have witnessed abuse use five disclosure strategies: (a) using self-harming behaviours as a call for help, (b) not disclosing it to anyone, (c) talking to friends, (d) talking to informal adult supports, or (e) talking to mandated service providers such as the police and social workers (Ungar, Barter, McConnell, Tutty, & Fairholm, 2009). Consequently, some youth do provide outward signs that abuse has or is occurring.

Sibling Abuse *Sibling abuse* "is pandemic and can have fatal results" (Kiselica & Morrill-Richards, 2007, p. 148). It is estimated that as many as 40% of children in the United States "engage in physical aggression against siblings, and as many as 85% engage in verbal aggression against siblings on a regular basis" (p. 148). In Canada, it is known that 32% of sexual assaults against minors are committed by family members, which includes both sibling and parental abuse (Department of Justice Canada, 2009). Reasons for sibling abuse are complicated, but they include rivalry for dominance and power struggles for resources. Regardless, across cultures it has been found that, when individuals experience sibling abuse, the chances increase during their lifetimes of becoming either victims or perpetrators in abusive relationships (Cunradi, Caetano, & Schafer, 2002).

Sibling abuse takes three dominant forms: sexual, physical, and psychological. Sexual abuse is almost always perpetuated on sisters by brothers. It may be a one-time act, but often it is continued over years. Physical abuse is inflicting harm by physical actions such as hitting, kicking, biting, scratching, or using objects such as hoses, coat hangers, belts, knives, and even guns. Psychological abuse includes constant, intense, or exaggerated teasing or contempt and downgrading and may be a part of the other two types of abuse. Whereas sibling abuse usually declines with age, it leaves its mark on those who experience it. The victims may become more violent with those less powerful than they are as time goes by.

A Québec study including 72 children (ages 5 to 16) referred to Child Protection Services between 1996 and 1999 evaluated its subjects for alleged sexual abuse. The researchers found that penetration was more frequent between siblings (70.8%) than in the father–daughter (34.8%) or stepfather–stepdaughter (27.3%) incest groups (Cyr, Wright, McDuff, & Perron, 2002). In an American study, researchers found that, in a survey of 1616 sexually abusive youths (aged 5 to 21), 38.8% of the victims were familial relative from within the same household (Ryan, Miyoshi, Metzner, Krugman, & Fryer, 1996).

Worling (1995) compared 32 12- to 19-year-old male sex offenders near Toronto who had assaulted younger siblings with 28 matched subjects who had assaulted only non-sibling children. He found that sibling incest was more strongly related to "marital discord, parental rejection, physical discipline, negative family atmosphere, dissatisfaction with family relationships, childhood sexual abuse, and presence of a younger child in the family" (p. 633).

Spouse and Partner Abuse *Spouse and partner abuse* is frequently referred to as "domestic violence" or "marital/partner violence"—that is, the "aggression that takes place in intimate relationships, usually between adults" (Kemp, 1998, p. 225). It is the attempt by one individual to "control the thoughts, beliefs, or behaviors of an intimate partner or to punish the partner for resisting one's control" (Peterman & Dixon, 2003, p. 41).

In 2006, over 38 000 incidents of spousal abuse were reported to police in Canada, representing 15% of police-reported violent allegations (Ogrodnik, 2008). Spousal abuse reported to police is most prevalent in Nunavut and Québec (20% each) and least prevalent in British Columbia, Nova Scotia, and New Brunswick (8% each) (Ogrodnik, 2008). Based on a survey of 24 000 Canadians, about 7% of adults in Canada (approximately 653 000 women and 546 000 men) experienced some form of violence in their common-law/married relationship in the five years prior to data collection for the 2004 General Social Survey (Department of Justice Canada, 2009).

Not surprisingly, 83% of the victims of police-reported spousal violence are women; only 17% of victims are men. These percentages remain constant throughout all provinces and territories. On an encouraging note, there was a steady decline in police-reported spousal violence between 1998 and 2006 (Ogrodnik, 2008).

There are many kinds of spousal and partner abuse. For example, abuse may include psychological, economic, physical, and/or sexual forms (Schecter & Ganley, 1995). It is not confined to a particular economic class, family structure, sexual orientation, or ethnic group. The worst form of spouse and partner abuse is known as battering, "violence which includes severe physical assault or risk of serious injury" (Kemp, 1998, p. 225). However, other forms of domestic violence include grabbing, slapping, pushing, and throwing things at one another (O'Leary & Murphy, 1999).

Seniors are also abused by spouses, adult children, or their caregivers. While 1% of seniors have been physically assaulted in Canada, another 7% have experienced either emotional or financial abuse. Spouses are implicated in most cases of elder abuse (Ogrodnik, 2008). Elders remain the least likely age group to be victimized, however, and if physical injuries are sustained, they are usually considered minor (Ogrodnik, 2008).

Lastly, of the 4490 murders that were solved in Canada between 1994 and 2003, 38% were family related. Nearly half (47%) of these were committed by a spouse. Youth under the age of 18 represented 25% of the murder victims during that time period (Ogrodnik, 2008).

Case Example: What Would *You* Do?

Charlene always wore long-sleeved blouses and long, flowing skirts to her job at a school. They were trendy clothes in some ways and antiquated in other ways. Every now and then she would wear a scarf around her neck, and on occasion she sported sunglasses.

Madge, Charlene's best friend, noticed one day that Charlene had a bruise below her scarf.

She began to notice other physical marks as the months passed. Finally, she confronted Charlene about whether she was being abused. Charlene denied the accusation.

1. What do you think Madge should do now?

2. Would entering counselling be helpful to Charlene at this point in time? Why or why not?

PREVENTING AND TREATING INTERPERSONAL ABUSE

Prevention programs in the interpersonal abuse arena are mainly educational in nature. They focus on teaching listening skills and appropriate behavioural interactions. A number have an Adlerian base (Gladding, 2007). Although they may take multiple forms, prevention programs usually stress cooperation, collaboration, and self-esteem. One such program is marriage enrichment.

Treatment for interpersonal abuse is prevalent. The four most common treatments for spouse or partner abuse are marital therapy, anger management training, individual therapy, and domestic conflict containment programs. Marital therapy may take the form of conjoint or couples therapy, but usually in abuse cases it does not because of the potential danger of violence. Therefore, recommended services are mostly gender-specific programs for the offender.

There are also a number of counselling approaches for dealing with sibling abuse. Most involve the direct participation of parents/guardians, children, and others involved and stress the importance of providing good supervision for children, giving children appropriate sexual education, and making sure homes are as violence-proof as possible (Wiehe, 2000).

Prevention and treatment of child abuse and neglect is complicated because it involves legal, developmental, and psychological issues (Pistorello & Follette, 1998; Wilcoxon et al., 2007). All provinces and territories require mental health workers and other professional helpers to report child abuse and neglect. "Failure to report child abuse usually constitutes unprofessional conduct that can lead to disciplinary action by a regulation board, possible conviction of a crime, and a civil lawsuit for damages" (Leslie, 2004, p. 48). Thus, before treatment can begin in most cases, legal issues must be resolved. In addition, developmental and psychological matters must be dealt with. For instance, when sexual abuse occurs early in life, children may blame themselves for it. Similarly, children of divorce often first find themselves at fault before they come to realize they have been victimized. Child sexual abuse is often not treated until adulthood, when other complications, such as couple intimacy, overlay the original problems.

Therefore, counsellors must deal with a plethora of current and historical issues in working with child abuse. Anger and feelings of betrayal on the part of the abuser must often be dealt with before working with the family as a whole in correcting the problem and preventing it from happening again. Furthermore, because of legal issues involved, the abuser may be separated from the family, which makes the job of working with the family even more difficult and challenging. There are specific organizations, such as the Community Child Abuse Council (www.childabusecouncil.on.ca) and the Canadian Society for the Investigation of Child Abuse (www.csicainfo.com), that provide support and information. Furthermore, the Childhelp National Child Abuse Hotline (call 1-800-4-A-CHILD) is devoted to the prevention of child abuse. The hotline provides services to the United States, its territories, and Canada, and is staffed 24 hours a day, 7 days a week with professional crisis counsellors. Through the use of interpreters, the organization provides service in 170 languages (see www.childhelp.org/pages/hotline).

There is no one treatment modality that works best in helping children who have been abused physically or sexually resolve the traumas of their experiences and make adequate and necessary adjustments (Hyde, Bentovim, & Monck, 1995; Oates & Bross, 1995). Rather, a variety of treatments have been used with members of this population and follow-up studies, for the most part, have not taken place or have been inconclusive (Greenwalt, Sklare, & Portes, 1998).

Intrapersonal Abuse

Substance Abuse *Substance abuse* is the habitual misuse of intoxicating and addicting substances, such as alcohol, drugs, and tobacco (i.e., nicotine). In this definition, drugs are defined as any substance other than food that can affect the way a person's mind and body works, including stimulants, depressants, and hallucinogens. Abuse of substances damages people mentally, physically, emotionally, socially, and spiritually. For example, the abuse of alcohol is frequently involved in disorderly or heinous behaviour from public drunkenness to date rape (Fagan, 2006). Indeed, substance abuse is "one of the major public health issues in today's society" and cuts across "gender, socioeconomic levels, ethnicity, age, religion, profession, geography, and most dimensions of human existence and background" (Stevens & Smith, 2005, p. iii). Alcohol and drug issues among the aged, adults, and adolescents are treated every day by counsellors in nursing and retirement homes, mental health clinics, colleges and universities, and public schools (Hinkle, 1999).

The Nature of Substance Abuse   Abuse of substances is one of the most frequently occurring mental health problems in Canada. The term *abuse* here refers to the use of a drug for the sole purpose of euphoria or recreation (Weigel, Donovan, Krug, & Dixon, 2007). For instance, in regard to alcohol, 9.3% of Canadians drink heavily, either infrequently or one or more times a week (Health Canada, 2009a). The problem is greater within gay and lesbian communities (Peterkin & Risdon, 2003) and with Aboriginal Canadians (Lix, Bruce, Sarkar, & Young, 2009).

Between "12% to 30% of all hospitalized patients abuse alcohol," and "health care costs among alcoholic families are twice as great as those of nonalcoholic families" (Steenbarger, 1998, p. 81). In addition, alcohol abuse among some populations, such as older adults, is often unrecognized, misdiagnosed, or attributed to the aging process (Williams et al., 2005). Tragically, in adolescents, alcohol abuse is often undertreated with "only 1 in 10 adolescents" receiving "any type of formal help . . . as compared to 1 in 5 adults" (Fagan, 2006, p. 326).

In 2002, the death, illness, and economic costs of substance abuse in Canada were estimated at approximately $40 billion. Tobacco accounted for $17 billion (42.7% of total cost), alcohol $14.6 billion (36.6%), and illegal drugs $8.2 billion (20.7%) (Rehm et al., 2006).

The Canadian Alcohol and Drug Use Monitoring Survey (CADUMS) is an ongoing national survey of alcohol and illicit drug use among Canadians 15 years of age and older. The survey began in 2008 and the results are based on telephone interviews, with 16 672 responses from across the 10 provinces. Derived from and similar to the Canadian Addiction Survey (CAS) of 2004, CADUMS is designed to provide detailed national and provincial estimates of alcohol and drug-related behaviours and outcomes (Health Canada, 2009a).

The main findings from CADUMS (Health Canada, 2009a) are as follows:

1. *Alcohol.* The lifetime prevalence rate for consumption was 90.2%, while 77.3% had consumed alcohol in the past year. The average age that youth begin drinking was 15.6 years. In the year prior to the survey, 4.2% were considered heavy infrequent drinkers while 5.1% were heavy frequent drinkers. *Heavy drinkers* was defined as five or more drinks for men and four or more drinks for women in one occasion, and *frequent use* was one or more times per week. More males (81.4%) reported drinking as compared to females (73.5%). For youth between 15 and 24 years of age, 78.4% drank alcohol in the year prior to the survey. Incidence of heavy infrequent drinking for 15- to 24-year-olds was five times higher than for adults 25 years and older (12.7% vs. 2.6%)., while for heavy frequent drinking, the rate was four times higher (13.5% vs. 3.6%).

2. *Cannabis.* The lifetime prevalence rate was 43.9%, while 11.4% had used cannabis in the year prior to the survey. The average age that youth begin use was 15.5 years. Prevalence usage for youth 15 to 24 years old was four times higher than for adults 25 years and older (32.7% vs. 7.3%). More males (14.4%) reported past year cannabis use as compared to females (8.6%).

3. *Other illicit drugs.* Usage in the year prior to the survey for the following drugs was as follows: (a) cocaine/crack 1.6%, (b) speed 1.1%, (c) hallucinogens 2.1%, (d) ecstasy 1.4%, and (e) methamphetamines 0.2%. In 2008, 12.1% of Canadians used one of six drugs (i.e., cannabis, cocaine or crack, speed, ecstasy, hallucinogens, or heroin).

4. *Abuse of psychoactive pharmaceutical drugs.* CADUMS also asked questions about three commonly used classes of drugs for therapeutic purposes: (a) opioid pain relievers, such as Oxycontin; (b) stimulants, such Ritalin and Dexedrine; and (c) tranquillizers and sedatives, such as Valium and Ativan. In 2008, 28.4% of respondents stated that they had used one or more of these drugs in the year prior to the survey, but only 2% said they used the drug to get high. For youth between 15 and 24, however, the recreational use of one or more of these drugs to get high rose to 9.4%.

For more information about substance abuse in Canada, visit the website of the Canadian Centre on Substance Abuse (www.ccsa.ca).

Whereas Americans reportedly see the use of drugs as the greatest problem they face (Centre on Addiction and Substance Abuse, 1995), in Canada, we are arguably more relaxed. An Angus Reid poll conducted with 1010 Canadian adults on April 8 and 9, 2010, found that 53% of the respondents believed marijuana should be legalized (Angus Reid Global Monitor, 2010).

Canada was the first nation in the world (i.e., July 2002) to regulate the use of cannabis for medical reasons and, in the 2004 federal election, the Marijuana Party received 0.3% of the popular vote. Furthermore, in November 2004, former prime minister Paul Martin re-introduced a bill that would allow anyone in possession of 15 grams or less of marijuana to face a fine instead of criminal charges. This motion, however, never came to a vote in the House of Commons. Current prime minister Stephen Harper appeared in a YouTube video on March 16, 2010, and implied that his government has no intention of legalizing marijuana (Angus Reid Global Monitor, 2010).

Although Canadian attitudes are often fairly relaxed around cannabis use, fewer than 7% of respondents were in favour of legalizing ecstasy, cocaine/crack, heroin, and crystal meth. Furthermore, there was a decrease in support for the legalization of the above mentioned illicit drugs (with the exception of marijuana, which remained at 53%) between 2008 and 2010 (Angus Reid Global Monitor, 2010).

The 2008 British Columbia Adolescent Health Survey found that youth are waiting longer than they did in the previous year to try alcohol and marijuana (Smith, Stewart, Poon, Saewyc, & McCreary Centre Society, 2010). Also encouraging is a conclusion drawn again from a researcher in British Columbia:

> Most young people who use alcohol or other drugs during their teen years do not have substance use problems and do not end up with abuse problems as adults either. If, however, a young teen is already using alcohol or other drugs, it can be worrisome. Youth who begin alcohol or drug use at young ages are more likely to develop substance abuse problems as they get older. (Saewyc, 2009, p. 8)

Where substance abuse problems do occur, however, more people are affected than just the addicted individual. Regarding alcohol abuse, for example, it is estimated that there are up to four times as many other people adversely affected. These include family members, friends, or associates (Fagan, 2006; Vick, Smith, & Herrera, 1998; Williams et al., 2005). Thus, what looks like intrapersonal abuse is also interpersonal in nature.

Often people who abuse one substance abuse other substances as well. *Polysubstance abuse* (the abuse of two or more substances simultaneously) is a growing phenomenon. In addition, abuse of substances often becomes a way of life related to social conditions. For example, many people begin smoking as adolescents in response to an unsatisfactory life rooted in poverty and hopelessness. Peer pressure, poor school performance, parental smoking, minority ethnic status, and an external locus of control make smoking more likely until addiction occurs (Hilts, 1996).

Addiction, which is often the result of substance abuse, is a complex, progressive behaviour pattern having biological, psychological, sociological, and behavioural components (Scott, 2000). It has been defined "as a persistent and intense involvement with and stress upon a single behavior pattern, with a minimization or even exclusion of other behaviors, both personal and interpersonal" (L'Abate, 1992, p. 2). A primary characteristic of addicts is that they become preoccupied with one object that controls their behaviours, thus limiting their other actions over time. Some subgroups in society may be more vulnerable to addictive behaviour, or have unique needs in regard to treatment, because of the stress they experience as a part of being a minority culture, such as their sexual orientation (Matthews, Selvidge, & Fisher, 2005).

Preventing Substance Abuse   Substance abuse and addiction prevention programs usually are tied into a community effort to prevent abuse on a global level. In preventing abuse, there are two factors that must be considered. The first is a *risk factor,* which is "typically defined as anything that increases the probability of a person using drugs" (Burrow-Sanchez, 2006, p. 284). For example, living in poverty, failing in school, or associating with drug users are all risk factors. In contrast, there is a so-called *protective factor,* which is "anything that protects or decreases the probability of a person using drugs" (p. 284). Examples of protective factors are a well-monitored and stable family, an association with friends who do not use drugs, and high achievement in school. *Triggers,* or environmental events, are involved in both risk and protective behaviours.

To try to protect and prevent substance abuse, a number of programs have been developed, some of which are more sophisticated and successful than others. One program, the "Just Say No" campaign, which was sponsored by local governments, focused on trying to help preteens and teenagers say "no" when offered a cigarette or a potentially addictive or dangerous substance. Children learned through this program how to be assertive and how to refuse offers of harmful drugs in an appropriate way. For example, they learned that they could simply ignore or walk away from drug-related situations as well as say "No, thanks" or make an excuse for refusing an offer of drugs.

"School-based drug prevention programs that are targeted, evidence-based, interactive, youth-focused, and engaging have been shown to have success in reducing drug abuse" (National Crime Prevention Centre [NCPC], 2009, p. 15). Public Safety Canada has outlined the important components of a substance abuse prevention program (NCPC, 2009), while York University has provided several great resources, including links to program materials suited for use in Canadian grade schools (York Region Health Connection, 2008). Several youth-friendly websites are also included on York University's list (e.g., Mothers Against Drunk Driving at www.maddyouth.ca and Ontario Students Against Impaired Driving at www.osaid.org).

There are also effective educational programs for teens who use tobacco and for potential and real cocaine addicts (see Canadian Association for School Health, n.d.).

These programs focus on both external and internal factors important to individuals in this age bracket. External factors include the impact of smoking on one's breath, teeth, and clothes, as well as monetary costs. Internal factors include such variables as lifestyle choices, time management, and nutrition. For younger individuals, external factors may be more effective in influencing their decisions to never begin smoking, or to stop smoking or doing drugs, whereas for older adolescents internal factors are more powerful.

A common element in approaches to substance abuse and addiction prevention involves group pressure and dynamics. In setting up preventive programs, counsellors are wise to use their knowledge of groups. The reason is that most people, especially adolescents, who get involved in the use of substances do so because their friends use drugs, they are bored, or they are under considerable stress (National Centre on Addiction and Substance Abuse at Columbia University, 2003). Therefore, when a group perceives drugs as hazardous to their health or dangerous, members of such a group are less likely to engage in experimenting with these substances. The group norm becomes one of discouraging members from trying drugs (Serritella, 1992).

Thus, educational and support groups are a valuable tool for counsellors to employ in warding off abuse and addictive behaviours in preventive programs (Gladding, 2008). To investigate what the Canadian government is doing regarding drug prevention and treatment, visit their comprehensive website (Health Canada, 2009b).

Treating Substance Abuse Approximately 25% of counselling cases relate to substance abuse and addiction problems either directly or indirectly. As indicated earlier, people who abuse or are addicted to substances of any type are difficult to work with because of the dysfunctional dynamics that surround them. Counsellors work with addicted persons as well as substance abusers in a number of ways, but three are most dominant: outpatient, residential, and in-patient, with outpatient being the most common (Burrow-Sanchez, 2006).

In providing treatment, it is important to remember that someone who is either addicted or a substance abuser must be "dry," or not currently taking an addictive substance, before any effective treatment can be started. Being dried out for a period of 30 or more days gives the person a "clean" body and mind to use in doing something different and positive. For example, families often organize themselves around alcohol abuse in a systemic way and enable family members to drink excessively (Bateson, 1971; Steinglass, 1979). In the alcoholic family system, there is an *overresponsible–underresponsible phenomenon*, with the overresponsible person(s) being a so-called *codependent* (Berenson, 1992). "An essential characteristic of someone who is codependent is that they continually invest their self-esteem in the ability to control and influence behavior and feelings in others as well as in themselves, even when faced with adverse consequences such as feelings of inadequacy after failure" (Springer, Britt, & Schlenker, 1998, p. 141). In such a situation, it is easier and more productive to work with the overfunctioning person(s) and modify that phenomenon than to try to get the underfunctioning person(s) to change.

Among the most prevalent factors affecting treatment for substance abuse are "motivation, denial, dual diagnosis, matching, control, and relapse" (L'Abate, 1992, p. 11). *Motivation* has to do with a desire to change, which most substance abusers do not wish to do because of their self-centredness and comfort. *Denial* is basically minimizing the effects of substance abuse on either oneself or others; it minimizes the harm that is being done. A *dual diagnosis* is one in which an abuser has more than one aspect of personality that is open to treatment. For instance, a substance abuser may be impulsive or depressed in addition to being addicted. *Matching* concerns the right treatment for a disorder. Some substance abuses, such as overdosing with cocaine, require specialized treatment. *Control* has to do with the regulation of behaviour, which substance abusers tend to disregard. Finally, *relapse* is the recidivism or reoccurrence of dysfunctional behaviours once they have been treated. It is discouraging to have substance abusers go through structured programs and end up acting the way they did before.

Treatment strategies for substance abusers may be aimed at individuals. For example, to lower resistance in substance abuse cases, *motivational interviewing* (MI) (Miller & Rollnick, 2002) may be tried. "MI is a brief counseling intervention designed to reduce a client's ambivalence toward change while increasing his or her motivation to engage in the behavior-change process" (Burrow-Sanchez, 2006, p. 286). MI techniques are largely drawn from person-centred counselling and include skills such as active listening, reflection, and reframing in order to help clients feel understood and to reinforce client "behaviors that are congruent with the desired behavior change" (p. 286).

In addition to MI, a bibliotherapeutic approach may work with some individuals (Hipple, Comer, & Boren, 1997). In this approach, abusers and addicts read books or view and listen to media and discuss ideas related to what they have experienced. For example, in working with adolescents, substance abusers might be asked to read *Go Ask Alice* by Anonymous, a nonfiction novel about teen drug abuse, or *Imitate the Tiger* by Jan Cheripko, a novel on teenage alcohol abuse. They would then discuss their reactions with a counsellor, including how they are like or not like the main characters of the book and what insights they gleaned from the reading.

In working with adolescents, especially with regard to alcohol and other substance use, Pollock (2006) cautions that counsellors need to remember the following:

- Working with adolescents is a treatment specialty.
- For counselling to be effective with adolescents, family and other significant people in the adolescent's life should be included.
- Adolescents need to be educated as to what counselling is.
- Because adolescents do not respond well to many adult treatments, therapeutic techniques need to be specifically tailored to them.
- Although relationship skills are important, the counsellor cannot function well trying to be the adolescent's friend.

- Counselling works best with adolescents if it is centred around "problem solving, skill building, and just being heard" (p. 331).

- "Therapeutic moments" are much more uneven with adolescents than with adults.

Specific Treatments

Treating Alcohol Abuse There are a number of treatment approaches for working with those who abuse alcohol, especially adults. However, the most well-known approach is Alcoholics Anonymous (AA). Founded in the 1930s, AA is the oldest successful treatment program in the world for working with alcoholics (AA World Services, 2002). It is "both a fellowship and a rehabilitation program" (Warfield & Goldstein, 1996, p. 196). Alcoholics suffer from what AA describes as "character defects" (AA World Services, 2002). "These are feelings, beliefs, and behaviors that dispose them to seek a sense of well-being by abusing alcohol" (Warfield & Goldstein, 1996, p. 197). AA meetings are conducted in small-group settings where literature—for example, *The Big Book* (AA World Services, 2002)—is used along with group discussion. The website for the Canadian chapter of AA is found at www.aacanada.com.

A key component in AA is the use of a 12-step program that has at its basis a spiritual foundation. Group discussions in AA meetings centre on helping members realize they need and have the support of others and a dependence on a higher power. The spiritual dimension in AA results in an emphasis on members admitting their powerlessness over alcohol (or other substances). Members who abstain from the use and abuse of alcohol are never "cured"; rather, they are "in recovery." There is also an emphasis in AA on responsibility, forgiveness, restitution (when possible), affirmation, ritual, and fellowship.

AA "has been adapted to treat many other problems such as narcotic addiction, cocaine abuse, overeating, compulsive gambling, compulsive sexual behavior, and the pain of children of alcoholics" (James & Hazler, 1998, p. 124). Some counsellors are uncomfortable with the spiritual qualities of AA (Bristow-Braitman, 1995) and prefer to discuss needed recovery qualities in cognitive-behavioural or humanistic language. Rational emotive behaviour therapy (REBT) has led the way in setting up recovery groups that are non-spiritual in nature.

Along with treating the person who is abusing alcohol, the counsellor also needs to work with the family and community. The support or scapegoating that abusers of alcohol receive from family and community systems in which they live makes a tremendous difference in their ability to abstain from the use of alcohol. AA and other recovery programs, such as Women for Sobriety, have special groups and programs for family members of persons who are substance abusers.

In the gay and lesbian communities, individuals are "at risk" because alcohol is seen as a way of coping with stigmatization. In addition, one of the most accepting social places for gays and lesbians to meet is a bar (Matthews et al., 2006). Therefore, when working with members of these groups in any setting, counsellors need to be sure to draw others into the conversation and even into the treatment plan.

Treating Nicotine Addictions *Nicotine addiction* is another prevalent problem. According to the Canadian Cancer Society (CCS) (2009), the most recent statistics available (i.e., 2005) reveal that a just under 5 million Canadians (19%) aged 15 and older were smokers. In 2005, 18% of youth between ages 15 and 19 smoked tobacco (CCS, 2009). "Smoking is the number one preventable cause of death in Canada" (CCS, 2009, para. 17). In 2008, 21% of Canadians aged 12 and older reported that they smoked either occasionally or daily, but this is down from 26% in 2001 (Statistics Canada, 2009).

Furthermore, "approximately 80% of alcoholics smoke" in addition to drinking, increasing their risk for a premature death or injury (Barker, 1997, p. 53). Most adults and adolescents who become nicotine dependent usually want to quit smoking. They often go to extraordinary lengths to achieve their goal of smoking cessation but unfortunately, as a group, they are not successful in the long run.

Counsellors can help improve the success rate of nicotine-addicted individuals in a number of ways (Singleton & Pope, 2000). One successful technique that counsellors use is *telephone counselling*, which has a success rate comparable to group smoking-cessation programs (Lichtenstein, Zhu, & Tedeschi, 2010). Telephone counselling consists of a 15- to 30-minute phone call where counsellors give positive, nonjudgmental feedback to those who are trying to quit smoking. The idea behind the strategy is to promote self-efficacy.

The best approaches incorporate aspects of cognitive-behaviour therapy and pharmacotherapy (Alderson, 2007). *Skills training* is helpful, for example. In this approach coping skills are taught, such as reframing and thought stopping, after clients have learned to recognize the cognitive, emotional, and environmental triggers that tend to produce the urge to smoke. Among the most successful skills are the use of self-statements concerned with the financial and health benefits of discontinuing smoking, as well as oral substitutes, increased physical activity, and the buddy system. Finally, self-help materials that are brief and factual, such as informational booklets related to smoking, can be useful. Booklets of this nature guide the smoker through the process of quitting and maintaining nonsmoking behaviour. The home page of the Canadian Cancer Society (2010) is an excellent place for finding such resources.

A recent designer drug (i.e., designed specifically to treat nicotine addiction) called Champix has demonstrated impressive results, although severe negative side effects have also been reported in some cases (Health Canada, 2009c). Older pharmaceuticals that have proven helpful for smoking cessation include Buproprion (also called Wellbutrin and Zyban) and various forms of nicotine-replacement therapies (e.g., patch, inhaler, gum) (Alderson, 2007).

Treating Illegal Drug Addiction Health Canada (2007) estimates that nearly 125 000 Canadians inject drugs, particularly cocaine, heroin, and steroids. Although these numbers are small proportionate to our population, cocaine and heroin use are both associated with crime and potentially serious health issues (Fischer, Rehm, Patra, & Cruz, 2006). Furthermore, as reported earlier, more than 12% of Canadians used cannabis, cocaine or crack, speed, ecstasy, hallucinogens, or heroin in 2008 (Health Canada, 2009a).

Individuals who are addicted to drugs other than alcohol or nicotine, such as cocaine, often receive treatment based on the AA model. However, because of society's greater disapproval of these drugs and their illegality, the context in which treatment is offered is often not the same. For example, one context in which treating illegal drug abuse is provided is jail, because many drug abusers are tried as criminals and incarcerated.

A prototype of a jail treatment program that works well is "Stay 'n Out" in Staten Island, New York. "Its secret is a captive audience; participants don't have any choice about showing up for therapy. It's be there—or you're off to a meaner cellblock" (Alter, 1995, pp. 20–21). Although the ethical dimensions of this program are debatable, the results are a recidivism rate of only 25%, much lower than the average. A substance abuse program such as Stay 'n Out saves money for communities to use in other ways because recovering addicts require lower health care and criminal justice costs.

Treating Substance Abuse Families Families play a large part in promoting or enabling substance abuse behaviours, and it is difficult to help substance abusers without including everyone in the family (Doweiko, 1990). "Students from homes in which parents are chemically dependent or abuse alcohol or other drugs (CDs) are at risk for a wide range of developmental problems" (Buelow, 1995, p. 327). Many families that abuse alcohol tend to be isolated, and children within them consequently suffer from a lack of positive role models. As children get older, they seem to be particularly affected for the worse from growing up in these families.

Substance abuse is used by these young people as a way to relieve stress, reduce anxiety, and structure time (Robinson, 1995). It is also an attempt by young adults to protect and stabilize dysfunctional families by keeping their attention off overall dynamics and on predictable problematic behaviours (Stanton & Todd, 1982). Substance abuse may serve as a substitute for sex and promote *pseudo-individuation* (a false sense of self). These complex and interrelated factors make it difficult to help people caught up in substance abuse patterns to change behaviours without an intensive social action approach designed to change dysfunctional systems (Lee & Walz, 1998).

Treatment services can take the form of providing information, but often counsellors must be confrontational with the family as a whole over the effects of substance abuse on the family as a unit as well as its individual members. Such an intervention cannot be made without an intensive systems approach that involves a number of people and agencies (Kaufman & Kaufman, 1992; Morgan, 1998).

Counsellors who realize the dysfunctional impact of substance abuse, especially in regard to alcohol and drug misuse in families, can work to help clients deal with feelings such as anger and defense mechanisms such as denial within a family context. They can also help the family take responsibility for their behaviours (Krestan & Bepko, 1988). In essence, they can help the family get back on track as a functional system by getting "involved in the treatment process" and "helping the abusing member overcome . . . addiction rather than serving as a force that maintains it" (Van Deusen, Stanton, Scott, Todd, & Mowatt, 1982, p. 39). In the process, families and their individual members are assisted in regard to resolving developmental issues as well.

Treating Women and Minority Cultural Groups in Substance Abuse

According to Health Canada (2009a), the percentage of Canadian women 15 years of age and older who report heavy use of alcohol is 2.8% (infrequently) and 2.6% (frequently), totalling 5.4%. Not all of these women would be considered dependent on alcohol, however, as Health Canada defines heavy drinking as four or more drinks for women on one occasion.

Nonetheless, those who have become addicted to alcohol may find it difficult to seek and obtain appropriate treatment because of societal rebuke and chastisement and because of barriers to treatment faced by women, such as the need for child care, cost, family opposition, and inadequate diagnosis (Van der Wade, Urgenson, Weltz, & Hanna, 2002). Although female alcohol abusers constitute about one-third of the membership in Alcoholics Anonymous, "there is little empirical evidence on the benefits of AA and NA to the female alcoholic or addict" (Manhal-Baugus, 1998, p. 82). Therefore, new theories and alternative treatment strategies are developing for women that reflect the broader context of women's lives, especially difficulties they face regarding alcohol addiction. These programs draw on community resources in a different way from traditional approaches. One of these programs is Women for Sobriety, a mutual help group based on a cognitive-behaviour modification approach that helps teach women to change their thinking so they may overcome feelings of helplessness, powerlessness, guilt, and dependence. It has 13 affirmations that promote positive thinking in a supportive relationship environment run by women for women (Manhal-Baugus, 1998).

In addition to gender differences, cultural differences may play a part in the recovery process. There may be special considerations for treating members of minority cultures. For instance, Aboriginal Canadians may find spiritual elements different from that of non-Aboriginal Canadian traditions important in helping them. Therefore, counsellors who work with this population may want to consult a medicine man or medicine woman before trying to work with people or groups seeking recovery (Vick et al., 1998). The same principle of seeking culturally appropriate support systems rings true in treating other culturally specific groups as well.

Affiliation, Certification, and Education of Substance Abuse Counsellors

Canadian counsellors wanting to become certified as addictions counsellors have a few options open to them. One option is with the Canadian Addictions Counsellors Certification Federation (n.d.), which was formed (under a different name) in 1985. It is a voluntary, nonprofit organization. Another choice is through the Canadian Council of Professional Certification (CCPC, n.d.). The CCPC certifies counsellors at two levels of demonstrated competency, either the Associate Addictions Counsellor or the higher level of Certified Addiction Counsellor II. A third possibility is training at the University of Lethbridge's addictions counselling program, the only baccalaureate degree of its kind available in Canada (Thibodeau, Solowoniuk, & Nixon, 2010).

Addictions counsellors often have a minimum of a master's degree in applied psychology (e.g., counselling, clinical) or clinical social work. In most cases, they will require additional training through the customary means available to them (psychologists require formal or informal training in the area and supervised practice). In accord with ethics requirements, professional counsellors need to demonstrate competence before practising in a specialized area.

Some counsellors in the field are also *recovering counsellors*, meaning that they were abusers in the past but are now "dry." Their academic credentials vary depending on the organization that hires them.

The effectiveness of the two groups appears to be about the same but the ways they work are distinct. Recovering counsellors are more likely to engage in activities that are consistent with the philosophy described in the 12 steps of Alcoholics Anonymous (Culbreth & Borders, 1999). Thus, they are "prone to be involved in community education programs, socialize with clients away from the work environment, and visit clients in the hospital," whereas non-recovering counsellors do not and are more prone to see alcohol and drug problems on a continuum rather than as a yes or no diagnosis. With the trend being for more professional counsellors than paraprofessionals to enter the field in the future, a number of procedures will change, including the way supervision is delivered (Culbreth & Borders, 1999). In addition, as this transition occurs, counsellors presently in the field will need intensive training to learn even more treatment interventions so they can work effectively with diverse clients presenting complex issues (Thombs & Osborn, 2001).

Compulsive Gambling

Moderate gambling, like moderate use of alcohol, is an accepted part of North American society and usually causes little concern. Nonetheless, legalized gambling increases the likelihood of crime, political corruption, and compulsive gambling. *Compulsive gambling* is an irrepressible obsession with gambling that manifests in an inability to stop, even when the individual attempts to do so. Those most at risk are youth, the elderly, and low-income individuals (Barmaki, 2010).

However, compulsive gambling is a serious social problem (Barmaki, 2010; Maske, 2007). In such cases gambling is not glitzy, glamorous, or fun. It is pathological and may tragically take the form of illegal and dehumanizing activities, as in the case of Michael Vick and dog fight betting (Frankel, 2010). Compulsive gambling is found in about 2.5% of the population. It leaves in its wake broken homes, shattered dreams, empty lives, and financial ruin.

Compulsive gambling parallels alcohol and drug addiction in numerous ways. Compulsive gamblers lose control over their behaviour. They commonly lie and cheat in order to continue their gambling. Like other addicts, they frequently try, unsuccessfully, to cut down or quit.

Compulsive gambling revolves around the "action" that occurs when placing a bet. In compulsive gamblers, there is an aroused, euphoric state comparable to the "high" sought by drug users. With it is an accompanied change in brain chemistry and often a "rush," which is sometimes characterized by sweaty palms, rapid heartbeat, and nausea experienced during the period of anticipation. Just like in other addictions, compulsive gamblers develop tolerance for the action. Thus they must increase the size of their bets or the odds against them to create the same amount of excitement.

Treatment for Compulsive Gambling Compulsive gambling is treatable, just like other addictive behaviours. However, many problem gamblers are reluctant to seek treatment because they do not understand the nature of the addiction involved and they do not want to lose self-esteem from admitting they cannot handle their problem.

One major source of help is Gamblers Anonymous (www.gamblersanonymous.org/mtgdirCAN.html). It follows the same pattern as Alcoholics Anonymous, including the same 12-step treatment program. The success rate is comparable to that for other addictions. However, sometimes the nature of treatment is longer and more complicated because a number of compulsive gamblers also suffer from other addictions such as alcoholism, drug abuse, compulsive shopping, or bulimia.

A recent extensive review of the literature also provides support for the use of cognitive-behavioural therapy in both group and individual formats for the successful treatment of compulsive gambling. Specifically, the techniques include various forms of desensitization, aversion therapy, multimodal therapy, psychoeducation, cognitive-restructuring, and relapse prevention (Hodgins & Peden, 2008).

Work Addiction (Workaholism)

Work is like any other activity or substance in that it can become all-consuming to the point where the person in the midst of it abandons other opportunities that could be beneficial. Robinson, Flowers, and Ng (2006) define *workaholism* as "a compulsive and progressive, potentially fatal disorder characterized by self-imposed demands, compulsive overworking, inability to regulate work habits, and overindulgence in work to the exclusion and detriment of intimate relationships and major life activities" (p. 213). Workaholism negatively affects families of those involved and can lead to mental health problems in marriages, including marital dissatisfaction associated with overcontrolling tendencies in a spouse and impaired communication (Robinson, 2001; Robinson et al., 2006).

While the popular press is intrigued by the concept of workaholism, very little research has actually been undertaken to understand it better (Burke, 2009). Not surprisingly, the opinions and observations concerning it are varied and conflicting, and some view it positively from an organization perspective (Burke, 2006; 2009).

Treating Work Addiction Robinson (1995, p. 33) recommends the following steps for working with clients who are addicted to work, especially those who are recovering.

- *"Help them slow down their pace."* Give them examples of how they can make a conscious effort to slow down their daily lives through deliberate means.

- *"Teach them to learn to relax."* Learning meditation or yoga, reading an inspirational book, or even soaking in a hot tub is healthy and helpful in moderation.

- *"Assist them in evaluating their family climate."* Interactions with family members, especially of a positive nature, can be meaningful and relaxing. Therefore, it behooves recovering addicts to explore ways they "can strengthen family ties."

- *"Stress the importance of celebrations and rituals."* Activities such as celebrations and rituals are the glue that hold families together and make life personally rich and rewarding.

- *"Help them [clients] get back into the social swing."* This strategy involves devising a plan for developing social lives and friendship. If successful, it "explores ways of building social networks outside of work."

- *"Address living in the now."* By appreciating the present, recovering addicts can enjoy experiences more and not become anxious about or preoccupied with the future.

- *"Encourage clients to nurture themselves."* Often individuals who have become addicts find it hard, if not impossible, to indulge themselves even in healthy ways. However, the practice of self-nurturing can be beneficial.

- *"Stress the importance of proper diet, rest, and exercise."* It is hard to function if a person is running on a deficit either physically or emotionally. Therefore, getting clients to balance their lives in regard to diet, rest, and exercise can go a long way to helping them recover from their addiction.

- *"Help clients grieve the loss of their childhoods"* and *"address self-esteem."* Many addicts feel ashamed, saddened, angry, or even determined by their past. Helping them realize they can recover from past times and experiences can go a long way in assisting clients to become functional.

- *"Inform clients [that] 12-step programs [are] available as a complement to the individual work you do with them."* Almost all addicts in recovery can benefit from a 12-step program that emphasizes human relationships in concert with a higher power.

COUNSELLING PEOPLE WITH DISABILITIES

Disabilities are prevalent in Canadian life. In 2006, 4.4 million Canadians (14.3%) stated that they have a disability, and the percentage increased with age from a low of 3.7% for children 14 years old and younger to 56.3% for those 75 and over. Overall, more females (15.2%) than males (13.4%) report a disability in Canada; however, more male children ages 0 to 14 report a disability (4.6%) than female children in this age group (2.7%). Interestingly, the percentage of disabled Canadians is lowest in Nunavut (8.4%) and highest in Nova Scotia (20.0%). The three most common forms of reported disability were lack of mobility, pain, and reduced agility (Human Resources and Skills Development Canada, 2010).

A population-based study comprised of Canadians with physical, sensory, and cognitive abilities revealed that disability had a significant effect on their perception of unmet health needs. The greatest deterrent was cost. Despite the fact that health care throughout Canada is publicly funded, disabled individuals (aged 20 to 64) perceived that affordability of services was a problem for them (McColl, Jarzynowska, & Shortt, 2010).

Disabled people are often economically disadvantaged, and they are less likely to be employed. Furthermore, they tend to require health care services more than non-disabled users. Many expenses of health care are hidden: transportation costs, attendant fees, and physician administrative fees for completing forms (often $25 to $30 per form). These fees might not be burdensome for a non-disabled Canadian, but for someone on a fixed disability income or pension, they may be unmanageable (McColl et al., 2010).

Counsellors in all walks of life work with people who have disabilities. *Rehabilitation counselling*, a specialty in the counselling profession, especially focuses on serving individuals with disabilities. *Rehabilitation* is defined as the re-education of individuals with disabilities who have previously lived independent lives. A related area, *habilitation*, focuses on educating clients who have been disabled from early life and have never been self-sufficient (Bitter, 1979). Rehabilitation counselling is a multidimensional task whose success is dependent on many things. "The rehabilitation counselor is expected to be a competent case manager as well as a skilled therapeutic counselor" (Cook, Bolton, Bellini, & Neath, 1997, p. 193). The ultimate goals of rehabilitation services are successful employment, independent living, and community participation (Bolton, 2001).

The Nature of Disabilities

A *disability* is a condition whereby individuals have difficulties with daily living activities or where they experience a physical, mental, or health problem that reduces the kind or amount of activities they can perform (Statistics Canada, 2003). Clients who have disabilities include those whose manifestations are physical, emotional, mental, and behavioural, including a wide variety of diagnoses such as alcoholism, arthritis, blindness, cardiovascular disease, deafness, cerebral palsy, epilepsy, mental retardation, drug abuse, neurological disorders, orthopedic disabilities, psychiatric disabilities, renal failure, speech impairments, and spinal cord conditions.

Unfortunately, people who have disabilities often encounter others who have misconceptions and biases about their limitations. These others may even harass people who are disabled about their disabilities, especially if the individuals have other characteristics, such as a minority sexual orientation (e.g., being lesbian) (Hunt, Matthews, Milsom, & Lammel, 2006). This type of treatment is cruel and may affect the person's "everyday social interactions" (Leierer, Strohmer, Leclere, Cornwell, & Whitten, 1996, p. 89). As a result, a large percentage of people with disabilities tend to withdraw from mainstream interactions with others and are unemployed or unable to achieve an independent-living status (Blackorby & Wagner, 1996).

A disability, of course, is not always for life. "Disability can be temporary or episodic, meaning that people are not necessarily affected by disability continuously" (Galarneau & Radulescu, 2009, p. 14). Between 1999 and 2004, for example, only 13% of Canadians with disabilities reported that they were affected by their disability for all six years.

As the disability period increases, however, the more likely the person will (a) be a woman, (b) have less education, (c) be older, and (d) live alone (Galarneau & Radulescu, 2009). According to a 2006 survey, 42% of disabled people between the ages of 15 and 64 were unable to work, and those who did so worked fewer hours per year compared to able Canadians (Galarneau & Radulescu, 2009). Furthermore, Canadian men and women who were disabled for that six-year period (1999–2004) reported earning up to nearly 20% less compared to the non-disabled (Galarneau & Radulescu, 2009).

People with disabilities may suffer from low self-esteem, lack of confidence in decision making, social stigma, a restricted range of available occupations, and few successful role models (Enright, 1997). They may also have limited early life experiences.

A *handicap*, which is linked to but distinct from a disability, is "an observable or discernible limitation that is made so by the presence of various barriers" (Schumacher, 1983, p. 320). An example of a person who is disabled and who has a handicap is someone who is a quadriplegic assigned to a third-floor apartment in a building without an elevator, or a partially deaf person receiving instructions orally. Counsellors help clients in these types of situations overcome handicaps and effectively cope with their disabilities.

Affiliation, Certification, and Education of Disability Counsellors

Rehabilitation counselling is the most prevalent specialty working with persons with disabilities and the one with which most who work in this area affiliate. The Commission on Rehabilitation Counselor Certification (CRCC; visit www.crccertification.com) is an internationally recognized certification program. Once certified, the rehabilitation practitioner receives the credential of being a Canadian Certified Rehabilitation Counselor (CCRC). The CRCC is the world's largest rehabilitation counselling organization with over 16 000 current certificants and over 35 000 certified rehabilitation counsellors since it was incorporated in 1974.

Another avenue available is the Vocational Rehabilitation Association of Canada (VRA; visit http://vracanada.com). Its website describes it as the leading national organization that represents professionals who focus on helping individuals return to gainful employment. Membership is open to anyone working in the rehabilitation field, and it offers various professional designations to qualified members (e.g., Registered Rehabilitation Professional, Registered Community Support Specialist).

Working with People with Disabilities

A distinguishing aspect of counselling with people who are disabled is the historical link with the *medical model* of delivering services (Ehrle, 1979). The prominence of the medical model is easy to understand when one recalls how closely professionals who were first involved with persons with disabilities treated those who were physically challenged. Even today, those who specialize as rehabilitation counsellors are required to have knowledge of medical terminology (Emener & Cottone, 1989, p. 577).

Yet different models of helping people who are disabled have emerged (Smart & Smart, 2006). There are four that are most prominent. The most popular of these is the *biomedical model,* which carries with it the prestige of the medical community. This model is steeped in the language of medicine but is silent in the language of social justice. According to this model, "disabilities are objective conditions that exist in and of themselves" (p. 30). They are considered deficiencies residing within an individual who is totally responsible for the problem. This model pathologizes the individual with the disability. Whereas the model may work best with acute injuries, it is "less useful with mental and psychiatric disabilities" and much stronger "when dealing with physical disabilities" (p. 31).

The second conception of disability is the *environmental and functional model*. Its focus is more appropriate for chronic disabilities (i.e., what most disabilities are). In this model, people carry a label with them (i.e., "disabled"). The label may lead to some degree of social prejudice and discrimination, yet it also places the blame for disabilities outside the individual.

The *sociopolitical model* is the third model and is sometimes referred to as the *minority model*. It assumes that persons with disabilities are a minority group rather than people with pathologies. "The hallmarks of this model include self-definition, the elimination (or reduction) of the prejudice and discrimination (sometimes referred to as 'handicapism') [and] rejection of medical diagnoses and categories" (p. 34).

The fourth model is the *peer counsellor model*. It assumes that people with direct experience with disabilities are best able to help those who have recently acquired disabilities.

In working with a client with disabilities to develop or to restore adjustment, the role of the counsellor is to assess the client's current level of functioning and the environmental situation, which either hinder or enhance functionality. After such an assessment is made, counsellors use a wide variety of counselling theories and techniques. Virtually all of the affective, behavioural, cognitive, and systemic theories of counselling are employed. Systems theories in rehabilitation work for the disabled have become especially popular in recent years (Cottone, Grelle, & Wilson, 1988; Guzman, Yassi, Baril, & Loisel, 2008; Hershenson, 1996).

The actual theories and techniques used are dictated by the skills of counsellors as well as the needs of clients. For example, a client with disabilities who has sexual feelings may need a psychoeducational approach on how to handle these emotions, whereas another client with disabilities who is depressed may need a more cognitive or behavioural intervention (Boyle, 1994). An action-oriented approach such as Gestalt psychodrama can be especially powerful in helping clients to become more involved in the counselling process and to accept responsibility for their lives (Coven, 1977). Furthermore, techniques such as role-playing, fantasy enactment, and psychodrama can be learned and used by clients to help in their adjustment.

A counsellor who works with clients who have disabilities must also be a professional with a clear sense of purpose (Wright, 1980; 1987). There are several competing, but not necessarily mutually exclusive, ideas about what roles and functions counsellors should assume, especially rehabilitation counsellors. In the late 1960s, Muthard and Salomone conducted the first systematic investigation of rehabilitation counsellors' work activities (Bolton & Jaques, 1978). They found eight major activities that characterize the counsellor's role and noted a high degree of importance attached to affective counselling, vocational counselling, and placement duties (Muthard & Salomone, 1978). In this survey, rehabilitation counsellors reported spending about 33% of their time in counselling activities, 25% in clerical duties, and 7% in client placement.

Clients with Specific Disabilities

There are a number of treatment modalities for clients with disabilities. Almost all theories used in counselling are employed with members of this population. In addition, Hershenson (1992b) has proposed a way of helping counsellors perform their tasks even better. He has devised a practical way to conceptualize a disability and provide appropriate services. He contends that disabilities result from one of four forces: supernatural or fate, medical, natural, or societal. Therefore, treatment can be based on explanations and techniques emphasizing faith (for the supernatural), logic (for the medical and natural), and power (for the societal). If the rehabilitation counsellor and client agree on the nature of cause and treatment, services can be provided in a more accepting and therapeutic way.

In a study on causal attributions and choices of rehabilitation approaches that support Hershenson's model, Williams, Hershenson, and Fabian (2000) found that undergraduates who attributed a client's disability to fate chose to get the person to accept the disability as one's lot in life. Where disabilities were attributed to natural or medical causes, medical or retraining services were the preferred choices of treatment. Finally, where socially imposed barriers were seen as the cause of the disability, the removal of these barriers was advocated.

Physical Disabilities Physical injuries such as spinal cord damage or blindness produce a major loss for an individual and consequently have a tremendous physical and emotional impact (Krause & Anson, 1997). Counselling and rehabilitation in such cases require concentration on both the client's and the family's adjustment to the situation.

Livneh and Evans (1984) point out that clients who have physical disabilities go through 12 phases of adjustment that may distinguish them from others: shock, anxiety, bargaining, denial, mourning, depression, withdrawal, internalized anger, externalized aggression, acknowledgment, acceptance, and adjustment/adaptation. There are behavioural correlates that accompany each phase and intervention strategies appropriate for each. For example, the client who is in a state of shock may be immobilized and cognitively disorganized. Intervention strategies most helpful during this time include comforting the person (both physically and verbally), listening and attending, offering support and reassurance, allowing the person to vent feelings, and referring the person to institutional care if appropriate.

People involved in helping a person with physical disabilities may need help themselves working through the recovery process and should be included as much as possible in developing detailed medical, social, and psychological evaluations. Therefore, counsellors should offer carefully timed supportive counselling, crisis intervention, and confrontation with these individuals while simultaneously helping the person with an injured spinal cord develop an internal locus of control for accepting responsibility for his or her life (Povolny, Kaplan, Marme, & Roldan, 1993). In addition to serving as a counsellor, a professional who works with individuals who are physically disabled must be an advocate, a consultant, and an educator. The task is comprehensive and involves a complex relationship among job functions.

Mental Disabilities Clients with mental disabilities include those who have mild to severely limited cognitive abilities. In cases involving children, the counsellor's tasks and techniques may be similar to those employed with an adult or adolescent with physical disabilities (supportive counselling and life-planning activities), but young clients with mental deficiencies require more and different activities. Parents must be helped as well in working through their feelings about their child with a disability and finding ways of promoting positive interactions that encourage maximum development (Huber, 1979).

When working with adolescents who have mental difficulties due to head injuries, a counsellor must address social issues as well as therapeutic activities (Bergland & Thomas, 1991). As a general rule, increased time and effort in attending to psychosocial issues are required for working with anyone who has been mentally impaired, regardless of the client's age or the cause of the impairment (Kaplan, 1993).

ADD or ADHD Attention deficit disorder (ADD) and attention deficit/hyperactivity disorder (AD/HD) are disorders that interfere with learning and day-to-day functioning for many individuals. These disabilities have different impacts throughout the lifespan. They are found in various forms (e.g., AD/HD, which affects between 3% and 5% of school-age children, has three subtypes: inattentive, hyperactivity-impulsivity, or a combination of the two) (Brown, 2000).

Regardless, difficulties such as "distractibility, impulsivity, disorganization, and interpersonal problems that persist and sometimes worsen with age" are among the symptoms and results that occur with individuals with AD/HD (Schwiebert, Sealander, & Dennison, 2002, p. 5). Heightened levels of frustration, anxiety, distress, depression, and diminished self-concepts are other results that may happen with any of these disorders.

Since ADD and AD/HD have become more widely known in recent years, a number of strategies for working with people who are so impaired have been developed by clinicians in educational and community settings. For instance, counsellors may help students with AD/HD prepare for postsecondary education and vocational entry by giving them cues in mnemonic form on how to behave in certain situations. One such cue is the mnemonic SLANT, which may be used to help those who have learning problems focus on classroom lectures (Mercer & Mercer, 2001, p. 165). The letters stand for

S = "Sit up straight"
L = "Lean forward"
A = "Activate thinking and Ask questions"
N = "Name key information and Nod your head to validate the teacher/speaker"
T = "Track the teacher or speaker"

Overall, counsellors who work with clients with ADD and AD/HD need to be aware that many facets of a client's personality may be shaped by the multiple effects of these disorders and that treatment may be a long-term process that is multidimensional in nature (Erk, 2000). Interventions for children or adolescents with AD/HD include, but are not limited to, (a) parent counselling and training, (b) client education, (c) individual and group counselling, and (d) social skills training (Brown, 2000).

Medical treatment may also be necessary. Proper medication "often results in increased attentiveness and decreased impulsivity and overactivity" (Brown, 2000). Stimulant medications, such as methylphenidate (Ritalin), dextroamphetamine (Dexedrine), and pemoline (Cylert), are usually the first medications chosen for AD/HD. However, not all children who have AD/HD need medication. In addition, if medications are prescribed, they should always be given first in small dosages. Counsellors need to be up to date on the latest medications and other treatments for this disorder in order to enhance the lives of clients they serve and their families.

HIV/AIDS Counsellors in a variety of settings provide services for persons with HIV/AIDS (All & Fried, 1994; Glenn, Garcia, Li, & Moore, 1998). HIV is now considered a chronic illness. "People living with HIV may develop impairments as the disease progresses, and may be considered to have a disability when social, economic, political or other barriers hinder their full and effective participation in society on an equal basis with others" (UNAIDS, 2009, p. 1).

A large percentage of people who are HIV-positive or who have AIDS are already socially stigmatized, so counsellors must first examine their own attitudes and feelings before attempting to deal with this special population. Their job is to then assist clients in dealing with psychosocial tasks, such as maintaining a meaningful quality of life, coping with loss of function, and confronting existential or spiritual issues. Common client emotions include shock, anger, anxiety, fear, resentment, and depression. Therefore, counsellors must help clients face these emotions as well. In addition, practical considerations such as preparing for treatment or death must be handled in a sensitive and caring way (Dworkin & Pincu, 1993).

Minority Groups with Disabilities In dealing with minority groups, such as female workers with disabilities, counsellors must be aware of the developmental processes typical in such populations and be prepared with appropriate counselling techniques for the problems peculiar to each group. Counselling women who are disabled, for example, involves four interrelated elements: "(a) job or skill training or education; (b) family support services; (c) trait-and-factor job matching and placement services; and (d) soft counselling support services" (Hollingsworth & Mastroberti, 1983, p. 590).

Berwald and Houtstra (2003), two social workers in Edmonton, described a group that they had led annually for the past five years for women with any form of disability. By combining feminism and social work practice, Berwald and Houtstra reported that the group members improved significantly (i.e., statistically) and that feedback from the members was favourable.

The counsellor who works with clients who have disabilities must be versatile. He or she must not only provide services directly but must also coordinate services with other professionals and monitor clients' progress in gaining independence and self-control. Thus, a counsellor needs skills from an array of theories and techniques and adaptability in shifting professional roles. A recent book dealing with the multicultural aspects of disabilities is available for those working in this area (Bryan, 2007).

SUMMARY AND CONCLUSION

Mental health counselling originated in the 1970s. Mental health counsellors work with a number of treatment disorders, as well as in primary prevention. Most mental health counsellors in Canada have training as psychologists, social workers, psychiatric nurses, and in specialized areas such as rehabilitation counselling or addictions counselling.

Community counsellors work in settings that are varied. As a group, community counsellors identify themselves strongly as counsellors even though some will become more identified with a specialty through training as time goes by.

In the realm of private practice, there are opportunities and pitfalls. Counsellors who are specialists as well as generalists set up individual as well as group practices. They must either have business and counselling abilities to be successful or they must hire business managers. There are a number of difficulties associated with private practice, such as finding support and supervision groups for oneself. There are numerous rewards as well, such as setting one's own hours and skirting the headaches of managed care regulations if desired. Overall, private practice continues to be a popular alternative for counsellors.

The specialty areas of substance abuse counselling and counselling with those who have disabilities are unique and yet interrelated. They emphasize the dynamics behind psychological adjustments, prevention programs, and treatment strategies.

The treatment of substance abusers is an important focus in counselling. The consumption of substances, such as alcohol, tobacco, and drugs, has a deleterious impact on individuals, families, and society in general. To work with members of this population, counsellors must focus on prevention and treatment. Prevention can come through educational programs, especially for children and youth. Treatment programs are usually more focused on adults and include systemic, spiritually focused groups, such as Alcoholics Anonymous, as well as programs run by professionals for those who are incarcerated or in treatment facilities.

Counselling with people who are disabled is like substance abuse counselling in that it focuses on both prevention and the provision of services. Counsellors who work in this area see themselves as distinct because they focus mainly on helping individuals with disabilities. Counselling with those who are disabled and rehabilitation counselling are similar to other types of counselling in that professionals employ many of the theories and techniques that other counsellors use. It is more the nature of the clientele being served, a need to know more medical terminology, and an occasional need to help place clients in specific settings, such as work or workshops, that set this counselling apart. Counsellors should remember that in working with people who have disabilities, most do not define themselves by their disability. Furthermore, they need to be aware that, as counsellors, they have feelings and thoughts about those with disabilities that they need to pay attention to if they are to empower and not impose their values on the clients they serve (Smart & Smart, 2006).

Your Personal Reflections

1. As you learned in this chapter, mental health counsellors are a generic group, and they have differing backgrounds (e.g., psychology, social work, psychiatric nursing). Which training appeals to you most, and why? What are the drawbacks of training in that field?

2. Do you know someone who has either attempted or committed suicide? Try to put yourself in that person's place. What might keep you from taking your own life? What would make such an act attractive?

3. You have most likely read a number of books or seen television shows and movies that portray individuals with various mental disorders. What is your opinion about how realistically these characters are presented? As you ponder this question, reflect also on the life of Clifford Beers, as presented in Chapter 1, and his struggle in getting the general public to understand mental disorders.

4. Because emotional abuse is so common, you have likely seen it expressed in a number of ways on various occasions. Describe the signs of abuse you have seen from the list presented earlier in the chapter. What has been your reaction to witnessing emotional abuse?

5. With so many types of prevention programs set up locally and nationally, why do you think there are still so many young adolescents who pick up the smoking habit?

6. Robinson has laid out some excellent ideas for slowing down the pace of life and enjoying people (see the section on work addiction in this chapter). How might you use these ideas in other venues of counselling besides dealing with workaholics?

Classroom Activities

1. In a team with four other classmates, devise a primary prevention plan for some underserved group in your community, (e.g., people living in poverty, older or abused persons). Note the number of resources you must coordinate to make your plan successful. Present your plan to the whole class.

2. Conduct a literature review of healthy development for the past five years. What are the latest trends? How can these trends be related to the work of mental health or community counsellors?

3. Visit an EAP program counsellor. What services offered in the program surprise you? Ask the EAP counsellor to assess the effectiveness of the program in which he or she works.

4. What do you see as the advantages and limitations of being a community counsellor? Make a list. Discuss your opinions with fellow classmates.

5. Invite a counsellor in private practice to speak to your class about what his or her work is like. Ask the counsellor about the business side of private practice as well as the clinical side of this specialty.

6. In pairs, discuss what services or facilities are still not accessible to people who have mobility impairments where you live. Discuss your findings when the entire class reconvenes.

7. Attend an open meeting of Alcoholics Anonymous, or interview a substance abuse counsellor about the services he or she presently provides. Inform the class about what you experienced at the AA meeting or what you found out from your interview with the substance abuse counsellor.

8. As a class, generate ideas about what you consider to be the most pressing societal needs in the next decade. Describe how substance abuse and disability counselllors can help alleviate problems associated with these needs. Apply your ideas to a specific setting in which you hope to be employed.

9. Khan and Cross (1984) found similarities and differences in the value systems held by three professional mental health groups: psychiatrists, psychologists, and social workers. Discuss with class members how values affect the delivery of counselling services in substance abuse and disability counselling.

10. Investigate the educational training of rehabilitation counsellors and the certification they obtain compared to substance abuse counsellors. How do these groups differ? In what ways are they alike?

Chapter 21
Counselling the Economically Disadvantaged in Canada

PRACTICE REFLECTION

One of the most rewarding jobs I had soon after graduating with a BA in psychology was working as a child and youth care worker. My co-workers were mostly caring, compassionate souls who really wanted to make a difference in the lives of children and teenagers. I was one of them. In the compulsory care facility I worked in, youth who had committed criminal offenses were given up to three months' detention. Unfortunately, at times this made me feel more like a guard than like the role I really wanted to play. There were instances where youth became uncontrollable, needing to be restrained and sometimes placed in a padded room for their own safety.

Sadly, many of these young people would leave the facility with positive aspirations, only to return weeks or months later. My co-workers and I thought some were definitely headed for the adult justice system. As staff, we were not assigned to work with specific youth in the centre during a shift at work, although the general practice was that male staff worked with males and female staff with females. Nonetheless, most of us developed favourites, young people with whom we developed good rapport and tended to engage more in conversation.

I remember having such a positive relationship with a 15-year-old called Sean. Sean was a tough kid from another city, and sure enough, he returned for a second bout of incarceration a few months after his release. Always full of attitude and narcissism, he was happy to see that I was still working there. Over the next few months, we had many conversations about his impoverished family and his struggles with each family member, particularly his father. We talked about his hopes, his dreams, his wants, and his needs. Mostly, it felt like being an older brother to him as there were only seven years between us.

Most of the time, we never learned what happened to these youth after they left the centre. Did they get through their adolescence without continuing their criminal behaviour? Did they set goals and attain them eventually? Sean wanted to be a movie star back then and, with his inflated ego, it wouldn't have surprised me if he tried to do it.

A few years ago, I ran into Sean while spending some time in a nearby city. The look of astonishment was overwhelming, and both of us embraced like long lost friends. Sean was working as a firefighter, happily married and the father of a young daughter. He was now helping people instead of assaulting them and stealing their property. Before we departed, he told me that I had made a difference in his life back then. He knew that someone cared about what happened to him.

I left with both a glow and a sadness. How many children out there are not getting what they need to grow up to become productive, healthy citizens? How many are living in poverty?

A sight rarely seen before 1980 in Canada has now become commonplace. Walk through the downtown of any major city and notice the hungry desperate eyes tracking you, wondering if you might help with their next meal ticket or their next fix. Some cities, like Winnipeg, have enacted civil legislation to protect innocent eyes from seeing a reality that only becomes painful if you think about what it means sociologically. In other cities, like Calgary, panhandlers, or beggers if you will, are still allowed legally to give voice to their plight in public. Not all are homeless of course, and most who are homeless are quiet on the public front, instead choosing to starve out whatever existence they can afford. Perhaps they haven't hit the proverbial "rock bottom"; perhaps they still have too much pride left to keep them from begging. For now, they remain quiet, humble, and increasingly desperate.

Many onlookers do their best to resurrect denial in order to believe that everything is okay, that everybody in our great nation is self-determined and that no one ends up there without making a rational free choice to be impoverished. Even worse, stories abound that these individuals are actually rich misers who would make most of us drool over their fortunes. As you learned in Chapter 9, denial is a powerful defense mechanism. It is so powerful, in fact, that it can keep victims from really feeling the abuse they are experiencing.

How is it that the Canadian Charter of Rights and Freedoms that guarantees certain rights to all who live here—such as the right to be secure and to not be deprived thereof—are not upheld? What about Article 25 of the Universal Declaration of Human Rights, a document ratified by the United Nations (n.d.) on December 10, 1948, which states that "everyone has the right to a standard of living adequate for the health and well-being of himself and of his family, including food, clothing, housing and medical care . . . ?" Given that the Canadian government had a role in creating this declaration, how is it that our prosperous country has a notorious reputation with the United Nations for our lack of responsiveness to an ongoing epidemic—the growing problem of homelessness and poverty, and the gross disparity between the rich and the poor?

This chapter moves into a form of diversity that affects more than 10% of our population, a percentage greater than many of the diverse groups described in Chapter 5. Frighteningly, the percentage of impoverished individuals is greatest among our most vulnerable: our children. Further, the founders of this country—our Indigenous people—suffer poverty at a rate higher than those who settled here from afar. The story is just as telling when we enlighten ourselves to discover that many of other impoverished inhabitants in Canada are also overrepresented in this underclass: women, ethnic minority groups, and recent immigrants.

This chapter is about the economically disadvantaged and the consequences that arise when governments are unable, or even worse, are uninterested, in taking appropriate and constructive action. Despite a promise by our federal government in 1987 to end poverty by the year 2000, several factors have actually led to the problem being worse now than even then.

Isn't counselling those who cannot afford to see us an oxymoron? Is counselling appropriate when basic needs are not being met? Given, however, that ethics codes in Canada impel us toward social action and social justice, what will be our response in the counselling profession?

POVERTY IN CANADA

At the root of homelessness is poverty and the shocking reality is that [in Canada] we are now tolerating a level of poverty that leaves so many without a roof over their heads. Beyond the root cause of poverty we also tolerate a housing situation in our cities that provides little or no accommodation the poor can afford. The formula is simple:

combine a growing number of poor and a growing number of expensive housing units and we have people on the streets. Add to this a failure to recognize that the mentally ill cannot manage on their own, economically or even with the simplest of life's demands, and we have even more people on the streets. (Murphy, 2000, p. 19)

CANADA HELPED DRAFT THE UNITED NATIONS DECLARATION OF HUMAN RIGHTS IN 1948 (Hobbins, 1989), a document that contains reference to housing as a fundamental human right under Article 25 (United Nations, n.d.). Nonetheless, unlike the United States and the United Kingdom, Canada has not developed a federal strategy to address the issues of poverty or homelessness, despite strong urgings from the United Nations (Hulchanski, n.d.).

Paul Martin co-chaired a Liberal task force regarding the federal housing program in 1990 under Prime Minister Brian Mulroney's Progressive Conservative government. The housing study contains many excellent recommendations, but most were never implemented (the study is available at www.housingagain.web.ca). In 1998, the UN Committee on Economic, Social and Cultural Rights rebuked Canada's failure to initiate a policy to help its poorest citizens in the previous five years, despite the strong economic growth that was then occurring (Murphy, 2000).

Nonetheless, every Canadian province and territory is taking steps to reduce poverty (Canadian Social Research Links, n.d.). The Minister of Housing and Urban Affairs in Alberta recently announced that the provincial government would be providing $188 million in 2010 for social housing projects (Kleiss, 2010). One example of a local initiative is that, in 2008, a foundation in the City of Calgary began a program to eliminate homelessness within 10 years (Calgary Homeless Foundation, 2010).

One should not assume, however, that poverty inevitably leads to a lack of happiness or negative sense of oneself. A recent study found that many people overestimate the impact of income on life satisfaction (Aknin, Norton, & Dunn, 2009).

It is difficult to get a notion of the extent of the poverty situation in Canada without having a clear idea of what defines it. Overall, however, it is believed that Canada's poverty rates are among the highest in the industrialized world (Raphael, 2009). The next section begins this discussion.

Defining Poverty

Canada does not have an official poverty measure and there is no internationally accepted definition to adopt (Dagan, 2010). Although Statistics Canada can provide us the unemployment rate and the consumer price index, they have refused to implement a measure of poverty as they believe that this is not their responsibility. Instead, they have stated that politicians need to first agree on a definition of poverty (Fellegi, 1997).

Low-Income Cut-Off   Statistics Canada most often uses the *low-income cut-off* (LICO) to estimate those who are struggling financially. In brief, the method looks at people who devote a larger share of their income to necessities (i.e., food, shelter, and clothing) than the average family; that is, more than 20 percentage points above the average family (Dagan, 2010). The LICO is sometimes referred to as the *poverty line* in Canada (Council of Canadians with Disabilities, 2010). Singh (2008) reported that, according to the 2006 Canadian Census, about 11.4% of Canadians live below the poverty line, representing about 3.5 million people.

The worst victims of poverty are children. About 18% of Canadian children live in families with incomes below the poverty line. These figures have not changed since 1989, when the Canadian government pledged to end child poverty by 2000 (Singh, 2008). Most of these children are being raised by single mothers. The 2008 Child Poverty Report Card indicated that British Columbia had the highest overall poverty rate in the country for the fifth year in a row at 16.1%, with a child poverty rate of 21.9% (Dagan, 2010).

The greatest financial hardships are faced by new immigrants to Canada. In 1980, recent immigrants earned about 85 cents to every dollar compared to their Canadian-born counterparts; in 2006, this had diminished to 63 cents. New immigrant women experienced an even worse scenario in 2006: They were earning 56 cents for every dollar earned by Canadian-born counterparts (Singh, 2008).

For those with disabilities, the poverty rate ranges from a high of 10.3% for those with a hearing loss to 22.3% for those with any cognitive or psychological impairment (Council of Canadians with Disabilities, 2010). The Conference Board of Canada (2009) ranked Canada 15th out of 17 countries regarding poverty among working-class people, and on their "report card" gave Canada a "D" grade for its inadequate efforts.

Market Basket Measure   Another method of measuring low income in Canada is called the market basket measure. *Market basket measure* (MBM) is "the cost of a specified basket of goods and services that a family would consume" (Human Resources and Skills Development Canada 2010, section 11, para. 1). According to the MBM, 10.1% of Canadians experienced low income in 2007, affecting 11.9% of children under age 18.

Basic Needs Poverty Measure   A more rigorous estimate is the *basic needs poverty measure* (BNPM). It is published by the Fraser Institute, considered to be a conservative and libertarian "think tank." Various data sources are used to calculate this measure, which considers the cost of basic essentials (e.g., food, shelter, clothing, health care, personal care, basic furnishings, transportation, laundry, home insurance) for various communities across Canada. Based on family size, it then looks at how many households are unable to afford these essentials. As of 2004, the BNPM was 4.9%, representing about 1.6 million Canadians (Sarlo, 2006).

Number of Homeless in Canada   It is estimated that more than 1 billion people are poorly housed in the world, with over 100 million living on the street (Begin, Casavant, Chenier, & Dupuis, 1999). Various surveys and statistics have shown that the number of homeless people in Canada, the United States, and Europe has steadily increased since the 1970s and is far beyond anything experienced one or two generations earlier (Pohl, 2001).

Canada has no official data on homelessness (Begin et al., 1999), but whatever number is estimated is considered seriously flawed because it is impossible to enumerate those who are mobile and have no fixed address (Hulchanski, n.d.). Nonetheless, Canada's National Secretariat on Homelessness estimated that there are 150 000 homeless people; other reports suggest the number may be as high as 300 000 in Canada (Echenberg & Jensen, 2008).

The percentage of seniors who are homeless is growing, and a higher percentage of older women than men experience severe mental illness (Stergiopoulos & Herrmann, 2003). Approximately 30% of the homeless population are women (Begin et al., 1999) and the link between abuse of women and homelessness is well established (Sev'er, 2002). A study in Toronto of homeless women between the ages of 18 and 44 revealed that they are 10 times more likely to die prematurely than women in the general population (Cheung & Hwang, 2004).

In the 1990s, about 30 000 people used a Toronto-funded emergency shelter at least once during any given year, with an estimated 25 000 of these being first-time users (Hulchanski, n.d.). On any given night in Toronto in 1997, emergency shelters reported an average of 6500 occupants (Begin et al., 1999). An enumeration of the homeless in Calgary on the night of May 14, 2008, found that 4060 people experienced absolute homelessness, which was an increase of 18.2% from two years earlier (Echenberg & Jensen, 2008).

One cannot assume that homeless people are not employed (Human Resources and Skills Development Canada, 2010). A study from Calgary in 1997 found that 45% of homeless individuals interviewed were working, although in unstable, low-paying jobs (Begin et al., 1999). Many individuals who live in homeless shelters across Canada are employed in low-paying work (Alliance to End Homelessness Ottawa, 2007).

Recent History of Poverty in Canada

The United Nations declared 1987 to be the International Year of Shelter for the Homeless, and this act alone stimulated interest in the area by researchers and field workers (Begin et al., 1999). Canada subsequently hosted several regional and national conferences on homelessness (Hulchanski, 2009).

Before 1980, large numbers of Canadians were housed in poor conditions, but they were not homeless. There were some transient single men who were helped by organizations such as the Salvation Army, and although they were often thought of as homeless, they generally had poor-quality housing in rooming houses and flophouses (Hulchanski, 2009). The word "homelessness" did not come into common usage in developed countries until the early to mid 1980s (Hulchanski, 2009).

The beginnings of cutbacks to social housing and related programs began in 1984 and, unlike many other countries, Canada ignored the call to action germinating from the 1987 United Nations declaration. In fact, the federal government ceased all construction of new social housing in 1993. In 1996, they pulled further away from low-income housing by transferring this responsibility to the provinces (Hulchanski, 2009).

Although panhandlers are often housed, some do rely on handouts to afford basic necessities (Hulchanski, n.d.). Partly in consequence of poverty, Canadian cities have experienced an increase in public begging, and this has led to civic actions being taken in some places. For example, in 1995, Winnipeg became the first city to enact a bylaw prohibiting begging, an act that could result in a fine of up to $1000 or six months in jail (Pohl, 2001). According to the Alberta Minister of Housing and Urban Affairs, giving money to panhandlers is usually ill-advised, as upward of 80% of the monies received are used for drugs, alcohol, gambling, and other destructive habits (Schneider, 2010).

Pohl (2001) wrote that the poor people themselves cannot be blamed for the extent of poverty and homelessness experienced in Canadian cities. Even in cases where poverty is the result of personal failures, nearly everyone has faced failure at one time or another. Becoming homeless, however, is an unjust and inhumane consequence (Hulchanski, 2009).

In regard to child poverty, the House of Commons Standing Committee on Human Resources, Skills and Social Development and the Status of Persons with Disabilities (HUMA) submitted a motion in the House of Commons (unanimously passed on November 24, 2009) that stated the following:

> That, with November 24th, 2009 marking the 20th anniversary of the 1989 unanimous resolution of this House to eliminate poverty among Canadian children by the year 2000, and not having achieved that goal, be it resolved that the Government of Canada, taking into consideration the Committee's work in this regard, and respecting provincial and territorial jurisdiction, develop an immediate plan to eliminate poverty in Canada for all. (Etoka, 2009)

Only time will tell if the Canadian government acts on this motion. Their record to date by all accounts has been discouraging.

Causes of Poverty and Homelessness

Poor Wages Most people in Canada who work for minimum wage and live independently are living below the poverty line. The minimum wages in Canada are shown in Table 21.1.

Table 21.1 Minimum Wages (Per Hour) in Canada as of July 1, 2010			
Alberta	$8.80	Nunavut	$10.00
British Columbia	$8.00	Ontario	$10.25
Manitoba	$9.00	Prince Edward Island	$8.70
New Brunswick	$8.50	Québec	$9.50
Newfoundland	$10.00	Saskatchewan	$9.25
Northwest Territories	$9.00	Yukon	$8.93
Nova Scotia	$9.20		

Figures from About.com: Canada online. (2010).

Between 1980 and 2005, the gap between top wage earners and the lowest increased from $83 000 to $105 400. However, a closer examination reveals that it was mostly the top 20% of wage earners who had experienced an increase in their salaries (Dagan, 2010). More individuals have become ineligible for social assistance (also known by many as *welfare*) due to tightening eligibility rules (Dagan, 2010).

Welfare is considered the last resort for people in Canada who have no income or inadequate income. Like minimum wage, there are 13 social assistance programs in Canada, and the amount of entitlement depends on the Canadian province or territory. Statistics reveal that most people on welfare in the 1990s were poorer than those in the 1980s (Hulchanski, n.d.).

Furthermore, wages for most Canadians on welfare in 2007 were substantially below the poverty line (Dagan, 2010). A report from 1999 found that only 9% of single people on welfare in Newfoundland were above the poverty line, and the highest rate was 70% in Ontario. For single-parent families, the lowest was in Alberta (50%) and the highest in Newfoundland (70%). For two-parent families on welfare, the lowest was in Québec (45%) and the highest in Prince Edward Island (62%) (Hulchanski, n.d.). When individuals leave welfare to enter the work force, the lack of educational opportunity or training leaves them in unstable, low-paid jobs, thus perpetuating the poverty cycle (Lightman, Mitchell, & Herd, 2008).

Case Example: What Would *You* Do?

Madeleine, aged 35, enters your counselling office and immediately strikes you as very anxious and worried. Bill, Madeleine's boss, laid her off yesterday from her $9.00 an hour retail job because sales were down and he could no longer afford to keep her. Nonetheless, Madeleine explains to you that her co-worker, Geraldine, was not laid off and that Geraldine has worked there for only five months, compared to Madeleine's year and a half. Although Madeleine's rent is only $500.00 per month, she has exactly $225.81 to her name. Madeleine is unskilled and the economy is in recession. She doesn't know how she is going to pay the bills and feed herself.

1. What suggestions would you make, assuming that this takes place in the province or territory of your permanent residence in Canada, to help Madeleine deal with her financial crisis?

2. Given that Madeleine had more seniority than Geraldine yet she was the one let go, how would you help her understand how this could happen? What strategies might you use to help Madeleine maintain positive self-esteem?

3. What could you envision as a possible long-term plan for Madeleine to escape poverty?

Deinstitutionalization of the Mentally Ill The Library of Parliament reported that the number of beds in Canadian mental hospitals decreased from 47 633 to 15 011 between 1960 and 1976, while the number of beds in psychiatric units in general hospitals rose only from 844 to 5836 during this same time period (Begin et al., 1999). This deinstitutionalization effort was meant to have a positive impact on mentally ill individuals and was made possible through the introduction of pharmaceuticals (Pohl, 2001). Unfortunately, many of these people could not make it on their own for various reasons and consequently became poor and in some cases homeless and destitute (Begin et al., 1999; Pohl, 2001).

Decrease in the Number of Low-Income Housing Projects (Pohl, 2001). As mentioned earlier, cutbacks to housing projects began in 1984. By 1993, the federal government had ceased construction of affordable housing for the poor and transferred all responsibility to provinces to 1996 (Hulchanski, 2009). Provinces have not created sufficient low-cost housing for those in need. "A significant component of the homelessness problem is that housing has not been a high priority for governments at any level" (Canadian Association of Housing and Renewal Officials, as cited in Hulchanski, 2009, para. 24).

Correlates of Poverty in Adults

Houselessness The term homelessness has come to mean a cluster of social problems and, as a result, the United Nations now uses the term *houselessness* to refer to only the housing problem aspect in their data collection efforts (Hulchanski, n.d.). Most people who are houseless are not chronically so and most who use shelters do so on a one-time-only basis. Nonetheless, the chronically houseless do occupy about half of the shelter beds at any given time (Laird, 2007).

Houselessness is categorized in several ways. One approach is to use three categories: the absolute houseless, the concealed houseless, and those at risk of becoming houseless (Hulchanski, n.d.). Another typology by the European Federation of National Associations Working with the Homeless uses the following categories: (a) rooflessness (for those living on the street or in emergency shelters), (b) houselessness (for those living in various shelters or institutions), (c) insecure housing (for those living with fear of eviction or violence), and (d) inadequate housing (living in unfit conditions) (Echenberg & Jensen, 2008). Yet another typology uses the terms chronic homelessness, cyclical homelessness, and temporary homelessness (Echenberg & Jensen, 2008).

The houseless are often stereotyped by outsiders as lazy, mentally ill, middle-aged, and male. The reality, however, is that houselessness is not limited to any age, gender, cultural group, or intellectual level (Reid, Berman, & Forchuk, 2005). The average age of houselessness has declined significantly in recent decades. While in the 1950s the average age was about 50, the average today is mid to low thirties (Pohl, 2001).

Homelessness has been linked to several physical and mental health problems, but essentially people without housing do not require medical or psychiatric treatment because of their lack of housing—instead, "they require housing" (Hulchanski, n.d., para. 30). Only after people are housed can they be treated for illnesses with some measure of success. There is empirical support that mentally ill individuals have fewer hospitalizations and experience a greater sense of well-being when they are provided with permanent housing and support (Nelson, Aubry, & Lafrance, 2007). "Care by a mental health specialist is positively associated with improved outcomes" (Stergiopoulos, Dewa, Rouleau, Yoder, & Chau, 2008, p. 61.).

Without a home, people are turned into human scavengers, where their entire focus in the psychological, social, and emotional sense is invested in hour-to-hour survival— essentially, they enter a different world from the rest of us. Hulchanski (n.d.) describes it as a "nightmare world" (para. 39), and for many of us, it only takes a couple of months without sufficient funds to end up on the street (Hulchanski, n.d.).

The majority of homeless individuals want to get off the street. Unfortunately, exiting is difficult given the obstacles they face. Very few people choose to live without a roof over their head (Hulchanski, n.d.).

Physical and Mental Illness The two most common illnesses believed to be associated with homelessness are mental illness and substance dependency, and research provides clear evidence that both are, in fact, overrepresented among homeless individuals. It is virtually impossible to determine which came first—the illness or the loss of a place to live. Research suggests that approximately 20% to 35% of homeless individuals experience mental illness (Pohl, 2001; Stuart & Arboleda-Florez, 2000). Contrary to popular perception, however, less than 10% suffer from schizophrenia; as is true of the general population, affective disorders are more common (Frankish, Hwang, & Quantz, 2005).

Case Example: What Would *You* Do?

Your final client of the day arrives a few minutes late, looking particularly dishevelled and smelling badly from stale perspiration. His name is Sam, and he looks to be in his mid-fifties. As he tries to tell you his story, you notice that his thoughts are confused; as he begins to tell you one thing, he switches naturally into an entirely different topic without giving you any transition. For 30 minutes, you listen and at the end of it still have little idea as to what Sam is looking for. You know he doesn't have an address that he can provide, and he seems not to have any family to speak of. He keeps muttering to himself that he is tired, but it is as though he doesn't know you are hearing him.

1. What response makes the most sense to you at this point?

2. What emergency services are there where you reside that can intervene? If there are no services that you can think of, how might the police be helpful in this instance?

3. When clients cannot articulate their goals and appear to have little insight as to what they want from counselling, does it become unethical to offer counselling? Why or why not?

Beyond these illnesses, it is well established that homeless people experience a disproportionate level of physical disease and physical risk (Hulchanski, n.d.). Sleeping in cold, damp conditions, compounded by a poor diet and inadequate sanitation, increases the risk of health problems. Exposure to cold over a protracted period places undue stress on the heart with concomitant increases in the incidence of cardiovascular disease and cancer. Homeless individuals experience an increased risk of infections, tuberculosis, HIV/AIDS, and other physical illnesses.

The homeless are more likely to be at physical risk because of violence and at greater risk of accidents. They also experience high rates of both criminal victimization and harassment (Huey, 2010).

Individuals living on the street also experience significantly higher degrees of morbidity and mortality compared to those who are housed (Pauly, 2008). While deaths due to freezing sometimes occur, deaths more often result from overdoses, liver disease, and injury (Begin et al., 1999). Several barriers exist that make it difficult for individuals to access health services (e.g., no health care card, inability to pay for prescriptions, healthcare providers reluctant to provide care due to their personal appearance) (Forchuk, Brown, Schofield, & Jensen, 2008).

Shame In a recent Canadian study, 17 students from poor families reported themes of shame and stigma because of their low socioeconomic status. They attempted to "pass" as middle class to reduce this shame. This created stress, however as class is not simply about money but is also about sharing the norms, values, and experiences that define a designated class (Beagan, 2007).

Substance Abuse Regarding the percentage of homeless people addicted to substances, the research is less clear, with estimates in the range of 30% to 50% (Paulsen, 2007; Pohl, 2001). When treatment for substance abuse is sought, the majority of clients return to using within a year of program completion (Paulsen, 2007). Those who are chronically homeless often report experiences of severe childhood trauma, and they tend to attribute their continuing homelessness to substance abuse problems (Morrell-Bellai, Goering, & Boydell, 2000).

Criminal Involvement A study in Ontario revealed that mentally ill individuals on welfare and unstably housed were the mostly likely mentally ill people to become legally involved (Sheldon, Aubry, Arboleda-Florez, Wasylenki, & Goering, 2006). Women are now the fastest growing criminal population in Canada, which has in part been attributed to cutbacks to social services (Balfour, 2006).

Correlates of Poverty in Children and Adolescents

Runaways Police records in 1995 indicated that 75% of the 56 749 missing children in Canada were runaways and, while 90% returned home within 60 days of leaving, the remaining never did. Children and adolescents run away from home for a multitude of reasons. In 1992, a study conducted in the Ottawa-Carleton area found that 75% of the street children interviewed ran way because of sexual assault, physical abuse, and/or psycho-emotional abuse (Begin et al., 1999).

A study of 405 youth interviewed on the streets of Calgary (aged 12 to 17) found that 70% were currently homeless or on the run. The two major reasons they provided for running away were poor communication at home (53%) and some form of abuse (33%) (Kufeldt & Nimmo, 1987).

Another study conducted in Calgary in 1994 found that more than half of the homeless children interviewed had been part of the child welfare system, and most had experienced abuse at home (Begin et al., 1999). Further to this, Aboriginal children in Canada are twice as likely as non-Aboriginal children to be placed in foster care (Trocme, Knoke, & Blackstock, 2004).

Street Involvement Current estimates suggest that about 150 000 youth live on the street in Canada (Krusi, Fast, Small, Wood, & Kerr, 2010). Research reveals that street kids are less healthy physically and psychologically than other groups of young people. They also lack a coherent set of medium- and long-range goals (Taylor, Lydon, Bougie, & Johannesen, 2004).

Without the support from positive adult role models, street youth are more likely to engage in risky sexual behaviours and to abuse substances (Kelly & Caputo, 2007; Smart & Adlaf, 1991). Researchers who conducted interviews with 38 young drug users in Vancouver concluded that early intervention is needed to reduce the likelihood that these youth will become initiated into negative social networks (Fast, Small, Wood, & Kerr, 2009). On a similar note, there appear to be stages of becoming a street youth that shape engagement within street culture (Karabanow, 2006).

A cluster analysis study comprised of 211 street youths in Toronto created a typology with eight distinct types of street youth: *entrepreneurs, drifters, partiers, retreatists, fringers, transcenders, vulnerables,* and *sex workers.* The authors suggested that each type would be best served through programming targeted at their unique style of street existence (Adlaf & Zdanowicz, 1999).

Economically disadvantaged neighbourhoods are the commonly accepted "havens" for youth gangs (Dupere, Lacourse, Willms, Vitaro, & Tremblay, 2007). Economic strain is associated with increased likelihood of youths engaging in criminal behaviour (Baron, 2007; 2008). The most consistent predictors of criminal activity and incarceration for a sample of 390 homeless adolescents were not having a secure shelter and the length of time they were on the street (McCarthy & Hagan, 1992). Furthermore, street youth are much more likely to become victim to a host of crimes compared to non-street youth (Baron, Forde, & Kennedy, 2007; Gatez, 2004).

Emotional Difficulties and Suicide Attempts In a study of 1112 children 12 years of age living in Québec, those raised in welfare families were more likely to experience behavioural problems compared to those whose families had never been poor. Maternal supervision was controlled in the study, suggesting a bona fide difference between the two groups (De Civita, Pagani, Vitaro, & Tremblay, 2007). Another study using participants in the National Longitudinal Study of Youth found that economically disadvantaged children at time 1 (aged three to four) were associated with undesirable personality change (family-level variables were controlled, such as cognitive and emotional support) at time 2 (aged five or six), compared to non-disadvantaged children (Hart, Atkins, & Matsuba, 2008). "Poor children feel deprived, part of the 'poor group,' embarrassed, hurt, picked on, inadequate and responsible" (Robinson, McIntyre, & Officer, 2005, p. 342). Poverty places children at increased risk for psychic and physical risk (Eisler & Schissel, 2004).

A 1992 survey of Ottawa street youth noted that 92% had attempted suicide (Begin et al., 1999). Homeless female youth in Canada also display increased suicidal behaviour compared to female youth in general (Votta & Farrell, 2009). Neighbourhood disadvantage is an important factor in explaining youth suicide (Dupere, Leventhal, & Lacourse, 2009).

Delayed Biological Growth Researchers interviewed 1929 mothers of toddlers (2.5 to 4 years) from the Québec Longitudinal Study of Child Development, with data also obtained from birth records. The toddlers who came from poor families were more likely to have growth delay even after neonatal conditions and mother characteristics were controlled (Ehounoux, Zunzunegui, Seguin, Nikiema, & Gauvin, 2009). Women with low incomes were more likely to have babies with lower birth weights, and they were also less likely to attend prenatal programs as compared to women with higher incomes (Canning, Frizzell, & Courage, 2010).

Case Example: What Would *You* Do?

You have been hired as a street-based youth worker. Every day on your shift, you ride with one other worker in a bus that has the inscription "Out Reach" in large print painted on both exterior sides. Further, you are told to spend most of your time within a four-block radius of where most of the street kids congregate. The problem is, you and your colleague are usually sitting alone in the bus and few youth actually come to visit. Both of you know that you need to immerse yourself with the street youth if this outreach project is to be successful.

1. What would you see as the most difficult parts of this job for you?

2. How would you go about establishing rapport with the young people who have a completely different lifestyle from the way you were raised?

3. How would you respond if a few youths began smoking marijuana in your presence? Would your response be any different if the drug was crack cocaine? What about crystal meth?

PROPOSED SOLUTIONS TO POVERTY IN CANADA

The following statement comes from the chair of the Canadian Senate Committee on Cities:

> We believe that eradicating poverty and homelessness is not only the humane and decent priority of a civilized democracy, but absolutely essential to a productive and

expanding economy benefitting from the strengths and abilities of all its people. (Eggleton, n.d., para. 12)

While the poor wait for solutions to be implemented, a Charter challenge has been launched. In effect, the legal argument is that the crisis of homelessness violates sections 7 and 15 of the *Canadian Charter of Rights and Freedoms*, the sections that pertain to the right to security of the person and to equality for disadvantaged groups (Hulchanski, 2009). Hulchanski (2009) recommends that action be taken on three levels: (a) the level of individuals and families, (b) the community level, and (c) the macro federal and provincial level. Without intervention at all three levels, Hulchanski believes that efforts will be unlikely to succeed.

The following is a list of possible solutions that have been advanced in the literature:

1. *Build more low-income housing.* One of the clearest solutions suggested is that more low-income dwellings need to be built in Canadian cities (Pohl, 2001). One idea among many is to use the annual surpluses from the Canadian Mortgage and Housing Corporation (CMHC) for new housing initiatives (Shapcott, 2006).

2. *Ensure all Canadians have adequate housing* (Hulchanski, n.d.).

3. *Create additional outreach services.* Two ideas include installing telephone street help lines and opening various physical and mental health care services for the poor (Hulchanski, n.d.).

4. *Offer housing support services.* These are services that provide episodic support to people so that they can continue to live independently (e.g., budgeting help, offering rent payments, cleaning services, counselling services, social supports) (Hulchanski, n.d.).

5. *Implement local living wage policies.* The New Westminster City Council (a city near Vancouver) approved a policy on April 28, 2010, providing for a minimum hourly wage to keep families above the poverty line (Dagan, 2010).

Goldberg and Green (2009) recently provided 10 further recommendations:

1. Legislate welfare as a human right for those in need.

2. Set income assistance thresholds at the provincial level.

3. Increase income assistance rates immediately.

4. Index income assistance rates and increase annually according to cost of living.

5. Establish appropriate minimum wages.

6. Increase the Canada Child Tax Benefit.

7. Develop affordable quality child care.

8. Provide training and educational opportunities for those on welfare.

9. Establish and provide appropriate financial allowances for refugees and immigrants.

10. Address housing affordability.

Finally, below is an extract of 10 recommendations from a list of 25 made in Ministers of Parliament Paul Martin and Joe Fontana's task force report published in 1990 (Martin & Fontana, 1990). The task force recommended that the Conservative government do the following:

1. Initiate consultations and negotiations with the provinces to create a new social program aimed at providing an income supplement for those below the poverty line.

2. Increase funding for the Federal Cooperative Housing program to create 5000 new cooperative housing units annually.

3. Ensure that an adequate number of affordable housing units are made available through the Canada Mortgage and Housing Corporation (CMHC) for those with special needs.

4. Urge the Minister of State (Housing) to develop a national formula that curbs the reductions in annual funding for provinces for housing.

5. Take immediate steps to lower the Bank of Canada prime interest rate.

6. Review the Canadian Real Estate Association's use of RRSP funds for home purchases.

7. Recommend that the Minister of State (Housing) convene a national housing forum to discuss a national housing policy.

8. Set the year 2000 as the target date to eliminate sub-standard housing on reserves.

9. Eliminate the Goods and Services Tax (GST).

10. Begin consultations with Canadians and provincial governments to reform the entire tax system.

COUNSELLING THE ECONOMICALLY DISADVANTAGED IN CANADA

Counsellors working with economically disadvantaged clients must have the ability to "distinguish unconscious depression from conscious despair, paranoia from adaptive wariness, and a sick [individual] from a sick nation" (Grier & Cobbs, 1992, p. 158). Unfortunately, graduate students are generally not provided specialized training in working with economically disadvantaged clientele (Caldwell, 2009). There are, however, several considerations when working with this population. The Arthur and Collins (2009) model of culture-infused counselling will serve as the organizational structure for the remainder of this chapter. As the preceding sections have focused on *awareness of the client's culture*, the bulk of this discussion concerns the other three areas: *cultural self-awareness*, *the working alliance*, and *engaging in social justice*.

The Arthur and Collins (2009) framework is again reproduced below from Chapter 4:

Table 21.2 rthur and Collins (2009) Multicultural Competence Framework

	Cultural Self-Awareness	Awareness of Client's Culture	Working Alliance	Engage in Social Justice
Attitudes and Beliefs (i.e., Self-Awareness)				
Knowledge				
Skills				

Cultural Self-Awareness

Often, individuals living in poverty believe that other people are looking down on them as lazy, dependent individuals who cannot think for themselves. This perception is thought to lead to low self-esteem and a sense of powerlessness (Liu & Estrada-Hernandez, 2010). It is crucial that counsellors do not inadvertently perpetuate this notion by believing stereotypes themselves. Counsellors generally come from the middle- to upper-classes, and it is difficult for many to relate to those who are economically disadvantaged (Bienvenu & Ramsey, 2006). Consequently, counsellors must be aware of their own upward mobility and desire to attain a higher social class or income (Liu & Estrada-Hernandez, 2010). Counsellors are encouraged to admit their biases about the attributions of poverty and about ethnic and racial stereotypes (Armstrong, 2007).

It is important to not generalize when working with economically disadvantaged people. Each person's situation is unique, and so is her or his worldview (Liu & Estrada-Hernandez, 2010). Nonetheless, many impoverished clients have a present-time orientation, an external locus of control, and limited practice with delaying gratification (Bienvenu & Ramsey, 2006).

Working Alliance

Working with Impoverished Adult Clients While it is important to instill hope with clients who are poor, it does not mean distorting the situation for the client. Rather, counsellors should help clients reframe their economic plight: Being poor is a situational event and not a character flaw (Liu & Estrada-Hernandez, 2010).

Narrative therapists have long worked with disenfranchised individuals, and some writers highly recommend its use with the economically disadvantaged (Fraenkel, Hameline, & Shannon, 2009). The emphasis on storytelling is appealing to many people who have suffered severe hardships.

Marital and family therapy is often indicated with economically disadvantaged clients because of the increased likelihood of mental health issues arising from prolonged financial strain (Grimes & McElwain, 2008). Grimes and McElwain (2008) suggest that counsellors use a solution-focused approach, asking (a) deconstruction questions (i.e., externalize the problem of poverty); (b) opening space questions (i.e., looking for unique outcomes); (c) preference questions (i.e., further exploring the unique outcomes identified); (d) story development questions (i.e., if the unique outcomes were positive, having client elaborate their story); (e) meaning questions (i.e., asking questions that emphasize a client's personal qualities that contributed to positive outcomes); and (f) questions to extend the story into the future (i.e., encouraging clients to make predictions about the future).

Waldegrave (20005) purports that counsellors will soon discover that most family problems result from events external to the family. Waldegrave provided unemployment and bad housing as examples of such events.

Rojano (2004) developed a particular form of family therapy specially designed for economically disadvantaged clients, known as *community family therapy*. Its focus is to help improve the family's economic position by incorporating aspects of structural, strategic, and ecosystems approaches to counselling practice.

Working with Impoverished Child and Adolescent Clients Research indicates that young homeless people trust neither counsellors nor the counselling process, nor do they like counselling (Cormack, 2009). The 16- to 21-year olds that Cormack (2009) interviewed would have preferred to see a counsellor outside of the counselling office, such as going for a walk or having coffee somewhere. They also preferred that counsellors spend some time in the client's environment. Boundaries were also raised as an issue, and Cormack recommends that counsellors adapt the 50-minute counselling hour to whatever the client prefers from the outset. Other suggestions include using creative approaches like art therapy, drama therapy, and group therapy.

Specific techniques have been developed to work with boys from impoverished families (Cervantes & Englar-Carlson, 2008). Such approaches do not pathologize behaviour by introducing diagnoses from the DSM-IV-TR system. Instead, the focus is on sociocultural factors. As is commonly found in a systems approach, clients are viewed as the "bearers" of their family's difficulties.

Researchers have also developed strategies for school counsellors who work with impoverished children in their school (Daniels, 1992; Stawser, Markos, Yamaguchi, & Higgins, 2000; Walsh & Buckley, 1994). Under the rubric of direct facilitation, school counsellors can establish an area where children can help themselves to clothing, snacks, and school supplies. They can also provide services or referrals to their parents. Under indirect facilitation strategies, school counsellors can establish a case management team to address the needs of children who are economically disadvantaged, and they can organize an after-school program. Another idea (among many others) is they can provide parents with medical and nutritional information.

Improving the Working Alliance Some suggestions for improving the working alliance suggested in the literature include the following:

1. *Move beyond the usual "boundaries" of practice.* Many economically disadvantaged clients face transportation difficulties. Counsellors may need to travel to accommodate their clients' needs (Grimes & McElwain, 2008). Other worthwhile ideas are to have a mobile counselling unit housed in a recreational vehicle or to offer unconventional approaches to typical counselling practice, such as facilitating a two-hour support group meeting around someone's kitchen table (Caldwell, 2009). A recent study of Honduran counsellors found that there were few boundaries between "real life" and "work life" in how they practised their profession. The counsellors were self-sacrificing and dedicated to personal moral principles (Sells et al., 2007).

2. *Establish and discuss the external stressors.* By talking about external stressors and their impact, clients see that the counsellor understands that much of being economically disadvantaged is outside a client's direct control (Grimes & McElwain, 2008). Also, the counsellor must let clients know that socioeconomic disparities exist and that they are unjust (Amstrong, 2007; Caldwell, 2009).

3. *Empower clients.* The theme of failure will likely arise, and it is important to help economically disadvantaged clients see that the problem is not themselves but is rather the situation (Grimes & McElwain, 2008). For example, clients can be empowered by focusing on their strengths, such as their persistence in dealing with adversity and their ability to be a good caregiver (Amstrong, 2007; Bienvenu & Ramsey, 2006).

4. *Assess how deeply entrenched the client is in poverty/homelessness.* A study by Snow and Anderson (1987) found a distinct difference between short-term homeless individuals using shelters and those who were chronically homeless. After four years on the street, it was common that homeless men were far more likely to embrace a positive identity as a homeless person. A later study found that 40% of their homeless sample described themselves as "happy," suggesting that such individuals may experience inertia in wanting to make any change to their living situation (Sumerlin & Norman, 1992).

5. *Provide appropriate employment/career counselling.* Wilgosh and Mueller (1993) stress the importance of work-skills training for economically disadvantaged clients. Economically disadvantaged clients intending to pursue postsecondary study will need extra encouragement and support (Cunningham & Tidwell, 1990). Many will experience something referred to by Piorkowski (1983) as *survivor guilt,* a condition where the student feels badly for becoming more successful than his or her family.

6. *Limit the use of humour.* Humour is usually only therapeutic when counsellors refer to themselves or to some situation they have encountered with economically disadvantaged clients (Lewis, 1992).

7. *Be sensitive to language.* Caldwell (2009) discussed the devaluing process that occurs when those who are privileged talk about the economically disadvantaged. Such terms as impoverished, homeless, and minority, for example, evoke emotional responses and may imply a dispositional quality to these constructs. This chapter has

been no exception to this use of language for the sake of simplicity, but in actual counselling practice, it is important to always keep in mind the other—the client sitting before you.

Engaging in Social Justice

Collaboration with Other Agencies and Organizations   Many agencies have layers of bureaucracy that economically disadvantaged clients have trouble navigating (Liu & Estrada-Hernandez, 2010). Helping clients navigate this terrain is an important aspect of counselling them (Bienvenu & Ramsey, 2006; Liu & Estrada-Hernandez, 2010). Furthermore, building interdisciplinary teams is another means of creative effective collaboration (Caldwell, 2009).

Providing Pro Bono Counselling to the Economically Disadvantaged
Many circles have criticized the social work profession for abandoning the poor (Bembry, Anderson, & Yaggy, 2002), and such criticism should be owned by all counselling specialities. No-cost counselling provided by trained volunteers that are supervised by professional counsellors is just one example of providing help where needed.

Advocacy Skills   Counsellors need to become advocates for their economically disadvantaged clients (Bienvenu & Ramsey, 2006). Advocacy is generally not taught by graduate schools in counselling psychology, although it remains an integral part of social work education. Counsellors who work with the economically disadvantaged will need to identify and confront oppression, including policies that unfairly marginalize their clients (Liu & Estrada-Hernandez, 2010). Bienvenu and Ramsey (2006) suggest that counsellors must become leaders in the community, both politically and socially.

You are now working as a professional counsellor in a private practice setting. A friend of yours makes frequent disparaging remarks regarding economically disadvantaged individuals. You have heard everything from "Why don't they look for a job instead of asking for handouts?" to "If they sought help for their mental illnesses and substance abuse problems, they wouldn't be where they are."

1. What do you believe is appropriate to say to your friend? To what extent can you see yourself speaking up?

2. What is the harm in saying nothing about these remarks?

3. What, if any, are your ethical obligations if you are (a) a social worker or (b) a psychologist?

Researching the Economically Disadvantaged The economically disadvantaged are underrepresented in research (Caldwell, 2009). By including them or focusing on them in research, greater exposure is provided. As is often clichéd in feminist discourse, the personal is political.

Counselling in the Global Quest to End Poverty Frank (2005) wrote that counselling practice and the counselling posture (e.g., unconditional positive regard, empathy, genuineness) have much to offer the international mandate to eradicate poverty. Counselling provides an excellent model of the human capacity to help others.

SUMMARY AND CONCLUSION

Although there is no internationally accepted definition of poverty, the low-income cut-off method currently used by Statistics Canada reveals that, in 2006, more than 10% of adults had annual incomes below the poverty line. Furthermore, current estimates suggest that between 150 000 and 300 000 Canadian inhabitants are homeless. Children, however, are the hardest hit, with about 18% living in poverty nationwide. While much rhetoric over many years has occurred within the federal government regarding the need to rectify this situation, even strong rebuke by the United Nations has not led to appreciable differences in the plight of today's poor living in Canada.

There are many reasons why Canada's economically disadvantaged have ended up where they are, including low wages and welfare benefits, deinstitutionalization of the mentally ill, and a decrease in the number of low-income housing projects. Unfortunately, there is a ripple effect from poverty, particularly when it becomes chronic. Homeless individuals experience a myriad of problems in greater proportion than those who have a regular safe place to sleep, including problems such as physical illness, mental illness, shame, substance abuse, and criminal involvement. Without question, the psychosocial costs incurred from allowing Canadian inhabitants to become homeless are tragic.

Graduate students in counselling generally receive little to no training in how to work with the economically disadvantaged, and their relative place of privilege does little to build a strong working alliance with the impoverished client sitting before them—unless steps are taken to build the necessary empathy that is fundamental to all human relationships. Counsellors will need to move beyond the usual boundaries of counselling practice to be effective in working with economically disadvantaged clients. Besides offering help to clientele, an equally important mandate is required of counsellors who work with the poor: engagement in social justice efforts and advocacy.

In closing this final chapter, it is helpful to remember that the counselling profession has a strong message to offer this struggling world and our clients who sometimes find themselves mired with adversity in one form or another. That message is to *really* listen, to *really* hear, to *really* feel, and to *really* care about what happens— and then to move beyond this to collaboratively find viable, realistic solutions. Ultimately, in this, a counsellor is expected to be a true role model of what a genuine loving being ought to look like. No small challenge, but on the other hand, what could be more purposeful and meaningful in life?

Your Personal Reflections

1. Instead of giving money to a panhandler, what responses do you believe are personally and morally appropriate? How do you currently deal with panhandlers?

2. If you eventually open a private practice, to what extent could you see yourself offering pro bono work to impoverished clients? What are the benefits and possible drawbacks to doing so?

3. If you wake up tomorrow and poverty is gone, what is it that has changed? How are people viewing the impoverished differently? What are individuals, communities, and all levels of government doing differently?

4. Have you ever written anything that was published in a newspaper or article that addressed a human rights issue or violation of human rights? What do you see as the personal obstacles to doing this? What do you see as the personal benefits of doing this?

5. From everything you have learned from this text, what stands out for you? What made the greatest impression, both positive and negative?

6. Do you now feel more inspired or less inspired to become a professional counsellor? Why or why not?

Classroom Activities

1. In groups of three or four, review the list of 25 recommendations that Paul Martin and Joe Fontana spearheaded in 1990 to deal with growing homeless problem in Canada (http://action.web.ca/home/housing/resources.shtml?x=67127&AA_EX_Session=fd83bd 77975ac7a2110113d712acd060). Which of these recommendations would still be viable today? Afterward, discuss these recommendations as a class.

2. In class, discuss recommendations for eradicating poverty in Canada in 10 years or less.

3. Referring back to Chapter 3, what ethical guidelines might be violated as you begin working with an impoverished clientele? How can these guidelines be adapted or changed to accommodate working with the economically disadvantaged?

4. Work on a group project to write a letter to the editor of your local newspaper regarding recommendations for reducing or eradicating poverty in your community.

5. In class, discuss encounters you have had with impoverished individuals. What happened? What thoughts went through your head? How did you feel? What did you do?

References

AA World Services, Inc. (2002). *Alcoholics Anonymous: The story of how many thousands of men and women have recovered from alcoholism* (4th ed.). New York: Author.

About.com: Canada online. (2010, July 1). *Minimum wage in Canada.* Retrieved from **http://canadaonline.about.com/library/bl/blminwage.htm**.

Abudabeth, N., & Aseel, H. A. (1999). Transcultural counseling and Arab Americans. In J. McFadden (Ed.), *Transcultural counseling* (2nd ed., pp. 283–296). Alexandria, VA: American Counseling Association.

ACES-ASCA Joint Committee on the Elementary School Counselor. (1966). The elementary school counselor: Preliminary statement. *Personnel and Guidance Journal, 44,* 658–661.

ACT, Inc. (1998). *DISCOVER.* Hunt Valley, MD: Author.

Adams, M. V. (n.d.). *What is Jungian analysis?* Retrieved from **www.jungnewyork.com/whatisit.shtml**.

Addington, J., Addington, D., Jones, B., & Ko, T. (2001). Family intervention in an early psychosis program. *Psychiatric Rehabilitation Skills, 5*(2), 272–286.

Addington, J., & Tran, L. (2009). Using the Brief Core Schema Scales with individuals at clinical high risk of psychosis. *Behavioural and Cognitive Psychotherapy, 37*(2), 227—231.

Adelman, H. S., & Taylor, L. (2002). School counselors and school reform: New directions. *Professional School Counseling, 5,* 235–248.

Adlaf, E. M., & Zdanowicz, Y. M. (1999). A cluster-analytic study of substance problems and mental health among street youths. *The American Journal of Drug and Alcohol Abuse, 25*(4), 639–660.

Adler, A. (1927). *Understanding human nature.* Greenwich, CT: Fawcett.

Adler, A. (1931). *What life should mean to you.* Boston: Little, Brown.

Adler, A. (1956). *The individual psychology of Alfred Adler: A systematic presentation in selections from his writings* (H. L. Ansbacher & R. R. Ansbacher, Eds.). New York: Norton.

Adler, A. (1964). *Social interest: A challenge to mankind.* New York: Capricorn.

Ahmad, F., Shik, A., Vanza, R., Cheung, A. M., George, U., & Stewart, D. E. (2004). Voices of South Asian women: Immigration and mental health. *Women & Health, 40*(4), 113–130.

Ahn, H., & Wampold, B. E. (2001). Where oh where are the specific ingredients? A meta-analysis of component studies in counseling and psychotherapy. *Journal of Counseling Psychology, 48,* 251–257.

Aiken, L. R., Jr., & Groth-Marnat, G. (2006). *Psychological testing and assessment* (12th ed.). Boston: Allyn & Bacon.

Aknin, L. B., Norton, M. I., & Dunn, E. W. (2009). From wealth to well-being? Money matters, but less than people think. *The Journal of Positive Psychology, 4*(6), 523–527.

Akos, P., Cockman, C. R., & Strickland, C. A. (2007). Differentiating classroom guidance. *Professional School Counseling, 10,* 455–463.

Akos, P., Hamm, J. V., Mack, S. G., & Dunaway, F. (2007). Utilizing the development influence of peers in middle school groups. *Journal for Specialists in Group Work, 32,* 51–60.

Alaggia, R. (2010). An ecological analysis of child sexual abuse disclosure: Considerations for child and adolescent mental health. *Journal of the Canadian Academy of Child and Adolescent Psychiatry/Journal de l'Academie canadienne de psychiatrie de l'enfant et de l'adolescent, 19*(1), 32–39.

Albee, G. W., & Gullotta, T. P. (1997). *Primary prevention works.* Thousand Oaks, CA: Sage.

Alberta Learning Information Service. (2008). *Alberta occupational profiles: Psychologist (section under salary).* Retrieved from **http://alis.alberta.ca/occinfo/Content/RequestAction.asp?aspAction=GetHTMLProfile&format=html&occPro_ID=71002221&SNT_ID=25**.

Alberta Learning Information Service. (2009). *Alberta occupational profiles: Social worker.* Retrieved from **http://alis.alberta.ca/occinfo/Content/RequestAction.asp?aspAction=GetHTMLProfile&format=html&occPro_ID=71002779&SNT_ID=25**.

Alberti, R. E., & Emmons, M. L. (2001). *Your perfect right: Assertive and equality in your life and relationships* (8th ed.). San Luis Obispo, CA: Impact.

Alderson, K. (2002). *Breaking out: The complete guide to building and enhancing a positive gay identity for men and women.* Toronto, ON: Insomniac Press.

Alderson, K. (2004). *Grade power: The complete guide to improving your grades through self-hypnosis.* Toronto, ON: Insomniac Press.

Alderson, K. (2007). *"Breathe, Freedom!" Lessons on kicking the crap out of cigarettes.* Calgary, AB: Kevin Alderson, publisher.

Alderson, K. G. (2004). Hands-on career counselling with gay, lesbian, and bisexual individuals. *Building Tomorrow Today Consultation Proceedings, 10,* 25–31.

Alderson, K. G. (2009). From madness to mainstream: Working with gay men today. In N. Arthur & S. Collins (Eds.), *Culture-infused counselling: Celebrating the Canadian mosaic* (2nd ed.) (pp. 395–422). Calgary, AB: Counselling Concepts.

Alderson, K. G., Orzeck, T. L., & McEwen, S. C. (2009). Alberta high school counsellors' knowledge of homosexuality and their attitudes toward gay males. *Canadian Journal of Education, 32*(1), 85–116.

Alderson, K. G. (2010). From madness to mainstream: Working with gay men today. In N. Arthur & S. Collins (Eds.), *Culture-infused counselling: Celebrating the Canadian mosaic* (2nd ed.) (pp. 395–422). Calgary, AB: Counselling Concepts.

Aldridge, D. (1994). Single-case research designs for the creative art therapist. *Arts in Psychotherapy, 21,* 333–342.

Ali, S. R., & Saunders, J. L. (2006). College expectations of rural Appalachian youth: An exploration of social cognitive career theory factors. *Career Development Quarterly, 55.*

All, A. C., & Fried, J. H. (1994). Psychosocial issues surrounding HIV infection that affect rehabilitation. *Journal of Rehabilitation, 60,* 8–11.

Allan, J., & Brown, K. (1993). Jungian play therapy in elementary schools. *Elementary School Guidance and Counseling, 28,* 30–41.

Allan, L. J., & Johnson, J. A. (2009). Undergraduate attitudes toward the elderly: The role of knowledge, contact and aging anxiety. *Educational Gerontology, 35*(1), 1–14.

Allen, G. (1977). *Understanding psychotherapy: Comparative perspectives.* Champaign, IL: Research Press.

Allen, M., Bromley, A., Kuyken, W., & Sonnenberg, S. J. (2009). Participants' experiences of mindfulness-based cognitive therapy: "It changed me in just about every way possible." *Behavioural and Cognitive Psychotherapy, 37*(4), 413–430.

Allen, M. B., Blashki, G., & Gullone, E. (2006). Mindfulness-based psychotherapies: A review of conceptual foundations, empirical evidence and practical considerations. *Australian and New Zealand Journal of Psychiatry, 40*(4), 285–294.

Allen, V. B. (1986). A historical perspective of the AACD ethics committee. *Journal of Counseling and Development, 64,* 293.

Alliance to End Homelessness Ottawa. (2007). *Housing works: A special report 2007.* Retrieved from **www.endhomelessnessottawa.ca.**

Alter, G. (1995, May 29). What works. *Newsweek,* 18–24.

Altmaier, E. M., Greiner, M., & Griffin-Pierson, S. (1988). The new scholarship on women. *Journal of Counseling and Development, 66,* 345–346.

Altmann, H. A., Nysetvold, I., & Downe, A. G. (1986). Evaluation of peer counselling in the elementary school. *Canadian Journal of Counselling, 20*(2), 85–90.

Alyn, J. H. (1988). The politics of touch in therapy: A response to Willison and Masson. *Journal of Counseling and Development, 66,* 432–433.

Ambler, D. A. (1989). Designing and managing programs: The administrator role. In U. Delworth, G. R. Hanson, & Associates (Eds.), *Student services: A handbook for the profession* (2nd ed., pp. 247–264). San Francisco: Jossey-Bass.

American Educational Research Association, American Psychological Association, and National Council on Measurement in Education. (1999, March). *Standards for educational and psychological tests* (Rev.). Washington, DC: American Educational Research Association.

American Psychiatric Association. (1994). *Diagnostic and statistical manual of mental disorders* (4th ed.). Washington, DC: Author.

American Psychiatric Association. (2000). *Diagnostic and statistical manual of mental disorders* (4th ed., text revision), *DSM-IV-TR.* Washington, DC: Author.

Americans with Disabilities Act. (1990, July 26). Public Law 101–336. Washington, DC: Government Printing Office.

Amos, W. E., & Williams, D. E. (1972). *Community counseling: A comprehensive team model for developmental services.* St. Louis, MO: Warren H. Green.

Amundson, N. (2006). Challenges for career interventions in changing contexts. *International Journal for Educational and Vocational Guidance, 6*(1), 3–14.

Amundson, N. E. (1996). Supporting clients through a change in perspective. *Journal of Employment Counseling, 33,* 155–162.

Anastasi, A. (1982). *Psychological testing* (5th ed.). New York: Macmillan.

Anastasi, A. (1992b). What counselors should know about the use and interpretation of psychological tests. *Journal of Counseling and Development, 70,* 610–615.

Anastasi, A., & Urbina, S. (1997). *Psychological testing* (7th ed.). Upper Saddle River, NJ: Prentice Hall.

Ancis, J. R., Sedlacek, W. E., & Mohr, J. J. (2000). Student perceptions of campus cultural climate by race. *Journal of Counseling and Development, 78,* 180–185.

Anderson, C. M., & Stewart, S. (1983). *Mastering resistance: A practical guide to family therapy.* New York: Guilford.

Anderson, D. (2007). Multicultural group work: A force for developing and healing. *Journal for Specialists in Group Work, 32*(3), 224–244.

Anderson, H., & Goolishian, H. (1992). The client is the expert: A not knowing approach to therapy. In S. McNamee & K. Gergen (Eds.), *Therapy as social construction* (pp. 25–39). Newbury Park, CA: Sage.

Anderson, H. D. (1995). Collaborative language systems: Toward a postmodern therapy. In R. H. Mikesell, D.-D. Lusterman, & S. H. McDanial (Eds.), *Integrating family therapy: Handbook of family psychology and systems theory* (pp. 27–44). Washington, DC: American Psychological Association.

Andronico, M. P. (Ed.). (1996). *Men in groups: Insights, interventions, and psychoeducational work.* Washington, DC: American Psychological Association.

Angus Reid Global Monitor. (2010, April 18). *Canadian majority would legalize marijuana.* Retrieved from **www.angus-reid.com/polls/view/canadian_majority_would_legalize_marijuana1.**

Anton, J. L. (1978). Intensive experimental designs: A model for the counselor/researcher. *Personnel and Guidance Journal, 56,* 273–278.

Anton, W. D., & Reed, J. R. (1991). *College adjustment scales professional manual.* Odessa, FL: Psychological Assessment Resources.

Aplin, J. C. (1985). Business realities and organizational consultation. *Counseling Psychologist, 13,* 396–402.

Arch, J. J., & Craske, M. G. (2008). Acceptance and commitment therapy and cognitive behavioral therapy for anxiety disorders: Different treatments, similar mechanisms? *Clinical Psychology: Science and Practice, 15*(4), 263–279.

Arellano-Morales, L. (2009). The use of multiracial feminism within counseling. In I. Marini & M. A. Stebnicki (Eds.),

The professional counselor's desk reference (pp. 345–354). New York, NY: Springer.

Armstrong, K. L. (2007). Advancing social justice by challenging socioeconomic disadvantage. In C. C. Lee (Ed.), *Counseling for social justice* (2nd ed.) (pp. 15–30). Alexandria, VA: American Counseling Association.

Arredondo, P. (1998). Integrating multicultural counseling competencies and universal helping conditions in culture-specific contexts. *Counseling Psychologist, 26,* 592–601.

Arredondo, P., Rosen, D. C., Rice, T., Perez, P. & Tovar-Gamero, Z. G. (2005). Multicultural counseling: A 10–year content analysis of the Journal of Counseling & Development. *Journal of Counseling and Development, 83,* 155–161.

Arredondo, P., Toporek, R., Brown, S., Jones, J., Locke, D. C., Sanchez, J., et al. (1996). *Operationalization of the multicultural counseling competencies.* Alexandria, VA: Association for Multicultural Counseling and Development.

Arthur, G. L., & Swanson, C. D. (1993). *Confidentiality and privileged communication.* Alexandria, VA: American Counseling Association.

Arthur, N. (2009). Learners in cross-cultural transition: Counselling international students. In N. Arthur & S. Collins (Eds.), *Culture-infused counselling: Celebrating the Canadian mosaic* (2nd ed.) (pp. 423–446). Calgary, AB: Counselling Concepts.

Arthur, N., & Collins, S. (Eds.) (2009). *Culture-infused counselling: Celebrating the Canadian mosaic* (2nd ed.). Calgary, AB: Counselling Concepts.

Arthur, N., & Lalande, V. (2009). Diversity and social justice implications for outcome approaches to evaluation. *International Journal for the Advancement of Counselling, 31*(1), 1–16.

Arthur, N., Merali, & Djuraskovic, I. (2009). Facilitating the journey between cultures: Counselling immigrants and refugees. In N. Arthur & S. Collins (Eds.), *Culture-infused counselling: Celebrating the Canadian mosaic* (2nd ed.) (pp. 285–314). Calgary, AB: Counselling Concepts.

Ary, D. (1996). *Introduction to research in education* (5th ed.). New York: Harcourt Brace.

Ashby, J. S., & Rice, K. G. (2002). Perfectionism, dysfunctional attitudes, and self-esteem: A structural equations analysis. *Journal of Counseling and Development, 80,* 197–203.

Aslanian, C. B., & Brickell, H. M. (1980). *Americans in transition: Life changes as reasons for adult learning.* New York: College Entrance Examination Board.

Association for Specialists in Group Work. (1992). Professional standards for the training of group workers. *Journal for Specialists in Group Work, 17,* 12–19.

Association for Specialists in Group Work. (1998). Best practice guidelines. *Journal for Specialists in Group Work, 23,* 237–244.

Association for Specialists in Group Work. (2000). Professional standards for the training of group workers. *Journal for Specialists in Group Work, 25,* 327–342.

Astramovich, R. L., & Coker, K. (2007). Program evaluation: The accoutability bridge model for counselors. *Journal of Counseling and Development, 85,* 162–172.

Astramovich, R. L., & Harris, K. R. (2007). Promoting self-advocacy among minority students in school counseling. *Journal of Counseling and Development, 85,* 269–276.

Atlas, G., & Morier, D. (1994). The sorority rush process: Self-selection, acceptance criteria, and the effect of rejection. *Journal of College Student Development, 35,* 346–353.

Aubrey, R. F. (1977). Historical development of guidance and counseling and implications for the future. *Personnel and Guidance Journal, 55,* 288–295.

Aubrey, R. F. (1979). Relationship of guidance and counseling to the established and emerging school curriculum. *School Counselor, 26,* 150–162.

Aubrey, R. F. (1983). The odyssey of counseling and images of the future. *Personnel and Guidance Journal, 61,* 78–82.

Auld, J. (2008). Milton H. Erickson and hypnosis: Reflections. *Australian Journal of Clinical and Experimental Hypnosis, 36*(2), 163–168.

Aust, C. F. (1990). Using client's religious values to aid progress in therapy. *Counseling and Values, 34,* 125–129.

Austin, J. T. (1994). Minnesota Multiphasic Personality Inventory (MMPI-2). *Measurement and Evaluation in Counseling and Development, 27,* 178–185.

Auvenshine, D., & Noffsinger, A. L. (1984). *Counseling: An introduction for the health and human services.* Baltimore: University Park Press.

Azar, B. (1994, June). Could "policing" test use improve assessment? *APA Monitor, 25,* 16.

Bachelor, A. (1995). Clients' perception of the therapeutic alliance: A qualitative analysis. *Journal of Counseling Psychology, 42*(3), 323–337.

Bachman, R. W. (1975). Elementary school children's perceptions of helpers and their characteristics. *Elementary School Guidance and Counseling, 10,* 103–109.

Baggerly, J., & Parker, M. (2005). Child-centered group play therapy with African American boys at the elementary school level. *Journal of Counseling and Development, 83,* 387–396.

Bagley, C., & Tremblay, P. (1998). On the prevalence of homosexuality and bisexuality, in a random community survey of 750 men aged 18 to 27. *Journal of Homosexuality, 36*(2), 1–18.

Bailey, W. R., Deery, N. K., Gehrke, M., Perry, N., & Whitledge, J. (1989). Issues in elementary school counseling: Discussion with American School Counselor Association leaders. *Elementary School Guidance and Counseling, 24,* 4–13.

Baker, E. L., & Nash, M. R. (2008). Psychoanalytic approaches to clinical hypnosis. In M. R. Nash & A. J. Barnier (Eds.), *The Oxford handbook of hypnosis: Theory, research, and practice* (pp. 439–456). New York, NY: Oxford University Press.

Baker, S. B., & Gerler, E. R., Jr. (2008). *School counseling for the twenty-first century* (4th ed.). Upper Saddle River, NJ: Merrill/Prentice Hall.

Baker, S. B., & Shaw, M. C. (1987). *Improving counseling through primary prevention.* Upper Saddle River, NJ: Prentice Hall.

Baker, S. B., Swisher, J. D., Nadenichek, P. E., & Popowicz, C. L. (1984). Measured effects of primary prevention strategies. *Personnel and Guidance Journal, 62,* 459–464.

Balfour, G. (2006). Re-imagining a feminist criminology. *Canadian Journal of Criminology and Criminal Justice, 48*(5), 735–752.

Balkin, R. S., & Roland, C. B. (2007). Reconceptualizing stabilization for counseling adolescents in brief psychiatric hospitalization: A new model. *Journal of Counseling and Development, 85*, 64–72.

Bandura, A. (1976). Effecting change through participant modeling. In J. D. Krumboltz & C. E. Thoresen (Eds.), *Counseling methods* (pp. 248–265). New York: Holt, Rinehart & Winston.

Bandura, A. (1977). *Social learning theory.* Oxford, UK: Prentice-Hall.

Bandura, A. (1982). The psychology of chance encounters and life paths. *American Psychologist, 37*, 747–755.

Bandura, A. (2001). Social cognitive theory: An agentic perspective. *Annual Review of Psychology, 52*, 1–25.

Bandura, A. (2004). Model of causality in social learning theory. In A. Freeman, M. Mahoney, P. DeVito, & D. Martin (Eds.), *Cognition and psychotherapy* (2nd ed.) (pp. 25–44). New York, NY: Springer.

Barber, J. (2008). Reclaiming the cognitive unconscious: Integrating hypnotic methods and cognitive-behavioral therapy. In M. R. Nash & A. J. Barnier (Eds.), *The Oxford handbook of hypnosis: Theory, research, and practice* (pp. 457–465). New York, NY: Oxford University Press.

Barber, J. G., Blackman, E. K., Talbot, C., & Saebel, J. (2004). The themes expressed in suicide calls to a telephone help line. *Social Psychiatry and Psychiatric Epidemiology, 39*(2), 121–125.

Barber, T. X. (2009). The necessary and sufficient conditions for hypnotic behavior. *American Journal of Clinical Hypnosis, 51*(4), 363–375.

Bardick, A. D., Bernes, K. B., Magnusson, K. C., & Witko, K. D. (2004). Junior high career planning: What students want. *Canadian Journal of Counselling, 38*(2), 104–117.

Bardick, A. D., Bernes, K. B., Magnusson, K. C., & Witko, K. D. (2006). Junior high school students' career plans for the future: A Canadian perspective. *Journal of Career Development, 32*(3), 250–271.

Barker, S. B. (1997). Nicotine addiction: An interview with Lori Karan. *Journal of Addiction and Offender Counseling, 17*, 50–55.

Barkley, W. M. (1982). Introducing research to graduate students in the helping professions. *Counselor Education and Supervision, 21*, 327–331.

Barlett, M. L. (2006). The efficacy of no-suicide contracts with clients in counseling on an outpatient basis. *Dissertation Abstracts International: Section B: The Sciences and Engineering, 67*(6–B), 3438.

Barlow, C. A., & Phelan, A. M. (2007). Peer collaboration: A model to support counsellor self-care. *Canadian Journal of Counselling, 41*(1), 3–15.

Barmaki, R. (2010). Gambling as a social problem: On the social conditions of gambling in Canada. *Journal of Youth Studies, 13*(1), 47–64.

Baron, S. W. (2007). Street youth, gender, financial strain, and crime: Exploring Broidy and Agnew's extension to general strain theory. *Deviant Behavior, 28*(3), 273–302.

Baron, S. W. (2008). Street youth, unemployment, and crime: Is it that simple? Using general strain theory to untangle the relationship. *Canadian Journal of Criminology and Criminal Justice, 50*(4), 399–434.

Baron, S. W., Forde, D. R., & Kennedy, L. W. (2007). Disputatiousness, aggressiveness, and victimization among street youths. *Youth Violence and Juvenile Justice, 5*(4), 411–425.

Barrett-Kruse, C., Martinez, E., & Carll, N. (1998). Beyond reporting suspected abuse: Positively influencing the development of the student within the classroom. *Professional School Counseling, 1*, 57–60.

Barrow, J. C., & Prosen, S. S. (1981). A model of stress and counseling interventions. *Personnel and Guidance Journal, 60*, 5–10.

Bartlett, W. E., Lee, J. L., & Doyle, R. E. (1985). Historical development of the Association for Religious and Values Issues in Counseling. *Journal of Counseling and Development, 63*, 448–451.

Baruch, D. E., Kanter, J. W., Busch, A. M., & Juskiewicz, K. L. (2009). Enhancing the therapy relationship in acceptance and commitment therapy for psychotic symptoms. *Clinical Case Studies, 8*(3), 241–257.

Bateson, G. H. (1971). The cybernetics of "self": A theory of alcoholism. *Psychiatry, 34*, 1–18.

Bauer, N. S., Lozano, P., & Rivara, F. P. (2007). The effectiveness of the Olweus Bullying Prevention Program in public middle schools: A controlled trial. *Journal of Adolescent Health, 40*(3), 266-274.

Bauman, S., & Waldo, M. (1998). Existential theory and mental health counseling: If it were a snake it would have bitten! *Journal of Mental Health Counseling, 20*, 13–27.

Baydoun, R. B., & Neuman, G. A. (1992). The future of the General Aptitude Test Battery (GATB) for use in public and private testing. *Journal of Business and Psychology, 7*(1), 81–91.

Beagan, B. L. (2007). Experiences of social class: Learning from occupational therapy students. *Canadian Journal of Occupational Therapy/ Revue Canadienne D'Ergotherapie, 74*(2), 125–133.

Beale, A. V., & Nugent, D. G. (1996). The pizza connection: Enhancing career awareness. *Elementary School Guidance and Counseling, 30*, 294–303.

Beale, A. V., & Scott, P. C. (2001). "Bullybusters": Using drama to empower students to take a stand against bullying behavior. *Professional School Counseling, 4*, 300–305.

Beane, J. A. (1986). The self-enhancing middle-grade school. *School Counselor, 33*, 189–195.

Beatch, R., Bedi, R. P., Cave, D. G., Domene, J. F., Harris, G. E., Haverkamp, B. E., & Mikhail, A-M. (2009, December). Counselling psychology in a Canadian context: Final report from the executive committee for a Canadian understanding of counselling psychology. *Counselling Psychology Section of the Canadian Psychological Association.* Retrieved from **www.cpa.ca/sections/counselling**.

Beaton, J., Dienhart, A., Schmidt, J., & Turner, J. (2009). Clinical practice patterns of Canadian couple/marital/family therapists. *Journal of Marital & Family Therapy, 35*(2), 193–203.

Beaver, M. L. (1991). Life review/reminiscent therapy. In P. K. H. Kim (Ed.), *Serving the elderly: Skills for practice* (pp. 67–89). New York: Aldine de Gruyter.

Beck, A. T., & Weishaar, M. (2008). Cognitive therapy. In R. J. Corsini & D. Wedding (Eds.), *Current psychotherapies* (8th ed., pp. 263–294). Belmont, CA: Thomson Brooks/Cole.

Becky, D., & Farren, P. M. (1997). Teaching students how to understand and avoid abusive relationships. *School Counselor, 44,* 303–308.

Becvar, D. S. (1982). The family is not a group: Or is it? *Journal for Specialists in Group Work, 7,* 88–95.

Becvar, D. S., & Becvar, R. J. (2006). *Family therapy: A systematic integration* (6th ed.). Boston: Allyn & Bacon.

Bédard, L., & Spain, A. (1999, November 11–17). Diversification of career choices: The relational aspect. *Zoom: On women and non-traditional occupations, Montreal international forum* (pp. 99–107). Retrieved from **emploique-bec.net/publications/pdf/06_etude_emp-zoom1999.pdf**

Bedi, R. P., Davis, M. D., & Arvay, M. J. (2005). The client's perspective on forming a counselling alliance and implications for research on counsellor training. *Canadian Journal of Counselling, 39*(2), 71–85.

Bedi, R. P., Davis, M. D., & Williams, M. (2005). Critical incidents in the formation of the therapeutic alliance from the client's perspective. *Psychotherapy: Theory, Research, Practice, Training, 42*(3), 311–323.

Beers, C. (1908). *A mind that found itself.* New York: Longman Green.

Befrienders International. (2007). *Befrienders Worldwide.* Retrieved August 7, 2007, from **www.befrienders.org/index.asp.**

Begin, P., Casavant, L., Miller Chenier, N., & Dupuis, J. (1999, January). *Homelessness.* Library of Parliament. Retrieved from **www2.parl.gc.ca/content/lop/research publications/prb991e.htm.**

Beharry, P., & Crozier, S. (2008). Using phenomenology to understand experiences of racism for second-generation South Asian women. *Canadian Journal of Counselling, 42*(4), 262–27

Beitel, M., Hutz, A., Sheffield, K. M., Gunn, C., Cecero, J. J., & Barry, D. C. (2009). Do psychologically-minded clients expect more from counselling? *Psychology and Psychotherapy: Theory, Research and Practice, 82*(4), 369–383.

Beiten, B. K., & Allen, K. R. (2005). Resilience in Arab American couples after September 11, 2001: A systems perspective. *Journal of Marital and Family Therapy, 31,* 251–267.

Bemak, F. (1998, February 13). *Counseling at-risk students.* Presentation at Wake Forest University Institute for Ethics and Leadership in Counseling, Winston-Salem, NC.

Bemak, F., & Keys, S. (2000). *Violence and aggressive youth: Intervention and prevention strategies for changing times.* Thousand Oaks, CA: Sage.

Bembry, J. X., Anderson, B. K., Yaggy, E. O'D. (2002). Mental health care for the poor: The pro bono counseling project. *Journal of Health Care for the Poor and Underserved, 13*(3), 273–279.

Benjamin, A. (1987). *The helping interview* (4th ed.). Boston: Houghton Mifflin.

Benshoff, J. M., & Paisley, P. O. (1996). The structured peer consultation model for school counselors. *Journal of Counseling and Development, 74,* 314–318.

Benson, L. T., & Deeter, T. E. (1992). Moderators of the relation between stress and depression in adolescence. *School Counselor, 39,* 189–194.

Berdie, R. F. (1966). Student personnel work: Definition and redefinition. *Journal of College Student Personnel, 7,* 131–136.

Berenson, B. G., & Mitchell, K. M. (1974). *Confrontation: For better or worse.* Amherst, MA: Human Resource Development Press.

Berenson, D. (1992). The therapist's relationship with couples with an alcoholic member. In E. Kaufman & P. Kaufman (Eds.), *Family therapy of drug and alcohol abuse* (pp. 224–235). Boston: Allyn & Bacon.

Berg, B. (1986). *The assertiveness game.* Dayton, OH: Cognitive Counseling Resources.

Berg, B. (1989). *The anger control game.* Dayton, OH: Cognitive Counseling Resources.

Berg, B. (1990a). *The anxiety management game.* Dayton, OH: Cognitive Counseling Resources.

Berg, B. (1990b). *The depression management game.* Dayton, OH: Cognitive Counseling Resources.

Berg, B. (1990c). *The self-control game.* Dayton, OH: Cognitive Counseling Resources.

Berg-Cross, L. (2002). *Couples therapy* (2nd ed.). Thousand Oaks, CA: Sage.

Bergland, M. M., & Thomas, K. R. (1991). Psychosocial issues following severe head injury of adolescence: Individual and family perceptions. *Rehabilitation Counseling Bulletin, 35,* 5–22.

Bergman, J. S. (1985). *Fishing for barracuda.* New York: Norton.

Bergmann, U. (2010). EMDR's neurobiological mechanisms of action: A survey of 20 years of searching. *Journal of EMDR Practice and Research, 4*(1), 22–42.

Berkel, L. A., & Constantine, M. G. (2005). Relational variables and life satisfaction in African American and Asian American college women. *Journal of College Counseling, 8,* 5–13.

Bernard, J. M., & Goodyear, R. K. (2004). *Fundamentals of clinical supervision* (3rd ed.). Boston: Allyn & Bacon.

Berne, E. (1964). *Games people play.* New York: Grove.

Berrios, R., & Lucca, N. (2006). Qualitative methodology in counseling research: Recent contributions and challenges for a new century. *Journal of Counseling & Development, 84,* 174–186.

Berube, E., & Berube, L. (1997). Creating small groups using school and community resources to meet student needs. *School Counselor, 44,* 294–302.

Berwald, C., & Houtstra, T. (2003). Joining feminism and social group work practice: A women's disability group. *Social Work with Groups: A Journal of Community and Clinical Practice, 25*(4), 71–83.

Betsworth, D. G., & Fouad, N. A. (1997). Vocational interests: A look at the past 70 years and a glance at the future. *Career Development Quarterly, 46,* 23–47.

Betz, N., & Fitzgerald, L. (1987). *The career psychology of women.* New York: Academic Press.

Bienvenu, C., & Ramsey, C. J. (2006). The culture of socioeconomic disadvantage: practical approaches to counseling. In C. C. Lee (Ed.), *Multicultural issues in counseling:*

New approaches to diversity (3rd. ed.) (pp. 345–353). Alexandria, VA: American Counseling Association.

Birren, J. E., Schaie, K. W., & Gatz, M. (Eds.). (1996). *Handbook of the psychology of aging* (4th ed.). San Diego: Academic Press.

Bishop, J. B. (1990). The university counseling center: An agenda for the 1990s. *Journal of Counseling and Development, 68,* 408–413.

Bishop, J. B. (1992). The changing student culture: Implications for counselors and administrators. *Journal of College Student Psychotherapy, 6,* 37–57.

Bishop, J. B., Gallagher, R. P., & Cohen, D. (2000). College students' problems: Status, trends, and research. In D. C. Davis and K. M. Humphrey (Eds.), *College counseling: Issues and strategies for a new millennium* (pp. 89–110). Alexandria, VA: American Counseling Association.

Bishop, S. R. (2002). What do we really know about Mindfulness-Based Stress Reduction? *Psychosomatic Medicine, 64*(1), 71–83.

Bitter, J. A. (1979). *Introduction to rehabilitation.* St. Louis: Mosby.

Blackman, J. S. (2003). *101 defenses: How the mind shields itself.* New York, NY: Routledge.

Blackorby, J., & Wagner, M. (1996). Longitudinal postschool outcomes of youth with disabilities: Findings from the national longitudinal transition study. *Exceptional Children, 62,* 399–413.

Blake, R. (1975). Counseling in gerontology. *Personnel and Guidance Journal, 53,* 733–737.

Blake, R. (1982). Assessing the counseling needs of older persons. *Measurement and Evaluation in Guidance, 15,* 188–193.

Blanck, G., & Blanck, R. (1979). *Egopsychology II: Psychoanalytic developmental psychology.* New York: Columbia University Press.

Blanton, P. G. (2002). The use of Christian meditation with religious couples: A collaborative language systems perspective. *Journal of Family Psychotherapy, 13*(3–4), 291–307.

Blatner, A. (2000). *Foundations for psychodrama: History, theory, and practice* (4th ed). New York: Springer.

Blimling, G. S., & Miltenberger, L. J. (1981). *The resident assistant.* Dubuque, IA: Kendall/Hunt.

Bloch, D. P. (1988). *Reducing the risk: Using career information with at-risk youth.* Eugene, OR: Career Information Systems.

Bloch, D. P. (1989). Using career information with dropouts and at-risk youth. *Career Development Quarterly, 38,* 160–171.

Bloland, P. A. (1986). Student development: The new orthodoxy? Part 1. *ACPA Developments, 13,* 1, 13.

Bloland, P. A. (1992, December). Qualitative research in student affairs. *CAPS Digest,* EDO-CG-92–26.

Bloom, M. (1996). *Primary prevention practices.* Thousand Oaks, CA: Sage.

Blue, A., Darou, W., & Ruano, C. (2009). Engaging the Elder within: Bridging and honouring the cultural spaces in counselling with First Nations. In N. Arthur & S. Collins (Eds.), *Culture-infused counselling: Celebrating the Canadian mosaic* (2nd ed) (pp. 259–284). Calgary, AB: Counselling Concepts.

Bobo, M., Hildreth, B. L., & Durodoye, B. (1998). Changing patterns in career choices among African-American, Hispanic, and Anglo children. *Professional School Counseling, 1*(4), 37–42.

Boeree, C. G. (2006). *Carl Jung, 1875–1961.* Retrieved from **http://webspace.ship.edu/cgboer/jung.html**.

Boesch, R., & Cimbolic, P. (1994). Black students' use of college and university counseling centers. *Journal of College Student Development, 35,* 212–216.

Bohlmeijera, E., Prengera, R., Taala, E., & Cuijpersb, P. (2010). The effects of mindfulness-based stress reduction therapy on mental health of adults with a chronic medical disease: A meta-analysis. *Journal of Psychosomatic Research, 68,* 539–544

Bolles, R. N., & Nelson, J. E. (2007). *What color is your parachute?* Berkeley, CA: Ten Speed Press.

Bolton, B. (2001). Measuring rehabilitation outcomes. *Rehabilitation Counseling Bulletin, 44,* 67–75

Bolton, B., & Jaques, M. E. (1978). Rehabilitation counseling research: Editorial introduction. In B. Bolton & M. E. Jaques (Eds.), *Rehabilitation counseling: Theory and practice* (pp. 163–165). Baltimore: University Park Press.

Bolton, R. (1979). *People skills: How to assert yourself, listen to others, and resolve conflicts.* Upper Saddle River, NJ: Prentice Hall.

Bonebrake, C. R., & Borgers, S. B. (1984). Counselor role as perceived by counselors and principals. *Elementary School Guidance and Counseling, 18,* 194–199.

Borders, L. D. (Ed.). (1994). *Supervision: Exploring the effective components.* Greensboro, NC: ERIC/CASS.

Borders, L. D. (2002). School counseling in the 21st century: Personal and professional reflections. *Professional School Counseling, 5,* 180–185.

Borders, L. D., & Brown, L. L. (2005). *The new handbook of counseling supervision.* Mahwah, NJ: Erlbaum.

Borders, L. D., & Drury, S. M. (1992). Comprehensive school counseling programs: A review for policymakers and practitioners. *Journal of Counseling and Development, 70,* 487–498.

Borders, L. D., & Leddick, G. R. (1987). *Handbook of counseling supervision.* Alexandria, VA: Association for Counselor Education and Supervision.

Borders, L. D., & Leddick, G. R. (1988). A nationwide survey of supervision training. *Counselor Education and Supervision, 27,* 271–283.

Borders, S., & Paisley, P. O. (1992). Children's literature as a resource for classroom guidance. *Elementary School Guidance and Counseling, 27,* 131–139.

Borgen, W. A. (1997). People caught in changing career opportunities: A counseling perspective. *Journal of Employment Counseling, 34,* 133–143.

Borgen, W., & Hiebert, B. (2006). Career guidance and counselling for youth: What adolescents and young adults are telling us. *International Journal for the Advancement of Counselling, 28*(4), 389–400.

Bowen, M. (1978). *Family therapy in clinical practice.* New York: Aronson.

Bowman, J. T., & Reeves, T. G. (1987). Moral development and empathy in counseling. *Counselor Education and Supervision, 26,* 293–298.

Bowman, R. P. (1986). Peer facilitator programs for middle graders: Students helping each other grow up. *School Counselor, 33,* 221–229.

Boy, A. V., & Pine, G. J. (1968). *The counselor in the schools: A reconceptualization.* Boston: Houghton Mifflin.

Boyer, S. P., & Sedlacek, W. E. (1989). Noncognitive predictors of counseling center use by international students. *Journal of Counseling and Development, 67,* 404–407.

Boyle, P. S. (1994). Rehabilitation counselors as providers: The issue of sexuality. *Journal of Applied Rehabilitation Counseling, 25,* 6–10.

Bradley, L. J. (1984). Lifespan career assessment for counselors and educators. *Counseling and Human Development, 16,* 1–16.

Bradley, M. K. (1978). Counseling past and present: Is there a future? *Personnel and Guidance Journal, 57,* 42–45.

Bradley, R. W. (1994). Tests and counseling: How did we ever become partners? *Measurement and Evaluation in Counseling and Development, 26,* 224–226.

Bram, A. D. (2010). The relevance of the Rorschach and patient-examiner relationship in treatment planning and outcome assessment. *Journal of Personality Assessment, 92*(2), 91–115.

Brammer, L. M., & MacDonald, G. (2003). *The helping relationship* (8th ed.). Boston: Allyn & Bacon.

Brandt, R. (1959). *Ethical theory.* Upper Saddle River, NJ: Prentice Hall.

Breti, D. (1998). *Internment camps in British Columbia.* Retrieved from **www.britishcolumbia.com/general/details.asp?id=44**.

Brewer, J. M. (1932). *Education as guidance.* New York: Macmillan.

Brinson, J. A. (1996). Cultural sensitivity for counselors: Our challenge for the twenty-first century. *Journal of Humanistic Education and Development, 34,* 195–206.

Bristow-Braitman, A. (1995). Addiction recovery: 12–step program and cognitive-behavioral psychology. *Journal of Counseling and Development, 73,* 414–418.

Brooks, G. R. (2010). *Beyond the crisis of masculinity: A transtheoretical model for male-friendly therapy.* Washington, DC: American Psychological Association.

Brosseau, J. (1973). Consulting: A potpourri? *Canadian Counsellor, 7*(4), 259–267.

Brown, D. (1985). Career counseling: Before, after or instead of personal counseling. *Vocational Guidance Quarterly, 33,* 197–201.

Brown, D. (1989). The preservice training and supervision of consultants. *Counseling Psychologist, 13,* 410–425.

Brown, D. (1993). Training consultants: A call to action. *Journal of Counseling and Development, 72,* 139–143.

Brown, D. (1997). Implications of cultural values for cross-cultural consultation with families. *Journal of Counseling and Development, 76,* 29–35.

Brown, D. (2002). The role of work and cultural values in occupational choice, satisfaction, and success: A theoretical statement. *Journal of Counseling and Development, 80,* 48–56.

Brown, D. (2007). *Career information, career counseling, and career development* (9th ed.). Boston: Allyn & Bacon.

Brown, D., Pryzwansky, W. B., & Schulte, A. C. (2005). *Psychological consultation* (6th ed.). Boston: Allyn & Bacon.

Brown, J. A. (1983). Consultation. In J. A. Brown & R. H. Pate, Jr. (Eds.), *Being a counselor: Directions and challenges* (pp. 124–146). Pacific Grove, CA: Brooks/Cole.

Brown, M. B. (2000). Diagnosis and treatment of children and adolescents with attention-deficit/hyperactivity disorder. *Journal of Counseling and Development, 78,* 195–203.

Brown, M. B. (2006). School-based health centers: Implications for counselors. *Journal of Counseling and Development, 84,* 187–191.

Brown, N. M. (1990). Men nurturing men. *Family Therapy Networker, 14,* 11.

Brown, N. W. (1998). *Psychoeducational groups.* Muncie, IN: Accelerated Development.

Brown, R. D. (1986). Editorial. *Journal of College Student Personnel, 27,* 99.

Brown, S. L. & May, K. M. (2009). Counseling with women. In C. M. Ellis & J. Carlson (Eds.), *Cross cultural awareness and social justice in counseling* (pp. 61–88). New York, NY: Routledge/Taylor & Francis.

Brown, T. (1980). Counsellor role: Canadian scene. *Canadian Counsellor, 14*(3), 181–185.

Brown, T., & Helms, J. (1986). The relationship between psychological development issues and anticipated self-disclosure. *Journal of College Student Personnel, 27,* 136–141.

Bryan, W. V. (2007). *Multicultural aspects of disabilities: A guide to understanding and assisting minorities in the rehabilitation process* (2nd ed.). Springfield, IL: Charles C. Thomas.

Bubenzer, D., Zimpfer, D., & Mahrle, C. (1990). Standardized individual appraisal in agency and private practice: A survey. *Journal of Mental Health Counseling, 12,* 51–66.

Buelow, G. (1995). Comparing students from substance abusing and dysfunctional families: Implications for counseling. *Journal of Counseling and Development, 73,* 327–330.

Bullis, R. K. (1993). *Law and the management of a counseling agency or private practice.* Alexandria, VA: American Counseling Association.

Bunch, B. J., Lund, N. L., & Wiggins, F. K. (1983). Self-disclosure and perceived closeness in the development of group process. *Journal for Specialists in Group Work, 8,* 59–66.

Bundy, M. L., & Poppen, W. A. (1986). School counselors' effectiveness as consultants: A research review. *Elementary School Guidance and Counseling, 20,* 215–222.

Burch, M. A., & Skovholt, T. M. (1982). Counseling services and men in need: A problem in person-environment matching. *AMHCA Journal, 4,* 89–96.

Burck, H. D., & Peterson, G. W. (1975). Needed: More evaluation, not research. *Personnel and Guidance Journal, 53,* 563–569.

Burgess, A. W., & Holstrom, L. L. (1974). Rape trauma syndrome. *American Journal of Psychiatry, 131,* 981–986.

Burke, C. A. (2010). Mindfulness-based approaches with children and adolescents: A preliminary review of current research in an emergent field. *Journal of Child and Family Studies, 19,* 133–144.

Burke, J. F. (1989). *Contemporary approaches to psychotherapy and counseling.* Pacific Grove, CA: Brooks/Cole.

Burke, K. L. (1993). The negative stereotyping of student athletes. In W. D. Kirk & S. V. Kirk (Eds.), *Student athletes: Shattering the myths and sharing the realities* (pp. 93–98). Alexandria, VA: American Counseling Association.

Burke, M. T., Hackney, H., Hudson, P., Miranti, J., Watts, G. A., & Epp, L. (1999). Spirituality, religion, and CACREP curriculum standards. *Journal of Counseling and Development, 77,* 251–257.

Burke, M. T., & Miranti, J. G. (1995). *Counseling: The spiritual dimension.* Alexandria, VA: American Counseling Association.

Burke, R. J. (Ed.) (2006). *Research companion to working time and work addiction. Research companion to working time and work addiction.* Northampton, MA: Edward Elgar.

Burke, R. J. (2009). Work addiction: Causes, consequences, and choices. In A. Browne-Miller (Ed.), *The Praeger international collection on addictions, Vol 4: Behavioral addictions from concept to compulsion* (pp. 3–25). Santa Barbara, CA: Praeger/ABC-CLIO.

Burrow-Sanchez, J. J. (2006). Understanding adolescent substance abuse: Prevalence, risk factors, and clinical implications. *Journal of Counseling and Development, 84,* 283–290.

Butcher, J. N. (1994). The MMPI-2: A new standard for personality assessment and research in counseling settings. *Measurement and Evaluation in Counseling and Development, 27,* 131–150.

Butcher, J. N., Williams, C. L., & Fowler, R. D. (2001). *Essentials of MMPI-2 and MMPI-A interpretation* (2nd ed.). Minneapolis: University of Minnesota Press.

Butler, K. (1990). Spirituality reconsidered. *Family Therapy Networker, 14,* 26–37.

Butler, R. N. (1998). *Aging and mental health: Positive psychosocial and biomedical approaches* (5th ed.). Boston: Allyn & Bacon.

Butler, R. N. (2001). Ageism. In G. L. Maddox (Ed.), *Encyclopedia of aging* (Vol. A-L, 3rd ed., p. 38). New York: Springer.

Butler, R. N. (2005). Ageism: Looking back over my shoulder. *Generations, 29,* 84–86.

Bynner, J. M. (1997). Basic skills in adolescents' occupational preparation. *Career Development Quarterly, 45,* 300–321.

Cahill, S. P., Carrigan, M. H., & Frueh, B. C. (1999). Does EMDR work? And if so, why?" A critical review of controlled outcome and dismantling research. *Journal of Anxiety Disorders, 13*(1–2), 5–33.

Cairns, S. L., Massfeller, H. F., & Deeth, S. C. (2010). Why do postsecondary students seek counselling? *Canadian Journal of Counselling, 44*(1), 34–50.

Caldwell, L. D. (2009). Counseling with the poor, underserved, and underrepresented. In C. M. Ellis & J. Carlson (Eds.), *Cross cultural awareness and social justice in counseling* (pp. 283–300). New York, NY: Routledge/Taylor & Francis.

Calgary Homeless Foundation. (2010). *Leading the 10 year plan to end homelessness.* Retrieved from **www.calgaryhomeless.com**.

Callis, R. (1985). Minnesota School Attitude Survey, Lower and Upper Forms. *Journal of Counseling and Development, 63,* 382.

Campbell, A., & Katona, G. (1953). The sample survey: A technique for social science research. In L. Festinger & D. Katz (Eds.), *Research methods in the behavioral sciences* (pp. 15–55). New York: Dryden.

Campbell, C. (1993a). Strategies for reducing parent resistance to consultation in the schools. *Elementary School Guidance and Counseling, 28,* 83–90.

Campbell, C. A. (1993b). Play, the fabric of elementary school counseling programs. *Elementary School Guidance and Counseling, 28,* 10–16.

Campbell, C. A., & Dahir, C. A. (1997). *Sharing the vision: The national standard for school counseling programs.* Alexandria, VA: American School Counselors Association.

Campbell, D. (1974). *If you don't know where you're going you'll probably end up somewhere else.* Niles, IL: Argus.

Campbell, D. T., & Stanley, J. C. (1963). *Experimental and quasi-experimental designs for research.* Chicago: Rand McNally.

Campbell, M. A., Doucette, N. L., & French, S. (2009). Validity and stability of the Youth Psychopathic Traits Inventory in a nonforensic sample of young adults. *Journal of Personality Assessment, 91*(6), 584–592.

Canadian Addictions Counsellors Certification Federation. (n.d.). *Home page.* Retrieved from **www.caccf.ca/**

Canadian Association for School Health. (n.d.). Tobacco and schools: Resources and information on the Internet for students, teachers, public health nurses and principals. *Schoolfile.* Retrieved from **www.schoolfile.com/hctrp2 .htm**.

Canadian Association for Social Work Education. (2009, December 7). *Home page.* Retrieved from **www.caswe-acfts.ca/en**.

Canadian Association of Social Workers. (2005a). *Code of ethics 2005.* Retrieved from **www.casw-acts.ca**.

Canadian Association of Social Workers. (2005b). *Guidelines for ethical practice 2005.* Retrieved from **www.casw-acts.ca**.

Canadian Association of Social Workers. (2009, August 18). *CASW Presents the Social Work Profession.* Retrieved from **www.casw-acts.ca**.

Canadian Cancer Society. (2009, December 10). *Facts on tobacco and cancer.* Retrieved from **www.cancer.ca/ontario/ prevention/quit%20smoking/od-ontario%20tobacco% 20stats.aspx**.

Canadian Cancer Society. (2010, March 24). *Publications.* Retrieved from **www.cancer.ca/canada-wide/publications .aspx**.

Canadian Career Development Foundation. (2006). *Home page.* Retrieved from **http://ccdf.ca**.

Canadian Career Information Association. (2005). *Home page.* Retrieved from **www.ccia-acadop.ca**.

Canadian Child Welfare Research Portal. (2009). *Timelines for the CIS-2008*. Retrieved from **www.cwrp.ca/cis-2008/timelines-cis-2008**.

Canadian Children's Rights Council. (1998–2010). *Child and teen suicides: Youth suicides in Canada and elsewhere*. Retrieved from **www.canadiancrc.com/Youth_Suicide_in_Canada.aspx**.

Canadian Council of Professional Certification. (n.d.). *About CCPC certification*. Retrieved from **www.ccpcprofessionals.com**.

Canadian Counselling and Psychotherapy Association. (2002, May). 2003 CCPA accreditation procedures and standards for counsellor education programs at the master's level. Retrieved from **www.ccpa-accp.ca/en/accreditation/standards**.

Canadian Counselling and Psychotherapy Association. (2007, January). *Code of ethics*. Retrieved from **www.ccacc.ca/en/resources/codeofethics**.

Canadian Counselling and Psychotherapy Association. (2009). *Cognica*. Retrieved from **www.ccacc.ca/en/resources/cognica**.

Canadian Counselling and Psychotherapy Association. (2009). *Who are counsellors?* Retrieved from **www.ccacc.ca/en/theprofession/whoarecounsellors**.

Canadian Counselling and Psychotherapy Association. (2009a). *History*. Retrieved from **www.ccacc.ca/en/aboutus/history**.

Canadian Counselling and Psychotherapy Association. (2009b). *Status of regulation*. Retrieved from **www.ccpa-accp.ca/en/page/?p=591**.

Canadian Counselling and Psychotherapy Association. (2009c). *Who are counsellors?* Retrieved from **www.ccacc.ca/en/theprofession/whoarecounsellors**.

Canadian Education Association. (2010). *Home page*. Retrieved from **http://cea-ace.ca/home.cfm**.

Canadian Encyclopedia. (2010). *South Asians*. Retrieved from **www.thecanadianencyclopedia.com/index.cfm?PgNm=TCE&Params=A1ARTA0007574**.

Canadian Group Psychotherapy Association. (n.d.- a). *Training*. Retrieved from **www.cgpa.ca/Training**.

Canadian Group Psychotherapy Association. (n.d.-b). *Training standards*. Retrieved from **www.cgpa.ca/Training-Standards**.

Canadian Institute for Health Information. (2006a). *Psychologists*. Retrieved from **secure.cihi.ca/cihiweb/products/Psychologists.pdf**

Canadian Institute for Health Information. (2006b). *Social workers*. Retrieved from **secure.cihi.ca/cihiweb/products/Social_workers.pdf**

Canadian Mental Health Association, Ontario (n.d.). Senior and mental health. Retrieved from **www.ontario.cmha.ca/seniors.asp**.

Canadian Mental Health Association. (2009). *Our history*. Retrieved from **www.cmha.ca/bins/content_page.asp?cid=7-135&lang=1**.

Canadian Professional Counsellor's Association. (n.d.). *Home page*. Retrieved from **www.cpca-rpc.ca**.

Canadian Psychological Association. (2000). *Canadian code of ethics for psychologists*. Retrieved from **www.cpa.ca/.../Canadian%20Code%20of%20Ethics%20for%20Psycho.pdf**.

Canadian Psychological Association. (2001). Guidelines for non-discriminatory practice (Rev. ed.). Ottawa, ON: Author. Retrieved from **www.cpa.ca/publications**.

Canadian Psychological Association. (2004, June). *Mutual recognition agreement*. Retrieved from **www.cpa.ca/documents/MRA.pdf**.

Canadian Psychological Association. (2009, November). *Definition of counselling psychology*. Retrieved from **www.cpa.ca/sections/counselling**.

Canadian Psychological Association. (2009). *Draft revision of the accreditation standards and procedures for doctoral programmes and internships in professional psychology, 2009*. Retrieved from **www.cpa.ca/accreditation/2009draftrevisionoftheaccreditationstandardsandproceduresfordoctoralprogrammesandinternshipsinprofessionalpsychology**.

Canadian Social Research Links. (n.d.). *Provincial and territorial anti-poverty strategies and poverty reduction campaigns*. Retrieved from **www.canadiansocialresearch.net/antipoverty.htm**.

Canaff, A. L. (1997). Later life career planning: A new challenge for career counselors. *Journal of Employment Counseling, 34*, 85–93.

Canino, G. (2004). Are somatic symptoms and related distress more prevalent in Hispanic/Latino Youth? Some methodological considerations. *Journal of Clinical Child and Adolescent Psychology, 33*(2), 272–275.

Canning, P. M., Frizzell, L. M., & Courage, M. L. (2010). Birth outcomes associated with prenatal participation in a government support programme for mothers with low incomes. *Child Care, Health & Development, 36*(2), 225–231.

Canon, H. J. (1985). Ethical problems in daily practice. In H. J. Canon & R. D. Brown (Eds.), *Applied ethics in student services* (pp. 5–15). San Francisco: Jossey-Bass.

Canon, H. J. (1988). Nevitt Sanford: Gentle prophet, Jeffersonian rebel. *Journal of Counseling and Development, 66*, 451–457.

Canon, H. J. (1989). Guiding standards and principles. In U. Delworth, G. R. Hanson, & Associates (Eds.), *Student services: A handbook for the professional* (2nd ed., pp. 57–79). San Francisco: Jossey-Bass.

Caplan, G. (1964). *Principles of preventive psychiatry*. New York: Basic Books.

Caplan, G. (1970). *The theory and practice of mental health consultation*. New York: Basic Books.

Caplan, G., & Caplan, R. (1993). *Mental health consultation and collaboration*. San Francisco: Jossey-Bass.

Capuzzi, D. (1994). *Suicide prevention in the schools*. Alexandria, VA: American Counseling Association.

Capuzzi, D. (Ed.). (2008). *Youth at risk: A preventive resource for counselors, teachers, and parents* (4th ed) Alexandria, VA: American Counseling Association.

Carey, J. C., & Dimmit, C. (2006). Resources for school counselors and counselor educators: The Center for School Counseling and Outcome Research. *Professional School Counseling, 9*, 416–420.

Carey, J. C., Williams, K. S., & Wells, M. (1988). Relationships between dimensions of supervisors' influence and counselor trainees' performance. *Counselor Education and Supervision, 28*, 130–139.

Carkhuff, R. R. (1969). *Helping and human relations* (Vols. 1 & 2). New York: Holt, Rinehart & Winston.

Carkhuff, R. R. (1972). *The art of helping*. Amherst, MA: Human Resource Development Press.

Carkhuff, R. R. (2000). *The art of helping* (8th ed.). Amherst, MA: Human Resource Development Press.

Carkhuff, R. R., & Anthony, W. A. (1979). *The skills of helping*. Amherst, MA: Human Resource Development Press.

Carkhuff, R. R., & Berenson, B. G. (1967). *Beyond counseling and psychotherapy*. New York: Holt, Rinehart & Winston.

Carlson, J., & Ardell, D. E. (1988). Physical fitness as a pathway to wellness and effective counseling. In R. Hayes & R. Aubrey (Eds.), *New directions for counseling and human development* (pp. 383–396). Denver: Love.

Carlson, J., & Dinkmeyer, D., Jr. (2001). *Consultation: Creating school-based interventions*. New York: Brunner/Mazel.

Carlson, J., Watts, R. E., & Maniacci, M. (Eds.). (2006). *Adlerian therapy: Theory and practice*. Washington, DC: American Psychological Association.

Carlson, J. G. (1989). Rebuttal. The MBTI: Not ready for routine use in counseling. A reply. *Journal of Counseling and Development, 67,* 489.

Carmichael, K. D. (1994). Sand play as an elementary school strategy. *Elementary School Guidance and Counseling, 28,* 302–307.

Carnegie Task Force on Meeting the Needs of Young Children. (1994). *Starting points: Meeting the needs of our youngest children.* New York: Author.

Carney, J. V., & Hazler, R. J. (1998). Suicide and cognitive-behavioral counseling: Implications for mental health counselors. *Journal of Mental Health Counseling, 20,* 28–41.

Carr, A. (1998). Michael White's narrative therapy. *Contemporary Family Therapy, 20*(4), 485–503.

Carr, A. (2009). Thematic review of family therapy journals in 2008. *Journal of Family Therapy, 31*(4), 405–427.

Carrese, M. A. (1998). Managing stress for college success through self-hypnosis. *Journal of Humanistic Education and Development, 36,* 134–142.

Carroll, L., Gilroy, P. J., & Ryan, J. (2002). Counseling transgendered, transsexual, and gender-variant clients. *Journal of Counseling and Development, 80,* 131–139.

Carroll, M. R., & Levo, L. (1985). The association for specialists in group work. *Journal of Counseling and Development, 63,* 453–454.

Carruthers, W. L., Sweeney, B., Kmitta, D., & Harris, G. (1996). Conflict resolution: An examination of the research literature and a model for program evaluation. *School Counselor, 44,* 5–18.

Carson, R. C., Butcher, J. N., & Mineka, S. (2000). Mood disorder and suicide. In *Abnormal psychology and modern life* (11th ed., pp. 209–267). Boston: Allyn & Bacon.

Carter, B., & McGoldrick, M. (1999). *The expanded family life cycle: Individual, family, and social perspectives* (3rd ed.). Boston: Allyn & Bacon.

Carter, R. T. (1990). The relationship between racism and racial identity among white Americans: An exploratory investigation. *Journal of Counseling and Development, 69,* 46–50.

Casey, J. M. (1996). Gail F. Farwell: A developmentalist who lives his ideas. *School Counselor, 43,* 174–180.

Cashwell, C. S., & Vacc, N. A. (1996). Family functioning and risk behaviors: Influences on adolescent delinquency. *School Counselor, 44,* 105–114.

Castonguay, L. G., Constantino, M. J., & Holtforth, M. G. (2006). The working alliance: Where are we and where should we go? *Psychotherapy: Theory, Research, Practice, Training, 43*(3), 271–279.

Cautilli, J., & Skinner, L. (1996, September). Combating youth violence through wrap-around service. *Counseling Today, 12.*

Cavanagh, M. E. (1990). *The counseling experience.* Prospect Heights, IL: Waveland.

Cecil, J. H., & Cobia, D. C. (1990). Educational challenge and change. In H. Hackney (Ed.), *Changing contexts for counselor preparation in the 1990s* (pp. 21–36). Alexandria, VA: Association for Counselor Education and Supervision.

Center on Addiction and Substance Abuse. (1995). *American adolescence.* New York: Columbia University Press.

Cervantes, J. M., & Englar-Carlson, M. (2008). Surviving in a sea with few lifeboats: Counseling boys from impoverished families. In M. S. Kiselica, M. Englar-Carlson, & A. M. Horne (Eds.), *Counseling troubled boys: A guidebook for professionals* (pp. 69–96). New York, NY: Routledge/Taylor & Francis Group.

Chan, J. G. (2003). An examination of family-involved approaches to alcoholism treatment. *The Family Journal, 11*(2), 129–138.

Chandler, C. K., Holden, J. M., & Kolander, C. A. (1992). Counseling for spiritual wellness: Theory and practice. *Journal of Counseling and Development, 71,* 168–175.

Chang, D. F., Tong, H., Shi, Q., & Zeng, Q. (2005). Letting a hundred flowers bloom: Counseling and psychotherapy in the People's Republic of China. *Journal of Mental Health Counseling, 27,* 104–116.

Chansonneuve, D. (2007). Addictive behaviours among Aboriginal people in Canada. *Aboriginal Healing Foundation.* Retrieved from **www.aboriginalcanada.gc.ca/acp/site.nsf/eng/ao26134.html**.

Chao, R., & Good, G. E. (2004). Nontraditional students' perspectives on college education: A qualitative study. *Journal of College Counseling, 7,* 5–12.

Chappell, N. L. (2009). Aging and mental health. *Social Work in Mental Health, 7*(1–3), 122–138.

Charpentier, M., Queniart, A., & Jacques, J. (2008). Activism among older women in Quebec, Canada: Changing the world after age 65. *Journal of Women & Aging, 20*(3–4), 343–360.

Chauvin, J. C., & Remley, T. P., Jr. (1996). Responding to allegations of unethical conduct. *Journal of Counseling and Development, 74,* 563–568.

Cheboud, E., & France, H. (n.d.). *Counselling African-Canadians.* Retrieved from **www.educ.uvic.ca/faculty/hfrance/african-Canadian.htm**.

Chen, X. (2007). *Part-time undergraduates in post secondary education 2003–04*. Washington, DC: U.S. Department of Education.

Chen-Hayes, S. F. (1997). Counseling lesbian, bisexual, and gay persons in couple and family relationships: Overcoming the stereotypes. *Family Journal, 5*, 236–240.

Cheon, H.-S., & Murphy, M. J. (2007) The self-of-the-therapist awakened. *Journal of Feminist Family Therapy, 19*(1), 1–16.

Chernin, J., Holden, J. M., & Chandler, C. (1997). Bias in psychological assessment: Heterosexism. *Measurement and Evaluation in Counseling and Development, 30*, 68–76.

Cheston, S. E. (1991). *Making effective referrals: The therapeutic process*. New York, NY: Gardner Press.

Cheston, S. E. (2000). A new paradigm for teaching counseling theory and practice. *Counselor Education and Supervision, 39*, 254–269.

Cheung, A. M., & Hwang, S. W. (2004). Risk of death among homeless women: A cohort study and review of the literature. *Canadian Medical Association Journal, 170*(8), 1243–1247.

Chew, A. L. (1984). Training counselors to interpret psychoeducational evaluations: A course model. *Counselor Education and Supervision, 24*, 114–119.

Chickering, A. W., & Reisser, L. (1993). *Education and identity* (2nd ed.). San Francisco: Jossey-Bass.

Child Abuse. (2007). American Academy of Pediatrics (Retrieved December 28, 2007 from **www.aap.org/publiced/BK0_ChildAbuse.htm**.

Childers, J. H., Jr., & Couch, R. D. (1989). Myths about group counseling: Identifying and challenging misconceptions. *Journal for Specialists in Group Work, 14*, 105–111.

Chiesa, A., & Serretti, A. (2009). Mindfulness-based stress reduction for stress management in healthy people: A review and meta-analysis. *The Journal of Alternative and Complementary Medicine, 15*(5), 593–600.

Chisolm, M. S. (1998, May 15). Colleges need to provide early treatment of students' mental illnesses. *Chronicle of Higher Education, 44*, B6–B7.

Chojnacki, J. T., & Gelberg, S. (1994). Toward a conceptualization of career counseling with gay/lesbian/bisexual persons. *Journal of Career Development, 21*, 3–9.

Chope, R. C. (2006). *Family matters: The influence of the family in career decision making*. Austin, TX: Pro-Ed.

Christenbury, L. (Ed.). (1995). *Books for you*. Chicago: National Council of Teachers of English.

Christenbury, L., Beale, A. V., & Patch, S. S. (1996). Interactive bibliocounseling: Recent fiction and nonfiction for adolescents and their counselors. *School Counselor, 44*, 133–145.

Christopher, J. C. (1996). Counseling's inescapable moral visions. *Journal of Counseling and Development, 75*, 17–25.

Chung, R., C-Y. (2005). Women, human rights, and counseling: Crossing international boundaries. *Journal of Counseling and Development, 83*, 262–268.

Chung, R., C-Y., & Bemak, F. (2002). The relationship of culture and empathy in cross-cultural counseling. *Journal of Counseling and Development, 80*, 154–159.

Chusmir, L. H. (1990). Men who make nontraditional career choices. *Journal of Counseling and Development, 69*, 11–16.

Ciarrochi, J., & Robb, H. (2005). Letting a little nonverbal air into the room: insights from acceptance and commitment therapy part 2: Applications. *Journal of Rational-Emotive & Cognitive-Behavior Therapy, 23*(2), 107–130.

Citizenship and Immigration Canada. (2009, February 20). *News release: Canada welcomes a record high number of newcomers in 2008*. Retrieved from **www.cic.gc.ca/english/department/media/releases/2009/2009–02–20.asp**.

Claiborn, C. D. (1979). Counselor verbal intervention, nonverbal behavior and social power. *Journal of Counseling Psychology, 26*, 378–383.

Clark, A. J. (2010a). Empathy and sympathy: Therapeutic distinctions in counseling. Journal of Mental Health Counseling, 32(2), 95–101.

Clark, D. R., McGrath, P. J., & MacDonald, N. (2007). Members' of Parliament knowledge of and attitudes toward health research and funding. *Canadian Medical Association Journal, 177*(9), 1045–1051.

Clarke, N. E., & Crowe, N. M. (2000). Stakeholder attitudes toward ADA title I: Development of an indirect measurement method. *Rehabilitation Counseling Bulletin, 43*, 58–65.

Clay, D. L., Anderson, W. P., & Dixon, W. A. (1993). Relationship between anger expression and stress in predicting depression. *Journal of Counseling and Development, 72*, 91–94.

Clemens, E. (2007). Developmental counseling and therapy as a model for school counselor consultation with teachers. *Professional School Counseling, 10*, 352–359.

Cleveland, P. H., & Lindsey, E. W. (1995). Solution-focused family interventions. In A. C. Kilpatrick & T. P. Holland (Eds.), *Working with families* (pp. 145–160). Boston: Allyn & Bacon.

Cobia, D. C., Sobansky, R. R., & Ingram, M. (2004). Female survivors of childhood sexual abuse: Implications for couples' therapists. *The Family Journal: Counseling and Therapy for Couples and Families, 12*, 312–318.

Cochran, J. L. (1996). Using play and art therapy to help culturally diverse students overcome barriers to school success. *School Counselor, 43*, 287–298.

Cochran, S. V. (2005). Evidence-based assessment with men. *Journal of Clinical Psychology, 61*(6), 649–660.

Cochran, S. V., & Rabinowitz, F. E. (2003). Gender-sensitive recommendations for assessment and treatment of depression in men. *Professional Psychology: Research and Practice, 34*, 132–140.

Cohen, G. D. (2000). *The creative age*. New York: Avon.

Cohen, J. (1990). Things I have learned (so far). *American Psychologist, 45*, 1304–1312.

Cohen, K. R. (2002). Accreditation standards and procedures for doctoral programmes and internships in professional psychology (4th ed.) *Canadian Psychological Association*. Retrieved from **www.cpa.ca/cpasite/userfiles/Documents/Accreditation/Accreditation%20Manual%20Jan08.pdf**.

Cohen, M. N. (1998, April 17). Culture, not race, explains human diversity. *Chronicle of Higher Education*, B4–B5.

Colangelo, N., & Pulvino, C. J. (1980). Some basic concerns in counseling the elderly. *Counseling and Values, 24,* 68–73.

Colbert, R. D., Vernon-Jones, R., & Pransky, K. (2006). The school change feedback process: Creating a new role for counselors in education reform. *Journal of Counseling and Development, 84,* 72–82.

Cole, C. G. (1982). Career guidance for middle junior high school students. *Vocational Guidance Quarterly, 30,* 308–314.

Cole, C. G. (1988). *Guidance in middle level schools: Everyone's responsibility.* Columbus, OH: National Middle School Association.

Coleman, H. L. K. (1998). General and multicultural counseling competency: Apples and oranges? *Journal of Multicultural Counseling and Development, 26,* 147–156.

Coll, K. M., Thobro, P., & Hass, R. (2004). Relational and purpose development in youth offenders. *Journal of Humanistic Counseling, Education and Development, 43,* 41–49.

College of Alberta Psychologists. (2005). *Standards of practice 2005.* Retrieved from **www.cap.ab.ca/frmPage .aspx?Page=Index**.

College of Alberta Psychologists. (2009). *Documents/online forms: Legislation and court decisions.* Retrieved from **www.cap.ab.ca/documents.aspx?DocTypeCode=Leg**.

Collins, B. G., & Collins, T. M. (1994). Child and adolescent mental health: Building a system of care. *Journal of Counseling and Development, 72,* 239–243.

Collins, S., & Arthur, N. (2009). Culture-infused counselling: A framework for multicultural competence. In N. Arthur & S. Collins (Eds.), *Culture-infused counselling: Celebrating the Canadian mosaic* (2nd ed.) (pp. 45–65). Calgary, AB: Counselling Concepts.

Collins, W. L. (2005). Embracing spirituality as an element of professional self-care. *Social Work & Christianity, 32*(3), 263–274.

Collison, B. B. (1981). Counseling adult males. *Personnel and Guidance Journal, 60,* 219–222.

Collison, B. B. (1982). Needs assessment for guidance program planning: A procedure. *School Counselor, 30,* 115–121.

Combs, A. (1982). *A personal approach to teaching: Beliefs that make a difference.* Boston: Allyn & Bacon.

Commission on Substance Abuse at Colleges and Universities. (1994). *Rethinking rites of passage: Substance abuse on America's campuses.* New York: Center on Addictionand Substance Abuse at Columbia University.

Compass, B. E., Connor-Smith, J. K., Saltzman, H., Thomsen, A. H., & Wadsworth, M. E. (2001). Coping with stress during childhood and adolescence: Problems, progress, and potential in theory and research. *Psychological Bulletin, 127,* 87–127.

Conference Board of Canada. (2009). *How Canada performs: A report card on Canada.* Retrieved from **www.conferenceboard.ca/HCP/default.aspx**.

Conference Board of Canada. (2010). *NATCON overview.* Retrieved from **www.natcon.org**.

Conoley, J. C. (1981). Emergent training issues in consultation. In J. C. Conoley (Ed.), *Consultation in schools: Theory,* *research procedures* (pp. 223–263). New York: Academic Press.

Conoley, J. C., & Conoley, C. W. (1992). *School consultation: Practice and training* (2nd ed.). Boston: Allyn & Bacon.

Constantine, M. G., Hage, S. M., Kindaichi, M. M., & Bryant, R. M. (2007). Social justice and multicultural issues: Implications for the practice and training of counselors and counseling psychologists. *Journal of Counseling and Development, 85,* 24–29.

Conyne, R. K. (1975). Environmental assessment: Mapping for counselor action. *Personnel and Guidance Journal, 54,* 150–154.

Conyne, R. K. (1998). What to look for in groups: Helping trainees become more sensitive to multicultural issues. *Journal for Specialists in Group Work, 23,* 22–32.

Conyne, R. K., & Cook, E. (2004). *Ecological counseling: An innovative approach to conceptualizing person-environment interaction.* Alexandria, VA: American Counseling Association.

Cook, A. S., & McBride, J. S. (1982). Divorce: Helping children cope. *School Counselor, 30,* 89–94.

Cook, D., Bolton, B., Bellini, J., & Neath, J. (1997). A statewide investigation of the rehabilitation counselor generalist hypothesis. *Rehabilitation Counseling Bulletin, 40,* 192–201.

Cook, D. W. (1989). Systematic need assessment: A primer. *Journal of Counseling and Development, 67,* 462–464.

Cook, E. P. (Ed.). (1993). *Women, relationships, and power: Implications for counseling.* Alexandria, VA: American Counseling Association.

Cook, E. P., Heppner, M. J., & O'Brien, K. M. (2002). Career development of women of color and White women: Assumptions, conceptualizations, and interventions from an ecological perspective. *Career Development Quarterly, 50,* 291–305.

Cooper, D. L., Healy, M., & Simpson, J. (1994). Student development through involvement: Specific changes over time. *Journal of College Student Development, 35,* 98–101.

Copeland, A. D. (1974). *Textbook of adolescent psychopathology and treatment.* Springfield, IL: Thomas.

Coppock, M. W. (1993). Small group plan for improving friendships and self-esteem. *Elementary School Guidance and Counseling, 28,* 152–154.

Corcoran, J., & Pillai, V. (2009). A review of the research on solution-focused therapy. *British Journal of Social Work, 39*(2), 234–242.

Corey, G. (2008). *Theory and practice of group counseling* (7th ed). Belmont, CA: Thomson Brooks/Cole.

Corey, G. (2009). *Theory and practice of counseling and psychotherapy* (8th ed). Belmont, CA: Brooks/Cole.

Corey, G., Corey, M. S., & Callanan, P. (2007). *Issues and ethics in the helping professions* (7th ed.). Belmont, CA: Thomson Brooks/Cole.

Cormack, J. (2009). Counselling marginalised young people: A qualitative analysis of young homeless people's views of counselling. *Counselling & Psychotherapy Research, 9*(2), 71–77.

Cormier, L. S., & Cormier, W. H. (1998). *Fundamental skills and cognitive behavioral interventions* (4th ed.). Pacific Grove, CA: Brooks/Cole.

Cormier, L. S., & Hackney, H. (2008). Counseling strategies and interventions (7th ed.). Boston: Pearson/Allyn & Bacon.

Corsini, R. J. (2008). Introduction. In R. J. Corsini & D. Wedding (Eds.), *Current psychotherapies* (8th ed., pp. 1–13). Belmont, CA: Thomson Brooks/Cole.

Corsini, R. J., & Wedding, D. (Eds.). (2008). *Current psychotherapies* (8th ed.). Belmont, CA: Thomson Brooks/Cole.

Costa, L., & Altekruse, M. (1994). Duty-to-warn guidelines for mental health counselors. *Journal of Counseling and Development, 72,* 346–350.

Cote, S. M., Vaillancourt, T., LeBlanc, J. C., Nagin, D. S., & Tremblay, R. E. (2006). The development of physical aggression from toddlerhood to pre-adolescence: A nationwide longitudinal study of Canadian children. *Journal of Abnormal Child Psychology, 34*(1), 71–85.

Cottone, R. R., Grelle, M., & Wilson, W. C. (1988). The accuracy of systemic versus psychological evidence in judging vocational evaluator recommendations: A preliminary test of a systemic theory of vocational rehabilitation. *Journal of Rehabilitation, 54,* 45–52.

Couch, R. D. (1995). Four steps for conducting a pregroup screening interview. *Journal for Specialists in Group Work, 20,* 18–25.

Council for Accreditation of Counseling and Related Educational Programs. (2001). *CACREP accreditation manual.* Alexandria, VA: Author.

Council for the Advancement of Standards in Higher Education. (2006). *CAS professional standards for higher education* (6th ed.). Washington, DC: Author.

Council of Canadians with Disabilities. (2010). *As a matter of fact: Poverty and disability in Canada.* Retrieved from **www.ccdonline.ca/en/socialpolicy/poverty-citizenship/ poverty-disability-canada**.

Counsellors Network. (2008). *Home page.* Retrieved from **www.cscounsellorsnetwork.com/education_associations .cfm**.

Cowen, E. L. (1982). Primary prevention research: Barrier opportunities. *Journal of Primary Prevention, 2,* 131–141.

Cowan, E. W., & Presbury, J. H. (2000). Meeting client resistance and reactance with reverence. *Journal of Counseling and Development, 78,* 411–419.

Cox, B. J., & Waller, L. L. (1991). *Bridging the communication gap with the elderly.* Chicago: American Hospital Association.

Cox, H. G. (1995). *Later life: The realities of aging* (5th ed.). Upper Saddle River, NJ: Prentice Hall.

Cox, R. P., & Anderson, H. (2003). Theories and concepts: How to understand families and health. In R. P. Cox (Ed.), *Health related counseling with families of diverse cultures: Family, health, and cultural competencies* (pp. 73–115). Westport, CT: Greenwood Press/Greenwood.

Cozby, P. C. (2001). *Methods in behavioral research* (7th ed.). Palo Alto, CA: Mayfield.

Craig, M. P., Contreras, M., & Peterson, N. (2000). Multicultural career exploration with adolescent females. In N. Peterson & R. C. Gonzalez (Eds.), *Career counseling*

models for diverse populations (pp. 20–35). Pacific Grove, CA: Brooks/Cole.

Crane, R. (2009). *Mindfulness-based cognitive therapy.* Hove, UK: Routledge.

Crawford, R. L. (1994). *Avoiding counselor malpractice.* Alexandria, VA: American Counseling Association.

Crawford, R. L., & Phyfer, A. Q. (1988). Adult children of alcoholics: A counseling model. *Journal of College Student Development, 29,* 105–111.

Creamer, D. G., & Associates (1990). *College student development: Theory and practices for the 1990s.* Alexandria, VA: American College Personnel Association.

Crespi, T. D., & Howe, E. A. (2000, March). Families in crisis: Considerations and implications for school counselors. *Counseling Today, 42*(9), 6.

Creswell, J. W. (2002). *Educational research: planning, conducting, and evaluating quantitative and qualitative research* (2nd ed.). Upper Saddle River, NJ: Merrill/ Prentice Hall.

Crites, J. O. (1969). *Vocational psychology.* New York: McGraw-Hill.

Crites, J. O. (1981). *Career counseling: Models, methods, and materials.* New York: McGraw-Hill.

Crodzki, L. (2002, May/June). Practice strategies. *Family Therapy Magazine, 1,* 43–44.

Cronbach, L. J. (1979). The Armed Services Vocational Aptitude Battery: A test battery in transition. *Personnel and Guidance Journal, 57,* 232–237.

Crosbie-Burnett, M., & Newcomer, L. L. (1989). A multimodal intervention for group counseling with children of divorce. *Elementary School Guidance and Counseling, 23,* 155–166.

Croteau, J. M., Anderson, M. Z., Distefano, T. M., & Kampa-Kokesch, S. (2000). Lesbian, gay, and bisexual vocational psychology: Reviewing foundations and planning construction. In R. M. Perez, K. A. Debord, & K. J. Bieschke (Eds.), *Handbook of counseling and psychotherapy with lesbian, gay, and bisexual clients* (pp. 383–408). Washington, DC: American Psychological Association.

Culbreth, J. R., & Borders, L. D. (1999). Perceptions of the supervisory relationship: Recovering and nonrecovering substance abuse counselors. *Journal of Counseling and Development, 77,* 330–338.

Cunningham, J. V., & Tidwell, R. (1990). Cognitive-developmental counseling: Preparing low-income students for college. *School Counselor, 37*(3), 225–232.

Cunradi, C., Caetano, R., & Schafer, J. (2002). Socioeconomic predictors of intimate partner violence among White, Black, and Hispanic couples in the United States. *Journal of Family Violence, 17,* 377–389.

Curtis, J. M. (1981). Indications and contraindications in the use of therapist's self-disclosure. *Psychological Reports, 49,* 449–507.

Curtis, R., & Sherlock, J. J. (2006). Wearing two hats: Counselors working as managerial leaders in agencies and schools. *Journal of Counseling and Development, 84,* 120–126.

Cutcliffe, J. R. (2005). Toward an understanding of suicide in First-Nation Canadians. *Crisis: The Journal of Crisis Intervention and Suicide Prevention, 26*(3), 141–145.

Cyr, M., Wright, J., McDuff, P., & Perron, A. (2002). Intrafamilial sexual abuse: Brother-sister incest does not differ from father-daughter and stepfather-stepdaughter incest. *Child Abuse & Neglect, 26*(9), 957–973.

Dagan, R. (2010, April 29). *Poverty in Canada: Resources.* Retrieved from **http://intraspec.ca/povertyCanada.php**.

Daigle, M. S. (2007). Mental health and suicide prevention services for Canadian prisoners. *International Journal of Prisoner Health, 3*(2), 163–171.

Daigneault, I., Hebert, M., & McDuff, P. 2009). Men's and women's childhood sexual abuse and victimization in adult partner relationships: A study of risk factors. *Child Abuse & Neglect, 33*(9), 638–647.

Dalton, A. L., & Galambos, N. L. (2009). Affect and sexual behavior in the transition to university. *Archives of Sexual Behavior, 38*(5), 675–687.

Daniel, T., & Ivey, A. E. (2007). *Microcounseling: Making skills work in a multicultural world.* Springfield, IL: Thomas.

Daniels, J. (1992). Empowering homeless children through school counseling. *Elementary School Guidance & Counseling, 27*(2), 104–112.

Daniels, J. A. (2002). Assessing threats of school violence: Implications for counselors. *Journal of Counseling and Development, 80*, 215–218.

Daniels, M. H., Mines, R., & Gressard, C. (1981). A meta-model for evaluating counseling programs. *Personnel and Guidance Journal, 5*(9), 578–582.

Daniluk, J. C., & Haverkamp, B. E. (1993). Ethical issues in counseling adult survivors of incest. *Journal of Counseling and Development, 72*, 16–22.

Das, A. K. (1998). Frankl and the realm of meaning. *Journal of Humanistic Education and Development, 36*, 199–211.

Dattilio, F. M. (1993). A practical update on the treatment of obsessive-compulsive disorders. *Journal of Mental Health Counseling, 15*, 244–259.

Daugherty, D. A., Murphy, M. J., & Paugh, J. (2001). An examination of the Adlerian construct of social interest with criminal offenders. *Journal of Counseling and Development, 79*, 465–471.

Dauvergne, M. (2003, spring). Family violence against seniors. Canadian Social Trends (Statistics Canada – Catalogue No. 11–008). Retrieved from **www.statcan.gc.ca/pub/11–008–x/2002004/article/6496–eng.pdf**.

Davenport, D. S., & Yurich, J. M. (1991). Multicultural gender issues. *Journal of Counseling and Development, 70*, 64–71.

Davidson, J. P., III. (1986, March). *Developing an effective evaluation plan.* Paper presented at the Jefferson County (Alabama) Model School Program, Birmingham, AL.

Davidson, P. R., & Parker, K. C. H. (2001). Eye movement desensitization and reprocessing (EMDR): A meta-analysis. *Journal of Consulting and Clinical Psychology, 69*(2), 305–316.

Davis, D. C. (1998). The American College Counseling Association: A historical view. *Journal of College Counseling, 1*, 7–9.

Davis, H. V. (1988). *Frank Parsons: Prophet, innovator, counselor.* Carbondale: University of Southern Illinois Press.

Davis, T., & Ritchie, M. (1993). Confidentiality and the school counselor: A challenge for the 1990s. *School Counselor, 41*, 23–30.

Day, R. W., & Sparacio, R. T. (1980). Structuring the counseling process. *Personnel and Guidance Journal, 59*, 246–249.

Day, S. X. (2008). *Theory and design in counseling and psychotherapy* (2nd ed.). Boston: Lahaska Press.

Dean, L. A. (1994, June). Chimney building. *Visions, 2*, 3–4.

DeAngelis, T. (1992, November). Best psychological treatment for many men: Group therapy. *APA Monitor, 23*, 31.

De Civita, M., Pagani, L. S., Vitaro, F., & Tremblay, R. E. (2007). Does maternal supervision mediate the impact of income source on behavioral adjustment in children from persistently poor families? *The Journal of Early Adolescence, 27*(1), 40–66.

Deegan, W. L., & O'Banion, T. (Eds.). (1989). *Perspectives on student development.* San Francisco: Jossey-Bass.

Del Prete, T. (1998). Getting back in touch with students: Should we risk it? *Professional School Counseling, 1*(4), 62–65.

DeLaszlo, V. S. (1994). *The basic writings of C. G. Jung.* New York: Modern Library.

DeLucia-Waack, J. L. (1996). Multiculturalism is inherent in all group work. *Journal for Specialists in Group Work, 21*, 218–223.

DeLucia-Waack, J. L. (1999). Supervision for counselors working with eating disorders groups: Countertransference issues related to body image, food, and weight. *Journal of Counseling and Development, 77*, 379–388.

Delve, C. I., Mintz, S. D., & Stewart, G. M. (1990). *Community service as values education.* San Francisco: Jossey-Bass.

Denzin, N. K., & Lincoln, Y. S. E. (2000). *Handbook of qualitative research* (2nd ed.). Thousand Oaks, CA: Sage.

Department of Justice Canada. (2009, May). *Family violence: Department of Justice Canada overview paper.* Retrieved from **www.justice.gc.ca/eng/pi/fv-vf/facts-info/fv-vf/fv-vf.pdf**.

Department of Justice Canada. (n.d.). *Canada's court system.* Retrieved from **www.justice.gc.ca/eng/dept-min/pub/ccs-ajc/pdf/courten.pdf**.

Depp, C. A., & Jeste, D. V. (2010). Phenotypes of successful aging: Historical overview. In C. A. Depp & D. V. Jeste (Eds.), *Successful cognitive and emotional aging* (pp. 1–14). Arlington, VA: American Psychiatric.

DeRidder, L. M. (1993). Teenage pregnancy: Etiology and educational interventions. *Educational Psychology Review, 5*, 87–103.

deShazer, S. (1984). The death of resistance. *Family Process, 23*, 11–17.

deShazer, S. (1991). *Putting differences to work.* New York: Norton.

DeVoe, M. W., & McClam, T. (1982). Service coordination: The school counselor. *School Counselor, 30*, 95–100.

Dewing, M., & Leman, M. (2006, March 16). Library of Parliament, Parliamentary Information and Research Service: *Canadian multiculturalism.* Retrieved from **www.parl.gc.ca/information/library/PRBpubs/936–e.htm**.

De Wit, D. J., Lipman, E., Manzano-Munguia, M., Bisanz, J., Graham, K., Offord, D. R., ... Shaver, K. (2007). Feasibility of a randomized controlled trial for evaluating the effectiveness of the Big Brothers Big Sisters community match program at the national level. *Children and Youth Services Review, 29*(3), 383–404.

Dickson, G. L., & Parmerlee, J. R. (1980). The occupation family tree: A career counseling technique. *School Counselor, 28,* 99–104.

Di Giunta, L., Eisenberg, N., Kupfer, A., Steca, P., Tramontano, C., & Caprara, G. V. (2010). Assessing perceived empathic and social self-efficacy across countries. *European Journal of Psychological Assessment, 26*(2), 77–86.

Dimeff, L. A., & Koerner, K. (2007). *Dialectical behaviour therapy in clinical practice: Applications across disorders and settings.* New York, NY: Guilford Press.

Dinkmeyer, D. (1973a). Elementary school counseling: Prospects and potentials. *School Counselor, 52,* 171–174.

Dinkmeyer, D. (1989). Beginnings of "Elementary School Guidance and Counseling." *Elementary School Guidance and Counseling, 24,* 99–101.

Dinkmeyer, D., & Losoncy, L. E. (1980). *The encouragement book: Becoming a positive person.* Upper Saddle River, NJ: Prentice Hall.

Dinkmeyer, D. C. (1971). The "C" group: Integrating knowledge and experience to change behavior. *Counseling Psychologist, 3,* 63–72.

Dinkmeyer, D. C. (1973b). The parent C group. *Personnel and Guidance Journal, 52,* 4.

Dinkmeyer, D. C., & Caldwell, C. E. (1970). *Developmental counseling and guidance: A comprehensive school approach.* New York: McGraw-Hill.

Dinkmeyer, D. C., & Carlson, J. (1973). *Consulting: Facilitating human potential and processes.* Upper Saddle River, NJ: Prentice Hall.

Dinkmeyer, D. C., & Muro, J. J. (1979). *Group counseling: Theory and practice* (2nd ed.). Itasca, IL: F. E. Peacock.

Dinkmeyer, D. C., Jr., & Carlson, J. (2006). Consultation: Creating school-based interventions (3rd ed.). New York: Routledge.

Divorce Magazine.com. (2010). *Canadian divorce statistics.* Retrieved from **www.divorcemag.com/statistics/statsCAN.shtml.**

Dixon, D. N., & Glover, J. A. (1984). *Counseling: A problem-solving approach.* New York: Wiley.

Dixon, W. A. (2000). Problem-solving appraisal and depression: Evidence for a recovery model. *Journal of Counseling and Development, 78,* 87–91.

Dixon, W. A., & Reid, J. K. (2000). Positive life events as a moderator of stress-related depressive symptoms. *Journal of Counseling and Development, 78,* 343–347.

Doan, R. E. (1998). The king is dead: Long live the king: Narrative therapy and practicing what we preach. *Family Process, 37*(3), 379–385.

Doan, R. E., & Scherman, A. (1987). The therapeutic effect of physical fitness on measures of personality: A literature review. *Journal of Counseling and Development, 66,* 28–36.

Dobson, J. E., & Campbell, N. J. (1986). Laboratory outcomes of personal growth groups. *Journal for Specialists in Group Work, 11,* 9–15.

Dollarhide, C. T. (1997). Counseling for meaning in work and life: An integrated approach. *Journal of Humanistic Education and Development, 35,* 178–187.

Donigian, J., & Malnati, R. (1997). *Systemic group therapy: A triadic model.* Pacific Grove, CA: Brooks/ Cole.

Donnay, D. A. C. (1997). E. K. Strong's legacy and beyond: 70 years of the Strong Interest Inventory. *Career Development Quarterly, 46,* 2–22.

Dorn, F. J. (1984). The social influence model: A social psychological approach to counseling. *Personnel and Guidance Journal, 62,* 342–345.

Dougherty, A. M. (1986). The blossoming of youth: Middle graders "on the grow." *School Counselor, 33,* 167–169.

Dougherty, A. M. (2005). *Psychological consultation and collaboration in school and community settings* (4th ed.). Pacific Grove, CA: Brooks/Cole.

Doweiko, H. E. (1990). *Concepts of chemical dependency.* Pacific Grove, CA: Brooks/Cole.

Drapela, V. J. (1983). Counseling, consultation, and supervision: A visual clarification of their relationship. *Personnel and Guidance Journal, 62,* 158–162.

Dreikurs, R. R. (1950). *Fundamentals of Adlerian psychology.* Chicago: Alfred Adler Institute.

Dreikurs, R. R. (1967). *Psychodynamics, psychotherapy, and counseling.* Chicago: Alfred Adler Institute.

Dreikurs, R. R., & Mosak, H. H. (1966). The tasks of life: I. Adler's three tests. *Individual Psychologist, 4,* 18–22.

Dreikurs, R. R., & Soltz, V. (1964). *Children: The challenge.* New York: Hawthorne.

Drug Rehab Services. (n.d.). *Heroin addiction in Canada.* Retrieved from **www.drugrehab.ca/heroin-addiction.html.**

Drummond, R. J., & Jones, K. D. (2006). *Appraisal procedures for counselors and helping professionals* (6th ed.). Upper Saddle River, NJ: Merrill/Prentice Hall.

Dryden, W. (1994). Reason and emotion in psychotherapy: Thirty years on. *Journal of Rational Emotive and Cognitive Behavior Therapy, 12,* 83–89.

Dumont, F., & LeComte, C. (1975). The effects of lighting and interpersonal distance on counseling interactions. *Canadian Counsellor, 9*(1), 9–19.

Dupere, V., Lacourse, E., Willms, J. D., Vitaro, F., & Tremblay, R. E. (2007). Affiliation to youth gangs during adolescence: The interaction between childhood psychopathic tendencies and neighborhood disadvantage. *Journal of Abnormal Child Psychology, 35*(6), 1035–1045.

Dupere, V., Leventhal, T., & Lacourse, E. (2009). Neighborhood poverty and suicidal thoughts and attempts in late adolescence. *Psychological Medicine, 39*(8), 1295–1306.

Dustin, D., & Ehly, S. (1984). Skills for effective consultation. *School Counselor, 31,* 23–29.

Duvall, J., & Young, K. (2009). Keeping faith: A conversation with Michael White. *Journal of Systemic Therapies, 28*(1), 1–18.

Duys, D. K., & Hobson, S. M. (2004). Reconceptualizing self-esteem: Implications of Kegan's constructive-developmental model for school counselors. *Journal of Humanistic Counseling, Education, and Development, 43,* 152–162.

Dworkin, S., & Pincu, L. (1993). Counseling in the era of AIDS. *Journal of Counseling and Development, 71,* 275–281.

Dye, H. A., & Borders, L. D. (1990). Counseling supervisors: Standards for preparation and practice. *Journal of Counseling and Development, 69,* 27–29.

Dyer, W. W., & Vriend, J. (1977). A goal-setting checklist for counselors. *Personnel and Guidance Journal, 55,* 469–471.

Dykeman, C., Daehlin, W., Doyle, S., & Flamer, H. S. (1996). Psychological predictors of school-based violence: Implications for school counselors. *School Counselor, 44,* 35–47.

Echenberg, H., & Jensen, H. (2008, December 29). *Defining and enumerating homelessness in Canada.* Library of Parliament, Parliamentary Information and Research Services. Retrieved from **www2.parl.gc.ca/content/lop/researchpublications/ prb0830–e.htm.**

Edgemon, A. W., Remley, T. P., Jr., & Snoddy, H. N. (1985). Integrating the counselor's point of view. *School Counselor, 32,* 296–301.

Education Trust. (1997). *The national guidance and counseling reform program.* Washington, DC: Author.

Egan, G. (2007). *The skilled helper* (8th ed.). Belmont, CA: Thomson Brooks/Cole.

Eggleton, A. (n.d.). *In from the margins: A call to action to end poverty in Canada.* Senate Subcommittee on Cities. Retrieved from **http://senatorarteggleton.ca/Default.aspx? tabid=236.**

Ehounoux, N. Z., Zunzunegui, M.-V., Seguin, L., Nikiema, B., & Gauvin, L.(2009). Duration of lack of money for basic needs and growth delay in the Quebec longitudinal study of child development birth cohort. *Journal of Epidemiology and Community Health, 63*(1), 45–49.

Ehrle, R. A. (1979). Rehabilitation counselors on the threshold of the 1980s. *Counselor Education and Supervision, 18,* 174–180.

EI group. (2010). Canadian history timeline. *Schools in Canada.com.* Retrieved from **www.schoolsincanada.com/ Canadian-History-Timeline.cfm.**

Eichhorn, D. H. (1968). Middle school organization: A new dimension. *Theory into Practice, 7,* 111–113.

Eisler, L., & Schissel, B. (2004). Privation and vulnerability to victimization for Canadian youth: The contexts of gender, race, and geography. *Youth Violence and Juvenile Justice, 2*(4), 359–373.

Elam, G. A., & Kleist, D. M. (1999). Research on the long-term effects of child abuse. *The Family Journal: Counseling and Therapy for Couples and Families, 7,* 154–160.

Elkind, D. (1986). Stress and the middle grader. *School Counselor, 33,* 196–206.

Ellerman, C. P. (2010). *Enchantments of the clinic: Power, eroticism, and illusion in the clinical relationship.* Lanham, MD: Jason Aronson.

Ellis, A. (1962). *Reason and emotion in psychotherapy.* New York: Stuart.

Ellis, A. (1971). *Growth through reason.* Palo Alto, CA: Science and Behavior Books.

Ellis, A. (1980). Foreword. In S. R. Walen, R. DiGiuseppe, & R. L. Wesslon (Eds.), *A practitioner's guide to rational-emotive therapy* (pp. vii–xii). New York: Oxford University Press.

Ellis, A. (1984). Must most psychotherapists remain as incompetent as they are now? In J. Hariman (Ed.), *Does psychotherapy really help people?* Springfield, IL: Thomas.

Ellis, A. (2008). Rational-emotive behavior therapy. In R. J. Corsini & D. Wedding (Eds.), *Current psychotherapies* (8th ed., pp. 187–222). Belmont, CA: Thomson Brooks/Cole

Elmore, P. B., Ekstrom, R. B., Diamond, E. E., & Whittaker, S. (1993). School counselors' test use patterns and practices. *School Counselor, 41,* 73–80.

Elmore, T. M., & Roberge, L. P. (1982). Assessment and experiencing: On measuring the marigolds. *Measurement and Evaluation in Guidance, 15,* 95–102.

Elstein, A. S., Shulman, A. S., & Sprafka, S. A. (1978). *Medical problem solving: An analysis of clinical reasoning.* Cambridge, MA: Harvard University Press.

Emener, W. G., & Cottone, R. R. (1989). Professionalization, deprofessionalization, and reprofessionalization of rehabilitation counseling according to criteria of professions. *Journal of Counseling and Development, 67,* 576–581.

Emerson, S., & Markos, P. A. (1996). Signs and symptoms of the impaired counselor. *Journal of Humanistic Education and Development, 34,* 108–117.

Engels, D. W., Jacobs, B. C., & Kern, C. W. (2000). Life-career developmental counseling. In D. C. Davis & K. M. Hemphrey (Eds.), *College counseling: Issues and strategies for a new millennium* (pp. 187–203). Alexandria, VA: American Counseling Association.

Engen, H. B., Lamb, R. R., & Prediger, D. J. (1982). Are secondary schools still using standardized tests? *Personnel and Guidance Journal, 60,* 287–290.

English, H. B., & English, A. C. (1956). *A comprehensive dictionary of psychological and psychoanalytical terms.* New York: Longman Green.

Engstrom, C. M., & Sedlacek, W. E. (1991). A study of prejudice toward university student-athletes. *Journal of Counseling and Development, 70,* 189–193.

Enns, C. Z. (1993). Twenty years of feminist counseling and therapy. *Counseling Psychologist, 21,* 3–87.

Enns, C. Z. (1994). Archetypes and gender: Goddesses, warriors, and psychological health. *Journal of Counseling & Development, 73*(2), 127–133.

Enns, C. Z. (1996). Counselors and the backlash: "Rape hype" and "false-memory syndrome." *Journal of Counseling and Development, 74,* 358–367.

Enns, C. Z., & Hackett, G. (1993). A comparison of feminist and nonfeminist women's and men's reactions to nonsexist and feminist counseling: A replication and extension. *Journal of Counseling and Development, 71,* 499–509.

Enright, M. S. (1997). The impact of short-term career development programs on people with disabilities. *Rehabilitation Counseling Bulletin, 40,* 285–300.

Erdberg, P. (1996). The Rorschach. In C. S. Newmark (Ed.), *Major psychological assessment instruments* (2nd ed.). Boston: Allyn & Bacon.

Erdman, P., & Lampe, R. (1996). Adapting basic skills to counsel children. *Journal of Counseling and Development, 74,* 374–377.

Erford, B. T. (2008). *Therapeutic dinosaur games.* Alexandria, VA: American Counseling Association.

Erickson, M. (1954). Special techniques of brief hypnotherapy. *Journal of Clinical and Experimental Hypnosis, 2,* 109–129.

Erickson, M. H. (2009). Further clinical techniques of hypnosis: Utilization techniques. *American Journal of Clinical Hypnosis, 51*(4), 341–362.

Erickson, R. C. (1987). Spirituality and depth psychology. *Journal of Religion & Health, 26*(3), 198–205.

Eriksen, K., & Kress, V. E. (2006). The DSM and the professional counseling identity: Bridging the gap. *Journal of Mental Health Counseling, 28,* 202–217.

Erikson, E. H. (1958). *Young man Luther.* New York: Norton.

Erikson, E. H. (1963). *Childhood and society* (2nd ed.). New York: Norton.

Erikson, E. H. (1968). *Identity, youth and crisis.* New York: Norton.

Erk, R. R. (2000). Five frameworks for increasing understanding and effective treatment of attention-deficit/ hyperactivity disorder: Predominately inattentive type. *Journal of Counseling and Development, 78,* 389–399.

Erkel, R. T. (1990, May/June). The birth of a movement. *Family Therapy Networker, 14,* 26–35.

Errebo, N., Knipe, J., Forte, K., Karlin, V., & Altayli, B. (2008). EMDR-HAP training in Sri Lanka following the 2004 tsunami. *Journal of EMDR Practice and Research, 2*(2), 124–139.

Erwin, T. M. (2006). A qualitative analysis of the Lesbian Connection's discussion forum. *Journal of Counseling and Development, 84,* 95–107.

Espelage, D. L., Bosworth, K., & Simon, T. R. (2000). Examining the social context of bullying behaviors in early adolescence. *Journal of Counseling and Development, 78,* 326–333.

Etchison, M., & Kleist, D. M. (2000). Review of narrative therapy: Research and review. *Family Journal, 8*(1), 61–67.

Etoka, G. (2009, November 17). *House of Commons Committees – HUMA (40–2) – Minutes of Proceedings.* Retrieved from **www2.parl.gc.ca/HousePublications/Publication. aspx?DocId=4238408&Language=E&Mode=1&Parl= 40&Ses=2**.

Evans, D. R., Hearn, M. T., Uhlemann, M. R., & Ivey, A. E. (2008). *Essential interviewing* (7th ed.). Belmont, CA: Thomson Brooks/Cole.

Evans, J. E., & Hines, P. L. (1997). Lunch with school counselors: Reaching parents through their workplace. *Professional School Counseling, 1,* 45–47.

Evans, K. M. (2010). ACA Advocacy Competencies and women. In M. Ratts, R. L. Toporek, & J. A. Lewis (Eds.), *ACA advocacy competencies: A social justice framework for counselors* (pp. 85–96). Alexandria, VA: American Counseling Association.

Evans, K. M., Kincade, E. A., Marbley, A. F., & Seem, S. R. (2005). Feminism and feminist therapy: Lessons from the past and hopes for the future. *Journal of Counseling and Development, 83,* 269–277.

Evans, N. J., Carr, J., & Stone, J. E. (1982). Developmental programming: A collaborative effort of residence life and counseling center staff. *Journal of College Student Personnel, 23,* 48–53.

Evans, S., Ferrando, S., Findler, M., Stowell, C., Smart, C., & Haglin, D. (2008). Mindfulness-based cognitive therapy for generalized anxiety disorder. *Journal of Anxiety Disorders, 22*(4), 716–721.

Evelyn, J. (2002, June 14). Nontraditional students dominate undergraduate enrollments, study finds. *Chronicle of Higher Education 48*(40), A34.

Everal, R. D., Altrows, K. J., & Paulson, B. L. (2006). Creating a future: A study of resilience in suicidal female adolescents. *Journal of Counseling and Development, 84,* 461–470.

Everly, G. S., Lating, J. M., & Mitchell, J. T. (2000). Innovations in group intervention: Critical Incident Stress Debriefing (CISD) and Critical Incident Stress Management (CISM). In A. R. Roberts (Eds.), *Crisis intervention handbook: Assessment, treatment, and research.* New York: Oxford Press.

Ewing, D. B. (1990). Direct from Minnesota: E. G. Williamson. In P. P. Heppner (Ed.), *Pioneers in counseling and development: Personal and professional perspectives* (pp. 104–111). Alexandria, VA: American Counseling Association.

Eysenck, H. J. (1952). The effects of psychotherapy: An evaluation. *Journal of Consulting Psychology, 16,* 319–324.

Exner, J. E. (2003). *The Rorschach: A comprehensive system* (4th ed.). New York: Wiley.

Fagan, R. (2006). Counseling and treating adolescents with alcohol and other substance use problems and their families. *The Family Journal: Counseling and Therapy for Couples and Families, 14,* 326–333.

Faiver, C., Eisengart, S., & Colonna, R. (2004). *The counselor intern's handbook* (3rd ed.). Pacific Grove, CA: Brooks/Cole.

Fall, K. A., Holden, J. M., & Marquis, A. (2010). *Theoretical models of counseling and psychotherapy* (2nd ed.). New York, NY: Routledge/Taylor & Francis.

Fall, M., & VanZandt, C. E. Z. (1997). Partners in research: School counselors and counselor educators working together. *Professional School Counseling, 1,* 2–3.

Fallon, M. V. (1997). The school counselor's role in first generation students' college plans. *School Counselor, 44,* 384–393.

Fals-Stewart, W. (2003). The occurrence of partner physical aggression on days of alcohol consumption: A longitudinal diary study. *Journal of Consulting and Clinical Psychology, 71,* 41–51.

Fast, D., Small, W., Wood, E., & Kerr, T. (2009). Coming 'down here': Young people's reflections on becoming entrenched in a local drug scene. *Social Science & Medicine, 69*(8), 1204–1210.

Faust, V. (1968). *History of elementary school counseling: Overview and critique.* Boston: Houghton Mifflin.

Fauth, J., & Hayes, J. A. (2006). Counselors' stress appraisal as predictors of countertransference behavior with male clients. *Journal of Counseling and Development, 84,* 430–439.

Fellegi, I. P. (1997, September). *On poverty and low income.* Statistics Canada. Retrieved from **www.statcan .gc.ca/pub/13f0027x/13f0027x1999001–eng.htm**.

Fenske, R. H. (1989). Evolution of the student services professional. In U. Delworth, G. R. Hanson, & Associates (Eds.), *Student services: A handbook for the profession* (2nd ed., pp. 25–56). San Francisco: Jossey-Bass.

Ferguson, G. A. (1992). Psychology in Canada: 1939–1945. *Canadian Psychology, 33*(4), 697–705.

Ferro, A., Basile, R., & Slotkin, P. (2008). Countertransference and the characters of the psychoanalytic session. *The Scandinavian Psychoanalytic Review, 31*(1), 3–10.

Filbert, K. M., & Flynn, R. J. (2010). Developmental and cultural assets and resilient outcomes in First Nations young people in care: An initial test of an explanatory model. *Children and Youth Services Review, 32*(4), 560–564.

Fischer, A. R., Jome, L. M., & Atkinson, R. A. (1998). Back to the future of multicultural psychotherapy with a common factors approach. *Counseling Psychologist, 26*, 602–606.

Fischer, B., Rehm, J., Patra, J., & Cruz, M. F. (2006). Changes in illicit opioid use across Canada. *Canadian Medical Association Journal, 175*(11), 1385–1387.

Fishman, C. H. (1988). *Treating troubled adolescents: A family therapy approach.* New York: Basic Books.

Fitzpatrick, M. R., & Irannejad, S. (2008). Adolescent readiness for change and the working alliance in counseling. *Journal of Counseling & Development, 86*(4), 438–445.

Fleming, J. S., & Rickord, B. (1997). Solution-focused brief therapy: One answer to managed mental health care. *Family Journal, 5*, 286–294.

Flowers, P., & Buston, K. (2001). "I was terrified of being different": Exploring gay men's accounts of growing-up in a heterosexist society. *Journal of Adolescence, 24.*

Flynn, R. J. (1994). Evaluating the effectiveness of career counselling: Recent evidence and recommended strategies. *Canadian Journal of Counselling, 28*(4), 270–280.

Fogle, D. O. (1979). Preparing students for the worst: The power of negative thinking. *Personnel and Guidance Journal, 57*, 364–367.

Fong, M. L. (1992). When a survey isn't research. *Counselor Education and Supervision, 31*, 194–195.

Fong, M. L., & Cox, B. G. (1983). Trust as an underlying dynamic in the counseling process: How clients test trust. *Personnel and Guidance Journal, 62*, 163–166.

Forchuk, C., Brown, S. A., Schofield, R., & Jensen, E. (2008). Perceptions of health and health service utilization among homeless and housed psychiatric consumer/survivors. *Journal of Psychiatric and Mental Health Nursing, 15*(5), 399–407.

Ford, D., & Urban, H. (1998). *Systems of psychotherapy: A comparative study* (2nd ed.). New York: Wiley.

Ford, D. Y., Harris, J. J., III, & Schuerger, J. M. (1993). Racial identity development among gifted Black students. *Journal of Counseling and Development, 71*, 409–417.

Forrest, D. V. (1983). Depression: Information and interventions for school counselors. *School Counselor, 30*, 269–279.

Forrest, L. (1989). Guiding, supporting, and advising students: The counselor role. In U. Delworth, G. R. Hanson, & Associates (Eds.), *Student services: A handbook for the profession* (2nd ed., pp. 265–283). San Francisco: Jossey-Bass.

Forsyth, D. R., & Strong, S. R. (1986). The scientific study of counseling and psychotherapy. *American Psychologist, 41*, 113–119.

Fortin, L. M., Carney, J. V., Rundle, M. F., Mackie, K., & Roberts, W. B. Jr. (2007). But I was just kidding!: The school counselor's role in responding to student threats and the potential for violence. In S. M. Dugger & L. Carlson (Eds.), *Critical incidents in counseling children* (pp. 399-410). Alexandria, VA: American Counseling Association.

Foster, S. (1996, December). Characteristics of an effective counselor. *Counseling Today,* 21.

Fouad, N. A., & Byars-Winston, A. M. (2005). Cultural context of career choice: Meta-analysis of race/ethnicity differences. *Career Development Quarterly, 53*, 223–233.

Fouad, N. A., & Mohler, C. J. (2004). Cultural validity of Holland's theory and the Strong Interest Inventory for five racial/ethnic groups. *Journal of Career Assessment, 12*(4), 423–439.

Fox, M. (1994). *The reinvention of work: A new vision of livelihood for our time.* San Francisco: Harper.

Fraenkel, P., Hameline, T., & Shannon, M. (2009). Narrative and collaborative practices in work with families that are homeless. *Journal of Marital and Family Therapy, 35*(3), 325–342.

Frank, O. (2005). Counselling and the global agenda to eradicate poverty: what framework to apply for multicultural understanding and interpretation? *International Journal for the Advancement of Counselling, 27*(1), 35–46.

Frankel, R. (2010, September 24). *Rebecca's war dog of the week: The fate of Michael Vick's fighting dogs.* Retrieved from **http://ricks.foreignpolicy.com/posts/2010/09/24/ rebecca_s_war_dog_of_the_week_the_fate_of_michael _vick_s_fighting_dogs.**

Frankish, C. J., Hwang, S. W., & Quantz, D. (2005). Homelessness and health in Canada: Research lessons and priorities. *Canadian Journal of Public Health, 96*(2), S23–S29.

Frankowski, B. L. (2004). Sexual orientation and adolescents. *Pediatrics, 113*, 1827–1832.

Freeman, F. H., Knott, K. B., & Schwartz, M. K. (1996). *Leadership education: A source book.* Greensboro, NC: Center for Creative Leadership.

Freeman, S. C. (1990). C. H. Patterson on client-centered career counseling: An interview. *Career Development Quarterly, 38,* 291–301.

Freud, A. (1936). *The ego and the mechanisms of defense* (J. Strachey, Trans.). New York: International Universities Press.

Freud, A. (1958). Adolescence. *Psychoanalytic Study of the Child, 13,* 255–278.

Frey, D. H. (1972). Conceptualizing counseling theories. *Counselor Education and Supervision, 11,* 243–250.

Frey, D. H. (1978). Science and the single case in counseling research. *Personnel and Guidance Journal, 56,* 263–268.

Frey, L. L., Beesley, D., & Liang, Y-S. (2009). The Client Evaluation of Counseling Inventory: Initial validation of an instrument measuring counseling effectiveness. *Training and Education in Professional Psychology, 3*(1), 28–36.

Friedan, B. (1994). *The fountain of age.* New York: Touchstone.

Friedberg, R. D. (1996). Cognitive-behavioral games and workbooks: Tips for school counselors. *Elementary School Guidance and Counseling, 31,* 11–19.

Friedlander, M. L., Wildman, J., Heatherington, L., & Skowron, E. A. (1994). What we do and don't know about the process of family therapy. *Journal of Family Psychology, 8,* 390–416.

Friedman, H. S. (1978). The relative strength of verbal versus nonverbal cues. *Personality and Social Psychology Bulletin, 4*(1), 147–150.

Frieman, B. B. (1994). Children of divorced parents: Action steps for the counselor to involve fathers. *The School Counselor, 28*, 197–205.

Friskopp, A., & Silverstein, S. (1995). *Straight jobs gay lives.* New York: Scribner.

Froehle, T. C. (1985). Guest editorial. *Counselor Education and Supervision, 24*, 323–324.

Frone, M. R. (2003). Work-family balance. In J. C. Quick & L. E. Terrick (Eds.), *Handbook of occupational health psychology* (pp. 143–162). Washington, DC: American Psychological Association.

Fuqua, D. R., & Newman, J. L. (1985). Individual consultation. *Counseling Psychologist, 13*, 390–395.

Furlong, M. J., Atkinson, D. R., & Janoff, D. S. (1979). Elementary school counselors' perceptions of their actual and ideal roles. *Elementary School Guidance and Counseling, 14*, 4–11.

Gade, E., Fuqua, D., & Hurlburt, G. (1988). The relationship of Holland's personality types to educational satisfaction with a Native-American high school population. *Journal of Counseling Psychology, 35*, 183–186.

Gadit, A. A. M. (2007). Mental health model: Comparison between a developed and a developing country. *Journal of Medicine, 1*(1). Retrieved from **www.scientificjournals .org/journals2007/articles/1047.htm.**

Gale, A. U. (1998). Carl McDaniels: A life of transitions. *Journal of Counseling and Development, 76*, 202–207.

Galarneau, D., & Radulescu, M. (2009, May). Employment among the disabled. *Statistics Canada.* Retrieved from **www.statcan.gc.ca/pub/75–001–x/2009105/article/../pdf/ 10865–eng.pdf.**

Galassi, J. P., & Gulledge, S. A. (1997). The middle school counselor and teacher-advisor programs. *Professional School Counseling, 1*, 55–60.

Galfo, A. J., & Miller, E. (1976). *Interpreting educational research* (3rd ed.). Dubuque, IA: Wm. C. Brown.

Gallessich, J. (1974). Training the school psychologist for consultation. *Journal of School Psychology, 12*, 138–149.

Gallessich, J. (1982). *The profession and practice of consultation.* San Francisco: Jossey-Bass.

Gallessich, J. (1985). Toward a meta-theory of consultation. *Counseling Psychologist, 13*, 336–354.

Galvin, M., & Ivey, A. E. (1981). Researching one's own interviewing style: Does your theory of choice match your actual practice? *Personnel and Guidance Journal, 59*, 536–542.

Ganje-Fling, M. A., & McCarthy, P. (1996). Impact of childhood sexual abuse on client spiritual development: Counseling implications. *Journal of Counseling and Development, 74*, 253–258.

Gardner, H. (1993). *Frames of mind: The theory of multiple intelligences.* New York: Basic Books.

Garner, R., Martin, D., & Martin, M. (1989). The PALS program: A peer counseling training program for junior high school. *Elementary School Guidance and Counseling, 24*, 68–76.

Garrett, M. T. (2006). When eagle speaks: Counseling Native Americans. In C. C. Lee (Ed.), *Multicultural issues in counseling* (3rd ed., pp. 25–54). Alexandria, VA: American Counseling Association.

Garrett, M. T., & Carroll, J. J. (2000). Mending the broken circle: Treatment of substance dependence among Native Americans. *Journal of Counseling and Development, 78*, 379–388.

Gasser, C. E., Larson, L. M., & Borgen, F. H. (2007). Concurrent validity of the 2005 Strong Interest Inventory: An examination of gender and major field of study. *Journal of Career Assessment, 15*(1), 23–43.

Gatez, S. (2004). Safe streets for whom? Homeless youth, social exclusion, and criminal victimization. *Canadian Journal of Criminology and Criminal Justice, 46*(4), 423–455.

Gati, I., & Saka, N. (2001). High school students' career-related decision-making difficulties. *Journal of Counseling and Development, 79*, 331–340.

Gaushell, H., & Lawson, D. (1994, November). *Counselor trainee family-of-origin structure and current intergenerational family relationships: Implications for counselor training.* Paper presented at the Southern Association of Counselor Education and Supervision Convention, Charlotte, NC.

Gay, L. R., Mills, G. E., & Airasian, P. (2006). *Educational research* (8th ed.). Upper Saddle River, NJ: Merrill/Prentice Hall.

Gazda, G. M. (1989). *Group counseling: A developmental approach* (4th ed.). Boston: Allyn & Bacon.

Gazda, G. M., Ginter, E. J., & Horne, A. M. (2001). *Group counseling and group psychotherapy: Theory and application.* Boston: Allyn & Bacon.

Geis, G. L., & Chapman, R. (1971). Knowledge of results and other possible reinforcers in self-instructional systems. *Educational Technology, 2*, 38–50.

Geist, R. A. (2009). Empathic understanding: The foundation of self-psychological psychoanalysis. In W. J. Coburn & N. VanDerHeide (Eds.), *Self and systems: Explorations in contemporary self psychology* (pp. 63–74). Hoboken, NJ: Wiley-Blackwell.

Gelso, C., & Fretz, B. (2001). *Counseling psychology* (2nd ed). Toronto, ON: Harcourt College.

Gelso, C. J. (1979). Research in counseling: Methodological and professional issues. *Counseling Psychologist, 8*, 7–36.

Gelso, C. J. (1985). Rigor, relevance, and counseling research: On the need to maintain our course between Scylla and Charybdis. *Journal of Counseling and Development, 63*, 551–553.

Gemignani, M., & Gliiberto, M. (2005). Counseling and psychotherapy in Italy: A profession in constant change. *Journal of Mental Health Counseling, 27*, 168–184.

Geraghty, M. (1997, August 1). Campuses see steep increase in students seeking counseling. *Chronicle of Higher Education,* A32.

Gerdes, H., & Mallinckrodt, B. (1994). Emotional, social, and academic adjustment of college students: A longitudinal study of retention. *Journal of Counseling and Development, 72*, 281–288.

Gergen, K. J. (1985). The social constructionist movement in modern psychology. *American Psychologist, 40*(3), 266–275.

Gergen, K. J. (2009). *An invitation to social construction* (2nd ed.). Thousand Oaks, CA: Sage.

Gerler, E. R. (1987). Classroom guidance for success in overseas schools. *International Quarterly, 5*, 18–22.

Gerler, E. R., & Anderson, R. F. (1986). The effects of classroom guidance on children's success in school. *Journal of Counseling and Development, 65*, 78–81.

Gerler, E. R., Drew, N. S., & Mohr, P. (1990). Succeeding in middle school: A multimodal approach. *Elementary School Guidance and Counseling, 24*, 263–271.

Gerler, E. R., Jr. (1985). Elementary school counseling research and the classroom learning environment. *Elementary School Guidance and Counseling, 20*, 39–48.

Gerrard, N. (1991). Racism and sexism, together, in counselling: Three women of colour tell their stories. *Canadian Journal of Counselling, 25*(4), 555–566.

Geroski, A. M., Rodgers, K. A., & Breen, D. T. (1997). Using the DSM-IV to enhance collaboration among school counselors, clinical counselors, and primary care physicians. *Journal of Counseling and Development, 75*, 231–239.

Gerstein, L. H., & Hotelling, K. (1987). Length of group treatment and changes in women with bulimia. *Journal of Mental Health Counseling, 9*, 162–173.

Gibb, B. E., & Abela, J. R. Z. (2008). Emotional abuse, verbal victimization, and the development of children's negative inferential styles and depressive symptoms. *Cognitive Therapy and Research, 32*(2), 161–176.

Gibbons, M. M., & Shoffner, M. F. (2004). Perspective first-generation college students: Meeting their needs through social cognitive career theory. *Professional School Counseling, 8*, 91–97.

Gibson, D. M., & Myers, J. E. (2000). Gender and infertility: A relational approach to counseling women. *Journal of Counseling and Development, 78*, 400–410.

Gibson, G., & Chard, K. M. (1994). Quantifying the effects of community mental health consultation interventions. *Consulting Psychology Journal: Practice and Research, 46*(4), 13–25.

Giles, T. A. (1983). Counseling services and men in need: A response to Burch and Skovholt. *AMHCA Journal, 5*, 39–43.

Gilkey, S. L., Carey, J., & Wade, S. L. (2009). Families in crisis: Considerations for the use of web-based treatment models in family therapy. *Families in Society, 90*(1), 37–45.

Gill, S. J. (1982). Professional disclosure and consumer protection in counseling. *Personnel and Guidance Journal, 60*, 443–446.

Gillies, R. M. (1993). Action research in school counseling. *School Counselor, 41*, 69–72.

Gilligan, C. (1982). *In a different voice: Psychological theory and women's development.* Cambridge, MA: Harvard University Press.

Gill-Wigal, J., Heaton, J., Burke, J., & Gleason, J. (1988). When too much is too much. *Journal of College Student Development, 29*, 274–275.

Gingerich, W. (2006). Obituary: Steve de Shazer. *Research on Social Work Practice, 16*(5), 549–550.

Ginter, E. J. (1989). Slayers of monster watermelons found in the mental health patch. *Journal of Mental Health Counseling, 11*, 77–85.

Ginter, E. J. (2001). Private practice. In D. C. Locke, J. E. Myers, & E. L. Herr (Eds.), *The handbook of counseling* (pp. 355–372). Thousand Oaks, CA: Sage.

Ginzberg, E. (1972). Toward a theory of occupational choice: A restatement. *Vocational Guidance Quarterly, 20*, 169–176.

Ginzberg, E., Ginsburg, S. W., Axelrad, S., & Herma, J. L. (1951). *Occupational choice.* New York: Columbia University Press.

Giordano, F. G., Schwiebert, V. L., & Brotherton, W. D. (1997). School counselors' perceptions of the usefulness of standardized test, frequency of their use, and assessment training needs. *School Counselor, 44*, 198–205.

Gladding, S. T. (1990a). Coming full cycle: Reentry after the group. *Journal for Specialists in Group Work, 15*, 130–131.

Gladding, S. T. (1990b). Let us not grow weary of theory. *Journal for Specialists in Group Work, 15*, 194.

Gladding, S. T. (1995). Humor in counseling: Using a natural resource. *Journal of Humanistic Education and Development, 34*, 3–12.

Gladding, S. T. (2002a). *Becoming a counselor: The light, the bright, and the serious.* Alexandria, VA: American Counseling Association.

Gladding, S. T. (2002b). Reflections on counseling after the crisis. In G. R. Walz and C. J. Kinkman (Eds.). *Helping people cope with tragedy and grief.* (pp 9–12), Greensboro, NC: ERIC/CASS and NBCC.

Gladding, S. T. (2004). *Counseling as an art: The creative arts in counseling* (3rd ed.). Alexandria, VA: American Counseling Association.

Gladding, S. T. (2005). *Counseling theories: Essential concepts and applications.* Upper Saddle River, NJ: Pearson Merrill Prentice Hall.

Gladding, S. T. (2006). *The counseling dictionary* (2nd ed). Upper Saddle River, NJ: Pearson.

Gladding, S. T. (2007). *Family therapy: History, theory, and practice* (4th ed.). Upper Saddle River, NJ: Merrill/Prentice Hall.

Gladding, S. T. (2008). *Groups: A counseling specialty* (5th ed.). Upper Saddle River, NJ: Merrill/ Prentice Hall.

Gladding, S. T., & Gladding, C. (1991). The ABCs of bibliotherapy for school counselors. *School Counselor, 39*, 7–13.

Gladding, S. T., & Hood, W. D. (1974). Five cents, please. *School Counselor, 21*, 40–43.

Gladding, S. T., Lewis, E. L., & Adkins, L. (1981). Religious beliefs and positive mental health: The GLA scale and counseling. *Counseling and Values, 25*, 206–215.

Gladding, S. T., & Newsome, D. (2004). *Community and agency counseling.* (2nd ed.). Upper Saddle River, NJ: Merrill/Prentice Hall.

Gladstein, G. A., & Apfel, F. S. (1987). A theoretically based adult career counseling center. *Career Development Quarterly, 36*, 178–185.

Glass, G. V. (1976). Primary, secondary, and meta-analyses of research. *Educational Researcher, 5*, 3–8.

Glasser, W. (1965). *Reality therapy: A new approach to psychiatry.* New York: Harper & Row.

Glasser, W. (1980). Reality therapy: An explanation of the steps of reality therapy. In W. Glasser (Ed.), *What are you doing? How people are helped through reality therapy*. New York: Harper & Row.

Glasser, W. (1981). *Stations of the mind*. New York: Harper & Row.

Glasser, W. (1984). *Control theory: A new explanation of how we control our lives*. New York: Harper & Row.

Glasser, W. (1988, November). *Reality therapy*. Workshop presented at the Alabama Association for Counseling and Development, Fall Conference, Birmingham.

Glasser, W. (1998). *Choice theory*. New York: HarperCollins.

Glasser, W. (2000). School violence from the perspective of William Glasser. *Professional School Counseling, 4*, 77–80.

Glasser, W. (2005, February). *Reality therapy today*. Presentation at the Wake Forest University Counseling Winter Forum. Winston-Salem, NC..

Glasser, W., & Wubbolding, R. (1995). Reality therapy. In R. Corsini & D. Wedding (Eds.), *Current psychotherapies* (5th ed., pp. 293–321). Itasca, IL: F. E. Peacock.

Glenn, M., Garcia, J., Li, L., & Moore, D. (1998). Preparation of rehabilitation counselors to serve people living with HIV/AIDS. *Rehabilitation Counseling Bulletin, 41*, 190–200.

Gloria, A. M., & Kurpius Robinson, S. E. (2000). I can't live without it: Adolescent substance abuse from a cultural and contextual framework. In D. Capuzzi & D. R. Gross (Eds.), *Youth at risk* (3rd ed., pp. 409–439). Alexandria, VA: American Counseling Association.

Gloria, A. M., & Rodriguez, E. R. (2000). Counseling Latino university students: Psychosociocultural issues for consideration. Journal of Counseling and Development, 78, 145–154.

Glosoff, H. L., Herlihy, B., & Spence, E. B. (2000). Privileged communication in the counselor-client relationship. *Journal of Counseling and Development, 78*, 454–462.

Glosoff, H. L., & Koprowicz, C. L. (1990). *Children achieving potential*. Alexandria, VA: American Counseling Association.

Gold, J., & Pitariu, G. V. (2004). Opening the eyes of counselors to the emotional abuse of men: An overlooked dynamic in dysfunctional families. *Journal of Humanistic Counseling, Education and Development, 43*, 178–187.

Gold, L. (1979). Adler's theory of dreams: An holistic approach to interpretation. In B. B. Wolman (Ed.), *Handbook of dreams: Research, theories, and applications*. New York: Van Nostrand Reinhold.

Goldberg, A. E. (2010). *Lesbian and gay parents and their children: Research on the family life cycle*. Washington, DC: American Psychological Association.

Goldberg, J. R. (1994, June). Spirituality, religion and secular values: What role in psychotherapy? *Family Therapy News, 25*(9), 16–17.

Goldberg, M., & Green, D. A. (2009, April). *Understanding the link between welfare policy and the use of food banks: An economic security project report*. Canadian Centre for Policy Alternatives. Retrieved from **www.policyalternatives.ca/publications/reports/understanding-link-between-welfare-policy-and-use-food-banks**.

Goldiamond, I. (1976). Self-reinforcement. *Journal of Applied Behavior Analysis, 9*, 509–514.

Goldin, E., & Bordan, T. (1999). The use of humor in counseling: The laughing cure. *Journal of Counseling and Development, 77*, 405–410.

Goldin, E., Bordan, T., Araoz, D. L., Gladding, S. T., Kaplan, D., Krumbolz, J., et al. (2006). Humor in counseling: Leader perpectives. *Journal of Counseling and Development, 84*, 397–404.

Goldin, P. R., & Gross, J. J. (2010). Effects of mindfulness-based stress reduction (MBSR) on emotion regulation in social anxiety disorder. *Emotion, 10*(1), 83–91.

Goldman, L. (1971). *Using tests in counseling* (2nd ed.). New York: Appleton-Century-Crofts.

Goldman, L. (1972a). Introduction. *Personnel and Guidance Journal, 51*, 85..

Goldman, L. G. (1976). A revolution in counseling research. *Journal of Counseling Psychology, 23*, 543–552.

Goldman, L. G. (1977). Toward more meaningful research. *Personnel and Guidance Journal, 55*, 363–368.

Goldman, L. G. (1978). Science, research, and practice: Confusing the issues. *Personnel and Guidance Journal, 56*, 641–642.

Goldman, L. G. (1979). Research is more than technology. *Counseling Psychologist, 8*, 41–44.

Goldman, L. G. (1986). Research and evaluation. In M. D. Lewis, R. L. Hayes, & J. A. Lewis (Eds.), *The counseling profession* (pp. 278–300). Itasca, IL: F. E.Peacock.

Goldman, L. G. (1992). Qualitative assessment: An approach for counselors. *Journal of Counseling and Development, 70*, 616–621.

Goldman, L. (1994a). The marriage between tests and counseling redux: Summary of the 1972 article. *Measurement and Evaluation in Counseling and Development, 26*, 214–216.

Goldman, L. (1994b). The marriage is over . . . for most of us. *Measurement and Evaluation in Counseling and Development, 26*, 217–218.

Goldstein, A. P. (1973). *Structural learning therapy: Toward a psychotherapy for the poor*. New York: Academic Press.

Goldstein, E. G. (2009). The relationship between social work and psychoanalysis: The future impact of social workers. *Clinical Social Work Journal, 37*(1), 7–13.

Good, G. E., & Brooks, G. R. (Eds.). (2005). *The new handbook of psychotherapy and counseling with men: A comprehensive guide to settings, problems, and treatment approaches* (Rev. & abridged ed.). San Francisco, CA: Jossey-Bass.

Goodman, J. (2010). Advocacy for older clients. In M. J. Ratts, R. L. Toporek, & J. A. Lewis (Eds.), *ACA advocacy competencies: A social justice framework for counselors*. (pp. 97–106). Alexandria, VA: American Counseling Association.

Goodman, J.T. (2010). Mental health. The Canadian Encyclopedia. Retrieved from **www.thecanadianencyclopedia.com/index.cfm?PgNm=TCE&Params=A1ARTA0005235**.

Goodnough, G. E., & Ripley, V. (1997). Structured groups for high school seniors making the transition to college and to military service. *School Counselor, 44*, 230–234.

Goodyear, R. K. (1976). Counselors as community psychologists. *Personnel and Guidance Journal, 54*, 512–516.

Goodyear, R. K. (1981). Termination as a loss experience for the counselor. *Personnel and Guidance Journal, 59,* 349–350.

Goodyear, R. K., & Bradley, F. O. (1980). The helping process as contractual. *Personnel and Guidance Journal, 58,* 512–515.

Gordon, H. M., & Connolly, D. A. (2010). Failing to report details of an event: A review of the directed forgetting procedure and applications to reports of childhood sexual abuse. *Memory, 18*(2), 115–128.

Gorton, G. E. (2005). Milton Hyland Erickson, 1901–1980. *The American Journal of Psychiatry, 162*(7), 1255.

Gottfredson, L., & Saklofske, D. H. (2009). Intelligence: Foundations and issues in assessment. *Canadian Psychology/Psychologie canadienne, 50*(3), 183–195.

Gottfredson, L. S. (1981). Circumscription and compromise: A developmental theory of occupational aspirations. *Journal of Counseling Psychology, 28,* 545–579.

Gottfredson, L. S. (2005). Applying Gottfredson's theory of circumscription and compromise in career guidance and counseling. In S. D. Brown & R. W. Lent (Eds.), *Career development and counseling: Putting theory and research to work* (pp. 71–100). Hoboken, NJ: Wiley.

Goud, N. (1990). Spiritual and ethical beliefs of humanists in the counseling profession. *Journal of Counseling and Development, 68,* 571–574.

Gougeon, C. (1989). Guidelines for special issues training sessions in secondary school peer counselling programs. *Canadian Journal of Counselling, 23*(1), 120–126.

Government of Alberta Health and Wellness. (2009). *Alberta regulation 82/2003, Health Professions Act: Social Workers Profession Regulation.* Retrieved from **www.qp.alberta.ca/574.cfm?page=2003_082.cfm&leg_type=Regs&isbncln=9780779731916.**

Grady, M. A. J. M., & Ephross, P. H. (1977). A comparison of two methods for collecting social histories of psychiatric hospital patients. *Military Medicine, 142*(7), 524–526.

Granello, D. H. (2004). Assisting beginning counselors in becoming gay affirmative: A workshop approach. *Journal of Humanistic Counseling, Education and Development, 43,* 50–64.

Grant, B. (1992). The moral nature of psychotherapy. In M. T. Burke & J. G. Miranti (Eds.), *Ethical and spiritual values in counseling* (pp. 27–35). Alexandria, VA: American Counseling Association.

Green, A., & Keys, S. G. (2001). Expanding the developmental school counseling paradigm: Meeting the needs of the 21st century student. *Professional School Counseling, 5,* 84–95.

Greenberg, L. S., & Goldman, R. N. (2008). *Emotion-focused couples therapy: The dynamics of emotion, love, and power.* Washington, DC: American Psychological Association.

Greenberg, L. S., James, P. S., & Conry, R. F. (1988). Perceived change processes in emotionally focused couples therapy. *Journal of Family Psychology, 2*(1), 5–23.

Greenberg, L., Warwar, S., & Malcolm, W. (2010). Emotion-focused couples therapy and the facilitation of forgiveness. *Journal of Marital and Family Therapy, 36*(1), 28–42.

Greene, M. (2006). Helping build lives: Career and life development of gifted and talented students. *Professional School Counseling, 10*(1), 34–42.

Greenwalt, B. C., Sklare, G., & Portes, P. (1998). The therapeutic treatment provided in cases involving physical child abuse: A description of current practices. *Child Abuse and Neglect, 22,* 71–78.

Gregory, R. A., & Britt, S. (1987). What the good ones do: Characteristics of promising leadership development programs. *Campus Activities Programming, 20,* 33–35.

Grewal, S., Bottorff, J. L., & Hilton, B. A. (2005). The influence of family on immigrant South Asian women's health. *Journal of Family Nursing, 11*(3), 242–263.

Grier, W., & Cobbs, P. (1992). *Black rage.* New York, NY: Basic.

Grigoriadis, S., & Robinson, G. E. (2007). Gender issues in depression. *Annals of Clinical Psychiatry, 19*(4), 247–255.

Grimes, M. E. & McElwain, A. D. (2008). Marriage and family therapy with low-income clients: Professional, ethical, and clinical issues. *Contemporary Family Therapy, 30*(4), 220–232.

Grites, T. J. (1979). Between high school counselor and college advisor: A void. *Personnel and Guidance Journal, 58,* 200–204.

Grosch, W. N., & Olsen, D. C. (1994). *When helping starts to hurt.* New York: Norton.

Grosse, S. J. (2002). Children and post traumatic stress disorder: What classroom teachers should know. In G. R. Walz & C. J. Kirkman (Eds.), *Helping people cope with tragedy and grief* (pp. 23–27). Greensboro, NC: ERIC & NBCC.

Grossman, P., Tiefenthaler-Gilmer, U., Raysz, A., & Kesper, U. (2007). Mindfulness training as an intervention for fibromyalgia: Evidence of postintervention and 3-year follow-up benefits in well-being. *Psychotherapy and Psychosomatics, 76*(4), 226–233.

Groth-Marnat, G. (1997). *Handbook of psychological assessment* (3rd ed.). New York: Wiley.

Guerney, L. (1983). Client-centered (nondirective) play therapy. In C. E. Schaeffer & K. J. O'Connor (Eds.), *Handbook of play therapy* (pp. 21–64). New York: Wiley.

Guerra, P. (1998, January). Advocating for school counseling. *Counseling Today,* 20.

Guindon, M. H., & Hanna, F. J. (2002). Coincidence, happenstance, serendipity, fate, or the hand of God: Case studies in synchronicity. *Career Development Quarterly, 50,* 195–208.

Guthmann, R. A. (1998). New-patient self-history questionnaires in primary care. *Journal of the American Board of Family Practice, 11*(1), 23–27.

Gutow, M. R., Rynkewitz, S., & Reicher, S. R. (2009). Responding to community needs utilizing a consultative approach. *Canadian Journal of School Psychology, 24*(3), 222–236.

Guy, J. D. (1987). *The personal life of the psychotherapist.* New York: Wiley.

Guzman, J., Yassi, A., Baril, R., & Loisel, P. (2008). Decreasing occupational injury and disability: The convergence of systems theory, knowledge transfer and action research. *Work: Journal of Prevention, Assessment & Rehabilitation, 30*(3), 229–239.

Gysbers, N. C. (2001). School guidance and counseling in the 21st century: Remember the past into the future. *Professional School Counseling, 5,* 96–105.

Gysbers, N. C., & Guidance Program Field Writers. (1990). *Comprehensive guidance programs that work.* Ann Arbor, MI: ERIC/CAPS.

Gysbers, N. C., & Henderson, P. (2006a). Comprehensive guidance and counseling evaluation programs: Program + Personnel = Results. In G. R. Waltz, J. C. Bleuer, & R. K. Yep (Eds.), Vistas: Compelling perspectives on counseling 2006 (pp. 187–190). Alexandria, VA: American Counseling Association.

Gysbers, N. C., & Henderson, P. (2006b). *Developing and managing your school guidance and counseling program* (4th ed). Alexandria, VA: American Counseling Association.

Gysbers, N. C., Heppner, J. A., & Johnstone, J. A. (2003). *Career counseling: Process, issues, & techniques* (2nd ed.). Boston: Allyn & Bacon.

Haase, R. F. (1970). The relationship of sex and instructional set to the regulation of interpersonal interaction distance in a counseling analogue. *Journal of Counseling Psychology, 17,* 233–236.

Haase, R. F., & DiMattia, D. J. (1976). Spatial environments and verbal conditioning in a quasi-counseling interview. *Journal of Counseling Psychology, 23,* 414–421.

Haberstroh, S., Duffey, T., Evans, M., Gee, R., & Trepal, H. (2007). The experience of online counseling. *Journal of Mental Health Counseling, 29,* 269–282.

Hackett, G. (1981). Survey research methods. *Personnel and Guidance Journal, 59,* 599–604.

Hackney, H. (1978). The evolution of empathy. *Personnel and Guidance Journal, 57,* 35–38.

Hackney, H., & Wrenn, C. G. (1990). The contemporary counselor in a changed world. In H. Hackney (Ed.), *Changing contexts for counselor preparation in the 1990s* (pp. 1–20). Alexandria, VA: Association for Counselor Education and Supervision.

Hadley, R. G., & Mitchell, L. K. (1995). *Counseling research and program evaluation.* Pacific Grove, CA: Brooks/Cole.

Hage, S. M. (2006). Profiles of women survivors: The development of agency in abusive relationships. *Journal of Counseling and Development, 84,* 83–94.

Haggard-Grann, U. (2007). Assessing violence risk: A review and clinical recommendation. *Journal of Counseling and Development, 85,* 294–301.

Hagger-Johnson, G. (2003). Internet research. *The Psychologist, 16*(8), 403.

Hall, A. S., & Torres, I. (2002). Partnerships in preventing adolescent stress: Increasing self-esteem, coping, and support through effective counseling. *Journal of Mental Health Counseling, 24,* 97–109.

Hall, C. S. (1954). *A primer of Freudian psychology.* New York: New American Library.

Hansen, J. C. (2005). Assessment of interests. In S. D. Brown & R. W. Lent (Eds.), *Career development and counseling: Putting theory and research to work* (pp. 281–304). Hoboken, NJ: John Wiley.

Hamachek, D. E. (1988). Evaluating self-concept and ego development within Erikson's psychosocial framework: A formulation. *Journal of Counseling and Development, 66,* 354–360.

Hamann, E. E. (1994). Clinicians and diagnosis: Ethical concerns and clinical competence. *Journal of Counseling and Development, 72,* 259–260.

Hammerschlag, C. A. (1988). *The dancing healers.* San Francisco: Harper & Row.

Hanna, C. A., Hanna, F. J., Giordano, F. G., & Tollerud, T. (1998). Meeting the needs of women in counseling: Implications of a review of the literature. *Journal of Humanistic Education and Development, 36,* 160–170.

Hanna, G. S. (1988). Using percentile bands for meaningful descriptive test score interpretations. *Journal of Counseling and Development, 66,* 477–483.

Hansen, F. T., & Amundson, N. (2009). Residing in silence and wonder: Career counselling from the perspective of 'being.' *International Journal for Educational and Vocational Guidance, 9*(1), 31–43.

Hansen, J. C., & Prather, F. (1980). The impact of values and attitudes in counseling the aged. *Counseling and Values, 24,* 74–85.

Hansen, J. C., Rossberg, R. H., & Cramer, S. H. (1994). *Counseling: Theory and process* (5th ed.). Boston: Allyn & Bacon.

Hansen, J. C., Stevic, R. R., & Warner, R. W. (1986). *Counseling: Theory and process* (4th ed.). Boston: Allyn & Bacon.

Hansen, J. C., Warner, R. W., & Smith, E. J. (1980). *Group counseling* (2nd ed.). Chicago: Rand McNally.

Hansen, J-I. C. (1994). Multiculturalism in assessment. *Measurement and Evaluation in Counseling and Development, 27,* 67.

Hansen, J. T. (1998). Do mental health counselors require training in the treatment of mentally disordered clients? A challenge to the conclusions of Vacc, Loesch, and Guilbert. *Journal of Mental Health Counseling, 20,* 183–188.

Hansen, J. T. (2006). Counseling theories within a postmodernist epistemology: New roles for theories in counseling practice. *Journal of Counseling and Development, 84,* 291–297.

Hansen, J-I. C., & Dik, B. J. (2005). Evidence of 12–year predictive and concurrent validity for SII Occupational Scale scores. *Journal of Vocational Behavior, 67*(3), 365–378.

Hanson, P. (1972). What to look for in groups: An observation guide. In J. Pfeiffer & J. Jones (Eds.), *The 1972 annual handbook for group facilitators* (pp. 21–24). San Diego: Pfeiffer.

Hanson, R. K., & Morton-Bourgon, K. E. (2009). The accuracy of recidivism risk assessments for sexual offenders: A meta-analysis of 118 prediction studies. *Psychological Assessment, 21*(1), 1–21.

Hanson, W. E., & Claiborn, C. D. (2006). Effects of test interpretation style and favorability in the counseling process. *Journal of Counseling and Development, 84,* 349–357.

Harding, A. K., Gray, L. A., & Neal, M. (1993). Confidentiality limits with clients who have HIV: A review of ethical and legal guidelines and professional policies. *Journal of Counseling and Development, 71,* 297–304.

Hare-Mustin, R. T. (1983). An appraisal of the relationship between women and psychotherapy. *American Psychologist, 38,* 593–599.

Hargus, E., Crane, C., Barnhofer, T., & Williams, J. M. G. (2010). Effects of mindfulness on meta-awareness and specificity of describing prodromal symptoms in suicidal depression. *Emotion, 10*(1), 34–42.

Harman, R. L. (1977). Beyond techniques. *Counselor Education and Supervision, 17,* 157–158.

Harris, A. H. S., Thoresen, C. E., & Lopez, S. J. (2007). Integrating positive psychology into counseling: Why and (when appropriate) how. *Journal of Counseling and Development, 85,* 3–13.

Harris, F. (1994, April). Everyday ethics. *ACCA Visions, 2,* 7–8, 10.

Harris-Bowlsbey, J. (1992, December). Building blocks of computer-based career planning systems. *CAPS Digest,* EDO-CG-92–7.

Harris-Bowlsbey, J., Dikel, M. R., & Sampson, J. P. (Eds.). (2002). *The Internet: A tool for career planning* (2nd ed.). Alexandria, VA: American Counseling Association.

Hart, D., Atkins, R., & Matsuba, M. K. (2008). The association of neighborhood poverty with personality change in childhood. *Journal of Personality and Social Psychology, 94*(6), 1048–1061.

Hartman, D. E. (2009). Test review: Wechsler Adult Intelligence Scale IV (WAIS IV): Return of the gold standard. *Applied Neuropsychology, 16*(1), 85–87.

Hartung, P. J., & Blustein, D. L. (2002). Reason, intuition, and social justice: Elaborating on Parsons' career decision-making model. *Journal of Counseling and Development, 80,* 41–47.

Hashimi, J. (1991). Counseling older adults. In P. K. H. Kim (Ed.), *Serving the elderly: Skills for practice* (pp. 33–51). New York: Aldine de Gruyter.

Hausdorf, P. A., LeBlanc, M. M., & Chawla, A. (2002). Cognitive ability testing and employment selection: Does test content relate to adverse impact? *Applied H.R.M. Research, 7*(1–2), 41–48.

Havighurst, R. J. (1959). Social and psychological needs of the aging. In L. Gorlow & W. Katkovsky (Eds.), *Reading in the psychology of adjustment* (pp. 443–447). New York: McGraw-Hill.

Hawes, D. J. (1989). Communication between teachers and children: A counselor consultant/ trainer model. *Elementary School Guidance and Counseling, 24,* 58–67.

Hay, C. E., & Kinnier, R. T. (1998). Homework in counseling. *Journal of Mental Health Counseling, 20,* 122–132.

Hayes, R. L. (1981). High school graduation: The case for identity loss. *Personnel and Guidance Journal, 59,* 369–371.

Hayes, R. L. (1993). Life, death, and reconstructive self. *Journal of Humanistic Education and Development, 32,* 85–88.

Hayes, S. C., Strosahl, K. D., & Wilson, K. G. (1999). Acceptance and commitment therapy: An experiential approach to behavior change. New York, NY: Guilford Press.

Hayduk, P., & Jewell, L. (2005). An introduction to counselling in Canada. Chapter 1: History of and trends in counselling in Canada. *Resources, Psych388, Canadian Supplement, Chapter 1, Athabasca University.* Retrieved from **http://psych.athabascau.ca**.

Hayman, P. M., & Covert, J. A. (1986). Ethical dilemmas in college counseling centers. *Journal of Counseling and Development, 64,* 318–320.

Health Canada. (2002). Canada's aging population. Retrieved from **www.phac-aspc.gc.ca/seniors-aines/pubs/fed_paper/pdfs/fedpager_e.pdf**.

Health Canada. (2002). *A report on mental illnesses in Canada.* Retrieved from **www.phac-aspc.gc.ca/publicat/miic-mmac/pdf/men_ill_e.pdf**.

Health Canada. (2006a, December 7). *Mental health – mental illness.* Retrieved from **www.hc-sc.gc.ca/hl-vs/iyh-vsv/diseases-maladies/mental-eng.php**.

Health Canada. (2006b, March 6). *Suicide prevention: First Nations, Inuit, and Aboriginal health.* Retrieved from **www.hc-sc.gc.ca/fniah-spnia/promotion/suicide/index-eng.php**.

Health Canada. (2007, May 7). *Reducing the harm associated with injection drug use in Canada.* Retrieved from **http://hc-sc.gc.ca/hc-ps/pubs/adp-apd/injection/summary-sommaire-eng.php**.

Health Canada. (2009a, July 31). *Canadian Alcohol and Drug Use Monitoring Survey: Summary of results for 2008.* Retrieved from **www.hc-sc.gc.ca/hc-ps/drugs-drogues/stat/_2008/summary-sommaire-eng.php**.

Health Canada. (2009b, October 29). *Drug prevention and treatment.* Retrieved from **www.hc-sc.gc.ca/hc-ps/drugs-drogues/index-eng.php**.

Healy, C. C., & Woodward, G. A. (1998). The Myers-Briggs Type Indicator and career obstacles. *Measurement and Evaluation in Counseling and Development, 31,* 74–85.

Heath, D. H. (1980). Wanted: A comprehensive model of healthy development. *Personnel and Guidance Journal, 58,* 391–399.

Heisel, M. J. (2006). Suicide and its prevention among older adults. *The Canadian Journal of Psychiatry / La Revue canadienne de psychiatrie, 51*(3), 143–154.

Helwig, A. (2002, Summer). New Orleans workshop highlights. *NECA Newsletter, 2.*

Henderson, S. J. (2000). "Follow your bliss": A process for career happiness. *Journal of Counseling and Development, 78,* 305–315.

Hendrick, S. S. (1988). Counselor self-disclosure. *Journal of Counseling and Development, 66,* 419–424.

Henriksen, E. M. (1991). A peer helping program for the middle school. *Canadian Journal of Counselling, 25*(1), 12–18.

Heppner, P. P. (1990). Life lines: Institutional perspectives [Feature editor's introduction]. *Journal of Counseling and Development, 68,* 246.

Heppner, P. P., & Anderson, W. P. (1985). On the perceived nonutility of research in counseling. *Journal of Counseling and Development, 63,* 545–547.

Heppner, P. P., Wampold, B. E., & Kivlighan, D. M., Jr. (2008). *Research design in counseling* (3rd ed). Belmont, CA: Thomson Brooks/Cole.

Herdt, G. (1997). *Same sex, different cultures.* Boulder, CO: Westview Press.

Herlihy, B. (1996). When a colleague is impaired: The individual counselor's response. *Journal of Humanistic Education and Development, 34,* 118–127.

Herlihy, B., & Sheeley, V. L. (1987). Privileged communication in selected helping professions: A comparison among statutes. *Journal of Counseling and Development, 64,* 479–483.

Herman, K. C. (1993). Reassessing predictors of therapist competence. *Journal of Counseling and Development, 72,* 29–32.

Herman, W. E. (1997). Values acquisition: Some critical distinctions and implications. *Journal of Humanistic Education and Development, 35,* 146–155.

Hermann, M. A., & Herlihy, B. R. (2006). Legal and ethical implications of refusing to counsel homosexual clients. *Journal of Counseling and Development, 84,* 414–418.

Herr, E. L. (1997). Super's life-span, life-space and its outlook for refinement. *Career Development Quarterly, 45,* 238–246.

Herr, E. L. (2002). School reform and perspectives on the role of school counselors: A century of proposals for change. *Professional School Counseling, 5,* 220–234.

Herr, E. L., Cramer, S. H., & Niles, S. G. (2004). *Career guidance and counseling through the lifespan: Systematic approaches* (6th ed.). Boston: Allyn & Bacon.

Herr, E. L., & Niles, S. G. (1994). Multicultural career guidance in the schools. In P. Pedersen & J. C. Carey (Eds.), *Multicultural counseling in schools* (pp. 177–194). Boston: Allyn & Bacon.

Herring, R. D. (1998). *Career counseling in schools: Multicultural and developmental perspectives.* Alexandria, VA: American Counseling Association.

Herring, R. D., & White, L. M. (1995). School counselors, teachers, and the culturally compatible classroom: Partnerships in multicultural education. *Journal of Humanistic Education and Development, 34,* 52–64.

Hershenson, D. B. (1982). A formulation of counseling based on the healthy personality. *Personnel and Guidance Journal, 60,* 406–409.

Hershenson, D. B. (1992a). A genuine copy of a fake Dior: Mental health counseling's pursuit of pathology. *Journal of Mental Health Counseling, 14,* 419–421.

Hershenson, D. B. (1992b). Conceptions of disability: Implications for rehabilitation. *Rehabilitation Counseling Bulletin, 35,* 154–159.

Hershenson, D. B. (1996). A systems reformulation of a developmental model of work adjustment. *Rehabilitation Counseling Bulletin, 40,* 2–10.

Hershenson, D. B., & Berger, G. P. (2001). The state of community counseling: A survey of directors of CACREP-accredited programs. *Journal of Counseling and Development, 79,* 188–193.

Hershenson, D. B., Power, P. W., & Seligman, L. (1989). Mental health counseling theory: Present status and future prospects. *Journal of Mental Health Counseling, 11,* 44–69.

Hershey, C. O., & Grant, B. J. B. (2002). Controlled trial of a patient-completed history questionnaire: Effects on quality of documentation and patient and physician satisfaction. *American Journal of Medical Quality, 17*(4), 126–135.

Hertlein, K. M., & Ricci, R. J. (2004). A Systematic research synthesis of EMDR studies: Implementation of the platinum standard. *Trauma, Violence, & Abuse, 5*(3), 285–300.

Hetzel, R. D., Barton, D. A., & Davenport, D. S. (1994). Helping men change: A group counseling model for male clients. *Journal for Specialists in Group Work, 19,* 52–64.

Hick, S. (1998). *Canada's unique social history.* Retrieved from **www.socialpolicy.ca/cush/m5/m5–t7.stm**.

Hick, S. F., & Chan, L. (2010). Mindfulness-based cognitive therapy for depression: Effectiveness and limitations. *Social Work in Mental Health, 8*(3), 225–237.

Hill, A., & Brettle, A. (2005). The effectiveness of counselling with older people: Results of a systematic review. *Counselling & Psychotherapy Research, 5*(4), 265–272.

Hill, C. (2004). *Helping skills: Facilitating exploration, insight, and action* (2nd ed). Washington, DC: American Psychological Association.

Hill, C. E. (1982). Counseling process research: Philosophical and methodological dilemmas. *Counseling Psychologist, 10,* 7–19.

Hill, C. E. (1991). Almost everything you ever wanted to know about how to do process research on counseling and psychotherapy but didn't know who to ask. In C. E. Watkins, Jr., & L. J. Schneider (Eds.), *Research in counseling* (pp. 85–118). Hillsdale, NJ: Erlbaum.

Hill, C. E., Carter, J. A., & O'Farrell, M. K. (1983). A case study of the process and outcomes of time-limited counseling. *Journal of Counseling Psychology, 30,* 3–18.

Hill, C. L., & Ridley, C. R. (2001). Diagnostic decision making: Do counselors delay final judgment? *Journal of Counseling and Development, 79,* 98–104.

Hill, E. W. (2002). Enhancing family therapy with analytical psychology. *Contemporary Family Therapy: An International Journal, 24*(3), 437–456.

Hilton, B. A., Grewal, S., Popatia, N., Bottorff, J. L., Johnson, J. L., Clarke, H., … Sumel, P. (2001). The desi ways: Traditional health practices of South Asian women in Canada. *Health Care for Women International, 22*(6), 553–567.

Hilts, P. J. (1996). *Smokescreen: The truth behind the tobacco industry cover-up.* Reading, MA: Addison-Wesley.

Hine, C. (2008). Internet research as emergent practice. In S. N. Hesse-Biber & P. Leavy (Eds.), *Handbook of emergent methods* (pp. 525–541). New York, NY: Guilford Press.

Hines, M. (1988). Similarities and differences in group and family therapy. *Journal for Specialists in Group Work, 13,* 173–179.

Hinkelman, J. M., & Luzzo, D. A. (2007). Mental health and career development of college students. *Journal of Counseling and Development, 85,* 143–147.

Hinkle, J. S. (1994a). DSM-IV: Prognosis and implications for mental health counselors. *Journal of Mental Health Counseling, 16,* 174–183.

Hinkle, J. S. (1994b, September). *Psychodiagnosis and treatment planning under the DSM-IV.* Workshop presentation of the North Carolina Counseling Association, Greensboro, NC.

Hinkle, J. S. (1994c). *Psychodiagnosis and treatment planning using the DSM-IV.* Greensboro, NC: Author.

Hinkle, J. S. (1999). A voice from the trenches: A reaction to Ivey and Ivey (1998). *Journal of Counseling and Development, 77*, 474–483.

Hinson, J. A., & Swanson, J. L. (1993). Willingness to seek help as a function of self-disclosure and problem severity. *Journal of Counseling and Development, 71*, 465–470.

Hinterkopf, E. (1998). *Integrating spirituality in counseling: A manual for using the experiential focusing method.* Alexandria, VA: American Counseling Association.

Hipple, T., Comer, M., & Boren, D. (1997). Twenty recent novels (and more) about adolescents for bibliotherapy. *Professional School Counseling, 1*, 65–67.

Hitchcock, A. A. (1984). Work, aging, and counseling. *Journal of Counseling and Development, 63*, 258–259.

Hobbins, A. J. (1989). René Cassin and the daughter of time: the first draft of the Universal Declaration of Human Rights. *Fontanus, 2*, 7–26. Retrieved from **http://digitool .library.mcgill.ca/R/?func=dbin-jump-full&object_id= 19018&local_base=GEN01–MCG02**.

Hobfoll, S. E, Watson, P., Bell, C. C., Bryant, R. A., Brymer, M. J., Friedman, M. J., ... Ursano, R. J. (2007). Five essential elements of immediate and mid–term mass trauma intervention: Empirical evidence. *Psychiatry: Interpersonal & Biological Processes, 70*(4), 283–315.

Hobson, S. M., & Kanitz, H. M. (1996). Multicultural counseling: An ethical issue for school counselors. *School Counselor, 43*, 245–255.

Hodgins, D. C., & Peden, N. (2008). Cognitive-behavioral treatment for impulse control disorders. *Revista Brasileira de Psiquiatria, 30*(Suppl1), S31–S40. **www.hc-sc.gc.ca/ ahc-asc/media/advisories-avis/_2009/2009_01–eng.php**.

Hodgkinson, H. L., Outtz, J. H., & Obarakpor, A. M. (1992). *The nation and the states: A profile and data book of America's diversity.* Washington, DC: Institute for Educational Leadership.

Hoffman, M. A., Phillips, E. L., Noumair, D. A., Shullman, S., Geisler, C., Gray, J., ... Ziegler, D. (2006). Toward a feminist and multicultural model of consultation and advocacy. *Journal of Multicultural Counseling and Development, 34*(2), 116–128.

Hoffman, R. M. (2006). Gender self-definition and gender self-acceptance in women: Intersections with feminist, womanist, and ethnic identities. *Journal of Counseling and Development, 84*, 358–372.

Hofmann, S. G. (2008). Acceptance and commitment therapy: New wave or Morita therapy? *Clinical Psychology: Science and Practice, 15*(4), 280–285.

Hofmann, S. G., & Asmundson, G. J. G. (2008). Acceptance and mindfulness-based therapy: New wave or old hat? *Clinical Psychology Review, 28*(1), 1–16.

Hogan, T. P. (2007). *Psychological testing: A practical introduction* (2nd ed). New York: Wiley.

Hohenshil, T. H. (1993). Assessment and diagnosis in the *Journal of Counseling and Development. Journal of Counseling and Development, 72*, 7.

Hohenshil, T. H. (1996). Role of assessment and diagnosis in counseling. *Journal of Counseling and Development, 75*, 64–67.

Hohenshil, T. H. (2000). High tech counseling. *Journal of Counseling and Development, 78*, 365–368.

Hohenshil, T. H., & Hohenshil, S. B. (1989). Preschool counseling. Journal of Counseling and Development, 67, 430–431.

Holden, J. (1993). *Behavioral consequences on behavior.* Unpublished manuscript, University of North Texas, Denton.

Holden, J. (2001). Cognitive-behavioral counseling. In D. C. Locke, J. E. Myers, & E. L.

Holden, R. R., & Troister, T. (2009). Developments in the self-report assessment of personality and psychopathology in adults. *Canadian Psychology/Psychologie canadienne, 50*(3), 120–130. Herr (Eds.), *The handbook of counseling* (pp. 131–150). Thousand Oaks, CA: Sage.

Holiday, M., Leach, M. M., & Davidson, M. (1994). Multicultural counseling and intrapersonal value conflict: A case study. *Counseling and Values, 38*, 136–142.

Holland, J. L. (1994). *Self-directed search.* Odessa, FL: Psychological Assessment Resources.

Holland, J. L. (1997). *Making vocational choices: A theory of vocational preferences and work environments* (3rd ed.). Odessa, FL: Psychological Assessment Resources.

Holland, J. L., & Gottfredson, G. D. (1976). Using a typology of persons and environments to explain careers: Some extensions and clarifications. *Counseling Psychologist, 6*, 20–29.

Hollander, S. K. (1989). Coping with child sexual abuse through children's books. *Elementary School Guidance and Counseling, 23*, 183–193.

Hollingsworth, D. K., & Mastroberti, C. J. (1983). Women, work, and disability. *Personnel and Guidance Journal, 61*, 587–591.

Hollis, J. W. (1997). *Counselor preparation 1996–1998* (9th ed.). Muncie, IN: Accelerated Development.

Holmes, T. H., & Rahe, R. H. (1967). The social readjustment rating scale. *Journal of Psychosomatic Research, 11*, 213–218.

Hood, A. B., & Johnson, R. W. (2007). *Assessment in counseling* (4th ed.). Alexandria, VA: American Counseling Association.

Hopper, S., Kaklauskas, F., & Greene, L. R. (2008). Group psychotherapy. In M. Hersen & A. M. Gross (Eds.), *Handbook of clinical psychology, vol 1: Adults* (pp. 647–662). Hoboken, NJ: John Wiley & Sons.

Horne, A. M. (2000). *Family counseling and therapy* (3rd ed.). Itasca, IL: F. E. Peacock.

Horne, A. M., & Mason, J. (1991, August). *Counseling men.* Paper presented at the Annual Convention of the American Psychological Association, San Francisco.

Horton, N. (1994, October 10). United States has most educated population. *Higher Education and National Affairs, 43*, 3.

Horvath, A. O. (2000). The therapeutic relationship: From transference to alliance. *Journal of Clinical Psychology, 56*(2), 163–173.

Horvath, A. O. (2001). The therapeutic alliance: Concepts, research and training. *Australian Psychologist, 36*(2), 170–176.

Horvath, A. O. (2005). The therapeutic relationship: Research and theory: An introduction to the Special Issue. *Psychotherapy Research, 15*(1–2), 3–7.

Horvath, A. O. (2006). The alliance in context: Accomplishments, challenges, and future directions. *Psychotherapy: Theory, Research, Practice, Training, 43*(3), 258–263.

Hosie, T. W. (1994). Program evaluation: A potential area of expertise for counselors. *Counselor Education and Supervision, 33,* 349–355.

Hosie, T. W., West, J. D., & Mackey, J. A. (1988). Employment and roles of mental health counselors in substance-abuse centers. *Journal of Mental Health Counseling, 10,* 188–198.

Hotchkiss, L., & Borow, H. (1996). Sociological perspective on work and career development. In D. Brown, L. Brooks, & Associates (Eds.), *Career choice and development* (3rd ed.). San Francisco: Jossey-Bass.

House, E. R. (1978). Assumptions underlying evaluation models. *Educational Researcher, 7,* 4–12.

House, R. M., & Hayes, R. L. (2002). School counselors: Becoming key players in school reform. *Professional School Counseling, 5,* 249–256.

House, R. M., & Miller, J. L. (1997). Counseling gay, lesbian, and bisexual clients. In D. Capuzzi & D. R. Gross (Eds.), *Introduction to the counseling profession* (2nd ed., pp. 397–432). Boston: Allyn & Bacon.

Houston, B. K. (1971). Sources, effects and individual vulnerability of psychological problems for college students. *Journal of Counseling Psychology, 18,* 157–161.

Howard, G. S. (1985). Can research in the human sciences become more relevant to practice? *Journal of Counseling and Development, 63,* 539–544.

Howell, T. M., & Yuille, J. C. (2004). Healing and treatment of Aboriginal offenders: A Canadian example. *American Journal of Forensic Psychology, 22*(4), 53–76.

Hoyt, K. B. (1994). Youth apprenticeship "American style" and career development. *Career Development Quarterly, 42,* 216–223.

Hoyt, K. B. (2005). *Career education: History and future.* Broken Arrow, OK: National Career Development Association.

Huber, C. H. (1979). Parents of the handicapped child: Facilitating acceptance through group counseling. *Personnel and Guidance Journal, 57,* 267–269.

Huber, C. H. (1980). Research and the school counselor. *School Counselor, 27,* 210–216.

Huber, C. H. (1983). A social-ecological approach to the counseling process. *AMHCA Journal, 5,* 4–11.

Huber, C. H. (1989). Paradox-orthodox: Brief pastoral psychotherapy. *Individual Psychology, 45,* 230–237.

Hudson, P. (1998, April/May). Spirituality: A growing resource. *Family Therapy News, 29*(2), 10–11.

Huey, L. (2010). False security or greater social inclusion? Exploring perceptions of CCTV use in public and private spaces accessed by the homeless. *British Journal of Sociology, 61*(1), 63–82.

Huey, W. C. (1986). Ethical concerns in school counseling. *Journal of Counseling and Development, 64,* 321–322.

Huffman, S. B., & Myers, J. E. (1999). Counseling women in midlife: An integrative approach to menopause. *Journal of Counseling and Development, 77,* 258–266.

Hulchanski, J. D. (2009, February 18). Growing home: Housing and homelessness in Canada. Keynote address at University of Calgary conference. *Growing Home: Housing and Homelessness in Canada.* Retrieved from **www.cprn.org/documents/51110_EN.pdf**.

Hulchanski, J. D. (n.d.). *Homelessness in Canada: Question and answer.* Retrieved from **www.raisingtheroof.org/lrn-home-QandA-index.cfm**.

Hulse-Killacky, D. (1993). Personal and professional endings. *Journal of Humanistic Education and Development, 32,* 92–94.

Hulse-Killacky, D., Killacky, J., & Donigian, J. (2001). *Making task groups work in your world.* Upper Saddle River, NJ: Prentice Hall.

Human Resources and Skills Development Canada. (2006, July 25). *Workplace equity for Aboriginals peoples and visible minorities groups: Working together.* Retrieved from **www.rhdcc-hrsdc.gc.ca/eng/lp/lo/lswe/we/special_projects/RacismFreeInitiative/WorkplaceEquityAMVM.shtml**.

Human Resources and Skills Development Canada. (2009, August 7). *Welcome to the National Occupational Classification.* Retrieved from **www5.hrsdc.gc.ca/noc/english/noc/2006/welcome.aspx**.

Human Resources and Skills Development Canada. (2010, May 3). *Canadians in context: Household and family.* Retrieved from **www4.hrsdc.gc.ca/.3ndic.1t.4r@-eng.jsp?iid=37**.

Human Resources and Skills Development Canada. (2010, June 4). *Canadians in context – people with disabilities.* Retrieved from **www4.hrsdc.gc.ca/.3ndic.1t.4r@-eng.jsp?iid=40**.

Human Resources and Skills Development Canada. (2010, August 13). *Financial security – low income incidence.* Retrieved from **www4.hrsdc.gc.ca/.3ndic.1t.4r@-eng.jsp?iid=23**.

Humes, C. W., II. (1972). Accountability: A boon to guidance. *Personnel and Guidance Journal, 51,* 21–26.

Humes, C. W., II. (1980). Counseling IEPs. *School Counselor, 28,* 87–91.

Hummell, D. L., Talbutt, L. C., & Alexander, M. D. (1985). *Law and ethics in counseling.* New York: Van Nostrand Reinhold.

Hunsley, J., Lee, C. M., & Aubry, T. (1999). Who uses psychological services in Canada? *Canadian Psychology/Psychologie canadienne, 40*(3), 232–240.

Hunt, B., Matthews, C., Milsom, A., & Lammel, J. A. (2006). Lesbians with physical disabilities: A qualitative study of their experiences with counseling. *Journal of Counseling and Development, 84,* 163–173.

Hunt-Meeks, S. (1983). The anthropology of Carl Jung: Implications for pastoral care. *Journal of Religion & Health, 22*(3), 191–211.

Hunter, S. V. (2006). Understanding the complexity of child sexual abuse: A review of the literature with implications for family counseling. *The Family Journal: Counseling and Therapy for Couples and Families, 14,* 349–358.

Husband, R., & Foster, W. (1987). Understanding qualitative research: A strategic approach to qualitative methodology. *Journal of Humanistic Education and Development, 26,* 50–63.

Huskey, H. H. (1994, April). Counseling the senior student. *Visions, 2,* 10–11

Hutchins, D. E., & Vaught, C. G. (1997). *Helping relation-ships and strategies* (3rd ed.). Pacific Grove, CA: Brooks/Cole.

Hutchins, J. (1995, December). Barrett calls for MFT mediation for false memory families. *Family Therapy News, 26,* 21.

Hutchins, R. M. (1936). *The higher learning in America.* New Haven, CT: Yale University Press.

Hutchinson, N. L., Freeman, J. G., & Quick, V. E. (1996). Group counseling intervention for solving problems on the job. *Journal of Employment Counseling, 33,* 2–19.

Huynh, M., Vandvik, I. H., & Diseth, T. H. (2008). Hypno-therapy in child psychiatry: The state of the art. *Clinical Child Psychology and Psychiatry, 13*(3), 377–393.

Hyde, C., Bentovim, A., & Monck, E. (1995). Some clinical and methodological implications of a treatment outcome study of sexually abused children. *Child Abuse and Neglect, 19,* 1387–1399.

Hyer, L. (1995). Review of Eye movement desensitization and reprocessing: Basic principles, protocols, and proce-dures. *Psychotherapy: Theory, Research, Practice, Train-ing, 32*(4), 711–712.

Hyer, L., & Brandsma, J. M. (1997). EMDR minus eye movements equals good psychotherapy. *Journal of Trau-matic Stress, 10*(3), 515–522.

Imbimbo, P. V. (1994). Integrating personal and career coun-seling: A challenge for counselors. *Journal of Employ-ment Counseling, 31,* 50–59.

Ingersoll, R. E. (1994). Spirituality, religion, and counseling: Dimensions and relationships. *Counseling and Values, 38,* 98–111.

Institute of Marriage and Family Canada. (2009, November 27). *Canadian divorce statistics.* Retrieved from **www.imfcanada.org/default.aspx?go=article&aid= 1182&tid=8.**

International Centre for Excellence in Emotionally Focused Therapy. (2007). *Welcome.* Retrieved from **www.iceeft. com/home.htm.**

Israelashvili, M. (1998). Preventive school counseling: A stress inoculation perspective. *Professional School Coun-seling, 1,* 21–25.

Isaac, M., Elias, B., Katz, L. Y., Belik, S-L., Deane, F. P., Enns, M. W., ... The Swampy Cree Suicide Prevention Team. (2009). Gatekeeper training as a preventative intervention for suicide: A systematic review. *The Cana-dian Journal of Psychiatry / La Revue canadienne de psy-chiatrie, 54*(4), 260–268.

Ivey, A. E. (1971). *Microcounseling.* Springfield, IL: Thomas.

Ivey, A. E. (1980). *Counseling and psychotherapy: Skills, theories, and practice.* Upper Saddle River, NJ: Prentice Hall.

Ivey, A. E. (1989). Mental health counseling: A developmen-tal process and profession. *Journal of Mental Health Counseling, 11,* 26–35.

Ivey, A. E., & Goncalves, O. F. (1988). Developmental ther-apy: Integrating developmental processes into the clinical practice. *Journal of Counseling and Development, 66,* 406–413.

Ivey, A. E., & Ivey, M. B. (1990). Assessing and facilitating children's cognitive development: Developmental counsel-ing and therapy in a case of child abuse. *Journal of Coun-seling and Development, 68,* 299–305.

Ivey, A. E., & Ivey, M. B. (1998). Reframing DSM-IV: Posi-tive strategies from developmental counseling and theory: *Journal of Counseling and Development, 76,* 334–350.

Ivey, A. E., & Ivey, M. B. (2007). *Intentional interviewing and counseling* (7th ed.). Belmont, CA: Thomson Brooks/Cole.

Ivey, A. E., Ivey, M. B., Myers, J. E., & Sweeney, T. J. (2005). *Developmental counseling and therapy: Promot-ing wellness over the lifespan.* Boston: Lahaska.

Iwasaki, M. (2005). Mental health and counseling in Japan: A path toward societal transformation. *Journal of Mental Health Counseling, 27,* 129–141.

Jackson, A. P., & Scharman, J. S. (2002). Constructing family-friendly careers: Mothers' experiences. *Journal of Counsel-ing and Development, 80,* 180–187.

Jackson, D. N., & Hayes, D. H. (1993). Multicultural issues in consultation. *Journal of Counseling and Development, 72,* 144–147.

Jacobs, E. E., Harvill, R. L., & Masson, R. L. (2006). *Group counseling* (5th ed.). Belmont, CA: Thomson Brooks/Cole.

Jacobs, M. (1994). Psychodynamic counselling: An identity achieved? *Psychodynamic Counselling, 1*(1), 79–92.

Jacobson, N. S., & Gurman, A. S. (Eds.). (2003). *Clinical handbook of couple therapy* (3rd ed.). New York: Guilford.

James, M. D., & Hazler, R. J. (1998). Using metaphors to soften resistance in chemically dependent clients. *Journal of Humanistic Education and Development, 36,* 122–133.

James, R. K. (2008). *Crisis intervention strategies* (6th ed.). Belmont, CA: Thomson Brooks/Cole.

James, R. K., & Gilliland, B. E. (2003). *Theories and strate-gies in counseling and psychotherapy* (5th ed). Toronto, ON: Pearson.

James, R. K., & Gilliland, B. E. (n.d.). *Jungian therapy com-panion website material.* Boston, MA: Allyn and Bacon. Retrieved from **wps.ablongman.com/wps/media/ objects/208/213942/jungian.pdf**

Jencius, M., & Rotter, J. C. (1998, March). *Applying natural-istic studies in counseling.* Paper presented at the Ameri-can Counseling Association Conference, Indianapolis, IN.

Jennissen, T., & Lundy, C. (n.d.). *Keeping sight of social justice: 80 years of building CASW.* Retrieved from **www.casw-acts.ca/aboutcasw/building_e.pdf.**

Jepsen, D. A. (1982). Test usage in the 1970s: A summary and interpretation. *Measurement and Evaluation in Guid-ance, 15,* 164–168.

Jesser, D. L. (1983). Career education: Challenges and issues. *Journal of Career Education, 10,* 70–79.

Jewish Family Services. (2002). *Teens and gambling.* Buf-falo, NY: Author.

Johnson, C. S. (1985). The American College Personnel Association. *Journal of Counseling and Development, 63,* 405–410.

Johnson, D. H., Nelson, S. E., & Wooden, D. J. (1985). Fac-ulty and student knowledge of university counseling cen-ter services. *Journal of College Student Personnel, 26,* 27–32.

Johnson, D. W., & Johnson, F. P. (2006). *Joining together* (9th ed.). Boston: Allyn & Bacon.

Johnson, L. S. (1979). Self-hypnosis: Behavioral and phenomenological comparisons with heterohypnosis. *International Journal of Clinical and Experimental Hypnosis, 27*(3), 240–264.

Johnson, M., & Scarato, A. M. (1979). A knowledge base for counselors of women. *Counseling Psychologist, 8,* 14–16.

Johnson, S. M. (2003). The revolution in couple therapy: A practitioner-scientist perspective. *Journal of Marital & Family Therapy, 29*(3), 365–384.

Johnson, W., & Kottman, T. (1992). Developmental needs of middle school students: Implications for counselors. *Elementary School Guidance and Counseling, 27,* 3–14.

Johnson, W. B., & Hayes, D. N. (1997). An identity-focused counseling group for men. *Journal of Mental Health Counseling, 19,* 295–303.

Jolliff, D. (1994). Group work with men. *Journal for Specialists in Group Work, 19,* 50–51.

Jome, L. M., Surething, N. A., & Taylor, K. K. (2005). Relationally oriented masculinity, gender nontraditional interests, and occupational traditionality of employed men. *Journal of Career Development, 32,* 183–197.

Jones, K. D., & Robinson, E. H. (2000). Psychoeducational groups: A model for choosing topics and exercises appropriate to group stages. *Journal for Specialists in Group Work, 25,* 356–365.

Jones, R. M. (1979). Freudian and post-Freudian theories of dreams. In B. B. Wolman (Ed.), *Handbook of dreams: Research, theories, and applications.* New York: Litton.

Jongsma, A. E., Jr., & Peterson, L. M. (1995). *The complete psychotherapy treatment planner.* New York: Wiley.

Jordan, J. V. (1995). A relational approach to psychotherapy. *Women and Therapy, 16,* 51–61.

Jordan, K. (2002). Providing crisis counseling to New Yorkers after the terrorist attack on the World Trade Center. *The Family Journal: Counseling and Therapy for Couples and Families, 10,* 139–144.

Jourard, S. M. (1958). *Personal adjustment: An approach through the study of healthy personality.* New York: Macmillan.

Jourard, S. M. (1964). *The transparent self: Self-disclosure and well-being.* Princeton, NJ: Van Nostrand.

Jourard, S. M. (1968). *Disclosing man to himself.* Princeton, NJ: Van Nostrand.

Jourdan, A. (2006). The impact of the family environment on the ethnic identity development of multiethnic college students. *Journal of Counseling and Development, 84,* 328–340.

Joynt, D. F. (1993). *A peer counseling primer.* Danbury, CT: Author.

Juhnke, G. A. (1996). The adapted-SAD PERSONS: A suicide assessment scale designed for use with children. *Elementary School Guidance and Counseling, 30,* 252–258.

Kabat-Zinn, J. (1984). An outpatient program in behavioral medicine for chronic pain patients based on the practice of mindfulness meditation: Theoretical considerations and preliminary results. *ReVISION, 7*(1), 71–72.

Kabat-Zinn, J. (1990). *Full catastrophe living: Using the wisdom of your body and mind to face stress and pain.* New York, NY: Random House.

Kabat-Zinn, J. (2003). Mindfulness-based interventions in context: Past, present, and future. *Clinical Psychology: Science and Practice, 10,* 144–156.

Kadison, R., & DiGeronimo, T. F. (2004). *College of the overwhelmed: The campus mental health crisis and what to do about it.* San Francisco: Jossey-Bass.

Kahn, W. J. (1976). Self-management: Learning to be our own counselor. *Personnel and Guidance Journal, 55,* 176–180.

Kahnweiler, W. M. (1979). The school counselor as consultant: A historical review. *Personnel and Guidance Journal, 57,* 374–380.

Kampfe, C. M. (2002). Older adults' perceptions of residential relocation. *Journal of Humanistic Counseling, Education and Development, 41,* 103–113.

Kamphaus, R. W., Beres, K. A., Kaufman, A. S., & Kaufman, N. L. (1996). The Kaufman Assessment Battery for Children (K-ABC). In C. S. Newmark (Ed.), *Major psychological assessment instruments* (2nd ed.). Boston: Allyn & Bacon.

Kampwirth, T. J. (2006). *Collaborative consultation in the schools* (3rd ed.). Upper Saddle River, NJ: Merrill/ Prentice Hall.

Kapes, J. T., & Whitfield, E. A. (2001). *A counselor's guide to career assessment instruments* (4th ed.). Columbus, OH: National Career Development Association.

Kaplan, A. (1964). *The conduct of inquiry.* San Francisco: Chandler.

Kaplan, R., & Manicavasagar, V. (1998). Adverse effect of EMDR: A case report. *Australian and New Zealand Journal of Psychiatry, 32*(5), 731–732.

Kaplan, R. M., & Saccuzzo, D. P. (2005). *Psychological testing: Principles, applications, and issues* (6th ed.). Belmont, CA: Thomson Brooks/ Cole.

Kaplan, S. P. (1993). Five year tracking of psychosocial changes in people with severe traumatic brain injury. *Rehabilitation Counseling Bulletin, 36,* 151–159.

Karabanow, J. (2006). Becoming a street kid: Exploring the stages of street life. *Journal of Human Behavior in the Social Environment, 13*(2), 49–72.

Kassam, A. (2006). Encounters with the north: Psychiatric consultation with Inuit youth. *Journal of the Canadian Academy of Child and Adolescent Psychiatry / Journal de l'Academie canadienne de psychiatrie de l'enfant et de l'adolescent, 15*(4), 174–178.

Katz, L. Y., Fotti, S. A., & Postl, L. (2009). Cognitive-behavioral therapy and dialectical behavior therapy: Adaptations required to treat adolescents. *Psychiatric Clinics of North America, 32*(1), 95–109.

Katz, M. R. (1975). *SIGI: A computer-based system of interactive guidance and information.* Princeton, NJ: Educational Testing Service.

Katz, M. R. (1993). *Computer-assisted career decision-making: The guide in the machine.* Hillsdale, NJ: Erlbaum.

Kaufman, E., & Kaufman, P. (Eds.). (1992). *Family therapy of drug and alcohol abuse.* Boston: Allyn & Bacon.

Kay, A. (2006). *Life's a bitch and then you change careers. 9 steps to get out of your funk and on to the future.* New York: STC Paperbacks.

Keat, D. B., II (1990). Change in child multimodal counseling. *Elementary School Guidance and Counseling, 24,* 248–262.

Keeling, R. P. (1993). HIV disease: Current concepts. *Journal of Counseling and Development, 71*, 261–274.

Kees, N. L. (2005). Women's voices, women's lives: An introduction to the special issue on women and counseling. *Journal of Counseling and Development, 83*, 259–261.

Keirsey, D., & Bates, M. (1984). *Please understand me: Character and temperament types.* Del Mar, CA: Prometheus Nemesis Book Company.

Kelly, E. W., Jr. (1995). *Spirituality and religion in counseling and psychotherapy.* Alexandria, VA: American Counseling Association.

Kelly, K., & Caputo, T. (2007). Health and street/homeless youth. *Journal of Health Psychology, 12*(5), 726–736.

Kelly, K. R. (1988). Defending eclecticism: The utility of informed choice. *Journal of Mental Health Counseling, 10*, 210–213.

Kelly, K. R., & Hall, A. S. (1994). Affirming the assumptions of the developmental model for counseling men. *Journal of Mental Health Counseling, 16*, 475–482.

Kemp, A. (1998). *Abuse in the family: An introduction.* Pacific Grove, CA: Brooks/Cole.

Kemp, J. T. (1984). Learning from clients: Counseling the frail and dying elderly. *Personnel and Guidance Journal, 62*, 270–272.

Kendall, P. C. (1990). *Coping cat workbook.* Philadelphia: Temple University.

Kerka, S. (1991). Adults in career transition. *ERIC Digest,* ED338896.

Kerlinger, F. N., & Lee, H. B. (2000). *Foundations of behavioral research* (4th ed.). New York: Harcourt.

Kern, C. W., & Watts, R. E. (1993). Adlerian counseling. *Texas Counseling Association Journal, 21*, 85–95.

Kernberg, O. (1975). *Borderline conditions and pathological narcissism.* New York: Aronson.

Kernes, J. L., & McWhirter, J. J. (2001). Counselors' attribution of responsibility, etiology, and counseling strategy. *Journal of Counseling and Development, 79*, 304–313.

Kerr, B. A., Claiborn, C. D., & Dixon, D. N. (1982). Training counselors in persuasion. *Counselor Education and Supervision, 22*, 138–147.

Keyes, C. L. M., & Lopez, S. J. (2002). Toward a science of mental health: Positive directions in psychodiagnosis and treatment. In C. R. Snyder & S. J. Lopez (Eds.), *The handbook of positive psychology* (pp. 45–62). New York: Oxford University Press.

Keys, S. G., & Bemak, F. (1997). School-family-community linked services: A school counseling role for changing times. *School Counselor, 44*, 255–263.

Keys, S. G., Bemak, F., Carpenter, S. L., & King-Sears, M. E. (1998). Collaborative consultant: A new role for counselors serving at-risk youths. *Journal of Counseling and Development, 76*, 123–133.

Khan, J. A., & Cross, D. G. (1984). Mental health professionals: How different are their values? *AMHCA Journal, 6*, 42–51.

Khan, S. B., Alvi, S. A., & Kirkwood, K. J. (1990). Validity of Holland's model: A confirmatory factor analysis. *Canadian Journal of Counselling, 24*(3), 178–185.

Kilgore, H., Sideman, L., Amin, K., Baca, L., & Bohanske, B. (2005). Psychologists' attitudes and therapeutic approaches toward gay, lesbian, and bisexual issues continue to improve: An update. *Psychotherapy: Theory, Research, Practice, Training, 42*(3), 395–400.

Kim, B., Lee, S-H., Kim, Y. W., Choi, T. K., Yook, K., Suh, S. Y., ... Yook, K-H. (2010). Effectiveness of a mindfulness-based cognitive therapy program as an adjunct to pharmacotherapy in patients with panic disorder. *Journal of Anxiety Disorders, 24*(6), 590–595.

Kim, B. S. K. (2007). Adherence to Asian and European American cultural values and attitudes toward seeking professional psychological help among Asian American college students. *Journal of Counseling Psychology, 54*(4), 474–480.

Kim, J. S. (2008). Examining the effectiveness of solution-focused brief therapy: A meta-analysis. *Research on Social Work Practice, 18*(2), 107–116.

Kim, Y. W., Lee, S-H., Choi, T. K., Suh, S. Y., Kim, B., Kim, C. M., ...Yook, K-H. (2009). Effectiveness of mindfulness-based cognitive therapy as an adjuvant to pharmacotherapy in patients with panic disorder or generalized anxiety disorder. *Depression and Anxiety, 26*(7), 601–606.

Kimmel, D. C. (1988). Ageism, psychology, and public policy. *American Psychologist, 43*, 175–178.

Kingsland, L. J., & Carr, R. A. (1986). Peer programs in postsecondary institutions in Canada. *Canadian Journal of Counselling, 20*(2), 114–121.

Kinnier, R. T., Brigman, S. L., & Noble, F. C. (1990). Career indecision and family enmeshment. *Journal of Counseling and Development, 68*, 309–312.

Kinsey, A. C., Pomeroy, W. B., & Martin, C. E. (1948). *Sexual behavior in the human male.* Philadelphia, PA: W. B. Saunders.

Kiracofe, N. M., & Wells, L. (2007). Mandated disciplinary counseling on campus: Problems and possibilities. *Journal of Counseling and Development, 85*, 259–268.

Kirk, W. D., & Kirk, S. V. (1993). The African American student athlete. In W. D. Kirk & S. V. Kirk (Eds.), *Student athletes: Shattering the myths and sharing the realities* (pp. 99–112). Alexandria, VA: American Counseling Association.

Kirmayer, L. J., Groleau, D., Guzder, J., Blake, C., & Jarvis, E. (2003). Cultural consultation: A model of mental health service for multicultural societies. *The Canadian Journal of Psychiatry / La Revue canadienne de psychiatrie, 48*(3), 145–153.

Kisch, R. M. (1977). Client as "consultant-observer" in the role-play model. *Personnel and Guidance Journal, 55*, 494–495.

Kiselica, M. S., & Look, C. T. (1993). Mental health counseling and prevention: Disparity between philosophy and practice? *Journal of Mental Health Counseling, 15*, 3–14.

Kiselica, M. S., & Morrill-Richards, M. (2007). Sibling maltreatment: The forgotten abuse. *Journal of Counseling and Development, 85*, 148–161.

Kiselica, M. S., & Pfaller, J. (1993). Helping teenage parents: The independent and collaborative roles of counselor educators and school counselors. *Journal of Counseling and Development, 72*, 42–48.

Kiselica, M. S., & Robinson, M. (2001). Bringing advocacy counseling to life: The history, issues, and human dramas of social justice working in counseling. *Journal of Counseling and Development, 79,* 387–397.

Kitchener, K. S. (1985). Ethical principles and ethical decisions in student affairs. In H. J. Canon & R. D. Brown (Eds.), *Applied ethics in student services* (pp. 17–29). San Francisco: Jossey-Bass.

Kitchener, K. S. (1994, May). Doing good well: The wisdom behind ethical supervision. *Counseling and Human Development,* 1–8.

Kivlighan, D. M. Jr., & Luiza, J. W. (2005). Examining the credibility gap and the mum effect: Rex stockton's contributions to research on feedback in counseling groups. *Journal for Specialists in Group Work, 30*(3), 253–269.

Klaw, E., & Humphreys, K. (2004). The role of peer-led mutual help groups promoting health and well-being. In J. L. DeLucia-Waack, D. A. Gerrity, C. R. Kalodner, & M. T. Riva (Eds.), *Handbook of group counseling and psychotherapy* (pp. 630–640). Thousand Oaks, CA: Sage.

Klein, F. (1978). *The bisexual option.* New York: Arbor House.

Kleiss, K. (2010, July 10). *Alberta pledges 188 million to house homeless.* Calgary Herald. Retrieved from **www.calgaryherald.com/news/Alberta+pledges+188M+ homeless/3256023/story.html**.

Kleist, D. M., & White, L. J. (1997). The values of counseling: A disparity between a philosophy of prevention in counseling and counselor practice and training. *Counseling and Values, 41,* 128–140.

Kline, W. B. (1986). The risks of client self-disclosure. *AMHCA Journal, 8,* 94–99.

Knapp, S., & Vandecreek, L. (1982). *Tarasoff:* Five years later. *Professional Psychology, 13,* 511–516.

Knowles, D. (1979). On the tendency of volunteer helpers to give advice. *Journal of Counseling Psychology, 26,* 352–354.

Kohlberg, L. (1969). *Stages in the development of moral thought and action.* New York: Holt, Rinehart & Winston.

Kohlberg, L. (1984). *Essays on moral development: Vol. 2. The psychology of moral development: The nature and validity of moral stages.* New York: Harper & Row.

Kolenc, K. M., Hartley, D. L., & Murdock, N. L. (1990). The relationship of mild depression to stress and coping. *Journal of Mental Health Counseling, 12,* 76–92.

Komives, S. R., Woodard, D. B., Jr., & Delworth, U. (1996). *Student services: A handbook for the profession* (3rd ed.). San Francisco: Jossey-Bass.

Konrad, S. (2005). Counselling considersations with specific groups: Counselling First Nations Canadians. Retrieved from **http://psych.athabascau.ca/html/Resources/Psych388/ CanadianSupplement/Chapter4/03_firstnations.shtml**.

Koons, C. R. (2008). Dialectical behavior therapy. *Social Work in Mental Health, 6*(1–2), 109–132.

Kopla, M., & Keitel, M. A. (Eds.). (2003). *Handbook of counseling women.* Thousand Oaks, CA: Sage.

Koppel, M. S. (1999). A Jungian perspective on therapy at the end of life. *Pastoral Psychology, 48*(1), 45–56.

Kosculek, J. F. (2000). The Ticket to Work and Work Incentives Improvement Act (WIIA) of 1999. *Rehabilitation Counselors Bulletin, 43,* 1–2.

Koski, L., Xie, H., & Finch, L. (2009). Measuring cognition in a geriatric outpatient clinic: Rasch analysis of the Montreal Cognitive Assessment. *Journal of Geriatric Psychiatry and Neurology, 22*(3), 151–160.

Kottler, J. A. (1991). *The complete therapist.* San Francisco: Jossey-Bass.

Kottler, J. A. (1993). *On being a therapist.* San Francisco: Jossey-Bass.

Kottler, J. A. (1994a). *Advanced group leadership.* Pacific Grove, CA: Brooks/Cole.

Kottler, J. A. (1994b). Working with difficult group members. *Journal for Specialists in Group Work, 19,* 3–10.

Kottler, J. A., Sexton, T. L., & Whiston, S. C. (1994). *The heart of healing.* San Francisco: Jossey-Bass.

Kovacs, A. L. (1965). The intimate relationship: A therapeutic paradox. *Psychotherapy, 2,* 97–103.

Kovacs, A. L. (1976). The emotional hazards of teaching psychotherapy. *Psychotherapy, 13,* 321–334.

Kraus, K., & Hulse-Killacky, D. (1996). Balancing process and content in groups: A metaphor. *Journal for Specialists in Group Work, 21,* 90–93.

Krause, J. S., & Anson, C. A. (1997). Adjustment after spinal cord injury: Relationship to participation in employment or educational activities. *Rehabilitation Counseling Bulletin, 40,* 202–214.

Krauskopf, C. J. (1982). Science and evaluation research. *Counseling Psychologist, 10,* 71–72.

Krebs, E., Hurlburt, G., & Schwartz, C. (1988). Vocational self-estimates and perceived competencies of native high school students: Implications for vocational guidance counselling. *Canadian Journal of Counselling, 22*(4), 212–225.

Kress, V. E., & Shoffner, M. F. (2007). Focus groups: A practical and applied research approach for counselors. *Journal of Counseling and Development, 85,* 189–195.

Kress, V. E. W., Eriksen, K. P., Rayle, A. D., & Ford, S. J. W. (2005). The DSM-IV-TR and culture: Considerations for counselors. *Journal of Counseling and Development, 83,* 97–104.

Krestan, J., & Bepko, C. (1988). Alcohol problems and the family life cycle. In B. Carter & M. McGoldrick (Eds.), *The changing family life cycle* (2nd ed., pp. 483–511). New York: Gardner.

Krieshok, T. S. (1987). Review of the Self-Directed Search. *Journal of Counseling and Development, 65,* 512–514.

Krieshok, T. S. (1998). An anti-introspectivist view of career decision making. *Career Development Quarterly, 46,* 210–229.

Krumboltz, J. D. (1966a). Behavioral goals of counseling. *Journal of Counseling Psychology, 13,* 153–159.

Krumboltz, J. D. (Ed.). (1966b). *Revolution in counseling.* Boston: Houghton Mifflin.

Krumboltz, J. D. (1979). *Social learning and career decision making.* New York: Carroll.

Krumboltz, J. D. (1991). *Manual for the Career Beliefs Inventory.* Palo Alto, CA: Consulting Psychologists Press.

Krumboltz, J. D. (1992, December). Challenging troublesome career beliefs. *CAPS Digest,* EDO-CG-92-4.

Krumboltz, J. D. (1994). Integrating career and personal counseling. *Career Development Quarterly, 42,* 143–148.

Krumboltz, J. D. (1996). A learning theory of career counseling. In M. Savickas & B. Walsh (Eds.), *Integrating career theory and practice* (pp. 233–280). Palo Alto, CA: CPP Books.

Krumboltz, J. D., & Levin, A. S. (2004). *Luck is no accident.* Atascadero, CA: Impact Publishers.

Krumboltz, J. D., & Mitchell, L. K. (1979). Relevant rigorous research. *Counseling Psychologist, 8*, 50–52.

Krusi, A., Fast, D., Small, W., Wood, E., & Kerr, T. (2010). Social and structural barriers to housing among street-involved youth who use illicit drugs. *Health & Social Care in the Community, 18*(3), 282–288.

Kubler-Ross, E. (1969). *On death and dying.* New York: Macmillan.

Kuder, F. (1939). *Manual for the Preference Record.* Chicago: Science Research Associates.

Kuder, F. (1977). *Activity interest and occupational choice.* Chicago: Science Research Associates.

Kufeldt, K., & Nimmo, M. (1987). Kids on the street they have something to say: Survey of runaway and homeless youth. *Journal of Child Care, 3*(2), 53–61.

Kuh, G. D. (1996). *Student learning outside the classroom: Transcending artificial boundaries.* Washington, DC: George Washington University.

Kuh, G. D., Bean, J. R., Bradley, R. K., & Coomes, M. D. (1986). Contributions of student affairs journals to the literature on college students. *Journal of College Student Personnel, 27*, 292–304.

Kunkel, M. A., & Newsom, S. (1996). Presenting problems for mental health services: A concept map. *Journal of Mental Health Counseling, 18*, 53–63.

Kurpius, D. J. (1978). Consultation theory and process: An integrated model. *Personnel and Guidance Journal, 56*, 335–338.

Kurpius, D. J. (1986a). Consultation: An important human and organizational intervention. *Journal of Counseling and Human Service Professions, 1*, 58–66.

Kurpius, D. J. (1986b). The helping relationship. In M. D. Lewis, R. L. Hayes, & J. A. Lewis (Eds.), *The counseling profession* (pp. 96–129). Itasca, IL: F. E. Peacock.

Kurpius, D. J. (1988). *Handbook of consultation: An intervention for advocacy and outreach.* Alexandria, VA: American Counseling Association.

Kurpius, D. J., & Brubaker, J. C. (1976). *Psycho-educational consultation: Definitions-functions-preparation.* Bloomington: Indiana University Press.

Kurpius, D. J., & Fuqua, D. R. (1993). Fundamental issues in defining consultation. *Journal of Counseling and Development, 71*, 598–600.

Kurpius, D. J., Fuqua, D. R., & Rozecki, T. (1993). The consulting process: A multidimensional approach. *Journal of Counseling and Development, 71*, 601–606.

Kurpius, D. J., & Robinson, S. E. (1978). An overview of consultation. *Personnel and Guidance Journal, 56*, 321–323.

Kurtz, P. D., & Tandy, C. C. (1995). Narrative family interventions. In A. C. Kilpatrick & T. P. Holland (Eds.), *Working with families* (pp. 177–197). Boston: Allyn & Bacon.

Kushman, J. W., Sieber, C., & Heariold-Kinney, P. (2000). This isn't the place for me: School dropout. In D. Capuzzi & D. R. Gross (Eds.), *Youth at risk* (3rd ed., pp. 471–507). Alexandria, VA: American Counseling Association.

Kutcher, S., & McLuckie, A. (2009). Evergreen: Towards a child and youth mental health framework for Canada. *Journal of the Canadian Academy of Child and Adolescent Psychiatry, 18*(2), 89–91.

L'Abate, L. (1992). Introduction. In L. L'Abate, G. E. Farrar, & D. A. Serritella (Eds.), *Handbook of differential treatments for addiction* (pp. 1–4). Boston: Allyn & Bacon.

L'Abate, L., Farrar, G. E., & Serritella, D. A. (Eds.). (1992). *Handbook of differential treatments for addiction.* Boston: Allyn & Bacon.

L'Abate, L., & Thaxton, M. L. (1981). Differentiation of resources in mental health delivery: Implications of training. *Professional Psychology, 12*, 761–767.

LaBarge, E. (1981). Counseling patients with senile dementia of the Alzheimer type and their families. *Personnel and Guidance Journal, 60*, 139–142.

LaCross, M. B. (1975). Non-verbal behavior and perceived counselor attractiveness and persuasiveness. *Journal of Counseling Psychology, 22*, 563–566.

Ladd, E. T. (1971). Counselors, confidences, and the civil liberties of clients. *Personnel and Guidance Journal, 50*, 261–268.

LaFountain, R. M., & Bartos, R. B. (2002). *Research and statistics made meaningful in counseling and student affairs.* Pacific Grove, CA: Brooks/ Cole.

LaFountain, R. M., Garner, N. E., & Eliason, G. T. (1996). Solutionfocused counseling groups: A key for school counselors. *School Counselor, 43*, 256–267.

Laird, G. (2007). *Shelter-homelessness in a growth economy: Canada's 21st century paradox. A report for the Sheldon Chumir Foundation for Ethics in Leadership.* Retrieved from **www.chumirethicsfoundation.ca/files/pdf/SHELTER.pdf**.

Laker, D. R. (2002). The career wheel: An exercise for exploring and validating one's career choices. *Journal of Employment Counseling, 39*, 61–71.

Lalande, V. (2004). Counselling psychology: A Canadian perspective. *Counselling Psychology Quarterly, 17*(3), 273–286.

Lalande, V., & Laverty, A. (2010). Creating connections: Best practices in counselling girls and women. In N. Arthur & S. Collins (Eds.), *Culture-infused counselling: Celebrating the Canadian mosaic* (2nd ed) (pp. 339–362). Calgary, AB: Counselling Concepts.

Lalande, V., & Magnusson, K. (2007). Measuring the impact of career development services in Canada: Current and preferred practices. *Canadian Journal of Counselling, 41*(3), 133–145.

Lalande, V. M., Crozier, S. D., & Davey, H. (2000). Women's career development and relationships: A qualitative inquiry. *Canadian Journal of Counselling, 34*(3), 193–203.

Lam, C. S., Hilburger, J., Kornbleuth, M., Jenkins, J., Brown, D., & Racenstein, J. M. (1996). A treatment matching model for substance abuse rehabilitation clients. *Rehabilitation Counseling Bulletin, 39*, 202–216.

Lambert, J. E., & Williams, R. A. (2009). Theory and practice of counseling families. In I. Marini & M. A. Stebnicki (Eds.), *The professional counselor's desk reference* (pp. 591–603). New York, NY: Springer.

Lambert, M. J., Masters, K. S., & Ogles, B. M. (1991). Outcome research in counseling. In C. E. Watkins, Jr., & L. J. Schneider (Eds.), *Research in counseling* (pp. 51–83). Hillsdale, NJ: Erlbaum.

Lambie, G. W. (2007). The contribution of ego development level to burnout in school counselors: Implications for professional school counseling. *Journal of Counseling and Development, 85*, 82–88.

Lampropoulos, G. K., Schneider, M. K., & Spengler, P. M. (2009). Predictors of early termination in a university counseling training clinic. *Journal of Counseling & Development, 87*(1), 36–46.

Landis, L. L., & Young, M. E. (1994). The reflective team in counselor education. *Counselor Education and Supervision, 33*, 210–218.

Landreth, G. L. (2002). *Play therapy: The art of the relationship* (2nd ed.). New York: Brunner-Routledge.

Langer, N. (2004). Resiliency and spirituality: Foundations of strengths perspective counseling with the elderly. *Educational Gerontology, 30*(7), 611–617.

Lanning, W. (1992, December). Ethical codes and responsible decision-making. *ACA Guidepost, 35*, 21.

Lapan, R. T., Gysbers, N. C., & Petroski, G. F. (2001). Helping seventh graders be safe and successful: A statewide study of the impact of comprehensive guidance and counseling programs. *Journal of Counseling and Development, 79*, 320–330.

Latimer, J., & Foss, L. C. (2005). The sentencing of aboriginal and non-aboriginal youth under the young offenders act: A multivariate analysis. *Canadian Journal of Criminology and Criminal Justice, 47*(3), 481–500.

Latner, J. D., & Wilson, G. T. (2000). Cognitive-behavioral therapy and nutritional counseling in the treatment of bulimia nervosa and binge eating. *Eating Behaviors, 1*(1), 3–21.

Lau, M. A., Bishop, S. R., Segal, Z. V., Buis, T., Anderson, N. D., Carlson, L., ... Devins, G. (2006). The Toronto Mindfulness Scale: Development and validation. *Journal of Clinical Psychology, 62*(12), 1445–1467.

Laux, J. M., Salyers, K. M., & Kotova, E. (2005). A psychometric evaluation of the SASSI-3 in a college sample. *Journal of College Counseling, 8*, 41–51.

Law, H. (2008). Narrative coaching and psychology of learning from multicultural perspectives. In S. Palmer & A. Whybrow (Eds.), *Handbook of coaching psychology: A guide for practitioners* (pp. 174–192). New York, NY: Routledge/Taylor & Francis.

Lawler, A. C. (1990). The healthy self: Variations on a theme. *Journal of Counseling and Development, 68*, 652–654.

Lawrence, G., & Kurpius, S. E. R. (2000). Legal and ethical issues involved when counseling minors in nonschool settings. *Journal of Counseling and Development, 78*, 130–136.

Lawson, A. W. (1994). Family therapy and addictions. In J. A. Lewis (Ed.), *Addiction: Concepts and strategies for treatment* (pp. 211–232). Gathersburg, MD: Aspen.

Lawson, D. (1989). Peer helping programs in the colleges and universities of Quebec and Ontario. *Canadian Journal of Counselling, 23*(1), 41–54.

Lawson, D. (1994). Identifying pretreatment change. *Journal of Counseling and Development, 72*, 244–248.

Lawson, G., Venart, E., Hazler, R. J., & Kottler, J. A. (2007). Toward a culture of counselor wellness. *Journal of Humanistic Counseling, Education and Development, 46*, 5–19.

Layne, C. M., & Hohenshil, T. H. (2005). High tech counseling: Revisited. *Journal of Counseling and Development, 83*, 222–226.

Lazarus, A. A. (1985). Behavior rehearsal. In A. S. Bellack & M. Hersen (Eds.), *Dictionary of behavior therapy techniques* (p. 22). New York: Pergamon.

Lazarus, A. A. (2008). Multimodal therapy. In R. J. Corsini & D. Wedding (Eds.), *Current psychotherapies* (8th ed., pp. 368–401). Belmont, CA: Thomson Brooks/ Cole.

Lazarus, A. A., & Beutler, L. E. (1993). On technical eclecticism. *Journal of Counseling and Development, 71*, 381–385.

Lazarus, A. P. (1989). *The practice of multimodal therapy: Systematic, comprehensive, and effective psychotherapy.* Baltimore: Johns Hopkins University Press.

Lazarus, R. S., & Folkman, S. (1984). *Stress, appraisal, and coping.* New York, NY: Springer-Verlag.

Leaman, D. R. (1978). Confrontation in counseling. *Personnel and Guidance Journal, 56*, 630–633.

Learner, B. (1981). Representative democracy, "men of zeal," and testing legislation. *American Psychologist, 36*, 270–275.

Learning Strategies Development. (2006). *Mindfulness-based stress reduction: What is mindfulness?* Retrieved from **www.bewell-dowell.org/sos/mindfulness_stress_reduction_grad.html**.

Leatherdale, S. T., Hammond, D., & Ahmed, R. (2008). Alcohol, marijuana, and tobacco use patterns among youth in Canada. *Cancer Causes & Control, 19*(4), 361–369.

Ledesma, D., & Kumano, H. (2009). Mindfulness-based stress reduction and cancer: A meta-analysis. *Psycho-Oncology, 18*(6), 571–579.

Lee, C. C. (1989). AMCD: The next generation. *Journal of Multicultural Counseling and Development, 17*, 165–170.

Lee, C. C. (1998). Professional counseling in a global context: Collaboration for international social action. In C. C. Lee & G. R. Walz (Eds.), *Social action: A mandate for counselors* (pp. 293–306). Alexandria, VA: American Counseling Association.

Lee, C. C. (2001). Culturally responsive school counselors and programs: Addressing the needs of all students. *Professional School Counseling, 4*, 257–261.

Lee, C. C. (Ed.). (2006a). *Counseling for social justice* (2nd ed.). Alexandria, VA: American Counseling Association.

Lee, C. C. (Ed.). (2006b). *Multicultural issues in counseling: New approaches to diversity* (3rd ed.). Alexandria, VA: American Counseling Association.

Lee, C. C., & Walz, G. R. (Eds.). (1998). *Social action: A mandate for counselors.* Alexandria, VA: American Counseling Association.

Lee, C. M. (2007). From clinical trials to professional training: A graduate course in evidence-based interventions for children, youth, and families. *Training and Education in Professional Psychology, 1*(3), 215–223.

Lee, R. M., & Robbins, S. B. (2000). Understanding social connectedness in college women and men. *Journal of Counseling and Development, 78*, 484–491.

Leech, N. L., & Kees, N. L. (2005). Researching women's groups: Findings, limitations, and recommendations. *Journal of Counseling and Development, 83*, 367–373.

Leedy, P. D., & Ormrod, J. E. (2001). *Practical research* (7th ed.). Upper Saddle River, NJ: Merrill/ Prentice Hall.

Lefrancois, G. R. (1987). *The lifespan* (2nd ed.). Belmont, CA: Wadsworth/Thomson.

Lehman, C. (1993, January 30). Faith-based counseling gains favor: Approach combines spirituality, sciene. *The Washington Post*, pp. B7–B8.

Leibert, T. W. (2006). Making change visible: The possibilities in assessing mental health counseling outcomes. *Journal of Counseling and Development, 84*, 108–113.

Leierer, S. J., Strohmer, D. C., Leclere, W. A., Cornwell, B. J., & Whitten, S. L. (1996). The effect of counselor disability, attending behavior, and client problem on counseling. *Rehabilitation Counseling Bulletin, 40*, 92–96.

Lenhardt, A. M. C. (1997). Grieving disenfranchised losses: Background and strategies for counselors. *Journal of Humanistic Education and Development, 35*, 208–218.

Leonard, M. M., & Collins, A. M. (1979). Woman as footnote. *Counseling Psychologist, 8*, 6–7.

Leong, F. T. L. (Ed.). (1995). *Career development and vocational behavior of racial and ethnic minorities*. Hillsdale, NJ: Erlbaum.

Lerner, S., & Lerner, H. (1983). A systematic approach to resistance: Theoretical and technical considerations. *American Journal of Psychotherapy, 37*, 387–399.

Leslie, R. S. (2004, July/August). Minimizing liability. *Family Therapy Magazine, 3*(4), 46–48.

Levant, R. F., Richmond, K., Majors, R. G., Inclan, J. E., Rossello, J. M., Heesacker, M., ... Sellers, A. (2003). A multicultural investigation of masculinity ideology and alexithymia. *Psychology of Men & Masculinity, 4*(2), 91–99.

Levenson, A. J. (1981). Ageism: A major deterrent to the introduction of curricula in aging. *Gerontology and Geriatrics Education, 1*, 161–162.

Levine, E. (1983). A training model that stresses the dynamic dimensions of counseling. *Personnel and Guidance Journal, 61*, 431–433.

Levin, M., & Hayes, S. C. (2009). Is acceptance and commitment therapy superior to established treatment comparisons? *Psychotherapy and Psychosomatics, 78*, 380.

LeVine, R. A., & Campbell, D. T. (1972). *Ethnocentrism: Theories of conflict, attitudes and group behavior*. New York, NY: Wiley.

Levinson, H. (2009). How organizational consultation differs from counseling. In H. Levinson, A. M. Freedman, & K. H. Bradt (Eds.), *Consulting psychology: Selected articles by Harry Levinson* (pp. 209–210). Washington, DC: American Psychological Association.

Lewin, S. S., Ramseur, J. H., & Sink, J. M. (1979). The role of private rehabilitation: Founder, catalyst, competitor. *Journal of Rehabilitation, 45*, 16–19.

Lewing, R. J., Jr., & Cowger, E. L., Jr. (1982). Time spent on college counselor functions. *Journal of College Student Personnel, 23*, 41–48.

Lewis, J., & Lewis, M. (1989). *Community counseling*. Pacific Grove, CA: Brooks/Cole.

Lewis, J. A., Hayes, B. A., & Bradley, L. J. (Eds.). (1992). *Counseling women over the life span*. Denver: Love.

Lewis, J. A., & Lewis, M. D. (1977). *Community counseling: A human service approach*. New York: Wiley.

Lewis, R. A., & Gilhousen, M. R. (1981). Myths of career development: A cognitive approach to vocational counseling. *Personnel and Guidance Journal, 59*, 296–299.

Lewis, R. E., & Borunda, R. (2006). Lived stories: Participatory leadership in school counseling. *Journal of Counseling and Development, 84*, 406–413.

Lewis, W. (1996). A proposal for initiating family counseling interventions by school counselors. *School Counselor, 44*, 93–99.

Lewis, W. M. (1992). Practical counseling techniques: A training guide for counseling homeless families. In C. Solomon & P. Jackson-Jobe (Eds.), *Helping homeless people: Unique challenges and solutions* (pp. 85–99). Alexandria, VA: American Association for Counseling.

Lichtenstein, E., Zhu, S-H., & Tedeschi, G. J. (2010). Smoking cessation quitlines: An underrecognized intervention success story. *American Psychologist, 65*(4), 252–261.

Liddle, B. J. (1999). Gay and lesbian clients' ratings of psychiatrists, psychologists, social workers, and counselors. *Journal of Gay & Lesbian Psychotherapy, 3*, 81–93.

Lieberman, M. A. (1991). Group methods. In F. H. Kanfer & A. P. Goldstein (Eds.), *Helping people change: A textbook of methods* (4th ed.). Boston: Allyn & Bacon.

Lieberman, M. A. (1994). Self-help groups. In H. I. Kaplan & B. J. Sadock (Eds.), *Comprehensive group psychotherapy* (3rd ed.). Baltimore: Williams & Wilkins.

Lightman, E. S., Mitchell, A., & Herd, D. (2008). Globalization, precarious work, and the food bank. *Journal of Sociology and Social Welfare, 35*(2), 9–28.

Lim, I. M. (2010). Key factors in California middle schools gang prevention programs. *Dissertation Abstracts International Section A: Humanities and Social Sciences, 70*(8-A), 2891.

Lindemann, E. (1944). Symptomatology and management of acute grief. *American Journal of Psychiatry, 101*, 141–148.

Lindemann, E. (1956). The meaning of crisis in individual and family. *Teachers College Record, 57*, 310.

Linley, P. A. (2006). Counseling psychology's positive psychological agenda: A model for integration and inspiration. *The Counseling Psychologist, 34*(2), 313–322.

Lipnevich, A. A., & Smith, J. K. (2009). Russian and American perspectives on self-regulated learning. *The International Journal of Creativity & Problem Solving, 19*(1), 83–100.

Lippert, L. (1997). Women at midlife: Implications for theories of women's adult development. *Journal of Counseling and Development, 76*, 16–22.

Littrell, J. M. (2001). Allen E. Ivey: Transforming counseling theory and practice. *Journal of Counseling and Development, 79*, 105–118.

Littrell, J. M., & Peterson, J. S. (2001). Transforming the school culture: A model based on an exemplary counselor. *Professional School Counseling, 4*, 310–313.

Liu, W. M., & Estrada-Hernandez, N. (2010). Counseling and advocacy for individuals living in poverty. In M. J. Ratts, R. L. Toporek, & J. A. Lewis (Eds.), *ACA advocacy competencies: A social justice framework for counselors* (pp. 43–53). Alexandria, VA: American Counseling Association.

Lively, K. (1998, May 15). At Michigan State, a protest escalated into a night of fires, tear gas, and arrests. *Chronicle of Higher Education, 44,* A46.

Livneh, H., & Antonak, R. F. (2005). Psychosocial adaptation to chronic illness and disability: A primer for counselors. *Journal of Counseling and Development, 83,* 12–20.

Livneh, H., & Evans, J. (1984). Adjusting to disability: Behavioral correlates and intervention strategies. *Personnel and Guidance Journal, 62,* 363–368.

Livneh, H., & Sherwood-Hawes, A. (1993). Group counseling approaches with persons who have sustained myocardial infarction. *Journal of Counseling and Development, 72,* 57–61.

Lix, L. M., Bruce, S., Sarkar, J., & Young, T. K. (2009, October). Risk factors and chronic conditions among Aboriginal and non-Aboriginal populations. *Statistics Canada.* Retrieved from **www.statcan.gc.ca/pub/82–003–x/2009004/article/10934–eng.pdf**

Locke, D. C. (1990). A not so provincial view of multicultural counseling. *Counselor Education and Supervision, 30,* 18–25.

Locke, D. C. (1998, Spring). Beyond U.S. borders. *American Counselor, 1,* 13–16.

Locke, W. S., & Gibbons, M. M. (2008). On her own again: The use of narrative therapy in career counseling with displaced new traditionalists. *The Family Journal, 16*(2), 132–138.

Lockhart, E. J., & Keys, S. G. (1998). The mental health counseling role of school counselors. *Professional School Counseling, 1*(4), 3–6.

Loesch, L. (1977). Guest editorial. *Elementary School Guidance and Counseling, 12,* 74–75.

Loesch, L. (1984). Professional credentialing in counseling: 1984. *Counseling and Human Development, 17,* 1–11.

Logan, W. L. (1997). Peer consultation group: Doing what works for counselors. *Professional School Counseling, 1,* 4–6.

London, M. (1982). How do you say good-bye after you've said hello? *Personnel and Guidance Journal, 60,* 412–414.

Long, L. L., & Young, M. E. (2007). *Counseling and therapy for couples* (2nd ed.). Belmont, CA: Thomson Brooks/Cole.

Lonigan, C. J., Elbert, J. C., & Johnson, S. B. Empirically supported psychosocial interventions for children: An overview. *Journal of Clinical Child Psychology, 27*(2), 138–145.

Lopez, F. G. (1986). Family structure and depression: Implications for the counseling of depressed college students. *Journal of Counseling and Development, 64,* 508–511.

Lopez, S. J., Edwards, L. M., Pedrotti, J. T., Prosser, E. C., LaRue, S., Spalitto, S. V., et al. (2006). Beyond the DSM-IV: Assumptions, alternatives, and alterations. *Journal of Counseling and Development, 84,* 259–267.

Lowman, R. L. (1993). The interdomain model of career assessment and counseling. *Journal of Counseling and Development, 71,* 549–554.

Loxley, J. C., & Whiteley, J. M. (1986). *Character development in college students.* Alexandria, VA: American Counseling Association.

Luber, M. (Ed). (2010). *Eye movement desensitization and reprocessing (EMDR) scripted protocols: Special populations.* New York, NY: Springer.

Luborsky, E. B., O'Reilly-Landry, M., & Arlow, J. A. (2008). Psychoanalysis. In R. J. Corsini & D. Wedding (Eds.), *Current psychotherapies* (8th ed., pp. 15–62). Belmont, CA: Thomson Brooks/ Cole.

Lucas, M. S., Skokowski, C. T., & Ancis, J. R. (2000). Contextual themes in career decision making of female clients who indicate depression. *Journal of Counseling and Development, 78,* 316–325.

Luft, J. (1970). *Group process: An introduction to group dynamics.* Palo Alto, CA: National Press Books.

Lundervold, D. A., & Belwood, M. F. (2000). The best kept secret in counseling: Single-case (N = 1) experimental design. *Journal of Counseling and Development, 78,* 92–102.

Lusky, M. B., & Hayes, R. L. (2001). Collaborative consultation and program evaluation. *Journal of Counseling and Development, 79,* 26–38.

Luzzo, D. A., & McWhirter, E. H. (2001). Sex and ethnic differences in the perception of educational and career-related barriers and levels of coping efficacy. *Journal of Counseling and Development, 79,* 61–67.

Lyddon, W. J., Clay, A. L., & Sparks, C. L. (2001). Metaphor and change in counseling. *Journal of Counseling and Development, 79,* 269–274.

Lynch, A. Q. (1985). The Myers-Briggs Type Indicator: A tool for appreciating employee and client diversity. *Journal of Employment Counseling, 22,* 104–109.

Lynch, R. K., & Maki, D. (1981). Searching for structure: A trait-factor approach to vocational rehabilitation. *Vocational Guidance Quarterly, 30,* 61–68.

Lynch, R. T., & Gussel, L. (1996). Disclosure and self-advocacy regarding disability-related needs: Strategies to maximize integration in postsecondary education. *Journal of Counseling and Development, 74,* 352–357.

Lynch, T. R., Trost, W. T., Salsman, N., & Linehan, M. M. (2007). Dialectical behavior therapy for borderline personality disorder. *Annual Review of Clinical Psychology, 3,* 181–205.

Lynn, S. J., & Frauman, D. (1985). Group psychotherapy. In S. J. Lynn & J. P. Garske (Eds.), *Contemporary psychotherapies: Models and methods* (pp. 419–458). Upper Saddle River, NJ: Merrill/Prentice Hall.

Maag, J., & Kotlash, J. (1994). Review of stress inoculation training with children and adolescents: Issues and recommendations. *Behavior Modification, 18,* 443–469.

MacCluskie, K. C. (1998). A review of eye movement desensitization and reprocessing (EMDR): Research findings and implications for counsellors. *Canadian Journal of Counselling, 32*(2), 116–137.

Madanes, C. (1984). *Behind the one-way mirror: Advances in the practice of strategic therapy.* San Francisco: Jossey-Bass.

Magnuson, S. (1996). Charlotte's web: Expanding a classroom activity for a guidance lesson. *Elementary School Guidance and Counseling, 31,* 75–76.

Mahalik, J. R., Good, G. E., & Englar-Carlson, M. (2003). Masculinity scripts, presenting concerns, and help seeking:

Implications for practice and training. *Professional Psychology: Research and Practice, 34*(2), 123–131.

Maholick, L. T., & Turner, D. W. (1979). Termination: The difficult farewell. *American Journal of Psychotherapy, 33,* 583–591.

Manassis, K. (2005). Family Involvement in psychotherapy: What's the evidence? In J. L. Hudson & R. M. Rapee (Eds.), *Psychopathology and the family* (pp. 283–300). New York, NY: Elsevier Science.

Manhal-Baugus, M. (1998). The self-in-relation theory and Women for Sobriety: Female-specific theory and mutual help group for chemically dependent women. *Journal of Addiction and Offender Counseling, 18,* 78–87.

Mann, D. (1986). Dropout prevention: Getting serious about programs that work. *NASSP Bulletin, 70,* 66–73.

Manthei, R. J. (1983). Client choice of therapist or therapy. *Personnel and Guidance Journal, 61,* 334–340.

Maples, M. F., & Abney, P. C. (2006). Baby boomers mature and gerontological counseling comes of age. *Journal of Counseling and Development, 84,* 3–9.

Maples, M. F., Dupey, P., Torres-Rivera, E., Phan, L. T., Vereen, L., & Garrett, M. T. (2001). Ethnic diversity and the use of humor in counseling: Appropriate or inappropriate? *Journal of Counseling and Development, 79,* 53–60.

Maples, M. F., Packman, J., Abney, P., Daugherty, R. F., Casey, J. A., & Pirtle, L. (2005). Suicide by teenagers in middle school: A postvention team approach. *Journal of Counseling and Development, 83,* 397–405.

Maples, M. R., & Luzzo, D. A. (2005). Evaluating DISCOVER's effectiveness in enhancing college students' social cognitive career development. *Career Development Quarterly, 53,* 274–285.

Margolin, G. (1982). Ethical and legal considerations in marital and family therapy. *American Psychologist, 37,* 788–801.

Marino, T. M. (1994, December). Starving for acceptance. *Counseling Today, 37,* 1, 4.

Marino, T. W. (1996, July). Looking for greener pastures. *Counseling Today,* 16.

Marinoble, R. M. (1998). Homosexuality: A blind spot in the school mirror. *Professional School Counseling, 1,* 4–7.

Marken, R. (1981). *Methods in experimental psychology.* Pacific Grove, CA: Brooks/Cole.

Markham, A. N., & Baym, N. K. (Eds.) (2009). *Internet inquiry: Conversations about method.* Thousand Oaks, CA: Sage.

Marks, L. I., & McLaughlin, R. H. (2005). Outreach by college counselors: Increasing student attendance at presentations. *Journal of College Counseling, 8,* 86–96.

Marotta, S. A. (2000). Best practices for counselors who treat posttraumatic stress disorder. *Journal of Counseling and Development, 78,* 492–495.

Marotta, S. A., & Asner, K. K. (1999). Group psychotherapy for women with a history of incest: The research base. *Journal of Counseling and Development, 77,* 315–323.

Marquis, R. A., & Flynn, R. J. (2009). The SDQ as a mental health measurement tool in a Canadian sample of looked-after young people. *Vulnerable Children and Youth Studies, 4*(2), 114–121.

Marshall, E. A., & Uhlemann, M. R. (1996). Counseling in Canada. In W. Evraiff (Ed.), *Counseling in Pacific Rim countries: Past – present – future* (pp. 17–30). San Mateo, CA: Lake Press.

Martin, D., & Martin, M. (1989). Bridging the gap between research and practice. *Journal of Counseling and Development, 67,* 491–492.

Martin, P., & Fontana, J. (1990). *National Liberal task force on housing.* National Liberal Caucus, Parliament of Canada, Ottawa, ON. Retrieved from **http://action.web.ca/ home/housing/resources.shtml?x=67127&AA_EX_ Session=fd83bd77975ac7a2110113d712acd060.**

Maske, M. (2007, July 18). Falcons' Vick indicted in dog fighting case. *Washington Post,* p. E1.

Maslow, A. H. (1962). *Toward a psychology of being.* Princeton, NJ: Van Nostrand.

Mason, O., & Hargreaves, I. (2001). A qualitative study of mindfulness-based cognitive therapy for depression. *British Journal of Medical Psychology, 74,* 197–212.

Mastercard Worldwide. (2006, December). *Masterindex of Canadian women consumers.* Retrieved from **www.mastercard.com/ca/wce/PDF/15860_MasterIndex-06–EN.pdf.**

Mathewson, R. H. (1949). *Guidance policy and practice.* New York: Harper.

Mathiasen, R. E. (1984). Attitudes and needs of the college student-client. *Journal of College Student Personnel, 25,* 274–275.

Maticka-Tyndale, E. (2008). Commentary: Sexuality and sexual health of Canadian adolescents: Yesterday, today and tomorrow. *Canadian Journal of Human Sexuality, 17*(3), 85–95.

Matthews, C. R. (2005). Infusing lesbian, gay, and bisexual issues into counselor education. *Journal of Humanistic Counseling, Education and Development, 44,* 168–184.

Matthews, C. R., Lorah, P., & Fenton, J. (2006). Treatment experiences of gays and lesbians in recovery from addiction: A qualitative inquiry. *Journal of Mental Health Counseling, 28,* 110–132.

Matthews, C. R., Selvidge, M. M. D., & Fisher, K. (2005). Addictions counselors' attitudes and behaviors toward gay, lesbian, and bisexual clients. *Journal of Counseling and Development, 83,* 57–65.

Matthews, D. B., & Burnett, D. D. (1989). Anxiety: An achievement component. *Journal of Humanistic Education and Development, 27,* 122–131.

Maultsby, M. C., Jr. (1984). *Rational behavior therapy.* Upper Saddle River, NJ: Prentice Hall.

Maultsby, M. C., Jr. (1986). Teaching rational self-counseling to middle graders. *School Counselor, 33,* 207–219.

Maxfield, L. (2009). Twenty years of EMDR. *Journal of EMDR Practice and Research, 3*(3), 115–116.

Maxwell, M. (2007). Career counseling is personal counseling: A constructivist approach to nurturing the development of gifted female adolescents. *Career Development Quarterly, 55,* 206–224.

May, J. C. (2005). Family attachment narrative therapy: Healing the experience of early childhood maltreatment. *Journal of Marital and Family Therapy, 31,* 221–237.

May, K. M. (1996). Naturalistic inquiry and counseling: Contemplating commonalities. *Counseling and Values, 40,* 219–229.

May, R. (1975). *The courage to create.* New York: Norton.

May, R. (2005). How do we know what works? *Journal of College Student Psychotherapy, 19*(3), 69–73.

May, R., Remen, N., Young, D., & Berland, W. (1985). The wounded healer. *Saybrook Review, 5,* 84–93.

Maynard, P. E., & Olson, D. H. (1987). Circumplex model of family systems: A treatment tool in family counseling. *Journal of Counseling and Development, 65,* 502–504.

Mays, D. T., & Franks, C. M. (1980). Getting worse: Psychotherapy or no treatment: The jury should still be out. *Professional Psychology, 2,* 78–92.

McAuliffe, G., & Lovell, C. (2006). The influence of counselor epistemology on the helping interview: A qualitative study. *Journal of Counseling and Development, 84,* 308–317.

McBride, M. C., & Martin, G. E. (1990). A framework for eclecticism: The importance of theory to mental health counseling. *Journal of Mental Health Counseling, 12,* 495–505.

McCarthy, B., & Hagan, J. (1992). Surviving on the street: The experiences of homeless youth. *Journal of Adolescent Research, 7*(4), 412–430.

McCarthy, C. J., Brack, C. J., Lambert, R. G., Brack, G., & Orr, D. P. (1996). Predicting emotional and behavioral risk factors in adolescents. *School Counselor, 43,* 277–286.

McCarthy, M., & Sorenson, G. (1993). School counselors and consultants: Legal duties and liabilities. *Journal of Counseling and Development, 72,* 159–167.

McCarthy, P., DeBell, C., Kanuha, V., & McLeod, J. (1988). Myths of supervision: Identifying the gaps between theory and practice. *Counselor Education and Supervision, 28,* 22–28.

McClure, B. A. (1990). The group mind: Generative and regressive groups. *Journal for Specialists in Group Work, 15,* 159–170.

McClure, B. A. (1994). The shadow side of regressive groups. *Counseling and Values, 38,* 77–89.

McClure, B. A., & Russo, T. R. (1996). The politics of counseling: Looking back and forward. *Counseling and Values, 40,* 162–174.

McColl, M. A., Jarzynowska, A., & Shortt, S. E. D. (2010). Unmet health care needs of people with disabilities: Population level evidence. *Disability & Society, 25*(2), 205–218.

McCollum, E. E. (2007). Introduction to the special issue. *Journal of Family Psychotherapy, 18*(3), 1–9.

McCormick, J. F. (1998). Ten summer rejuvenators for school counselors. *Professional School Counseling, 1,* 61–63.

McCormick, N. B. (2010). Preface to sexual scripts: Social and therapeutic implications. *Sexual and Relationship Therapy, 25*(1), 91–95.

McCormick, R. M. (1997). Healing through interdependence: The role of connecting in First Nations healing practices. *Canadian Journal of Counselling, 31*(3), 172–184.

McCormick, R. M. (2000). Aboriginal traditions in the treatment of substance abuse. *Canadian Journal of Counselling, 34*(1), 25–32.

McCormick, R. M., Neumann, H., Amundson, N. E., & McLean, H. B. (1999). First Nations Career/Life Planning Model: Guidelines for practitioners. *Journal of Employment Counseling, 36*(4), 167–176.

McCoy, G. A. (1994, April). A plan for the first group session. *ASCA Counselor, 31,* 18.

McCracken, J. E., Hayes, J. A., & Dell, D. (1997). Attributions of responsibility for memory problems in older and younger adults. *Journal of Counseling and Development, 75,* 385–391.

McCullough, J. J. (2010). The regions of Canada: Quebec. *J. J.'s complete guide to Canada.* Retrieved from **www. filibustercartoons.com/New%20Canada%20Guide/ index.php?page=quebec.**

McDade, S. A. (1989). Leadership development: A key to the new leadership role of student affairs professionals. *NASPA Journal, 27,* 33–41.

McDanial, S. H., & Gergen, K. J. (1993). Harold A. Goolishian (1924–1991): Obituary. *American Psychologist, 48*(3), 292.

McDaniels, C. (1984). The work/ leisure connection. *Vocational Guidance Quarterly, 33,* 35–44.

McDonald, M. (2000, May). *The governance of health research involving human subjects (HRIHS).* Depository Services, Government of Canada. Retrieved from dsp-psd.pwgsc.gc.ca/collection_2008/lcc-cdc/JL2–45–2000E.pdf

McEneaney, A. M. S., & Gross, J. M. (2009). Introduction to the special issue: Group interventions in college counseling centers. *International Journal of Group Psychotherapy, 59*(4), 455–460.

McEwan, K. L., Donnelly, M., Robertson, D., & Hertzman, C. (1991). *Mental health problems among Canada's seniors: Demographic and epidemiologic considerations.* Ottawa: Health and Welfare Canada.

McFadden, J. (Ed.). (1999). *Transcultural counseling* (2nd ed.). Alexandria, VA: American Counseling Association.

McFadden, J., & Lipscomb, W. D. (1985). History of the Association for Non-white Concerns in Personnel and Guidance. *Journal of Counseling and Development, 63,* 444–447.

McGannon, W., Carey, J., & Dimmitt, C. (2005). *The current status of school counseling outcome research* (Research Monograph No. 2). Amherst: Center for School Counseling Outcome Research, University of Massachusetts, School of Education.

McGoldrick, M., Gerson, R., & Petry, S. (2008). *Genograms: Assessment and intervention* (3rd ed.). New York: Norton.

McGowan, A. S. (1995). "Suffer the little children": A developmental perspective. *Journal of Humanistic Education and Development, 34,* 50–51.

McHugh, M. C., Koeske, R. D., & Frieze, I. H. (1986). Issues to consider in conducting nonsexist psychological research. *American Psychologist, 41,* 879–890.

McKirnan, D., Stokes, J., Doll, L., & Burzette, R. (1995). Bisexually active males: social characteristics and sexual behavior. *Journal of Sex Research, 32,* 65–76.

McLean, R., & Marini, I. (2008). Working with gay men from a narrative counseling perspective: A case study. *Journal of LGBT Issues in Counseling, 2*(3), 243–257.

McLeod, J. (1995). *Doing counselling research*. Thousand Oaks, CA: Sage.

McMahon, M., & Patton, W. (1997). Gender differences in children and adolescents' perceptions of influences on their career development. *School Counselor, 44*, 368–376.

McNally, R. J. (1999). EMDR and Mesmerism: A comparative historical analysis. *Journal of Anxiety Disorders, 13*(1–2), 225–236.

McWey, L. M. (2004). Predictors of attachment styles of children in foster care: An attachment theory model for working with families. *Journal of Marital and Family Therapy, 30*, 439–452.

McWhirter, J. J., McWhirter, B. T., McWhirter, A. M., & McWhirter, E. H. (1994). High- and low-risk characteristics of youth: The five Cs of competency. *School Counselor, 28*, 188–196.

McWhirter, J. J., McWhirter, B. T., McWhirter, E. H., & McWhirter, R. J. (2004). *At-risk youth: A comprehensive response* (3rd ed.). Belmont, CA: Thomson Brooks/Cole.

McWilliams, N. (2009). Some thoughts on the survival of psychoanalytic practice. *Clinical Social Work Journal, 37*(1), 81–83.

Means, B. L. (1973). Levels of empathic response. *Personnel and Guidance Journal, 52*, 23–28.

Meehl, P. (1973). *Psychodiagnosis: Selected papers*. New York: Norton.

Mehrabian, A. (1970). Some determinants of affiliation and conformity. *Psychological Reports, 27*, 19–29.

Mehrabian, A. (1971). *Silent messages*. Belmont, CA: Wadsworth.

Meichenbaum, D. (1993). Changing conceptions of cognitive behavior modification: Retrospect and prospect. *Journal of Consulting and Clinical Psychology, 61*, 202–204

Meichenbaum, D. (1996a). Stress inoculation training for coping with stressors. *The Clinical Psychologist, 49*, 4–7.

Meier, S. T., & Davis, S. R. (2008). *The elements of counseling* (6th ed.). Belmont, CA: Thomson Brooks/ Cole.

Melnyk, B. M. (2009). The latest evidence on the effectiveness of behavioral counseling interventions with adults. *Worldviews on Evidence-Based Nursing, 6*(4), 250–254.

Mencken, F. C., & Winfield, I. (2000). Job search and sex segregation: Does sex of social contact matter? *Sex Roles, 42*, 847–865.

Mercer, C. D., & Mercer, A. R. (2001). *Teaching students with learning problems* (6th ed.). Upper Saddle River, NJ: Prentice Hall.

Merchant, N., & Dupuy, P. (1996). Multicultural counseling and qualitative research: Shared worldview and skills. *Journal of Counseling and Development, 74*, 537–541.

Merriam, S. B. (2002). Assessing and evaluating qualitative research. In S. B. Merriam (Ed.), *Qualitative research in practice* (pp. 18–33). San Francisco: Jossey-Bass.

Merta, R. J. (1995). Group work: Multicultural perspectives. In J. G. Ponterotto, J. M. Casas, L. A. Suzuki, & C. M. Alexander (Eds.), *Handbook of multicultural counseling* (pp. 567–585). Thousand Oaks, CA: Sage.

Mertens, D. M. (1998). *Research methods in education and psychology*. Thousand Oaks, CA: Sage.

Metz, A. J., & Guichard, J. (2009). Vocational psychology and new challenges. *Career Development Quarterly, 57*, 310–318.

Meyer, D. F. (2005). Psychological correlates of help seeking for eating-disorder symptoms in female college students. *Journal of College Counseling, 8*, 20–30.

Meyer, D. F., & Russell, R. K. (1998). Caretaking, separation from parents, and the development of eating disorders. *Journal of Counseling and Development, 76*, 166–173.

Meyer, G. J., Finn, S. E., Eyde, L. D., Kay, G. G., Moreland, K. L., Dies, R. R., et al. (2001). Psychological testing and psychological assessment: A review of evidence and issues. *American Psychologist, 56*, 128–165.

Meyer, W., Bockting, W. O., Cohen-Kettenis, P., Coleman, E., DiCeglie, D., Devor, H., et al. (2001). *The Harry Benjamin International Gender Dysphoria Association's Standards of care for gender identity disorders* (6th ed.). Retrieved from **www.wpath.org/publications_standards.cfm**.

Michaels, S. (1996). The prevalence of homosexuality in the United States. In R. P. Cabaj & T. S. Stein (Eds.), *Textbook of homosexuality and mental health* (pp. 43–63). Washington, DC: American Psychiatric Press.

Middleton, R. A., Flowers, C., & Zawaiza, T. (1996). Multiculturalism, affirmative action, and section 21 of the 1992 Rehabilitation Act amendments: Fact or fiction? *Rehabilitation Counseling Bulletin, 40*, 11–30.

Miller, C. P., & Forrest, A. W. (2009). Ethics of family narrative therapy. *The Family Journal, 17*(2), 156–159.

Miller, E., & Reid, C. (2009). Counseling older adults: Practical implications. In I. Marini & M. A. Stebnicki (Eds.), *The professional counselor's desk reference* (pp. 777–787). New York, NY: Springer.

Miller, G. A., Wagner, A., Britton, T. P., & Gridley, B. E. (1998). A framework for understanding the wounding of healers. *Counseling and Values, 42*, 124–132.

Miller, G. M. (1982). Deriving meaning from standardized tests: Interpreting test results to clients. *Measurement and Evaluation in Guidance, 15*, 87–94.

Miller, J. B., & Stiver, I. R. (1997). The healing connection: How women form relationships in therapy and in life. Northvale, NJ: Aronson.

Miller, K. L., Miller, S. M., & Stull, J. C. (2007). Predictors of counselor educators' cultural discriminatory behavior. *Journal of Counseling and Development, 85*, 325–336.

Miller, L. D., & McLeod, E. (2001). Children as participants in family therapy: Practice, research, and theoretical concerns. *The Family Journal, 9*(4), 375–383.

Miller, M. J. (1985). Analyzing client change graphically. *Journal of Counseling and Development, 63*, 491–494.

Miller, M. J. (1998). Broadening the use of Holland's hexagon with specific implications for career counselors. *Journal of Employment Counseling, 35*, 2–6.

Miller, M. J. (2002). Longitudinal examination of a three-letter holland code. *Journal of Employment Counseling, 39*, 43–48.

Miller, M. J., Scaggs, W. J., & Wells, D. (2006). The Relevancy of Holland's theory to a nonprofessional occupation. *Journal of Employment Counseling, 43*(2), 62–69.

Miller, W. R., & Brown, S. A. (1997). Why psychologists should treat alcohol and drug problems. *American Psychologist, 52,* 1269–1279.

Miller, W. R., & Rollnick, S. (2002). *Motivational interviewing: Preparing people for change* (2nd ed). New York: Guilford.

Minuchin, P., Colapinto, J., & Minuchin, S. (1999). *Working with families of the poor.* New York: Guilford.

Minuchin, S. (1974). *Families and family therapy.* Cambridge, MA: Harvard University Press.

Minuchin, S., & Fishman, H. C. (1981). *Family therapy techniques.* Cambridge, MA: Harvard University Press.

Minuchin, S., Montalvo, B., Guerney, B., Rosman, B., & Schumer, F. (1967). *Families of the slums.* New York: Basic Books.

Mitchell, R. (2001). *Documentation in counseling records* (2nd ed.). Alexandria, VA: American Counseling Association.

Mitchell, R. (2007). *Documentation in counseling records: An overview of ethical, legal, and clinical issues* (3rd ed.). Alexandria, VA: American Counseling Association.

Miwa, Y., & Hanyu, K. (2006). The effects of interior design on communication and impressions of a counselor in a counseling room. *Environment and Behavior, 38,* 484–502.

Mohai, C. E. (1991). *Are school-based drug prevention programs working?* Ann Arbor, MI: CAPS Digest (EDO-CG-91-1).

Moleski, S. M., & Kiselica, M. S. (2005). Dual relationships: A continuum ranging from the destructive to the therapeutic. *Journal of Counseling and Development, 83,* 3–11.

Mollen, D. (2006). Voluntarily childfree women: Experiences and counseling consideration. *Journal of Mental Health Counseling, 28,* 269–284.

Monk, G. (1998). Narrative therapy: An exemplar of the postmodern breed of therapies. *Counseling and Human Development, 30*(5), 1–14.

Moore, D., & Haverkamp, B. E. (1989). Measured increases in male emotional expressiveness following a structured group intervention. *Journal of Counseling and Development, 67,* 513–517.

Moore, D., & Leafgren, F. (Eds.). (1990). *Problem solving strategies and interventions for men in conflict.* Alexandria, VA: American Counseling Association.

Moore, D. D., & Forster, J. R. (1993). Student assistance programs: New approaches for reducing adolescent substance abuse. *Journal of Counseling and Development, 71,* 326–329.

Moos, R. (1973). Conceptualization of human environments. *American Psychologist, 28,* 652–665.

Moradi, B., & DeBlaere, C. (2010). Women's experiences of sexist discrimination: Review of research and directions for centralizing race, ethnicity, and culture. In H. Landrine & N. F. Russo (Eds.), *Handbook of diversity in feminist psychology* (pp. 173–210). New York, NY: Springer US.

Morgan, J. I., & Skovholt, T. M. (1977). Using inner experience: Fantasy and daydreams in career counseling. *Journal of Counseling Psychology, 24,* 391–397.

Morgan, J. P., Jr. (1994). Bereavement in older adults. *Journal of Mental Health Counseling, 16,* 318–326.

Morgan, O. J. (1998). Addiction, family treatment, and healing resources: An interview with David Berenson. *Journal of Addiction and Offender Counseling, 18,* 54–62.

Mori, S. (2000). Addressing the mental health concerns of international students. *Journal of Counseling and Development, 78,* 137–144.

Morran, D. K. (1982). Leader and member self-disclosing behavior in counseling groups. *Journal for Specialists in Group Work, 7,* 218–223.

Morrell-Bellai, T., Goering, P. N., & Boydell, K. M. (2000). Becoming and remaining homeless: A qualitative investigation. *Issues in Mental Health Nursing, 21*(6), 581–604.

Morrill, W. H., Oetting, E. R., & Hurst, J. C. (1974). Dimensions of counselor functioning. *Personnel and Guidance Journal, 53,* 354–359.

Morrissey, M. (1998, January). The growing problem of elder abuse. *Counseling Today,* 14.

Morse, C. L., & Russell, T. (1988). How elementary counselors see their role: An empirical study. *Elementary School Guidance and Counseling, 23,* 54–62.

Mosak, H., & Maniacci, M. P. (2008). Adlerian psychotherapy. In R. J. Corsini & D. Wedding (Eds.), *Current psychotherapies* (8th ed., pp. 63–106). Belmont, CA: Thomson Brooks/Cole.

Moser, C. A., & Kalton, G. (Eds.). (1972). *Survey methods in social investigation* (2nd ed.). New York: Basic Books.

Moss, E. L., & Dobson, K. S. (2006). Psychology, spirituality, and end-of-life care: An ethical integration? *Canadian Psychology/Psychologie canadienne, 47*(4), 284–299.

Mostert, D. L., Johnson, E., & Mostert, M. P. (1997). The utility of solution-focused, brief counseling in schools: Potential from an initial study. *Professional School Counseling, 1,* 21–24.

Mudore, C. F. (1997). Assisting young people in quitting tobacco. *Professional School Counseling, 1,* 61–62.

Mullen, P. E., Martin, J. L., Anderson, J. C., Romans, S. E., & Herbison, G. P. (1995). The long-term impact of physical, emotional, and sexual abuse of children: A community study. *Child Abuse and Neglect, 20,* 7–21.

Munro, J. N., & Bach, T. R. (1975). Effect of time-limited counseling on client change. *Journal of Counseling Psychology, 22,* 395–398.

Muro, J. J. (1981). On target: On top. *Elementary School Guidance and Counseling, 15,* 307–314.

Murphy, B. (2000). *On the street: How we created homelessness.* Winnipeg, MB: J. Gordon Shillingford.

Murray, H. A. (1938). *Explorations in personality.* New York: Oxford University Press.

Muthard, J. E., & Salomone, P. R. (1978). The role and function of the rehabilitation counselor. In B. Bolton & M. E. Jaques (Eds.), *Rehabilitation counseling: Theory and practice* (pp. 166–175). Baltimore: University Park Press.

Myers, I. B. (1962). *Manual for the Myers-Briggs Type Indicator.* Palo Alto, CA: Consulting Psychologists Press.

Myers, I. B. (1980). *Gifts differing.* Palo Alto, CA: Consulting Psychologists Press.

Myers, J., & Sweeney, T. J. (2005). *Counseling for wellness: Theory, research, and practice.* Alexandria, VA: American Counseling Association.

Myers, J. E. (1983). A national survey of geriatric mental health services. *AMHCA Journal, 5,* 69–74.

Myers, J. E. (1995). From "forgotten and ignored" to standards and certification: Gerontological counseling comes of age. *Journal of Counseling and Development, 74,* 143.

Myers, J. E. (1998). Combatting ageism: The rights of older persons. In C. C. Lee & G. Walz (Eds.), *Social action for counselors.* Alexandria, VA: American Counseling Association.

Myers, J. E., Poidevant, J. M., & Dean, L. A. (1991). Groups for older persons and their caregivers: A review of the literature. *Journal for Specialists in Group Work, 16,* 197–205.

Myers, J. E., Sweeney, T. J., & Witmer, J. M. (2000). The wheel of wellness: Counseling for wellness: A holistic model for treatment planning. *Journal of Counseling and Development, 78,* 251–266.

Myers, J. E., Shoffner, M. F., & Briggs, M. K. (2002). Developmental counseling and therapy: An effective approach to understanding and counseling children. *Professional School Counseling, 5,* 194–202.

Myers, J. E., & Truluck, M. (1998). Human beliefs, religious values, and the counseling process: A comparison of counselors and other mental health professionals. *Counseling and Values, 42,* 106–123.

Myers, S. (2000). Empathetic listening: Reports on the experience of being heard. *Journal of Humanistic Psychology, 40,* 148–173.

Myrick, R. D. (1997). Traveling together on the road ahead. *Professional School Counseling, 1,* 4–8.

Myrick, R. D. (2003). *Developmental guidance and counseling: A practical approach* (4th ed.). Minneapolis: Educational Media Corporation.

Nahon, D., & Lander, N. R. (2008). Recruitment and engagement in men's psychotherapy groups: An integrity model, value-based perspective. *International Journal of Men's Health, 7*(3), 218–236.

Napier, A., & Whitaker, C. (1978). *The family crucible.* New York: Harper & Row.

Nasser-McMillan, S. C., & Hakim-Larson, J. (2003). *Counseling* considerations among Arab Americans. *Journal of Counseling and Development, 81,* 150–159.

National Center on Addiction and Substance Abuse at Columbia University. (2003). *CASA 2003 teen survey: High stress, frequent boredom, too much spending money: Triple threat that hikes risk of teen substance abuse.* New York: Author.

National Center on Addiction and Substance Abuse at Columbia University. (2007). *Wasting the best and brightest.* New York: Author.

National Crime Prevention Centre. (2009). School-based drug abuse prevention: Promising and successful programs. *Public Safety Canada.* Retrieved from **www.publicsafety.gc.ca/res/cp/res/2009–01–drg-abs-eng.aspx**.

National Occupational Information Coordinating Committee. (1994). *Program guide: Planning to meet career development needs in school-to-work transition programs.* Washington, DC: U.S. Government Printing Office.

Negy, C. (2004). *Cross-cultural psychotherapy: Toward a critical understanding of diverse clients.* Reno, NV: Bent Tree Press.

Nelligan, A. (1994, Fall). Balancing process and content: A collaborative experience. *Together, 23,* 8–9.

Nelson, G., Aubry, T., & Lafrance, A. (2007). A review of the literature on the effectiveness of housing and support, assertive community treatment, and intensive case management interventions for persons with mental illness who have been homeless. *American Journal of Orthopsychiatry, 77*(3), 350–361.

Nelson, J. A. (2006). For parents only: A strategic family therapy approach in school counseling. *The Family Journal: Counseling and Therapy for Couples and Families, 14,* 180–183.

Nelson, M. L. (1996). Separation versus connection: The gender controversy: Implications for counseling women. *Journal of Counseling and Development, 74,* 339–344.

Nelson, R. C., & Shifron, R. (1985). Choice awareness in consultation. *Counselor Education and Supervision, 24,* 298–306.

Ness, M. E. (1989). The use of humorous journal articles in counselor training. *Counselor Education and Supervision, 29,* 35–43.

Neugarten, B. L. (1978). The rise of the young-old. In R. Gross, B. Gross, & S. Seidman (Eds.), *The new old: Struggling for decent aging* (pp. 47–49). New York: Doubleday.

Neumann, H., McCormick, R. M., Amundson, N. E., & McLean, H. B. (2000). Career counselling First Nations youth: Applying the First Nations Career-Life Planning Model. *Canadian Journal of Counselling, 34*(3), 172–185.

Newman, J. L. (1993). Ethical issues in consultation. *Journal of Counseling and Development, 72,* 148–156.

Newman, J. L., Fuqua, D. R., Gray, E. A., & Simpson, D. B. (2006). Gender differences in the relationship of anger and depression in a clinical sample. *Journal of Counseling and Development, 84,* 157–162.

New York Association for Analytical Psychology. (2008). *About Jungian analysis: Frequently asked questions.* Retrieved from **www.nyaap.org/index.php/id/4**.

Nicholas, D. R., Gobble, D. C., Crose, R. G., & Frank, B. (1992). A systems view of health, wellness, and gender: Implications for mental health counseling. *Journal of Mental Health Counseling, 14,* 8–19.

Nichols, M. (1988). *The self in the system: Expanding the limits of family therapy.* New York: Brunner/ Mazel.

Nichols, M., & Schwartz, R. C. (2006). *Family therapy: Concepts and methods* (7th ed.). Boston: Allyn & Bacon.

Nichols, M. P. (1998). The lost art of listening. *IAMFC Family Digest, 11*(1), 1–2, 4, 11.

Niles, S. G., & Harris-Bowlsbey, J. H. (2005). *Career development interventions in the 21st century* (2nd ed.). Upper Saddle River, NJ: Merrill/Prentice Hall.

Nims, D. R. (1998). Searching for self: A theoretical model for applying family systems to adolescent group work. *Journal for Specialists in Group Work, 23,* 133–144.

Nisson, J. E., Love, K. M., Taylor, K. J., & Slusher, A. L. (2007). A content and sample analysis of quantitative articles published in the *Journal of Counseling & Development* between 1991 and 2000. *Journal of Counseling and Development, 85,* 357–363.

Noll, V. (1997). Cross-age mentoring program for social skills development. *School Counselor, 44,* 239–242.

Norcross, J. C., & Beutler, L. E. (2008). Integrative psychotherapies. In R. J. Corsini & D. Wedding (Eds.), *Current psychotherapies* (8th ed., pp. 481–511). Belmont, CA: Thomson Brooks/Cole.

Nuttgens, S.A., & Campbell, A.J. (2010). Multicultural considerations for counselling First Nation clients. *Canadian Journal of Counselling, 44(2),* 115–129.

Nwachuku, U., & Ivey, A. (1991). Culture-specific counseling: An alternative model. *Journal of Counseling and Development, 70,* 106–111.

Nystul, M. S. (2006). *The art and science of counseling and psychotherapy* (3rd ed.). Upper Saddle River, NJ: Merrill/Prentice Hall.

Oakland, T. (1982). Nonbiased assessment in counseling: Issues and guidelines. *Measurement and Evaluation in Guidance, 15,* 107–116.

Oates, R. K., & Bross, D. C. (1995). What have we learned about treating child physical abuse? A literature review of the last decade. *Child Abuse and Neglect, 19,* 463–473.

Oberman, A. H. (2009). Review of Mindfulness-based cognitive therapy. *The Family Journal, 17(4),* 380.

O'Brien, B. A., & Lewis, M. (1975). A community adolescent self-help center. *Personnel and Guidance Journal, 54,* 212–216.

OCCOPPQ. (2009). *Historique.* Retrieved from **www.occoppq.qc.ca/ordre/historique.shtml**.

Odell, M., & Quinn, W. H. (1998). Therapist and client behaviors in the first interview: Effect on session impact and treatment duration. *Journal of Marital and Family Therapy, 24,* 369–388.

O'Donnell, J. M. (1988). The holistic health movement: Implications for counseling theory and practice. In R. Hayes & R. Aubrey (Eds.), *New directions for counseling and human development* (pp. 365–382). Denver: Love.

Oetting, E. R. (1976). Planning and reporting evaluative research: Part 2. *Personnel and Guidance Journal, 55,* 60–64.

Offet-Gartner, K. (2009). Engaging in culturally competent research. In N. Arthur & S. Collins (Eds.), *Culture-infused counselling: Celebrating the Canadian mosaic* (2nd ed.) (pp. 209–244). Calgary, AB: Counselling Concepts.

Ogrodnik, L. (Ed.). (2008, October). Family violence in Canada: A statistical profile 2008. *Canadian Centre for Justice Statistics, Statistics Canada.* Retrieved from **www.statcan.gc.ca/pub/85-224-x/85-224-x2008000-eng.pdf**.

O'Hanlon, W. H., & Weiner-Davis, M. (1989). *In search of solutions: A new direction in psychotherapy.* New York: Norton.

Ohlsen, M. M. (1977). *Group counseling* (2nd ed.). New York: Holt, Rinehart & Winston.

Ohlsen, M. M. (1983). *Introduction to counseling.* Itasca, IL: F. E. Peacock.

Okun, B. F. (1990). *Seeking connections in psychotherapy.* San Francisco: Jossey-Bass.

Okun, B. R. (1997). *Effective helping: Interviewing and counseling techniques* (5th ed.). Belmont, CA: Thomson.

Okun, B. F., Fried, J., & Okun, M. L. (1999). *Understanding diversity: A learning-as-practice primer.* Pacific Grove, CA: Brooks/Cole.

Oldham, J.M., & Morris, L. B. (1995). *New personality self-portrait: Why you think, work, love, and act the way you do.* New York: Bantam.

O'Leary, K. D., & Murphy, C. (1999). Clinical issues in the assessment of partner violence. In R. Ammerman & M. Hersen (Eds.), *Assessment of family violence: A clinical and legal sourcebook* (pp. 46–94). New York: Wiley.

Olsen, L. D. (1971). Ethical standards for group leaders. *Personnel and Guidance Journal, 50,* 288.

Olson, D. H. (1986). Circumplex model VII: Validation studies and FACES III. *Family Process, 25,* 337–351.

Onedera, J. D., & Greenwalt, B. (2007). Choice theory: An interview with Dr. William Glasser. *The Family Journal: Counseling and Therapy for Couples and Families, 15,* 79–86.

O'Neil, J. M., & Carroll, M. R. (1988). A gender role workshop focused on sexism, gender role conflict, and the gender role journey. *Journal of Counseling and Development, 67,* 193–197.

Oon, Z. (2008). A critical presentation of the life and work of Franz Anton Mesmer MD and its influence on the development of hypnosis. *European Journal of Clinical Hypnosis, 8(1),* 32–40.

Openlander, P., & Searight, R. (1983). Family counseling perspectives in the college counseling center. *Journal of College Student Personnel, 24,* 423–427.

Osborn, D. S., Howard, D. K., & Leierer, S. J. (2007). The effect of a career development course on the dysfunctional career thoughts of racially and ethnically diverse college freshment. *Career Development Quarterly, 55,* 365–377.

Osborne, J. L., Collison, B. B., House, R. M., Gray, L. A., Firth, J., & Lou, M. (1998). Developing a social advocacy model for counselor education. *Counselor Education and Supervision, 37,* 190–202.

Osborne, W. L. (1982). Group counseling: Direction and intention. *Journal for Specialists in Group Work, 7,* 275–280.

Osborne, W. L., Brown, S., Niles, S., & Miner, C. U. (1997). *Career development assessement and counseling.* Alexandria, VA: ACA.

Osipow, S. H., & Fitzgerald, L. F. (1996). *Theories of career development* (4th ed.). Boston: Allyn & Bacon.

Ost, L-G. (2008). Efficacy of the third wave of behavioral therapies: A systematic review and meta-analysis. *Behaviour Research and Therapy, 46(3),* 296–321.

Ostlund, D. R., & Kinnier, R. T. (1997). Values of youth: Messages from the most popular songs of four decades. *Journal of Humanistic Education and Development, 36,* 83–91.

Otani, A. (1989). Client resistance in counseling: Its theoretical rationale and taxonomic classification. *Journal of Counseling and Development, 67,* 458–461.

Ottawa Divorce.com. (2007). *Canadian divorce statistics.* Retrieved from **www.ottawadivorce.com/statistics.htm**.

Ottens, A. J., & Klein, J. F. (2005). Common factors: Where the soul of counseling and psychotherapy resides. *Journal* of *Humanistic Counseling, Education and Development, 44,* 32–45.

Otwell, P. S., & Mullis, F. (1997). Counselor-led staff development: An efficient approach to teacher consultation. *Professional School Counseling, 1,* 25–30.

Pace, D., Stamler, V. L., Yarris, E., & June, L. (1996). Rounding out the Cube: Evolution to a global model for counseling centers. *Journal of Counseling and Development, 74,* 321–325.

Pachis, B., Rettman, S., & Gotthoffer, D. (2001). *Counseling on the net 2001.* Boston: Allyn & Bacon.

Pack-Brown, S. P., Whittington-Clark, L. E., & Parker, W. M. (1998). *Images of me: A guide to group work with African-American women.* Boston: Allyn & Bacon.

Page, S. A., & King, M. C. (2008). No-suicide agreements: Current practices and opinions in a Canadian urban health region. *The Canadian Journal of Psychiatry / La Revue canadienne de psychiatrie, 53*(3), 169–176.

Paisley, P. O., & Hubbard, G. T. (1994). *Developmental school counseling programs: From theory to practice.* Alexandria, VA: American Counseling Association.

Paisley, P. O., & McMahon, H. G. (2001). School counseling for the 21st century: Challenges and opportunities. *Professional School Counseling, 5,* 106–115.

Paivo, A., & Ritchie, P. (1996). Psychology in Canada. *Annual Review of Psychology, 47,* 341–370.

Palladino Schultheiss, D. E., Palma, T. V., & Manzi, A. J. (2005). Career development in middle childhood: A qualitative inquiry. *Career Development Quarterly, 53,* 246–262.

Paradise, L. V., & Kirby, P. C. (2005). The treatment and prevention of depression: Implications for counseling and counselor training. *Journal of Counseling and Development, 83,* 116–119.

Paramore, B., Hopke, W. E., & Drier, H. N. (1999). *Children's dictionary of occupations.* Bloomington, IL: Meridian Education Corp.

Parlett, M., & Denham, J. (2007). Gestalt therapy. In W. Dryden (Ed.), *Dryden's handbook of individual therapy* (5th ed.) (pp. 227–255). Thousand Oaks: Sage.

Parent, G. & Cousineau, M. (2003). Conséquences à long terme d'un mass murder: le cas de Polytechnique, neuf ans plus tard. *The International Journal of Victimology, 1*(3), Retrieved from **www.jidv.com/njidv/index.php? option=com_content&view=article&id=189: consequences-a-long-terme-dun-mass-murder-le-cas- de-polytechnique-neuf-ans-plus-tard&catid=109: jidv03&Itemid=391**.

Parham, T. A., White, J. L., & Ajamu, A. (2000). *The psychology of Blacks: An African centered perspective.* Upper Saddle River, NJ: Prentice Hall.

Parikh, S. V., Segal, Z. V., Grigoriadis, S., Ravindran, A. V., Kennedy, S. H., Lam, R. W., & Patten, S. B. (2009). Canadian Network for Mood and Anxiety Treatments (CANMAT) clinical guidelines for the management of major depressive disorder in adults. II. Psychotherapy alone or in combination with antidepressant medication. *Journal of Affective Disorders, 117*(Suppl 1), S15–S25.

Parker, M. (1994, March). SIG updates. *Career Developments, 9,* 14–15.

Parker, R. M., & Szymanski, E. M. (1996). Ethics and publications. *Rehabilitation Counseling Bulletin, 39,* 162–163.

Parker, W. M., Archer, J., & Scott, J. (1992). *Multicultural relations on campus.* Muncie, IN: Accelerated Development.

Parsons, F. (1909). *Choosing a vocation.* Boston: Houghton Mifflin.

Parsons, R. D. (1996). *The skilled consultant: A systematic approach to the theory and practice of consultation.* Boston: Allyn & Bacon.

Partin, R. (1993). School counselors' time: Where does it go? *School Counselor, 40,* 274–281.

Patel, S. R., Carmody, J., & Simpson, H. B. (2007). Adapting mindfulness-based stress reduction for the treatment of obsessive-compulsive disorder: A case report. *Cognitive and Behavioral Practice, 14*(4), 375–380.

Paterson, D. J., & Darley, J. (1936). *Men, women, and jobs.* Minneapolis: University of Minnesota Press.

Paterson, J., Robertson, S. E., & Bain, H. C. (1979). Canada. In V. J. Drapella (Eds.), *Guidance and counseling around the world* (pp. 24–40). Washington, DC: University of America Press.

Paterson, J. G., & Janzen, H. L. (1993). School counselling in the social, political and educational context of Canada. *International Journal for the Advancement of Counselling, 16*(3), 151–168.

Patry, M. W., Stinson, V., & Smith, S. M. (2009). Supreme Court of Canada addresses admissibility of posthypnosis witness evidence: R. v. Trochym (2007). *Canadian Psychology/Psychologie canadienne, 50*(2), 98–105.

Patterson, C. H. (1971). Are ethics different in different settings? *Personnel and Guidance Journal, 50,* 254–259.

Patterson, G. R. (1971). *Families: Applications of social learning to family life.* Champaign, IL: Research Press.

Patterson, L. E., & Welfel, E. R. (2005). *Counseling process* (6th ed.). Pacific Grove, CA: Brooks/Cole.

Patterson, W., Dohn, H., Bird, J., & Patterson, G. (1983). Evaluation of suicide patients: The SAD PERSONS scale. *Psychosomatics, 24,* 343–349.

Paul, E. L., & Brier, S. (2001). Friendsickness in the transition to college: Precollege predictors and college adjustment correlates. *Journal of Counseling and Development, 79,* 77–89.

Paul, G. L. (1967). Strategy of outcome research in psychotherapy. *Journal of Consulting Psychology, 31,* 109–118.

Paul, G. L. (1967). Outcome research in psychotherapy. *Journal of Consulting Psychology, 31,* 109–118.

Paulsen, M. (2007, January 8). *Seven solutions to homelessness.* Retrieved from **http://thetyee.ca/Views/2007/01/ 08/HomelessSolutions**.

Paulson, B. L., & Worth, M. (2002). Counseling for suicide: Client perspectives. *Journal of Counseling and Development, 80,* 86–93.

Pauly, B. (2008). Harm reduction through a social justice lens. *International Journal of Drug Policy, 19*(1), 4–10.

Peach, L., & Reddick, T. L. (1991). Counselors can make a difference in preventing adolescent suicide. *School Counselor, 39,* 107–110.

Pearson Education. (2010). *WAIS IV scoring assistant with Canadian norms.* Retrieved from **www.pearsonassessmentsupport .com/support/index.php?View=entry&EntryID=2319**.

Pearson, J. E. (1988). A support group for women with relationship dependency. *Journal of Counseling and Development, 66,* 394–396.

Pearson, Q. M. (1998). Terminating before counseling has ended: Counseling implications and strategies for counselor relocation. *Journal of Mental Health Counseling, 20,* 55–63.

Pearson, Q. M. (2000). Opportunities and challenges in the supervisory relationship: Implications for counselor supervision. *Journal of Mental Health Counseling, 22,* 283.

Peck, M. S. (1978). *The road less traveled.* New York: Simon & Schuster.

Pedersen, P. (1987). Ten frequent assumptions of cultural bias in counseling. *Journal of Multicultural Counseling and Development, 15,* 16–22.

Pedersen, P. (1990). The constructs of complexity and balance in multicultural counseling theory and practice. *Journal of Counseling and Development, 68,* 550–554.

Pedersen, P. (Ed.). (1999). *Multiculturalism as a fourth force.* Philadelphia, PA: Brunner/Mazel.

Pedersen, P. B. (1977). The triad model of cross-cultural counselor training. *Personnel and Guidance Journal, 56,* 94–100.

Pedersen, P. B. (1978). Four dimensions of cross-cultural skill in counselor training. *Personnel and Guidance Journal, 56,* 480–484.

Pedersen, P. B. (1982). Cross-cultural training for counselors and therapists. In E. Marshall & D. Kurtz (Eds.), *Interpersonal helping skills: A guide to training methods, programs, and resources.* San Francisco: Jossey-Bass.

Pedersen, P., Lonner, W. J., & Draguns, J. G. (Eds.). (1976). *Counseling across cultures.* Honolulu: University of Hawaii Press.

Peer, G. G. (1985). The status of secondary school guidance: A national survey. *School Counselor, 32,* 181–189.

Peloquin, K., & Lafontaine, M-F. (2010). Measuring empathy in couples: Validity and reliability of the Interpersonal Reactivity Index for Couples. *Journal of Personality Assessment, 92*(2), 146–157.

Pence, E., Paymar, M., Ritmeester, T., & Shepard, M. (1998). *Education groups for men who batter: The Duluth model.* New York: Springer.

Pender, D. A., & Prichard, K. K. (2009). ASGW best practice guidelines as a research tool: A comprehensive examination of the Critical Incident Stress Debriefing. *Journal for Specialists in Group Work, 34*(2), 175–192.

Penedo, F. J., & Dahn, J. R. (2005). Exercise and well-being: A review of mental and physical health benefits associated with physical activity. *Current Opinions in Psychiatry, 18,* 189–193.

Pepler, D., Jiang, D., Craig, W., & Connolly, J. (2008). Developmental trajectories of bullying and associated factors. *Child Development, 79*(2), 325–338.

Pergolizzi, F., Richmond, D., Macario, S., Gan, Z., Richmond, C., & Macario, E. (2009). Bullying in middle schools: Results from a four-school survey. *Journal of School Violence, 8*(3), 264–279.

Perry, W. G., Jr. (1970). *Forms of intellectual and ethical development in the college years.* New York: Holt, Rinehart & Winston.

Perusse, R., Goodnough, G. E., & Lee, V.V. (2009). Group counseling in the schools. *Psychology in the Schools, 46*(3), 225–231.

Peterkin, A., & Risdon, C. (2003). *Caring for lesbian and gay people: A clinical guide.* Toronto, ON: University of Toronto Press.

Peterman, L. M., & Dixon, C. G. (2003). Domestic violence between same-sex partners: Implications for counseling. *Journal of Counseling and Development, 81,* 40–47.

Peters, H. J. (1980). *Guidance in the elementary schools.* New York: Macmillan.

Petersen, S. (2000). Multicultural perspective on middle-class women's identity development. *Journal of Counseling and Development, 78,* 63–71.

Peterson, C., & Seligman, M. E. P. (2004). *Character strength and virtues: A handbook and classification.* Washington, DC: American Psychological Association.

Peterson, K. S., & O'Neal, G. (1998, March 25). Society more violent; so are its children. *USA Today,* p. 3A.

Peterson, N., & Gonzalez, R. C. (Eds.). (2000). *Career counseling models for diverse populations.* Pacific Grove, CA: Brooks/Cole.

Peterson, N., & Priour, G. (2000). Battered women: A group vocational counseling model. In N. Peterson & R. C. Gonzalez (Eds.), *Career counseling models for diverse populations* (pp. 205–218). Pacific Grove, CA: Brooks/Cole.

Petrocelli, J. V. (2002). Processes and stages of change: Counseling with the transtheoretical model of change. *Journal of Counseling and Development, 80,* 22–30.

Pettersen, N., & Turcotte, M. (1996). Utilization in Canada of the General Aptitude Test Battery. *Canadian Psychology/Psychologie canadienne, 37*(4), 181–194.

Phelps, R. E., Tranakos-Howe, S., Dagley, J. C., & Lyn, M. K. (2001). Encouragement and ethnicity in African American college students. *Journal of Counseling and Development, 79,* 90–97.

Piazza, N. J., & Baruth, N. E. (1990). Client record guidelines. *Journal of Counseling and Development, 68,* 313–316.

Piercy, F. P., & Lobsenz, N. M. (1994). *Stop marital fights before they start.* New York: Berkeley.

Pietrofesa, J. J., Hoffman, A., & Splete, H. H. (1984). *Counseling: An introduction* (2nd ed.). Boston: Houghton Mifflin.

Pinson-Milburn, N. M., Fabian, E. S., Schlossberg, N. K., & Pyle, M. (1996). Grandparents raising grandchildren. *Journal of Counseling and Development, 74,* 548–554.

Pinto, R. P. & Morrell, E. M. (1988). Current approaches and future trends in smoking cessation programs. *Journal of Mental Health Counseling, 10,* 95–110.

Piorkowski, G. K. (1983). Survivor guilt in the university setting. *Personnel & Guidance Journal, 61*(10), 620–622.

Piotrowski, C., & Keller, J. (1989). Psychological testing in outpatient mental health facilities: A national study. *Professional Psychology: Research and Practice, 20,* 423–425.

Pistole, M. C. (1997a). Attachment theory: Contributions to group work. *Journal for Specialists in Group Work, 22,* 7–21.

Pistole, M. C. (1997b). Using the genogram to teach systems thinking. *Family Journal, 5,* 337–341.

Pistole, M. C., & Roberts, A. (2002). Mental health counseling: Toward resolving identity confusion. *Journal of Mental Health Counseling, 24,* 1–19.

Pistorello, J., & Follette, V. M. (1998). Childhood sexual abuse and couples' relationships: Female survivors' reports in therapy group. *Journal of Marital and Family Therapy, 24,* 473–485.

Phelan, J. (2003). Child and youth care family support work. *Child & Youth Services, 25*(1–2), 67–77.

Phillips, R. D. (2010). How firm is our foundation? Current play therapy research. *International Journal of Play Therapy, 19*(1), 13–25.

Pires, P., & Jenkins, J. M. (2007). A growth curve analysis of the joint influences of parenting affect, child characteristics and deviant peers on adolescent illicit drug use. *Journal of Youth and Adolescence, 36*(2), 169–183.

Podemski, R. S., & Childers, J. H., Jr. (1980). The counselor as change agent: An organizational analysis. *School Counselor, 27,* 168–174.

Pohl, R. (2001, November). *Homelessness in Canada.* Street Level Consulting and Counselling. Retrieved from **www.streetlevelconsulting.ca/homepage/homelessness InCanada_Part1.htm**.

Polanski, P. J., & Hinkle, J. S. (2000). The mental status examination: Its use by professional counselors. *Journal of Counseling and Development, 78,* 357–364.

Polansky, J., Horan, J. J., & Hanish, C. (1993). Experimental construct validity of the outcomes of study skills training and career counseling as treatments for the retention of at-risk students. *Journal of Counseling and Development, 71,* 488–492.

Pollack, W. S., & Levant, R. F. (Eds.). (1998). *New psychotherapies for men.* New York: Wiley.

Pollock, S. L. (2006). Internet counseling and its feasibility for marriage and family counseling. *The Family Journal: Counseling and Therapy for Couples and Families, 14,* 65–70.

Ponterotto, J. G., & Casas, J. M. (1987). In search of multicultural competence within counselor education programs. *Journal of Counseling and Development, 65,* 430–434.

Ponterotto, J. G., & Sabnani, H. B. (1989). "Classics" in multicultural counseling: A systematic five-year content analysis. *Journal of Multicultural Counseling and Development, 17,* 23–37.

Ponzetti, J. J., Jr., & Cate, R. M. (1988). The relationship of personal attributes and friendship variables in predicting loneliness. *Journal of College Student Development, 29,* 292–298.

Ponzo, Z. (1978). Age prejudice of "act your age." *Personnel and Guidance Journal, 57,* 140–144.

Ponzo, Z. (1985). The counselor and physical attractiveness. *Journal of Counseling and Development, 63,* 482–485.

Pope, M., & Sweinsdottir, M. (2005). Frank, We Hardly Knew Ye: The Very Personal Side of Frank Parsons. *Journal of Counseling and Development, 83,* 105–115.

Popenhagen, M. P., & Qualley, R. M. (1998). Adolescent suicide: Detection, intervention, and prevention. *Professional School Counseling, 1,* 30–35.

Posthuma, B. W. (2002). *Small groups in counseling and therapy: Process and leadership* (4th ed.). Boston: Allyn & Bacon.

Povolny, M. A., Kaplan, S., Marme, M., & Roldan, G. (1993). Perceptions of adjustment issues following a spinal cord injury: A case study. *Journal of Applied Rehabilitation Counseling, 24,* 31–34.

Powers, M. B., Zum Vorde Sive Vording, M. B., & Emmelkamp, P. M. G. (2009). Acceptance and commitment therapy: A meta-analytic review. *Psychotherapy and Psychosomatics, 78*(2), 73–80.

Poznanski, J. J., & McLennan, J. (2003). Becoming a psychologist with a particular theoretical orientation to counseling practice. *Australian Psychologist, 38*(3), 223–226.

Pozzebon, J. A., Visser, B. A., Ashton, M. C., Lee, K., & Goldberg, L. R. (2010). Praissman, S. (2008). Mindfulness-based stress reduction: A literature review and clinician's guide. *Journal of the American Academy of Nurse Practitioners, 20*(4), 212–216.

Prediger, D. J. (Ed.). (1993). *Multicultural assessment standards: A compilation for counselors.* Alexandria, VA: Association for Assessment in Counseling.

Prediger, D. J. (1994). Tests and counseling: The marriage that prevailed. *Measurement and Evaluation in Counseling and Development, 26,* 227–234.

Presbury, J. H., Echterling, L. G., & McKee, J. E. (2002). *Ideas and tools for brief counseling.* Upper Saddle River, NJ: Prentice Hall.

Pressly, P. K., & Heesacker, M. (2001). The physical environment and counseling: A review of theory and research. *Journal of Counseling and Development, 79,* 148–160.

Prieto, L. R., & Scheel, K. R. (2002). Using case documentation to strengthen counselor trainees' case conceptualization skills. *Journal of Counseling and Development, 80,* 11–21.

Prochaska, J. O. (1999). How do people change, and how can we change to help many more people? In M. A. Hubble, B. L. Duncan, & S. D. Miller (Eds.), *The heart and soul of change: What works in therapy* (pp. 227–255). Washington, DC: American Psychological Association.

Prochaska, J. O., & DiClemente, C. C. (1992). The transtheoretical approach. In J. C. Norcross & M. R. Goldfried (Eds.), *Handbook of psychotherapy integration* (pp. 300–334). New York: Basic Books.

Prout, H. T., & Brown, D. T. (Eds.) (2007). Counseling and psychotherapy with children and adolescents: *Theory and practice for school and clinical settings* (4th ed.). Hoboken, NJ: John Wiley & Sons.

Psychologists' Association of Alberta (2010). Fee schedule (based upon a 50 minute session) as of January 1, 2010. Retrieved from **www.psychologistsassociation.ab.ca/ pages/Recommended_Fee_Schedule**.

Psychometric characteristics of a public-domain self-report measure of vocational interests: The Oregon Vocational Interest Scales. *Journal of Personality Assessment, 92*(2), 168–174.

Public Health Agency of Canada. (2010, January 12). *Emergency response services.* Retrieved from **www.phac-aspc.gc.ca/emergency-urgence/index-eng.php**.

Pull, C. B. (2009). Current empirical status of acceptance and commitment therapy. *Current Opinion in Psychiatry, 22*(1), 55–60.

Pulver, C. A., & Kelly, K. R. (2008). Incremental validity of the Myers-Briggs Type Indicator in predicting academic major selection of undecided university students. *Journal of Career Assessment, 16*(4), 441–455.

Purkey, W. W., & Schmidt, J. J. (1987). *The inviting relationship*. Upper Saddle River, NJ: Prentice Hall.

Puterbaugh, D. T. (2006). Communication counseling as a part of a treatment plan for depression. *Journal of Counseling and Development, 84*, 373–380.

Pyle, K. R. (2000). A group approach to career decision making. In N. Peterson & R. C. Gonzalez (Eds.), *Career counseling models for diverse populations* (pp. 121–136). Pacific Grove, CA: Brooks/Cole.

Qualls, S. H., & Anderson, L. N. (2009). Family therapy in late life. *Psychiatric Annals, 39*(9), 844–850.

Quirttana, S. M., & Kerr, J. (1993). Relational needs in late adolescent separation-individuation. *Journal of Counseling and Development, 71*, 349–354.

RCMP Public Affairs Directorate. (1993). *Native spirituality guide*. Retrieved from **dsp-psd.pwgsc.gc.ca/Collection/ JS62–80–1998E.pdf**

Ragle, J., & Krone, K. (1985). Extending orientation: Telephone contacts by peer advisors. *Journal of College Student Personnel, 26*, 80–81.

Rainey, L. M., Hensley, F. A., & Crutchfield, L. B. (1997). Implementation of support groups in elementary and middle school student assistant programs. *Professional School Counseling, 1*, 36–40.

Rainsford, C. (2002). Counselling older adults. *Reviews in Clinical Gerontology, 12*(2), 159–164.

Raj, R. (2002). Towards a transpositive therapeutic model: Developing clinical sensitivity and cultural competence in the effective support of transsexual and transgendered clients. *International Journal of Transgenderism, 6*(2), No Pagination Specified.

Rak, C. F., & Patterson, L. E. (1996). Promoting resilience in at-risk children. *Journal of Counseling and Development, 74*, 368–373.

Randolph, D. L., & Graun, K. (1988). Resistance to consultation: A synthesis for counselor-consultants. *Journal of Counseling and Development, 67*, 182–184.

Raney, S., & Cinarbas, D. C. (2005). Counseling in developing countries: Turkey and India as examples. *Journal of Mental Health Counseling, 27*, 149–160.

Raphael, D. (2009). Poverty, human development, and health in Canada: Research, practice, and advocacy dilemmas. *CJNR: Canadian Journal of Nursing Research, 41*(2), 7–18.

Rayle, A. D. (2006). Mattering to others: Implications for the counseling relationship. *Journal of Counseling and Development, 84*, 483–487.

Reardon, R. C., Bullock, E. E., & Meyer, K. E. (2007). A Holland perspective on the U.S. workforce from 1960 to 2000. *Career Development Quarterly, 55*, 262–274.

Ree, M. J., & Craigie, M. A. (2007). Outcomes following mindfulness-based cognitive therapy in a heterogeneous sample of adult outpatients. *Behaviour Change, 24*(2), 70–86.

Reese, R. J., Conoley, C. W., & Brossart, D. F. (2006). The attractiveness of telephone counseling: An empirical investigation of current perceptions. *Journal of Counseling and Development, 84*, 54–60.

Rehm, J., Baliunas, D., Brochu, S., Fischer, B., Gnam, W., Patra, J., ... Single, E. (2006, March). The costs of substance abuse in Canada 2002: Highlights. *Canadian Centre on Substance Abuse (CCSA)*. Retrieved from **www.ccsa.ca/2006%20CCSA%20Documents/ ccsa-011332–2006.pdf**.

Reid, S., Berman, H., & Forchuk, C. (2005). Living on the streets in Canada: A feminist narrative study of girls and young women. *Issues in Comprehensive Pediatric Nursing, 28*(4), 237–256.

Remer, R. (1981). The counselor and research: An introduction. *Personnel and Guidance Journal, 59*, 567–571.

Remley, T. P., Jr. (1985). The law and ethical practices in elementary and middle schools. *Elementary School Guidance and Counseling, 19*, 181–189.

Remley, T. P., Jr. (1991). *Preparing for court appearances*. Alexandria, VA: American Counseling Association.

Remley, T. P., Jr. (1992, Spring). You and the law. *American Counselor, 1*, 33.

Remley, T. P., Jr., & Sparkman, L. B. (1993). Student suicides: The counselor's limited legal liability. *School Counselor, 40*, 164–169.

Resnikoff, R. D. (1981). Teaching family therapy: Ten key questions for understanding the family as patient. *Journal of Marital and Family Therapy, 7*, 135–142.

Reupert, A. (2006). The counsellor's self in therapy: An inevitable presence. International Journal for the Advancement of Counselling, 28(1), 95–105.

Ribak-Rosenthal, N. (1994). Reasons individuals become school administrators, school counselors, and teachers. *School Counselor, 41*, 158–164.

Rice, K. G., & Dellwo, J. P. (2002). Perfectionism and self-development: Implications for college adjustment. *Journal of Counseling and Development, 80*, 188–196.

Rice, K. G., & Whaley, T. J. (1994). A short term longitudinal study of within-semester stability and change in attachment and college student adjustment. *Journal of College Student Development, 35*, 324–330.

Richardson, E. H. (1981). Cultural and historical perspectives in counseling American Indians. In D. W. Sue (Ed.), *Counseling the culturally different* (pp. 216–249). New York: Wiley.

Richardson, R. C., & Norman, K. I. (1997). "Rita dearest, it's OK to be different": Teaching children acceptance and tolerance. *Journal of Humanistic Education and Development, 35*, 188–197.

Richter-Antion, D. (1986). Qualitative differences between adult and younger students. *NASPA Journal, 23*, 58–62.

Ridley, C. R. (2005). *Overcoming unintentional racism in counseling and therapy: A practitioner's guide to intentional intervention* (2nd ed.). Thousand Oaks, CA: Sage.

Rimm, D. C., & Cunningham, H. M. (1985). Behavior therapies. In S. J. Lynn & J. P. Garske (Eds.), *Contemporary psychotherapies: Models and methods* (pp. 221–259). Upper Saddle River, NJ: Prentice Hall.

Ringwalt, C. L., Ennett, S., Johnson, R., Rohrbach, L. A., Simons-Rudolph, A., Vincus, A., & Thorne, J. (2003). Factors associated with fidelity to substance use prevention curriculum guides in the nation's middle schools. *Health Education & Behavior, 30*(3), 375-391.

Riordan, R. J., & Beggs, M. S. (1987). Counselors and self-help groups. *Journal of Counseling and Development, 65*, 427–429.

Ritchie, M. H. (1986). Counseling the involuntary client. *Journal of Counseling and Development, 64,* 516–518.

Ritchie, M. H. (1989). Enhancing the public image of school counseling: A marketing approach. *School Counselor, 37,* 54–61.

Ritchie, M. H., & Partin, R. L. (1994). Parent education and consultation activities of school counselors. *School Counselor, 41,* 165–170.

Ritter, K. Y. (1982). Training group counselors: A total curriculum perspective. *Journal for Specialists in Group Work, 7,* 266–274.

Riva, M. T., Lippert, L., & Tackett, M. J. (2000). Selection practices of group leaders: A national survey. *Journal for Specialists in Group Work, 25,* 157–169.

Rivera, E. T., Phan, L. T., Hadduv, C. D., Wilbur, J. R., & Arredondo, P. (2006). Honesty in multicultural counseling: A pilot study of the counseling relationship. *Revista Interamericana de Psicologia, 40*(1), 37–45.

Roark, M. L. (1987). Preventing violence on college campuses. *Journal of Counseling and Development, 65,* 367–371.

Roberti, J. W., & Storch, E. A. (2005). Psychosocial adjustment of college students with tattoos and piercings. *Journal of College Counseling, 8,* 14–19.

Roberts, A. R. (2000). *Crisis intervention handbook: Assessment, treatment, and research.* New York: Oxford Press.

Roberts, D., & Ullom, C. (1989). Student leadership program model. *NASPA Journal, 27,* 67–74.

Robertson, S. E., & Borgen, W. A. (2001–2002). 2003 CCA accreditation procedures and standards for counsellor education programs at the master's level. Canadian Counselling and Psychotherapy Association. Retrieved from **www.ccpa-accp.ca/en/accreditation**.

Robinson, B. E. (1995, July). Helping clients with work addiction: Don't overdo it. *Counseling Today, 38,* 31–32.

Robinson, B. E. (2001). Workaholism and family functioning: A profile of familial relationships, psychological outcomes, and research considerations. *Contemporary Family Research, 23,* 123–135.

Robinson, B. E., Flowers, C., & Ng, K-M (2006). The relationship between workaholism and marital disaffection: Husbands' perspective. *The Family Journal: Counseling and Therapy for Couples and Families, 14,* 213–220.

Robinson, E. H., III. (1994). Critical issues in counselor education: Mentors, models, and money. *Counselor Education and Supervision, 33,* 339–343.

Robinson, F. P. (1950). *Principles and procedures of student counseling.* New York: Harper.

Robinson, L. M., Mcintyre, L., & Officer, S. (2005). Welfare babies: Poor children's experiences informing healthy peer relationships in Canada. *Health Promotion International, 20*(4), 342–350.

Robinson, R. (2008). Reflections on the debriefing debate. *International Journal of Emergency Mental Health, 10*(4), 253–259.

Robinson, S. E., & Gross, D. R. (1986). Counseling research: Ethics and issues. *Journal of Counseling and Development, 64,* 331–333.

Robinson, S. E., & Kinnier, R. T. (1988). Self-instructional versus traditional training for teaching basic counseling skills. *Counselor Education and Supervision, 28,* 140–145.

Robinson, T. L., & Howard-Hamilton, M. (2000). *The convergence of race, ethnicity, and gender: Multiple identities in counseling.* Upper Saddle River, NJ: Merrill/Prentice Hall.

Rodenburg, R., Benjamin, A., de Roos, C., Meijer, A. M., & Stams, G. J. (2009). Efficacy of EMDR in children: A meta-analysis. *Clinical Psychology Review, 29*(7), 599–606.

Rodgers, R. F. (1980). Theories underlying student development. In D. G. Creamer (Ed.), *Student development in higher education* (pp. 10– 96). Cincinnati, OH: American College Personnel Association.

Rodgers, R. F. (1989). Student development. In U. Delworth, G. R. Hanson, & Associates (Eds.), *Student services: A handbook for the profession* (2nd ed., pp. 117–164). San Francisco: Jossey-Bass.

Rodriguez Rust, P. C. (2002). Bisexuality: The state of the union. *Annual Review of Sex Research, 13,* 180–240.

Roehlke, H. J. (1988). Critical incidents in counselor development: Examples of Jung's concept of synchronicity. *Journal of Counseling and Development, 67,* 133–134.

Rogers, C. R. (1964). Toward a science of the person. In T. W. Wann (Ed.), *Behaviorism and phenomenology: Contrasting bases for modern psychology* (pp. 109–140). Chicago: University of Chicago Press.

Rogers, C. R. (1967). The conditions of change from a client-centered view. In B. Berenson & R. Cankhuff (Eds.), *Sources of gain in counseling and psychotherapy* (pp. 71–86). New York: Holt, Rinehart & Winston.

Rogers, C. R. (1970). *Carl Rogers on encounter groups.* New York: Harper & Row.

Rogers, C. R. (1987). The underlying theory: Drawn from experience with individuals and groups. *Counseling and Values, 32,* 38–46.

Rogers, J. R. (1990). Female suicide: The trend toward increased lethality in method of choice and its implications. *Journal of Counseling and Development, 69,* 37–38.

Rogers, J. R. (2001). Theoretical grounding: The "missing link" in suicide research. *Journal of Counseling and Development, 79,* 16–25.

Rojano, R. (2004). The practice of Community Family Therapy. *Family Process, 43*(1), 59–77.

Roloff, M. E., & Miller, G. R. (Eds.). (1980). *Persuasion: New directions in theory and research.* Beverly Hills, CA: Sage.

Ronnestad, M. H., & Skovholt, T. M. (1993). Supervision of beginning and advanced graduate students of counseling and psychotherapy. *Journal of Counseling and Development, 71,* 396–405.

Rosen, S., & Tesser, A. (1970). On the reluctance to communicate undesirable information: The MUM effect. *Sociometry, 33,* 253–263.

Rosenthal, H. (2005). *Before you see your first client.* Philadelphia: Brunner-Routledge.

Rosenthal, J. A. (2001). *Statistics and data interpretation for the helping professions.* Pacific Grove, CA: Brooks/Cole.

Rossi, P. H., & Freeman, H. E. (1999). *Evaluation: A systematic approach* (6th ed.). Beverly Hills, CA: Sage.

Rottinghaus, P. J., Coon, K. L., Gaffey, A. R., & Zytowski, D. G. (2007). Thirty-year stability and predictive validity of vocational interests. *Journal of Career Assessment, 15*(1), 5–22.

Rowe, C. E. Jr. (2009). "Psychophobia" is a major current issue affecting psychoanalytic training and practice. *Clinical Social Work Journal, 37*(1), 79–80.

Rowley, W. J., & MacDonald, D. (2001). Counseling and the law: A cross-cultural perspective. *Journal of Counseling and Development, 79,* 422–429.

Royal Canadian Mounted Police Public Affairs Directorate. (1993). *Native spirituality guide.* Retrieved from **www.rcmp-grc.gc.ca/pubs/abo-aut/spirit-spiritualite-eng.htm**.

Roysircar, G. (2009). The big picture of advocacy: Counselor, heal society and thyself. Journal of Counseling & Development, 87(3), 288–294.

Rubin, S. G. (1990). Transforming the university through service learning. In C. I. Delve, S. D. Mintz, & G. M. Stewart (Eds.), *Community services as values education* (pp. 111–124). San Francisco: Jossey-Bass.

Rudolph, J. (1989). The impact of contemporary ideology and AIDS on the counseling of gay clients. *Counseling and Values, 33,* 96–108.

Rueth, T., Demmitt, A., & Burger, S. (1998, March). *Counselors and the DSM-IV: Intentional and unintentional consequences of diagnosis.* Paper presented at the American Counseling Association Convention, Indianapolis, IN.

Ruiz, F. J. (2010). A review of Acceptance and Commitment Therapy (ACT) empirical evidence: Correlational, experimental psychopathology, component and outcome studies. *International Journal of Psychology & Psychological Therapy, 10*(1), 125–162.

Rule, W. R. (1982). Pursuing the horizon: Striving for elusive goals. *Personnel and Guidance Journal, 61,* 195–197.

Rumberger, R. W. (1987). High school dropouts. *Review of Educational Research, 57,* 101–122.

Runyan, D. K., Dunne, M. P., & Zolotor, A. J. (2009). Introduction to the development of the ISPCAN child abuse screening tools. *Child Abuse & Neglect, 33*(11), 842–845.

Ryan, G., Miyoshi, T. J., Metzner, J. L., Krugman, R. D., & Fryer, G. E. (1996). Trends in a national sample of sexually abusive youths. *Journal of the American Academy of Child and Adolescent Psychiatry, 35*(1), 17–25.

Ryan, W., & Smith, J. D. (2009). Antibullying programs in schools: How effective are evaluation practices? *Prevention Science, 10*(3), 248–259.

Rybak, C. J., & Brown, B. M. (1997). Group conflict: Communication patterns and group development. *Journal for Specialists in Group Work, 22,* 31–42.

Ryder, A. G., Yang, J., Zhu, X., Yao, S., Yi, J., Heine, S. J., & Bagby, R. M. (2008). The cultural shaping of depression: Somatic symptoms in China, psychological symptoms in North America? *Journal of Abnormal Psychology, 117*(2), 300–313.

Sack, R. T. (1985). On giving advice. *AMHCA Journal, 7,* 127–132.

Sack, R. T. (1988). Counseling responses when clients say "I don't know." *Journal of Mental Health Counseling, 10,* 179–187.

Sadlier, R. (n.d.). *Historica: Black history, Canada.* Retrieved from **http://blackhistorycanada.ca**.

Saewyc, E. M. (2009). Alcohol and other drug use among BC students: Myths and realities. *Visions: BC's Mental Health and Addictions Journal, 5*(2), 8–9. Retrieved from **www.heretohelp.bc.ca/publications/visions**.

Saewyc, E. M., Taylor, D., Homma, Y., & Ogilvie, G. (2008). Trends in sexual health and risk behaviours among adolescent students in British Columbia. *Canadian Journal of Human Sexuality, 17*(1–2), 1–13.

Saidla, D. D. (1990). Cognitive development and group stages. *Journal for Specialists in Group Work, 15,* 15–20.

Salisbury, A. (1975). Counseling older persons: A neglected area in counselor education and supervision. *Counselor Education and Supervision, 4,* 237–238.

Salomone, P. R., & McKenna, P. (1982). Difficult career counseling cases. I: Unrealistic vocational aspirations. *Personnel and Guidance Journal, 60,* 283–286.

Salomone, P. R., & Sheehan, M. C. (1985). Vocational stability and congruence: An examination of Holland's proposition. *Vocational Guidance Quarterly, 34,* 91–98.

Salvendy, J. (1999). *About us – history of the CGPA: The beginnings of CGPA.* Retrieved from **www.cgpa.ca/History-of-the-CGPA**.

Same sex rights: Canada timeline. (2007, March 1). CBC News Online. Retrieved from **www.cbc.ca/news/background/samesexrights/timeline_canada.html**.

Sampson, J. P., Kolodinsky, R. W., & Greeno, B. P. (1997). Counseling on the information highway: Future possibilities and potential problems. *Journal of Counseling and Development, 75,* 203–212.

Sampson, J. P., Jr., & Bloom, J. W. (2001). The potential for success and failure of computer applications in counseling and guidance. In D. C. Locke, J. E. Myers, & E. L. Herr (Eds.), *The handbook of counseling* (pp. 613–627). Thousand Oaks, CA: Sage.

Samuel, E. (2004). Racism in peer-group interactions: South Asian students' experiences in Canadian academe. *Journal of College Student Development, 45*(4), 407–424.

Sandeen, A. (1988). *Student affairs: Issues, problems and trends.* Ann Arbor, MI: ERIC/CAPS.

Sanderson, J., Kosutic, I., Garcia, M., Melendez, T., Donoghue, J., Perumbilly, S., ... Anderson, S. (2009). The measurement of outcome variables in couple and family therapy research. *American Journal of Family Therapy, 37*(3), 239–257.

Sanford, N. (1962). *The American college.* New York: Wiley.

Sanford, N. (1979). Freshman personality: A stage in human development. In N. Sanford & J. Axelrod (Eds.), *College and character.* Berkeley, CA: Montaigne.

Saraceni, R., & Russell-Mayhew, S. (2007). Images and ideals: Counselling women and girls in a "thin-is-in" culture. *Canadian Journal of Counselling, 41*(2), 91–106.

Sarlo, C. (2006, November 1). *Poverty in Canada: 2006 update.* Retrieved from **www.fraserinstitute.org/research-news/display.aspx?id=13293**.

Saunders, T., Driskell, J. E., Johnston, J. H., & Salas, E. (1996). The effect of stress inoculation training on anxiety and performance. *Journal of Occupational Psychology, 1*(2), 170–186.

Savage, T. A., Harley, D. A., & Nowak, T. M. (2005). Applying social empowerment strategies as tools for self-advocacy in counseling lesbian and gay male clients. *Journal of Counseling and Development, 83,* 131–137.

Savickas, M. L. (1989). Annual review: Practice and research in career counseling and development, 1988. *Career Development Quarterly, 38,* 100–134.

Savickas, M. L. (1998). Interpreting interest inventories: A case example. *Career Development Quarterly, 46,* 307–319.

Savickas, M. L. (2005). The theory and practice of career construction. In S. D. Brown & R. W. Lent (Eds.), *Career development and counseling: Putting theory and research to work* (pp. 42–70). New York: Wiley.

Savin-Williams, R. C. (2005). *The new gay teenager.* Cambridge, MA: Harvard University Press.

Scarborough, J. L. (1997). The SOS Club: A practical peer helper program. *Professional School Counseling, 1,* 25–28.

Schechter, L. R. (2008). From 9/11 to Hurricane Katrina: Helping others and oneself cope following disasters. *Traumatology, 14*(4), 38–47.

Schecter, S., & Ganley, A. (1995). *Domestic violence: A national curriculum for family preservation practitioners.* San Francisco: Family Violence Prevention Fund.

Schein, E. H. (1978). The role of the consultant: Content expert or process facilitator? *Personnel and Guidance Journal, 56,* 339–343.

Schellenberg, R. C., Parks-Savage, A., & Rehfuss, M. (2007). Reducing levels of elementary school violence with peer mediation. *Professional School Counseling, 10,* 475–481.

Scher, M. (1981). Men in hiding: A challenge for the counselor. *Personnel and Guidance Journal, 60,* 199–202.

Scher, M., & Stevens, M. (1987). Men and violence. *Journal of Counseling and Development, 65,* 351–355.

Schmidt, J. A. (1974). Research techniques for counselors: The multiple baseline. *Personnel and Guidance Journal, 53,* 200–206.

Schmidt, J. J. (2004). *A survival guide for the elementary/middle school counselor* (2nd ed). San Francisco: Jossey-Bass.

Schmidt, J. J. (2007). *Counseling in schools: Comprehensive programs of responsive services for all students* (5th ed.). Boston: Allyn & Bacon.

Schmidt, J. J., & Osborne, W. L. (1981). Counseling and consultation: Separate processes or the same? *Personnel and Guidance Journal, 60,* 168–170.

Schmidt, J. J., & Osborne, W. L. (1982). The way we were (and are): A profile of elementary counselors in North Carolina. *Elementary School Guidance and Counseling, 16,* 163–171.

Schneller, G., & Chalungsooth, P. (2002, June). Development of a multilingual tool to assess client presenting problems. *American College Counseling Association Visions,* 5–7.

Schneider, K. (2010, July 10). *Homeless handouts targeted.* Calgary Sun. Retrieved from **www.calgarysun.com/news/alberta/2010/07/06/14620696.html?keepThis=true&TB_iframe=true&height=500&width=850**.

Schneider, K. J., & Krug, O. T. (2010). *Existential-humanistic therapy.* Washington, DC: American Psychological Association.

Schofield, W. (1964). *Psychotherapy: The purchase of friendship.* Upper Saddle River, NJ: Prentice Hall.

Schrank, F. A. (1982). Bibliotherapy as an elementary school counseling tool. *Elementary School Guidance and Counseling, 16,* 218–227.

Schubert, S., & Lee, C. W. (2009). Adult PTSD and its treatment with EMDR: A review of controversies, evidence, and theoretical knowledge. *Journal of EMDR Practice and Research, 3*(3), 117–132.

Schuh, J. J., Shipton, W. C., & Edman, N. (1986). Counseling problems encountered by resident assistants: An update. *Journal of College Student Personnel, 27,* 26–33.

Schulz, W. E., Sheppard, G. W., Lehr, R., & Shepard, B. (2006). *Counselling ethics: Issues and cases.* Ottawa, ON: Canadian Counselling Association

Schumacher, B. (1983). Rehabilitation counseling. In M. M. Ohlsen (Ed.), *Introduction to counseling* (pp. 313–324). Itasca, IL: F. E. Peacock.

Schutz, W. (1971). *Here comes everybody: Bodymind and encounter culture.* New York: Harper & Row.

Schwiebert, V. L., Myers, J. E., & Dice, C. (2000). Ethical guidelines for counselors working with older adults. *Journal of Counseling and Development, 78,* 123–129.

Schwiebert, V. L., Sealander, K. A., & Dennison, J. L. (2002). Strategies for counselors working with high school students with attention-deficit/hyperactivity disorder. *Journal of Counseling and Development, 80,* 3–10.

Scott, C. G. (2000). Ethical issues in addiction counseling. *Rehabilitation Counseling Bulletin, 43,* 209–214.

Scrignar, C. B. (1997). *Post-traumatic stress disorder, diagnosis, treatment and legal issues* (3rd ed.). New York: Bruno.

Sears, R., Rudisill, J., & Mason-Sear, C. (2006). *Consultation skills for mental health professionals.* New York: Wiley.

Sears, S. (1982). A definition of career guidance terms: A National Vocational Guidance Association perspective. *Vocational Guidance Quarterly, 31,* 137–143.

Sears, S. J., & Granello, D. H. (2002). School counseling now and in the future: A reaction. *Professional School Counseling, 5,* 164–171.

Seiler, G., & Messina, J. J. (1979). Toward professional identity: The dimensions of mental health counseling in perspective. *AMHCA Journal, 1,* 3–8.

Segal, Z. V., Williams, J. M. G., & Teasdale, J. D. (2002). *Mindfulness-based cognitive therapy for depression: A new approach to preventing relapse.* New York, NY: Guilford.

Seligman, L. (1984). Temporary termination. *Journal of Counseling and Development, 63,* 43–44.

Seligman, L. (1999). Twenty years of diagnosis and the DSM. *Journal of Mental Health Counseling, 21,* 229–239.

Seligman, M. E. P., & Csikszentmihalyi, M. (2000). Positive psychology: An introduction. *American Psychologist, 55*(1), 5–14.

Sells, J. N., Giordano, F. G., Bokar, L., Klein, J., Sierra, G. P., & Thumc, B. (2007). The effect of Honduran counseling practices on the North American counseling profession: The power of poverty. *Journal of Counseling & Development, 85*(4), 431–439.

Selvini-Palazzoli, M., Boscolo, L., Cecchin, G., & Prata, G. (1978). *Paradox and counterparadox.* New York: Monson.

Semple, R. J., Lee, J., Rosa, D., & Miller, L. F. (2010). A randomized trial of mindfulness-based cognitive therapy for children: Promoting mindful attention to enhance social-emotional resiliency in children. *Journal of Child and Family Studies, 19*(2), 218–229.

Senour, M. N. (1982). How counselors influence clients. *Personnel and Guidance Journal, 60,* 345–349.

Serritella, D. A. (1992). Tobacco addiction. In L. L'Abate, G. E. Farrar, & D. A. Serritella (Eds.), *Handbook of differential treatments for addiction* (pp. 97–112). Boston: Allyn & Bacon.

Service Canada. (2007, March 31). *Job futures: Welcome to Canada's career and education planning tool.* Retrieved from **www.jobfutures.ca/en/home.shtml**.

Service Canada. (2007a, March 31). Job futures: Psychologists (NOC 4151). Retrieved from **www.jobfutures.ca/noc/print/4151.html**.

Service Canada. (2007b, March 31). Job futures: Social workers (NOC 4152). Retrieved from **www.jobfutures.ca/noc/print/4152.html**.

Service Canada. (2009, March 11). *Old Age Security (OAS) Program.* Retrieved from **www.hrsdc.gc.ca/eng/isp/oas/oasrates.shtml**.

Seto, A., Becker, K. W., & Akutsu, M. (2006). Counseling Japanese men on fathering. *Journal of Counseling and Development, 84,* 488–492.

Sev'er, A. (2002). A feminist analysis of flight of abused women, plight of Canadian shelters: Another road to homelessness. *Journal of Social Distress & the Homeless, 11*(4), 307–324.

Sexton, T. L. (1993). A review of the counseling outcome research. In G. R. Walz & J. C. Bleuer (Eds.), *Counselor efficacy* (pp. 79–119). Ann Arbor, MI: ERIC/CAPS.

Sexton, T. L. (1996). The relevance of counseling outcome research: Current trends and practical implications. *Journal of Counseling and Development, 74,* 590–600.

Sexton, T. L., & Whiston, S. C. (1996). Integrating counseling research and practice. *Journal of Counseling and Development, 74,* 588–589.

Shanks, J. L. (1982). Expanding treatment for the elderly: Counseling in a private medical practice. *Personnel and Guidance Journal, 61,* 553–555.

Shapcott, M. (2006, September). *Executive summary from "blueprint to end homelessness in Toronto."* Wellesley Institute. Retrieved from **www.wellesleyinstitute.com/news/affordable-housing-news/the-blueprint-to-end-homelessness-in-toronto**.

Shapiro, D., Walker, L., Manosevitz, M., Peterson, M., & Williams, M. (2008). *Surviving a licensing board complaint: What to do, what not to do: Practical tips from the experts.* Phoenix, AZ: Zeig, Tucker & Theisen.

Shapiro, D. H. (1992). Adverse effects of meditation: A preliminary investigation of long-term meditators. *International Journal of Psychosomatics, 39,* 62–67.

Shapiro, F., & Maxfield, L. (2002). In the blink of an eye. *The Psychologist, 15*(3), 120–124.

Shapiro, J. L., Peltz, L. S., & Bernadett-Shapiro, S. (1998). *Brief group treatment: Practical training for therapists and counselors.* Pacific Grove, CA: Brooks/Cole.

Sharf, R. S., & Bishop, J. B. (1979). Counselors' feelings toward clients as related to intake judgments and outcome variables. *Journal of Counseling Psychology, 26*(3), 267–269.

Shariff, A. (2009). Ethnic identity and parenting stress in South Asian families: Implications for culturally sensitive counselling. *Canadian Journal of Counselling, 43*(1), 35–46.

Sharkin, B. S. (1997). Increasing severity of presenting problems in college counseling centers: A closer look. *Journal of Counseling and Development, 75,* 275–281.

Sharpley, C. F. (2007). So why aren't counselors reporting n = 1 research designs? *Journal of Counseling and Development, 85,* 349–356.

Shaw, H. E., & Shaw, S. F. (2006). Critical ethical issues in online counseling: Assessing current practices with an ethical intent checklist. *Journal of Counseling and Development, 84,* 41–53.

Shavinina, L. V. (2008). How can we better identify the hidden intellectually-creative abilities of the gifted? *Psychology Science, 50*(2), 112–133.

Sheehy, G. (1976). *Passages: Predictable crises of adult life.* New York: Bantam.

Sheehy, R. S. & Horan, J. J. (2004). The effects of stress-inoculation training for first year law students. *International Journal of Stress Management, 11,* 41–55

Sheeley, V. L. (1983). NADW and NAAS: 60 years of organizational relationships. In B. A. Belson & L. E. Fitzgerald (Eds.), *Thus, we spoke: ACPA-NAWDAC, 1958–1975.* Alexandria, VA: American College Personnel Association.

Sheeley, V. L., & Eberly, C. G. (1985). Two decades of leadership in measurement and evaluation. *Journal of Counseling and Development, 63,* 436–439.

Sheeley, V. L., & Herlihy, B. (1989). Counseling suicidal teens: A duty to warn and protect. *School Counselor, 37,* 89–97.

Sheldon, C. T., Aubry, T. D., Arboleda-Florez, J., Wasylenki, D., & Goering, P. N. (2006). Social disadvantage, mental illness and predictors of legal involvement. *International Journal of Law and Psychiatry, 29*(3), 249–256.

Shelton, C., & Allen, J. (2006). Middle school challenges: Reflection, relationships, and responsibility. In J. Pelliteri, R. Stern, C. Shelton, & B. Muller-Ackerman (Eds.), *Emotionally intelligent school counseling* (pp. 95-104). Mahwah, NJ: Lawrence Erlbaum.

Sheppard, G. (n.d.). *Notebook on ethics, legal issues, and standards for counsellors: A few interesting decisions from case law.* Retrieved from **www.ccpa-accp.ca/en/resources/notebookonethics.**

Sherrard, P. A. D., & Amatea, E. S. (1994). Through the looking glass: A preview. *Journal of Mental Health Counseling, 16,* 3–5.

Sherry, A., Lyddon, W. J., & Henson, R. K. (2007). Adult attachment and developmental personalities styles: An empirical study. *Journal of Counseling and Development, 85,* 337–348.

Shertzer, B., & Linden, J. D. (1979). *Fundamentals of individual appraisal, assessment techniques for counselors.* Boston: Houghton Mifflin.

Shertzer, B., & Stone, S. C. (1980). *Fundamentals of counseling* (3rd ed.). Boston: Houghton Mifflin.

Shertzer, B., & Stone, S. C. (1981). *Fundamentals of guidance* (4th ed.). Boston: Houghton Mifflin.

Shields, M. (2006). *Unhappy on the job. Statistics Canada, Health Reports, 17*(4), Catalogue 82–003. Retrieved from **www.stats-can.ca/english/ads/82–003–XPE/pdf/17–4b.pdf**.

Shulman, L. (1999). *The skills of helping individuals, families, groups, and communities* (4th ed.). Itasca, IL: F. E. Peacock.

Siegal, J. C., & Sell, J. M. (1978). Effects of objective evidence of expertness and nonverbal behavior on client perceived expertness. *Journal of Counseling Psychology, 25*, 188–192.

Sielski, L. M. (1979). Understanding body language. *Personnel and Guidance Journal, 57*, 238–242.

Sills, C. (Ed.) (2006). *Contracts in counselling and psychotherapy* (2nd ed.). Thousand Oaks, CA: Sage.

Silverman, W. K., & Hinshaw, S. P. (2009). The second special issue on evidence-based psychosocial treatments for children and adolescents: A 10-year update. *Journal of Clinical Child & Adolescent Psychology, 37*(1), 1–7.

Simner, M. L. (1994). Recommendations by the Canadian Psychological Association for improving the North American safeguards that help protect the public against test misuse. Ottawa, ON: Canadian Psychological Association. Retrieved from **www.cpa.ca/publications**.

Simon, G. M. (1989). An alternative defense of eclecticism: Responding to Kelly and Ginter. *Journal of Mental Health Counseling, 2*, 280–288.

Simon, L., Gaul, R., Friedlander, M. L., & Heatherington, L. (1992). Client gender and sex role: Predictors of counselors' impressions and expectations. *Journal of Counseling and Development, 71*, 48–52.

Simone, D. H., McCarthy, P., & Skay, C. L. (1998). An investigation of client and counselor variables that influence the likelihood of counselor self-disclosure. *Journal of Counseling and Development, 76*, 174–182.

Singh, A. A., & Salazar, C. F. (2010). Process and action in social justice group work: Introduction to the special issue. The Journal for Specialists in Group Work, 35(2), 93–96.

Singh, G. (2008, April 3). *South Asians become Canada's biggest visible minority.* Retrieved from **www.thaindian.com/newsportal/world-news/south-asians-become-canadas-biggest-visible-minority_10033906.html**.

Singh, G. (2008, May 2). *11.4 percent Canadians live below poverty line.* Thaindian News. Retrieved from **www.thaindian.com/newsportal/world-news/114–percent-canadians-live-below-poverty-line_10044198.html**.

Singleton, M. G., & Pope, M. (2000). A comparison of successful smoking cessation interventions for adults and adolescents. *Journal of Counseling and Development, 78*, 448–453.

Sinick, D. (1980). Attitudes and values in aging. *Counseling and Values, 24*, 148–154.

Skinner, B. F. (1953). *Science and human behavior.* New York: Macmillan.

Sklare, G., Keener, R., & Mas, C. (1990). Preparing members for "here-and-now" group counseling. *Journal for Specialists in Group Work, 15*, 141–148.

Sklare, G., Petrosko, J., & Howell, S. (1993). The effect of pre-group training on members' level of anxiety. *Journal for Specialists in Group Work, 18*, 109–114.

Skovholt, T. M., & McCarthy, P. R. (1988). Critical incidents: Catalysts for counselor development. *Journal of Counseling and Development, 67*, 69–72.

Skowron, E.A., & Platt, L. F. (2005). Differentiation of self and child abuse potential in young adulthood. *The Family Journal: Counseling and Therapy for Couples and Families, 13*, 281–290.

Sladeczek, I. E., & Heath, N. L. (1997). Consultation in Canada. *Canadian Journal of School Psychology, 13*(2), 1–14.

Sladeczek, I. E., Madden, L., Illsley, S. D., Finn, C., & August, P. J. (2006). American and Canadian perceptions of the acceptability of conjoint behavioural consultation. *School Psychology International, 27*(1), 57–77.

Slavik, S. (1991). Early memories as a guide to client movement through life. *Canadian Journal of Counseling, 25*, 331–337.

Smart, D. W., & Smart, J. F. (1997). DSM-IV and culturally sensitive diagnosis: Some observations for counselors. *Journal of Counseling and Development, 75*, 392–398.

Smart, J. F., & Smart, D. W. (2006). Models of disability: Implications for the counseling profession. *Journal of Counseling and Development, 84*, 29–40.

Smart, R. G., & Adlaf, E. M. (1991). Substance use and problems among Toronto street youth. *British Journal of Addiction, 86*(8), 999–1010.

Smead, R. (1995). *Skills and techniques for group work with children and adolescents.* Champaign, IL: Research Press.

Smith, A., Stewart, D., Poon, C., Saewyc, E. & McCreary Centre Society (2010). What a difference a year can make: Early alcohol and marijuana use among 16 to 18 year old BC students. Vancouver, BC: *McCreary Centre Society.* Retrieved from **www.mcs.bc.ca**.

Smith, E. M. J., & Vasquez, M. J. T. (1985). Introduction. *Counseling Psychologist, 13*, 531–536.

Smith, H. B., Sexton, T. H., & Bradley, L. J. (2005). The practice research network: Research into practice, practice into research. *Counseling and Psychotherapy Research, 5*, 285–290.

Smith, M. L. (1981). Naturalistic research. *Personnel and Guidance Journal, 59*, 585–589.

Snider, M. (1992). *Process family therapy.* Boston: Allyn & Bacon.

Snider, P. D. (1987). Client records: Inexpensive liability protection for mental health counselors. *Journal of Mental Health Counseling, 9*, 134–141.

Snow, D. A., & Anderson, L. (1987). Identity work among the homeless: The verbal construction and avowal of personal identities. *American Journal of Sociology, 92*, 1336–1371.

Snyder, B. A. (2005). Aging and spirituality: Reclaiming connection through storytelling. *Adultspan Journal, 4*, 49–55.

Snyder, B. A., & Daly, T. P. (1993). Restructuring guidance and counseling programs. *School Counselor, 41*, 36–42.

Solomon, C. (1982). Special issue on political action: Introduction. *Personnel and Guidance Journal, 60*, 580.

Solsberry, P. W. (1994). Interracial couples in the United States of America: Implications for mental health counseling. *Journal of Mental Health Counseling, 16,* 304–316.

Sommers-Flanagan, J., & Sommers-Flanagan, R. (1998). Assessment and diagnosis of conduct disorder. *Journal of Counseling and Development, 76,* 189–197.

Sparks, J. A., & Duncan, B. L. (2010). Common factors in couple and family therapy: Must all have prizes? In B. L. Duncan, S. D. Miller, B. E. Wampold, & M. A. Hubble (Eds.), *The heart and soul of change: Delivering what works in therapy* (2nd ed.). (pp. 357–391). Washington, DC: American Psychological Association.

Sperry, L., Carlson, J., & Lewis, J. (1993). Health counseling strategies and interventions. *Journal of Mental Health Counseling, 15,* 15–25.

Splete, H. H. (1982a). Consultation by the counselor. *Counseling and Human Development, 15,* 1–7.

Splete, H. H. (1982b). Planning for a comprehensive career guidance program in the elementary schools. *Vocational Guidance Quarterly, 30,* 300–307.

Springer, C. A., Britt, T. W., & Schlenker, B. R. (1998). Codependency: Clarifying the construct. *Journal of Mental Health Counseling, 20,* 141–158.

Springer, C. A., & Lease, S. H. (2000). The impact of multiple AIDS related bereavement in the gay male population. *Journal of Counseling and Development, 78,* 297–304.

Sprinthall, N. A. (1981). A new model for research in service of guidance and counseling. *Personnel and Guidance Journal, 59,* 487–496.

Sprinthall, N. A. (1984). Primary prevention: A road paved with a plethora of promises and procrastinations. *Personnel and Guidance Journal, 62,* 491–495.

Sprinthall, N. A., Hall, J. S., & Gerler, E. R., Jr. (1992). Peer counseling for middle school students experiencing family divorce: A deliberate psychological education model. *Elementary School Guidance and Counseling, 26,* 279–294.

Spruill, D. A., & Fong, M. L. (1990). Defining the domain of mental health counseling: From identity confusion to consensus. *Journal of Mental Health Counseling, 12,* 12–23.

Spokane, A. R., & Catalano, M. (2000). The Self-Directed Search: A theory-driven array of self-guided career interventions. In C. E. Watkins, Jr., & V. I. Campbell (Eds.), *Testing and assessment in counseling practice* (2nd ed., pp. 339–370). Mahwah, NJ: Erlbaum.

Spokane, A. R., & Cruza-Guet, M. C. (2005). Holland's theory of vocational personalities in work environments. In S. D. Brown & R. W. Lent (Eds.), *Career development and counseling: Putting theory and research to work* (pp. 24–41). Hoboken, NJ: John Wiley & Sons

St. Clair, K. L. (1989). Middle school counseling research: A resource for school counselors. *Elementary School Guidance and Counseling, 23,* 219–226.

Stadler, H. (1986). Preface to the special issue. *Journal of Counseling and Development, 64,* 291.

Staley, W. L., & Carey, A. L. (1997). The role of school counselors in facilitating a quality twenty-first century workforce. *School Counselor, 44,* 377–383.

Stamm, M. L., & Nissman, B. S. (1979). *Improving middle school guidance.* Boston: Allyn & Bacon.

Stanard, R. P., Sandhu, D. S., & Painter, L. C. (2000). Assessment of spirituality in counseling. *Journal of Counseling and Development, 78,* 204–210.

Stanton, M., & Todd, T. (1982). *The family therapy of drug abuse and addiction.* New York: Guilford.

Statistics Canada (2003, May 13). *2001 Census: analysis series. Religions in Canada.* [Catalogue no. 96F0030XIE2001015]. Retrieved from **www12.statcan.ca/english/census01/ Products/Analytic/companion/rel/contents.cfm.**

Statistics Canada. (2003, April 4). *Definitions: Disability.* Retrieved from **www.statcan.gc.ca/pub/89–577–x/ 4065024–eng.htm.**

Statistics Canada. (2003, September). *Ethnic diversity study: Portrait of a multicultural society.* Retrieved from **www.statcan.gc.ca/bsolc/olc-cel/olc-cel?catno=89–593– X&CHROPG=1&lang=eng.**

Statistics Canada. (2004, March 16). *Spotlight: Black population.* Retrieved from **www.statcan.gc.ca/pub/11–002– x/2004/03/07604/4155366–eng.htmStatisticsCanada.** (2005, December 13). *The daily: Divorce and the mental health of children.* Retrieved from **www.statcan.gc.ca/ daily-quotidien/051213/dq051213c-eng.htm.**

Statistics Canada. (2006, March 7). *The daily: Women in Canada.* Retrieved from **www.statcan.gc.ca/daily-quotidien/ 060307/dq060307a-eng.htm.**

Statistics Canada. (2007a, August 16). *The Arab community in Canada.* Retrieved from **www.statcan.gc.ca/pub/89– 621–x/89–621–x2007009–eng.htm.**

Statistics Canada. (2007b, March 15). *The Chinese community in Canada.* Retrieved from **www.statcan.gc.ca/ pub/89–621–x/89–621–x2006001–eng.htm.**

Statistics Canada. (2007c, August 16). *The Latin American community in Canada.* Retrieved from **www.statcan.gc.ca/ pub/89–621–x/89–621–x2007008–eng.htm.**

Statistics Canada. (2007a, July 17). *Age and sex.* Retrieved from **www12.statcan.gc.ca/census-recensement/2006/ rt-td/as-eng.cfm.**

Statistics Canada. (2007b, February 12). *Spotlight: Deaths. Life expectancy.* Retrieved from **www42.statcan .ca/smr04/2007/02/smr04_04307_05–eng.htm.**

Statistics Canada. (2007d, July 16). *The South Asian community in Canada.* Retrieved from **www.statcan.gc.ca/pub/89– 621–x/89–621–x2007006–eng.htm.**

Statistics Canada. (2008, April 2). *The daily: 2006 census: Ethnic origin, visible minorities, place of work and mode of transportation.* Retrieved from **www.statcan.gc.ca/ daily-quotidien/080402/dq080402a-eng.htm.**

Statistics Canada. (2008, July 25). *Canada at a glance 2009: Demography.* Retrieved from **www45.statcan.gc.ca/ 2009/cgco_2009_001–eng.htm.**

Statistics Canada. (2009, June 25). *Canadian Community Health Survey 2008.* Retrieved from **www.statcan .gc.ca/daily-quotidien/090625/dq090625b-eng.htm.**

Statistics Canada. (2009, July 21). *Police reported crime statistics, 2008.* Retrieved from **www.statcan.gc.ca/ daily-quotidien/090721/dq090721a-eng.htm.**

Statistics Canada. (2009, November 23). *The daily: Study: Quality of employment in the Canadian immigrant labour market.* Retrieved from **www.statcan.gc.ca/daily-quotidien/091123/dq091123b-eng.htm.**

Statistics Canada. (2009a, December 11). *Ethnic origins, 2006 counts, for Canada, provinces and territories – 20% sample data*. Retrieved from **www12.statcan.ca/census-recensement/2006/dp-pd/hlt/97–562/pages/page.cfm?Lang=E&Geo=PR&Code=01&Data=Count&Table=2&StartRec=1&Sort=3&Display=All&CSDFilter=5000#Notes**.

Statistics Canada. (2009b, December 31). *Immigrant status (4) for the population of Canada, provinces and territories, 1911 to 2006 censuses - 20% sample data*. Retrieved from **www12.statcan.gc.ca/census-recensement/2006/dp-pd/tbt/Rp-eng.cfm?LANG=E&APATH=3&DETAIL=0&DIM=0&FL=A&FREE=0&GC=0&GID=0&GK=0&GRP=1&PID=89423&PRID=0&PTYPE=88971,97154&S=0&SHOWALL=0&SUB=0&Temporal=2006&THEME=72&VID=0&VNAMEE=&VNAMEF=**.

Statistics Canada. (2009c, December 23). *Quarterly demographic estimates: Highlights*. Retrieved from **www.statcan.gc.ca/pub/91–002–x/2009003/aftertoc-aprestdm1–eng.htm**.

Statistics Canada. (2009d, November 18). *The report at a glance: Population growth and age structure*. Retrieved from **www.statcan.gc.ca/pub/91–209–x/2004000/rprt-eng.htm#a4**.

Statistics Canada. (2009a, March 31). *2006 census: Family portrait: Continuity and change in Canadian families and households in 2006: National portrait: Census families. Same-sex married couples counted for the first time*. Retrieved from **www12.statcan.ca/census-recensement/2006/as-sa/97–553/p4–eng.cfm**.

Statistics Canada. (2009b, March 30). *Suicides and suicide rate, by sex and by age group (both sexes)*. Retrieved from **www40.statcan.ca/l01/cst01/hlth66a-eng.htm**.

Statistics Canada. (2010, January 3). *Population projections of visible minority groups, Canada, provinces and regions 2001–2017: Demography division*. Retrieved from **www.statcan.gc.ca/cgi-bin/af-fdr.cgi?l=eng&loc=www.statcan.gc.ca/pub/91–541–x/91–541–x2005001–eng.pdf&t=Population%20Projections%20of%20Visible%20Minority%20Groups,%20Canada,%20Provinces%20and%20Regions**.

Statistics Canada. (2010, February 23). *The daily: Deaths*. Retrieved from **www.statcan.gc.ca/daily-quotidien/100223/dq100223a-eng.htm**.

Statton, J. E., & Wilborn, B. (1991). Adlerian counseling and the early recollections of children. *Individual Psychology, 47*, 338–347.

Steen, S., Bauman, S., & Smith, J. (2008). The preparation of professional school counselors for group work. *Journal for Specialists in Group Work, 33*(3), 253–269.

Steen, S., & Kaffenberger, C. J. (2007). Integrating academic interventions into small group counseling in elementary school. *Professional School Counseling, 10*, 516–519.

Steenbarger, B. N. (1998). Alcohol abuse and college counseling: An overview of research and practice. *Journal of College Counseling, 1*, 81–92.

Steinglass, P. (1979). Family therapy with alcoholics: A review. In E. Kaufman & P. N. Kaufman (Eds.), *Family therapy of drug and alcohol abuse* (pp. 147–186). New York: Gardner.

Stergiopoulos, V., & Herrmann, N. (2003). Old and homeless: A review and survey of older adults who use shelters in an urban setting. *The Canadian Journal of Psychiatry / La Revue canadienne de psychiatrie, 48*(6), 374–380.

Stevens, P., & Smith, R. L. (2005). *Substance abuse counseling: Theory and practice* (3rd ed.). Upper Saddle River, NJ: Merrill/Prentice Hall.

Stevens-Smith, P., & Hughes, M. M. (1993). *Legal issues in marriage and family counseling*. Alexandria, VA: American Counseling Association.

Stevens-Smith, P., & Remley, T. P., Jr. (1994). Drugs, AIDS, and teens: Intervention and the school counselor. *School Counselor, 41*, 180–184.

Stewart, D., Cornish, P., & Somers, K. (1995). Empowering students with learning disabilities in the Canadian postsecondary educational system. *Canadian Journal of Counselling, 29*(1), 70–79.

Stewart, S. E., Manion, I. G., & Davidson, S. (2002). Emergency management of the adolescent suicide attemptor: A review of the literature. *Journal of Adolescent Health, 30*(5), 312–325.

Stinnett, N. (1998). *Good families*. New York: Doubleday.

Stinnett, N., & DeFrain, J. (1985). *Secrets of strong families*. Boston: Little, Brown.

Stockton, R., Barr, J. E., & Klein, R. (1981). Identifying the group dropout: A review of the literature. *Journal for Specialists in Group Work, 6*, 75–82.

Stone, C. B. (2005). *School counseling principles: Ethics and law*. Alexandria, VA: American School Counselors Association.

Stone, G. L., & Archer, J., Jr. (1990). College and university counseling centers in the 1990s: Challenges and limits. *Counseling Psychologist, 18*, 539–607.

Stones, M. J. & Kozma, A. (1981). The Canadian origin of functional age research. *Canadian Psychology/Psychologie canadienne, 22*(1), 104–106.

Strahan, R. F., & Kelly, A. E. (1994). Showing clients what their profiles mean. *Journal of Counseling and Development, 72*, 329–331.

Strawser, S., Markos, P. A., Yamaguchi, B. J., & Higgins, K. (2000). A new challenge for school counselors: Children who are homeless. *Professional School Counseling, 3*(3), 162–171.

Street, S., & Isaacs, M. (1998). Selfesteem: Justifying its existence. *Professional School Counseling, 1*, 46–50.

Stripling, R. O. (1978). ACES guidelines for doctoral preparation in counselor education. *Counselor Education and Supervision, 17*, 163–166.

Strong, E. K., Jr. (1943). *Vocational interests of men and women*. Stanford, CA: Stanford University Press.

Strong, S. R. (1982). Emerging integrations of clinical and social psychology: A clinician's perspective. In G. Weary & H. Mirels (Eds.), *Integrations of clinical and social psychology* (pp. 181–213). New York: Oxford University Press.

Strong, T. (2008). Externalising questions: A micro-analytic look at their use in narrative therapy. *The International Journal of Narrative Therapy and Community Work, 3*, 59–71.

Stuart, H. L., & Arboleda-Florez, J. (2000). Homeless shelter users in the postdeinstitutionalization era. *The Canadian Journal of Psychiatry / La Revue canadienne de psychiatrie, 45*(1), 55–62.

Stude, E. W., & McKelvey, J. (1979). Ethics and the law: Friend or foe? *Personnel and Guidance Journal, 57,* 453–456.

Studer, J. R., Oberman, A. H., & Womack, R. H. (2007). Producing evidence to show counseling effectiveness in the schools. *Professional School Counseling, 9*(5), 385–391.

Stufflebeam, D. L., Foley, W. J., Gephart, W. J., Guba, E. G., Hammond, R. L., Merriman, H. D., et al. (1971). *Educational evaluation and decision-making.* Bloomington, IN: Phi Delta Kappa.

Stum, D. (1982). DIRECT: A consultation skills training model. *Personnel and Guidance Journal, 60,* 296–302.

Sue, D. W. (1978a). Counseling across cultures. *Personnel and Guidance Journal, 56,* 451.

Sue, D. W. (1978b). Editorial. *Personnel and Guidance Journal, 56,* 260.

Sue, D. W. (1992, Winter). The challenge of multiculturalism. *American Counselor, 1,* 6–14.

Sue, D. W., Arredondo, P., & McDavis, R. J. (1992). Multicultural counseling competencies and standards: A call to the profession. *Journal of Counseling and Development, 70,* 477–486.

Sue, D. W., Ivey, A. E., & Pedersen, P. (1996). *A theory of multicultural counseling and therapy.* Pacific Grove, CA: Brooks/Cole.

Sue, D., & Sue, D. W. (1991). Counseling strategies for Chinese Americans. In C. C. Lee & B. L. Richardson (Eds.), *Multicultural issues in counseling: New approaches to diversity* (pp. 79–90). Alexandria, VA: American Association for Counseling.

Sullivan, K. R., & Mahalik, J. R. (2000). Increasing career self-efficacy for women: Evaluating a group intervention. *Journal of Counseling and Development, 78,* 54–62.

Sumerlin, J. R., & Norman, R. L. Jr. (1992). Self-actualization and homeless men: A known-groups examination of Maslow's hierarch of needs. *Journal of Social Behavior and Personality, 7,* 469–481.

Sunich, M. F., & Doster, J. (1995, June). Cocaine—Part II. *Amethyst Journal, 1,* 1–2.

Super, D. E. (1954a). Career patterns as a basis for vocational counseling. *Journal of Counseling Psychology, 1,* 12–19.

Super, D. E. (1954b). Guidance: Manpower utilization or human development? *Personnel and Guidance Journal, 33,* 8–14.

Super, D. E. (1957). *The psychology of careers.* New York: Harper.

Super, D. E. (1983). Synthesis: Or is it distillation? *Personnel and Guidance Journal, 61,* 511–514.

Super, D. E. (1990). A life-span, life-space approach to career development. In D. Brown, L. Brooks, & Associates (Eds.), *Career choice and development: Applying contemporary theories to practice* (2nd ed., pp. 197–261). San Francisco: Jossey-Bass.

Super, D. E., Thompson, A. S., & Lindeman, R. H. (1988). *Adult career concerns inventory.* Palo Alto, CA: Consulting Psychologists Press.

Sussman, N. M., & Rosenfeld, H. M. (1982). Influence of culture, language, and sex on conversational distance. *Journal of Personality and Social Psychology, 42*(1), 66–74.

Sutcher, H. (2008). Hypnosis, hypnotizability and treatment. *American Journal of Clinical Hypnosis, 51*(1), 57–67.

Suzuki, L. A., & Kugler, J. F. (1995). Intelligence and personality assessment. In J. G. Ponterotto, J. M. Casas, L. A. Suzuki, & C. M. Alexander (Eds.), *Handbook of multicultural counseling* (pp. 493–515). Thousand Oaks, CA: Sage.

Suzuki, L. A., Meller, P. J., & Ponterotto, J. G. (Eds.). (2001). *Handbook of multicultural assessment: Clinical, psychological, and educational applications* (2nd ed.). San Francisco: Jossey-Bass.

Swanson, J. L., & Hansen, J. C. (1988). Stability of vocational interests over 4–year, 8–year, and 12–year intervals. *Journal of Vocational Behavior, 33,* 185–202.

Swartz-Kulstad, J. L., & Martin, W. E., Jr. (1999). Impact on culture and context on psychosocial adaptation: The cultural and contextual guide process. *Journal of Counseling and Development, 77,* 281–293.

Sweeney, T. J. (1998). *Adlerian counseling* (4th ed.). Muncie, IN: Accelerated Development.

Swim, J. K., Becker, J. C., Lee, E., & Pruitt, E-R. (2010). Sexism reloaded: Worldwide evidence for its endorsement, expression, and emergence in multiple contexts. In H. Landrine & N. F. Russo (Eds.), *Handbook of diversity in feminist psychology* (pp. 137–171). New York, NY: Springer.

Sylvania, K. C. (1956). Test usage in counseling centers. *Personnel and Guidance Journal, 34,* 559–564.

Talbutt, L. C. (1981). Ethical standards: Assets and limitations. *Personnel and Guidance Journal, 60,* 110–112.

Talbutt, L. C. (1983). The counselor and testing: Some legal concerns. *School Counselor, 30,* 245–250.

Tamminen, A. W., & Smaby, M. H. (1981). Helping counselors learn to confront. *Personnel and Guidance Journal, 60,* 41–45.

Tang, M., Fouad, N. A., & Smith, P. L. (1999). Asian Americans' career choices: A path model to examine factors influencing their career choices. *Journal of Vocational Behavior, 54*(1), 142–157.

Tate, D. S., & Schwartz, C. L. (1993). Increasing the retention of American Indian students in professional programs in higher education. *Journal of American Indian Education, 32,* 21–31.

Taub, D. J. (1998). Promoting student development through psychoeducational groups: A perspective on the goals and process matrix. *Journal for Specialists in Group Work, 23,* 196–201.

Taylor, D. M., Lydon, J. E., Bougie, E., & Johannesen, K. (2004). "Street kids": Towards an understanding of their motivational context. *Canadian Journal of Behavioural Science/Revue canadienne des sciences du comportement, 36*(1), 1–16.

Taylor, J. G., & Baker, S. B. (2007). Psychosocial and moral development of PTSD-diagnosed combat veterans. *Journal of Counseling and Development, 85,* 364–369.

Taylor, J. (2005). A thumbnail map for solution-focused brief therapy. *Journal of Family Psychotherapy, 16*(1), 27–33.

Tedeschi, G. J., Zhu, S-H, Anderson, C. M., Cummins, S., & Ribner, N. G. (2005). Putting it on the line: Telephone counseling for adolescent smokers. *Journal of Counseling and Development, 83,* 416–424.

Tennyson, W. W., & Strom, S. M. (1986). Beyond professional standards: Developing responsibleness. *Journal of Counseling and Development, 64,* 298–302.

Terres, C. K., & Larrabee, M. J. (1985). Ethical issues and group work with children. *Elementary School Guidance and Counseling, 19,* 190–197.

Terry, L. L. (1989). Assessing and constructing a meaningful system: Systemic perspective in a college counseling center. *Journal of Counseling and Development, 67,* 352–355.

Teyber, E. (2000). *Interpersonal process in psychotherapy: A relational approach.* Belmont, CA: Wadsworth/ Thomson.

The Association of Social Workers of Northern Canada. (2006). *Welcome!* Retrieved from **www.socialworknorth .com/index.php?option=com_content&task=view&id= 36&Itemid=72**.

Thibodeau, S. C., Solowoniuk, J. D., & Nixon, G. L. (2010). A unique addictions counselling program: An untapped resource in Canada. Manuscript submitted to the *Canadian Journal of Counselling.*

Thiessen, V. (2009). The pursuit of postsecondary education: A comparison of first nations, African, Asian, and European Canadian youth. *Canadian Review of Sociology, 46*(1), 5–37.

Thomas, A. J. (1998). Understanding culture and worldview in family systems: Use of the multicultural genogram. *The Family Journal, 6,* 24–32.

Thomas, A. R., Solorzano, L., & Cobb, H. C. (2007). Culturally responsive counselling and psychotherapy with children and adolescents. In H. T. Prout & D. T. Brown (Eds.), *Counseling and psychotherapy with children and adolescents* (4th ed.) (pp. 64–93). Hoboken, NJ: John Wiley & Sons.

Thomas, G. P., & Ezell, B. (1972). The contract as counseling technique. *Personnel and Guidance Journal, 51,* 27–31.

Thomas, J. T. (2010). *The ethics of supervision and consultation: Practical guidance for mental health professionals.* Washington, DC: American Psychological Association.

Thomas, S. C. (1996). A sociological perspective on contextualism. *Journal of Counseling and Development, 74,* 529–536.

Thomas, V. (1994). Value analysis: A model of personal and professional ethics in marriage and family counseling. *Counseling and Values, 38,* 193–203.

Thombs, D. L., & Osborn, C. J. (2001). A cluster analysis study of clinical orientations among chemical dependency counselors. *Journal of Counseling and Development, 79,* 450–458.

Thompson, A. (1990). *Guide to ethical practice in psychotherapy.* New York: Wiley.

Thompson, B. (1996). *Personal Preferences Self-Description Questionnaire.* College Station, TX: Psychometrics Group.

Thompson, B. (2002). 'Statistical,' 'practical,' and 'clinical': How many kinds of significance do counselors need to consider? *Journal of Counseling and Development, 80,* 64–71.

Thoresen, C. E. (1978). Making better science, intensively. *Personnel and Guidance Journal, 56,* 279–282.

Thornburg, H. D. (1978). *The bubblegum years: Sticking with kids from 9 to 13.* Tucson: HELP Books.

Thornburg, H. D. (1986). The counselor's impact on middle-grade students. *School Counselor, 33,* 170–177.

Thorndike, R. M. (1997). *Measurement and evaluation in psychology and education* (6th ed.). Upper Saddle River, NJ: Merrill/Prentice Hall.

Thorndike, R. M. (2005). *Measurement and evaluation in psychology and education* (7th ed.). Upper Saddle River, NJ: Merrill/Prentice Hall.

Thurman, C. (1983). Effects of a rational-emotive treatment program on Type A behavior among college students. *Journal of College Student Personnel, 24,* 417–423.

Thyer, B. A. (2008). Respondent learning theory. In B. A. Thyer, K. M. Sowers, & C. N. Dulmus (Eds.), *Comprehensive handbook of social work and social welfare, volume 2: Human behavior in the social environment* (pp. 39–67). Hoboken, NJ: John Wiley & Sons.

Ting, S-M. R. (2009). Meta-analysis on dating violence prevention among middle and high schools. *Journal of School Violence, 8*(4), 328–337.

Tinsley, H. E. A., & Bradley, R. W. (1986). Test interpretation. *Journal of Counseling and Development, 65,* 462–466.

Tiwari, S. K., & Wang, J. (2008). Ethnic differences in mental health service use among White, Chinese, South Asian and South East Asian populations living in Canada. *Social Psychiatry and Psychiatric Epidemiology, 43*(11), 866–871.

Todd, T. C. (1986). Structural-strategic marital therapy. In N. S. Jacobson & A. S. Gurman (Eds.), *Clinical handbook of marital therapy* (pp. 71–105). New York: Guilford.

Tomes, H. (1996, August). Are we in denial about child abuse? *APA Monitor, 27,* 55.

Tomine, S. (1986). Private practice in gerontological counseling. *Journal of Counseling and Development, 64,* 406–409.

Tomlinson, S. M., & Evans-Hughes, G. (1991). Gender, ethnicity, and college students' responses to the Strong-Campbell Interest Inventory. *Journal of Counseling and Development, 70,* 151–155.

Toneatto, T., & Nguyen, L. (2007). Does mindfulness meditation improve anxiety and mood symptoms? A review of the controlled research. *The Canadian Journal of Psychiatry / La Revue canadienne de psychiatrie, 52*(4), 260–266.

Tonso, K. L. (2009). Violent masculinities as tropes for school shooters: The Montreal Massacre, the Columbine Attack and rethinking schools. *American Behavioral Scientist, 52*(9), 1266–1285.

Toub, G. (2010). A brief introduction to Jungian therapy. Retrieved from **www.4therapy.com/consumer/conditions/ item.php?uniqueid=7580&categoryid=493&**.

Tracey, T. J. (1983). Single case research: An added tool for counselors and supervisors. *Counselor Education and Supervision, 22,* 185–196.

Tracey, T. J. (1991). Counseling research as an applied science. In C. E. Watkins, Jr., & L. J. Schneider (Eds.), *Research in counseling* (pp. 3–32). Hillsdale, NJ: Erlbaum.

Tran, K., Kaddatz, J., & Allard, P. (2005, August). *South Asians in Canada: Unity through diversity.* Retrieved from **www.statcan.gc.ca/kits-trousses/pdf/social/edu04_0128a-eng.pdf**.

Trepper, T. S., Dolan, Y., McCollum, E. E., & Nelson, T. (2006). Steve de Shazer and the future of solution-focused therapy. *Journal of Marital & Family Therapy, 32*(2), 133–139.

Trocmé, N., Fallon, B., MacLaurin, B., Daciuk, J., Felstiner, C., Black, T., ... Cloutier, R. (2005). Canadian incidence study of reported child abuse and neglect – 2003. *Minister of Public Works and Government Services Canada.* Retrieved from **www.phac-aspc.gc.ca/cm-vee/csca-ecve/pdf/childabuse_final_e.pdf**.

Trocme, N., Knoke, D., & Blackstock, C. (2004). Pathways to the overrepresentation of Aboriginal children in Canada's child welfare system. *Social Service Review, 78*(4), 577–599.

Trotzer, J. P. (1988). Family theory as a group resource. *Journal for Specialists in Group Work, 13,* 180–185.

Truax, C., & Mitchell, K. (1971). Research on certain therapist interpersonal skills in relation to process and outcome. In A. E. Bergin & S. L. Garfield (Eds.), *Handbook of psychotherapy and behavior change: An empirical analysis.* New York: Wiley.

Truax, C. B., & Carkhuff, R. R. (1967). *Toward effective counseling and psychotherapy: Training and practice.* Chicago: Aldine.

Trusty, J., Robinson, C. R., Plata, M., & Ng, K-M. (2000). Effects of gender, socioeconomic status, and early academic performance on postsecondary educational choice. *Journal of Counseling and Development, 78,* 463–472.

Tucker, D. (2002). *"Precarious" non-standard employment-A review of the literature.* Wellington, New Zealand: Labour Market Policy Group, Department of Labour. Retrieved from **www.dol.govt.nz/publications-browse .asp?BrowseBy=Date&Year=2002**.

Tuckman, B. (1965). Developmental sequence in small groups. *Psychological Bulletin, 63,* 384–399.

Tuckman, B. W., & Jensen, M. A. (1977). Stages of small group development revisited. *Group and Organizational Studies, 2,* 419–427.

Turner, J., & Helms, D. (1994). *Lifespan development* (5th ed.). Chicago: Holt, Rinehart.

Turock, A. (1978). Effective challenging through additive empathy. *Personnel and Guidance Journal, 57,* 144–149.

Turock, A. (1980). Immediacy in counseling: Recognizing clients' unspoken messages. *Personnel and Guidance Journal, 59,* 168–172.

Tuten, T. L., Urban, D. J., & Bosnjak, M. (2002). Internet surveys and data quality: A review. In B. Batinic, U-D Reips, & M. Bosnjak (Eds.), *Online social sciences* (pp. 7–26). Ashland, OH: Hogrefe & Huber.

Tyler, L. E. (1984). What tests don't measure. *Journal of Counseling and Development, 63,* 48–50.

Tylka, T. L., & Subich, L. M. (2002). Exploring young women's perceptions of the effectiveness and safety of maladaptive weight control techniques. *Journal of Counseling and Development, 80,* 101–110.

Tymchuk, A. J. (1986). Guidelines for ethical decision making. *Canadian Psychology, 27,* 36–43.

Tymofievich, M., & Leroux, J. A. (2000). Counselors' competencies in using assessments. *Measurement and Evaluation in Counseling and Development, 33,* 50–59.

Tysl, L. (1997, January). Counselors have a responsibility to promote the counseling profession. *Counseling Today,* 16.

Umansky, D. L., & Holloway, E. L. (1984). The counselor as consultant: From model to practice. *School Counselor, 31,* 329–338.

UNAIDS. (2009, April). *Disability and HIV policy brief.* Retrieved from aids.about.com/od/legalissues/a/disability.htm

Ungar, M., Barter, K., McConnell, S. M., Tutty, L. M., & Fairholm, J. (2009). Patterns of abuse disclosure among youth. *Qualitative Social Work: Research and Practice, 8*(3), 341–356.

Ungersma, A. J. (1961). *The search for meaning.* Philadelphia: Westminster.

United Nations. (n.d.). *The Universal Declaration of Human Rights.* Retrieved from **www.un.org/en/documents/ udhr/index.shtml**.

University of Waterloo. (n.d.). *Career development emanual.* Retrieved from **www.cdm.uwaterloo.ca/index2.asp**.

Urbina, S. (2005). *Essentials of psychological testing.* New York: Wiley.

U.S. Department of Health and Human Services, National Institute of Mental Health. (1999). *Mental health: A report of the Surgeon General–Executive Summary.* Rockville, MD: Author.

U.S. Department of Health, Education, and Welfare. (1974). Vocational rehabilitation program: Implementation provisions, rules and regulations. *Federal Register, 39,* 42470–42507.

U.S. Employment Service. (1939). *Dictionary of occupational titles.* Washington, DC: Author.

Uysal, A., & Oner-Ozkan, B. (2007). A self-presentational approach to transmission of good and bad news. *Social Behavior and Personality, 35*(1), 63–78.

Vacc, N., Loesch, L., & Guilbert, D. (1997). The clientele of certified clinical mental health counselors. *Journal of Mental Health Counseling, 19,* 165–170.

Vacc, N. A., & Juhnke, G. A. (1997). The use of structured clinical interviews for assessment in counseling. *Journal of Counseling and Development, 75,* 470–480.

Vacc, N. A., Juhnke, G. A., & Nilsen, K. A. (2001). Community mental health service providers' code of ethics and the *Standards for Educational and Psychological Testing. Journal of Counseling and Development, 79,* 217–224.

Vacc, N. A., & Loesch, L. C. (2001). *A professional orientation to counseling* (3rd ed.). Philadelphia: Brunner-Routledge.

Vacha-Haase, T., & Thompson, B. (2002). Alternative ways of measuring counselees' Jungian psychological-type preferences. *Journal of Counseling and Development, 80,* 173–179.

Vaihinger, H. (1911). *The philosophy of "as if."* New York: Harcourt, Brace, & World.

Valle, R. (1986). Cross-cultural competence in minority communities: A curriculum implementation strategy. In M. R. Miranda & H. H. L. Kitano (Eds.), *Mental health research and practice in minority communities: Development of culturally sensitive training programs* (pp. 29–49). Rockville, MD: National Institute of Mental Health. (ERIC Document Reproduction Service No. ED278754)

VanBoven, A. M., & Espelage, D. L. (2006). Depressive symptoms, coping strategies, and disordered eating among college women. *Journal of Counseling and Development, 84,* 341–348.

Van Buren, J. (1992). Gender-fair counseling. In J. A. Lewis, B. Hayes, & L. J. Bradley (Eds.), *Counseling women over the life span* (pp. 271–289). Denver: Love.

Van Buren, J. B., Kelly, K. R., & Hall, A. S. (1993). Modeling nontraditional career choices: Effects of gender and school location on response to a brief videotape. *Journal of Counseling and Development, 72,* 101–104.

Vancouver Community Network. (2009). *Multicultural organization database*. Retrieved from **www.vcn.bc.ca/ multicultural/welcome.html**.

Van der Wade, H., Urgenson, F. T., Weltz, S. H., & Hanna, F. J. (2002). Women and alcoholism: A biopsychosocial perspective and treatment approaches. *Journal of Counseling and Development, 80,* 145–153.

Van Deusen, J. M., Stanton, M. D., Scott, S. M., Todd, S. C., & Mowatt, D. T. (1982). Getting the addict to agree to involve the family of origin: The initial contact. In M. D. Stanton, T. C. Todd, & Associates (Eds.), *The family therapy of drug abuse and addiction* (pp. 39–59). New York: Guilford.

van Deurzen, E. (2002). Existential therapy. In W. Dryden (Ed.), *Handbook of individual therapy* (4th ed.) (pp. 179–208). London, UK: Sage.

Van Dussen, D. J., & Weaver, R. R. (2009). Undergraduate students' perceptions and behaviors related to the aged and to aging processes. *Educational Gerontology, 35*(4), 340–355.

Van Hoose, W. H., & Kottler, J. (1985). *Ethical and legal issues in counseling and psychotherapy* (2nd ed.). San Francisco: Jossey-Bass.

Vandenbos, G. R., Cummings, N., & Deleon, P. H. (1992). A century of psychotherapy: Economic and environmental influences. In D. K. Freedheim (Ed.), *History of psychotherapy: A century of change* (pp. 65–102). Washington, DC: American Psychological Association.

Vanlaar, W., Mayhew, D., & Marcoux, K., Wets, G., Brijs, T., & Shope, J. (2009). An evaluation of graduated driver licensing programs in North America using a meta-analytic approach. *Accident Analysis and Prevention, 41*(5), 1104–1111

Vargas, A. M., & Borkowski, J. G. (1986). Physical attractiveness, social influences, and counseling processes. In F. J. Dorn (Ed.), *The social influence process in counseling and psychotherapy* (pp. 95–105). Springfield, IL: Charles C Thomas.

Varlami, E., & Bayne, R. (2007). Psychological type and counselling psychology trainees' choice of counselling orientation. *Counselling Psychology Quarterly, 20*(4), 361–373.

Vereen, L. G., Butler, S. K., Williams, F. C., Darg, J. A., & Downing, T. K. E. (2006). The use of humor when counseling African American college students. *Journal of Counseling and Development, 84,* 10–15.

Vernon, A. (1989). *Thinking, feeling, and behaving: An emotional education curriculum for children (Grades 1–6)*. Champaign, IL: Research Press.

Vick, R. D., Smith, L. M., & Herrera, C. I. R. (1998). The healing circle: An alternative path to alcoholism recovery. *Counseling and Values, 42,* 133–141.

Vickio, C. J. (1990). The goodbye brochure: Helping students to cope with transition and loss. *Journal of Counseling and Development, 68,* 575–577.

Victoria Holocaust Remembrance and Education Society. (2002). *A webography: The history of racism in Canada*. Retrieved from **www.hopesite.ca/remember/history/ racism_canada_1.html**.

Viney, L. L., Henry, R. M., & Campbell, J. (2001). The impact of group work on offender adolescents. *Journal of Counseling and Development, 79,* 373–381.

Vogel, D. L., Wade, N. G., & Hackler, A. H. (2007). Perceived public stigma and the willingness to seek counseling: The mediating roles of self-stigma and attitudes toward counseling. *Journal of Counseling Psychology, 54*(1), 40–50.

Voight, N. L., Lawler, A., & Fulkerson, K. F. (1980). Community-based guidance: A "Tupperware party" approach to mid-life decision making. *Personnel and Guidance Journal, 59,* 106–107.

Vontress, C. E. (1966). Counseling the culturally different adolescent: A school-community approach. In J. C. Gowan & G. Demos (Eds.), *The disadvantaged and potential dropout* (pp. 357–366). Springfield, IL: Thomas.

Vontress, C. E. (1967). The culturally different. *Employment Service Review, 4,* 35–36.

Vontress, C. E. (1996). A personal retrospective on cross-cultural counseling. *Journal of Multicultural Counseling and Development, 16,* 73–83.

Vontress, E. E. (2008). Existential therapy. In J. Frew & M. D. Spiegler (Eds.), *Contemporary psychotherapies for a diverse world* (pp. 141–176). Boston, MA: Lahaska Press.

Votta, E., & Farrell, S. (2009). Predictors of psychological adjustment among homeless and housed female youth. *Journal of the Canadian Academy of Child and Adolescent Psychiatry / Journal de l'Academie canadienne de psychiatrie de l'enfant et de l'adolescent, 18*(2), 126–132.

Vriend, J., & Dyer, W. W. (1973). Counseling the reluctant client. *Journal of Counseling Psychology, 20,* 240–246.

Wade, J. C. (1998). Male reference group identity dependence: A theory of male identity. *Counseling Psychologist, 26,* 349–383.

Wahl, K. H., & Blackhurst, A. (2000). Factors affecting the occupational and educational aspirations of children and adolescents. *Profesional School Counseling, 3,* 367–374.

Wakefield, J. C. (1992). The concept of mental disorder: On the boundary between biological facts and social values. *American Psychologist, 47,* 373–388.

Waldegrave, C. (2005). "Just therapy" with families on low incomes. *Child Welfare: Journal of Policy, Practice, and Program, 84*(2), 265–276.

Waldo, M. (1985). Curative factor framework for conceptualizing group counseling. *Journal for Counseling and Development, 64,* 52–58.

Waldo, M. (1989). Primary prevention in university residence halls: Paraprofessional-led relationship enhancement groups for college roommates. *Journal of Counseling and Development, 67,* 465–471.

Waldo, M., & Bauman, S. (1998). Regrouping the categorization of group work: A goal and process (GAP) matrix for groups. *Journal for Specialists in Group Work, 23,* 164–176.

Waldo, M., Horswill, R. K., & Brotherton, W. D. (1993). Collaborating with state departments to achieve recognition of mental health counselors. *Journal of Mental Health Counseling, 15,* 342–346.

Walen, S. R., DiGuiseppe, R., & Dryden, W. (1992). *A practitioner's guide to rational-emotive therapy*. New York: Oxford University Press.

Walker-Staggs, J. (2000). DISCOVER. In N. Peterson & R. C. Gonzalez (Eds.), *Career counseling models for diverse populations* (pp. 112–120). Pacific Grove, CA: Brooks/Cole.

Wall, J. E., & Walz, G. R. (Eds.). (2004). *Measuring up: Assessment issues for teachers, counselors, and administators*. Greensboro, NC: CAPS Press.

Wallace, W. A., & Hall, D. L. (1996). *Psychological consultation: Perspectives and applications*. Pacific Grove, CA: Brooks/Cole.

Walls, R. T., & Fullmer, S. L. (1996). Comparing rehabilitated workers with the United States workforce. *Rehabilitation Counseling Bulletin, 40*(2), 153–164.

Walsh, M. E., & Buckley, M. A. (1994). Children's experiences of homelessness: Implications for school counselors. *Elementary School Guidance & Counseling, 29*(1), 4–15.

Walsh, R. (2000). Asian psychotherapies. In R. J. Corsini & D. Wedding (Eds.), *Current psychotherapies* (6th ed., pp. 407–444). Itasca, IL: F. E. Peacock.

Walsh, R. A., & McElwain, B. (2002). Existential psychotherapies. In D. J. Cain & J. Seeman (Eds.), *Humanistic psychotherapies: Handbook of research and practice* (pp. 253–278). Washington, DC: American Psychological Association.

Walsh, W. B., & Osipow, S. H. (1994). *Career counseling for women*. Hillsdale, NJ: Erlbaum.

Walsh, W. B., & Savickas, M. (Eds.). (2005). *Handbook of vocational psychology* (3rd ed.). Hillsdale, NJ: Erlbaum.

Walsh, W. M., & Keenan, R. (1997). Narrative family therapy. *Family Journal, 5*, 332–336.

Walter, J., & Peller, J. (1992). *Becoming solution-focused in brief therapy*. New York: Brunner/Mazel.

Ward, D. E. (1982). A model for the more effective use of theory in group work. *Journal for Specialists in Group Work, 7*, 224–230.

Ward, D. E. (1984). Termination of individual counseling: Concepts and strategies. *Journal of Counseling and Development, 63*, 21–25.

Ward, D. E. (2002). Like old friends, old familiar terms and concepts need attention. *Journal for Specialists in Group Work, 27*, 119–121.

Ward, V., & Bezanson, L. (1991). Career counselling of girls and women: Guidelines for professional practice. *Canadian Journal of Counselling, 25*(4), 476–484.

Warfield, R. D., & Goldstein, M. B. (1996). Spirituality: The key to recovery from alcoholism. *Counseling and Values, 40*, 196–205.

Wark, D. M. (2008). What we can do with hypnosis: A brief note. *American Journal of Clinical Hypnosis, 51*(1), 29–36.

Wastell, C. A. (1996). Feminist development theory: Implications for counseling. *Journal of Counseling and Development, 74*, 575–581.

Watkins, C. (2001). Comprehensive guidance programs in an international context. *Professional School Counseling, 4*, 262–270.

Watkins, C. E., Jr. (1983a). Burnout in counseling practice: Some potential professional and personal hazards of becoming a counselor. *Personnel and Guidance Journal, 61*, 304–308.

Watkins, C. E., Jr. (1983b). Counselor acting out in the counseling situation: An exploratory analysis. *Personnel and Guidance Journal, 61*, 417–423.

Watkins, C. E., Jr. (1985). Early recollections as a projective technique in counseling: An Adlerian view. *AMHCA Journal, 7*, 32–40.

Watkins, C. E., Jr. (1990a). The effects of counselor self-disclosure: A research review. *Counseling Psychologist, 18*, 477–500.

Watkins, C. E., Jr. (1990b). The testing of the test section of the *Journal of Counseling and Development:* Historical, contemporary, and future perspectives. *Journal of Counseling and Development, 69*, 70–74.

Watkins, C. E., Jr., & Schneider, L. J. (1989). Self-involving versus self-disclosing counselor statements during an initial interview. *Journal of Counseling and Development, 67*, 345–349.

Watkins, C. E., Jr., & Schneider, L. J. (1991). Research in counseling: Some concluding thoughts and ideas. In C. E. Watkins, Jr., & L. J. Schneider (Eds.), *Research in counseling* (pp. 287–299). Hillsdale, NJ: Erlbaum.

Watkins, E. (1983). Project retain: A client centered approach to student retention. *Journal of College Student Personnel, 24*, 81.

Watson, J. C. (2005). College student-athletes' attitudes toward help-seeking behavior and expectations of counseling services. *Journal of College Student Development, 46*, 442–429.

Watts, R. E. (2000a). Adlerian counseling: A viable approach for contemporary practice. *TCA Journal, 28*(1), 11–23.

Watts, R. E. (2000b). Entering the new millennium: Is Individual Psychology still relevant? *Journal of Individual Psychology, 56*(1), 21–30.

Watzlawick, P., Weakland, J. H., & Fisch, R. (1974). *Change: Principles of problem formation and problem resolution*. New York: W.W. Norton.

Waxer, P., & White, R. (1973). Introducing psychological consultation to a university community. *Canadian Psychologist/Psychologie canadienne, 14*(3), 256–265.

Webb, W. (1992). Empowering at-risk children. *Elementary School Guidance and Counseling, 27*, 96–103.

Webster, S. R., Vogel, D. L., Wie, M., & McLain, R. (2006). African American men, gender role conflict, and psychological distress: The role of racial identity. *Journal of Counseling and Development, 84*, 419–429.

Wechsler, D. (1997). *Wechsler Adult Intelligence Scale—Third Edition*. San Antonio, TX: Psychological Corporation.

Weigel, D. J., Donovan, K. A., Krug, K. S., & Dixon, W. A. (2007). Prescription opioid abuse and dependence: Assessment strategies for counselors. *Journal of Counseling and Development, 85*, 211–215.

Weikel, W. J., & Palmo, A. J. (1989). The evolution and practice of mental health counseling. *Journal of Mental Health Counseling, 11*, 17–25.

Weiner, I. B. (1992). *Psychological disturbance in adolescence* (3rd ed.). New York, NY: Wiley.

Weinrach, S. G. (1980). Unconventional therapist: Albert Ellis. *Personnel and Guidance Journal, 59*, 152–160.

Weinrach, S. G. (1987). Microcounseling and beyond: A dialogue with Allen Ivey. *Journal of Counseling and Development, 65*, 532–537.

Weinrach, S. G. (1996). The psychological and vocational interest patterns of Donald Super and John Holland. *Journal of Counseling and Development, 75*, 5–16.

Weinrach, S. G., Ellis, A., MacLaren, C., DiGiuseppe, R., Vernon, A., Wolfe, J., et al. (2001). Rational emotive behavior therapy successes and failures: Eight personal perspectives. *Journal of Counseling and Development, 79,* 259–268.

Weinrach, S. G., & Thomas, K. R. (1998). Diversity-sensitive counseling today: A postmodern clash of values. *Journal of Counseling and Development, 76,* 115–122.

Weiss, L. G., Saklofske, D. H., Coalson, D., & Engi Raiford, S. (2010). *WAIS-IV Clinical use and interpretation:* Scientist-practitioner perspectives. New York, NY: Academic Press.

Weist, M. D., Bryant, Y. U., Dantzler, J., Martin, S., D'Amico, M., Griffith, B., & Gallun, B. (2009). Evaluation of a state-wide initiative in the United States to prevent/reduce sexual harassment in schools. *Health Education, 109*(2), 112-124.

Weitzenhoffer, A. M. (2000). *The practice of hypnotism* (2nd ed.). Toronto, ON: John Wiley & Sons.

Welfel, E. R., Danzinger, P. R., & Santoro, S. (2000). Mandated reporting of abuse/maltreatment of older adults: A primer for counselors. *Journal of Counseling and Development, 78,* 284–292.

Welfel, E. R., & Lipsitz, N. E. (1983). Wanted: A comprehensive approach to ethics research and education. *Counselor Education and Supervision, 22,* 320–332.

Wendel, P. (1997, October). Cultural bias among minority counselors. *Counseling Today, 1,* 20.

Werner, J. L. (1978). Community mental health consultation with agencies. *Personnel and Guidance Journal, 56,* 364–368.

West, J. D., Bubenzer, D. L., Smith, J. M., & Hamm, T. L. (1997). Insoo Kim Berg and solution-focused therapy. *Family Journal, 5,* 286–294.

West, J. D., Hosie, T. W., & Mackey, J. A. (1987). Employment and roles of counselors in mental health agencies. *Journal of Counseling and Development, 66,* 135–138.

West, J. D., Hosie, T. W., & Zarski, J. J. (1987). Family dynamics and substance abuse: A preliminary study. *Journal of Counseling and Development, 65,* 487–490.

West, P. L., Mustaine, B. L., & Wyrick, B. (2002). Apples and oranges make a nice start for a fruit salad: A response to Culbreth and Borders (1999). *Journal of Counseling and Development, 80,* 72–76.

Westbrook, B. W. (1988). Suggestions for selecting appropriate career assessment instruments. *Measurement and Evaluation in Counseling and Development, 20,* 181–186.

Westbrook, F. D., Kandell, J. J., Kirkland, S. E., Phillips, P. E., Regan, A. M., Medvene, A., et al. (1993). University campus consultation: Opportunities and limitations. *Journal of Counseling and Development, 71,* 684–688.

Westcott, N. A. (1983). Application of the structured life-review technique in counseling elders. *Personnel and Guidance Journal, 62,* 180–181.

Westgate, C. E. (1996). Spiritual wellness and depression. *Journal of Counseling and Development, 75,* 26–35.

Wetter, D. W., Fiore, M. C., Gritz, E. R., Lando, H. A., Stitzer, M. L., Hasselblad, V., et al. (1998). The agency for health care policy and research smoking cessation clinical practice guideline. *American Psychologist, 53,* 657–669.

Whalen, D. (n.d.) The mental health needs of an aging population. *Canadian Mental Health Association.* Retrieved from **www.cmhanl.ca/pdf/Healthy%20Aging.pdf**.

Wheeler, C. D., & D'Andrea, L. M. (2004). Teaching counseling students to understand and use immediacy. *Journal of Humanistic Counseling, Education and Development, 43,* 117–128.

Wheeler, P. T., & Loesch, L. (1981). Program evaluation and counseling: Yesterday, today, and tomorrow. *Personnel and Guidance Journal, 59,* 573–578.

Whiston, S. C. (1996). Accountability through action research: Research methods for practitioners. *Journal of Counseling and Development, 74,* 616–623.

Whiston, S. C. (2002). Response to the past, present, and future of school counseling: Raising some issues. *Professional School Counseling, 5,* 148–155.

Whiston, S. C., & Quinby, R. F. (2009). Review of school counseling outcome research. *Psychology in the Schools, 46*(3), 267–272.

Whiston, S. C., & Sexton, T. L. (1998). A review of school counseling outcome research: Implications for practice. *Journal of Counseling and Development, 76,* 412–426.

Whitaker, C. (1977). Process techniques of family therapy. *Interaction, 1,* 4–19.

White, E. B. (1952). *Charlotte's web.* New York: Trophy.

White, J. (2007). Working in the midst of ideological and cultural differences: Critically reflecting on youth suicide prevention in indigenous communities. *Canadian Journal of Counselling, 41*(4), 213–227.

White, M. (1995). *Re-authoring lives.* Adelaide, Australia: Dulwich Centre Publications.

White, M. (2009). Narrative practice and conflict dissolution in couples therapy. *Clinical Social Work Journal, 37*(3), 200–213.

White, M., & Epston, D. (1990). *Narrative means to therapeutic ends.* New York: Norton.

Whiteley, J. M. (1982). *Character development in college students.* Alexandria, VA: American Counseling Association.

Whitmarsh, L., Brown, D., Cooper, J., Hawkins-Rodgers, Y., & Wentworth, D. K. (2007). Choices and challenges: A qualitative exploration of professional women's career patterns. *Career Development Quarterly, 55,* 225–236.

Wiehe, V. R. (2000). Sibling abuse. In H. Henderson (Ed.), *Domestic violence and child abuse resource sourcebook* (pp. 409–492). Detroit, MI: Omnigraphics.

Wiggins, J., & Weslander, D. (1979). Personality characteristics of counselors rated as effective or ineffective. *Journal of Vocational Behavior, 15,* 175–185.

Wiggins, J. D., Moody, A. D., & Lederer, D. A. (1983). Personality typologies related to marital satisfaction. *AMHCA Journal, 5,* 169–178.

Wihak, C., & Merali, N. (2003). Culturally sensitive counselling in Nunavut: Implications of Inuit traditional knowledge. *Canadian Journal of Counselling, 37*(4), 243–255. Retrieved from **http://cjc-rcc.ucalgary.ca/cjc/index.php/rcc/article/view/238/530**.

Wihak, C., & Merali, N. (2005). A narrative study of counsellors' understandings of Inuit spirituality. *Canadian Journal of Counselling, 39*(4), 245–259.

Wihak, C., & Price, R. E. (2006). *Counselling across cultures: Working with Aboriginal clients.* Retrieved from **www.natcon.org/archive/natcon/papers/natcon_papers_2006_e1.pdf**.

Wikipedia. (2009a, December 4). *École Polytechnique massacre.* Retrieved from **http://en.wikipedia.org/wiki/%C3%89cole_Polytechnique_Massacre**.

Wilcox-Matthew, L., Ottens, A., & Minor, C. W. (1997). An analysis of significant events in counseling. *Journal of Counseling and Development, 75,* 282–291.

Wilcoxon, S. A. (1985). Healthy family functioning: The other side of family pathology. *Journal of Counseling and Development, 63,* 495–499.

Wilcoxon, S. A. (1986). Engaging nonattending family members in marital and family counseling: Ethical issues. *Journal of Counseling and Development, 64,* 323–324.

Wilcoxon, S. A. (1987). Ethical standards: A study of application and utility. *Journal of Counseling and Development, 65,* 510–511.

Wilcoxon, S. A., & Fenell, D. (1983). Engaging the nonattending spouse in marital therapy through the use of therapist-initiated written communication. *Journal of Marital and Family Therapy, 9,* 199–203.

Wilcoxon, S. A., & Puleo, S. G. (1992). Professional-development needs of mental health counselors: Results of a national survey. *Journal of Mental Health Counseling, 14,* 187–195.

Wilcoxon, S. A., Remley, T. P., Jr., Gladding, S. T., & Huber, C. H. (2007). *Ethical, legal and professional issues in the practice of marriage and family therapy* (4th ed.). Upper Saddle River, NJ: Merrill/Prentice Hall.

Wilgosh, L., & Mueller, H. H. (1993). Work skills for disadvantaged and unprepared youth and adults. International Journal for the Advancement of Counselling, 16(2), 99–105.

Wilkerson, K., & Bellini, J. (2006). Interpersonal and organizational factors associated with burnout among school counselors. *Journal of Counseling and Development, 84,* 440–450.

Williams, C. B., & Freeman, L. T. (2002). Report of the ACA Ethics Committee: 2000–2001. *Journal of Counseling and Development, 80,* 251–254.

Williams, D. T., Hershenson, D. B., & Fabian, E. S. (2000). Causal attributions of disabilities and the choice of rehabilitation approach. *Rehabilitation Counseling Bulletin, 43,* 106–112.

Williams, J. E. (1962). Changes in self and other perceptions following brief educational-vocational counseling. *Journal of Counseling Psychology, 9,* 18–30.

Williams, J. M., Ballard, M. B., & Alessi, H. (2005). Aging and alcohol abuse: Increasing counselor awareness. *Adultspan Journal, 4,* 7–18.

Williams, J. M. G., Russell, I. T., Crane, C., Russell, D., Whitaker, C. J., Duggan, D. S., ... Silverton, S. (2010). Staying well after depression: Trial design and protocol. *BMC Psychiatry, 10,* ArtID 23.

Williams, J. M. G., & Swales, M. (2004). The use of mindfulness-based approaches for suicidal patients. *Archives of Suicide Research, 8*(4), 315–329.

Williamson, E. G. (1939). *How to counsel students: A manual of techniques for clinical counselors.* New York: McGraw-Hill.

Williamson, E. G. (1961). *Student personnel services in colleges and universities.* New York: McGraw-Hill.

Williamson, E. G. (1972). Trait-and-factor theory and individual differences. In B. Stefflre & W. H. Grant (Eds.), *Theories of counseling* (2nd ed, pp. 136–176). New York: McGraw-Hill.

Williamson, E. G., & Biggs, D. A. (1979). Trait-factor theory and individual differences. In H. M. Burks, Jr. & B. Stef-

flre (Eds.), *Theories of counseling* (3rd ed., pp. 91–131). New York: McGraw-Hill.

Willison, B., & Masson, R. (1986). The role of touch in therapy: An adjunct to communications. *Journal of Counseling and Development, 65,* 497–500.

Willoughby, T., & Perry, G. P. (2002). Working with violent youth: Application of the transtheoretical model of change. *Canadian Journal of Counselling, 36*(4), 312–326.

Wilmarth, R. R. (1985, Summer). Historical perspective, part two. *AMHCA News, 8,* 21.

Wilson, F. R., & Yager, G. G. (1981). A process model for prevention program research. *Personnel and Guidance Journal, 59,* 590–595.

Wilson, G. T. (2008). Behavior therapy. In R. J. Corsini & D. Wedding (Eds.), *Current psychotherapies* (8th ed., pp. 223–262). Belmont, CA: Thomson Brooks/Cole.

Wilson, K. B., & Senices, J. (2005). Exploring the vocational rehabilitation acceptance rates for Hispanics versus Non-Hispanics in the United States. *Journal of Counseling and Development, 83,* 86–96.

Wilson, R. J., Cortoni, F., & McWhinnie, A. J. (2009). Circles of support & accountability: A Canadian national replication of outcome findings. *Sexual Abuse: Journal of Research and Treatment, 21*(4), 412–430.

Winston, R. B., Jr., & Creamer, D. G. (1997). *Improving staffing practices in student affairs.* San Francisco: Jossey-Bass.

Winston, R. B., Jr., & Ender, S. C. (1988). Use of student paraprofessionals in divisions of college student affairs. *Journal of Counseling and Development, 66,* 466–473.

Wise, E. A., Streiner, D. L., & Walfish, S. (2010). A review and comparison of the reliabilities of the MMPI-2, MCMI-III- and PAI presented in their respective test manuals. *Measurement and Evaluation in Counseling and Development, 42*(4), 246–254.

Witmer, J. M., & Young, M. E. (1996). Preventing counselor impairment: A wellness model. *Journal of Humanistic Education and Development, 34,* 141–155.

Wittmer, J., & Adorno, G. (2000). *Managing your school counseling program: Developmental strategies* (2nd ed.). Minneapolis: Educational Media Corporation.

Wolfgang, A. (1985). The function and importance of nonverbal behavior in intercultural counseling. In P. Pedersen (Ed.), *Handbook of cross-cultural counseling and therapy* (pp. 99–105). New York, NY: Greenwood Press.

Wolgast, B. M., Lambert, M. J., & Puschner, B. (2003). The dose-response relationship at a college counseling center: Implications for setting session limits. *Journal of College Student Psychotherapy, 18*(2), 15–29.

Wong, S. E. (2008). Operant learning theory. In B. A. Thyer, K. M. Sowers, & C. N. Dulmus (Eds.), *Comprehensive handbook of social work and social welfare, volume 2: Human behavior in the social environment* (pp. 69–99). Hoboken, NJ: John Wiley & Sons.

Woody, R. H. (1988). *Fifty ways to avoid malpractice.* Sarasota, FL: Professional Resource Exchange.

Woody, R. H., Hansen, J. C., & Rossberg, R. H. (1989). *Counseling psychology.* Pacific Grove, CA: Brooks/Cole.

Wooten, H. R. (1994). Cutting losses for student-athletes in transition: An integrative transition model. *Journal of Employment Counseling, 31,* 2–9.

Worden, M. (2003). *Family therapy basics* (3rd ed.). Pacific Grove, CA: Brooks/Cole.

Wordpress.com. (2007, November 6). *Moments in time: The internment camps of Japanese Canadians in Canada during World War II*. Retrieved from **http://timeinmoments .wordpress.com/2007/11/06/the-internment-camps-of-japanese-canadians-in-canada-during-world-war-ii**.

World Health Organization. (2005–2010). *Mental health*. Retrieved from **www.wpro.who.int/sites/mnh**.

Worling, J. R. (1995). Adolescent sibling-incest offenders: Differences in family and individual functioning when compared to adolescent nonsibling offenders. *Child Abuse & Neglect, 19*(5), 633–643.

Wrenn, C. G. (1962). The culturally encapsulated counselor. *Harvard Educational Review, 32*, 444–449.

Wright, G. N. (1980). *Total rehabilitation*. Boston: Little, Brown.

Wright, G. N. (1987). Rehabilitation counselors' qualifications and client responsibilities structure their professional relationships. *Journal of Applied Rehabilitation Counseling, 18*, 18–20.

Wright, J., Sabourin, S., Mondor, J., McDuff, P., & Mamodhoussen, S. (2007). The clinical representativeness of couple therapy outcome research. *Family Process, 46*(3), 301–316.

Wubbolding, R. E. (1988). *Using reality therapy*. New York: Harper/ Collins.

Wubbolding, R. E. (1991). *Understanding reality therapy: A metaphorical approach*. New York: Harper.

Wubbolding, R. E. (1998). *Cycle of managing, supervising, counseling, and coaching using reality therapy*. Cincinnati: Center for Reality Therapy.

Wubbolding, R. E. (2000). *Reality therapy for the 21st century*. New York: Brunner-Routledge.

Wyatt, T., Daniels, M. H., & White, L. J. (2000). Noncompetition agreements and the counseling profession: An unrecognized reality for private practitioners. *Journal of Counseling and Development, 78*, 14–20.

Yalom, I. D. (2005). *The theory and practice of group psychotherapy* (5th ed.). New York: Basic Books.

Yalom, I. D., & Lieberman, M. (1971). A study of encounter group casualties. *Archives of General Psychiatry, 25*, 16–30.

Yates, T. M., & Wekerle, C. (2009). The long-term consequences of childhood emotional maltreatment on development: (Mal)adaptation in adolescence and young adulthood. *Child Abuse & Neglect, 33*(1), 19–21.

Yeh, C. J., & Hwang, M. Y. (2000). Interdependence in ethnic identity and self: Implications for theory and practice. *Journal of Counseling and Development, 78*, 420–429.

Yontef, G. (2007). The power of the immediate moment in gestalt therapy. [References]. *Journal of Contemporary Psychotherapy, 37*(1), 17–23.

Yontef, G., & Fairfield, M. (2008). Gestalt therapy. In K. Jordan (Ed.), *The quick theory reference guide: A resource for expert and novice mental health professionals* (pp. 83–106). Hauppauge, NY: Nova Science.

Yoon, E., & Jepsen, D. A. (2008). Expectations of and attitudes toward counseling: A comparison of Asian international and U.S. graduate students. *International Journal for the Advancement of Counselling, 30*(2), 116–127.

York Region Health Connection. (2008, August). *Health resources for schools: Substance abuse prevention*.

Retrieved from **http://search.york.ca/search?q= resource+substance+abuse+prevention&site=default_ collection& entqr=0&ud=1&sort=date%3AD%3AL% 3Ad1&output=xml_no_dtd&oe=UTF-8&ie=UTF-8& client=default_frontend&proxystylesheet=default_ frontend& btnG=Search**.

Young, J. S., Wiggins-Frame, M., & Cashwell, C. S. (2007). Spirituality and counselor competence: A national survey of American Counseling Association members. *Journal of Counseling and Development, 85*, 47–52.

Young, K. (2008). Narrative practice at a walk-in therapy clinic: Developing children's worry wisdom. *Journal of Systemic Therapies, 27*(4), 54–74.

Young, M. E. (2005). *Learning the art of helping: Building blocks and techniques* (3rd ed.). Upper Saddle River, NJ: Merrill/Prentice Hall.

Young, R. A. (1988). Ordinary explanations and career theories. *Journal of Counseling and Development, 66*, 336–339.

Young, R. A., & Nicol, J. J. (2007). Counselling psychology in Canada: Advancing psychology for all. *Applied Psychology: An International Review, 56*, 20–32.

Zanarini, M. C. (2009). Psychotherapy of borderline personality disorder. *Acta Psychiatrica Scandinavica, 120*(5), 373–377.

Zhang, D. (1995). Depression and culture. *Canadian Journal of Counselling, 29*(3), 227–233.

Zimpfer, D. (1996). Five-year follow-up of doctoral graduates in counseling. *Counselor Education and Supervision, 35*, 218–229.

Zimpfer, D., & DeTrude, J. (1990). Follow-up of doctoral graduates in counseling. *Journal of Counseling and Development, 69*, 51–5.

Zinck, K., & Littrell, J. M. (2000). Action research shows group counseling effective with at-risk adolescent girls. *Professional School Counseling, 4*, 50–59.

Zinker, J. C. (2009). Gestalt therapy is permission to be creative: A sermon in praise of the use of experiment in Gestalt therapy. *Gestalt Review, 13*(2), 123–124.

Zinnbauer, B. J., & Pargament, K. I. (2000). Working with the sacred: Four approaches to religious and spiritual issues in counseling. *Journal of Counseling and Development, 78*, 162–171.

Zins, J. E. (1993). Enhancing consultee problem-solving skills in consultative interactions. *Journal of Counseling and Development, 72*, 185–188.

Zunker, V. G. (2006). *Career counseling* (7th ed.). Pacific Grove, CA: Brooks/Cole.

Zur, O. (2009). Therapist self-disclosure: Standard of care, ethical considerations, and therapeutic context. In A. Bloomgarden & R. B. Mennuti (Eds.), *Psychotherapist revealed: Therapists speak about self-disclosure in psychotherapy* (pp. 31–51). New York, NY: Routledge/Taylor & Francis.

Zytowski, D. (1985). Frank! Frank! Where are you now that we need you? *Counseling Psychologist, 13*, 129–135.

Zytowski, D. G. (1992). Three generations: The continuing evolution of Frederic Kuder's interest inventories. *Journal of Counseling and Development, 71*, 245–248.

Zytowski, D. G., & Holmberg, K. S. (1988). Preferences: Frederic Kuder's contributions to the counseling profession. *Journal of Counseling and Development, 67*, 150–156.

Credits

Index

Alzheimer's disease, 116
AMCD. *See* Association for Multicultural Counselling and Development (AMCD)
American Association for Marriage and Family Therapy (AAMFT), 437
American Counselling Association (ACA), 16, 21–22, 118
   Code of Ethics, 77
American Family Therapy Association (AFTA), 438
American Mental Health Counselling Association (AMHCA), 13
American Psychiatric Association
   Diagnostic and Statistical Manual of Mental Disorders, 7, 38–40, 127, 391, 392
American Psychological Association (APA), 438, 473
   Division 17, 13
AMHCA. *See* American Mental Health Counselling Association (AMHCA)
Amplification, 228
Anal stage, 217. *See also* Psychosexual developmental stages
Analytical psychology, 226
Anglophones, 93
Animus, 227
Anxiety, 266
   hierarchical scale, 235, 236
   mental health counselling, 521
Anxiety disorders, 474
APA. *See* American Psychological Association (APA)
Apprenticeships in career counselling, 417
Aptitude tests, 379
Arab Canadians, counselling, 103–104
Arbuckle, Dugald, 12
Archetypes, 227
Arthur, Nancy, culture-infused counselling model, 88–89
ASD. *See* Acute stress disorder (ASD)
ASERVIC. *See* Association for Spiritual, Ethical, and Religious Values in Counselling (ASERVIC)
A-SPS. *See* Adapted-SAD PERSONS scale (A-SPS)
Assertiveness training, 235
Assessment, 390–391
Association for Adult Aging and Development (AAAD), 14
Association for Behavioural and Cognitive Therapies (ABCT), 237

Association for Multicultural Counselling and Development (AMCD), 14, 86–87
Association for Non-white Concerns in Personnel and Guidance (ANWC), 13, 87
Association for Religious and Value Issues in Counselling, 13
Association for Specialists in Group Work, 13
Association for Spiritual, Ethical, and Religious Values in Counselling (ASERVIC)
   "Summit on Spirituality," 131–132
Association of Counsellor Educators and Supervisors (ACES), 13
Attention deficit disorder (ADD), 549–550
Attention deficit/hyperactivity disorder (AD/HD), 549–550
   in children, 474
Attentiveness, 156
Attractiveness, 148–149
Attribution models, 36–37
Autonomy, in ethics, 53, 62
Axline, Virginia, play therapy, 473

B

Babe, 482
1984 *Badgley Report on Child Sexual Abuse,* 525
Bandura, Albert, 18, 411
BASIC ID (technical eclecticism), 214
Basic needs poverty measure (BNPM), 558
Beck, Aaron, cognitive therapy, 12, 238, 245
Beers, Clifford, *A Mind That Found Itself,* 9
Befrienders International, 20
Behavioral therapy, 233–237
   counsellor and, 234
   goals, 234
   human nature and, 233–234
   limitations of, 237
   strengths of, 236–237
   techniques, 234–236
Behavioural counselling, 233–237
Behavioural disputation, 240
Behavioural rehearsal, 235
Behavioural responses, 170–171
Bell, John, 436
Beneficence, in ethics, 53, 62
Berne, Eric, transactional analysis, 12
Bibliotherapy, 536
   elementary school children, 482
   secondary school children, 492

Binge drinking, 502
Biomedical model
   disability counselling, 546–547
Birth order, 222
Bisexuals, 125–128
   career counselling with, 426–428
   counselling with, 127–128
   defined, 126
BNPM. *See* Basic needs poverty measure (BNPM)
Books for You, 492
Bordin, Edward, 138
Boston's Vocational Bureau, 8
Bott, E.A., 10
Bowen, Murray, 454
Bowen systems theory, 454–457
Brewer, John, 490
   Education as Guidance, 11, 13
Brief Core Schema Scales, 373
Brief counselling approaches, 436
British Canadians, 92–93
2008 British Columbia Adolescent Health Survey, 533
Bruff v. North Mississippi Health Services, Inc., 77
Bullying
   anti-bullying programs, 487
   preventive counselling, 480–481, 487
Buproprion, 538
Burnout, 30–31
Burns, David, 238
Buros Institute of Mental Measurements, 371

C

CACGS. *See* Computer-assisted career guidance systems (CACGS)
CACREP. *See* Council for Accreditation of Counseling and Related Educational Programs (CACREP)
CADUMS. *See* Canadian Alcohol and Drug Use Monitoring Survey (CADUMS)
CAMFTE. *See* Commission on Accreditation for Marriage and Family Therapy Education (CAMFTE)
Canada
   Aboriginal people in, 82, 94–97
   counselling relationships, legal decisions on, 69–71
   immigrants in, 81–82
   spirituality and religion in, 131
   visible minorities in, 81–82

misperceptions and realities
about, 300
place in counselling, 300–302
stages in, 307–308, 310
theoretical approaches in
conducting, 306–307
types of, 303–306
Group work, 15
GSS. *See General Social Survey* (GSS)
Guidance
career, 402–403
definition of, 3–4
vocational, 8–9, 10, 402. *See also*
Career counselling
*Guidelines for Non-Discriminatory
Practice*, 372

H

Habilitation, 545
Haley, Jay, 435, 457, 460
Handicap defined, 546
Harper, Stephen, 533
Hartmann, Heinz, 216
Hayes, Steven C.
acceptance and commitment
therapy (ACT), 255
HDC. *See* Human Development
Center (HDC)
Health and wellness promotion
programs (HWPs), 515
Heavy drinkers
defined, 532
Helpful behaviors in initial interviews,
156–158
HELPING, 478
Helping, levels of, 31–32
Helping alliance. *See* Working alliance
Hiebert, Bryan, 401
Hincks, Clarence, 9
Hispanic Canadians, counselling,
102–103
HIV/AIDS, 550–551
Holland, John, 380, 406–407
RIASEC model, 406
Vocational Preference
Inventory, 29
Homelessness, 558–559, 562–563. *See
also* Houselessness; Poverty
causes of, 560–562
mental illness and, 563–564
substance abuse and, 563–564
Homework, 181–182, 453
Homicide
prevention programs, 492–493
Homophobia, 128
Homosexual individuals, 125–128
counselling with, 127–128

Honesty, 148
Houselessness, 562–563. *See also*
Homelessness
House-Tree-Person (HTP) Test, 382
Human Development Center
(HDC), 488
Humanistic counselling theories, 12
Humanistic theories, 262–273
Human nature
acceptance and commitment therapy (ACT) view of, 256
Adlerian view of, 222–223
behavioral view of, 233–234
Bowen systems theory view,
454–455
cognitive therapy (CT) view
of, 245
collaborative counselling view
of, 286
crisis counselling view of,
289–290
dialectical behaviour therapy
(DBT) view of, 254
emotion-focused couples and family therapy (EFCFT) view, 462
existential counselling view of,
266–267
Gestalt view of, 266–267
Jungian view of, 227
mindfulness-based cognitive therapy (MBCT) view of, 252
mindfulness-based stress reduction
(MBSR) view of, 250
narrative counselling view of, 279
person-centered view of, 262–263
psychoanalytic view of, 217–218
rational emotive behavioral
therapy (REBT) view of, 238
reality therapy (RT) view of,
241–242
solution-focused counselling view
of, 282–283
strategic (brief) counselling
view, 460
stress inoculation training (SIT)
view of, 248
structural family counselling view,
457–458
Human Resources and Skills
Development Canada, 403
Humour in counselling process,
176–177
Humphrey, George, 10
Hurricane Katrina, 17–18
HWPs. *See* Health and wellness
promotion programs (HWPs)

I

IAMFC. *See* International Association
of Marriage and Family
Counselors (IAMFC)
IBs. *See* Irrational Beliefs (iBs)
I Can't Talk About It, 482
ICEEFT. *See* International Centre for
Excellence in Emotionally
Focused Therapy (ICEEFT)
Id, 217
Identity, of counselling, 21–22
IEPs. *See* Individualized education
programs (IEPs)
Illegal drug addiction, 539
Imaginal disputation, 240
Immediacy in counselling process,
175–176
Immigrants, in Canada, 81–82
Immigration Act of 1967, 85
Implied rights, of clients, 73
Implosive therapy, 236
In a Different Voice (Gilligan), 120
Individual counselling sessions,
termination of, 193–194
Individual/group counselling
versus marriage/family
counselling, 443–444
Individualized education programs
(IEPs), 495
Individual psychology, 221. *See also*
Adlerian theory
Individuate, 226, 455
Inferiority complex, 222
Information-oriented first interview,
152–154
Informed consent, 56
Inherited and acquired cultures, 436
Initial interviews, 150–159
attentiveness, 156
conducting the interview, 155–159
door closers, 156
door openers, 155–156
empathy, 156
helpful behaviors, 156–158
non-helpful behaviors, 158–159
rapport, 155
SOLER (nonverbal
behaviors), 157
touching, 158
types of, 150–155
verbal and nonverbal behaviour,
156–158
Initiative in clients, 140–144
In loco parentis, 495–496
Inpatient settings, 5
Input evaluation, 348
Insurance companies, 392

Intelligence tests, 377–379
Interest/career inventory, 379–382
Internal consistency analysis, in
  reliability, 376
International Association for
  Educational and Vocational
  Guidance, 401
International Association of Marriage
  and Family Counselors
  (IAMFC), 438
International Centre for Excellence in
  Emotionally Focused Therapy
  (ICEEFT), 462
International counselling, 105–106
International Society for the
  Prevention of Child Abuse
  and Neglect, 373
Internet, 19–20
  and ethics, 65
Interpersonal abuse, 525–531. *See also*
  Intrapersonal abuse
  child abuse and neglect, 526–527
  childhood sexual abuse, 527
  defined, 525
  emotional abuse, 525–526
  physical abuse, 528
  prevention and treatment, 530–531
  psychological abuse, 528
  sexual abuse, 528
  sibling abuse, 528
  spouse and partner abuse, 528–529
Interpersonal empathy, 172
Interpersonal Reactivity Index, 373
Interpretation, 219–220
Interview, exit, 199
Interview, structured clinical, 390–391
Intrapersonal abuse, 531–544. *See also*
  Interpersonal abuse; Substance
  abuse
  compulsive gambling, 542–543
  work addiction (workaholism),
  543–544
Introvert, 227
Irrational Beliefs (iBs), 238
Irrational thinking, 238

J

Jacobson, Neil, 436
Job, 402
*Job Futures: Welcome to Canada's
  Career and Education Planning
  Tool,* 401
Johari window, 166
Johnson, Sue, 462
Jourard, Sidney, 12
*Journal for Counseling and
  Development,* 322

*Journal of Clinical Child and Adoles-
  cent Psychology,* 473
*Journal of Counselling and
  Development,* 42
*Journal of Employment
  Counseling,* 401
*Journal of Humanistic Counseling,
  Development and
  Education,* 520
Journal of Medicine, 520
*Journal of Multicultural Counselling
  and Development,* 87
*Journal of Technology in
  Counselling,* 20
Jung, Carl, 30, 112, 129, 226–227, 384
Jungian theory, 226–229
  counsellors and, 227
  goals, 227–228
  human nature and, 227
  limitations of, 229
  strengths of, 228–229
  techniques, 228
Justice, in ethics, 53, 62
"Just Say No" campaign, 534

K

Kabat-Zinn, Jon
  mindfulness-based stress reduction
  (MBSR), 250
Kegan, Robert, 481
Kerr, Michael, 454
Klein, Melanie, 216, 473
Kohlberg, Lawrence
  developmental stage theory, 471
  moral development models, 14
Kohut, Heinz, 216
KOIS. *See* Kuder Occupational
  Interest Survey (KOIS)
Krumboltz, John, *Revolution in
  Counselling,* 12
Kuder Career Planning System, 404
Kuder Occupational Interest Survey
  (KOIS), 381

L

Latency period, 217. *See also*
  Psychosexual developmental
  stages
Latino Canadians, 507
  counselling, 102–103
Lavender ceiling, 428
Law, 67–77
  civil and criminal liability, 72–73
  client rights and records, 73–74
  and counselling, 67–68
  counselling minors, 73
  counsellor in court, 75
  definition, 49, 67

ethics *vs.,* 75–77
  violations of, 57
Lazarus, Arnold, technical eclecticism
  (BASIC ID), 214
Leadership, 21
Leading in counselling process,
  169, 170
Learning theory, 12
Lecturing, 159
Lesbian Connection, 128
Lesbians, 125–128
  career counselling with, 426–428
  counselling with, 127–128
  defined, 126
Letter to engage a non-attending
  spouse, 446
Liability, of counsellors, 72–73
Liability insurance, 72
LICO. *See* Low-income cut-off
  (LICO)
Liddy, Roy, 10
*Life's a Bitch and Then You Change
  Careers: 9 Steps to Get Out
  of Your Funk and on to Your
  Future,* 405
Life tasks, 222–223
Lighting, 144
Linehan, Marsha M., dialectical be-
  haviour therapy (DBT), 254
The Lion King, 482
"Little adults." *See* Adolescents;
  Children
"Little Hans," 473
The Little Mermaid, 482
Locus of control, 90, 91
Locus of responsibility, 90, 91
Logotherapy, 266
Long-term relationships, 4
Low-income cut-off (LICO), 557–558
Low-income housing projects, 562

M

Macroscopic approach, 215
Madanes, Cloe, 460
Maintenance, 235
Majority-culture clients, 83
Malpractice, by counsellors, 72
Managed care, 392
  ethics in, 66
Managerial leadership, 21
Marital/partner violence. *See* Spouse
  and partner abuse
Maritime Guidance Association, 11
Market basket measure (MBM), 558
Marriage and family counselling,
  430–465
  Bowen systems theory, 454–457

Weakland, John, 460
Wechsler, David, 378
Wechsler intelligence tests, 378
Wellness, 18
WFC. *See* Work-family conflicts (WFC)
What Color Is Your Parachute? (Bolles and Nelson), 405
Whitaker, Carl, 435
White, Michael, 436
WHO. *See* World Health Organization (WHO)
Williams, Segal
    Mindfulness-based cognitive therapy (MBCT), 252
Williamson, E. G., 10, 37, 405
Wolpe, Joseph, systematic desensitization, 12
Women

career counselling with, 422–425
and substance abuse, 540–541
Women, counselling, 117–120
    concerns in, 118–119
    issues and theories of, 119–120
Women's movement, 12–13
Work addiction (workaholism), 543–544
Work-family conflicts (WFC), 419
Workforce, changes in, 399–400
Working alliance
    adult clients, 569–570
    children/adolescents clients, 570
    concept of, 138
    definition of, 138
    improvement, 570–572
World Health Organization (WHO)
    mental health defined by, 514
Worldviews, 90, 91

Wraparound programs, 493
Wubbolding, Robert, 241

Y

Yoga, 91
Young v. Bella, 71
Youth counselling
    common disorders, 474–475
    developmental stage theories and, 471–472
    evidence-based treatments, 473–474
    factors, 471
    history of, 473
    overview, 470–473
Youth Psychopathic Traits Inventory, 373